At the beginning of the twentieth century Scandinavia lay on the margin of European power politics. With the polarisation of international relations in the era of the two world wars, Denmark, Finland, Norway and Sweden became the point where the spheres of influence of three great powers – Great Britain, Germany and Russia – intersected. From the turn of the century the demands of modern warfare led the European powers to take a closer interest in Scandinavian affairs.

In this book, Patrick Salmon uses his extensive research in British, German and Scandinavian archives to examine the position of the Nordic countries in the great-power rivalries and conflicts of the period 1890–1940. However, it does not treat the Nordic countries merely as passive victims. It seeks to show that, despite the disparity in strength between the great powers and the small states of northern Europe, the latter had means of adapting to great-power pressures and even influencing the policies of their formidable neighbours.

Scandinavia and the great powers 1890–1940

Scandinavia and the great powers 1890–1940

PATRICK SALMON

University of Newcastle upon Tyne

CAMBRIDGE
UNIVERSITY PRESS

PUBLISHED BY THE PRESS SYNDICATE OF THE UNIVERSITY OF CAMBRIDGE
The Pitt Building, Trumpington Street, Cambridge CB2 1RP United Kingdom

CAMBRIDGE UNIVERSITY PRESS
The Edinburgh Building, Cambridge CB2 2RU, United Kingdom
40 West 20th Street, New York, NY 10011–4211, USA
10 Stamford Road, Oakleigh, Melbourne 3166, Australia

First published 1997

Printed in Great Britain at the University Press, Cambridge

Typeset in 9 ½/12 pt Plantin   [CE]

A catalogue record for this book is available from the British Library

Library of Congress cataloguing in publication data

Salmon, Patrick, 1952–
Scandinavia and the great powers 1890–1940 / Patrick Salmon.
    p.   cm.
Includes bibliographical references and index.
ISBN 0 521 41161 0
1. Scandinavia – History – 20th century.
2. Scandinavia – Foreign relations – Great Britain.
3. Great Britain – Foreign relations – Scandinavia.
4. Scandinavia – Foreign relations – Germany.
5. Germany – Foreign relations – Scandinavia.
6. Scandinavia – Foreign relations – Russia/Soviet Union.
7. Russia/Soviet Union – Foreign relations – Scandinavia. I. Title.
DL83.S35   1997
327.48′009′041 – dc21   96–53310 CIP

ISBN 0 521 41161 0 hardback

For Karen, Katie and Jessica

Contents

Tables

Preface

I have been working on this book for a long time, and on various aspects of Scandinavian history for much longer. I can now appreciate what Professor W. R. Mead meant when he wrote in the preface to his *Historical Geography of Scandinavia* (1981) of 'the recurrent fear that it is over ambitious – indeed naïve – to embark on such an undertaking'. I can also sympathise with his other reasons for writing more slowly than he had intended: the difficulty of keeping pace with Scandinavian scholarship, and concern for the opinion of colleagues in the Nordic countries and elsewhere. In some sections of the book I have been able to draw upon my own earlier publications. I owe much, however, to the work of others in the field, and am only too well aware of the limits of my own knowledge and expertise (my inability to read Finnish or Russian remains the most nagging defect).

During the writing of this book I have incurred many debts of gratitude. Research in foreign countries always involves expense, in the Nordic countries more than most. When I first visited Norway in 1976, as a penurious research student, Great Britain was in the grip of a sterling crisis and Norway was at the height of the oil boom. I recall going without food for longer periods than I could manage now. Since then I have become more affluent; the disparities between the British and Nordic currencies have diminished; and Norwegian cuisine has improved. At an age when I would not mind losing some weight, I can now visit Scandinavia without doing so. I am therefore grateful to a large number of organisations and individuals who have helped to sustain my research over a long period.

I would like to acknowledge first the support of three people who have acted as mentors at successive stages of my career: first Harry Hinsley, my doctoral supervisor at Cambridge; second Hans-Jürgen Schröder, who introduced me to the world of German scholarship at Mainz; and third Olav Riste, who gave me my first opportunities to visit Scandinavia and to publish my work, and who has continued to give me much encouragement.

I wish to thank the following bodies for financial support: the British Council; the Institut für Europäische Geschichte, Mainz; the Institutt for forsvarsstudier, Oslo; Norsk Forskningsråd; the Staff Travel Fund and the Small Grants Research Sub-Committee of the University of Newcastle upon Tyne.

The archivists and librarians of a large number of institutions provided invaluable assistance in making available the archival material in their care. I should particularly like to mention Herr Ernst-Wilhelm Norman, formerly of Utenriksdepartementets arkiv (Norway); Professor Wilhelm Carlgren, formerly of Utrikesdepartementets arkiv (Sweden); Herr Klaus Kjølsen of Udenrigsministeriet (Denmark); Frau Dr Maria Keipert of the Politisches Archiv des Auswärtigen Amtes in Bonn; the officials of the former Deutsches Zentralarchiv at Potsdam and of the Public Record Office in London; Mr Henry Gillett of the Bank of England Archive; and Mr Robert Firth of the Robinson Library, University of Newcastle upon Tyne. I am grateful to the late Lord Amery and Mr George Hohler for allowing me to consult papers in their possession.

It is a pleasure to thank the many other people who have given me advice, information or hospitality, and often all three. They include: Rolf Ahmann, David Aldridge, Karl Otmar Freiherr von Aretin, Tony Badger, Roald Berg, Kathy Burk, Dan Christensen, Maurice Cowling, Andrew Croft, Martin Dyrbye, Max Engman, Carl-Axel Gemzell, Philip Giltner, Klaas Hartmann, John Hiden, Sven Holtsmark, Kalervo Hovi, Merja-Liisa Hinkkanen, the late Walther Hubatsch, Alf Johansson, Sune Jungar, David Kirby, Hans Kirchhoff, Tom Kristiansen, Andrew Lambert, Aleksander Loit, Peter Ludlow, Thomas Magnusson, Alan Milward, Svend Aage Mogensen, Thomas Munch-Petersen, Timo Myllyntaus, Lutz Oberdörfer, Herbert Olbrich, Jukka Nevakivi, Torbjörn Norman, Mieczyslaw Nurek, Helge Pharo, the late Stephen Roskill, David Saunders, Harm Schröter, Magne Skodvin, Richard Smith, Zara Steiner, Esa Sundbäck, Martti Turtola, Donald Cameron Watt, Philip Williamson and Clemens Wurm.

I must also thank the organisers of various conferences in Scandinavia, whose invitations have enabled me to combine archival research with meeting colleagues in congenial surroundings. I am grateful in particular to Professor Olav Riste and other members of the research project *Norsk utenrikspolitikks historie* for taking the trouble, at their meeting in November 1995, to read and comment on a draft of part of my book. Odd-Bjørn Fure, author of the third volume of *Norsk utenrikspolitikks historie*, was kind enough to let me see draft chapters of his book prior to publication.

I have also received constant encouragement from Richard Fisher of Cambridge University Press. My greatest debt, however, is to my family: for their support and for keeping me in touch with real life.

Definitions

'Scandinavia' and 'the Nordic states'

The difficulty of defining these terms reflects real problems of national and regional identity. 'Scandinavia' refers to a geographically distinct region of Europe; 'the Nordic states' signifies four countries (Denmark, Norway, Sweden and Finland), not three (Denmark, Norway and Sweden) or five (the first four plus Iceland). Until the end of the First World War, 'Scandinavia' and 'the Scandinavian states' were identical. Following the emergence of an independent Finnish state, culturally but not (apart from a Swedish-speaking minority) ethnically related to Scandinavia, the term 'Nordic' came to be favoured as a means of referring to the states and societies which together composed 'Norden'.

The latter term, now universally employed in the countries concerned, remains virtually untranslatable. 'Northern Europe' and 'The North' are the nearest equivalents, but neither is sufficiently precise to make it wholly acceptable (though both crop up occasionally in this book). To outsiders, at least, 'Scandinavia' remains a term which refers to the whole region including Finland. I have followed this familiar though inconsistent usage but have tried to be consistent, when referring to its component states, in distinguishing between 'the Scandinavian states' (three) and 'the Nordic states' (four). Four, not five, because Iceland appears in the book only incidentally. There are a number of reasons for this. Iceland is widely separated geographically from the four continental Nordic countries; it is much smaller in terms of population, and has an entirely different and much less diversified economic structure. Finally, between 1918 and its achievement of full independence in 1944 Iceland was an independent kingdom in association with Denmark and was unable to conduct an independent foreign policy.

Place names and geographical features

The names of places and geographical features are generally those current in the periods and countries concerned except where there are obvious English equivalents, e.g. Gothenburg, Jutland, Copenhagen; the Sound, the Belts etc.

Kristiania (alternative spelling: Christiania) is used for the Norwegian capital before 1925, when it was renamed Oslo. Trondheim is preferred to Trondhjem.

The duchies of Schleswig/Slesvig and Holstein/Holsten, disputed for centuries between Germany and Denmark, present special problems. Schleswig (German) and Slesvig (Danish) are used interchangeably according to context. Holstein, the more 'German' of the two provinces, is given the German spelling throughout.

For Finland, Finnish-language place-names are preferred to Swedish – e.g. Helsinki, not Helsingfors – but sometimes Swedish equivalents are given in parentheses: e.g. Vaasa (Vasa).

Place-names in present-day Poland, Latvia, Estonia and Russia are given in the language appropriate to the period (usually German), but sometimes modern equivalents are given in parentheses: e.g. Reval (Tallinn).

Abbreviations

AA	Auswärtiges Amt
AB	Aktiebolag(et)
Abt.	Abteilung
ADAP	*Akten zur Deutschen Auswärtigen Politik*, series B (21 vols., Göttingen, 1966–83)
ADM	Admiralty
AEG	Allgemeine Elektrizitäts-Gesellschaft
AG	Aktiengesellschaft
AO	Auslands-Organisation (of NSDAP)
APA	Aussenpolitisches Amt (of NSDAP)
BA	Bundesarchiv, Koblenz
BASF	Badische Anilin und Sodafabrik
BD	Gooch, G. P., and H. W. V. Temperley (eds.), *British Documents on the Origins of the War, 1898–1914* (11 vols. in 13, London, 1926–38
Bd	Band (volume)
BDFA	Bourne, Kenneth, and Donald Cameron Watt (eds.) *British Documents on Foreign Affairs*, part I, series F
BEA	Bank of England Archive
BEF	British Expeditionary Force
BT	Board of Trade
BUL	Birmingham University Library
CAB	Cabinet
CAC	Churchill Archive Centre
CID	Committee of Imperial Defence
CIGS	chief of the imperial general staff
COS	chiefs of staff
CUL	Cambridge University Library
DAAD	Deutsche Akademische Austauschdienst
DBFP	*Documents on British Foreign Policy*, series 1–3
DCNS	deputy chief of the naval staff
DDF	*Documents diplomatiques français*, series 2 and 3 (Paris, 1930–53)
DDWV	Deutsch–Dänische Wirtschaftsvereinigung
DFDS	Det forenede Dampskib Selskab

DGFP	*Documents on German Foreign Policy*, series C and D
DMO	director of military operations
DNI	director of naval intelligence
DNO	director of naval operations
DNVP	Deutschnationale Volkspartei
DOT	Department of Overseas Trade
FBI	Federation of British Industries
FO	Foreign Office
GP	Lepsius, J., A. Mendelssohn-Bartholdy and F. Thimme (eds.), *Die grosse Politik der europäischen Kabinette 1871–1914* (40 vols. in 54, Berlin, 1922–7)
HaPol	Handelspolitische Abteilung
HPA	Handelspolitische Ausschuss
ICI	Imperial Chemical Industries
IG Farben	Interessengemeinschaft Farbenindustrie AG
IIC	Industrial Intelligence Centre
IWM	Imperial War Museum
LKAB	Luossavaara-Kiirunavaare Aktiebolag
MEW	Ministry of Economic Warfare
MP	member of parliament
NA	naval attaché
Nd	Norden
NG	Nordische Gesellschaft
NOT	Netherlands Overseas Trust
NSDAP	Nationalsozialistische Deutsche Arbeiterpartei
NUD	Utenriksdepartementet (Norway)
OKM	Oberkommando der Kriegsmarine
OKW	Oberkommando der Wehrmacht
PA	Politisches Archiv des Auswärtigen Amtes, Bonn
PEP	Political and Economic Planning
PID	Political Intelligence Department
PRO	Public Record Office
RA	Rigsarkiv, Copenhagen
RAO	Riksarkiv, Oslo
RDI	Reichsverband der Deutschen Industrie
RfdA	Reichsstelle für den Aussenhandel
RI	Reichsgruppe Industrie
RIIA	Royal Institute of International Affairs
RL	Robinson Library, University of Newcastle upon Tyne
RWM	Reichswirtschaftsministerium
SA	Stortingets arkiv, Oslo
SD	Sicherheitsdienst
SIS	Secret Intelligence Service
SKL	Seekriegsleitung

SS	Schutzstaffel
SUD	Utrikesdepartementet (Sweden)
T	Treasury
TGO	Trafikaktiebolag Grängesberg–Oxelösund
UM	Udenrigsministeriet (Denmark)
Vowi	Volkswirtschaftliche Abteilung (of IG Farben)
WO	War Office
ZfdA	Zentralstelle für den Aussenhandel
ZSta	Zentrales Staatarchiv, Potsdam

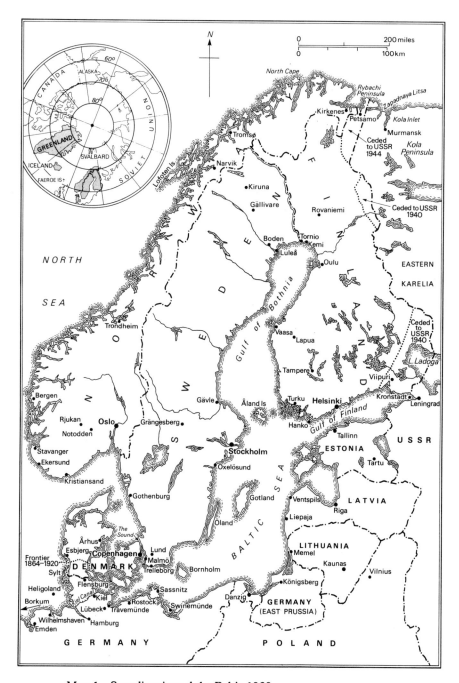

Map 1   Scandinavia and the Baltic 1939

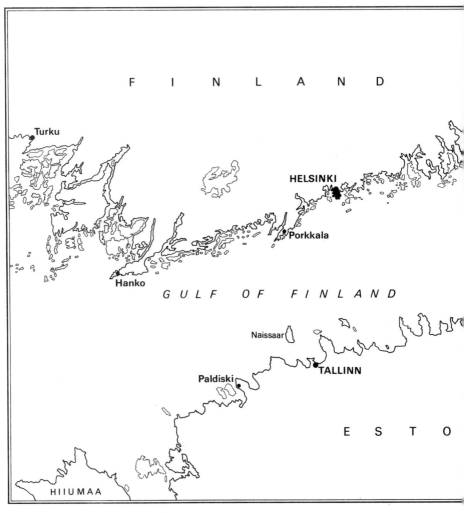

Map 2   The Gulf of Finland

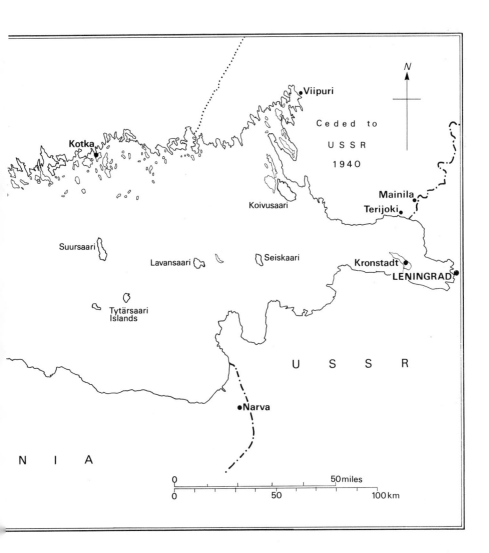

N

•Viipuri

Ceded to

USSR

1940

Kotka

Mainila

Terijoki

Koivusaari

Suursaari

Lavansaari

Seiskaari

Kronstadt

LENINGRAD

Tytärsaari
Islands

U S S R

•Narva

N I A

0   50 miles

0   50   100 km

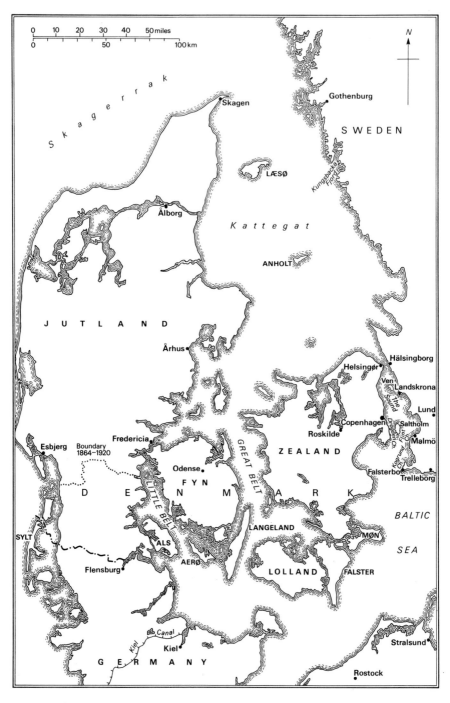

Map 3   Entrances to the Baltic

Introduction

Small states and great powers in the international system

The period bounded by the lapse of Bismarck's reinsurance treaty in 1890 and the German invasion of Denmark and Norway in 1940 was one in which the Nordic countries became enmeshed in international conflict to a degree unprecedented since the early nineteenth century. The progressive erosion of Scandinavian isolation, culminating in the traumatic years of war and occupation between 1939 and 1945 (from which only Sweden was spared), forms one of the main themes of this book. Another is the inability of the Nordic states to fulfil – either individually (apart, again, from Sweden) or collectively – one of the basic functions of any state: the protection of their citizens from external attack. There is another side to the story. Of the minor states of Europe, the Nordic countries were – and remain – among the most fortunate. They have enjoyed a large measure of internal stability and have had few rivalries among themselves. Rapid industrialisation, beginning in the nineteenth century, combined with periods of social democratic rule which were longer and more continuous than anywhere else in Europe, enabled the Nordic countries to construct societies which were, by the late twentieth century, among the most egalitarian and most prosperous in the world. Yet their very success made the Nordic countries vulnerable to external pressures.

The first half of the twentieth century was a period dominated by war and the anticipation of war. It was also a period of unprecedented ideological confrontation and economic competition among the European great powers. With their increasing integration in the world economy, Nordic economies became more dependent on fluctuations in the business cycle and more exposed to changes in economic policy on the part of their chief trading partners. As warfare came to require the total mobilisation of societies and economies, so Nordic economic resources became increasingly important to belligerents. Changes in the nature of warfare, especially at sea and in the air, also made Scandinavia less peripheral in strategic terms. The ideological confrontations of the inter-war period challenged traditional Scandinavian values as well as the embryonic Scandinavian 'middle way'.[1] Although the

[1] The term was first used by Marquis Childs in his celebrated study of Swedish social

1

Nordic experience proved less traumatic than that of other 'peripheral' regions of Europe such as the Balkan or Iberian peninsulas,[2] Scandinavia was unable to escape involvement in international conflict, and on the whole became less capable of doing so with the passage of time. Whilst Denmark, Norway and Sweden managed to remain neutral during the First World War, only Sweden managed to stay out of the Second World War. Or, to amplify the last point in a way that further accentuates the differing fortunes of the individual Nordic states, Norway and Denmark were occupied by Germany in 1940 and Sweden was not; Finland fought two wars against the Soviet Union between 1939 and 1944 and Sweden fought none at all. Yet the process was not wholly irreversible. In the Cold War era, despite the fact that all the Nordic states except Sweden had formal ties with one or other of the superpower blocs, the Nordic region again achieved a certain remoteness from international confrontation.

The subject matter of this book is wide ranging, and both the primary sources and secondary literature on the subject are now very extensive. Perhaps for this reason, and also perhaps because Nordic historians have been reluctant to generalise about the history of the Nordic countries as a whole,[3] there have been few large-scale surveys of the kind that is attempted here, though there have been a number of shorter ones.[4] For examples of books dealing primarily with the international position of all four Nordic states it was necessary until recently to go back to the period immediately following the Second World War. It was no coincidence that the first years of the Cold War should have seen the publication of such works as Rowland Kenney's *The Northern Tangle* (1946), *Scandinavia Between East and West*, edited by Henning Friis (1950), the survey of *The Scandinavian States and Finland* produced by the Royal Institute of International Affairs in 1951, or Nils Ørvik's *The Decline of Neutrality 1914–1941* (1953).[5] As G. M. Gathorne-Hardy wrote in the preface to the RIIA volume, 'it is obvious that the Scandinavian peninsula no longer occupies a remote grand-stand in which its inhabitants can be passive and neutral spectators of any future conflict, but

---

democracy, *Sweden: The Middle Way* (New Haven, Conn., 1936; revised and enlarged edn, 1938).

[2] This comparison is developed in Krister Wahlbäck, 'The Nordic Region in Twentieth-Century European Politics', in Bengt Sundelius (ed.), *Foreign Policies of Northern Europe* (Boulder, Colo., 1982), pp. 9–32.

[3] 'It is one of the mysteries of European historiography that serious comparative studies in Scandinavian history are so rare, at all events for epochs later than the Middle Ages': K.-G. Hildebrand, 'Economic Policy in Scandinavia During the Inter-War Period', *Scandinavian Economic History Review* 23 (1975), pp. 99–115 (p. 100).

[4] E.g. Wahlbäck, 'Nordic Region'; Henrik S. Nissen, 'The Nordic Societies', in Nissen (ed.), *Scandinavia During the Second World War* (Minneapolis, 1983), pp. 3–52.

[5] Even though it takes the form of a survey of Scandinavian institutions, the Friis volume is suffused with Cold War assumptions and fears. Ørvik's book has a wider geographical scope than the others, covering the United States as well as other non-Scandinavian neutrals, and is also less focused on Cold War concerns.

constitutes more than 1,200 miles of the front line dividing the forces of East and West'.[6]

A similar revival of interest appears to have taken place in the 1990s. The present decade has seen the publication of David Kirby's two-volume history of the *Baltic World* between 1492 and 1993,[7] as well as the two-volume collective work *In Quest of Trade and Security: The Baltic in Power Politics, 1500–1990*, edited by Göran Rystad, Klaus-Richard Böhme and Wilhelm Carlgren.[8] Both of these studies, like my own, were conceived before the end of the Cold War. All, however, have been written in the knowledge of the radical transformation of Europe that has resulted from the destruction of Soviet power. In the Baltic region the changes have been momentous. They include the recovery of independence by the three Baltic states, Estonia, Latvia and Lithuania; the end of Finland's forty-year 'special relationship' with the Soviet Union; and, with the entry of both Finland and Sweden into the European Union, the end of a tradition of Swedish neutrality dating back to the Napoleonic era. As Scandinavia and the Baltic attract a degree of attention greater even than that of the early post-war period, historians are in a position to offer explanations for the changes that have occurred.

This book therefore asks a number of questions about the Nordic experience in the twentieth century. How did Scandinavia succeed in preserving a certain measure of detachment from international confrontation despite its increasing economic, political and strategic integration in the international system? How, in other words, did Nordic societies as a whole manage to survive, and even prosper, in a period which was dominated by great-power conflict? Why did it nevertheless become more difficult for them to do so? Why, in particular, did the experiences of the individual Nordic states differ so widely and indeed become more divergent over time?

The answers to these questions are in part external to Scandinavia. They have to do with changes in the nature of warfare and in the international economy, as well as with the rivalries of the European great powers before and during the two world wars. The book therefore examines the changing place of Scandinavia in the political, economic and strategic calculations of policy makers in Britain, Germany and Russia – the powers to which Scandinavia was of most direct concern. It also focuses, however, on the Nordic states themselves. Their differing capacities to resist external pressures were based in part on elementary facts of geography and resource endowment. But they also

---

[6] RIIA, *The Scandinavian States and Finland: A Political and Economic Survey* (London, 1951), p. vii.

[7] David Kirby, *Northern Europe in the Early Modern Period: The Baltic World 1492–1772* (London, 1990); Kirby, *The Baltic World 1772–1993: Europe's Northern Periphery in an Age of Change* (London, 1995).

[8] Göran Rystad, Klaus-Richard Böhme and Wilhelm M. Carlgren (eds.), *In Quest of Trade and Security: The Baltic in Power Politics 1500–1990*, vol. I, *1500–1890* (Lund, 1994); vol. II, *1890–1990* (Lund, 1995).

depended on the skill with which each Nordic state managed its own external affairs: the extent, in other words, to which the leaders of each state were able to formulate and conduct effective foreign and security policies.

The distinction between the two perspectives – great-power and small-power – is vital. Scandinavia was, for long periods, a region of only marginal interest to the great powers. From this perspective, the main task is to explain why the region moved closer to the forefront of attention at times of international crisis and war. From the Nordic perspective, however, relations with the great powers were a matter of paramount concern, often indeed of life and death. If neither world war could have been won in Scandinavia (notwithstanding the dreams of some strategists, both amateur and professional), war could have spelt the end of an independent existence for one or more of the Nordic states. The experiences of Norway, Denmark and Finland during the Second World War were traumatic enough; and the fate of Estonia, Latvia and Lithuania between 1940 and 1991 was a sombre reminder of what could happen to small states in northern Europe.

Constraints and opportunities in Nordic policy making

This approach assumes that the Nordic states were not merely passive elements in the international system. It shares the view expressed by Michael Handel in his study of *Weak States in the International System* that, 'while the weak states are frequently more vulnerable than the great powers, they are not helpless'.[9] Clearly geography and resources exerted a powerful influence over the kinds of policy they were able to pursue. Given the prevailing state of military technology in the first half of the twentieth century, key points in the strategic geography of northern Europe such as the Baltic Straits, the Åland Islands and the Gulf of Finland were likely to be of concern to one or more of the great powers. In a long war, the supply of agricultural produce from Denmark or iron ore from Sweden might be of vital importance to the economic survival of one or other of the belligerents. But the Nordic states concerned had some influence over whether these matters of great-power interest constituted assets or liabilities. That British and German anxiety about the position of Denmark at the entrance to the Baltic did not result in a violation of Danish neutrality by either power during the First World War may have been due in part to skilful Danish diplomacy. The refusal of Finnish diplomacy to acknowledge Soviet anxiety about the security of Leningrad helped to precipitate the Soviet invasion of Finland in November 1939. Denmark's ability to keep both Britain and Germany supplied with agricultural produce helped to preserve Danish neutrality between 1914 and 1918, but carried much less weight with the belligerents at the beginning of the Second World War, and did nothing to deter Germany from invading the country in April 1940. Germany's

[9] Michael Handel, *Weak States in the International System* (London, 1981), p. 257.

Table 1 *Exports and imports as a percentage of the total output (GNP) of the Nordic countries*

	Denmark			Finland	
	Exports	Imports		Exports	Imports
1865	16	20.2	1865	11.7	18.6
1900	21.3	31.5	1900	20.1	27.8
1913	27.7	33.8	1913	25.1	30.9
1925	29.1	31.5	1925	25.7	25.4
1938	20.4	21.6	1938	21.8	22.0
1955	25.4	28.2	1955	16.2	16.2
1969	22.7	28.6	1969	20.2	20.7

	Norway			Sweden	
	Exports*	Imports		Exports	Imports
1865	25.5	27.1	1865	13.6	13.2
1900	29.6	34.9	1900	17.4	23.4
1914	35.2	36.2	1913	20.8	21.6
1925	30.1	30.4	1925	16.0	17.0
1939	28.2	27.8	1938	15.7	17.7
1955	38.4	41.2	1955	17.5	20.3
1969	37.9	35.8	1969	19.2	19.9

Sources and note: B. R. Mitchell, *International Historical Statistics: Europe 1750–1988* (New York, 1992), tables E1, J1; T. Bergh, T. J. Hanisch, E. Lange and H. Ø. Pharo, *Growth and Development: The Norwegian Experience 1830–1980* (Oslo, 1981), table 1, p. 162.
* Includes shipping services.

dependence on Swedish iron ore was a powerful bargaining counter for Sweden in its relations with the belligerents, but came close to being a liability when it tempted Britain and France into contemplating an invasion of Scandinavia early in 1940.

A further constraint was imposed by the openness of the Nordic economies. Klaus Knorr suggests that 'the main bases of national economic power consist of the volume and structure of a state's foreign economic transactions'.[10] A country is susceptible to external economic pressure (a) if its foreign trade is large relative to its gross national product; (b) if it exports a relatively limited range of products of which it does not enjoy a monopoly control; and (c) if its foreign trade is conducted with only a small number of trading partners.[11] By these criteria the Nordic countries have always been vulnerable.

Table 1 shows that the Nordic countries have been heavily dependent on foreign trade throughout the modern period, with exports and imports regularly constituting between 20 and as much as 40 per cent of GNP.

[10] Klaus Knorr, *The Power of Nations: The Political Economy of International Relations* (New York, 1975), p. 84.
[11] Ibid., pp. 84–93.

Table 2 Foreign trade of the Nordic countries by commodity groups (%)

Denmark

	1874	1880–4	1890–4	1900–4	1910–14	1921–5	1936–9	1946–9	1955–8	1967–70
Agricultural products	82.0	79.0	84.0	89.0	87.0	81.0	72.0	61.0	54.0	23.0
Industrial products	13.0	13.0	7.0	5.0	8.0	16.0	23.0	31.0	42.0	70.0
Other goods	5.0	8.0	9.0	6.0	5.0	3.0	5.0	8.0	4.0	7.0

Finland

	1870–9	1880–9	1890–9	1900–9	1910–14	1923–5	1935–7
Timber products	43.8	44.7	46.1	55.0	51.7	58.0	44.0
Paper & pulp	3.3	8.0	9.3	13.7	19.2	28.0	40.0
Agricultural products	22.9	23.1	24.3	17.6	17.0	9.0	7.0
Other goods	30.0	24.2	20.3	13.7	12.1	5.0	9.0

	1951–5	1966–70
Agriculture	2.7	4.8
Forestry	11.2	1.0
Timber industry	30.0	16.8
Paper industry	42.8	43.5
Metals & engineering	10.4	22.2
Other industry	2.9	11.7
Total industry	86.1	94.2

Norway

	1865	1875	1885	1895	1905	1925	1935	1946	1960	1970
Fishing & whaling products	21.8	20.1	16.4	17.4	15.6	13.8	9.9	11.2	6.7	7.0
Timber, pulp & paper products	23.6	19.0	19.7	20.4	21.9	23.6	13.8	13.2	9.8	7.7
Mining, metals & chemical products	2.9	3.3	3.2	2.4	3.4	12.8	17.2	10.5	17.5	16.5
Other industrial products	5.3	6.7	9.2	11.0	9.7	13.5	10.6	9.0	8.6	4.7
Shipping services	41.4	45.2	43.3	38.9	32.5	29.0	38.2	47.0	44.0	41.6
Other industrial products	5.0	5.7	8.2	9.9	16.9	7.3	10.3	9.1	13.4	22.5

Sweden	1881-5	1891-5	1901-5	1911-13	1924-5	1934-8	1947-50	1959-62	1967-70
Timber products	40.4	37.1	38.5	26.1	22.0	13.2	10.0	8.4	7.7
Iron & steel	16.2	9.5	10.2	9.3	5.3	7.2	5.4	7.8	8.9
Grain	11.7	4.7	0.4	0.3	—	—	—	—	—
Butter	6.3	12.0	8.9	6.0	—	—	—	—	—
Paper & pulp	4.6	8.3	12.9	17.6	27.2	28.3	33.3	23.0	15.8
Iron ore	—	0.4	5.0	8.0	7.9	9.5	7.0	7.6	4.0
Engineering products	2.6	3.1	6.7	10.5	14.3	21.3	27.0	37.5	42.7
Others	18.2	24.9	17.4	22.2	23.3	20.5	17.3	15.7	20.9

Sources: Based on Lennart Jörberg, 'The Nordic Countries 1850–1914', in Carlo M. Cipolla (ed.), *The Fontana Economic History of Europe*, vol. IV, part 2 (London, 1973), pp. 375–485, tables 13, 18, 22, 29; Lennart Jörberg and Olle Krantz, 'Scandinavia 1914–1970', in Cipolla (ed.), *The Fontana Economic History of Europe*, vol. VI, part 2 (London, 1976), pp. 377–459, table 12.

Although all four achieved a significant increase in self-sufficiency during the 1930s, the Second World War was followed by their full re-integration into the world economy, demonstrated most strikingly in the case of Norway.

Table 2 shows that despite the success of Scandinavian industrialisation, the Nordic economies before the Second World War were still relatively undiversified. Denmark's dependence on the export of agricultural produce and Finland's upon the export of timber products, paper and pulp are particularly striking. Their rapid transformation into fully industrialised economies was a phenomenon of the post-war period. The Norwegian and Swedish economies were more diversified; but Norway remained heavily reliant on shipping, while Swedish exports of timber, paper and pulp still outweighed exports of engineering products by a considerable margin. The Nordic countries therefore remained dependent on the export of a narrow range of primary or semi-finished products for which there were often wide fluctuations of demand and price.

Table 3 shows that until the Second World War the foreign trade of the Nordic countries was dominated by a small number of major trading partners: above all, Great Britain and Germany, with Germany as the chief source of imports and Britain as the chief export market. It also shows that this commercial duopoly was noticeably strengthened in the inter-war period, with the virtual elimination of Russia as a trading partner, the relative decline of intra-Scandinavian trade and, especially in the 1930s, the marginalisation of the United States. The limited range of export markets, together with the fact that demand for many Scandinavian export products was relatively inelastic, greatly restricted the Nordic countries' freedom of manoeuvre. The growth of self-sufficiency indicated by table 1 did little, before the Second World War, to reduce their dependence on Great Britain and Germany.

Yet there is only a partial correlation between the indicators identified by Knorr and the actual degree of vulnerability experienced by the Nordic countries. As table 1 shows, their economies have on the whole become more open, and thus ostensibly more exposed to pressure, since the Second World War. The fact that this position has not been exploited by their trading partners clearly reflects the more settled international environment and liberal international trading regime which have prevailed throughout the post-war period, as well as the strength derived by the Nordic countries from the increased diversification of their economies. Conversely, they were much more vulnerable to exploitation between the wars, a period in which the 'hegemonic stability' of the pre-war period had broken down and in which economic crisis and depression were endemic, while at the same time the Nordic economies had not yet attained as large a measure of diversity.[12]

Was there any correlation between economic dependence and political

[12] For a discussion of the theory of hegemonic stability, see Arthur A. Stein, 'The Hegemon's Dilemma: Great Britain, the United States and the International Economic Order', *International Organization* 38 (1984), pp. 355–86.

Table 3 *Foreign trade of the Nordic countries with main trading partners (%)*

| | | | **Denmark** | | |
| | | | **Exports** | | |
	Germany	UK	Norway & Sweden	USA	Others
1874	32.8	39.4	21.7	—	6.1
1900	17.3	59.1	12.7	1.8	9.1
1913	24.8	55.5	7.5	1.1	11.1
1925	20.5	55.5	11.4	0.5	12.0
1938	19.2	54.2	9.6	1.1	15.9
1955	16.8*	33.0	12.2	7.3	30.7

| | | | **Imports** | | |
	Germany	UK	Norway & Sweden	USA	Others
1874	35.6	24.9	15.5	1.7	22.3
1900	29.2	20.5	11.6	14.8	23.9
1913	38.4	15.8	9.4	10.2	26.3
1925	28.0	14.7	7.5	16.2	33.5
1938	24.0	33.8	8.9	7.7	25.7
1955	18.7*	25.6	12.1	7.9	35.7

| | | | **Finland** | | | |
| | | | **Exports** | | | |
	Germany	Russia/Soviet Union	Sweden	UK	USA	Others
1874	6.4	39.4	8.5	25.5	—	20.2
1900	8.7	29.2	3.6	29.7	—	28.7
1913	12.9	28.1	4.2	27.1	—	27.6
1925	13.4	7.7	4.3	37.0	5.3	32.3
1938	14.8	0.3	5.8	33.3	11.7	34.1
1955	9.2*	17.6	1.9	24.2	5.8	41.4

| | | | **Imports** | | | |
	Germany	Russia/Soviet Union	Sweden	UK	USA	Others
1874	26.1	44.4	9.2	14.8	5.6	—
1900	33.3	37.4	4.8	12.6	0.4	11.5
1913	41.0	28.3	5.7	12.3	—	12.7
1925	31.9	1.3	6.5	17.0	14.7	28.6
1938	20.3	0.8	14.2	17.1	9.0	38.7
1955	8.8*	14.4	4.8	19.9	5.2	46.8

(*cont.*)

Table 3(*cont.*)

Norway

Exports

	Denmark	France	Germany	Netherlands	Sweden	UK	USA	Others
1874	6.4	8.8	15.7	6.0	12.4	31.4	—	19.2
1900	4.2	4.7	13.3	6.4	8.7	42.8	1.2	18.8
1913	2.3	3.6	17.0	4.6	6.6	24.9	7.6	33.3
1925	4.4	6.9	10.2	2.7	5.9	28.8	10.6	30.5
1938	4.3	6.6	15.5	2.7	8.8	24.7	7.8	29.7
1955	5.3	4.2	11.2*	3.5	9.1	21.8	9.2	35.7

Imports

	Denmark	France	Germany	Netherlands	Sweden	UK	USA	Others
1874	10.8	4.8	26.3	3.7	7.0	29.6	1.1	16.8
1900	5.5	1.7	27.3	4.8	8.7	29.9	5.5	16.7
1913	5.1	2.2	31.9	3.8	8.3	26.4	7.1	15.2
1925	6.1	2.6	20.3	5.4	6.7	22.6	14.1	22.1
1938	3.5	3.0	18.4	3.3	11.5	16.2	10.0	34.1
1955	3.7	3.5	13.9*	5.3	16.2	20.2	8.6	28.6

Sweden

Exports

	Denmark	France	Germany	Netherlands	Norway	UK	USA	Others
1874	14.2	8.9	6.2	2.3	3.3	56.4	0.9	7.7
1900	12.3	7.7	16.6	7.7	1.8	43.2	—	10.7
1913	8.7	8.1	21.9	2.3	6.6	29.1	4.2	19.1
1925	6.2	6.2	15.1	4.1	4.8	27.0	10.5	26.1
1938	4.9	3.3	18.2	3.7	6.7	24.5	9.0	29.7
1955	5.8	5.2	13.3*	6.2	9.7	19.7	4.9	35.2

Imports

	Denmark	France	Germany	Netherlands	Norway	UK	USA	Others
1874	18.2	3.6	21.2	3.8	5.1	30.6	2.8	14.7
1900	12.0	1.8	35.7	2.1	4.2	33.7	1.7	8.8
1913	6.4	4.1	34.2	2.5	3.1	24.4	9.1	16.2
1925	8.6	3.4	26.1	4.1	3.4	20.1	15.1	19.2
1938	6.0	3.0	24.0	5.5	3.1	18.3	16.3	23.9
1955	3.6	4.9	21.9*	7.1	3.2	13.7	9.8	35.8

Source and note: Based on B. R. Mitchell, *International Historical Statistics: Europe 1750–1988* (New York, 1992), table E2.
* Indicates trade with West Germany.

dependence? 'It goes without saying', wrote the liberal German economist Wilhelm Röpke in 1942, 'that the strong mutual dependence of countries bound by bilateral trading may easily develop into a one-sided dependence, which starts by being economic and ends as political.'[13] Again the evidence is ambiguous. The Nordic experience tends to confirm Handel's assertion that the great powers 'have not always been able to translate their economic strength into political gains. When they have tried to use economic pressure to coerce weak states to accept their political demands, they have frequently failed.'[14] During the First World War, economic pressure of the most extreme kind was employed by the belligerents in order to compel the Scandinavian states to comply with their demands. Yet the latter had some success (Denmark most, Norway least) in neutralising these countervailing pressures. Until 1917 they were also able to 'borrow' strength from a much more powerful neutral, the United States. In the inter-war period Denmark is the clearest example of a country whose economic vulnerability made it increasingly deferential to the demands of a major trading partner. However, it deferred less to Great Britain, the country which bought most from Denmark, than to Germany. This was partly, of course, because Germany was a close and potentially menacing neighbour. It was also a result of German commercial policy. Although Germany bought less than Britain, its purchases were targeted towards products which were politically sensitive and could thus be used as a means of pressure on the Danish government. But the other three Nordic countries were not intimidated to the same degree. Indeed by the late 1930s Sweden, the strongest Nordic economy, was displaying a remarkable degree of confidence and self-assurance, especially towards Great Britain.

Nordic policy makers thus had some control over their own destinies. But the relationship between the various influences – geography, resources, the international environment and diplomatic skill – remains a highly complex one. Swedish diplomacy before and during the Second World War, for example, was frequently more adroit than that of Denmark and Norway, but Sweden was *able* to be more skilful because it enjoyed a more sheltered strategic position and because iron ore proved more of an asset than a liability in Sweden's relations with the belligerents. It would be hard to say whether the Swedes made their own luck, or whether their luck enabled them to be skilful. Erik Scavenius was a more effective Danish foreign minister during the First World War than Peter Munch at the beginning of the Second, but Denmark's military capacity was smaller (both relatively and absolutely) in 1939 than it had been in 1914, and Scavenius had to deal with the kaiser's Germany, Munch with Hitler's.

[13] Wilhelm Röpke, *International Economic Disintegration* (London, 1942), p. 40.
[14] Handel, *Weak States*, p. 259. For further discussion of this point, see T. Bergh, T. J. Hanisch, E. Lange and H. Ø. Pharo, *Growth and Development: The Norwegian Experience 1830–1980* (Oslo, 1981), pp. 154–7.

There is a further sense in which Nordic policy makers were unable to operate in a vacuum. They were products of a specific social, political, economic and cultural order within their own countries. Michael Handel plays down the domestic determinants of foreign policy in weak states. 'The international system', he writes, 'leaves them less room for choice in the decision-making process. Their smaller margin of error and hence greater preoccupation with survival makes the essential interests of weak states less ambiguous.' In addition, 'because of the reduced scale of complexity of bureaucratic and decision-making structures', there is less scope for 'bureaucratic politics' than in larger states.[15] However, Nikolaj Petersen, in an important study of Danish security policy before 1914, makes greater allowance for issues of perception, judgement or choice on the part of policy makers. Much, he suggests, will depend on their perceptions of what he terms their country's influence capability and stress sensitivity 'and the degree to which they can get these perceptions accepted in society at large'.[16] If they judge the situation wrongly, they will be put right by the external environment (in the most extreme circumstances, by being invaded) and be exposed to criticism from within the country for not safeguarding the national interest.[17]

There can be little doubt that the domestic circumstances of small states do influence their capacity to conduct effective external policies. They determine the political complexion of governments, the recruitment policies of bureaucracies and the political constituencies from which governments derive their support. In the case of Scandinavia in the first half of the twentieth century, the influence of domestic conditions on foreign policy was in some respects more negative than positive. These were decades in which the Nordic peoples were embarking on a great enterprise: the construction of modern, democratic societies in some of Europe's harshest geographical and climatic conditions. The qualities which made Scandinavians successful in this effort were not necessarily those which made them effective managers of their external affairs. The judgement of a British diplomat on Norwegian reactions to the signature of the Versailles treaty in 1919 was no doubt unduly negative, but nevertheless contained an element of truth:

The questions which really interest the average Norwegian and fill the columns of the daily press are of a more domestic nature and rarely soar above the level of a commercial or socialistic parochialism, absorption in which, in preference to a desire to make world-history, is commonly conceded to be the criterion of a nation's happiness.[18]

---

[15] Handel, *Weak States*, p. 3.

[16] Nikolaj Petersen, 'International Power and Foreign Policy Behavior: The Formulation of Danish Security Policy in the 1870–1914 Period', in Kjell Goldmann and Gunnar Sjöstedt (eds.), *Power, Capabilities, Interdependence: Problems in the Study of International Influence* (London and Beverly Hills, 1979), pp. 235–69 (p. 243).

[17] Compare the analysis in Carsten Holbraad, *Danish Neutrality: A Study in the Foreign Policy of a Small State* (Oxford, 1991), ch. 2.

[18] Esmond Ovey (British chargé d'affaires, Kristiania) to FO, 30 June 1919, *DBFP*, 1, III, pp. 2–4.

Parochialism, introspection, nationalism and even xenophobia were all symptoms of inward-looking societies with little knowledge of the outside world. And where knowledge existed, it was often expressed in legalistic or moralistic terms. Hence the prominence, for example, of Scandinavian international lawyers in the international peace movements of the nineteenth and twentieth centuries.

The implications for Scandinavia's external relations of the smallness and newness of Nordic societies were far-reaching. In Denmark and Sweden, the day-to-day conduct of foreign and security policies tended, well into the twentieth century, to remain the preserve of small, traditional elites. This brought advantages of continuity and experience but carried with it the danger that at a time of rapid social and political change, foreign policy might be used to fight domestic battles (for example the linkage between constitutional change, defence policy and pro-Germanism in Sweden before and during the First World War). It led to mistrust between conservative military men and democratic politicians, as well as between traditional diplomats and academic lawyers who intruded into their preserve. Of the noted jurist Hjalmar Hammarskjöld, prime minister of Sweden between 1914 and 1917, Count Wrangel, Sweden's minister in London during the First World War, scathingly remarked: 'The Hammarskjöld way of conducting policy might perhaps suit a peasant republic like that of the Boers, but is not appropriate to a diplomacy that counts the names of Axel Oxenstierna and Hugo Grotius among its practitioners.'[19] Such figures were still more prominent in Norway and Finland (independent from 1905 and 1917 respectively), where foreign services had to be improvised at short notice.

Small societies may be more vulnerable than larger ones to penetration from outside. Radicals of both the extreme left and the extreme right looked to larger states for protection and patronage: the Norwegian Labour Party in the early 1920s and the Finnish Communist Party (illegal throughout the inter-war period) to Moscow; Quisling and his associates to Berlin. Quisling was, among other things, a highly intelligent individual who felt himself to be too big for Norwegian society. The resentment of such figures may also be a source of vulnerability (witness also the careers of Scandinavian spies for the Soviet Union in the post-war era). Conspiratorial activity does not usually succeed in destabilising large states, but it may help to topple small ones, as Quisling's dealings with Nazi Germany did in 1939–40.

However, smallness can also be an asset. In societies relatively free from bureaucracy (to take up the point noted by Handel), and in capital cities where, at a certain level, almost everyone knew everyone else (something which is still true of the Nordic capitals today), governments could draw on ability and experience wherever it might be found. The knowledge of

[19] Note of February 1917, quoted in Wilhelm M. Carlgren, *Ministären Hammarskjöld. Tillkomst, söndring, fall. Studier i svensk politik 1914–1917* (Stockholm, 1967), p. 136.

economists, historians, international lawyers and political scientists, and the expertise and foreign connections of businessmen (like successive generations of the Wallenberg family in Sweden), could be placed at the service of the state. It was also possible to use the growing influence of parliaments and of democratic political parties to build a domestic consensus in support of the government's policies.

Externally, the task of Nordic statesmanship was to limit the consequences of dependence while maximising the benefits of modernisation. Internally, the task was to educate electorates in the realities of power. If policy makers found it difficult to construct a domestic consensus for policies designed to enhance the security of their countries – and often indeed shared the general dislike of spending money on armaments – the relative cohesion of Nordic societies nevertheless helped them to remain detached from international entanglements. Only Finland, with its deep social and political divisions after 1917, fell prey to irredentism and, if not adventurism, then certainly fatalism in its relations with the Soviet Union.

Here is another way in which domestic conditions and foreign policy interact. For Handel, the key variable in the external policy of small states is their ability to mobilise the strength of others: 'The diplomatic art of the weak states is to obtain, commit and manipulate, as far as possible, the power of other, more powerful states in their own interests . . . The most important condition for the security of the weak states, therefore, is their ability to appeal to other states for help and support.'[20] On the whole, however, this has not been typical of the Scandinavian experience. The Nordic states have been notable for their refusal either to seek outside support or to support one another. Nordic cooperation in matters of foreign and security policy has never progressed very far, and the occasions when external powers have come to their aid, as in the case of Germany in Finland in 1918, or Britain and France in Norway in 1940, have not usually been happy ones.

Robert L. Rothstein, in his study of *Alliances and Small States*, is closer to the mark when he writes that, within limits, a small power could 'affect its chances of survival, primarily by altering the expectations which the Great Powers held about its position and its likely response to external pressures'. It could do so by following 'a cautious and nonprovocative policy'; by appearing 'to represent a coherent national state without dissident minorities or irredentist neighbours'; and by maintaining sufficient military strength to 'turn itself into an unattractive target'. 'In sum, it could hope to improve its chances by appearing to be a substantially stronger and more unified state.' It is possible, therefore, for even a weak state to enhance its security not merely by 'borrowing' the military strength of others or relying on other 'institutions, processes or developments', but by standing on its own.[21] This is what Sweden has done

---

[20] Handel, *Weak States*, pp. 257–8.
[21] Robert L. Rothstein, *Alliances and Small States* (New York and London, 1968), pp. 194–5.

successfully for most of the twentieth century.[22] For Denmark and Norway the lesson of the Second World War was that they could not stand entirely alone, and in 1949 both states entered into security arrangements with the Western powers. Finland had much less choice when it signed a treaty of friendship and mutual cooperation with the Soviet Union in 1948, but there was nevertheless a realisation that Finnish security depended on a voluntary acknowledgement of the security interests of its powerful neighbour. And the commitments of Denmark and Norway to NATO, and of Finland to the Soviet Union, remained less far-reaching than those of the superpowers' other security partners. In each case, moreover, the experience of war or occupation helped to enhance rather than weaken national solidarity.

In the first half of the twentieth century, the outside world was encroaching upon Scandinavia to an unprecedented degree and making unprecedented demands on Nordic statesmanship. Rothstein suggests that the kinds of pressure exerted on small states vary according to the prevailing international system. In a balance-of-power situation (of the kind that prevailed for much of the nineteenth century), small states have little influence but are also largely left to their own devices.[23] A system in which international tension is high and the great powers are competing for influence – as in the periods leading up to the two world wars – is the one, according to Rothstein, in which the small state finds itself most ardently courted. Even the small amount of power which it represents may amount to a significant accretion of strength to one or other of the great powers, or at least be something worth denying to its rivals. Petersen has applied Rothstein's thesis to the position of Denmark immediately before the First World War;[24] it could also be applied to that of Finland at the beginning of the Second. Ostensibly, a display of heightened interest on the part of a great power enhances a smaller state's influence. In fact it merely deprives that state of 'the immunity of irrelevance'.[25] 'The belief that the increased influence of various Small Powers means increased security is essentially illusory and ephemeral . . . since it reflects the development of a situation which may be disastrous: an imminent or apparently imminent general war.'[26]

As in any small state, therefore, one of the most difficult tasks facing Nordic policy makers was to assess the significance of the messages conveyed by larger states. Great-power interest might be flattering but it might also be dangerous. If indifference was the norm, Scandinavians might underestimate the importance of apparently low-level or routine exchanges. The problem derives from what Sven Holtsmark has termed the 'asymmetry of expectations' which characterises the relationship between large and small states. Small states assign primary importance to such a relationship and will discuss even minor

---

[22] Though Swedish neutrality was 'Westward-leaning' throughout the Cold War period.
[23] Rothstein, *Alliances and Small States*, pp. 195–202.
[24] Petersen, 'Danish Security Policy', pp. 246–9.
[25] Rothstein, *Alliances and Small States*, p. 212.   [26] Ibid., p. 191.

matters pertaining to it at the highest political level. But for a great power it is a secondary relationship handled largely 'by the foreign policy bureaucracy, which will be allowed to play a relatively independent role and even to decide matters of primary importance to small powers'. Small states, instinctively expecting great powers to treat the relationship as seriously as they do themselves, tend to ignore 'the signals and decisions of the bureaucracy and signals from the lower political level, waiting in vain for clear-cut top-level statements'.[27]

The great powers and Scandinavia

This leads to a more detailed consideration of great-power policies towards the Nordic states. It was suggested earlier that the leaders of Britain, Germany and Russia tended to show interest in Scandinavia only at times of acute international crisis – in other words immediately before, during and after the two world wars. But Holtsmark's observations suggest that we also need to take account of the periods when Scandinavia was *not* at the forefront of attention: in other words, to devote attention to exchanges which were, from a great-power perspective, conducted at a relatively low level during the long periods which were largely free from dramatic political or military incident. We must also examine the interactions of those responsible for the conduct of relations between the Nordic states and their larger neighbours: the 'groups of decision-makers who conduct the day-to-day transactions with other politically constituted groups of decision-makers in other states'.[28] In Scandinavia, these were people who were close to the top of small and relatively informal policy-making establishments. Their opposite numbers in Britain, Germany or Russia were usually much more junior members of a more hierarchical 'foreign policy-making élite'.[29] As Holtsmark suggests, matters of high policy for one side were matters of low policy for the other. William Wallace, discussing the making of foreign policy in Britain, elaborates the point about low policy in a way which can be applied with equal validity to the other great powers:

Low policy issues are those in which few political values and few domestic interests are seen to be at stake: detailed and routine transactions between friendly governments, regular conversations with distant countries, technical agreements on matters to which governments attach little political significance and so on. Policy here is close to

---

[27] Sven G. Holtsmark, *Enemy Springboard or Benevolent Buffer? Soviet Attitudes to Nordic Cooperation 1920–1955* (Oslo, 1992), pp. 74–5. Hence, for example, the failure of the Finnish government to attach sufficient weight to the overtures for a Soviet–Finnish defence arrangement initiated by Boris Yartsev in April 1938. Ostensibly only a second secretary at the Soviet legation, Yartsev was in fact in direct communication with the Politburo, a connection of which even the Soviet Foreign Ministry was apparently unaware.

[28] Donald Cameron Watt, 'The Study of International History: Language and Reality', in Commission of History of International Relations, Cahier No. 1, *Problems and Discussions on the History of International Relations* (Madrid, 1990), pp. 20–1 (p. 21).

[29] Donald Cameron Watt, *Personalities and Policies* (London, 1965), pp. 1–15.

administration, although decisions are taken – within the assumptions laid down within the wider frameworks of sectoral and of high policy issues – which may be significant for small and uninfluential groups of British citizens, or for small and uninfluential foreign governments or foreign interests.[30]

It is important for our purposes to try to establish how decisions which might have been of vital interest to 'small and uninfluential foreign governments' were arrived at. This requires taking a closer look at the attitudes and actions of the officials concerned. These are the people to whom shorthand terms such as 'Britain', 'Germany' or 'Russia' usually refer. They pursued what they conceived to be the interests of their respective states in the light of a set of assumptions about the nature of those interests. Such assumptions were a compound of historical precedents and contemporary realities, of principles, prejudices and common sense, even of a kind of departmental folk-wisdom. They thus ranged, in the case of the British Foreign Office, from views on major policy issues such as the need to maintain a balance of power in Europe or to avoid undertaking military commitments on the Continent, to the presumption that Norwegians were 'legalistic', Swedes 'militaristic' or 'slow-witted' and so on. Without adding up to anything so precise as a 'policy' towards Scandinavia, such views inevitably coloured routine diplomatic exchanges in times of low international tension. In times of high tension, when politicians suddenly discovered an interest in Scandinavia and de-manded advice from their professional advisers, they acquired much greater significance.

Perhaps the most striking feature of relations between the Nordic countries and two of the powers concerned (Britain and Germany) though not with the third (Russia) is that they were largely economic in character. The scrutiny and management of commercial and financial transactions probably constituted by far the largest day-to-day task of the foreign policy bureau-cracies of Britain, Germany and the Nordic countries. It is not surprising that historians have attempted to relate such economic exchanges to the broader foreign policy and strategic goals of such countries as Britain and Germany, as well as to assess their importance for their political relations with Scandinavia, particularly during the era of economic depression and recovery in the 1930s. During this decade, both Britain and Germany intensified their economic relations with a number of weaker trading partners, using a variety of means to compel them to buy more British or German goods. In a period of rising international tension, such pressures frequently acquired political or strategic connotations. Nazi Germany's relations with the agrarian states of central and south-eastern Europe have been frequently discussed in this connection.

Scandinavia is in some ways a more interesting example since here the economic strengths of Britain and Germany were more evenly matched.

[30] William Wallace, *The Foreign Policy Process in Britain* (London, 1976), p. 12.

Albert O. Hirschman's *National Power and the Structure of Foreign Trade* of 1945 offered an analysis of the way in which Nazi Germany exploited its importance as a market for agricultural and raw material exports both to strengthen its strategic position in wartime and to enhance its political influence over the Danubian and Balkan states. In Scandinavia, by contrast, there prevailed what Hirschman termed an 'Anglo-German duopoly', and German influence was diminished by 'the presence of Great Britain as a big alternative market'.[31] Hirschman's analysis has been modified by the work of Harm Schröter, who shows that foreign trade alone is an insufficient indicator of the relative economic strengths of Germany and Great Britain. By examining cartel relationships in such major industries as coal, chemicals, iron and steel and the electrical industry (frequently invisible to those who rely mainly on the archives of government departments), Schröter provides a much more accurate picture of the extent of German penetration of Scandinavian economic life between the wars.[32] Sven Nordlund's study of foreign investment in Sweden reinforces this impression over a longer time-span, from the 1890s to 1945.[33]

The effect of such studies reinforces the suggestion made earlier that the scope for the political manipulation of economic relationships was more limited than governments sometimes believed. On the other hand, governments could derive much advantage from the routine mechanisms of bilateral trade, provided these were managed with sufficient skill. In the 1930s, for example, Germany employed a mixture of inducements and compulsion, through the exchange clearing system and other devices, to bind the economies of its smaller trading partners to a peacetime relationship which was readily adaptable to wartime conditions. Economic self-interest and fear proved a highly effective combination, one which Great Britain, Germany's chief rival, was unable to emulate.

We must reiterate, however, that momentous though their consequences might be for the Nordic countries, such policies were usually conducted with only a fraction of the attention and energy devoted to areas of more immediate concern. There was, and remains, a fundamental disparity of perception between large and small powers. Small states hanker after the world as it ought to be; great powers deal with the world as it is. This naturally leads the small states to favour an international regime which will protect their interests and enhance their prestige: hence the traditional Scandinavian support for international organisations and the rule of law. Yet this does not imply any monopoly of virtue on their part. President Paasikivi of Finland, a man who

[31] Albert O. Hirschman, *National Power and the Structure of Foreign Trade* (Berkeley and Los Angeles, 1945), pp. 110, 113.

[32] Harm Schröter, *Aussenpolitik und Wirtschaftsinteresse. Skandinavien im aussenwirtschaftlichen Kalkül Deutschlands und Grossbritanniens 1918–1939* (Frankfurt am Main, Berne and New York, 1983).

[33] Sven Nordlund, *Upptäckten av Sverige. Utländska direktinvestingar i Sverige 1895–1945* (Umeå, 1989).

knew what he was talking about, remarked that small countries would be imperialist too, if only they were big enough.[34] The virtues of the Nordic countries, such as they are, are a function of their size. Those who live in larger countries may envy but cannot imitate them.

[34] J. K. Paasikivi, *Meine Moskauer Mission 1939–1941* (Hamburg, 1966), p. 243.

1 The end of isolation: Scandinavia and the modern world

Both geographically and in the European imagination, Scandinavia lies on the northern margin of Europe. Havelock Ellis conveyed a characteristic nineteenth-century image when he described Norway as 'a land having, in its most characteristic regions, a year of but one day and night – the summer a perpetual warm sunlit day filled with the aroma of trees and plants, and the rest of the year a night of darkness and horror; a land which is on the extreme northern limit of European civilisation'.[1] The facts of Scandinavian life are harsh by European standards: Scandinavia is 'the western part of Siberia'.[2] It is a Siberia tempered by the Gulf Stream, and this moderating influence has made civilised existence possible in such high latitudes for centuries. Nevertheless, until very recent times the physical environment imposed rigid constraints on human activity in the far north of Europe.

Since the resources which could be exploited by primitive technology were so meagre, much of the population lived on the very edge of subsistence. In the late nineteenth century the Scandinavian countries were still among the poorest in Europe in terms of per capita income. It is only within the last hundred years that the physical constraints have been decisively overcome through the application of modern technology to every field of activity: communications, housing, agriculture and extractive and manufacturing industry.[3] The tyrannies of climate and terrain have to a large extent been overcome, but the habits of isolation and detachment have persisted into the late twentieth century. Scandinavians still feel different from, and sometimes superior to, other Europeans; the rest of Europe still takes notice of Scandinavia only intermittently. Yet the experience of Scandinavia in the twentieth century has been one of growing integration with the outside world, with all the benefits and penalties that this has entailed.

Escape from dependence on the physical environment led to greater dependence on the outside world. Scandinavian prosperity was built on foreign

---

[1] Preface to *The Pillars of Society, and Other Plays by Henrik Ibsen* (London, 1888), pp. vii–xxx (pp. vii–viii).
[2] Bernt Hagtvedt and Erik Rudeng, 'Scandinavia: Achievements, Dilemmas, Challenges', in Stephen R. Graubard (ed.), *Norden – The Passion for Equality* (Oslo, 1986), pp. 283–308 (p. 283).
[3] W. R. Mead, *An Economic Geography of the Scandinavian States and Finland* (London, 1958), pp. 295–8; Mead, *An Historical Geography of Scandinavia* (London, 1981), pp. 5–6.

trade, and as a result the Scandinavian countries became highly vulnerable to fluctuations in the international economy. Culturally, too, they tended to become dependent on those societies from which they borrowed models of technological or social development. The sources of many of their problems were external to the Scandinavian countries and beyond their control. But the characteristic pattern of Scandinavian modernisation – the sudden emergence of modern industrial societies superimposed upon traditional modes of thought and social organisation – complicated the task of responding to external pressures and constructing coherent foreign policies.

This chapter highlights some of the distinctive features of the Scandinavian experience and suggests that, well before 1914, modernisation had given rise to new and disturbing implications for relations between the Scandinavian states and the European great powers: the states with which they traded; from which they derived models of economic, social and political development; and with which they had to reckon in the formulation of their foreign and security policies. In the first instance their security policies had to be adjusted to meet the challenges of modern warfare in a changing constellation of great-power relationships. But there was also the more intangible question of the openness of Scandinavian societies to external influences, and the extent to which this conferred advantages on the great powers from which most such influences derived. Perhaps the most visible expression of Scandinavian concern was the debate over the control of natural resources: here Norwegian hydro-power and Swedish iron ore were the most contentious issues. To an increasing extent, however, the problem was defined in terms of the 'peaceful penetration' of German influence, which many Scandinavians came to perceive as a direct challenge to their political and cultural identity. And of course the rise of German power also had implications for the other great powers of the region. As this chapter will show, there was already a latent Anglo-German rivalry which was to become more explicit in the inter-war period.

Modernisation and dependence

Economic modernisation came late to Scandinavia.[4] When it did, in the second half of the nineteenth century, Scandinavian growth rates were

---

[4] Surveys of Scandinavian industrialisation include: A. Milward and S. B. Saul, *The Economic Development of Continental Europe 1780–1870* (London, 1973), pp. 467–535; L. Jörberg, 'The Nordic Countries 1850–1914', in Carlo M. Cipolla (ed.), *The Fontana Economic History of Europe*, vol. IV, part 2 (London, 1973), pp. 375–485; K.-G. Hildebrand, 'Labour and Capital in the Scandinavian Countries in the Nineteenth and Twentieth Centuries', in P. Mathias and M. M. Postan (eds.), *Cambridge Economic History of Europe*, vol. VII, part 1 (Cambridge, 1978), pp. 590–628. David Kirby, *The Baltic World 1772–1993: Europe's Northern Periphery in an Age of Change* (London, 1995), provides a vivid and comprehensive picture of the social, cultural and political consequences of modernisation in the Scandinavian and Baltic region (though, as its title suggests, it deals less with Norway than with the other Nordic countries).

among the fastest in Europe.[5] By the turn of the century Sweden, Denmark and Norway – followed at some distance by the Grand Duchy of Finland – had pulled away from the other countries of the European periphery, such as those of the Balkan or Iberian peninsulas, and were beginning to achieve levels of development approaching those of the western European 'core'.[6] The Scandinavian countries thus managed to avoid the semi-colonial relationship with the advanced economies of western Europe which was to be the fate of other 'peripheral' regions. If, as has been suggested, peripheralisation was the rule, Scandinavia is an exception which has to be explained.[7]

Scandinavia lacked many of the prerequisites for industrialisation. It lacked technology and capital; above all, if it was to follow the British or continental model of industrialisation, it lacked coal. The symptoms of stagnation and rural overpopulation were evident in the massive emigration of Swedes and Norwegians to North America. On the other hand, Scandinavia was rich in human capital. Though poor in terms of per capita income, the Scandinavian countries on the eve of industrialisation were, to use Lars G. Sandberg's term, 'impoverished sophisticates'.[8] Thanks to Lutheranism, their populations were literate; they were also both mobile and enterprising, as was demonstrated by the success of Scandinavian emigrants to the United States. In Sweden, Norway and Finland, though to a lesser extent in Denmark (always closer to continental influences), the peasantry had traditionally been free from serfdom. There were traditions of political activity (in Sweden the fourth, or peasants', estate of the Riksdag survived until 1866) and of cooperation: whether among Danish farmers, where it was fostered by the folk high schools and the cooperative movements of the nineteenth century; or among the fishing and ship-owning communities of the west coast of Norway. Such traditions compensated in part for the absence of fully developed banking systems and of advanced education in technology and commerce. In Norway and Finland, the two states which did not yet enjoy full political independence,

[5] For preliminary estimates, see Paul Bairoch, 'Europe's Gross National Product: 1800–1975', *Journal of European Economic History* 5 (1976), pp. 273–340. For a revision of Bairoch's figures in the light of improved data, see N. F. R. Crafts, 'Gross National Product in Europe 1870–1910: Some New Estimates', *Explorations in Economic History* 20 (1983), pp. 387–401.

[6] Sidney Pollard, *Peaceful Conquest: The Industrialization of Europe 1760–1970* (Oxford, 1981), pp. 232–3.

[7] Dieter Senghaas, *The European Experience: A Historical Critique of Development Theory* (Leamington Spa, 1985), pp. 16–17; Francis Sejersted, 'A Theory of Economic and Technological Development in Norway in the Nineteenth Century', *Scandinavian Economic History Review* 40 (1992), pp. 40–75.

[8] Lars G. Sandberg, 'The Case of the Impoverished Sophisticate: Human Capital and Swedish Economic Growth Before World War I', *Journal of Economic History* 39 (1979), pp. 225–41.

economic development was consciously linked to the growth of national consciousness by 'modernising elites'.[9]

These assets enabled the Scandinavian countries to benefit from the growth of demand for goods and services from the advanced industrial economies of western and central Europe, while at the same time retaining control over the modernisation process. Scandinavian economic growth was largely export-led. Fish, timber, iron ore, agricultural produce and shipping services were required in increasing quantities, first by Great Britain, later by Germany. Foreign demand encouraged the development of certain key sectors which in turn stimulated the growth of the economy as a whole. By exploiting foreign markets Scandinavian industries were able to escape the confines of their own small populations and achieve substantial economies of scale. Scandinavian entrepreneurs raised capital and invested in new technology – either bought from abroad or developed by Scandinavians – or identified gaps in the market which could be exploited with traditional technology (Norwegian shipping).

By the beginning of the twentieth century Sweden had moved beyond its early dependence on timber exports to become the most developed Scandinavian economy, with a large manufacturing sector which included advanced industries, such as engineering and electrical equipment.[10] The Danish experience was in some ways even more remarkable. Denmark went forward on the basis of 'high-technology agriculture' rather than large-scale manufacturing industry.[11] Economic development was intimately linked to national regeneration. After 1870 Danish agriculture underwent a complete reorientation and reorganisation in response to the collapse of demand for traditional exports – grain and cattle – together with the moral and political challenge of military defeat in 1864 and the loss of Schleswig-Holstein. An early expression of the new orientation towards England and determination to avoid dependence on Germany was the construction of a new east–west railway line and of a new port at Esbjerg on the west coast of Jutland. The transformation of Danish agriculture was accomplished through the introduction of new technology and the adoption of a new kind of organisation, the producer cooperative. The production of butter, mainly for sale to Great Britain, was followed by the development of the bacon industry. By deliberately orienting its trade towards Great Britain, which took as much as 68 per cent of Danish agricultural exports in the years immediately preceding the First World War, Denmark was taking full advantage of the international division of labour under free trade.[12] It was

[9] Sejersted, 'Theory of Economic and Technological Development'; Timo Myllyntaus, *The Gatecrashing Apprentice: Industrialising Finland as an Adopter of New Technology* (Helsinki, 1990).

[10] J. Kuuse, 'Foreign Trade and the Breakthrough of the Engineering Industry in Sweden 1890–1920', *Scandinavian Economic History Review* 25 (1977), pp. 1–36.

[11] Pollard, *Peaceful Conquest*, p. 235. See also N. F. R. Crafts, 'Patterns of Development in Nineteenth-Century Europe', *Oxford Economic Papers* 36 (1984), pp. 438–58 (p. 456).

[12] Birgit Nüchel Thomsen and B. Thomas, *Anglo-Danish Trade 1661–1963: A Historical Survey* (Århus, 1966), pp. 286–93.

not simply a matter of responding to the decline of British agriculture, but of creating a market in Britain through a vigorous marketing strategy which emphasised the high quality of Danish products.

The modernisation process was more problematic in Norway, despite the development of successful 'off-shore' industries such as shipping, fishing and whaling, and 'enclave' industries based on forest products.[13] Finland, meanwhile, remained much the least economically advanced of the four Nordic economies until well after the Second World War, its development conditioned by its position as part of the Russian empire. At the turn of the century industries which had produced a wide range of products – notably iron – for the Russian market collapsed when Russian industries modernised and when Finnish goods were excluded by the imposition of new tariff barriers.[14] Even though Finland found new outlets in western Europe, the structure of Finnish exports became less diversified and more dependent on a few products – sawn timber, butter, pulp and paper. In all four countries, moreover, modernisation created new internal tensions. These reduced the cohesion of Scandinavian societies and made them less capable of meeting external challenges either individually or collectively.

Like economic modernisation, the political transformation of Scandinavia was late, rapid and remarkably complete. Between the 1890s and the 1930s, political systems which, in the case of Denmark and Sweden at least, were conservative by western European standards had been transformed into a social democratic hegemony which was to survive largely unshaken until the economic upheavals of the late twentieth century.[15] This was due in part to the distinctive character of Scandinavian industrialisation, with scattered concentrations of industrial activity, often in remote and rural regions rather than in large cities, which contributed to the early development of nationally based and centralised working-class organisations. It also derived from the character of rural society. The roots of the industrial labour force were in the peasantry and relations between town and country were still very close. In Norway and Finland in particular, there existed large numbers of poor, semi-proletarianised fishermen, farmers and forestry workers who provided the social democrats with an important rural constituency. Most importantly, rural interests had their own political parties – the Agrarians in Norway, Sweden and Finland, and the Liberals (Venstre) and Radical Liberals (Det radikale Venstre) in Denmark – which were ideologically flexible and were eventually, in the inter-

[13] See especially Fritz Hodne, *The Norwegian Economy 1920–1980* (London and Canberra, 1983), pp. 58–69; T. Bergh, T. J. Hanisch, E. Lange and H. Ø. Pharo, *Growth and Development: The Norwegian Experience 1830–1980* (Oslo, 1981), pp. 89–91.

[14] Erkki Pihkala, 'Relations with Russia, Foreign Trade and the Development of the Finnish Economy 1860–1939', in Tapani Mauranen (ed.), *Economic Development in Hungary and Finland 1860–1939* (Helsinki, 1985), pp. 25–48.

[15] Francis G. Castles, *The Social Democratic Image of Society: A Study of the Achievements and Origins of Scandinavian Social Democracy in Comparative Perspective* (London, 1978).

war period, to conclude the 'crisis agreements' with the left which formed the foundation of social democratic hegemony.

The forces of conservatism in Scandinavian society were not prepared to give up without a fight. The principles of parliamentarism and democracy came early to Norway (in 1884) but late to Denmark and Sweden. Parliamentary government was established in Denmark in 1901, after a long struggle between King Christian IX and his prime minister Estrup on the one hand, and the Folketing on the other, and in Sweden only in 1917.[16] Here too the crown, in the person of Gustav V, conducted a determined rearguard action, backed by such conservative intellectuals as the explorer Sven Hedin and the geopolitician Rudolf Kjellén, and the prime minister from 1914 to 1917, Hjalmar Hammarskjöld. The conservatives and the crown capitulated only after the major election victory of the left in 1917, and in the shadow of the February revolution in Russia, to the formidable Liberal–Socialist alliance of which the Social Democrats under Hjalmar Branting became the main beneficiaries.[17] In both Denmark and Sweden defence was the battleground on which the constitutional and political struggle was fought between the forces of liberalism and parliamentarism on the one hand and those of monarchy and conservatism on the other.

The capitulation of the 'old right' may have been due to a realisation of the futility of rearguard actions. This does not mean, however, that Scandinavia was immune from the destabilising consequences of rapid economic change. Class conflict remained strong until the early 1930s (in Finland much longer), and the discontent of the rural and urban petite bourgeoisie expressed itself in ways which prefigured the right-wing radicalism of the inter-war years.[18] Nationalism, chauvinism and local and regional particularism tended, if anything, to gain in strength.[19] Living in small, isolated communities on the verge of subsistence, Scandinavians of the pre-industrial era had developed qualities of individualism, self-reliance and egalitarianism which did not always adapt readily to the demands of modern society. Deep cleavages developed between the countryside and the rapidly growing towns. Rural romantics represented the former as the home of simple national virtues, the latter as that of slums, disease and an alien cosmopolitanism.[20]

There was often a direct link between claims to national self-determination

---

[16] Troels Fink, *Estruptidens politiske historie 1875–1894* (2 vols., Odense, 1986).

[17] Douglas V. Verney, *Parliamentary Reform in Sweden 1866–1921* (Oxford, 1957); Leif Lewin, *Ideology and Strategy: A Century of Swedish Politics* (Cambridge, 1988), pp. 87–122.

[18] Tom Ericsson, *Mellan kapital och arbete. Småborgerligheten i Sverige 1850–1914* (Umeå, 1988), p. 181; Lewin, *Ideology and Strategy*, pp. 40–1.

[19] See the useful essays on Norwegian, Danish, Finnish and Icelandic nationalism in Rosalind Mitchison (ed.), *The Roots of Nationalism: Studies in Northern Europe* (Edinburgh, 1980). On Norway, see also Andreas Elviken, 'The Genesis of Norwegian Nationalism', *Journal of Modern History* 3 (1931), pp. 365–91.

[20] G. M. Gathorne-Hardy, *Norway* (London, 1925), pp. 171–2, 277–8; Ericsson, *Mellan kapital och arbete*; Aarne Reunala, 'The Forest and the Finns', in Max Engman and David Kirby (eds.), *Finland: People, Nation, State* (London, 1989), pp. 38–56.

and the process of economic modernisation. The Norwegian demand for a separate consular service which was the immediate occasion of the break-up of the Scandinavian union in 1905 was justified by reference to Norway's worldwide commercial and shipping interests. Sometimes Scandinavian nationalism led to conflict with non-Scandinavian powers. Danish and German nationalisms clashed in Slesvig and Holstein; Finnish nationalism flourished under the patronage of Alexander II only to fall foul of the tsarist government's policy of Russification from the 1890s onward.[21] Nationalism also set up barriers to communication and cooperation among the Scandinavian states themselves. The language conflict in Norway was in part an expression of class conflict and the urban–rural divide,[22] but its effect was also to make Norwegian speech less comprehensible to Swedes and Danes. The Finnish-speaking majority in Finland was intolerant of the Swedish-speaking minority on both historical and social grounds.

The political consequences of modernisation thus had important implications for Scandinavia's foreign relations. The divisive qualities of Scandinavian nationalism weakened the capacity to meet external challenges. The long hegemony of the left (liberals as well as socialists) gave the Scandinavian countries governments which wanted to live at peace with the rest of the world and were often reluctant to spend money on defence. More generally, the effort of constructing societies based on principles of social and economic equality, outstandingly successful as it was, may have led Scandinavians to take too little notice of ominous developments in the world outside.

Problems of Scandinavian security

The development of industrialised warfare in the late nineteenth and early twentieth centuries heightened the disparity in power between the European great powers and their smaller neighbours and posed new challenges for the security policies of the Scandinavian states. In the pre-industrial age Scandinavian states had been able to exert an independent influence on European affairs. Denmark had been a power of some regional importance – the 'guardian' of the entrances to the Baltic – whilst seventeenth-century Sweden had been a great power in its own right, the metropolis of a Baltic empire. The rise of Russia spelt the end of Swedish hegemony, and during the Napoleonic wars Great Britain and Prussia did not hesitate to intervene in Scandinavia and the Baltic in order to secure their strategic objectives. For the kingdom of Denmark–Norway the experience of these years was traumatic, with the naval defeat of 1801, the bombardment of Copenhagen and seizure of the Danish

---

[21] William Carr, *Schleswig-Holstein 1815–1848: A Study in National Conflict* (Manchester, 1963); C. Leonard Lundin, 'Finland', in Edward C. Thaden (ed.), *Russification in the Baltic Provinces and Finland 1855–1914* (Princeton, N. J., 1981), pp. 355–457.

[22] Einar Haugen, *Language Conflict and Language Planning: The Case of Modern Norwegian* (Cambridge, Mass., 1966).

fleet in 1807, and the imposition of a severe blockade, all at the hands of Great Britain. Any comfort the Danes might subsequently have derived from the outcome of the Schleswig-Holstein crisis in 1848–52 was dispelled by their crushing defeat at the hands of the forces of the German Confederation, led by Prussia and Austria, in 1864. Sweden's rulers, on the other hand, avoided the mistakes which had placed Denmark on the losing side in the Napoleonic wars and prudently chose Marshal Bernadotte of France (who in turn prudently changed sides) as their crown prince. The loss of Finland to Russia in 1809 was counterbalanced by union with Norway, formerly under the Danish crown, in 1814.

Unlike Denmark, Sweden did not entirely renounce its great-power ambitions. The 'system of strict and independent neutrality'[23] adopted by Bernadotte on his accession to the throne as King Karl XIV Johan in 1818 failed to satisfy his successors Oscar I (1844–59) and Karl XV (1859–72). Their dynastic ambitions to regain Finland, or even to establish a united Scandinavian kingdom, were fuelled by the 'Scandinavianism' widespread among the educated classes in Sweden, Denmark and, to a lesser extent, Norway. But there was no support in either Swedish or Norwegian society for an adventurist foreign policy. Karl XV's attempt to bring about an alliance with Denmark in 1863 was thwarted by opposition from his Swedish and Norwegian ministers and marked the end of any idea of using Swedish forces beyond the frontiers of the state.[24] Sweden's eclipse was confirmed by the outcomes of the Crimean war, the German–Danish war of 1864 and the Franco-Prussian war of 1870. After 1871 the overwhelming presence in the Baltic of Russia and of the new German empire was an inescapable fact of life. Abandoning the tradition of Russo-Swedish friendship which dated back to the days of Bernadotte and Alexander I, conservative Swedish opinion led by King Oscar II (1872–1907) and, initially, King Gustav V (1907–50) cultivated German friendship as a counterweight to what it now perceived as the Russian menace.

As the Scandinavian countries ceased to play an active role in European affairs, and as disagreements among themselves became fewer or were resolved peacefully – even the separation of Norway and Sweden in 1905 – there developed a distinctively Scandinavian view of international affairs. It was based in part on a feeling of moral superiority – smallness and weakness being readily equated with virtue – and in part on the assumption that cooperation in defence and foreign policies was both desirable and feasible. It seemed reasonable to assume that peoples with such close racial affinities, living in such a geographically distinct region on the northern margins of Europe, ought

---

[23] Memorandum of 1834 by Karl Johan, quoted in Krister Wahlbäck, *The Roots of Swedish Neutrality* (Stockholm, 1986), p. 10.

[24] Alf W. Johansson and Torbjörn Norman, 'Den svenska neutralitetspolitiken i historiskt perspectiv', in Bo Hugemark (ed.), *Neutralität och försvar. Perspektiv på svensk säkerhetspolitik 1809–1985* (Stockholm, 1986), pp. 11–43 (p. 14).

to be able to present a common front to the rest of the world. Yet fundamental differences of interest and perception, based on differing historical experiences and geostrategic locations, invariably prevented them from doing so. These differences were exacerbated, but were not created, by the processes of modernisation discussed earlier in this chapter. They were inherent in Scandinavian geography and history. Put most simply, Norway faces west, Sweden and Finland face east and Denmark faces south. Until the Second World War, Sweden and Finland feared Russia and generally looked to Germany as a counterweight; Denmark, fearing Germany, felt unable to rely on either Britain or Russia for support; Norway had little fear of either Russia or Germany but assumed in any case that, in the last resort, British self-interest and naval power formed a sufficient guarantee of Norwegian security. Hence the weakness of pan-Scandinavianism in the nineteenth century and of the various twentieth-century efforts in defence cooperation.

Quite apart from the question of cooperation, each Scandinavian state faced formidable problems in its pursuit of a credible defence policy. In the first instance, security depended on non-involvement in conflicts between the great powers. After 1815, both Sweden and Denmark pursued policies of neutrality. So too did Norway after 1905. But Scandinavian neutrality had no basis in international law (unlike, for example, that of Switzerland after 1815 or Belgium after 1830).[25] Even after 1871, when neutrality was clearly the overriding goal of Swedish policy, governments and monarchs refused to permit any formal constraint on their freedom of action.[26] Denmark and Norway, on the other hand, tried and failed, in 1903 and 1905–7 respectively, to obtain an international guarantee of their permanent neutrality.[27] In the case of Denmark, each of the great powers had a different conception of what neutrality would entail – whether, for instance, it obliged Denmark to close the Straits to the warships of belligerent powers or to keep them open – and preferred to keep the question undecided. In the case of Norway, too, they wished to keep their options open.

If the Scandinavian states were to remain neutral in time of war, they also had to avoid being seen to take sides in peacetime. Denmark's dynastic links with Russia; Norway's presumed orientation towards Great Britain; the strongly pro-German tendencies of many Swedes before 1914 – all served to deepen the suspicions of other great powers about their probable sympathies in wartime. Neutrality would also be threatened by the existence of issues likely to lead to conflict with neighbouring powers. No such issues confronted Sweden and Norway (although the incipient conflict *between* the two countries before 1905 clearly rendered them less capable of meeting external challenges).

---

[25] Pertti Luntinen, 'Neutrality in Northern Europe Before the First World War', in Jukka Nevakivi (ed.), *Neutrality in History* (Helsinki, 1993), pp. 107–14.

[26] Johansson and Norman, 'Den svenska neutralitetspolitiken', pp. 20–1.

[27] See ch. 2, pp. 66, 71–5.

Denmark, however, was in a highly vulnerable position as long as the Schleswig-Holstein question remained unsettled.

Above all, the Scandinavian states had to demonstrate the will and capacity to defend their neutrality against external aggression – or, more realistically, to prevent belligerents from using their territories as a means of attacking their enemies. Their ability to do so depended on their geographical location as well as on the state of their armed forces and their willingness to use them. It was also affected by the changes in military technology and in the European balance of power which, especially after 1890, increased the strength of the great powers relative to that of smaller powers, and at the same time led those great powers to take a more active interest in the affairs of northern Europe. Sweden, Denmark and newly independent Norway responded in sharply divergent ways to the worsening international climate.

Sweden enjoyed the most favoured strategic position in Scandinavia and had a long military tradition. However, its defensive position was not as strong as Karl Johan had hoped when he obtained Norway in compensation for the loss of Finland. On the one hand, it proved impossible to construct a common defence for the united kingdoms; on the other, Russia's frontier had moved westward. It now abutted on Swedish territory in the far north and encompassed the entire eastern shore of the Gulf of Bothnia. Tsarist Russia was the 'hereditary enemy'. Especially after Oscar I's break with the policy of friendship with Russia at the time of the Crimean war (through the conclusion of the treaty of 1855 with Great Britain and France), it came to be regarded by most Swedes in positions of authority, as well as by large sections of Swedish public opinion, as a real danger to Swedish security.[28] The Swedish capital was thought to be particularly exposed in view of Russia's possession of the Åland Islands, close to Stockholm at the entrance to the Gulf of Bothnia. Despite their demilitarisation under the terms of the treaty of Paris of 1856 (the 'Åland servitude'), Swedish opinion remained vigilant in its scrutiny of Russian activities on the islands. From the 1880s onward there developed in addition a growing belief in Russia's expansionist intentions in the far north. Railway construction in Finland, and later the policy of Russification, seemed to confirm fears that Russia aimed at the acquisition of an ice-free port on the Norwegian coast.[29] Meanwhile the industrial development of northern Sweden, combined with the insistence, in an age of increasing national consciousness, that no part of the realm must be surrendered to an invader without resistance, led to the emergence of a new military strategy aimed at defending Sweden's frontiers in the north. The key to the new defensive

[28] Folke Lindberg, *Den svenska utrikespolitikens historia*, vol. III, part 4, *1872–1914* (Stockholm, 1958), pp. 109–24; Eirik Hornborg, *Sverige och Ryssland genom tiderna* (Stockholm, 1941).

[29] Tuomo Polvinen, *Die finnischen Eisenbahnen in den militärischen und politischen Plänen Russlands vor dem Ersten Weltkrieg* (Helsinki, 1962).

system was the great fortress at Boden, 'the Gibraltar of the north', first proposed by the chief of the general staff in 1887 and finally approved by the Riksdag in 1900.

At the same time, Sweden's armed forces were modernised both on land and at sea. As a result of the military reforms begun in 1885 and completed with the introduction of universal conscription in 1901, they became the largest and best equipped in northern Europe. The protracted debate on defence was intimately bound up with the development of parliamentary politics in Sweden. Whilst the Liberals were able to exploit the Riksdag's budgetary powers to secure greater parliamentary influence over foreign policy and defence, conservatives, army and crown employed the defence issue as the principal means of resisting democratisation and constitutional change. Greeting a mass demonstration of farmers in February 1914 in his 'palace yard speech' (written by Sven Hedin), King Gustav V appealed to their patriotism and brought about the fall of the Staaff government. The task of its successor, led by Hjalmar Hammarskjöld, was to bring about 'a shift in the constitutional balance of power and rearmament on the largest possible scale'[30] – a task from which it was deflected only by the outbreak of war.[31] Only after the war, once it was clear that the armed forces would not be used in support of an adventurist foreign policy or a German alliance, were Liberals and Social Democrats largely reconciled to the idea of a strong defence.

Danish defence policy evolved in the shadow of 1864. It was influenced, too, by the growth of Anglo-German naval rivalry and the likelihood of a naval battle in the southern North Sea or in the entrances to the Baltic. Danish policy was not, however, merely fatalistic. Admittedly the experience of defeat and the overwhelming presence of Germany bred an attitude of 'defence nihilism' encapsulated in the phrase 'Hvad skal det nytte?' – 'What's the use?' Such views were held particularly strongly on the left, especially within the Radical Liberal Party, where the young historian and future foreign minister Peter Munch was their leading spokesman.[32] Until 1901, however, government was in the hands of conservatives who were prepared to expend considerable sums (in defiance of parliament) on defence measures. At first policy was still shaped by hopes of regaining the lost duchies, but this idea was hurriedly abandoned after the first Prussian victories of 1870. However, a more optimistic phase of Danish defence policy began in the mid-1880s and continued until the middle of the following decade. It was based on the assumption that, while the Jutland peninsula was indefensible, and the island of Zealand only just defensible, it might be possible for Copenhagen to hold out, if suitably fortified, until one or more of the other great powers intervened

---

[30] Lewin, *Ideology and Strategy*, p. 110.
[31] Still more far-reaching ambitions, both internally and externally, are suggested in Gösta Johanson, 'Efter borggårdstalet – nya kupp-planer', *Scandia* 59 (1993), pp. 71–111.
[32] Viggo Sjøqvist, *Peter Munch. Manden, politikeren, historikeren* (Copenhagen, 1976), pp. 60–70.

in their own interest. Starting in 1882, the Estrup government fortified Copenhagen regardless of parliamentary opinion. Danish self-confidence was such that, for a short time, in 1893–4, the government even showed some interest in overtures from France and Russia.[33]

Gradually, however, as hopes aroused in 1903 of a neutrality guaranteed by Germany and Russia disappeared, and as Germany became increasingly insistent on a 'correct' Danish attitude in time of war, there developed an emphasis on making Danish neutrality acceptable to Germany. Whilst the Danish population became more anti-German as a result of the Prussian government's hard-line policies in Slesvig, Liberal and Radical Liberal governments after 1901 pursued an increasingly German-oriented defence policy. The defence bill passed in 1909 implemented the recommendations of a defence commission which sat from 1902 to 1908. There was much greater emphasis on defence against attack from the sea, which would presumably come only from Germany's enemies. Copenhagen was to be strongly fortified on the sea side; the navy was to be equipped for coastal defence. It was tacitly admitted that Denmark could never be on the side of Germany's enemies in time of war.

When Karl Johan became crown prince of Sweden he regarded union with Norway as preferable to a reconquest of Finland.[34] Sweden's western frontier would be secured and the Scandinavian peninsula, separated from its neighbours by sea or intractable terrain, would form a natural strategic unity. However, he failed to reckon with the strength of Norwegian particularism, which placed considerable limitations on the king's authority over the Norwegian army and navy. Nor did Norwegian opinions on defence coincide with those of Sweden. Norwegians agreed with Karl Johan on the geographical remoteness of the Scandinavian peninsula but regarded Norway as the more secure of the two kingdoms.[35] Norwegian opinion was cool towards pan-Scandinavianism and mistrustful of Swedish adventurism under Oscar I and Karl XV.[36] Norwegians also tended to be less apprehensive than Swedes about Russia's intentions. And, they believed, if Russia were to attack Sweden or Norway, Great Britain would be obliged to intervene, both in its own interest and under the terms of the Anglo-French guarantee of the united kingdoms' territorial integrity in the treaty of 1855.

Norway appeared to gain little from the Swedish connection. Indeed as the union crisis deepened in the 1890s, Sweden came to be regarded as the chief threat to Norwegian security. After the 1895 crisis in particular, Norwegian

---

[33] Troels Fink, *Ustabil balance. Dansk udenrigs- og forsvarspolitik 1894–1905* (Århus, 1969), p. 13.

[34] Gerhard Munthe, '1905. Fred eller krig', *Historisk tidsskrift* (Norway) 59 (1980), pp. 164–75.

[35] Olav Riste, *Isolationism and Great Power Protection: The Historical Determinants of Norwegian Foreign Policy* (Oslo, 1984), p. 2.

[36] Theodore Jorgensen, *Norway's Relation to Scandinavian Unionism 1815–1871* (Northfield, Minn., 1935).

defence spending increased dramatically.[37] Four ironclads and a large number of other vessels provided Norway for the first time with a credible national defence, as opposed to local coastal defences.[38] Fortifications were built at Kristiania, Kristiansand, Bergen and Trondheim; the army was equipped with modern weaponry; the period of military service was increased, and conscription was introduced into the three northernmost counties for the first time. Although King Oscar II formally remained commander-in-chief, the Norwegian government took steps in the 1890s to gain full control of the military leadership and secured the loyalty of officers to the Norwegian authorities. Above all, a system of fortifications was built on the Swedish frontier. Its military value was debatable, but its political significance as a declaration of Norway's will to independence was clear. The Swedes refrained from using force against Norway in 1905 not for military reasons but because they realised that it would be politically counterproductive.[39]

Independent Norway devoted its diplomatic efforts between 1905 and 1907 to securing a status of permanent neutrality. In the event, Norway had to be content with a treaty of integrity (see ch. 2, pp. 71–5). This implied that the great powers – Britain and Germany in particular – wished to reserve the right to utilise Norwegian waters, and possibly even territory, in time of war. The increasingly visible presence in Norwegian fjords of units of the High Seas Fleet (accompanied every summer by Wilhelm II on the imperial yacht *Hohenzollern*) suggested that the threat was a real one. Britain could still be expected to react with vigour to any German move against Norway, but might itself occupy Norwegian territory. And, following the massive demonstration of German naval power off the coasts of Norway at the height of the Moroccan crisis in July 1911, there were, the British minister reported, 'many Norwegians who no longer regard British naval supremacy as indisputable'.[40] The case for a strong national defence was argued publicly by such prominent figures as Fridtjof Nansen, the celebrated explorer and statesman.[41] In 1912 a further 20 million kroner was allocated to the naval defence budget to pay for more coastal defences, two more ironclads and one submarine. Even though foreign observers tended to discount Norway's military capacity, its army was equipped and armed almost entirely by Norwegian factories, and was on the whole well prepared for the kind of fighting that might have resulted from an attack on Norwegian soil.[42]

---

[37] Trond Stenslund, 'Norges sjømilitære opprustning 1895–1902 og forholdet til Sverige', *Scandia* 61 (1995), pp. 29–44.

[38] Munthe, '1905', p. 165.

[39] Ibid., pp. 173–4.

[40] Sir M. Findlay (Kristiania): 'Annual Report, 1911', 19 March 1912, FO 371/1415 (*BDFA*, I, F, III, pp. 200–12).

[41] Reidar Omang, *Norsk utenrikstjeneste*, vol. II, *Stormfulle tider 1913–1928* (Oslo, 1959), p. 31.

[42] Generalmajor A. D. Dahl, 'Den britiske bedømmelse av Norges forsvarsberedskap', *Norges forsvar* 24 (1974), pp. 153–6.

Economic development and national sovereignty

On the eve of the First World War the Scandinavian countries were firmly integrated in the world economy. Communications between Scandinavia and the outside world had been radically improved, with the expansion of existing ports such as Copenhagen and Gothenburg, the construction of new ones at Esbjerg and Narvik, the establishment of ocean-going steamer services and the introduction in 1909 of direct ferry communications between Sweden and Germany. Complex patterns of trade, finance and investment linked Scandinavia with the leading industrial powers of western Europe – above all, Great Britain and Germany – as well as with the Russian empire and the United States. However, the progress that had been made by the beginning of the twentieth century, though considerable, had not led to any significant degree of economic diversification except in Sweden. Even in Sweden, nearly half the labour force was still engaged in agriculture in 1910. In Finland, as we have seen, the economy had become *less* diversified. Each country remained 'dangerously specialized in one or two primary commodities'.[43]

And if Scandinavians were largely successful in maintaining control over the modernisation process, there are signs that by the beginning of the twentieth century this position was becoming increasingly difficult to sustain. By the turn of the century much larger and more capital-intensive enterprises were being established in Scandinavia. The discovery of the basic process of steel production by Gilchrist Thomas in 1878, followed by its widespread adoption in Germany, made possible for the first time the economic exploitation of the high-grade phosphoric iron ores of northern Sweden. The great ore fields of Gällivare and Kiruna were opened up and linked, by an epic feat of railway construction, to the Atlantic at Narvik and the Baltic at Luleå. In Norway Birkeland and Eyde patented a method for the production of artificial nitrogen in 1904, and built the Norsk Hydro plant at Rjukan in Telemark, the first large-scale utilisation of Norway's vast reserves of hydro-electric power. Both the Swedish and the Norwegian enterprises required large amounts of foreign capital. In the case of Norway in particular, native ingenuity outran domestic capital supplies and the initiative for the development of hydro-power was taken by foreigners. Such developments opened up the prospect that Scandinavians might lose control over key sectors of the economy and be reduced to a semi-colonial status. They also exposed the Scandinavian countries to competition among the European great powers for control over Scandinavian resources and markets.

The intense Scandinavian debate on the implications of industrial development had many aspects. There were those, especially in Norway, who condemned the whole process and wished to return to an imagined rural idyll free from the evils of social and political unrest. Swedish conservatives, on the

---

[43] Pollard, *Peaceful Conquest*, p. 233.

other hand, preached a progressive nationalism.[44] The exploitation of Sweden's natural resources and the development of industry would, they hoped, counteract the alienation of the working class and the draining away of the labour force through emigration.[45] As Kjellén put it, the future for Sweden no longer lay in imperial expansion but in the exploitation of 'Lapland's natural treasures of ores and water power'.[46] Nevertheless, there was concern throughout Scandinavia that the process of modernisation should remain in Scandinavian hands. One aspect of this concern was the debate over tariff protection. Another was the way in which foreign control of certain key industries and resources in Norway and Sweden came to be regarded as a direct threat to national integrity and independence.

Tariffs

Dieter Senghaas has emphasised the importance of tariff policy as a means of avoiding 'peripheralisation'. He suggests that the characteristic Scandinavian strategy was a successful alternation between free trade and protection. An early phase of export-led growth, associated with free trade, was succeeded by a phase of industrialisation through import substitution (assisted by protectionist measures), and finally (in most cases well after the Second World War) by full commitment to the modern international free-trading system.[47] Even moderate tariffs could afford some protection in a predominantly free-trading system.[48] But tariffs remained a source of political contention. On the one hand, Scandinavia's export industries benefited from free trade. On the other, tariffs were required as a means of protecting industries which were oriented towards the domestic market or which faced foreign competition in the initial stages of development.

Even though export interests generally remained dominant, there were important variations from one country to another, reflecting differing traditions and the balance of social and economic forces within the country.[49] The debate was also profoundly influenced by the nature of the international regime. The change in the international climate brought about by Germany's return to protection in 1879 strengthened the hand of protectionist forces within Scandinavian society, especially in Sweden. After a prolonged and bitter

---

[44] Nils Elvander, *Harald Hjärne och konservatismen. Konservativ idédebatt i Sverige 1865–1922* (Stockholm, 1961).

[45] Franklin D. Scott, 'Sweden's Constructive Opposition to Emigration', *Journal of Modern History* 37 (1965), pp. 307–35; Arne Ruth, 'The Second New Nation: The Mythology of Modern Sweden', in Graubard, *Norden*, pp. 240–82.

[46] Rudolf Kjellén, *Stormakterna. Konturer kring samtidens storpolitik* (2nd edn, 2 vols., Stockholm, 1911), vol. I, p. 74.

[47] Senghaas, *European Experience*, pp. 32–3, 71–94.

[48] Sejersted, 'Theory of Economic and Technological Development', p. 57.

[49] Poul Drachmann, *The Industrial Development and Commercial Policies of the Three Scandinavian Countries* (Oxford, 1915).

struggle, a protectionist tariff was finally introduced in 1888.[50] Whilst Denmark remained firmly committed to free trade,[51] Norway moved towards protectionism first in the tariff of 1897 and later in the more far-reaching tariff of 1905 which, coinciding with the attainment of independence and the agitation over the concession laws (see pp. 37–9), marked a new phase of economic nationalism in the country.

Tariffs had far-reaching implications. They influenced the investment decisions of foreign companies. Direct investment might be attractive to such firms as a means of circumventing tariff barriers.[52] Another consequence of the growth of tariff protection was that it made Scandinavian economic cooperation more difficult. The Swedish economist Pontus Fahlbeck told a meeting of economists in Copenhagen in 1888 that the Scandinavian countries ought to create a protectionist customs union to avoid being reduced to vassal status among the great economic powers.[53] In practice, however, the increasing divergence in tariff policy, marked in particular by the demise of the inter-state treaty between Sweden and Norway in 1897 and the break-up of the union of the two kingdoms in 1905, reflected real differences in the economic interests of the three countries. Danish exports to Sweden, for example, declined drastically in the 1890s, while Swedish export interests turned increasingly away from Scandinavia and towards the two great Baltic markets of Germany and Russia.[54] Monetary policy was also affected by the growing economic disparities among the three countries. Fixed exchange rates, which had characterised the Scandinavian Monetary Union since its creation in 1873, were brought to an end, and the Union was deprived of much of its substance when it was renegotiated at Sweden's insistence following the break with Norway in 1905.[55]

If tariff protection often reflected a defensive mentality, by the 1890s it had been joined by a more outward-looking ethos, expressed in the promotion of Scandinavian commerce throughout the world. In an age of imperialism, small countries without colonial markets and large armed forces had to find other means of promoting their economic interests and preserving their national identities. The reform of the Danish consular service in 1893 led to the establishment of new consulates in developing countries in North and South America, south-east Asia and Australia, and allowed businessmen to enter the

[50] Lewin, *Ideology and Strategy*, pp. 33–52.
[51] Hans Kryger Larsen, 'Det nationale synspunkt på den økonomiske udvikling 1888–1914', in Ole Feldbæk (ed.), *Dansk identitetshistorie*, vol. III, *Folkets Danmark 1848–1940* (Copenhagen, 1992), pp. 468–511.
[52] Sven Nordlund, *Upptäckten av Sverige. Utländska direktinvestingar i Sverige 1895–1945* (Umeå, 1989), p. 16.
[53] Larsen, 'Det nationale synspunkt', p. 480; Nordlund, *Upptäckten av Sverige*, pp. 97–8.
[54] Nordlund, *Upptäckten av Sverige*, pp. 91–4.
[55] Eli F. Hecksher, Kurt Bergendal, Wilhelm Keilhau, Einar Cohn and Thorsteinn Thorsteinsson, *Sweden, Norway, Denmark and Iceland in the World War* (New Haven, Conn., 1930), pp. 129–31.

service.[56] A similar reform occurred in Sweden in 1906 following the dissolution of the union with Norway.[57] One of the main thrusts of Swedish export policy was towards the Far East, where a legation was established in Japan in 1906 with a member of the Wallenberg banking family as its first head. China was of particular interest as one of the few markets where the open door still stood open, and as a place where the inhabitants could be encouraged to look to a small, non-imperialist country like Sweden for know-how and capital.[58] A member of the British legation in Stockholm commented on these efforts:

The Swedes are a proud but lethargic nation, slow to change and adopt new methods, but their intelligence is undoubted, and I believe them to have realized that they can improve their position in the group of smaller Powers. At the bottom of their new inclination to 'hustle' is probably an instinctive feeling of jealousy and rivalry when contemplating the efforts of the Norwegians in endeavouring to develop their trade. The Swedes have no wish to be left behind; and fear of being so, and thus receiving a fresh blow to their national pride, has spurred them on to the efforts one sees made in all quarters.[59]

In Norway itself, the requirements of shipping and trade were so great, and there was apparently so little need to conduct an active foreign policy, that there was much support for amalgamating the diplomatic and consular services – a reform finally carried through in 1922.[60] Another characteristic expression of the new outlook was the establishment of a free port at Copenhagen in 1894. In part a defensive response to the free port at Hamburg and the construction of the Kiel Canal, the project also represented a vision (never fully realised) of Copenhagen as a centre of North Atlantic and Baltic commerce.[61] The great shipping lines – first the Danish DFDS and later the Norwegian–American and Swedish–American lines – were also symbols of national independence and prestige: most of all, perhaps, H. N. Andersen's East Asiatic Company, which from 1897 ran a direct service from Denmark to Siam and which, in the view of one contemporary commentator, enabled Denmark to rival Russia and Germany, with their great armies and navies, as a presence in the Far East.[62]

Tariffs themselves, of course, also served as active instruments of commer-

---

[56] Klaus Kjølsen, 'Denmark: The Royal Danish Ministry of Foreign Affairs', in Zara Steiner (ed.), *The Times Survey of Foreign Ministries of the World* (London, 1982), pp. 163–83 (p. 171).

[57] Wilhelm Carlgren, 'Sweden: The Ministry for Foreign Affairs', in Steiner, *Times Survey of Foreign Ministries*, pp. 455–69 (p. 462).

[58] Jan Larsson, *Diplomati och industriellt genombrott. Svensk exportsträvanden på Kina 1906–1916* (Uppsala, 1977).

[59] H. Dering to FO, 15 October 1906, FO 368/53, No. 35300.

[60] Erik-Wilhelm Norman, 'Norway: The Royal Norwegian Ministry of Foreign Affairs', in Steiner, *Times Survey of Foreign Ministries*, pp. 391–408 (pp. 394–8); Olav Riste, 'The Foreign Policy-Making Process in Norway: An Historical Perspective', in *Forsvarsstudier. Årbok for Forsvarshistorisk forskningssenter, Forsvarets høgskole 1982* (Oslo, 1983), pp. 232–45 (pp. 234–5).

[61] Larsen, 'Det nationale synspunkt', pp. 489–93.   [62] Ibid., p. 494.

cial diplomacy. They were, as we have seen, of little use to a country in a relatively weak bargaining position, like Norway after 1897. In Swedish hands they could prove a much more formidable weapon.[63] The introduction of the 1902 Bülow tariff in Germany faced Sweden with a menacing situation. Many of the new tariff's provisions were directly aimed against Swedish goods and seemed intended to force Sweden to adhere to the German commercial treaty system as well as to hinder the progress of Swedish industrialisation. At the same time, the existing Swedish industrial tariffs, dating from 1892, were in need of revision and offered little protection against imports of manufactured goods from Germany. The first Swedish venture into commercial diplomacy, which led to the signature of a provisional trade agreement with Germany in 1906, was neither very well prepared nor skilfully handled.[64] It was, however, a useful learning experience, and the 1906 treaty served as a holding operation while the Swedes devised a new tariff. Introduced in 1910, this provided for a much more differentiated treatment of manufactured goods, and was a direct inducement to German industry and the German government to negotiate for a new commercial treaty.

A further incentive was offered by the revision of the Swedish law on the export of iron ore (see pp. 39–40). The pressing need for iron ore on the part of the Ruhr iron and steel industry gave Sweden a powerful ally within Germany. In addition, the Swedes were effective negotiators. The Swedish delegation included businessmen and politicians as well as civil servants; the German comprised only officials of Prussia and the Reich, and industrial interests had little direct involvement in preparations for the negotiations. In the commercial treaty of 1911, the Germans obtained some reductions in the 1910 tariff (which had always been intended as a bargaining counter) but had to make important concessions to Swedish export interests. Sweden's success was due to the fact that Germany was more dependent on Swedish iron ore than Sweden on German industrial goods. Germany had no alternative source of iron ore, but Sweden could threaten to switch to Britain, for example, as a source of imports. As a small power, moreover, Sweden possessed strengths that Germany lacked: its greater internal solidarity; a less sharp division between the state and the private sector, and the capacity to display a united front even when internal divisions existed.[65]

Foreign capital: Norwegian hydro-power

The other great issue of debate was the role of foreign capital. By the turn of the century there were many in Norway and Sweden who regarded foreign

[63] Anders Lindberg, *Småstat mot stormakt. Beslutsystemet vid tillkomsten av 1911 års svensk–tyska handels- och sjöfartstraktat* (Lund, 1983).
[64] Yvonne Maria Werner, *Svensk–tyska förbindelser kring sekelskiftet 1900. Politik och ekonomi vid tillkomsten av 1906 års svensk–tyska handels- och sjöfartstraktat* (Lund, 1989).
[65] Anders Lindberg, *Småstat mot stormakt*, p. 279.

involvement in the economy as a direct threat to national sovereignty – and ultimately even national security. Their anxieties were aroused by the two cases of large-scale development discussed briefly above: the exploitation of Norwegian water power, especially by the new electro-chemical industry, and the opening up of the iron ore fields of northern Sweden. Here dependence was palpable. Foreign capital played a greater part than in earlier stages of economic development; foreign individuals or companies exerted a more direct influence on the exploitation of Scandinavian resources. The relationship between economic growth and national sovereignty was therefore raised in an acute form. In both cases the dilemma was resolved by the intervention of the state as legislator and, ultimately, as entrepreneur.

The first large-scale exploitation of Norway's vast hydro-electric resources came with the construction of the Norsk Hydro plant at Rjukan in Telemark for the production of artificial nitrates.[66] The plant was powered by what was then one of the largest hydro-electric stations in the world, equipped by the German, Swiss and Swedish electrical industries. The bulk of the capital was raised in Sweden – from the Wallenberg-owned Enskilda Bank – and in France, and by means of a partnership with the German chemical firm BASF. Other firms followed Norsk Hydro's example in the harnessing of Norwegian water power, including the British-owned pulp and paper firm of Borregaard, which was by 1909 the biggest industrial employer in Norway; and foreign capital was heavily involved in the new industries which refined metals such as aluminium, nickel and iron by thermo-electrolytic methods.[67]

A reaction against foreign ownership set in following Norway's achievement of independence in 1905.[68] Temporary measures in 1906–7 were followed by permanent restrictions, in the concession laws of 1909, on the sale and exploitation of waterfalls, forests and mineral deposits. One consequence which was expected – and which was acceptable to many of the laws' promoters[69] – was a slowing of the rate of Norwegian industrialisation. Foreign businessmen certainly threatened to stop investing in Norway if the concession laws were passed. The Swedish banker K. A. Wallenberg wrote in 1913 that the political situation in Norway was such that the Enskilda Bank was considering winding up rather than extending its interests there.[70] The head of a British-owned mining company was reported as saying that 'English Capitalists are so disgusted with Norwegian legislation that they would prefer to invest their money in Morocco, Spain or South America.'[71]

The British minister to Norway was sceptical of such claims: 'I have reported very fully on these matters to the FO for the past three years, and I

[66] Fritz Hodne, *An Economic History of Norway 1815–1870* (Bergen, 1975), pp. 294–8.
[67] Ibid., pp. 298–300.
[68] Ibid., pp. 311–15; Berge Furre, *Norsk historie 1905–1940* (Oslo, 1972), pp. 30–40.
[69] Gathorne-Hardy, *Norway*, pp. 274–81.
[70] Hodne, *Economic History of Norway*, p. 314.
[71] Quoted in Sir A. Herbert (British minister to Norway) to Dering (FO), 31 October 1909, FO 368/15.

have not ceased to urge the necessity for British Capitalists to look after the Norwegian water power. As usual, they have allowed the chance to go by.'[72] Moreover, Norwegian economic development was not impeded by the passing of the concession laws.[73] Growth was particularly strong in the period 1905–16. If there was a momentary slackening of growth and investment rates in the years 1907–9, which may have been caused by uncertainty about the new legislation, both resumed vigorously once the laws had reached their final shape and the Conservatives had been returned to power in the elections of 1909. One British firm withdrew from its timber-processing interests in Norway, but did so as much owing to low cellulose and paper prices as to political considerations. German interests withdrew from Norsk Hydro in 1911, but this was due to a series of disagreements with Sam Eyde.[74] The Wallenbergs actually increased their involvement in Norwegian industry after 1909, while the British minister in Kristiania reported in 1912 that 'German capitalists have been taking an increasing interest in Norwegian enterprise, chiefly in the development of the water-power in which Norway is so rich.'[75]

Foreign capital: Swedish iron ore

Swedish iron ore, the other natural resource whose exploitation was fiercely debated, cast its shadow over Scandinavian international relations in the first four decades of the twentieth century. This was inevitable given the richness of Sweden's ore deposits and the unique relationship which developed between the Swedish mining industry and the iron and steel industry of the Ruhr. By 1914 the essence of that relationship had been largely fixed both in terms of ownership of the means of production and transportation, and in relations between the Swedish and German states.

The existence of the extensive phosphoric iron ore deposits at Gällivare and Kiruna-Luossavaara in northern Sweden, with their high iron content (over 60 per cent), had been known at least since the sixteenth century, but large-scale exploitation was attempted only after the discovery of the basic process by Gilchrist Thomas in 1878, which permitted for the first time the utilisation of phosphoric ores in steel making. The new process was rapidly adopted by the German iron and steel industry. Drawing on the phosphoric ores of the Longwy-Briey basin in Lorraine, German steel manufacturers soon had to look farther afield. Exports of phosphoric ore from the important Grängesberg mine in central Sweden began in the late 1880s, and at the same time the first

[72] Ibid.
[73] Even Lange, 'The Concession Laws of 1906–1909 and Norwegian Industrial Development', *Scandinavian Journal of History* 2 (1977), pp. 311–30. See also Bergh et al., *Growth and Development*, pp. 103–5.
[74] Arthur Stonehill, *Foreign Ownership in Norwegian Enterprises* (Oslo, 1965), p. 37.
[75] Mansfeldt Findlay, 'Annual Report on Norway, 1911', 19 March 1912, FO 371/1415 (printed in *BDFA*, I, F, III, pp. 200–12).

serious attempts were made to develop the ore fields of the north.[76] In 1883 a British company obtained a concession to build a railway linking the mines with the Norwegian coast on the Ofot Fjord, and with the Baltic at Luleå. The section from Gällivare to Luleå was completed, and the first shipments were made in 1888, but the company ran into financial difficulties and was bought out by the Swedish state in 1891. The Swedish and Norwegian governments then went on, between 1898 and 1902, to complete the line, and the first shipments from the new Norwegian port of Narvik were made in 1903.[77] The main reason for the failure of the British company was the vociferous Swedish protectionist movement against foreign interests which, by threatening prohibitive export duties, forced the company into liquidation.[78]

By 1892 ownership of the northern Swedish mines was effectively in the hands of one company, the Luossavaara-Kiirunavaare Aktiebolag (LKAB), while the central Swedish phosphoric mines and railways were controlled from 1896 by the Trafikaktiebolag Grängesberg–Oxelösund (TGO).[79] The LKAB, lacking capital, had been offered to the state in 1890 and again in 1902. On the second occasion it nearly fell into the hands of the German steel industry before the TGO, seeking to extend the base of its operations by acquiring the much larger ore deposits of the north, purchased a controlling share in 1903.[80] The TGO was still largely in foreign hands, but the Swedish state possessed considerable power over its operations through its control of the railways, the only means by which the ore could be transported. Demands for the introduction of an export duty on iron ore in 1906 resulted in part from hostility towards foreign capital, in part from the desire to stimulate the Swedish iron smelting industry and to promote the export of iron instead of ore. The Swedish government was placed in an uncomfortable position between, on the one hand, domestic protectionist agitation and, on the other, pressure from foreign importers of ore, above all from Germany. The proposal for an export duty was defeated (the Swedish–German commercial treaty of 1906 contained an undertaking that no such duty would be imposed) and, after much hesitation, the government acquired a half share in the LKAB by an agreement of 1907. Control of both the mines and the railway thus passed into Swedish hands; and the state acquired a large measure of influence over the future development of the industry. The use to which such influence could be put was demonstrated, as we have seen, in the negotiations leading to the German–Swedish trade agreement of 1911.

---

[76] Martin Fritz, *Svensk järnmalmsexport 1883–1913* (Gothenburg, 1967).
[77] Hodne, *Economic History of Norway*, pp. 304–6.
[78] B. Jonsson, *Staten och malmfälten. En studie i svensk malmfältpolitik omkring sekelskiftet* (Stockholm, 1969), p. 367.
[79] For the process by which these companies were formed, see Nils Meinander, *Gränges. En kronika om svensk järnmalm* (Stockholm, 1968), pp. 15–156.
[80] Jonsson, *Staten och malmfälten*, p. 370.

Patterns of influence

As citizens of developing countries, Scandinavians were constantly looking abroad for foreign models of social, cultural and intellectual development and adopting them eclectically.[81] At the same time, they were fully aware of the dependence to which such borrowing, as well as the growth of foreign economic involvement in Scandinavia, might lead – though this could also be used as an argument for further development. As a Finnish journal wrote in 1911, 'To destroy a small nation, political dominance by a more powerful country is not needed. The latter's industry is enough for that. But even a small industrialised nation can surprisingly resist the oppression of a powerful country.'[82]

Yet there was no obvious correlation between economic influence on the one hand and political or cultural influence on the other. There was, rather, a relatively simple pattern of economic dependence and a more complex pattern based on a diverse range of influences which sometimes coincided with economic interests, but frequently did not. Between the 1870s and the eve of the First World War, a period in which the value of Scandinavian trade increased by between three and four times, Britain and Germany strengthened their dominant position in the commerce of the four Nordic countries. In the decade before 1913 the two countries supplied between them over 55 per cent of the total imports of the four Nordic countries and took nearly 56 per cent of their exports (table 4). But British influence was much less than might have been deduced from the value of Anglo-Scandinavian trade, while Germany's much greater influence was clearly due to more than commercial success alone. Other countries, notably France and the United States, at times exerted a considerable influence quite independently of their relatively minor role in Scandinavian commerce before 1914. And influence was a two-way process. Scandinavian technological innovation found many borrowers, and the remarkable flowering of Scandinavian culture towards the end of the nineteenth century many admirers, in the world at large.

Although early nineteenth-century romantics in both Germany and Scandinavia proclaimed the cultural and racial identity of the Germanic and Scandinavian peoples, and a few (like Bishop Grundtvig in Denmark) discovered a natural affinity with the English,[83] there was no innate disposition to follow particular foreign models, whether German, British or French. It was rather a matter of choice: the product of conscious decisions taken at many different levels – from courts and governments to individual businessmen,

---

[81] Hagtvet and Rudeng, 'Scandinavia: Achievements, Dilemmas, Challenges', pp. 286–9; Carl G. Gustavson, *The Small Giant: Sweden Enters the Industrial Era* (Athens, Ohio, and London, 1986), pp. 300–2.

[82] Quoted in Timo Myllyntaus, *Electrifying Finland: The Transfer of a New Technology into a Late Industrialising Economy* (London, 1991), p. 60.

[83] M. Gerhardt and W. Hubatsch, *Deutschland und Skandinavien im Wandel der Jahrhunderte* (Bonn, 1977), pp. 308–24.

Table 4 *The combined trade of Germany and the United Kingdom as a percentage of the total trade of the Nordic countries: averages over ten-year periods (1874–1913)*

	Exports to Germany and UK		
1874–83	1884–93	1894–1903	1904–13
51.5	52.0	56.1	55.7
	Imports from Germany and UK		
1874–83	1884–93	1894–1903	1904–13
52.1	53.0	54.1	55.1

Source: B. R. Mitchell, *International Historical Statistics: Europe 1750–1988* (New York, 1992), table E2.

scholars, scientists or trade unionists. The Swedish royal family, of French origin, switched from an ostentatiously pro-French to an equally pronounced pro-German orientation when Oscar II succeeded Karl XV in 1872.[84] The Swedish armed forces, in the aftermath of the Prussian victories of 1866 and 1870, adopted German-style uniforms and, in 1901, the German model of universal conscription. But Scandinavians looked first to France and later to Germany not merely because they were impressed by military success, but because France and, still more, Germany were regarded as appropriate models for modernising societies. The British model of economic development, based on the large-scale production of cheap and relatively low-quality goods such as textiles, on the intensive use of coal-powered energy and the concentration of manufacturing in large urban centres, was one which was neither easy nor, perhaps, desirable, for latecomers to emulate. The interventionist state of Napoleon III or of Prussia and Bismarckian Germany, which took upon itself the responsibility for economic growth – in particular through education – stood in many ways closer to Scandinavian political traditions, especially those of Sweden, than did the night-watchman state of nineteenth-century England.

The growth of German influence, though perhaps strongest in Sweden, was not confined to that country. Nor was it restricted to the more conservative sections of society such as the court and the aristocracy. In the late nineteenth century Germany stood for progress in all fields: technical, industrial and intellectual as well as military, and as a model for social legislation and political organisation for the left as well as the right. 'It is true', Heckscher remarks, 'that Hjalmar Branting's personal sympathies were for France, but the brand of socialism adopted was entirely German. The same is true of the trade unions, which took after the German model, and so far as one can see, no one in Sweden appears to have realized that the trade unions in England went back at least to the middle of the century and were possessed of considerably greater

[84] Folke Lindberg, *Kunglig utrikespolitik. Studier och essayer från Oskar II:s tid* (Stockholm, 1950), pp. 5–44.

stability.'[85] Danish Social Democrats and trade unionists were influenced equally strongly by their German mentors. There was, however, a kind of democratic antidote to German influence among the poorer members of society, which was provided by mass emigration to the United States – the only foreign country of which many ordinary people had either knowledge or experience.[86]

German cultural influence in Scandinavia had always been strong. Contacts between Scandinavia and the German-speaking world were close in the romantic era, and Scandinavian writers and artists, including Ibsen, Strindberg and Munch, continued to gravitate towards Germany. Increasingly, however, influence flowed in the opposite direction. Starting with Ibsen in the 1880s and followed by Bjørnstjerne Bjørnson, Jonas Lie and Knut Hamsun, Norwegian writers, too, were received enthusiastically in Germany as exponents of a new realism and naturalism.[87] There was, however, another German image of Scandinavia, a romanticised view of Scandinavian landscape, mythology and race, of which Kaiser Wilhelm II, among others, was an enthusiastic exponent.[88]

In other respects, too, the Scandinavian countries came to have more to offer to the outside world. This was true especially of Scandinavian science and technology, but also of social and political organisation. As Scandinavian societies became more sophisticated, influence became less and less of a one-way process. The transformation was accompanied by a growing self-confidence, particularly in Sweden. Sir Cecil Spring Rice, appointed British minister to Stockholm in 1908, was increasingly struck (and irritated) by the way in which, he felt, the Swedes combined their new mood with deference to Germany and a patronising belief in the impending doom of the British empire. 'This particular country is at the top of an optimistic wave', he wrote in August 1912; and some months later: 'There is absolutely no limit to Swedish confidence especially since the Olympic Games [held that year in Stockholm] and I believe they think the time has come to take a hand in the [diplomatic] game.'[89]

Sven Nordlund's study of foreign investment in Sweden refers to 'the intensifying rivalry between Britain and Germany over Sweden's raw materials'. British acquisitions in the Swedish timber industry and German purchases of iron ore mines were, he suggests, 'components of an informal

[85] E. F. Heckscher, 'A Survey of Economic Thought in Sweden 1875–1950', *Scandinavian Economic History Review* 1 (1953), pp. 105–25 (p. 118).

[86] Folke Lindberg, *Den svenska utrikespolitikens historia* III, 4, pp. 136–7.

[87] Gerhardt and Hubatsch, *Deutschland und Skandinavien*, pp. 387–93.

[88] Birgit Marschall, *Reisen und Regieren. Die Nordlandfahrten Kaiser Wilhelms II* (Heidelberg, 1991).

[89] Spring Rice to Henry Adams, 30 August 1912, printed in Stephen Gwynn (ed.), *The Letters and Friendships of Sir Cecil Spring Rice* (2 vols., London, 1929), vol. II, p. 170; Spring Rice to Lord Knollys, 15 October 1912, FO 800/241.

imperialist strategy regarding the Swedish market, with the aim of making Sweden a raw material satellite'.[90] To the extent that this was a deliberate strategy it was, as we have seen, only partially successful. In any case it resulted less from conscious 'imperialism' than from the efforts of firms to ensure continuing supplies of raw materials, as well as from normal commercial competition. Anglo-German rivalry was normally latent rather than explicit. There was, however, a growing imbalance between the two great industrial economies. German industry made increasing inroads into traditional British export markets. By the late nineteenth century British commerce was on the defensive in much of continental Europe, including Scandinavia. Germany for its part, as a relatively new industrial nation, faced difficulties in finding export markets overseas and thus concentrated its efforts on neighbouring small European states such as the Netherlands, Switzerland, and the Balkan and Scandinavian countries. In such markets the advantages of proximity and cultural affinity were combined with German industrial and commercial dynamism.

The figures for Scandinavian trade show a picture of significant though not catastrophic decline in British exports, with the share of Scandinavian imports supplied by Great Britain falling from an average of 23 per cent in 1874–83 to just under 20 per cent in 1904–13 (table 5).[91] Over the same period Germany's share rose from 29 to 35 per cent. The proportion of Scandinavian exports taken by each country changed less. In the decade before the First World War Britain still took nearly 38 per cent of the exports of the four Nordic countries, while Germany's share was just under 18 per cent. The balance varied from country to country. Some were more dependent than others on the British market. Over 50 per cent, and sometimes as much as 60 per cent, of all Danish exports went to Great Britain. Sweden, on the other hand, had reduced its export dependence on Britain from over 56 per cent in 1874 to less than 25 per cent by 1913. Both Denmark and Finland took around 40 per cent of their imports from Germany. There were also major exceptions to the general pattern. Britain remained by far the most important supplier of fuels – above all, coal – to Scandinavian markets, while Germany was the largest, and sometimes the only, market for important Scandinavian products such as Swedish iron ore. But the most striking change was the relative (and in some cases absolute) decline of Great Britain, and the rise of Germany, as exporters of manufactured goods to the Scandinavian countries.

[90] Nordlund, *Upptäckten av Sverige*, pp. 298–9.
[91] Scandinavian import statistics, on which these percentages are based, have to be treated with caution since they record the country of *purchase*, which may not necessarily be the country of *production*. The difference is of particular significance for Great Britain given its importance as an intermediary for the purchase of goods from the British empire and other overseas countries. For further discussion of this point, see Harm Schröter, *Aussenpolitik und Wirtschaftsinteresse. Skandinavien im aussenwirtschaftlichen Kalkül Deutschlands und Grossbritanniens 1918–1939* (Frankfurt am Main, Berne and New York, 1983), p. 465 (n. 33).

Table 5 *Trade with Germany and the United Kingdom as a percentage of the total trade of the Nordic countries: averages over ten-year periods (1874–1913)*

Exports							
1874–83		1884–93		1894–1903		1904–13	
Germany	UK	Germany	UK	Germany	UK	Germany	UK
15.2	36.3	14.3	37.7	13.9	42.2	17.8	37.9
Imports							
1874–83		1884–93		1894–1903		1904–13	
Germany	UK	Germany	UK	Germany	UK	Germany	UK
28.9	23.2	30.4	22.6	32.0	22.1	35.2	19.9

Source: B. R. Mitchell, *International Historical Statistics: Europe 1750–1988* (New York, 1992), table E2.

The decline was sharpest after the turn of the century and in the goods of highest value. In Denmark, for example, Britain's share of imports of finished metal goods, ships and machinery fell from over 33 per cent in the late 1890s to less than 16 per cent in the years 1910–13, while Germany's share rose from 35 to over 78 per cent.[92] The evidence of capital investment reinforces the impression that Britain was losing ground in Scandinavia not just to Germany, but even to France and the Scandinavian countries themselves. In Denmark, for instance, the main period of British investment was in the 1850s and 1860s, and was concerned mainly with railway construction.[93] After 1870 the bulk of the capital needed for agricultural and industrial development was raised in Germany and France (despite the fact that in 1873 Denmark was the only country other than Britain which was able to borrow at 3 per cent on the London Stock Exchange).[94] Of the 466 million kroners' worth of Danish bonds and shares held abroad in 1912, 213 million was in German hands and only 25 million in British.[95] French capital was prominent in the construction of the Swedish railway network; A. O. Wallenberg, the founder of Stockholms Enskilda Bank (the leading Swedish investment bank) was an ardent Francophile who had close links with the Paris money market.[96] In Norway there was a large amount of British investment, particularly in the wood-processing industry.[97] As in Sweden, however, British investors were also attracted to risky mining ventures

[92] Nüchel Thomsen and Thomas, *Anglo-Danish Trade*, pp. 199–200.
[93] Ibid., pp. 297–300.
[94] D. C. M. Platt, *Foreign Finance in Continental Europe and the United States 1815–1870* (London, 1984), p. 177.
[95] Nüchel Thomsen and Thomas, *Anglo-Danish Trade*, p. 298.
[96] Olle Gasslander, *History of Stockholms Enskilda Bank to 1914* (Stockholm, 1962); Folke Lindberg, *Den svenska utrikespolitikens historia* III, 4, pp. 126–8; Lars G. Sandberg, 'Banking and Economic Growth in Sweden Before World War I', *Journal of Economic History* 38 (1978), pp. 650–80; Hecksher, 'Economic Thought in Sweden', pp. 110–11.
[97] Stonehill, *Foreign Ownership in Norwegian Enterprises*, pp. 30–1.

such as Dunderland Iron Ore Company founded in 1902, which suspended production in 1908 having produced heavy losses and very little iron ore.[98] Nordlund's study shows that over half the total foreign investment in Swedish extractive and manufacturing industries between 1895 and 1914 was made by Danish and Norwegian firms, but that among the leading industrial nations, Germany accounted for 19 per cent and Great Britain only 11 per cent of the total.[99] In financial services such as insurance and banking, however, Britain retained a leading position. In Norway, for example, foreign companies, mainly British, held 21 per cent of the insurance market, and Norwegian fire accident and marine insurance companies were dependent to a large extent on the reinsurance facilities provided by London.[100] Banking links between London and Scandinavia were dominated by Hambros Bank, which enjoyed a close relationship with Norwegian and Danish governments throughout the nineteenth century.[101]

The diminishing British economic presence was a phenomenon by no means confined to Scandinavia, and was in fact less pronounced than in other European markets.[102] To some extent it was bound to follow from Britain's loss of industrial pre-eminence as other countries industrialised. The fact that it was accompanied by a shift of British exports to less developed overseas markets, and by a massive investment in the non-European world, above all North and South America, may be seen as a rational response to the changing nature of the world economy.[103] On the other hand, Britain's concentration on less developed markets may have reflected a growing uncompetitiveness in selling more advanced products to more prosperous and sophisticated consumers.

British diplomats in Scandinavia were certainly alert to the growth of German competition and critical of British lack of enterprise. Commenting in 1906 on the revival of Swedish commercial activity, the British chargé d'affaires in Stockholm expressed the hope that

British traders will make a supreme effort now, strike the iron while it is malleable, inundate Sweden with commercial travellers conversant, if possible, with the language, and will send their price lists here in Swedish as well as English with – what to me appears highly important – the equivalent of English prices clearly given in Swedish

[98] M. Flinn, 'Scandinavian Iron Ore Mining and the British Steel Industry 1870–1914', *Scandinavian Economic History Review* 1 (1953), pp. 31–46 (pp. 42–6); Hodne, *Economic History of Norway*, p. 303.

[99] Nordlund, *Upptäckten av Sverige*, table 8, p. 68.

[100] O. G. Adamson (ed.), *Industries of Norway* (Oslo, 1952), pp. 352–3.

[101] Hodne, *Economic History of Norway*, p. 215; Bo Bramsen and Kathleen Wain, *The Hambros 1779–1979* (London, 1979).

[102] Ross J. S. Hoffman, *Great Britain and the German Trade Rivalry 1875–1914* (Philadelphia, 1933; repr. New York and London, 1983), pp. 114–38.

[103] R. Floud and D. McCloskey (eds.), *The Economic History of Britain Since 1700* (2 vols., Cambridge, 1981), vol. II, pp. 25–6, 66–7. For the geographical distribution of British overseas investment, see Lance E. Davis and Robert A. Huttenback, *Mammon and the Pursuit of Empire: The Economics of British Imperialism* (abridged edn, Cambridge, 1988), pp. 39–44.

currency, with a view to capturing some of the orders which have slipped away from them into the hands of the indefatigable German.[104]

In Whitehall, both the Foreign Office and the Board of Trade were aware of the implications for German trade of the opening of the first direct rail and ferry link between Sweden and Germany, from Trelleborg to Sassnitz, in 1909.[105] In Kristiania, Sir Arthur Herbert was scathing, as we have seen, about the pusillanimity of British firms in the face of the Norwegian concession laws. He was also prepared to meet head-on the charge 'that His Majesty's officials resident abroad, do not do, what they reasonably, or unreasonably can to assist them in matters of trade', citing two recent examples of ventures he had supported but which had failed through lack of enterprise.[106] On occasion, the Foreign Office would intervene formally in support of British business. After 1908 the Wilson Line, which ran the only steamer service between Bergen and Hull, was successful on several occasions in persuading the Foreign Office to make representations against proposals to establish a state-subsidised Norwegian line in direct competition.[107] This was, however, a case of unfair competition rather than preferential treatment; there was much less official support than in Germany for the active promotion of British commercial interests abroad.[108] German cartel arrangements and tariff policies, moreover, made it possible to sell iron and steel products in foreign markets at prices 15–20 per cent lower than those paid at home.[109]

British officials were conscious of the political and strategic implications of Germany's growing commercial predominance. Scandinavian business interests frequently shared this concern but were also ready to play on it for their own purposes. Both Spring Rice in Stockholm and Herbert in Kristiania were particularly receptive to investment proposals which stressed the need to deny Germany control of strategic industries and raw materials.[110] In 1909 Spring Rice was approached by the Swedish scientist and financial speculator (and later pro-German activist) Professor Gösta Mittag-Leffler with a proposal for British investment in the Norwegian nitrates industry. The latter's reputation, together with scientific doubts, led the Foreign Office to oppose the scheme

---

[104] Dering to Grey, 15 October 1906, FO 368/53, No. 35300.

[105] Correspondence in FO 368/331.

[106] Herbert to Grey, 11 February 1910, FO 368/440, No. 5463. One of these was the Eyde initiative discussed in the following two paragraphs.

[107] Correspondence in FO 368/208, 368/314 and 368/440; Findlay, 'Annual Report on Norway, 1911', 19 March 1912, FO 371/1415 (*BDFA*, I, F, III, p. 211).

[108] Hoffman, *German Trade Rivalry*, pp. 51–62; D. C. M. Platt, 'The Role of the British Consular Service in Overseas Trade 1825–1914', *Economic History Review* 15 (1962–3), pp. 494–512; Platt, *Finance, Trade and Politics in British Foreign Policy 1815–1914* (Oxford, 1970); K. Schädlich, 'Wandlungen in der Aussenhandelsdiplomatie Grossbritanniens (1885–1910)', in F. Klein (ed.), *Neue Studien zum Imperialismus vor 1914* (Berlin, 1980), pp. 135–63.

[109] Nüchel Thomsen and Thomas, *Anglo-Danish Trade*, p. 197.

[110] David H. Burton, *Cecil Spring Rice: A Diplomat's Life* (London and Toronto, 1990), p. 145.

(though they used Swedish and Norwegian prejudice against foreign capital as a cover).[111]

A more promising approach was made, also in 1909, when Sam Eyde suggested to Herbert that British firms should subscribe to a share issue by the Notodden nitrates works, in order to establish a British presence in a firm hitherto dominated by French and German interests at a time when it was poised to undertake a new venture in the electric smelting of low-grade Norwegian iron ores:

> As in the first place Norwegian sympathies are decidedly English, and secondly they do not want for political reasons to have the whole country overrun by Germans, Eyde wishes to give the English capitalists and iron masters the first offer of coming in . . . There is not the slightest question that this is a fair and square offer, and if we do not profit by it, our Teuton friends will come in, and we shall never have a chance again.[112]

The Foreign Office put Eyde in touch with a number of leading industrialists, including Sir Andrew Noble, the chairman of Armstrongs, but without result. Eyde told Herbert that 'his mission had been fruitless, and that he would now turn to Germany which he, as a Norwegian and a patriot, was unwilling to do, as there was already enough German capital in the country'.[113] 'The iron people he said did not respond, and did not see the importance of controlling a new iron supply at their doors and were generally "slow".'[114] Eyde was evidently quite ruthless in his attempts to obtain capital wherever it might be found.[115] His aversion to German capitalists, however, was probably genuine. The problems over Norsk Hydro have been noted above, and Herbert's successor Mansfeldt Findlay reported in 1912 that 'There is nearly always friction when German and Norwegian capitalists attempt to work together, and last autumn means were found to replace the large German interest in the Notodden nitrate factory by other capital.'[116]

The Foreign Office files for the years leading up to the First World War are full of expressions of anxiety about the growth of German influence in Scandinavia. The annual report on Denmark for 1910 concluded with the reflection that

> One cannot . . . help being struck by the peaceful penetration which is being carried on commercially, artistically and in a literary manner, by Germany. Young Danes who wish to push themselves commercially go to Germany and establish connections there. Danish literary people turn to Germany for appreciation . . . Danish universities are shaping themselves more after German models. German shops are penetrating even into

---

[111] Correspondence in FO 368/15, Nos. 38559, 39509, 39835, 40208, 40343, 42809, 44254. For Spring Rice's interest in the electrical smelting of iron ore, see Gwynn, *Letters and Friendships of Spring Rice* II, pp. 144, 148.

[112] Herbert to Hardinge, 22 April 1909, FO 368/314, No. 16755.

[113] Herbert to FO, 11 February 1910, FO 368/440, No. 5463.

[114] Herbert to Dering, 31 October 1909, FO 368/315, No. 40343.

[115] Stonehill, *Foreign Ownership in Norwegian Enterprises*, pp. 35–9.

[116] Findlay, 'Annual Report on Norway, 1911', 19 March 1912, FO 371/1415 (*BDFA*, I, F, III, p. 211).

Copenhagen. Such peaceful penetration it is impossible to avoid. On the other hand, I am convinced that the Danish national feeling is as strong as ever it was. Denmark has no idea of allowing herself to be absorbed into her greater neighbour.[117]

Findlay, too, while noting the 'friction' between German and Norwegian capitalists, pointed to the way in which the growth of German influence seemed to flow ineluctably from the deepening relationship between the two countries, particularly in the field of education: 'Many Norwegians go to Germany for education, more especially to the excellent German mining and engineering schools. They come back speaking German fluently, and more or less influenced by German methods and mentality.'[118]

At the same time, however, British diplomats emphasised that Scandinavians were by no means resigned to their fate. Denmark's determination to avoid absorption was noted in the report quoted earlier. Swedes, too, were noticeably ambivalent in their attitudes towards Germany. Sir Cecil Spring Rice, summing up from Stockholm the events of the same year, 1910, noted: 'Sweden is conscious of the peaceful though not benevolent penetration of Germany in the world of commerce and finance; she does not like it, but she has to accept it.'[119] Both national pride and economic self-interest made Scandinavians resentful of German power even while they learned from Germany and admired much of what it stood for. The absence of a dynamic British commercial presence meant, however, that there was no effective counterweight. Politically, too, Britain seemed remote and ineffectual.[120]

That Scandinavia might be absorbed either formally or informally into a German-dominated economic sphere came to seem increasingly probable. It would be a mistake to see this as a clearly formulated and consistently pursued policy on the part of German industry or the German government. The evidence of German diplomatic activity and German–Scandinavian military contacts (discussed in chs. 2 and 3) suggests that official interest in Scandinavia was rather fitful and certainly less intense than that directed towards, for example, the Balkans in the immediate pre-war years. There are, however, a number of stray remarks and observations which, taken together, indicate an interest in formalising economic relations with Scandinavia on the analogy of the German Zollverein. The history of the Zollverein suggested, of course, that what began as a customs union ended as a political one. In 1902 Kaiser Wilhelm II minuted on a despatch from Stockholm that 'a Zollverein must be created' in order to 'draw Sweden across to us as a federal state'.[121] Reichenau,

---

[117] J. C. T. Vaughan (Copenhagen) to FO, enclosing report by Sir Alan Johnstone, 1 January 1911, FO 371/1360 (*BDFA*, I, F, XVII, pp. 377–88).

[118] 'Annual Report on Norway, 1911', 19 March 1912, FO 371/1415 (*BDFA*, I, F, III, p. 211).

[119] 'Annual Report, 1910', 31 January 1911, FO 371/1225 (*BDFA*, I, F, III, p. 129).

[120] Sir Conyngham Greene (Copenhagen) to FO, enclosing annual report for 1911, 1 January 1912, FO 371/1360 (*BDFA*, I, F, XVII, pp. 394–5).

[121] Marginal note on a despatch from Stockholm, quoted in Folke Lindberg, *Den svenska utrikespolitikens historia* III, 4, p. 153.

German minister to Sweden from 1911 to 1915, told a Swedish acquaintance that he wanted Sweden to become a part of Germany in the same way as, for example, Baden or Württemberg.[122] Admiral von Tirpitz wished Germany's 'representatives abroad to favour tactfully the interests of Scandinavian, Swiss and Dutch private persons in so far as these desired, and to look after them as if they were Germans':

These small States, so important for us and for the world, would have greeted the development of our power in a friendly way if they had found in us a natural support in any difficulty, and *if we had enabled them* to grasp the idea of 'Europe' as persistently and skilfully represented by us.[123]

The kaiser's credibility may have been undermined when he also called for a union of the 'Indo-Germanic races' against the Slav menace, but such fantasies were in tune with the mood of the time (they recalled the ideas of Joseph Chamberlain and Theodore Roosevelt) and had some resonance in Scandinavia itself.[124]

A number of Scandinavians responded positively to the idea of German hegemony, notably those conservative Swedes who favoured partnership with Germany as a means of achieving Swedish hegemony in northern Europe and who became (along with a number of Finns) pro-German activists after the outbreak of war. Kjellén argued that Sweden should look beyond Scandinavia and concentrate on peaceful economic and cultural expansion in Russia, but that as a small state Sweden must also seek security through alignment with a great power – and the only possible one was Germany.[125] Others advocated a Nordic confederation or Baltic league in close association with the Central Powers, and maintained links with such figures as Heinrich Class, the leader of the Pan-German League, and Friedrich Naumann, the National Liberal advocate of *Mitteleuropa*.[126]

Other Scandinavians were less sanguine. Peter Vedel, the former head of the Danish Foreign Ministry, wrote pessimistically in 1906 of the consequences of Denmark's growing deference towards Germany in matters of defence and economic policy.[127] If Denmark explicitly accepted that it lay within Germa-

---

[122] Diary of Professor Gösta Mittag-Leffler: entry for 22–5 June 1913, cited in Wilhelm M. Carlgren, *Neutralität oder Allianz. Deutschlands Beziehungen zu Schweden in den Anfangsjahren des Ersten Weltkrieges* (Stockholm, 1962), p. 22. The Liberal foreign minister Ehrensvärd, repudiating the advocates of an alliance with Germany, told the British minister that 'To ally herself with any Great Power would be, for a small state like Sweden, equivalent to becoming the vassal of that Power, and for his own part he honoured his country too highly to wish to see it occupy a position like Wurtemberg [*sic*]': Howard to Grey, 27 January 1914, FO 425/380, No. 5853.

[123] A. von Tirpitz, *My Memoirs* (2 vols., London, n.d. [1919]), vol. I, pp. 181–2.

[124] Speech at Ballholmen, Norway, reported in Findlay to Grey, 5 August 1913, FO 800/69.

[125] Elvander, *Harald Hjärne och konservatismen*, p. 274.

[126] L. Torbjörn Norman, 'Right-Wing Scandinavianism and the Russian Menace', in John Hiden and Aleksander Loit (eds.), *Contact or Isolation? Soviet–Western Relations in the Interwar Period* (Stockholm, 1991), pp. 329–49.

[127] Note of 17 December 1906, quoted in Viggo Sjøqvist, *Peter Vedel. Udenrigsministeriets*

ny's sphere of influence – perhaps even by concluding a military alliance – it would become a vassal state. There would be a gradual penetration of German capital, leading to the destruction of Danish industry and the disappearance of Denmark as an independent entity. The Danes would have to fight to preserve their language and nationality just as the inhabitants of North Slesvig were now doing. If the dynasty were to retain its throne at all, it would have to be satisfied, at best, with a position similar to that occupied by the king of Saxony. King Frederik VIII of Denmark expressed similar fears.[128]

Certainly, Denmark was by far the most exposed of all the Scandinavian countries, and the one towards which unofficial German efforts were most persistently directed. The kaiser, according to his chancellor Bülow, returned repeatedly to the idea of building a closer relationship with Denmark.[129] Bülow's confidant at the German Foreign Office, Friedrich von Holstein, while advising caution in the short term, described 'the plan of drawing Denmark within the outer ambit of the German Empire' as 'a great idea of the future'.[130] In the German–Danish military conversations of 1906–8 (ch. 3, pp. 103–8), demands for a closer economic relationship were explicitly linked to a proposal for a military alliance.[131] Tirpitz, for whom, 'from the point of view of naval policy, a close relationship with Denmark' was 'much more important, for example, than our alliance with Austria', would have been 'prepared to make territorial sacrifices [i.e. in Slesvig] for a naval and economic agreement with this Germanic cousin of ours'.[132] But German policy was far from consistent. Baron von Schoen, minister in Copenhagen from 1900 to 1905, was critical both of those 'German circles, which were bent on extension of power, and boasted of Germany's military strength', and thus undermined attempts to improve German–Danish relations, and of his own political superiors:

Little or nothing was done in responsible German quarters to counteract this unfortunate state of affairs, or, at all events, nothing likely to be of use. It was thought unnecessary to attach any great weight to our relations with our smaller neighbours; they were hardly taken into political consideration at all, and it was left to the local authorities in the country to deal with the uncomfortable state of affairs on the frontier as they thought best.[133]

---

direktør (2 vols., Århus, 1957–62), vol. II, *1865–1911*, p. 285. His remarks were prompted by knowledge of German–Danish military conversations: see pp. 103–8 in this volume.

[128] Viggo Sjøqvist, *Erik Scavenius. Danmarks udenrigsminister under to verdenskrige. Statsminister 1942–1945* (2 vols., Copenhagen, 1973), vol. I, *1877–1920*, p. 67.

[129] Bernhard Fürst von Bülow, *Denkwürdigkeiten* (4 vols., Berlin, 1930–1), vol. II, pp. 79–80.

[130] Memorandum of 6 February 1905, in Norman Rich and M. H. Fisher (eds.), *The Holstein Papers* (4 vols., Cambridge, 1955–63), vol. IV, *Correspondence 1897–1909*, pp. 324–5.

[131] Spring Rice speculated whether a similar linkage might not exist in the case of Sweden: 'I wonder if Sweden will be asked to enter into a military agreement as the price of an equitable commercial Treaty' (Spring Rice to Hardinge, 13 April 1909, FO 800/241).

[132] Tirpitz, *Memoirs* I, p. 181.

[133] Freiherr von Schoen, *The Memoirs of an Ambassador* (London, 1922), p. 11. For Schoen's scepticism as to the feasibility of an alliance with Denmark, see his letter to Holstein of 11 February 1905, Rich and Fisher, *Holstein Papers* IV, pp. 325–6.

Nevertheless, the atmosphere improved with the coming to power of the Liberals in Denmark in 1901. They and their Radical Liberal successors (as well as the increasingly influential Social Democratic Party) were dedicated to a policy of strict neutrality and seem to have accepted fatalistically that little could be done to prevent the gradual absorption of Denmark into the German sphere of influence.[134]

There seems little doubt that, if peace had continued beyond 1914, German commerce and capital, and German ideas, would have continued to penetrate further, into Scandinavia as a whole. As the German industrialist Hugo Stinnes put it, 'Let us have three to four years more of peaceful development and Germany will be the undisputed economic master of Europe.'[135] Sir Edward Grey, the British foreign secretary, wrote bitterly of the conduct of the Scandinavian states at the Hague Conference of 1907:

Many of the smaller Powers, notably Sweden, Norway and Denmark, clearly intimated that, even where their interests seemed to demand their going with us, they dare not do anything that might expose them to the ill-will of Germany . . . The dominating influence in the conference has clearly been *fear* of Germany . . . If the present position of Germany allows her to take up the domineering attitude she assumes here, what will be her bearing when . . . she gains a more complete hegemony in Europe and the world? One shudders to think of what would then become of British interests.[136]

In part, of course, Scandinavian fear of Germany derived from its position of military preponderance on the European continent. But, except in Denmark, there was little or no fear of a direct German attack; nor could anyone have anticipated the devastating effect that German submarine warfare was later to have on Scandinavian shipping. It is also true that Germany's leadership was far less confident – and probably less aggressive – than it appeared to hostile critics such as Grey. Scandinavian deference towards Germany was based not merely on fear but on the community of economic interest which had been built up between Germany and its European neighbours. Economic power underpinned Germany's claim to a controlling voice in the affairs of continental Europe – a continent from which Great Britain was drawing away economically even as it became more deeply entangled in its diplomatic and military alignments.

[134] Bjørn Svensson, *Tyskerkursen* (Copenhagen, 1983).
[135] Quoted in Wolfgang J. Mommsen, *Imperial Germany 1867–1918: Politics, Culture and Society in an Authoritarian State* (London, 1995), p. 91.
[136] Grey to Tyrrell, 11 October 1907, FO 800/69.

2 Scandinavia in European diplomacy 1890–1914

Towards the end of the nineteenth century the European great powers began to take a more active interest in Scandinavian affairs. Changes in military technology and in the balance of power in Europe as a whole, as well as within Scandinavia itself, heightened the strategic importance of northern Europe and raised questions about both the capacity and the willingness of the Scandinavian states to preserve their neutrality in the event of war. For much of the century Scandinavia and the Baltic had been of strategic interest only in the context of a war between Great Britain and Russia. The Crimean war showed that the Baltic was one of the few regions where British naval power could be brought to bear effectively against Russia, and its lessons were not entirely forgotten in the second half of the nineteenth century.[1] Moreover, 'the epoch in which an Anglo-Russian conflict seemed the most likely outcome of international relations' did not come to an end until the peaceful resolution of the Dogger Bank affair in 1904.[2] Already, however, Scandinavia and the Baltic had been profoundly affected by the revolution in the European balance of power brought about by the creation of the German empire in 1871.

The destabilising effects of this creation, limited until 1890 by Bismarck's conservatism and diplomatic skill, began to be revealed under his successors. Following the lapse of the Reinsurance treaty, the Scandinavian states began to feel the repercussions of the increasing polarisation of international relations between Germany, Austria-Hungary and Italy on the one hand, and France and Russia on the other. Denmark in particular acquired strategic importance as a potential link between Russia and France and a sensitive point on Germany's northern flank.[3] In 1893 the German chancellor Caprivi delivered a speech in which he reckoned as a matter of course that Denmark would be ranked alongside Russia and France as Germany's adversary in wartime.[4] The

---

[1] Andrew Lambert, *The Crimean War: British Grand Strategy Against Russia 1853–1856* (Manchester, 1990); Lambert, '"Part of a Long Line of Circumvallation to Confine the Future Expansion of Russia": Great Britain and the Baltic 1809–1890', in Göran Rystad, Klaus-Richard Böhme and Wilhelm M. Carlgren (eds.), *In Quest of Trade and Security: The Baltic in Power Politics 1500–1990*, vol. I, *1500–1890* (Lund, 1994), pp. 297–334.

[2] A. J. P. Taylor, *The Struggle for Mastery in Europe 1848–1918* (Oxford, 1954), p. 425.

[3] Viggo Sjøqvist, *Peter Vedel. Udenrigsministeriets direktør* (2 vols., Århus, 1957–62), vol. II, *1865–1911*, pp. 206–10.

[4] Troels Fink, *Ustabil balance. Dansk udenrigs- og forsvarspolitik 1894–1905* (Århus, 1969), p. 13.

completion of the Kiel Canal in 1895, followed by the construction of the German High Seas Fleet, raised for the first time the prospect of an Anglo-German naval war in which both Denmark and Norway might be in the front line. The building of strategic railways by Russia in Finland awoke Swedish fears of Russian aggression and revived British anxieties about Russian designs on the warm-water ports of the Norwegian coast which had been dormant since the 1850s.[5]

Nor was Scandinavia's role merely passive. The stability of northern Europe was threatened by the deepening crisis in Swedish–Norwegian relations which culminated in the emergence of an independent Norwegian state in 1905. The disappearance of the Scandinavian union, hitherto the keystone of the northern European balance of power, opened up the prospect of a political vacuum and raised the question of what was to replace the treaty of 1855 by which Britain and France had guaranteed the territories of the united kingdoms against Russia. The union crises of 1884 and 1895 provoked flurries of concern in Berlin, London and St Petersburg. The dissolution of the union in 1905 marked the beginning of a period of intense diplomatic activity which resulted in the signature of three international agreements: the Norwegian integrity treaty of 1907, and the Baltic and North Sea agreements of 1908. The history of these negotiations has attracted relatively little attention outside the Scandinavian countries themselves.[6] Some of the leading participants, like Grey, were at pains to deny their significance. But as Pertti Luntinen, the most recent historian of the negotiations, points out, their very blandness is a key to their significance.[7] The fact that they did little more than affirm the territorial status quo on the shores of the North Sea and the Baltic showed how difficult it was to achieve great-power consensus. It could be done only by shelving the really contentious issues. The agreements of 1907–8 contained no reference to Norwegian neutrality or to the legal status of the Danish Straits, nor even a definition of where the North Sea ended and the Baltic Sea began. The negotiations formed, in Folke Lindberg's words, 'part of the silent, hard struggle for influence in the Northern countries and for control of the Baltic, above all the entrances to this sea'.[8]

Scandinavia was drawn into great-power diplomacy after the turn of the

[5] Tuomo Polvinen, *Die finnischen Eisenbahnen in den militärischen und politischen Plänen Russlands vor dem Ersten Weltkrieg* (Helsinki, 1962); Paul Knaplund, 'Finmark in British Diplomacy 1836–1855', *American Historical Review* 30 (1925), pp. 478–502; C. F. Palmstierna, 'Sweden and the Russian Bogey: A New Light on Palmerston's Foreign Policy', *Nineteenth Century and After* 112 (1933), pp. 739–54; Jens Petter Nielsen, 'Ønsket tsaren seg en isfri havn i nord?', *Historisk tidsskrift* (Norway) 70 (1991), pp. 604–21.

[6] But see Paul Herre, *Die kleinen Staaten Europas und die Entstehung des Weltkrieges* (Munich, 1937); Walther Hubatsch, 'Zur deutschen Nordeuropa-Politik um das Jahr 1905', *Historische Zeitschrift* 188 (1959), pp. 594–605; David W. Sweet, 'The Baltic in British Diplomacy Before the First World War', *Historical Journal* 13 (1970), pp. 451–90; Detlef Grell, *Die Auflösung des Schwedisch–Norwegischen Union – 1905 – im Spiegel der europäischen Grossmachtspolitik. Unter besonderer Berücksichtigung der Akten des Auswärtigen Amtes* (Essen, 1984).

[7] Pertti Luntinen, *The Baltic Question 1903–1908* (Helsinki, 1975), p. 240.

[8] Folke Lindberg, *Scandinavia in Great Power Politics 1905–1908* (Stockholm, 1958), p. 37.

century as a result, in part, of Britain's gradual abandonment of isolation and its integration into the European alliance system. One of the initial effects of this process was to set Britain against both Russia and Germany and to open up the prospect of a Russo-German rapprochement which would have had profound implications for the balance of power in northern Europe. The Anglo-Japanese alliance of 1902 made Russia more interested in good relations with Germany, and gave Germany an opportunity to drive a wedge between Russia and France. The Anglo-French entente of 1904 gave implicit support to France against Germany as the price for settling colonial rivalries in Africa. To the extent that war with Germany was regarded as a real prospect, the price was an acceptable one. Britain had been alienated by the erratic nature of German foreign policy since 1896, in which violently anti-British gestures alternated with expressions of friendship which never developed into mutual trust, let alone a formal alliance. Germany's construction of a High Seas Fleet represented a direct challenge to British naval supremacy, despite the kaiser's protestations to the contrary, although it was only in the summer of 1904 that the British Admiralty made its first plans for war against Germany.[9]

What can be seen with hindsight as a transitional phase in which the old antagonism between Britain and Russia was being dismantled and replaced by a new Anglo-German antagonism seemed to Germany's leaders to mark a more profound transformation. In 1904, and still more in 1905 following the destruction of the Russian Baltic Fleet and France's humiliation in Morocco, the kaiser and his chancellor believed that they had within their grasp the continental alliance which both had long sought. An understanding between Russia and Germany would be followed by the adherence of France, if the latter could be sufficiently intimidated and made to realise the folly of reliance on Great Britain. These dreams may have been doomed to failure, but should not be discounted as motives for German actions. Issues of real importance were at stake. Russo-German rapprochement implied nothing less than the exclusion of British political influence and naval power from the Baltic. Acting in concert, the two continental powers could dominate the Danish Straits and close them to the Royal Navy at will. The Scandinavian states would be wholly under the influence of Germany and Russia. British naval mastery outside the Baltic might even be outflanked by a Russian or German naval presence on the Norwegian coast. Although such ambitions could not be realised to their fullest extent, even the degree of collaboration that was achieved between Germany and Russia had serious implications for Britain's position in northern Europe.

Scandinavia and the great powers

Until diplomatic attention came to focus on northern Europe in the first years of the twentieth century, the conduct of relations between the Scandinavian

---

[9] Arthur J. Marder, *British Naval Policy 1880–1905: The Anatomy of British Sea Power* (London, 1940), pp. 463–5, 479–82.

states and their larger neighbours was largely a matter of routine. The rapid economic and political changes of the late nineteenth and early twentieth centuries had little impact on policy making in Scandinavia before 1914. Public interest in foreign affairs was limited, expenditure on foreign services was meagre and the conduct of relations with foreign governments remained the preserve of a narrow elite. In Sweden, for example, there was little discussion of foreign affairs either in the press or in parliament until the early years of the twentieth century. The farmers who dominated the Swedish Riksdag in the late nineteenth century were largely indifferent to the subject and parsimonious in their attitude towards public spending. It is true that one formal means of consultation with the Riksdag existed in the form of the 'secret committee' (hemliga utskottet), but this met very infrequently and its last two meetings before 1914, in 1895 and 1905, were entirely taken up with the question of Norway.[10] Only after the outbreak of the First World War, when Sweden was faced with vital issues in its relations with the belligerents, did the Riksdag begin to demand a greater say in the decision-making process.

In both Denmark and Sweden, formal responsibility for the conduct of foreign policy lay with the crown. The real powers of the Danish king diminished greatly after the revolution of 1848, though at the beginning of the twentieth century there was still scope for royal interventions. The Swedish constitution of 1809 gave the king wide-ranging powers, including the right to declare war, make peace and conclude treaties, which were used extensively by King Karl XIV Johan. Karl XV's failure to bring about an alliance with Denmark in 1863 marked the end of an independent role for the king in the making of foreign policy. However, both Oscar II and Gustav V had strong views on foreign policy and a liking for high-level diplomacy, though the latter was irresolute and often merely the instrument of his formidable consort Victoria.[11] Effective power was thus in the hands of the government of the day – though most foreign ministers (who were almost invariably career diplomats) were 'content with a policy of muddling through'.[12] Paradoxically, the scope for royal diplomacy was greatest in the most democratic of the three Scandinavian countries. In newly independent Norway, where foreign policy procedures were less institutionalised and important issues were at stake, King Haakon VII played an important role in the negotiations for an integrity treaty between 1905 and 1907.[13]

[10] W. M. Carlgren, Neutralität oder Allianz. Deutschlands Beziehungen zu Schweden in den Anfangsjahren des Ersten Weltkrieges (Stockholm, 1962), p. 92.

[11] Folke Lindberg, Kunglig utrikespolitik. Studier och essayer från Oskar II:s tid (Stockholm, 1950); W. M. Carlgren, 'Gustaf V och utrikespolitiken', in Studier i modern historia tillägnade Jarl Torbacke den 18 augusti 1990 (Stockholm, 1990), pp. 41–57.

[12] Wilhelm Carlgren, 'Sweden: The Ministry for Foreign Affairs', in Zara Steiner (ed.), The Times Survey of Foreign Ministries of the World (London, 1982), pp. 455–69 (pp. 460–1).

[13] Tim Greve, Haakon VII of Norway (London, 1983), pp. 53–4; Roald Berg, '"Det land vi venter hjælp af". England som Norges beskytter 1905–1908', in Forsvarsstudier IV. Årbok for Forsvarshistorisk forskningssenter, Forsvarets høgskole 1985 (Oslo, 1985), pp. 111–68 (p. 134).

Until 1914 it was still possible to run foreign affairs with tiny foreign ministry establishments. The ministries themselves – Udenrigsministeriet in Denmark, Utrikesdepartementet in Sweden and Utenriksdepartementet in Norway – were largely staffed by middle-class civil servants (in Denmark, often the sons of officials and clergymen), while the membership of the diplomatic services, like that of other European states, was almost wholly aristocratic.[14] The same was true (though with a less aristocratic ethos) of Norway after 1905. Here there was strong support for the view that 'the foreign services should concentrate on looking after Norway's economic interests, to the virtual exclusion of all other activities normally associated with foreign policy'.[15] However, Norway was able to draw on the expertise of Norwegian diplomats who had risen high in the Swedish–Norwegian diplomatic service: men like Thor von Ditten, head of the Foreign Ministry in Stockholm from 1901 to 1903, or Fritz Wedel Jarlsberg, the united kingdoms' minister in Madrid, who served after 1905 as Norwegian ministers in, respectively, Berlin and Paris.[16] In all three countries, however, the growing volume of routine communications with foreign states meant that Foreign Ministry officials, and especially the permanent heads, were becoming overworked. When more important issues arose, it was frequently impossible for the necessary expertise to be found within the bureaucratic establishment: hence the growing practice of co-opting lay experts – particularly academic experts on international law – either as part-time consultants or as full-time officials.

Is it possible, against this background, to identify any attempt to pursue a clearly defined foreign policy on the part of any of the three Scandinavian states? In the case of Denmark, as we have seen, the predominant concern was to avoid involvement in war. In practice, this came increasingly to mean establishing a 'correct' relationship with Germany. Sweden's position was more ambivalent. Until 1905, the position of Norway in the Swedish–Norwegian union constituted the most important brake on the conduct of the union's foreign policy.[17] The Storting's constitutional powers over foreign policy were greater than those of the Riksdag. Its approval was required for offensive war, and it had the right to be notified of alliances and treaties. More importantly, both Norwegian opinion and the king's Norwegian ministers were reluctant to endorse what they perceived as Swedish adventurism and an increasing Swedish disregard for Norwegian interests. There was thus a danger that a more active foreign policy might jeopardise the existence of the union.

[14] Sjøqvist, *Vedel* II, pp. 236–59; Klaus Kjølsen, 'Denmark: The Royal Danish Ministry of Foreign Affairs', in Steiner, *Times Survey of Foreign Ministries*, pp. 163–83 (p. 170).
[15] Erik-Wilhelm Norman, 'Norway: The Royal Norwegian Ministry of Foreign Affairs', in Steiner, *Times Survey of Foreign Ministries*, pp. 391–408 (p. 395); Reidar Omang, *Norsk utenrikstjeneste*, vol. I, *Grunnleggende år* (Oslo, 1955).
[16] Erik-Wilhelm Norman, 'Norway', p. 393; Omang, *Norsk utenrikstjeneste* I, pp. 42–62, 113–23.
[17] Narve Bjørgo, Øystein Rian and Alf Kaartvedt, *Norsk utenrikspolitikks historie*, vol. I, *Selvstendighet og union. Fra middelalderen til 1905* (Oslo, 1995), pp. 233–5, 339–59.

The heritage of an imperial past still coloured Swedish attitudes and, especially after 1905, made Swedish statesmen sensitive to any hints at their country's diminished status. After the loss of Norway, Swedish thoughts turned intermittently to revenge, sometimes to Scandinavian hegemony. Official policy, however, remained cautious and unadventurous. According to one of its prime ministers, E. G. Boström (speaking in 1905), Sweden had 'no [foreign] policy in any real sense apart from protecting its neutrality'.[18] Wilhelm Carlgren has aptly described Sweden after 1905 as being afflicted with a kind of 'snow-blindness' towards the world at large after decades of preoccupation with the problem of Norway.[19]

Ironically, in view of Bjørnstjerne Bjørnson's famous dictum that the best foreign policy was to have no foreign policy, only Norway appears to have had a clear sense of purpose in its relations with the outside world. Roald Berg has shown that foreign policy was one of the elements employed by an elite of 'nation-builders' (scholars, politicians and journalists) in order to consolidate the independence won in 1905.[20] This effort entailed, among other things, protecting the country's economic resources (through the concession laws and the attempt to extend the limit of Norwegian territorial waters from three to four miles in order to exclude foreign fishing vessels); excluding or assimilating alien ethnic elements (the Sami (Lapp) and Finnish population in the far north of the country); and pursuing the long-term goal of establishing Norwegian sovereignty over the Arctic archipelago of Svalbard (Spitsbergen). As defined by Jørgen Løvland, Norway's first foreign minister, Norwegian foreign policy must be defensive but not passive.[21] Norway needed a strong foreign policy in order to keep the country out of great-power combinations and alliances which could drag it into war, and in order to secure its material interests through an energetic commercial policy. Deeply sceptical towards 'the European warlike states' (including Great Britain, Norway's *de facto* protector), Løvland was determined to secure international recognition of Norway's desire to avoid involvement in the impending great war either through a guarantee of its neutrality or, when that attempt failed, through the guarantee of integrity embodied in the treaty of 1907.

Turning to the great powers, we find policy towards the Scandinavian states governed by the relatively lowly position which they occupied in the perceived hierarchy of foreign policy interests. Sweden was, at best, a power of the middle rank, whilst the drastic decline in Denmark's international status was reflected in the halving in the size of its diplomatic service after 1848.[22]

---

[18] Quoted in W. M. Carlgren, *Ministären Hammarskjöld. Tillkomst, söndring, fall. Studier i svensk politik 1914–1917* (Stockholm, 1967), pp. 91–2.

[19] Carlgren, review of Yvonne-Maria Werner, *Svensk–tyska förbindelser kring sekelskiftet 1900* (Lund, 1989), in *Historisk tidskrift* (Sweden) 110 (1990), pp. 425–7.

[20] Roald Berg, *Norsk utenrikspolitikks historie*, vol. II, *Norge på egen hånd 1905–1920* (Oslo, 1995), pp. 317–18.

[21] Ibid., pp. 53–4.   [22] Kjølsen, 'Denmark', p. 171.

Nevertheless, Copenhagen was a more attractive diplomatic posting than either Stockholm or (after 1905) Kristiania. In the German diplomatic service it ranked second after Brussels in the hierarchy of European ministerial posts (these followed, of course, the seven ambassadorships in the major capitals) – much higher than the other Scandinavian capitals, and the only one regarded as a proving ground for diplomats destined for ambassadorial appointments.[23]

Denmark's importance had much to do with the close family ties between the Danish royal family and those of Russia, Germany and Great Britain. In the words of one American minister to Denmark, Copenhagen 'was not only a city of rumours, but a city of news. The pulse of Europe could be felt there because Europeans of distinction were passing and repassing continually.'[24] Future secretaries of state who served in Copenhagen included Kiderlen-Wächter, Schoen and Brockdorff-Rantzau. In the British and Russian diplomatic services, too, Copenhagen was a stepping-stone to higher places. The connections between the Danish and Russian royal families were particularly strong and made Copenhagen a favoured posting among Russian diplomats: Muraviev served there; so too did Isvolsky before becoming foreign minister in 1906.[25] Among Britain's representatives Edward Goschen, minister from 1900 to 1905, moved on to Vienna and then to Berlin; Conyngham Greene, appointed in 1910, became ambassador to Japan only two years later.[26]

But Stockholm, though often uncongenial climatically, socially and, to an increasing extent, politically, was also a post for able diplomats like Rennell Rodd (who liked the place) and Spring Rice (who came to detest it). Rodd went to Rome and Spring Rice to Washington.[27] And Stockholm was growing in importance. The appointment of Esme Howard to Stockholm in 1913 as Spring Rice's successor 'derived from the Foreign Office's determination to have a seasoned diplomat in what was becoming an increasingly sensitive post'.[28] If Swedish manners were too rigid for some British diplomats, the social life of Kristiania proved lively and relaxed for the first generation of diplomats accredited to the Norwegian capital,[29] though Arthur Herbert, Britain's first minister to Norway, was disconcerted, when presenting his credentials, by the informality of Norwegian government ministers.[30] His successor Mansfeldt Findlay was an imperious and embittered man, 'exiled' to

[23] Lamar Cecil, *The German Diplomatic Service 1871–1914* (Princeton, N. J., 1976), pp. 14–15.
[24] Maurice Francis Egan, *Ten Years near the German Frontier: A Retrospect and a Warning* (London, 1918), p. 10.
[25] Isvolsky, *The Memoirs of Alexander Iswolsky* (London, n.d. [c. 1920]), pp. 19–20.
[26] On Goschen's appointments, see Raymond A. Jones, *The British Diplomatic Service 1815–1914* (Waterloo, Ont., 1983), p. 195.
[27] Ibid.
[28] B. J. C. McKercher, *Esme Howard: A Diplomatic Biography* (Cambridge, 1989), p. 133.
[29] Ernst Günther, *Minnen från ministertiden i Kristiania åren 1905–1908* (Stockholm, 1923), pp. 65–9.
[30] F. Wedel Jarlsberg, *Reisen gjennem livet* (Oslo, 1932), p. 240.

Norway as a result of an unfortunate episode in his earlier career.[31] Though efficient and entirely upright, he was not, in the shrewd judgement of his wartime press attaché, 'suited for contact with the democratic, independent Norwegian people'.[32]

As long as the Scandinavian states remained a backwater, there was little incentive for the great powers to pay attention to Scandinavian affairs. In the absence of pressing political issues, and in view of the importance of economic and commercial affairs, the vast bulk of day-to-day official communications with the Scandinavian countries was handled in Britain by the Commercial and Sanitary Department of the Foreign Office and in Germany by Division II – the Handelspolitische Abteilung – of the Auswärtiges Amt. The Commercial Department was considered dull by Foreign Office officials, and was also regarded as the least efficient.[33] Though by the mid-1880s it dealt with 80 per cent of the Wilhelmstrasse's correspondence, Division II was also a decidedly low-status section.[34] But even in Division I, the Political Division, Scandinavian affairs took a low priority, being supervised by a counsellor whose miscellaneous responsibilities also covered Luxemburg, Portugal, Mexico and South America, Africa and the German colonies, as well as keeping watch over the international anarchist movement.[35] The Foreign Office's organisation after the reforms of 1906 was more rational, with Scandinavian political affairs being handled by the Western Department under one of the Office's most able officials, Eyre Crowe. In the Russian Foreign Ministry the division of responsibilities among departments was frequently confused, and there was little central direction. Isvolsky's reform programme after 1906 was well conceived but had little effect before the outbreak of war.[36] Differences of outlook between diplomats, whose careers were spent exclusively abroad, and Foreign Ministry officials were also greater than in Britain or Germany.[37] There was perhaps also more scope for initiative on the part of enterprising men on the spot, like Kroupensky in Kristiania or Isvolsky in Copenhagen.

Despite the widening responsibilities of foreign offices and diplomats, and the growing demand for a more open diplomacy, the making of foreign policy in every country remained an elite activity.[38] Apart from the small number of permanent officials who handled day-to-day relations with the Scandinavian countries, Scandinavian affairs engaged the attention of those elites only

---

[31] The 'Denshawi Outrage' in Egypt in 1906 is summarised in Rowland Kenney, *Westering* (London, 1939), pp. 217–19.

[32] Ibid., p. 127.

[33] Zara Steiner, *The Foreign Office and Foreign Policy 1898–1914* (Cambridge, 1969), p. 21 (n. 1).

[34] Cecil, *German Diplomatic Service*, pp. 9–10.   [35] Ibid., p. 12.

[36] G. H. Bolsover, 'Izvol'sky and Reform of the Russian Ministry of Foreign Affairs', *Slavonic and East European Review* 63 (1985), pp. 21–40.

[37] Dominic Lieven, *Russia's Rulers Under the Old Regime* (New Haven, Conn., and London, 1989), pp. 196–9.

[38] M. S. Anderson, *The Rise of Modern Diplomacy 1450–1919* (London, 1993), pp. 110–19, 128–48.

intermittently. In Great Britain, the German–Danish crisis of 1863–4 had been a unique occasion on which dynastic sympathies and strategic concerns coincided to produce acute disagreements over Scandinavian policy between crown, government and parliament.[39] In the 1880s British politicians like Gladstone, Joseph Chamberlain and W. E. Forster discovered, from their differing perspectives, interesting parallels between the Swedish–Norwegian constitutional conflict and the crisis over Irish Home Rule.[40] But when Scandinavian affairs did come to require attention after the turn of the century, politicians had more pressing concerns, both internal and external.

The distaste of Sir Edward Grey, foreign secretary in the Liberal government after 1906, for the negotiations which led to the Baltic and North Sea agreements of 1908 emerges clearly from his memoirs. 'It is not worthwhile to explain these negotiations', he wrote. 'What result they had at the time has been superseded by the war and its consequences. Nor did they have any important influence on the course of events before the war; but the records about them show how suspicious everyone was.'[41] Preoccupied with their programme of reform, with their domestic political difficulties and, to an increasing extent, with the Irish question, most members of the government had little time for foreign affairs in general, let alone those of northern Europe. In 1908, Zara Steiner notes, the Cabinet 'passed hastily over the Baltic and North Sea agreements . . . to consider a Licensing Bill'.[42]

Monarchs were a different matter. Partly owing to his close family connections with the Danish, and later with the Swedish and Norwegian, royal families, King Edward VII took an active interest in Scandinavia, and especially in the question of who was to succeed to the throne of the new kingdom of Norway.[43] Although his ministers did their best to limit his role, it was perhaps more important than some historians have suggested.[44] Certainly he seems to have intrigued against his nephew the kaiser almost as vigorously as the latter suspected.[45] The personal role of the tsar in the making of Russian foreign policy was potentially very great, and Nicholas II took a close interest in diplomatic activity and appointments.[46] He lacked the intelligence and determination of his father Alexander III, but the fluid diplomatic situation in

[39] W. E. Mosse, 'Queen Victoria and Her Ministers in the Schleswig-Holstein Crisis 1863–1864', *English Historical Review* 78 (1963), pp. 263–83; Keith A. P. Sandiford, 'The British Cabinet and the Schleswig-Holstein Crisis 1863–1864', *History* 58 (1973), pp. 360–83.

[40] Sir Horace Rumbold, *Further Recollections of a Diplomatist* (London, 1903), pp. 289–92; Paul Knaplund (ed.), *British Views on Norwegian–Swedish Problems 1880–1895: Selections from Diplomatic Correspondence* (Oslo, 1952), pp. x–xii, 41–3, 150–2, 201–2, 227–30.

[41] Viscount Grey of Falloden, *Twenty-Five Years* (2 vols., London, 1925), vol. I, p. 143.

[42] Steiner, *Foreign Office and Foreign Policy*, p. 86.

[43] Sir Sidney Lee, *King Edward VII* (2 vols., London, 1925–7), vol. II, pp. 315–26, 582–4.

[44] Steiner, *Foreign Office and Foreign Policy*, pp. 202–7.

[45] See e.g. Edward VII's conversation with Nansen, reported in Nansen to Løvland, 27 November 1906, in Reidar Omang (ed.), *Norge og stormaktene 1906–1914*, vol. I (Oslo, 1957), p. 118.

[46] Lieven, *Russia's Rulers*, p. 197.

Europe in the first years of the century, together with Russia's defeat in the Far East in 1904–5, made Scandinavia an attractive area for Russian diplomatic activity, and thus tended to make the tsar difficult to control.[47] Despite attempts to correct the institutional weakness of Russian government, notably with the establishment of the Council of Ministers in 1905, foreign policy remained susceptible to imperial interference.[48]

Russian policy was torn between, on the one hand, tsarist principles of conservatism and monarchical solidarity and, on the other, the *Realpolitik* of the professional diplomats and officials in the Foreign Ministry.[49] Both Bismarck and his successors played on Russian loyalty to the Bernadotte dynasty and hostility towards Norwegian 'republicanism'. On other questions, too, notably whether the Baltic should be a closed or an open sea, Russia was indecisive. From the point of view of power politics, however, the break-up of the Swedish–Norwegian union was in many ways advantageous to Russia. There were also some indications of an interest in the warm-water ports of northern Norway.[50] Nicholas II was intermittently attracted to the idea of overturning the status quo in northern Europe, while Isvolsky skilfully employed Scandinavian and Baltic issues in his diplomatic strategy of striking a balance between Germany and Great Britain. The outcome of the negotiations of 1905–8 was in some respects, though not all, a Russian success and a tribute to Isvolsky's resourcefulness.[51]

Monarchical diplomatic activity in Scandinavia was seen at its most vigorous in the person of Kaiser Wilhelm II of Germany. He paid frequent visits to all three Scandinavian countries, made forceful pronouncements on the destinies of Scandinavia and Germany, and intervened decisively in the international affairs of the region. In the light of Birgit Marschall's work on Wilhelm II's northern travels, the kaiser's enthusiasm for things Scandinavian can no longer be dismissed but must be regarded as a 'mirror' of the cultural preoccupations of Wilhelmine society.[52] His frequent visits to Scandinavia and his impulsive diplomatic interventions have also been interpreted as inconsequential gestures, and have been contrasted with the predominantly cautious official line towards Scandinavia maintained from the Bismarck era up to 1914.[53] In many respects such scepticism is justified.[54] But the kaiser was not an isolated figure in the German policy-making establishment.

[47] Ibid., p. 198.
[48] David M. McDonald, 'A Lever Without a Fulcrum: Domestic Factors and Russian Foreign Policy 1905–1914', in Hugh Ragsdale (ed.), *Imperial Russian Foreign Policy* (Cambridge, 1993), pp. 268–311.
[49] Sune Jungar, *Ryssland och den svensk–norska unionens upplösning* (Turku, 1969), p. 192.
[50] Ibid., pp. 45–9, 85–8.   [51] Luntinen, *Baltic Question*, pp. 75–83.
[52] Birgit Marschall, *Reisen und Regieren. Die Nordlandfahrten Kaiser Wilhelms II* (Heidelberg, 1991).
[53] Carlgren, *Neutralität oder Allianz*, pp. 25–6.
[54] For a discussion of the role of the kaiser's personality in German policy making, see Thomas A. Kohut, *Wilhelm II and the Germans: A Study in Leadership* (New York and Oxford, 1991).

Bernhard von Bülow, foreign minister from 1897 to 1900 and chancellor from 1900 to 1909, certainly distanced himself from the kaiser in his memoirs, and the latter's importance is played down by the editors of the German diplomatic documents, *Die grosse Politik*.[55] But fears of Russian and British ambitions in the north were widespread in the upper reaches of the German establishment – in the mind, for instance, of Friedrich von Holstein at the Wilhelmstrasse – and were not merely fantasies of the kaiser alone.[56] Wilhelm II for his part was capable of exercising restraint and changing tack when necessary. The kaiser and Bülow, moreover, were in agreement on the basic objectives of German diplomacy including, ultimately, the creation of a continental alliance of Germany, Russia and France directed against Great Britain.[57]

Germany, Russia and the Baltic 1903–1905

The question of whether the Baltic Sea could be kept open to the warships of all nations in time of war was the one issue vital to Britain, Germany and Russia alike. For Britain the matter was ostensibly clear-cut. Free access to the Baltic was one of the cardinal principles of British naval strategy and foreign policy. Between the seventeenth century and the Napoleonic wars, when the Royal Navy had been dependent on Baltic supplies, it had been a matter of life and death. In the modern age – an age not only of steam and ironclads, but also of dreadnoughts, mines and torpedoes – the principle was becoming unenforceable, but was one upon which Britain continued to insist with the utmost vigour.

Both Germany and Russia, on the other hand, hankered after a Baltic closed to foreign warships – a *mare clausum*. However, Russia was uncomfortably aware that in practice this might imply conceding mastery of the Baltic to Germany, especially after the destruction of the Russian Baltic Fleet at the hands of Japan in 1904. When the entente of 1907 opened up the prospect of collaboration with British naval power, Russia shifted towards the British position on an open Baltic. It was not yet clear how limited Britain's naval commitment to the Baltic would prove to be. Grey told the Russian foreign minister Sazonov in 1912 that Britain could not take the risk of affording Russia any naval support in a sea whose entrances were effectively controlled

---

[55] Bernhard Fürst von Bülow, *Denkwürdigkeiten* (4 vols., Berlin, 1930–1); Barbara Vogel, *Deutsche Russlandspolitik. Das Scheitern der deutschen Weltpolitik unter Bülow 1900–1906* (Düsseldorf, 1973), p. 8; A. J. P. Taylor, *Struggle for Mastery*, p. 578.

[56] E.g. Holstein memorandum of 22 February 1904, in Norman Rich and M. H. Fisher (eds.), *The Holstein Papers* (4 vols., Cambridge, 1955–63), vol. IV, *Correspondence 1897–1909*, pp. 282–4.

[57] Vogel, *Deutsche Russlandspolitik*, pp. 8–11, 44–8. For a persuasive assessment of Bülow's approach to foreign policy, see Katharine A. Lerman, 'Bismarck's Heir: Chancellor Bernhard von Bülow and the National Idea 1890–1918', in John Breuilly (ed.), *The State of Germany: The National Idea in the Making, Unmaking and Remaking of a Modern Nation-State* (London, 1992), pp. 103–27.

by Germany.[58] On the other hand, the Anglo-Russian naval conversations of May 1914 offered some encouragement to Russia (though their main effect was to alarm the Germans).

Germany enjoyed a uniquely favourable strategic position in the Baltic and the southern North Sea. Although Britain dominated the northern approaches to the North Sea and the Channel, the German navy had absolute command of Danish waters and was able to shift its vessels quickly between the North Sea and the Baltic through the Kiel Canal. But Germany too remained undecided as to where its strategic interests ultimately lay. Until the outbreak of war in 1914, the navy was uncertain whether to keep the Baltic entrances open and risk a British incursion, or to close them and gain security at the expense of its own freedom of manoeuvre (the option eventually chosen).[59]

In these circumstances the inadequacy of the Danish defence effort, discussed earlier, was crucial since Denmark stood astride the most important maritime entrances to the Baltic, including the Great Belt – the only route, until the widening of the Kiel Canal in 1914, navigable by the largest modern warships.[60] The break-up of the Scandinavian union was of international importance because it exposed Denmark's weakness and coincided with the growing tendency of military and especially naval planners to include Scandinavia in their strategic calculations. It also coincided with a particularly fluid period of great-power relations, between about 1902 and 1907, in which Scandinavia and the Baltic played a part in Germany's attempt to arrest the movement of Great Britain towards France and Russia, and to rectify the mistake made in 1890, when the Reinsurance treaty had been allowed to lapse, by restoring a German–Russian rapprochement.

The German attempt to bring about a Russo-German rapprochement was based on the hope that an acknowledgement of common interests in the Baltic region would serve as the basis for a wider understanding and as a means of weakening Russia's links with the Western powers. It hinged on the personal relationship between Kaiser Wilhelm II and Tsar Nicholas II and began in 1903 with an attempt to secure joint control of the Danish Straits. The initiative culminated in the famous meeting of the two emperors at Björkö (Koivusaari), off the coast of Finland, in July 1905, and ended with the collapse of Germany's Moroccan adventure in 1906.[61] In their correspondence and meetings, the kaiser alternately flattered and intimidated the tsar, playing on shared anti-British prejudices, and in particular on the tsar's fear of a

---

[58] Serge Sazonov, *Fateful Years 1909–1916* (London, 1928), pp. 60–2; Grey, *Twenty-Five Years* I, pp. 298–9.

[59] See ch. 4, pp. 126–7.

[60] For an analysis of the strategic significance of the various Baltic entrances, see the despatch of 6 March 1907 by Captain Dumas, the naval attaché in Berlin, in *BD* VIII, pp. 122–9. For a description of some of the technical aspects of navigating the seaways, see Gunnar Alexandersson, *The Baltic Straits* (The Hague, 1982), pp. 63–9.

[61] R. J. Sontag, 'German Foreign Policy 1904–1906', *American Historical Review* 33 (1928), pp. 278–301.

British naval assault on Russia in the Baltic. The legal status of the Baltic Straits in wartime and Denmark's capacity to defend its neutrality were the principal issues preoccupying the two monarchs. Although Bülow, abetted by Holstein, sought to exploit the kaiser's dynastic relationships, the latter's personal diplomacy was frequently too flamboyant and indiscreet for their purposes.[62] More implacably anti-British than the kaiser (or Holstein), and more consistent in his strategic conception of a continental bloc as the foundation of German world power, Bülow was also more conscious of the constraints on Germany's freedom of manoeuvre.[63] For Bülow the time was never right. Though tempted by the kaiser's vision, Bülow and Holstein were sufficiently realistic to acknowledge that no hypothetical improvement in German–Russian relations could outweigh the damage caused to Anglo-German relations by any overt attempt to bring Denmark and the Danish Straits under German control.[64] The chancellor's task was therefore to put a brake on the kaiser's impetuosity. It was not until the end of 1904, when Bülow's diplomatic calculations had been proved false and Germany faced isolation, that he was to abandon caution and actively seek an alliance with Russia.[65]

Although Wilhelm II had long dreamt of a continental alliance of Germany, Russia and France, his previous diplomatic interventions in Scandinavia had had an anti-Russian thrust. The Scandinavian union crisis of 1895 prompted the kaiser to write a long letter to the Swedish crown prince depicting the consequences of Norwegian independence. Sweden would be encircled by a predatory Russia and its only salvation would lie in joining a customs union with Germany.[66] The 'Germanic North' would then form a bloc protecting the whole of Europe against a 'Slavic–Czech invasion'. Wilhelm later responded to a request from Oscar II for not only moral but also material German assistance against a Russian intervention in the union conflict, with a suggestion that Sweden should join the triple alliance. The offer was not taken up (and it was regarded by the kaiser's advisers mainly as a means of evading the king's request), but in 1902, as we have seen in the last chapter, the kaiser was still thinking of exploiting Swedish fears of Russia to make Sweden a 'federal state' in a German-led Zollverein.

The deterioration of Anglo-Russian relations following the conclusion of the Anglo-Japanese alliance in 1902 prompted the kaiser to revive the idea of a continental league against what he now believed to be a prospective combina-

---

[62] Norman Rich, *Friedrich von Holstein: Politics and Diplomacy in the Era of Bismarck and Wilhelm II* (2 vols., Cambridge, 1965), vol. II, pp. 475, 679–80, 689.

[63] Ibid., p. 731; Peter Winzen, 'Prince Bülow's *Weltmachtpolitik*', *Australian Journal of Politics and History* 22 (1976), pp. 227–42.

[64] Bülow, *Denkwürdigkeiten* II, pp. 79–80; Holstein memorandum of 6 February 1905, Rich and Fisher, *Holstein Papers* IV, pp. 324–6.

[65] Winzen, '*Weltmachtpolitik*', pp. 239–41.

[66] Folke Lindberg, *Kunglig utrikespolitik*, pp. 160–75; M. Gerhardt and W. Hubatsch, *Deutschland und Skandinavien im Wandel der Jahrhunderte* (Bonn, 1977), p. 375.

tion of Japan, Great Britain and the United States.[67] It would be in the interest of both Germany and Russia to prevent a British (or Anglo-American) naval assault on the Baltic. This could be achieved, as the kaiser told the Russian ambassador before setting off for a visit to Copenhagen in April 1903, by a 'union of the northern realms – Denmark, Sweden, Norway, Germany and Russia – for the protection of the Baltic'.[68] Another solution, suggested by the tsar when the two emperors met at Darmstadt in November, was the permanent neutralisation of Denmark.[69] This was one which the Danish government itself favoured, encouraged by the suggestion of a Russian international law expert in an article published in the autumn of 1903 suggesting that Denmark could achieve neutral status merely by declaring itself neutral.[70] But while the Danes believed that neutrality did not imply closing the Straits, the tsar's interpretation was different. If, he told the kaiser, the Danes could not prevent the British or the Americans from entering the Belts and the Sound, 'they must empower us two, who are endangered by this state of affairs, to do it for them', using 'the Danish forts and Copenhagen as base of operations'.[71]

In encouraging the kaiser to broach the subject of neutralisation with King Christian IX of Denmark (who was to visit Berlin in December 1903), Nicholas II was, as Bülow immediately pointed out, inviting Germany to prevent an attack on his capital, and thus make Russia's enemies its own.[72] Having failed to prevent Wilhelm from raising the subject with the king of Denmark, Bülow was faced with the choice of alienating either Russia by dropping the proposal, or Britain and the United States by allowing it to go ahead.[73] The kaiser had limited Bülow's freedom of manoeuvre by reporting to the tsar Christian IX's positive response to the idea of 'an agreement secretly made between the 3 Sovereigns' by which Germany and Russia would guarantee Danish neutrality and, if necessary, 'help to defend it by force'.[74] He refused to bow to Bülow's objections: Germany must, he said, act as Russia's honest broker, and the question of Denmark was vital to Germany from the military point of view. 'It would mean a doubling of our strength in wartime if we could rely on Denmark!'[75]

Only the intervention of Admiral Büchsel, the chief of the naval staff, changed the kaiser's mind. Far from seeking Danish neutrality, Germany should, the Naval Staff argued, occupy Danish territory along the shores of the Great and Little Belts in order to tempt the British fleet into a battle in the narrow Danish waters, where Germany would enjoy the tactical advantage.[76]

---

[67] Fink, *Ustabil balance*, p. 125.   [68] *GP* XIX, 1, p. 68.   [69] *GP* XVIII, 1, p. 75.
[70] Fink, *Ustabil balance*, p. 15.   [71] *GP* XVIII, 1, p. 75 (English in original).
[72] *GP* XIX, 1, pp. 67–70.
[73] Metternich (London) to AA, 23 December 1903, ibid., pp. 78–80.
[74] Ibid., p. 71 (English in original).   [75] Ibid., p. 85.
[76] Walther Hubatsch, *Weserübung. Die deutsche Besetzung von Dänemark und Norwegen 1940* (Göttingen, 1960), pp. 2–3; Carl-Axel Gemzell, *Organization, Conflict and Innovation: A Study of German Naval Strategic Planning 1888–1940* (Lund, 1973), pp. 69–70.

The kaiser's apparent unfamiliarity with the main strategic plan of the German navy, on which it had been working since 1899 (see ch. 3, pp. 95–6), is revealing. Nevertheless, he was now prepared to fall in with the face-saving solution formulated by Holstein, that the initiative for the project should be made to come from Denmark.[77] Despite last-minute complications in January 1904 caused by the Danish government's belief, when it finally came to hear of the proposal, that it was still something that had to be taken seriously, the episode was brought to an untidy conclusion.[78] By the spring of 1904 the Russians, already at war with Japan and contemplating the journey to the Far East that would lead to the destruction of the Baltic Fleet at Tsushima, had lost interest in a closed Baltic; and it remains debatable whether any responsible Russian statesman shared the tsar's enthusiasm for closure.[79]

In October 1904, with Britain and Russia apparently close to war as a result of the Dogger Bank incident, and an estrangement between Britain and France confidently expected despite the entente they had signed in April, kaiser and chancellor were at last in agreement that the time was right to offer Russia an alliance.[80] The tsar, however, wished to 'initiate' the French into the alliance before it was signed. A Russian alliance would, furthermore, be anti-British; but Germany was, as Bülow insisted, in no position to antagonise Great Britain. It was precisely at this time, however, in November and December 1904, that the Germans were agitated by articles in the British press suggesting that there should be a preventive attack (on the analogy of Copenhagen in 1807) on their fleet.[81] On 3 December Büchsel presented to the kaiser a plan for dealing with a sudden British strike.[82] The first step would be an unannounced invasion of Denmark and the seizure of Danish waterways. The kaiser approved the plan and ordered the General Staff to alert two army corps in north Germany for a strike against Denmark: the chancellor and the Wilhelmstrasse were not informed of these preparations. Although the war scare passed, the German–Russian negotiations made no progress: whatever the tsar's personal inclinations, the Russians would not sacrifice their alliance with France. But if Russia could not be made to break with France, France might be forced to join with Russia and Germany. The opportunity came in 1905.

The climax of the kaiser's and Bülow's attempt at Russo-German rapprochement was reached when the two emperors met off the Finnish island of Björkö in July 1905.[83] Here at last, isolated from his ministers, the tsar signed the defensive alliance which he had been persuaded to shy away from at the end of

[77] *GP* XIX, 1, pp. 73–7.   [78] Fink, *Ustabil balance*, pp. 146–64.
[79] Jungar, *Ryssland*, p. 84; Jonathan Steinberg, 'Germany and the Russo-Japanese War', *American Historical Review* 75 (1970), pp. 1965–86 (p. 1968).
[80] A. J. P. Taylor, *Struggle for Mastery*, pp. 422–4.
[81] Marder, *British Naval Policy*, pp. 496–500; *GP* XIX, 2, pp. 351–80.
[82] Jonathan Steinberg, 'Russo-Japanese War', pp. 1978–9.
[83] *GP* XIX, 2, pp. 435–528.

1904.[84] From the German point of view the circumstances were uniquely propitious. The Moroccan crisis had led, on 6 June, to the fall of Delcassé, the architect of the entente; Germany had supported Russia in its war against Japan; the Russian Baltic Fleet had been destroyed at Tsushima on 27 May; Russia was in turmoil. But it was essential that the treaty be concluded before Russia made peace with Japan. Then, the Germans believed, there was a real chance that an intimidated France, humiliated over Morocco, its only ally crippled by war, could be persuaded to join Bülow's long-contemplated continental alliance. The scheme contained numerous miscalculations, of which the most crucial was the overestimation of the tsar's personal influence on Russian policy. Merely to obtain his signature, it was believed, was sufficient to ensure that the document could not be disavowed.[85]

Yet the fact that Björkö led nowhere (by the end of 1905 Russia's refusal to do anything that might jeopardise the alliance with France had become clear) should not lead us to underrate the expectations that were placed in it not merely by the kaiser, but above all by Bülow.[86] The latter's memoirs are misleading on this point.[87] He objected violently to the form of the treaty: the kaiser's insertion of the words 'en Europe' into the draft text had, he claimed, made it valueless to Germany since Russia would be under no obligation to attack India in the event of a war between Germany and Britain. But Bülow's melodramatic resignation threat had to do with much more than the wording of the treaty. He was probably trying to force a resolution of the much larger question of Germany's policy over Morocco and relations with France, and perhaps also to underline the constitutional point that only the chancellor could conclude agreements of this sort.[88] After the resignation episode had passed, both Bülow and Holstein recognised that what the kaiser had achieved was very much to Germany's advantage.[89] They did not imagine that the tsar could be overruled by his advisers. Even after the tsar's letters of October and November 1905 withdrawing from the treaty on the grounds of its incompatibility with Russia's obligations to France, Bülow sought to use the prospect of German participation in an international loan to Russia to bring about a change in Russian policy. The bitterness with which he ultimately forbade German participation, in March 1906, was a measure of Bülow's disillusionment.[90]

The treaty of Björkö can be fully understood only if its Scandinavian

---

[84] The existence of the treaty remained secret until after the First World War. The first detailed account (based on the recollections of the Russian statesman Count Witte) was published in E. J. Dillon, *The Eclipse of Russia* (New York, 1918).

[85] Vogel, *Deutsche Russlandspolitik*, p. 47.

[86] Kohut, *Wilhelm II*, pp. 188–9, supports the view that Björkö was more than an exercise in personal diplomacy on the part of the kaiser.

[87] Bülow, *Denkwürdigkeiten* II, pp. 137–51.

[88] Vogel, *Deutsche Russlandspolitik*, p. 224; Fink, *Ustabil balance*, p. 238.

[89] Fink, *Ustabil balance*, p. 239; *GP* XIX, 2, pp. 492–6; A. J. P. Taylor, *Struggle for Mastery*, p. 432.

[90] Vogel, *Deutsche Russlandspolitik*, pp. 227–31.

ramifications are taken into account. The meeting at Björkö was coloured by the crisis caused by Norway's secession from the Scandinavian union in June 1905, and by the two emperors' continuing preoccupation with the strategic position of Denmark. Scandinavia would, according to the kaiser, form an integral part of the new continental bloc. On 27 July he wrote to the tsar: 'Holland, Belgium, Denmark, Sweden will all be attracted to this new great centre of gravity . . . They will revolve in the orbit of the great block of Powers (Russia, Germany, France, Austria, Italy) and feel confidence in leaning on and revolving around this mass.'[91]

At Björkö, Wilhelm II sought to exploit the union crisis by playing on the tsar's fears of British designs on Norway. The kaiser, arriving at Björkö immediately after meeting the king of Sweden at Gävle, gave the tsar an account of their conversation.[92] The king had remarked, he said, that if Norway became independent Germany would be free to occupy Bergen, after which Great Britain might seize Kristiansand.[93] 'Emperor Nicholas was visibly disturbed at the prospect of a partition of Norway and the possibility of an English occupation, and said that in that case his harbours on the Murman coast would lose all value and there was an immediate danger that the Kattegat would be closed to Russia.'[94] The kaiser also hinted that British influence might be extended over Norway by other means. An opening had been created by Oscar II's refusal to agree to the Norwegian request for a Bernadotte prince as king of Norway. The alternative favoured by the Norwegians, Prince Carl of Denmark, happened to be the son-in-law of Edward VII.[95] Merely to mention the latter's interest in Prince Carl's candidature was sufficient to revive all of the tsar's apprehensions about British intrigues.

Although Edward VII did have a lively interest in the affair,[96] the kaiser's own expectations appear to have been equally far-reaching. He may originally have hoped to see a German prince, possibly one of his own sons, on the Norwegian throne – a possibility held out by the Swedish minister in Berlin, Arvid Taube, as early as 1903.[97] When this proved unrealisable he favoured first a Swedish prince, and then Prince Valdemar of Denmark, whose candidature had previously been suspect because it was backed by Russia. Finally the kaiser bowed to the inevitable. In Copenhagen on his return journey he ingratiated himself with Prince Carl and his young son Alexander

---

[91] Herman Bernstein (ed.) *The Willy–Nicky Correspondence: Being the Secret and Intimate Telegrams Exchanged Between the Kaiser and the Tsar* (New York, 1918), p. 191; see alternative version in Folke Lindberg, *Scandinavia*, p. 35.

[92] On this meeting, see Folke Lindberg, *Scandinavia*, pp. 32–4.

[93] Luntinen, *Baltic Question*, p. 57, suggests that the kaiser probably made up the story himself.

[94] *GP* XIX, 2, pp. 454–6.

[95] Norway's leaders deliberately chose Prince Carl in order to strengthen British self-interest, through his wife Princess Maud, in the welfare and security of Norway: Berg, *Norsk utenrikspolitikks historie* II, pp. 43–8.

[96] Lee, *Edward VII*, pp. 315–26.

[97] Hubatsch, 'Zur deutschen Nordeuropa-Politik', pp. 598–9.

(who were to become, respectively, King Haakon VII and King Olav V of Norway).[98] Thereafter the kaiser continued to display an ostentatious interest in the welfare of the new royal family on his annual visits to the west coast of Norway.[99]

Denmark also figured prominently in the discussions at Björkö. The two emperors returned to the idea which they had discussed in 1903, of guaranteeing Danish neutrality in such a way as to prevent a British naval incursion into the Baltic. The kaiser wished to crown his achievement by bringing Denmark into the alliance during his stay in Copenhagen. Bülow advised caution, and when the kaiser arrived there at the end of July he proved uncharacteristically silent on the subject. This was, he told the tsar, because the Danes were already resigned to a German–Russian preventive occupation in time of war.[100] However, Count Raben, the Danish foreign minister, surmised, perhaps more accurately, that the kaiser had originally wished to raise the question of closing the Straits 'but that he had refrained from this because of the attitude of British public opinion as well as a well-founded fear that he would not find the Northern monarchs to be favourably disposed listeners'.[101] In his conversation with Christian IX, however, the kaiser still 'mentioned the great idea you [Nicholas II] have – coinciding with mine – of a European "Zollverein" to knit the interests of Europes [sic] peoples closer together'.[102]

Behind the kaiser's overtures towards Denmark lay real fears about the country's strategic position. The war scare of late 1904 had reinforced the view of the Naval Staff that Germany must occupy Danish territory in the early stages of an Anglo-German naval war.[103] The army was, however, reluctant to consider any such modification of the Schlieffen Plan. In 1903, and as recently as December 1904, the kaiser had been impressed by Büchsel's argument, but by February 1905 he had come round to the army view and argued that the fleet should remain on the defensive.[104] This made it all the more important to 'bring about [a] closer relationship with Denmark': a message which he telegraphed twice to Bülow in the course of that month.[105] The prospect that Norway might come under British influence through Prince Carl's accession to the throne provided a further argument in favour of this course of action.[106]

After Björkö the kaiser renounced grand gestures towards Denmark, but German influence over that country was pursued by less overt means: through the Moltke–Lütken talks of 1906–7 and the economic and cultural penetration

---

[98] Hubatsch criticises the slackness of Bülow's policy on the throne affair, ibid., pp. 600–3.
[99] As reported e.g. in Leech (Kristiania) to FO, 2 August 1906, FO 371/99.
[100] Bernstein, *Willy–Nicky Correspondence*, pp. 117–20.
[101] Folke Lindberg, *Scandinavia*, p. 37.   [102] *GP* XIX, 2, p. 491 (English in original).
[103] See ch. 3, pp. 95–6.   [104] Gemzell, *Organization*, p. 70.
[105] Bülow, *Denkwürdigkeiten* II, pp. 79–80; Fink, *Ustabil balance*, pp. 235–6; Fink, *Spillet om dansk neutralitet 1905–1909. L. C. F. Lütken og dansk udenrigs- og forsvarspolitik* (Århus, 1959), pp. 23–4.
[106] Folke Lindberg, *Scandinavia*, pp. 33–4.

discussed in the previous chapter. After Björkö, too, there was no more talk of a continental bloc. In 1906 Germany suffered a decisive diplomatic defeat at the Algeçiras conference; Great Britain and France began staff talks; and, under the guidance of the new foreign minister, Isvolsky, Russia moved towards the understanding with Great Britain which the British had been seeking for years. This did not mean, however, that Russia and Germany had no common ground, or that they had ceased working together, if necessary against Britain's interests, should it suit them to do so. Scandinavia and the Baltic still offered considerable scope for such activity.

The Scandinavian crisis 1905–1908

In June 1905 Norway seceded unilaterally from the Scandinavian union. The break-up of the union was accompanied by much acrimony and even the threat of war between Norway and Sweden.[107] It also raised the question of what was to replace the treaty of 1855 by which Britain and France had guaranteed the territorial integrity of the united kingdoms in exchange for a Swedish undertaking not to cede territory to Russia.[108] As the Swedish–Norwegian crisis approached its climax in May–June 1905, the Swedish crown prince sounded British and German opinion. He found Britain ready to renew the guarantee for both Sweden and Norway if it was not directed explicitly against Russia, while both Britain and Germany favoured German participation. The Norwegians themselves made clear their desire for a great-power guarantee of Norwegian independence, but did not make an appeal to the great powers until November 1906. From the start, the Norwegians insisted that they wanted a treaty in which the powers would not only guarantee Norway's independence and integrity, but also recognise its neutrality.[109]

The distinction between integrity and neutrality was crucial, and was underlined at an early stage in the British deliberations on the Norwegian proposal. Sir Charles Hardinge, the permanent under-secretary of the Foreign Office, noted that 'the question of integrity is far more important than that of neutralization'.[110] Eyre Crowe, the head of the Western Department, minuted on 27 November that a guarantee of integrity alone 'need not be held to prevent one of the guaranteeing powers from temporarily occupying Norwegian territory without any intention of retaining it. Such a course might conceivably be convenient to Germany or even England in case of a war with Russia, or to Russia in the converse case.'[111] The Norwegians also wished to

---

[107] Raymond E. Lindgren, *Norway–Sweden: Union, Disunion and Scandinavian Integration* (Princeton, N. J., 1959).

[108] Ragnhild Hatton, 'Palmerston and Scandinavian Union"', in K. Bourne and D. C. Watt (eds.), *Studies in International History: Essays Presented to W. Norton Medlicott* (London, 1967), pp. 119–44.

[109] But they realised that they might not be able to achieve both: see memorandum by Arnold Ræstad, 5 May 1906, Omang, *Norge og stormaktene* I, pp. 72–8.

[110] Quoted in Luntinen, *Baltic Question*, p. 95.   [111] Quoted ibid.

include a reservation clause allowing Norway to go to the assistance of Sweden or Denmark if either should be attacked. This required the two other Scandinavian states to declare their neutrality or have it guaranteed, but it soon emerged that neither was prepared to take such a step (the Swedish crown prince declared that it would be tantamount to reducing Sweden to the status of 'Belgium or even Switzerland').[112] The great powers nevertheless had to consider the implications of Scandinavian neutrality for their own interests in the region. The juridical position of the Danish Straits was much less clear-cut than that of the Black Sea Straits, and there was considerable uncertainty as to whether Sweden and Denmark, if neutral, would be obliged to keep open or to close the entrances to the Baltic to belligerent warships in time of war.[113]

Although the latter interpretation did not seem plausible to British experts, it called to mind the ominous precedent of the Armed Neutralities of the eighteenth century, particularly that of 1780.[114] Even if the northern neutrals did not close the Straits themselves, the Germans were thought likely to do so either by force or through a secret understanding with Denmark. Well-founded rumours of German–Danish negotiations were rife early in 1907 – Hardinge believed an understanding might already exist – although they were later to be discounted (wrongly) by the Foreign Office.[115] The prospect of guaranteeing the neutrality of Norway alone was still more alarming. The director of naval intelligence (DNI), Captain Ottley, who had originally regarded Norwegian independence exclusively in the light of 'the slow glacial drift of Russian intrigue and Russian territorial expansion',[116] had shifted his ground significantly by 1907. Clearly reflecting the views of Sir John Fisher, the first sea lord, he told the Committee of Imperial Defence (CID) in February that 'Norwegian neutrality might handicap Great Britain in a war with Germany – if the latter occupied Denmark, Great Britain would need to seize a Norwegian port. The terms of the treaty might involve Great Britain in a war with Russia and France who would be obliged to defend Norwegian integrity.'[117]

The Foreign Office and the Admiralty were thus in agreement on the need for Britain to retain a free hand in respect of Norway in wartime. They came to regret the initial British support for a Russian counter-draft (in fact drafted jointly with the Germans) of the Norwegian treaty proposal which deleted the Scandinavian reservation but guaranteed Norway's independence, integrity *and* neutrality.[118] On 25 April 1907 the CID endorsed their misgivings by

---

[112] Folke Lindberg, *Scandinavia*, p. 48.

[113] The Russians, for instance, had reverted by 1905 to the view that Danish neutrality required the Danes to keep the Straits open for all kinds of ships at all times, but still left open the theoretical possibility of a treaty between Russia and the Scandinavian countries (on the model of the agreement of 1759 between Russia, Denmark and Sweden): Luntinen, *Baltic Question*, pp. 38–9.

[114] Hardinge memo, 18 February 1907, *BD* VIII, pp. 107–8; Sweet, 'Baltic', p. 462.

[115] Sweet, 'Baltic', pp. 462–3; Folke Lindberg, *Scandinavia*, pp. 79–81; Luntinen, *Baltic Question*, pp. 112–19; *BD* VIII, p. 108.

[116] Memo of 5 June 1905, CAB 17/59.

[117] CID, 95th meeting, 21 February 1907, CAB 2/2.   [118] Sweet, 'Baltic', p. 461.

coming down against the neutrality stipulation. British thinking on the subject had already been revealed by Fisher 'with his characteristic frankness' to Nansen, Norway's first minister in London. Fisher had, he said, told Grey that Britain should not commit herself to recognising Norwegian neutrality unless Sweden and Denmark were also declared neutral. If this were to happen,

he would regard it as a great advantage and as an important 'bulwark', but if Norway alone became neutral it would be a weakness. For if Germany occupied Denmark and closed the Belts in a war with England, it would be an urgent necessity for England to occupy a Norwegian harbour in order to create a base for operations in these waters.[119]

However, the Russian formula was accepted in June 1907 not only by the Germans and French but also by the Norwegians, who unexpectedly dropped their insistence on a Scandinavian reservation. At this point the British were given a pretext for vetoing the Norwegian treaty when the Russian government proposed the abrogation of the 'Åland servitude' of 1856 and signified its intention of refortifying the islands. Sir Edward Grey refused to sign the treaty on the ground that the whole Baltic problem had now been opened up, and that it must now be dealt with by a conference of the four great powers to revise the treaties of 1855 and 1856.

To explain why the Russians chose to link Norway and the Baltic by reviving the Åland question at this time, it is necessary to examine their response to the Norwegian crisis in a longer perspective. Between 1902 and 1904, as we have seen, Russia had favoured the permanent neutralisation of Denmark and possibly of Sweden and Norway as well, to be guaranteed jointly by Germany and itself, as a means of keeping a hostile naval power (i.e. Britain) out of the Baltic. The prospect of a Baltic *mare clausum* had thus weakened for a short time the traditional Russian antipathy towards Scandinavian integration. By 1904 the tsarist government, wishing to ensure the passage of the Baltic Fleet to the Far East, had lost interest in the idea, whilst in 1905 military defeat and internal collapse made it anxious that the Norwegian question should be settled as soon as possible.

The Russians were in a weak position but exploited it with some skill. They sought to win Norwegian confidence and make the Norwegians less inclined to seek the support of other great powers. Participation in a new guarantee treaty seemed to be one way of achieving this. In fact the Norwegians remained suspicious and placed all their hopes in Great Britain, showing no gratitude for Russian efforts on their behalf.[120] Nevertheless, Russian involvement would also ensure that the treaty, unlike its predecessor of 1855, had no anti-Russian edge. Support for Norwegian neutrality, provided it was not linked to that of the other Scandinavian states, would serve the same purpose and help to

---

[119] Nansen to Løvland, printed in Steiner Kjærheim (ed.), *Fridtjof Nansen. Brev* (4 vols., Oslo, 1961–6), vol. III, pp. 56–9. The story reached the Foreign Office via the Russian minister in Kristiania: Folke Lindberg, *Scandinavia*, pp. 65–6; Sweet, 'Baltic', p. 464.

[120] Berg, ' "Det land vi venter hjælp af" ', pp. 115–16, 130–4.

prevent the use of Norwegian territory by other powers in time of war.[121] In addition, Sweden would be isolated.[122] Even if it were not made a 'dependency of Russia, or almost like a Russian Grand Duchy', as the British feared,[123] it might be forced into an agreement with Germany and Russia which involved the exclusion of Britain from the Baltic.

This seems to have been very much what Isvolsky had in mind. His broader aim was to recreate a basis for Russo-German collaboration at a time when Russia was moving towards an Asian agreement with Great Britain. Germany and Russia were already in close consultation over the Norwegian treaty. Raising the Åland question in July 1907 gave Isvolsky the further 'occasion to collaborate with Germany which he so badly needed'.[124] But his objectives in northern Europe were important in their own right. Much more was at stake than the status of the Åland Islands themselves, either for reasons of Russian prestige or as a means of preventing the Finnish uprising which Isvolsky seems genuinely to have feared.[125] Nor is there any evidence of aggressive intentions towards Sweden. Isvolsky's ultimate aim was, he told the Germans, to 'éliminer toute influence étrangère de la mer Baltique'.[126] A conversation of July 1907 in which he 'described his plan as a new version of Catherine the Great's Neutrality League of 1780 directed against England' suggests that he had the same precedent in mind as the British Foreign Office.[127]

Grey's firm response to the Russian proposal indicated that Isvolsky had overreached himself. Anxious to prevent the possibility of British interference in Baltic affairs which his Åland proposal had created, Isvolsky rejected the idea of a conference. Grey then declared that he was prepared to revert to a separate treaty for Norway, despite the danger that Sweden would be condemned to isolation, but would consider only a guarantee of integrity, not neutrality. The other powers concerned were disinclined to credit Britain with genuine solicitude for Sweden. The Norwegians, the Germans and the Russians all suspected British designs on Norwegian ports in wartime, while a French diplomat remarked: 'England, even when she speaks of Sweden, thinks of Denmark.'[128] However all, with the exception of Sweden, rapidly fell in with the British proposal. Their reasons for doing so naturally differed. The Norwegians had little choice in the matter, but realised that the dropping of neutrality restored the Scandinavian option which they had originally sought.

[121] Jungar, *Ryssland*, pp. 84–8, 114, 194–5.
[122] Jungar quotes ibid., p. 114, a letter of 1907 from the Russian vice-consul in Hammerfest, Zur-Mühlen, to M. A. Taube, Isvolsky's adviser on northern European affairs, recalling a remark of Taube's from February 1905 that Russia's aim in Scandinavia was 'Divide et impera'. See also Dr Michael Freiherr von Taube, *Der grossen Katastrophe entgegen. Die russische Politik der Vorkriegszeit und das Ende des Zarenreichs (1904–1917)* (2nd edn, Leipzig, 1937), pp. 113–57.
[123] Hardinge minute, 29 June 1907, quoted in Sweet, 'Baltic', p. 465.
[124] Luntinen, *Baltic Question*, p. 90.
[125] Folke Lindberg, *Scandinavia*, p. 71; Luntinen, *Baltic Question*, pp. 84–9.
[126] Quoted in Folke Lindberg, *Scandinavia*, p. 74.   [127] Ibid., p. 99.
[128] Quoted ibid., p. 78; Isvolsky's views are reported in *GP* XXIII, 2, pp. 444–5.

Isvolsky accepted for the same reason that he had rejected the conference: to prevent the British from linking the Norwegian question with that of the Åland Islands. Whilst the French readily followed the British lead, the Germans were obliged reluctantly to follow the Russians in order to avoid an isolated opposition. Only Sweden remained unreconciled, interpreting the guarantee of Norwegian integrity as being directed against itself. Largely owing to Swedish hostility and suspicion, especially of Britain's motives, the signature of the Norwegian integrity treaty was delayed until 2 November 1907.

As Lindberg points out, British concern for Sweden's position was entirely genuine: not out of altruism but because 'it was in the *interest* of England to prevent the isolation and consequent weakening of Sweden'.[129] Britain's primary interest in northern Europe was stability. Hitherto this had been guaranteed by the 1855 treaty. Since it had proved impossible to replace that treaty with a guarantee for both Norway and Sweden, Britain had to rely on an improvement in relations between the two countries and guard against the possibility of a disgruntled and isolated Sweden falling in with a Russo-German combination in the Baltic. The meeting between the two emperors which took place at Swinemünde in August 1907 suggested that the prospect of such a combination was a real one. Nevertheless British policy was not guided solely by such considerations. Luntinen, who has had the opportunity to consult a wider range of British papers than Lindberg, places much greater emphasis on the aspect which aroused contemporary suspicions: naval warfare. The British decision to oppose neutrality was taken at a time when rumours of German–Danish negotiations were current. The views of Fisher and Hardinge, the heads respectively of the Admiralty and the Foreign Office, were identical on this point. Fisher's we have already seen. Hardinge wrote in a private letter to Sir Arthur Nicolson at St Petersburg:

If in time of war the Straits remain open that is all we want. If Germany tries to close them we shall regard ourselves as absolutely free to do what we like and even to ignore the integrity of Norway should we require a naval base on the Norwegian coast.[130]

In the light of Zara Steiner's work on the pre-1914 Foreign Office, Lindberg is surely wrong to discount Hardinge's influence or to draw a sharp distinction between the views of Grey and those of his permanent under-secretary.[131] Grey took the advice of the Admiralty, the Foreign Office and the CID fully into account. All were unanimous in opposing any commitment which might prevent the use of Norwegian territory by Britain in time of war.

The northern European crisis which had begun when Norway seceded from the union with Sweden ended on 23 April 1908, when the powers bordering the Baltic Sea and the North Sea signed two treaties in which, along with

---

[129] Folke Lindberg, *Scandinavia*, p. 132.   [130] *BD* VIII, pp. 164–5.
[131] Steiner, *Foreign Office and Foreign Policy*, pp. 92–3. See also Briton Cooper Busch, *Hardinge of Penshurst: A Study in the Old Diplomacy* (Hamden, Conn., 1980), pp. 122–3.

general expressions of goodwill and friendship, they undertook to respect and maintain the territorial status quo in the regions bordering on the two seas.[132] Grey's disparaging remarks on the Baltic and North Sea agreements tend to obscure their significance, as well as some important differences between them. Each of the two leading signatories of the North Sea agreement, Britain and Germany, regarded it as a sop to the other. Germany sought to compensate Britain for its exclusion from the Baltic, whilst for Britain acceptance of the agreement was a harmless way of reassuring Germany that it was not isolated.[133]

The Baltic agreement was more important. In a narrow sense it was, like the Norwegian integrity treaty, part of the diplomatic solution to the break-up of the Swedish–Norwegian union. It brought a formal end to the treaty of 1855 (which guaranteed the united kingdoms against Russia alone), and thus provided a renewed, more realistic guarantee of Swedish security. At the same time it represented a change in the juridical position of the two powers which had guaranteed the 1855 treaty. Britain and France were signatories of the North Sea agreement, but not of its Baltic counterpart. They could now resort only to the Åland convention of 1856 as the legal basis for their claim to a voice in Baltic affairs. Yet the Baltic agreement still fell short of the ambitions of Russia and Germany. They had looked to the formation at very least of a Baltic entente, and had contemplated much more: the exclusion of foreign fleets from the Baltic in wartime and, for Russia, an end to the 'Åland servitude'. Partly to compensate Britain for exclusion from the Baltic, and partly to divide it from France, the Germans had proposed a parallel North Sea agreement. But this had given Britain and France the opportunity to transform 'the narrow and potentially sinister Russo-German combination in the Baltic into a general exchange of innocuous guarantees'.[134]

Nevertheless, from the point of view of British naval interests, an opportunity had been lost. A well-informed contemporary British commentator remarked that the two agreements 'divide a problem that is essentially indivisible, and to that extent are unsatisfactory'.[135] Nothing had been done to settle the question of access to the Baltic in wartime. The status of the entrances to the Baltic remained undefined. The only statement that referred to them at all was one which defined the North Sea as extending 'jusqu'à son alliance avec les eaux de la Mer Baltique'. The Baltic and North Sea agreements, like the Norwegian integrity treaty, merely skirted round the issues of real importance. Just as the Norwegian treaty said nothing about

[132] Texts printed in *BD* VIII, pp. 175–6, 184. The signatories of the North Sea agreement were the United Kingdom, Denmark, France, Germany, the Netherlands and Sweden. Belgium and Norway were excluded because of their special positions under the treaties of 1830 and 1907 respectively. The signatories of the Baltic agreement were Germany, Denmark, Sweden and Russia.

[133] Sweet, 'Baltic', p. 470.   [134] Ibid., p. 477.

[135] Britannicus, 'The Northern Question', *North American Review* 188 (1908), pp. 237–47 (p. 247).

neutrality, so the Baltic and North Sea agreements made no mention of the Danish Straits. Certainly none of the great powers which signed the agreements acted as though they were of any practical significance. After 1908 Germany had no further hope of achieving a Baltic entente with Russia and turned instead to consolidating its hold over Denmark and strengthening its military links with Sweden. As for the North Sea agreement, the German foreign minister, Schoen, remarked even before it was concluded that 'in case of war it would prove necessary to ignore those treaty obligations which might interfere with Germany's military interests'.[136] Within little more than a year Russia was to resume its attempt to revise the status of the Åland Islands. Britain, meanwhile, was faced with the reality of German naval power and, quite irrespective of its legal position, tacitly abandoned its claim to naval influence in the Baltic in time of war.

The Russo-German exchanges over the Baltic which resulted ultimately in the Baltic and North Sea agreements were initiated by Isvolsky in July 1907 at a critical point in the Norwegian treaty negotiations: following the British rejection of his proposal to revise the Åland convention. They began on a high note with another successful imperial meeting – at Swinemünde in August 1907 – and led to the conclusion on 29 October of a secret treaty between Russia and Germany which was intended to form the basis of a Baltic entente. It expressed the interest of the two powers in maintaining the territorial status quo in the Baltic region, envisaged the participation of the two lesser Baltic powers, Sweden and Denmark, and provided for the revision of the Åland convention.[137] By late November 1907, with anti-British feeling in Sweden at its height in the aftermath of the Norwegian treaty, Swedish adherence to the Russo-German entente seemed imminent. From the beginning of December, however, the scheme unravelled as Britain and France grasped the opportunity to regain the diplomatic initiative.

The British government had regarded the increasing signs of Russo-German collaboration in the Baltic without undue alarm. Grey felt that Britain could have no objection to a status quo agreement as long as its maritime rights were not threatened. On 4 December 1907 the Germans admitted that negotiations for a Baltic agreement were in progress and proposed a parallel agreement for the North Sea. From the British point of view the least acceptable aspect of the German proposal was its presumed intention to split Britain from France. Grey insisted upon France's inclusion among the signatories, and once the Germans had given in on this point his attitude was calm, even patronising.[138] If they wished to show that they were not isolated, the Germans should be allowed to sign any agreements they liked, so long as they referred only to the status quo and were not used to drive a wedge between Britain and France. The response of France, hitherto largely indifferent to the problems of

[136] Quoted in Folke Lindberg, *Scandinavia*, p. 233.
[137] Text in *GP* XXIII, 2, pp. 483–5.
[138] For German reluctance to include France, see Folke Lindberg, *Scandinavia*, p. 188.

northern Europe, was more heated. The French government was alarmed by the evidence of Russo-German collaboration and by the fact that Russia had taken the lead. It had received 'written proof (German) that negotiations were initiated by M. Isvolski and that they went beyond maintenance of the status quo'.[139] As a result, on the one hand, of Grey's conciliatory response to the German North Sea proposals, and on the other of France's sharp diplomatic response to the perfidy of its Russian ally, the Russo-German Baltic scheme started to lose momentum from December 1907 onwards.

Quite apart, however, from the intervention of the Western powers, and despite Isvolsky's reference to the 'spirit of Björkö', this last phase of collaboration between Germany and Russia in the Baltic seems curiously lacking in substance.[140] On the German side the negotiations were conducted without the energy and high ambition which had marked the period up to 1905. Holstein had left office; the Moroccan adventure had ended in the *débâcle* of Algeçiras. Bülow and the kaiser played a less active part. The leading participant on the German side was Schoen, who left St Petersburg to become foreign minister in the autumn of 1907. He was more than a mere 'good-natured mediocrity'.[141] As a former minister in Copenhagen, where he had established a close friendship and working relationship with his Russian colleague, Isvolsky, Schoen took an active interest in Baltic affairs.[142] But his actions betrayed the growing caution with which Germany approached both Russia and Britain: he was anxious to avoid too close a relationship with Russia if this seemed likely either to alienate Britain or to enhance British influence in Scandinavia.

Concrete considerations of German security in the Baltic were also coming to occupy German minds. In 1909 Arvid Taube, the Swedish foreign minister and former minister in Berlin, recalled two conversations which revealed the contradictions in Germany's position at the time of the Baltic and North Sea negotiations in the previous year. The first was with the kaiser, who 'had usually shown him the greatest amiability' but on this occasion 'looked at him severely, and without any preparation asked him curtly why his Government objected to Russia fortifying the Åland Islands'.[143] 'At a later date' he had spoken to Schoen, who 'informed Count Taube that in the view of the German Government the objections of Sweden were very well founded, and, what was more, it would be a serious thing for Germany if the entrance to the Gulf of

---

[139] Bertie (Paris) to Hardinge, 28 December 1907, *BD* VIII, pp. 157–8; Sweet, 'Baltic', p. 471. In fact the French were in possession of an authentic German record of the Swinemünde meeting which had been either leaked or obtained by underhand means.

[140] Schoen to Bülow, 10 August 1907, *GP* XXII, pp. 68–72.

[141] G. P. Gooch, *Recent Revelations of European Diplomacy* (London, 1927), p. 29.

[142] For Schoen's assessment of Isvolsky, see *GP* XXII, pp. 21–4.

[143] Spring Rice (Stockholm) to FO, 17 August 1909, FO 371/745 (*BDFA*, I, F, III, pp. 14–15). Taube dated the conversation to 'about a month after the Swinemünde meeting' which would have been September 1907. However, it almost certainly took place at a dinner on 1 February 1908: Folke Lindberg, *Scandinavia*, p. 222.

Bothnia were blocked, as she received her supplies of Swedish iron-ore by sea'.[144]

The Russians, too, were strangely hesitant. For Isvolsky the abrogation of the Åland servitude was, he told Bülow at Swinemünde, 'a question of honour and of security' against 'nihilistic intrigues' in Finland.[145] He was supported in this by the tsar, who appears to have learned of the existence of the Åland convention for the first time only in 1906, and who obtained the kaiser's personal assurance of support on the question at Swinemünde.[146] Isvolsky was equally serious in his goal of achieving a Baltic entente which would not only act as a counterweight to Russia's Asian agreement with Great Britain, but serve to exclude all non-Baltic powers from a position of influence in the region.[147] Yet Russian ambitions foundered on the resistance of Sweden and the failure of the Germans, for the reasons indicated above, to apply sufficient pressure to make the Swedes give way. Isvolsky seems to have realised as soon as the negotiations with Sweden became drawn out – certainly by February 1908 – that his Åland goal was unattainable.[148] From an even earlier date – the point in December 1907 when the Germans included Denmark in the Baltic negotiations and brought out their North Sea proposals without consulting Russia – Isvolsky was concerned more with retrieving than exploiting the situation.[149] Nicolson wrote from St Petersburg in January: 'He appears to fear that matters are becoming too much involved and complicated, and he may regret that he ever embarked on a Baltic cruise with so impetuous and erratic a shipmate.'[150] It was the tsar himself who administered the *coup de grâce* to Isvolsky's scheme by renouncing, on 29 February, Russia's demand for the annulment of the Åland convention – possibly in response to an appeal from King Gustav V of Sweden.[151]

Sweden held the key to the Baltic situation despite the fact that both the Swedish government and Swedish public opinion felt their country to be weak and isolated after the loss of Norway. The signature of the Norwegian integrity treaty in November 1907 brought an end to the guarantee of 1855. Obliged to reappraise the entire basis of Swedish foreign policy and convinced that it could not maintain a position of isolated neutrality, the government came close to a decision to join the Russo-German pact. But this meant accepting the annulment of the Åland convention. The task of Russia – seconded with diminishing enthusiasm by Germany – was to convince the Swedes that it was a price worth paying. Russian military activities on the islands were, it was

[144] Spring Rice (Stockholm) to FO, 17 August 1909, FO 371/745 (*BDFA*, I, F, III, pp. 14–15).
[145] *GP* XXIII, 2, p. 474.
[146] Folke Lindberg, *Scandinavia*, pp. 221–2.
[147] Draft secret treaty, printed in *GP* XXIII, 2, pp. 463–4.
[148] Folke Lindberg, *Scandinavia*, pp. 276–81.   [149] Ibid., pp. 189–90.
[150] *BD* VIII, pp. 159–60.
[151] A story given by Michael von Taube in his memoirs, *Der grossen Katastrophe entgegen*, which Folke Lindberg (*Scandinavia*, pp. 276–81) does not believe.

argued, merely in the nature of a police action, directed solely against Finnish arms smugglers and in no way a threat to Swedish security.[152] King Gustav, who succeeded to the throne in December 1907, was readily persuaded. Bitterness over Norwegian independence had made him strongly anti-British, and he was eager to sign a Baltic pact with Germany, Russia and Denmark. Several members of the government, notably Trolle, the foreign minister, shared his view. But the Russian argument made no impression on other ministers, or upon the Swedish public.

At the end of December the Swedish Cabinet decided that it could not accept the annulment of the Åland convention as part of a Baltic agreement with Germany and Russia. By February 1908 its resolve had been strengthened by the shift of Swedish public opinion towards a pro-British stance. It was becoming clear to government and public alike that their anger with Britain over Norway had been misplaced. Germany, in whom they had placed their trust, was meanwhile urging them to make a concession on a question that was vital to Swedish security. They also realised that Britain and Sweden, as maritime powers, had a shared interest in an open Baltic. Towards the end of February Grey indicated Britain's support for Sweden's position on the Åland question in guarded but unmistakably positive terms. A few days later the tsar's statement acknowledged Russia's diplomatic defeat.

Sweden's resistance over the Ålands delayed not only the Baltic but also the North Sea negotiations, since the British insisted that the two agreements must be signed simultaneously. Britain's main concern was with ensuring the right of belligerent vessels to use the Straits. This could be done, it was thought, either by making specific reference to the Straits or by combining the two agreements in one. The latter solution would also ensure that France and Britain continued to have a voice in Baltic affairs. But there were disadvantages in both courses. To insist that the Baltic Straits must be mentioned in the agreement would enable Russia or Germany to demand the inclusion of the Straits of Dover and the Channel as an entrance to the North Sea. If France and Britain were to be treated as Baltic powers, Russia would have to be treated as a North Sea power. And as long as the Åland convention remained in force, Britain and France would continue to have a Baltic presence.

In February 1908 the British Cabinet accepted the principle of two separate treaties on condition that they contained a statement that where one sea ended the other began. Further reassurance was provided when Germany agreed to the inclusion of Sweden among the signatories of the North Sea agreement. Three powers – Germany, Sweden and Denmark – were therefore to be signatories of both agreements. Even though Denmark was by now regarded as being too much under German domination to be a reliable guarantor of the free navigation of the Straits, Sweden shared Britain's interest in an open Baltic, and was still capable of conducting an independent foreign policy.

[152] *GP* XXII, p. 71.

There are signs, moreover, that Swedish leaders recognised that British support was at least as important as that of Germany for the maintenance of Swedish neutrality, and came with fewer strings attached.[153] The period after 1907 saw a notable improvement in Anglo-Swedish relations, especially with the visit of King Edward VII to Stockholm in 1908.[154]

The outcome of the Baltic and North Sea negotiations was ostensibly a success for British diplomacy. Yet it left Britain's rights of naval access to the Baltic defined no more precisely than they had been before (an omission which was to be repeated, less excusably, in 1919). Indeed it could be argued that despite the failure of the kaiser's more spectacular efforts at Björkö and Algeçiras, and the conclusion of an Anglo-Russian entente in 1907, the net effect of the diplomatic manoeuvring of the period 1905–8 was greatly to diminish Britain's position in northern Europe. Admittedly Norwegian independence was achieved under British auspices, and the Norwegian integrity treaty of 1907 preserved Britain's freedom of manoeuvre in and around Norway in time of war. But the possibility of a German–Russian combination in the Baltic had not been precluded by the Anglo-Russian entente, and was in fact given a new lease of life by the protracted negotiations over Norway. Even though Isvolsky's Swinemünde proposal was watered down, the Baltic and North Sea agreements to which it led nevertheless marked the formal exclusion of Britain from a position of influence in the Baltic region. They were the diplomatic equivalent of the changes in naval strategy which were to keep the Royal Navy (apart from submarines) out of the Baltic for the duration of the First World War.

Not all historians would endorse this view of Britain's declining role in northern Europe. Walther Hubatsch believes that the Anglo-Russian entente of 1907 rendered German–Russian collaboration in the Baltic a dead letter, and that by 1909 all three Scandinavian countries had undergone a decisive orientation towards Great Britain.[155] The policy of the Danish government had reverted to a cautious neutrality following the inconclusive end of the Moltke–Lütken talks in 1908 (ch. 3, pp. 103–8), whilst the Danish population remained firmly in the Entente camp. Norway had been in the British sphere of influence since 1905, and even Sweden seemed to have come closer to Britain

---

[153] Gunnar Åselius, 'Storbritannien, Tyskland och den svenska neutraliteten 1880–1914: en omvärdering', *Historisk tidskrift* (Sweden) 114 (1994), pp. 228–66.

[154] See e.g. conversations with King Edward and Sir Charles Hardinge recorded in Arvid Lindman (ed. Nils F. Holm), *Dagbocksanteckningar* (Stockholm, 1972), pp. 15–17. See also Patrick Salmon, '"Between the Sea Power and the Land Power": Scandinavia and the Coming of the First World War', *Transactions of the Royal Historical Society*, 6th series, 3 (1993), pp. 23–49 (pp. 34–5).

[155] Walther Hubatsch, 'Deutschlands Seeflanke in Nordeuropa', in Hubatsch, *Kaiserliche Marine. Aufgaben und Leistungen* (Munich, 1975), pp. 124–36 (pp. 127–9). This view is held in a much more extreme form by Hubatsch's student Detlef Grell. In *Die Auflösung der Schwedisch–Norwegischen Union*, Grell argues (esp. pp. 91, 116–17) that Britain skilfully intrigued to split the Scandinavian union and put its own candidate on the Norwegian throne, by this means turning Norway into a docile instrument of British interests.

with the marriage of the Swedish crown prince to an English princess in 1905. Hubatsch highlights a point which Luntinen, with his predominantly Baltic perspective, does not, perhaps, fully appreciate. In the contest between continental and maritime power, how advantageous was it ultimately for Germany to dominate an enclosed inland sea? As the First World War was to show, Britain could respond to the threat of exclusion with that of encirclement, using its geographical position and naval superiority to control the flow of trade and the passage of naval vessels between the North Sea and the North Atlantic.

3   The war of the future: Scandinavia in the strategic plans of the great powers

This chapter is about a war that did not happen. It was a war of daring British assaults on Esbjerg and the Kiel Canal; of great naval battles in the entrances to the Baltic; of an Anglo-French drive from the German Baltic coast to Berlin; of a German–Swedish invasion of Finland, followed by an advance on St Petersburg. That this war existed only in the minds of politicians, publicists and naval and military planners is no reason why it should be ignored. Belief in the possibility of armed conflict in northern Europe reflected the fears produced by a period of profound international disturbance. It was also the result of attempts to come to terms with rapid changes in military technology, the implications of which could in many cases only be guessed at. Moreover, the implementation of ideas ventilated in the pre-1914 period was actively considered during the war itself.

Many of the plans for war in Scandinavia were expressions of institutional rivalries between the armed services of the great powers. Those produced by the British and German navies (discussed in the next two sections of this chapter) represented prolonged rearguard actions against the growing predominance of the military, and of the continental European theatre. Naval officers who favoured action in Scandinavia shared the common 'ideology of the offensive'[1] but wished to see it directed towards a theatre where, they believed, their own country or their own branch held the strategic advantage. Army officers in Germany and, to an increasing extent, in Britain as well wanted to avoid any diversion of resources or effort from the western and eastern fronts where, they believed, the best prospects for a successful offensive lay. Each side drew its own lessons from technological change. British critics of a naval offensive and amphibious operations on the Scandinavian or German coasts pointed to the hazards posed to the Royal Navy by Germany's strongly entrenched position and by new weapons such as mines, submarines and torpedoes. Their German counterparts poured scorn on the navy's assumption that the British would ever allow their superior forces to be exposed to such dangers. On the other hand, those critics did not admit that machine guns, trenches and barbed wire could have the same stultifying effect on a land offensive as the new naval weapons had on marine warfare. At the same time

[1] Jack Snyder, *The Ideology of the Offensive: Military Decision Making and the Disasters of 1914* (Ithaca, N. Y., and London, 1984).

they proved capable of persuading civilians of the merits of a continental strategy. The opinions of staff officers like Schlieffen or Henry Wilson carried more conviction than those of Admiral Büchsel or Admiral Jackie Fisher.

The intensification of Anglo-German naval rivalry following the launching of the first dreadnought in 1906 and Tirpitz's supplementary naval law of November 1907 concealed the fact that in each country the battle for resources and the setting of strategic priorities was being won by the army at the expense of the navy. With the establishment of the Committee of Imperial Defence (CID) in 1902 and of a General Staff in 1904, the beginning of military cooperation with France following the Moroccan crisis of 1905, and the creation of the British Expeditionary Force (BEF) in 1906, Britain moved decisively towards a continental commitment.[2] In Germany the Schlieffen plan for a lightning strike against France at the beginning of a two-front war received its definitive form in December 1905, whilst the army bills of 1912 and 1913 brought to an end the long period in which Tirpitz's navy had received the lion's share of military expenditure. By 1912, moreover, both the British and the German navies had, unknown to each other, tacitly abandoned plans for a major naval engagement in the southern North Sea or the entrances to the Baltic in the early phases of an Anglo-German war. In the same year the Royal Navy replaced its strategy of a close blockade of German ports with an 'open' blockade based on control of the approaches to the North Sea in the Channel and between Scotland and the Norwegian coast. In 1914 each side expected the other to take the offensive, neither fully comprehending that its own reluctant adoption of a defensive strategy had been paralleled on the other side of the North Sea.

Fears of another offensive that did not materialise – in this case a Swedish–German invasion of Finland – prompted Russian planning for the defence of St Petersburg, which forms the subject of the second section of this chapter. It is followed by a section discussing the overtures made by the German General Staff to Denmark in 1906–8 and to Sweden in 1910 – both expressions of the demand, at a time of hardening diplomatic alignments, for reassurance about the position of the Scandinavian countries in time of war. The last part of the chapter examines the strategy of economic warfare against Germany which was developed in Britain in the immediate pre-war years. Conceived as a means of exploiting Great Britain's economic and naval strengths, as well as avoiding a costly continental commitment, this strategy was to be adopted – albeit hesitantly and without full comprehension – by the British Cabinet after the outbreak of war. It became an adjunct of the continental commitment, not a substitute for it. It also became the means by which the Scandinavian countries – spared the horrors of war on their soil –

[2] J. McDermott, 'The Revolution in British Military Thinking from the Boer War to the Moroccan Crisis', in Paul Kennedy (ed.), *The War Plans of the Great Powers 1880–1914* (London, 1979), pp. 99–117.

were yet to become the objects of belligerent pressure as both sides sought to conscript them into an economic war of unprecedented scale.

The search for a naval offensive: Great Britain and Germany

Great Britain

The strength of Germany's strategic position was recognised in Britain even before the creation of a large German navy. During the Crimean war, the British and French navies had conducted campaigns in the Baltic with relative impunity.[3] Although the Royal Navy remained confident of its technical ability to mount Baltic operations against Russia, the mere existence of a united Germany after 1871 constituted a potential constraint on Britain's freedom of manoeuvre. A despatch from Stockholm during the Anglo-Russian crisis of 1885 pointed out that a neutral Germany was likely to 'raise troublesome questions' if any attempt was made to interfere with its Baltic trade, which had grown considerably since 1871.[4] Sweden and Denmark would probably take the same attitude under pressure from Germany and Russia. In 1904 there was some discussion of the possibility of British involvement in the Russo-Japanese war. Again Germany rather than Russia was regarded as the main obstacle to bringing British naval power to bear in the Baltic.[5] Of particular interest are the comments of Charles Ottley, the assistant director of naval intelligence (DNI), on a proposal from the youthful journalist and future Conservative minister Leo Amery to consider 'the possibility of getting Sweden to join us in an attempt to rescue Finland from the Russians', and thus to 'strike at the very heart of Russia' by bringing a hostile army to 'the gates of St Petersburg'.[6]

Ottley's principal reservation concerned the feasibility of Baltic operations in the face of German opposition: 'Altho' neutral at the outbreak of war, Germany may at any moment fling her sword into the Russian scale, and her geographical position is such that we should have her ships perpetually upon our flank, if we sought to send our transports through the Sound.' It would be preferable, he suggested, 'to send only our best and fastest warships into the Baltic, while we utilized the deep and convenient fiords on the Norwegian

[3] Andrew Lambert, *The Crimean War: British Grand Strategy Against Russia 1853–1856* (Manchester, 1990); Basil Greenhill and Ann Giffard, *The British Assault on Finland 1854–1855: A Forgotten Naval War* (London, 1988).
[4] Memorandum by Edmund W. Cope (British chargé d'affaires, Stockholm), 18 April 1885, in Paul Knaplund (ed.), *British Views on Norwegian–Swedish Problems 1880–1895: Selections from Diplomatic Correspondence* (Oslo, 1952), pp. 135–6.
[5] Keith Neilson, '"A Dangerous Game of American Poker": The Russo-Japanese War and British Policy', *Journal of Strategic Studies* 12 (1989), pp. 62–87 (pp. 67–8).
[6] L. S. Amery to A. J. Balfour (first lord of the Admiralty), 27 October 1904, in John Barnes and David Nicholson (eds.), *The Leo Amery Diaries*, vol. I, *1896–1929* (London, 1980), p. 50. Amery was to become one of the most active supporters of aid to Finland during the Soviet–Finnish Winter War of 1939–40.

Coast for the disembarkation of our troops'. Even so, 'we must not disregard the enormous value of the Kiel Canal, as enabling Germany to threaten our sea-communications from the East Coast of England across the North Sea, *as well as* with the Gulf of Bothnia'.[7] Such caution has to be borne in mind in considering the many schemes for naval operations against Germany which were discussed by the Admiralty, the War Office and the CID in the decade before the outbreak of war in 1914.[8]

Part of the problem lies in the personality of Admiral Sir John Fisher, first sea lord from 1904 to 1910, under whom most of the Admiralty's strategic ideas first saw the light of day. Jackie Fisher (who had served in the Baltic in 1855 as a fourteen-year-old cadet) was famous for his vehement statements about the need to launch a pre-emptive strike against the German fleet. He also spoke of the navy's power to land an army on the coasts of Schleswig-Holstein or Pomerania – only '90 miles from Berlin on that 14 miles of sandy beach, impossible of defence against a Battle Fleet sweeping with devastating shells the flat country for miles, like a mower's scythe'.[9] Yet such utterances have to be placed in context. Fisher, unlike most of the strategists discussed in this chapter, had experienced war and did not take its risks lightly. His rhetoric was intended to make war less likely by galvanising his superiors and by deterring Britain's enemies. But Fisher was also fighting his own battles against critics both within and outside the navy. For all their belligerence, the plans which emanated from the Admiralty were not adequately thought through either by Fisher himself or by his subordinates; and in the absence of a Naval Staff there was no way in which they could be incorporated into a coherent naval strategy. The navy's emphasis on combined operations in northern Europe derived, in part at least, from the need to hit upon some offensive-looking operation at a time when its position as the senior service was under threat from the army. Only by ensuring that the army remained 'a projectile to be fired by the navy'[10] could Fisher and his colleagues hope to arrest the momentum of the continental commitment.

[7] Memorandum of 28 October 1904, CAB 17/59. An unsigned letter to Amery of 31 October, ibid., expressed interest in the scheme, and stated that it was impracticable under existing conditions, but concluded: 'Meanwhile, you may be sure that the project is not being lost sight of.' In a letter to Amery of 3 November Balfour said that he had not been able to discuss the proposal in detail with his military advisers but regarded it as being 'well worth consideration': Barnes and Nicholson, *Amery Diaries* I, p. 51.

[8] Hans Branner, 'Østersøen og de danske stræder i engelsk krigsplanlægning 1904–1914', *Historie. Jyske samlinger* 9 (1972), pp. 493–535; Paul Hayes, 'Britain, Germany and the Admiralty's Plans for Attacking German Territory 1906–1915', in Lawrence Freedman, Hayes and Robert O'Neill (eds.), *War, Strategy and International Politics: Essays in Honour of Sir Michael Howard* (Oxford, 1992), pp. 95–116.

[9] Letter to Lord Esher of 25 April 1912, printed in Arthur J. Marder (ed.), *Fear God and Dread Nought: The Correspondence of Admiral of the Fleet Lord Fisher of Kilverstone* (2 vols., London, 1956), vol. II, *Years of Power 1904–1914*, pp. 453–5.

[10] Fisher memorandum of 20 May 1904, cited in Paul Haggie, 'The Royal Navy and War Planning in the Fisher Era', in Kennedy, *War Plans of the Great Powers*, pp. 118–32 (p. 126). See also a memorandum of August 1907 in which Fisher attributes the phrase to Sir Edward Grey, cited in Ruddock F. Mackay, *Fisher of Kilverstone* (Oxford, 1973), p. 382.

The Admiralty's earliest plans for a war against Germany, dating from the summer of 1904, envisaged operations against Heligoland and the German North Sea coast. The Moroccan crisis of 1905 (during which Fisher pointedly sent the Channel Fleet into the Baltic) made the prospect of war with Germany more real.[11] At the same time it led the Admiralty to take a much more optimistic view than in previous scenarios, which had been based on the assumption that Germany would be supported by either France or Russia or both.[12] A blockade of Germany's Baltic ports was now considered for the first time – either by means of a strong force sent specially through the Belts or by closing the Belts themselves, although, as the DNI put it, 'the latter form of blockade, since it would affect neutral interests a good deal, would require consideration'.[13] Admiral Sir Arthur Wilson, commander-in-chief of the Channel Fleet, suggested a further option: 'If Denmark were on our side, a very effective diversion might be made by assisting her to recover Schleswig and Holstein, including the port of Kiel, and in that case the fleet might operate very effectively in conjunction with a land force on the coast of the Little Belt or Kiel Bay.'[14] The Admiralty took up the idea[15] and suggested to the War Office in July 1905 that such an operation might oblige Germany to divert substantial forces from the French frontier.[16] The War Office's views fluctuated, but by October 1905 it had come down against the idea, believing that it would not tie down sufficient numbers of German troops and that the German coast would be too heavily defended.[17]

During the Algeçiras crisis in December 1905 and January 1906, when war with Germany still seemed imminent, a number of plans were developed, largely independently, at the War Office, the Admiralty and the CID. While the Admiralty under Fisher remained fixed on Schleswig-Holstein and the Baltic, Grierson, the director of military operations (DMO) believed that British forces should be deployed only in Belgium or France.[18] A discussion group at the CID established by its secretary, Sir George Clarke, at first took a middle course between the views of the two armed services[19] but later, in the absence of sufficiently persuasive Admiralty arguments, moved towards the War Office's preference for sending a force to the western front. In January 1906 (though the fact was unknown to most of the Cabinet), consultation with the

[11] Fisher to Julian Corbett, 28 July 1905, in Marder, *Fear God and Dread Nought*, p. 63; Marder, *British Naval Policy 1880–1905: The Anatomy of British Sea Power* (London, 1940), pp. 479–81.

[12] Marder, *British Naval Policy*, pp. 502–5.   [13] Charles Ottley, cited ibid., p. 503.

[14] Ibid., pp. 504–5.

[15] Undated Admiralty memorandum (probably late June 1905), quoted in Neil W. Summerton, 'The Development of British Military Planning for a War Against Germany 1904–1914' (Ph.D thesis, University of London, 1970), p. 30.

[16] Memorandum of July 1905, ADM 116/866B.

[17] Grant-Duff (WO) to Ballard, 7 September 1905, ADM 116/1043B; 'British Military Action in Case of War with Germany', sent to Admiralty c. 30 September 1905, ibid.; Callwell to Ballard, 3 October 1905, ibid.; revised memorandum, 'British Military Action in Case of War with Germany', ibid.; Summerton, 'British Military Planning', pp. 33–48.

[18] *DDF*, 2, VIII, pp. 197–8.   [19] Mackay, *Fisher of Kilverstone*, pp. 351–5.

French and Belgian General Staffs had taken place for the first time; in that month the CID authorised the War Office to start detailed planning for the despatch of an expeditionary force. This was the point at which the continental commitment was made in earnest. Fisher for his part merely withdrew the naval representative (Captain Ottley) from the CID group, whose deliberations in any case came to an end shortly afterwards. Lacking a Naval Staff, the Admiralty made no plans for the Schleswig and Baltic alternatives.

Towards the end of 1906, however, Fisher, aware that the absence of naval war plans made him vulnerable to his critics, established a planning committee headed by Captain G. A. Ballard, formerly director of naval operations (DNO).[20] The Ballard committee's secretary was Captain Maurice Hankey of the Royal Marines. Its work was assisted by Captain Slade (an enthusiast for amphibious operations who was to succeed Ottley as DNI when the latter became secretary of the CID in August 1907) and Ottley, as well as by the distinguished naval historian Julian Corbett.[21] The committee came up with four plans for war against Germany. The first was aimed at the 'destruction or enforced idleness' of German shipping by means of what was in fact, though not in name, a distant blockade in the North Sea and in the Channel. The second plan envisaged a close blockade of the German North Sea and Baltic coasts. Entering the Baltic would raise questions about 'the political status of the entrances to the Baltic' which the committee believed to be highly uncertain, especially as far as the Great Belt was concerned.[22] The third plan added the possibility of bombarding ports and coastal defences, as well as 'a series of large scale raids' on the German Baltic coast.[23]

Finally, the committee considered the need for a combined operation to counter a German occupation of the Danish islands of Zealand and Fyn at the beginning of a war against Great Britain. The plans for operations in Denmark were based on two alternative assumptions. Both cases assumed that the sea communications between Germany and Zealand could be cut and gave no consideration to the advantages enjoyed by Germany in those waters. If the Danes were friendly to the Germans the best course would be to prevent all food supplies from being imported into Zealand (this at a time when Britain strongly resisted any suggestion that food should be treated as contraband). If the Danes opposed the Germans a force should be landed in their support.

The plans of 1906–7 have been criticised for their 'almost complete refusal to face the naval realities of the day', whilst Ballard himself wrote in October 1911 that the plans and the internal discussions to which they led had revealed

---

[20] Summerton, 'British Military Planning', pp. 265–78; Haggie, 'Royal Navy', pp. 120–5.
[21] The plans are printed in their entirety in P. K. Kemp (ed.), *The Papers of Admiral Sir John Fisher* (2 vols., London, 1964), vol. II, pp. 316–468.
[22] Ibid., pp. 370–1.
[23] Ibid., p. 436. Summerton remarks ('British Military Planning', p. 273) that this proposal was 'so strangely out of keeping with their general attitude . . . that we may reasonably suspect the influence of Fisher and Slade'.

a state of 'indecision and chaos that would have been disastrous in war'.[24] Summerton points out, however, that the committee's preference was for 'a strategy of economic attrition by means of distant blockade' and that it was generally sceptical about the feasibility and desirability of combined operations.[25] This judgement is supported by the testimony of the committee's secretary, Maurice Hankey. For Hankey, the Ballard committee's activities were of value as an 'intensive study of five months' duration' which was to influence much of his work over the next twelve years.[26] He also emphasised that the committee's investigations of close blockade and Baltic operations were strictly secondary to 'the importance of the susceptibility of Germany to economic pressure, though we could not judge whether it would be possible to squeeze her into submission, or how long it would take, particularly in view of the assistance she could obtain from her continental neighbours'.[27]

Although the Admiralty did not consult the War Office on the plans of 1906–7, the army had not closed its mind to the Baltic. In 1907–8, probably as a result of the diplomatic activity surrounding the Norwegian integrity treaty and the Baltic and North Sea agreements, the attention of both departments was drawn to the problem of the status of the entrances to the Baltic.[28] Relations between the War Office and the Admiralty were also unusually good at this time since Major-General Ewart, DMO from October 1906, was on friendly terms with Slade, who became DNI in August 1907.[29] In that month Ewart began on his own initiative to look into the question of Denmark and of a British entry into the Baltic.[30] This formed the prelude to a far-reaching investigation of the possibility of sending a military expedition to the Danish island of Zealand, which took place under the auspices of the CID's 'invasion inquiry' and of its sub-committee on the 'Military Needs of the Empire' in 1908–9.[31] Despite Ewart's open-mindedness, the War Office ultimately turned against the idea once again. And while the Admiralty remained on the whole much more optimistic than the War Office about the prospects for success, the naval planners were by no means inclined to underestimate the risks entailed in such an operation.

The strength of Slade's commitment to a Baltic offensive is revealed in a secret minute submitted to Fisher in November 1907. A British naval presence in the Baltic would, he argued, serve several purposes: threatening Germany's Baltic coasts, protecting British trade and strengthening Sweden and Denmark

---

[24] Summerton, 'British Military Planning', p. 317; Ballard memorandum cited in Mackay, *Fisher of Kilverstone*, p. 375.

[25] Summerton, 'British Military Planning', p. 274.

[26] Lord Hankey, *The Supreme Command 1914–1918* (2 vols., London, 1961), vol. I, p. 40.

[27] Ibid. For an assessment of Hankey's ideas and influence, see Avner Offer, *The First World War: An Agrarian Interpretation* (Oxford, 1989), esp. pp. 246–9, 294–5.

[28] Summerton, 'British Military Planning', pp. 223–63.   [29] Ibid., pp. 220–1.

[30] Ibid., p. 386.

[31] For the circumstances of these inquiries, see ibid., pp. 381–6 and 404–7. See also Hans Branner, *Småstat mellem stormagt 3eslutningen om mineudlædning august 1914* (Copenhagen and Århus, 1972), pp. 121–3ʳ.

against German or Russian intimidation. A British presence might be secured in peacetime by frustrating German moves to pressurise Denmark into closing the Belts, or by encouraging Sweden's interest in dredging the Sound – an operation which would promote the economic welfare of the port of Malmö, but which would also permit the entry of British warships. In wartime, however, Britain 'must be prepared at any time after war has broken out to undertake a large combined operation against Denmark'.[32]

During 1908 Slade continued to press for a Baltic offensive. In a war against Germany alone it would be unnecessary to force an entry into the Baltic 'except perhaps at a late period of the war and after a decision has been arrived at with the German Fleet'. But in order to relieve pressure on France 'it would probably be necessary to run risks which would be quite unjustifiable if we were acting on our own account'. The threat of an attack on the Baltic coast would hold down more German forces 'than any we could hope to hold when acting in other directions'.[33] Operations on the island of Zealand would be in response to a threatened or actual German attempt to occupy Denmark in order to obtain command of the Belts and the Sound – a not implausible scenario in the light of the German navy's earlier plans and the rumours of German–Danish cooperation in 1906–7, but one which had little relevance by 1908.

By the spring of 1909 Baltic operations had been effectively ruled out at the highest levels – and this had been tacitly accepted even by Fisher. A General Staff memorandum of 28 November 1908 for the Military Needs of the Empire sub-committee made a formidable case for the view that the only effective assistance that could be afforded to France was direct military support on the western front.[34] Slade was persuaded of the need to send an expeditionary force to France and even Fisher gave an assurance that the Admiralty could guarantee the safe transport of the troops across the Channel. At the third meeting of the sub-committee, on 23 March 1909, Fisher 'made it clear that he did not wish to contest the General Staff's assessment of the Baltic question'.[35] Further evidence of the growing caution of naval thinking was given to a Danish naval officer by a British colleague in October 1910. The navy, he said, had given up the idea of attempting to enter the Kattegat or the Baltic, at least with large ships, and had rejected the idea of a landing at Esbjerg owing to the dangers posed by German submarines.[36]

---

[32] 'British Policy in the Baltic in the Event of War with Germany', 25 November 1907, HD 3/133. This document appears without explanation or comment in a file of miscellaneous Secret Service material released for public scrutiny by the Public Record Office in 1994. It is practically the only 'policy' item in the file; most of the rest are records of payments to British agents in various parts of the world.

[33] Memorandum of July 1908, cited in Branner, *Småstat mellem stormagt*, p. 122.

[34] Mackay, *Fisher of Kilverstone*, p. 405.   [35] Ibid., p. 407.

[36] Viggo Sjøqvist, *Erik Scavenius. Danmarks udenrigsminister under to verdenskrige. Statsminister 1942–1945* (2 vols., Copenhagen, 1973), vol. I, *1877–1920*, p. 76.

The definitive victory of the army's plan to send an expeditionary force to France was won at a celebrated meeting of the CID on 23 August 1911, held to discuss the military implications of the second Moroccan crisis.[37] Refusing to guarantee that the navy could protect the crossing of the expeditionary force to France, Fisher's successor as first sea lord, Sir Arthur Wilson, kept the Admiralty's war plans 'locked away in his own brain',[38] though he indicated that the navy's main task would be to impose a close blockade of the German coast. This would once again require the capture of the islands of Borkum and Heligoland, for which army cooperation was essential. After the lucid exposition of the army's plans by Sir Henry Wilson, the DMO, none of the ministers present was prepared to contemplate any diversion of forces from France in pursuit of such visionary schemes. Henceforth the navy's task was to enable a British expeditionary force to be transported to the continent. However, the strategy of economic pressure survived Arthur Wilson's botched presentation to become one of the principal instruments of British strategy upon the outbreak of war in 1914, and was to enmesh the Scandinavian neutrals in the Allied war effort more comprehensively than any of the operations imagined by the Admiralty in peacetime. Nor did consideration of Baltic schemes come to an end.

Winston Churchill, first lord of the Admiralty from 1911 to 1915, was an enthusiastic disciple of Fisher.[39] Yet that he had also become a supporter of the continental commitment was revealed, for example in his prescient memorandum 'The Military Aspect of the Continental Problem' of late 1911.[40] Churchill, like Fisher, was torn between sober assessment of the realities of Britain's strategic position and the impulse for bold, decisive action. At the beginning of the First World War that impulse was to lead him, via Borkum and the Baltic, to the Dardanelles. In 1939–40 it helped to lead Britain to disaster in Norway and Churchill to the premiership.

In 1913 a number of schemes were produced on Churchill's initiative, including plans for the capture of the German islands of Borkum, Sylt and Heligoland, the destruction of the locks at the western entrance of the Kiel Canal, and a landing at Esbjerg.[41] On 31 July 1914 Churchill sent these reports to Asquith, the prime minister, together with a number of other proposals for action on neutral territory. In order of priority they were the Dutch island of Ameland; Ekersund on the south-west coast of Norway; Læsø Channel (Denmark); Kungsbacka Fjord (south-west Sweden); and then, as 'less urgent' cases, Esbjerg, Sylt, Borkum and Heligoland. The naval and military experts charged with investigating these recommendations were not to concern themselves either with 'questions of violation of neutrality' or 'whether

---

[37] For accounts of this meeting, see Winston Churchill, *The World Crisis 1911–1918* (new edn, 2 vols., London, 1938), vol. I, pp. 38–42; Arthur J. Marder, *From the Dreadnought to Scapa Flow: The Royal Navy in the Fisher Era 1904–1919* (5 vols., London, 1961–70), vol. I, pp. 388–93; Offer, *First World War*, pp. 296–7.
[38] Churchill, *World Crisis* I, p. 41.   [39] Ibid., p. 53.   [40] Printed ibid., pp. 42–6.
[41] Marder, *Dreadnought to Scapa Flow* II, pp. 178–9.

the troops could be better employed elsewhere'.[42] Quite apart from these considerations, however, the experts found all of the proposals fraught with risk and offering little advantage.

But within a few months of the outbreak of war Borkum and the Baltic returned to the forefront as the main alternative to the Dardanelles for a flanking attack on the Central Powers.[43] Churchill was the leading advocate of a flanking strategy and, as he wrote in a section omitted from the published version of his *World Crisis*, he preferred action in the north to action in the south, regarding the Dardanelles as long as he was in office 'only as an interim operation'.[44] He made the capture of Borkum and the close blockade of the German North Sea coast the preliminary to an assault on the Baltic rather than a separate operation, but intended it also to force the High Seas Fleet to come out and give battle. The main purpose of an entry into the Baltic would be to secure command of that sea and make possible an amphibious landing by British and Russian troops on the German coast. In addition Churchill hoped to persuade Denmark and Holland to join in the war on the side of the Entente. This recalled the idea which had been pressed upon him by Sir Henry Wilson, the DMO at the time of the Moroccan crisis in 1911, of 'an offensive and defensive alliance of England, France, Belgium, Denmark and Russia'.[45]

At the end of 1914 the War Council rejected Borkum and the Baltic in favour of the Dardanelles, but Churchill revived the idea – again without success – on his return to government in July 1917. It has been suggested with justice that for Churchill 'this scheme had become a panacea for all the ills of British strategy': as had happened in the past and was to happen again in the future, Churchill's predilection for the offensive overrode his strategic judgement.[46]

Although interest in Scandinavia as a theatre of naval warfare declined in the immediate pre-war years, the British authorities remained vigilant in monitoring Germany's increasingly pervasive naval presence. 'During the summer months', the minister in Copenhagen reported, 'it is almost impossible to visit any creek or water-way without finding a German yacht . . . usually manned, so far as can be judged, by a naval crew.'[47] A report of October 1911 by Colonel Bridges, the British military attaché, suggested that the evidence for German naval activity in Denmark was more than anecdotal. Bridges contrasted the constant presence of the German navy in Danish and

[42] Ibid., p. 180; Martin Gilbert, *Winston S. Churchill*, vol. III, *1914–1916* (London, 1971), pp. 19–21.

[43] For a discussion of the competing projects, see Marder, *Dreadnought to Scapa Flow* II, pp. 176–98.

[44] Robin Prior, *Churchill's 'World Crisis' as History* (London, 1983), p. 47.

[45] C. E. Callwell, *Field-Marshal Sir Henry Wilson: His Life and Diaries* (2 vols., London, 1927), vol. I, p. 102; Churchill to Grey, 30 August 1911, printed in Churchill, *World Crisis* II, p. 47. See also David French, *British Strategy and War Aims 1914–1916* (London, 1986), p. 12.

[46] Tuvia Ben-Moshe, 'Churchill's Strategic Conception During the First World War', *Journal of Strategic Studies* 12 (1989), pp. 5–21 (p. 14).

[47] Vaughan (Copenhagen) to FO, 31 December 1910, FO 371/1109.

Norwegian waters with the increasingly infrequent visits of the Home Fleet, and suggested that 'The German tactics of patronage and peaceful penetration, so noticeable a few years back in Holland and Belgium, are now being applied to Scandinavia. In Denmark the poison is particularly virulent, and is concentrated towards the one end, the emasculation of the country.'[48] As a direct result of this report, the Admiralty and the Foreign Office persuaded the Treasury to approve in 1912 the creation of a new naval attaché's post for the three Scandinavian countries (previously divided between the attachés at St Petersburg and Berlin), in order to reflect 'the growing significance of the attitude of these countries from a naval point of view'.[49] Later that year the Home Fleet paid its first large-scale visit for several years to Scandinavian and Baltic waters, thus going some way to 'prevent the impression growing up that the NW Baltic exists as a Manoeuvre Area for the German fleet'.[50]

The German naval presence in Norwegian waters was particularly disturbing since Great Britain regarded Norway, unlike Denmark, as lying within its own naval sphere.[51] During the Norwegian integrity negotiations, as we have seen, both the Admiralty and the Foreign Office wished to retain the option of seizing a base on Norwegian territory to counteract a German thrust into Denmark. The situation was complicated by Wilhelm II's habit of spending a large part of every summer cruising off the west coast of Norway, 'the only country', he said, 'where he could rest in peace after the strain of work, and where the people really left him alone to enjoy the leisure and quiet he desired'.[52] However, the kaiser was invariably accompanied by large detachments of the German fleet. This, together with the fact that the Germans complied only nominally with the rules introduced by the Norwegian government between 1912 and 1914 to limit the number of foreign warships visiting their waters, reinforced the conviction growing among many Norwegians that it was Germany rather than Great Britain who intended to seize a base, or even occupy the whole country, upon the outbreak of war.[53]

Germany

The development of German strategic planning as it affected Scandinavia was influenced, as in Britain, by conflicting perceptions of the nature of a future war, and by deep rivalries both between and within the two armed services. In both army and navy there were three sources of authority. The Prussian

---

[48] Bridges to Sir C. Greene (Copenhagen), 11 October 1911, ibid.
[49] Admiralty to Treasury, 11 April 1912, FO 371/1360.
[50] Captain Hugh Watson (NA, Berlin) to Lord Granville, 27 September 1912, FO 371/1415.
[51] Tom Kristiansen, 'Mellom landmakter og sjømakter. Norges plass i britisk forsvars- og utenrikspolitikk 1905–1914' (Hovedoppgave i historie, University of Oslo, 1988), pp. 170–9.
[52] Speech in Ålesund, reported in Leech (Kristiania) to FO, 26 July 1906, FO 371/98.
[53] E.g. Findlay to FO, 8 November 1911, FO 371/1174; Findlay to FO, 26 February 1912, FO 371/1415; Findlay, 'Annual Report. Norway 1913', 3 March 1914 (pp. 3–4), FO 371/2056.

Ministry of War had its equivalent in the Imperial Naval Office (Reichs-marineamt), headed by a state secretary who represented the navy in the Reichstag. The Prussian General Staff carried out the task of planning in peacetime and held the high command in time of war. For the navy these tasks were fulfilled from 1889 to 1899 by the Naval Command (Oberkommando der Marine – OKM), and thereafter by its successor, the Admiralty Staff (Admiralstab). Finally there were the kaiser's naval and military cabinets. The internecine divisions produced by this complex bureaucratic structure were rendered all the more intractable by the absence of any coordinating authority comparable with the CID. Ultimate responsibility for both army and navy lay with the kaiser, but this naturally served merely to heighten the uncertainties. The traditional primacy of the army in Prussian state and society gave the General Staff a far-reaching autonomy. It planned and acted with little or no reference to other bodies, let alone the civilian authorities. In the last years of peace the army regained the priority, in terms of both budgets and strategy, which it had lost to the navy in the years of Tirpitz's ascendancy after 1897.

The navy, for its part, veered erratically in its strategic planning but came down ultimately, like its British counterpart, in favour of a defensive strategy. Its uncertainties were due in part to the conflict between perception of Britain's overwhelming naval superiority and the desire to seek a decisive battle with the British fleet. The Germans came to acknowledge the strength of Britain's strategic position while realising that their own defensive strengths in the German Bight and the Baltic made a British direct assault increasingly unlikely. The logical response to this insight would have been to concentrate on mines, torpedo-boats, submarines and commerce raiding to attack Britain's weak point – its reliance on overseas trade – and to protect Germany's coasts. Tirpitz had more than an inkling of this but, for both personal and political reasons, refused to divert resources away from his self-imposed task of building up a great battle fleet.[54]

As in Britain, pre-war discussions of action in Scandinavia appear to have focused exclusively on Denmark. Despite the regular presence of the High Seas Fleet in Norwegian waters, the German navy seems never to have considered the possibility of capturing Norwegian territory in the face of British naval superiority.[55] An occupation of Denmark figured prominently in the navy's strategic planning between 1892 (the date of Tirpitz's appointment as chief of staff) and 1905.[56] The idea was never looked upon with favour by the General

[54] Gary E. Weir, 'Tirpitz, Technology and Building U-boats 1897–1916', *International History Review* 6 (1984), pp. 174–90.

[55] Carl-Axel Gemzell, *Organization, Conflict and Innovation: A Study of German Naval Strategic Planning 1888–1940* (Lund, 1973), pp. 65–6.

[56] For discussions of German naval strategic planning before the First World War, see Walther Hubatsch, *Der Admiralstab und die obersten Marinebehörden in Deutschland 1848–1945* (Frankfurt am Main, 1958); Gemzell, *Organization*; Paul Kennedy, 'The Development of German Naval Plans Against England 1896–1914', in Kennedy, *War Plans*, pp. 170–98.

Staff, who regarded it as a diversion from Germany's main tasks on the western and eastern fronts. In the 1890s, however, Denmark, still resenting the loss of Slesvig, could be viewed as a potential ally of France and Russia. Until the completion of the Kiel Canal in 1895, the navy would be forced to concentrate in either in the North Sea or the Baltic in the event of a war with one or both of these powers. The attitude of Denmark was therefore important. A memorandum by the OKM of 1892 reflected Tirpitz's preoccupation with a decisive battle.[57] It recommended that, if Denmark was neutral, the fleet should go on the offensive against France in the North Sea. If Denmark intervened, the fleet should remain in the Baltic to wait for the enemy and fight in the narrow Danish waters. The entire country should be occupied to prevent the French and Russian fleets from joining up. Schlieffen, the chief of the general staff, responded that the army would not have enough troops available in a two-front war but did agree to arrange for some reconnaissance to be carried out in Denmark.

From 1896 onwards Britain was regarded as Germany's main naval enemy. In 1899 the newly constituted Admiralstab, under Bendemann, prepared a plan for war against England which returned to the idea of a battle in the Baltic approaches and an occupation of Denmark.[58] Again the idea was to 'compensate numerical inferiority at sea by superiority on land'.[59] The main battle fleet would be based at Kiel and the army would occupy Denmark immediately upon the outbreak of war. The British were expected to respond by sending a battle fleet into the Baltic. In Danish waters it would be weakened by torpedo-boat attacks and bombardment from the land, as well as by minefields. The German fleet could then be moved from the Baltic via the Kiel Canal in order to fight the decisive battle with Britain's reduced forces in the North Sea.

The kaiser authorised the army and navy to begin joint planning for an invasion of Denmark, and they continued to do so until 1905. From the start, however, Schlieffen's attitude was as negative as it had been in 1892. If Britain had 'one or perhaps even two allies on the continent, then the parts of the German army capable of offensive actions would be completely tied to operations on the country's borders'[60] – in other words in the east and west, not the north. Even if Germany was fighting Britain alone, Schlieffen could spare no more than one division and was prepared to contemplate only an occupation of the island of Fyn. The conclusion of the Anglo-French entente in 1904 reinforced the army's unfavourable judgement on the Danish plan. The navy, however, remained strongly committed to it. As we have seen, it was for the sake of this plan that Büchsel, chief of the admiralty staff from 1902 to 1908, persuaded the kaiser against the idea of Denmark's neutralisation in

---

[57] Gemzell, *Organization*, pp. 66–7.
[58] Kennedy, 'German Naval Plans', p. 177; Gemzell, *Organization*, pp. 69–70.
[59] Gemzell, *Organization*, p. 69.
[60] Quoted in Kennedy, 'German Naval Plans', p. 178.

December 1903.[61] In November 1904, at the time of the Anglo-German war scare, the kaiser accepted the navy's plan and ordered two army corps to be kept in readiness for an invasion of Denmark.

The German navy's preoccupation with Denmark represented a fundamental rejection of the Schlieffen plan. This was not merely because Schlieffen wished to confine the navy's role to the defence of the North Sea coast and winning naval supremacy in the Baltic.[62] In a memorandum written early in 1905 Büchsel challenged the idea of violating the neutrality of Holland and Belgium at the beginning of a war against France and Russia.[63] It was, he said, a vital necessity for Dutch and Belgian ports to be kept open since they handled so large a proportion of German foreign trade. A German invasion would merely ease the task of Great Britain in imposing a blockade. Clearly the navy was anticipating a long war of the kind that Schlieffen hoped to avoid by his bold thrust through the Low Countries into France. With Denmark the position was precisely the opposite. Of all the smaller states, Büchsel declared, Denmark would be the one most directly affected by an Anglo-German war, and the military situation required at all costs that Germany must violate Danish neutrality. Only in this way could the enemy be made to divide his forces and the danger of a British landing at Esbjerg be averted.

On 14 February 1905 Büchsel initiated discussions with the future foreign secretary Kiderlen-Wächter, acting on behalf of the chancellor, on the military and political implications of a German occupation of Denmark. The navy's requirements included the deployment of one division and two army corps to block the Great and Little Belts, the blocking of the Sound by sunken ships, and the preparation of notes to the Danish and Swedish governments. Both Bülow and Holstein now had serious reservations about the navy's plan. Bülow feared that a German occupation of Denmark would provoke a hostile Russian reaction. He also felt that, while it might be possible for Germany to get away with violating the neutrality of the Low Countries, it could not violate the neutrality of Denmark as well. Bülow came down on the side of the western front just as the CID in Britain was to do in 1911. The kaiser was persuaded to reverse his earlier decision. Büchsel wrote to Tirpitz in February 1905:

His Majesty the Kaiser has recently ordered that the navy has *not* to count upon the assistance of the army in a strategical defensive in its operations in the Belts. His Majesty the Kaiser has arrived at this alteration in the previous basis for the deployment of his fleet because on the one hand the Chancellor has recently expressed important doubts from a political standpoint while on the other hand the army cannot provide the troops necessary for the occupation of Danish territory without making success in another place questionable.[64]

This categorical statement did not prevent Büchsel from continuing to

[61] See ch. 2, pp. 66–7.   [62] Hubatsch, *Admiralstab*, p. 118.
[63] Summarised ibid., pp. 118–19, and printed in part, ibid., pp. 247–50.
[64] Quoted in Kennedy, 'German Naval Plans', p. 180, from Hubatsch, *Admiralstab*, p. 120.

hanker after an occupation of Denmark.[65] Yet the Danish strategy was opposed not merely by Schlieffen, whose plan for a two-front war was definitively adopted in December 1905, but also by some of the most powerful figures in the naval hierarchy, including Tirpitz, Admiral von Müller (chief of the Marinekabinett) and Prince Heinrich (chief of the High Seas Fleet).[66] Büchsel was therefore forced to acknowledge the need for a new strategy in the light of the General Staff's veto, the increasing concentration of British naval forces in the North Sea and the probability of French naval support for Britain. The emphasis was now to be strictly defensive.[67] In the operational plan which he drew up early in 1905, Büchsel argued that the Kattegat was of no value as a battleground without security from the land. Instead, the main German force should be kept in the North Sea to deal with the likelihood that Britain would begin a war with an assault on Germany's North Sea coast. Any British attempt to enter the Baltic could probably be dealt with either by the fleet in the North Sea or by Germany's remaining forces in the Baltic.

The possibility of a return to an offensive strategy occurred under Büchsel's two successors as chief of staff, Baudissin (1908–9) and Fischel (1909–11). It was based upon a growing realisation of German strength. A British assault on the German coastline or a close blockade seemed increasingly unlikely in view of the improvements in Germany's coastal defences since 1906. Germany might therefore risk taking the offensive to 'win access to the ocean' by seeking a battle with the British in the northern part of the North Sea. If it did not do so, Britain could, thanks to its geographical position, throttle Germany merely by remaining on the defensive. There was, however, a flaw in this strategy. The introduction of the new 'dreadnought'-type ships after 1906 had necessitated the widening of the Kiel Canal. This task was begun in 1909. Until it was completed (in July 1914), Germany's capacity to wage a vigorous offensive at the beginning of a war against Britain was circumscribed. If an offensive strategy were to be attempted, the High Seas Fleet, based at Wilhelmshaven, would have to be sent via the canal to Kiel, where the new battleships were based, and then escort them through Danish waters back into the North Sea – a lengthy journey which would deprive the German offensive of any element of surprise.

In these circumstances the new emphasis on a battle in the North Sea came to be questioned and attention returned to the Baltic entrances and the position of Denmark. In a marginal note on a memorandum by Fischel of August 1910, which justified the North Sea as the main theatre of operations, the kaiser wrote that no final decision had been made between the North Sea and the Baltic and rejected Fischel's view that operations in the Baltic

---

[65] Jonathan Steinberg, 'Germany and the Russo-Japanese War', *American Historical Review* 75 (1970), pp. 1965–86 (p. 1968); Gemzell, *Organization*, p. 70 (n. 64); Hubatsch, *Admiralstab*, p. 139.

[66] Hubatsch, *Admiralstab*, p. 127 (n. 69).   [67] Kennedy, 'German Naval Plans', p. 182.

entrances should be abandoned.[68] Holtzendorff, chief of the High Seas Fleet from 1909, came out strongly in favour of keeping the fleet in the Baltic and going out no further than the Skagerrak in order to tempt the British into a battle in Danish waters. Unlike earlier advocates of action in the Baltic entrances, Holtzendorff does not appear to have envisaged an occupation of Danish territory as a precondition for these operations. If it was merely a matter of passing warships through Danish waters on their way to the Kattegat and Skagerrak, Danish neutrality would not be violated. The General Staff's continuing opposition to an invasion of Denmark also had to be taken into account. Its argument, repeated on several occasions between 1911 and 1913, was that a war against Britain alone was improbable and that a war on several fronts would require all available land forces.[69] This line of reasoning was now welcomed by the Admiralty Staff as a means of undermining Holtzendorff's plans.

Fischel opposed Holtzendorff's idea of a 'waiting offensive', but it was not until after he was succeeded by Heeringen as chief of staff in 1911 that the Admiralty Staff's preference for the North Sea was able to prevail. Heeringen did not believe that the British would allow themselves to be drawn into the Baltic, but he did expect them to blockade the German North Sea coast. The fleet should therefore aim to bring the British to battle in the southern part of the North Sea – the strategy also favoured by Tirpitz. The kaiser was finally persuaded to take the same view as a result of the naval manoeuvre of September 1912. He was now, he said, firmly opposed to the idea that the fleet should await the battle with the British in the Kattegat or in Danish waters, and declared that the German Bight was 'our main theatre of war'.[70] In November 1912 German pre-war naval strategy reached its final form. It confirmed the decision in favour of the North Sea and embodied a 'tactically offensive, but strategically defensive plan which aimed at preventing a British attempt to blockade the North Sea ports while seeking to bring their forces to battle, if conditions were favourable, in the German Bight'.[71]

The seal was set upon the navy's abandonment of the Baltic as a theatre of operations against Great Britain by the Danish mining of the Great Belt, at Germany's request, in the first days of the First World War. This action was to be described by a retired admiral after the war as 'an unbelievable error' which had prevented Germany from taking an 'offensive–defensive course'.[72] It was an expression of the defensive mentality which had come to prevail in Germany's attitude towards its northern flank – a mentality which owed much to the growing weight of the army at the expense of the navy in the shaping of German strategy.

---

[68] Gemzell, *Organization*, p. 81.   [69] Ibid., p. 88 (n. 111).   [70] Quoted ibid., p. 86.
[71] Ibid., pp. 86–7; Hubatsch, *Admiralstab*, p. 152.
[72] Rear-Admiral aD Levetzow to Vice-Admiral Wolfgang Wegener, 21 March 1927, quoted in Gemzell, *Organization*, pp. 87–8.

Russia, Finland and the defence of St Petersburg

The Finnish theatre at first occupied a relatively unimportant position in Russia's plans for war against Germany and Austria-Hungary. Apart from a narrow belt along the northern coast of the Gulf of Finland, its terrain was thickly forested and unsuited to large-scale military operations. Finland was also remote from the central theatre in Poland, where the main battles between the three empires would be fought out. In the 1890s, following the conclusion of the alliance with France, the spirit of Russia's plans was offensive and self-confident. The Russians recognised, however, that the building of the Kiel Canal gave Germany the opportunity to concentrate its naval forces in the Baltic.[73] German forces might launch an attack on St Petersburg through the Baltic provinces of Courland and Livonia (which together approximate present-day Latvia), and Estonia, on the southern side of the Gulf of Finland. Hence the construction of naval bases at Libau (Liepaja) and Windau (Ventspils) (though Libau was also to serve as the base for Russia's ocean-going fleet). However, the capital might also be threatened from the north. A mobilisation plan of 1899 for the Finnish military district envisaged the possibility of enemy landings on the Finnish side of the Gulf and referred to the political unreliability of the local population.[74] Of more immediate importance were the numerical weakness of the forces at Russia's disposal in Finland, and the fact that the railway line from St Petersburg to Viborg (Viipuri) ran close to the shoreline and could easily be cut by attack from the sea. The problem of defending Finland was exacerbated by the abolition, for political reasons, of the separate Finnish army and the introduction in 1901 of conscription into the Russian army.[75] Russian troops were sent to Finland too slowly to provide an adequate substitute for the formerly autonomous Finnish forces.

The strategic position was transformed by the events of 1904–5: the destruction of the Russian Baltic Fleet by the Japanese at Tsushima and the outbreak of revolution throughout the empire, including Finland. A memorandum written for the General Staff by General Alekseev in 1908 gave a thoroughly pessimistic assessment of Russia's military prospects. Russia must reckon on Romania and Sweden being added to its enemies in the west, and had to face the danger of Finnish separatism at the very gates of St Petersburg. When the Baltic Fleet was rebuilt it must be based not at Libau, which could not be defended, but at Kronstadt. Reval (Tallinn) would become its main operational base, with Porkkala in Finland providing flanking support. In the

---

[73] Juhani Paasivirta, *Finland and Europe: The Period of Autonomy and the International Crises 1808–1914* (London, 1981), p. 173.

[74] Tuomo Polvinen, *Die finnischen Eisenbahnen in den militärischen und politischen Plänen Russlands vor dem Ersten Weltkrieg* (Helsinki, 1962), pp. 17–19.

[75] J. E. O. Screen, 'The Finnish Army 1881–1901: A National Force in a Russian Context', *Slavonic and East European Review* 70 (1992), pp. 453–76; Pertti Luntinen, *French Information on the Russian War Plans 1880–1914* (Helsinki, 1984), pp. 23, 26, 63–5.

short term, however, the elimination of Russian naval power in the Baltic meant that the security of the capital must depend almost exclusively on land forces.[76] Finland, formerly peripheral, was now central to St Petersburg's defence.

In 1905 the Grand Duchy's separate military administration was disbanded and its defences incorporated into the St Petersburg military district. The war plan of 1910, prepared by General Danilov, reflected a continuing consciousness of Russian weakness, especially in relation to Germany, in the aftermath of the Russo-Japanese war.[77] It was thoroughly defensive in spirit and anticipated the abandonment of much of Poland in the face of a German advance. The plans prepared for the St Petersburg district were in keeping with Danilov's pessimistic scenario. They assumed that the Germans and their Swedish allies would launch surprise attacks on the Finnish coast, possibly even before a formal declaration of war. The most likely landing points were thought to be either in south-west Finland, between Turku and Porkkala, or – at much greater risk to the attackers – in the vicinity of the island of Björkö, not far from St Petersburg itself. The aim in the former case would be to conquer the whole of Finland or at least to provoke a Finnish uprising; in the latter case it would be a direct attack on the Russian capital.

Even though the Russian General Staff, encouraged by Russia's rapid military revival, returned to an offensive strategy in 1912, Finland was still perceived as a weak point in the empire's defences.[78] The army expected to be faced in time of war with the dual task of repelling enemy assaults from the sea and repressing the Finnish civilian population. The general strike of 1905 had virtually paralysed transport and communications in the Grand Duchy: it would be catastrophic if these events were repeated at the same time as a foreign invasion. The Russian authorities responded with a vigorous programme of Russification. They suspected the loyalties of the Finnish pilot service, whose members guided shipping through the labyrinth of islands off the Finnish coast (including the Åland Islands). In 1912 the service was placed under the Russian Naval Ministry, with the result that the pilots resigned *en masse*.[79] The General Staff also considered detaching the districts of Finland nearest to St Petersburg and annexing them directly to the empire, although it had not succeeded in doing so by the outbreak of war.

Railways posed the most intractable problem for the Russian authorities and were also the chief source of suspicion of Russian intentions on the part of the Swedes. To the empire's habitual shortage of money for railway construction

---

[76] Luntinen, *Russian War Plans*, p. 105.

[77] Snyder, *Ideology of the Offensive*, pp. 166–72.

[78] See the discussion of the manoeuvre carried out between Helsinki and St Petersburg in May 1914, in John W. Steinberg, 'Russian General Staff Training and the Approach of War', in Frans Coetzee and Marilyn Shevin-Coetzee (eds.), *Authority, Identity and the Social History of the Great War* (Providence, R. I., and Oxford, 1995), pp. 275–303 (pp. 289–94).

[79] Luntinen, *Russian War Plans*, p. 150.

were added the problem of finding routes through Finland's inhospitable terrain, with its many lakes and rivers, and the need to find a *modus vivendi* with the autonomous Finnish government and Diet, whose priorities were quite different from those of the imperial government. Although the Finns played up the strategic value of railways when it suited them to do so, their main interest was economic: to facilitate trade between Finland and the outside world, and to improve communications in the sparsely settled interior and north of the country. Until the turn of the century the Finns had things mainly their own way. In the 1860s the Russian government won an early victory in the controversy over the gauge of the Grand Duchy's new railway system. However, the decision in favour of the empire's broad gauge as opposed to the narrower gauge that was standard in the rest of Europe was undermined when the frugal Finns built their lines to a specification which was incapable of taking the heavy Russian locomotives and rolling stock.[80] The Finns also succeeded in 1898 in winning the tsar's approval for the construction of a line to Tornio on the Swedish frontier at the head of the Gulf of Bothnia.

This situation was anathema to General Bobrikov, chief of staff of the St Petersburg military district, who became governor-general of Finland in August 1898. Bobrikov wished to make the Finnish railway system serve the military needs of the empire.[81] It was to be brought under Russian administration, with the use of the Russian language, to facilitate mobilisation in time of war. The construction of new lines was to be concentrated in eastern Finland to improve communications with the rest of the empire. Bobrikov was bitterly opposed to the line to Tornio, since it would bring Finns and Swedes closer together and facilitate a Swedish–German attack on Finland.[82] This was ironic since many Swedes regarded the construction of the line as evidence of Russia's expansionist ambitions in the far north of Sweden and Norway.[83] Bobrikov also demanded that railway communications must be secure from attack – hence the plan for a second line, running further inland, linking St Petersburg and Finland.

There was a temporary halt in Russian pressure on Finland following the assassination of Bobrikov in 1904 and the Russo-Japanese war, but it was resumed after 1907. The Grand Duchy's railways were placed under the Russian Ministry of Transport. Priority was given to the completion of the remaining gaps in the line that ran through the interior of Finland from St Petersburg to Vaasa (Vasa) on the Gulf of Bothnia – a project which alarmed the Swedes (see pp. 108–9). The line was also to be made suitable for use by the heavy Russian traffic. In 1911 the chief of the general staff, Zhilinskii, joined forces with the prime minister, Stolypin, in defeating the Finance

[80] Polvinen, *Die finnischen Eisenbahnen*, pp. 46–7.
[81] Tuomo Polvinen, *Imperial Borderland: Bobrikov and the Attempted Russification of Finland 1898–1904* (London, 1995).
[82] Polvinen, *Die finnischen Eisenbahnen*, p. 96.   [83] Ibid., pp. 261–4.

Ministry's preference for handing the construction work over to private contractors. The strategic importance of the line was too great, in Zhilinskii's view, for it to be left in private hands. The St Petersburg–Vaasa line was finally completed during the First World War – testimony to Russian fears of a Swedish–German invasion that never materialised.

It was easy to dismiss those fears, yet they were by no means wholly irrational.[84] Many observers shared the assumption that Sweden would join the German side on the outbreak of war. In May 1909, for example, the French minister in Stockholm reported the existence of a military pact between Sweden and Germany.[85] The fact that by 1912 the German navy had written off an attack in the Gulf of Finland as too costly was a tribute to the strength of Russia's newly constructed coastal defences and the rapid revival of Russian naval power.[86] Tsushima had been not merely a catastrophe but an opportunity to rebuild ships which would soon have been obsolete in any case.[87] Despite Russia's financial difficulties, its naval budget was larger than Germany's.[88] Although Russian strategic assessments were pessimistic and concentrated on building a strong defence in the Gulf of Finland, the efforts devoted to this purpose proved successful. An article in the *Marine-Rundschau* of April 1914, probably inspired by the German Admiralty Staff, wrote that 'a powerful Russian fleet, based on the strong position Reval–Porkkala, is a factor of extraordinary political and military significance and demands unceasing vigilance'.[89] This judgement was to be confirmed by the failure of Germany's naval forces to penetrate Russia's defences in the Gulf of Finland during the first two years of the war.[90]

Nor were Russian anxieties about Finnish loyalties groundless, even though the response – Russification – merely radicalised a population which had remained faithful to a succession of tsars throughout the nineteenth century.[91] The Japanese General Staff took an active interest in the Finnish revolutionary movement.[92] Leo Amery's interest in the same subject has been noted earlier. However, British ministers and officials, ignorant of Finnish conditions and anxious to improve relations with Russia, were more inclined to sympathise

[84] E.g. the remarks of a French officer in 1911, quoted in Luntinen, *Russian War Plans*, p. 132.

[85] Snyder, *Ideology of the Offensive*, p. 168.

[86] Hubatsch, *Admiralstab*, p. 154; Luntinen, *Russian War Plans*, pp. 150–3.

[87] Peter Gatrell, 'After Tsushima: Economic and Administrative Aspects of Russian Naval Rearmament 1905–1913', *Economic History Review* 43 (1990), pp. 255–70; Donald W. Mitchell, *A History of Russian and Soviet Sea Power* (New York, 1974), pp. 274–82.

[88] Walther Hubatsch, 'Die russische Marine im deutschen Urteil', in Hubatsch, *Kaiserliche Marine. Aufgaben und Leistungen* (Munich, 1975), pp. 92–123.

[89] Quoted ibid., pp. 118–19.

[90] See the comments of the Russian foreign minister, Serge Sazonov, *Fateful Years 1909–1916* (London, 1928), p. 61.

[91] C. Leonard Lundin, 'Finland', in Edward C. Thaden (ed.), *Russification in the Baltic Provinces and Finland 1855–1914* (Princeton, N. J., 1981), pp. 355–457.

[92] Olavi K. Fält and Antti Kujala (eds.), *Rakka Ryusui: Colonel Akashi's Report on His Secret Activities During the Russo-Japanese War* (Helsinki, 1988).

with the Russian predicament. Some saw Finland as another Ireland,[93] while Sir Edward Grey responded in December 1915 to a Swedish request for support for the Finns in their struggle to maintain their autonomy: 'Think if we had a foreign nation settled in Kensington.'[94] Yet there can be no doubt that the solutions adopted by the tsarist government exacerbated the problems they were intended to solve. Just as Russification alienated the Finns, so railway construction apparently confirmed Swedish fears of Russian intentions. Sweden, meanwhile, was in Russian eyes more firmly than ever in the German camp.

The German General Staff and Scandinavia

Germany and Denmark

Although the German General Staff had no interest in undertaking an invasion of Denmark in support of a naval offensive, it was preoccupied with the possibility that the country might be used as a jumping-off point for an invasion of Germany. In 1903 it was still reckoning that, in a war against France and Russia, Denmark might take the side of Germany's enemies and enable them to launch an attack on Kiel and the Canal.[95] It had much greater cause to worry when, at the time of the first Moroccan crisis in 1905, French newspapers carried reports that Britain had offered to support France by blocking the Elbe and landing 100,000 men in Schleswig-Holstein.[96] Since Schleswig-Holstein had virtually no harbours suitable for landing an invasion force, both the Danish and the German authorities came to believe that a landing might be attempted at the Danish port of Esbjerg. General von Moltke, who succeeded Schlieffen as chief of staff in December 1905, was keen to improve relations with Denmark. As a first step he wished to moderate the harsh policy of the Prussian government towards the Danish inhabitants of North Schleswig. This change of policy was actively supported by Bülow and the Wilhelmstrasse as well as by the kaiser. It was to bear fruit in an agreement (the so-called Optant convention) on the nationality of certain sections of the population of North Schleswig – the subject of a long-running dispute between Denmark and Germany – at the beginning of 1907. Moltke also responded

---

[93] George Maude, 'Finland in Anglo-Russian Diplomatic Relations 1899–1910', *Slavonic and East European Review* 48 (1970), pp. 557–81. For Finnish efforts to publicise their cause in Britain, see George Maude, 'The Finnish Question in British Political Life 1899–1914', *Turun historiallinen arkisto* 28 (1973), pp. 325–44.

[94] Erik Palmstierna, *Orostid. Politiska dagbocksanteckningar* (2 vols., Stockholm, 1952–3), vol. I, *1914–1916*, p. 174, quoted in Eino Lyytinen, *Finland in British Politics in the First World War* (Helsinki, 1980), p. 67.

[95] Troels Fink, *Spillet om dansk neutralitetet 1905–1909. L. C. F. Lütken og dansk udenrigs- og forsvarspolitik* (Århus, 1959), p. 19.

[96] These reports appear to have originated with the French foreign minister Delcassé, and it has been suggested that some such offer may have been made to him personally by King Edward VII: ibid., pp. 25–6.

with alacrity to a proposal made in February 1906 by the new chief of the Danish War Ministry, Captain L. C. F. Lütken, to hold informal discussions on the possibility of closer relations between Germany and Denmark.[97]

The Lütken–Moltke talks of 1906–8 took place against a background of complex events which had disturbing implications from the point of view of German security.[98] It was, as we have seen, a time of intense diplomatic activity, much of it centring, at least implicitly, on the position of Denmark and the entrances to the Baltic. It was also a period in which the General Staff was having to come to terms with the strategic implications of Britain's entente with France. If Britain chose to throw its weight behind the Dual Alliance in a future war, it could be expected to do so at the point where its naval power could be exploited most effectively. For the German General Staff, as for the British Admiralty, this meant Germany's exposed northern flank. German fears – and those of Moltke in particular – were focused principally on the Danish North Sea port of Esbjerg. The talks coincided, finally, with the deliberations of the Danish defence commission of 1902–8. Expert opinion in Denmark was polarised between the view of the army, which favoured the traditional policy of reliance on Great Britain and a relatively strong land defence, and belief of the navy that the growth of German naval power had radically altered Denmark's strategic position and placed it wholly in the German sphere of influence. If Germany was to be prevented from occupying Danish territory in time of war, it must be convinced that Denmark was capable of repelling any violation of its neutrality by Britain. This meant, among other things, strengthening Denmark's sea defences and in particular those of Copenhagen.

Captain Lütken was a capable and self-assured officer who was driven by the conviction that it was imperative for Denmark to establish an intimate relationship with Germany. As an army officer he was therefore very much isolated in his views. In the 1890s Lütken had tied his personal career to the rising Liberal Party, and in particular to its dominant personality, J. C. Christensen. Lütken was unsuccessful in his attempt to be appointed military attaché to Germany after the Liberals came to power in 1901, but was sent to Berlin for a period of 'study' in 1902–3, where he made a number of contacts with members of the General Staff including its future chief, Moltke. His chance came with the formation in January 1905 of a new government in which Christensen held the posts of prime minister and minister of defence. Christensen, like Lütken, believed that it was essential for Denmark to pursue a neutrality policy that was acceptable to Germany. In December 1905 he appointed Lütken to the top post in the Ministry of War.

The first conversation between Moltke and Lütken, held in Copenhagen on 18 February 1906, revealed Moltke's concern with the possibility of a British

---

[97] Ibid., p. 30.

[98] Unless otherwise stated, the present account is based on Fink, *Spillet*, which prints the most important Danish and German documents.

landing at Esbjerg.[99] He regarded this as more probable than an attempt to land on the island of Zealand. If, however, the Danish capital were to be threatened, Germany could offer practical support. Moltke also mentioned the possibility of blocking the Great Belt, both as a measure for the defence of Copenhagen and as a matter of importance to Germany in its own right – revealing an essentially defensive posture which was at odds, as we have seen, with the bulk of naval opinion. The General Staffs of the two countries could, he suggested, reach an agreement on measures for Denmark's defence without committing their governments to cooperation of a more far-reaching nature. Moltke's message was that, if the Danes could 'keep the English at arm's length' by convincing them that they were determined to defend their territory, Denmark might be able to preserve its neutrality: Germany would not be the first to break it. But Denmark must in no circumstances place itself on the side of Germany's enemies. Moltke also developed more general themes. He hinted at the possibility of an understanding on North Schleswig, and of tariff concessions to compensate Danish farmers for the loss of their trade with Great Britain. Denmark, finally, might help to pave the way for rapprochement between Germany and the other Scandinavian powers.

After a lengthy debate within the Danish government, the prime minister authorised Lütken in June 1906 to resume the conversations with a view to obtaining a public assurance from Germany that it would respect Denmark's neutrality in a future war on condition that Denmark mounted an effective defence to prevent the use of its territory by any other power. Such a unilateral declaration, had it been made, would have been as clear a demonstration as any that Danish neutrality had been compromised in Germany's favour. Christensen went further, however, when he suggested that a military convention might be concluded between the two countries if Denmark received 'substantial advantages in return'.[100] By this he meant no less than the return of North Schleswig to Denmark.

But Moltke's tone had changed by the time the two men met again at the beginning of July.[101] He was not interested in doing deals. Denmark, he said, was only making demands, not making offers. It would be scarcely capable of defending its neutrality in time of war; Germany could ask only one question of Denmark in the event of an Anglo-German war: friend or foe? Germany could not give any assurance that it would respect Danish neutrality since it was a matter of vital importance to close the Great Belt, and for this it would require Danish territory. Moltke then relented a little, hinting at the possibility of a change in border conditions in Schleswig after a war in which Denmark had taken Germany's side, or of an exchange of Schleswig for the Danish West Indies. He also suggested that there was no need for an open military convention: it was only necessary for secret agreements to be concluded

[99] Report of conversation by Captain Lütken, 19 February 1906, ibid., pp. 237–40.
[100] Instructions to Captain Lütken, 29 June 1906, ibid., pp. 260–1.
[101] Reports of conversations of 2 and 3 July 1906 by Lütken and Moltke, ibid., pp. 262–5.

between the General Staffs of the two countries. Lütken for his part appears to have gone much further than a mere assurance that Denmark would defend its neutrality. Once the defences of Copenhagen were completed in three to four years' time, he said, Denmark need not fear a British attack on its capital. It could then 'take Germany's side'.[102]

Moltke spoke in similar though more restrained terms in conversation with King Frederik VIII during the latter's visit to Berlin in November 1906.[103] Moltke continued to show an active interest in Denmark in the first months of 1907. This was a period during which German–Danish rapprochement was sealed by the signature of the Optant convention of 11 January 1907, but in which Britain was also alerted to the growing intimacy of German–Danish relations, notably through an article in *The Times* of 6 March which had been inspired by the French minister in Copenhagen. The German archives contain a brief summary of a draft military agreement between Germany and Denmark drawn up by the General Staff on 10 February 1907. It provided for Denmark to take responsibility for the security of Zealand and most of the Jutland peninsula, while Germany itself defended Esbjerg.[104] Although Fink suggests there is no indication that this draft was ever discussed outside the inner circles of the General Staff, it clearly formed the basis of Moltke's remarks when the two men met again in Berlin on 28 March 1907.[105]

This time Lütken came without instructions but he gave Moltke a categorical assurance that 'all *responsible* Danish statesmen' were convinced that 'Denmark could in no circumstances stand on the side of Germany's adversaries, and that if it proved impossible to maintain Denmark's neutrality in a German–British war, it would go along with Germany.' Moltke correctly took this statement to refer to J. C. Christensen and declared himself well satisfied with the assurance.[106] Without mentioning a formal treaty, he again stressed the importance of an effective defence for Esbjerg. If the Danes could not undertake the task, the Germans were ready to do it for them. As he had done at their first meeting, Moltke raised the prospect of economic compensation for Denmark if it joined the German side. Germany would take all of Denmark's agricultural exports for the duration of the war and would pay the top prices for them.

By April 1907 the exchanges between Lütken and Moltke were no longer secret. Well-informed articles, some originating with Lütken's opponents in the War Ministry, began to appear in the Danish press. Some members of the government, notably the foreign minister, Raben-Levetzau, were beginning to have doubts about Christensen's conspicuously pro-German course. However, in a letter of 25 May 1907 Lütken gave Moltke a categorical pledge that 'as long as Christensen was at the helm, Germany could rely on Denmark'. And,

[102] These words appear only in Moltke's account.
[103] Records of conversation, Fink, *Spillet*, pp. 272–4.   [104] Ibid., pp. 275–6.
[105] Ibid., p. 69.
[106] Report of conversation between Lütken and Moltke, ibid., pp. 279–82.

he went on, Christensen's policy would probably be continued even after his departure from power.

Moltke was apparently satisfied with this assurance. He continued to work for an improvement in German–Danish relations, bringing pressure to bear on obstructive local officials to speed up implementation of the Optant convention in North Schleswig. The two men met again in April 1908, shortly before signature of the Baltic and North Sea agreements. According to Lütken's brief diary entry for 14 April, Moltke again advised the Danes urgently to improve the sea fortifications of Copenhagen and to 'do something about Esbjerg'.[107] However, the basis of their collaboration was to be shattered by the fall of the Christensen ministry as a result of the Alberti scandal in October 1908. Lütken's influence declined with the fall of his patron; his pledge could not bind Christensen's successors. Asked on behalf of the new foreign minister if there were any agreements with Germany, Lütken replied truthfully enough: 'none at all'.[108] The new Neergaard government was notably less accommodating towards Germany than its predecessor. Instructions sent to the Danish minister in Berlin at the time of the Bosnian crisis in March 1909, when war seemed imminent, emphasised that, although Denmark would do its utmost to avoid coming into conflict with Germany, it would be obliged to resist if Germany tried to force it into an alliance before Britain had violated its neutrality.

Yet Moltke had reason to be satisfied with the outcome of his exchanges with Lütken. The Neergaard government took care to keep Moltke informed of its defence preparations at Copenhagen and Esbjerg, and seems to have gone some way towards convincing him that his fears of a British landing were exaggerated.[109] It also tried to pursue a more even-handed defence policy which, in addition to improving the sea defences of Copenhagen, envisaged the construction of a series of new forts lying at some distance from the city to secure the capital against a German attack from the land side. But this part of the plan had to be dropped from the defence ordinance of 1909 owing to the opposition of J. C. Christensen. The coming to power of the Radical Liberals under the leadership of C. T. Zahle in 1909–10 and again in 1913 brought a return to a more pro-German orientation. The new defence minister Peter Munch and the 32-year-old foreign minister Erik Scavenius admittedly broke with the Christensen–Lütken approach, which postulated a relatively strong defence as a means of convincing the Germans that Denmark was capable of resisting the violation of its neutrality by a power hostile to Germany. They argued instead that the best defence for Denmark was disarmament.[110]

This was partly because both men took a notably optimistic view of the

[107] Ibid., p. 216.   [108] Diary entry for 9 October 1908, ibid., p. 220.
[109] Memorandum by War Ministry, 18 March 1909, sent by Lütken to Moltke, ibid., pp. 312–16.
[110] Viggo Sjøqvist, *Peter Munch. Manden, politikeren, historikeren* (Copenhagen, 1976), pp. 60–70.

international situation in these years but it was also, for Scavenius at least, a result of rational calculation. No defence, however strong, would deter the great powers from intervening in Scandinavia if that was what they wished to do. In practice, however, their commitments on other fronts would be so great that they would never have sufficient forces available for operations in what was, for all of them, a strictly secondary theatre.[111] Accurate as this prediction was to prove, it was still vital to give Germany no pretext for violating Danish neutrality. Scavenius had no difficulty in establishing friendly relations with Ulrich von Brockdorff-Rantzau, who had been appointed German minister to Copenhagen in 1912. He also helped to stifle Danish expressions of indignation when the Prussian government renewed its harsh policy towards the Danish inhabitants of North Schleswig. There could be little doubt that the Radical government would go to great lengths to appease Germany if called upon to compromise its neutrality in time of crisis.

Germany and Sweden

Moltke's second major initiative before the First World War was towards Sweden in 1909–10. He wanted more from the Swedes than from the Danes – and ultimately obtained less. From the Danes an assurance of neutrality was sufficient, provided it could be guaranteed by Denmark's own efforts, supplemented if necessary by German support. The Swedes were to be persuaded to depart from neutrality in favour of an alliance with Germany against Russia. This, despite promising beginnings, was more than the Swedes could accept. Moltke's initiative reflected the deepening antagonism between Germany and Russia following the Bosnian crisis. Moltke and his diplomatic allies – Pückler, the German minister in Stockholm, and Kiderlen-Wächter, German foreign minister from August 1910 – sought to exploit the feelings of insecurity and isolation felt by the conservative Lindman government in Sweden in the aftermath of the Baltic and North Sea negotiations. In particular Moltke wished to win Sweden over to the German side in the event of war with Russia. To this end the Swedes had to be convinced of the reality of the Russian threat to themselves and be persuaded that they stood a good chance of success if they went to war.

In November 1909 the German military attaché in St Petersburg reported on the construction of a railway from the Russian capital to the port of Vaasa in Finland.[112] According to Swedish opinion (probably that of the Swedish military attaché), he said, the Russian aim was to concentrate troops at the port in order to threaten Sweden with an invasion. Vaasa was located at the narrowest point of the Gulf of Bothnia, and there were good rail connections on the Swedish side of the Gulf. This report gave Moltke an opportunity to press for a more active policy towards Sweden. As he wrote to Schoen on 12

---

[111] Sjøqvist, *Scavenius* I, pp. 60–1.   [112] Polvinen, *Die finnischen Eisenbahnen*, p. 266.

December 1909, Moltke did not believe for one moment that Russia had any aggressive intentions towards Sweden.[113] On the contrary, he suggested, Russian railway construction in Finland reflected fears that Sweden might join with Germany and the outbreak of a revolution in Finland to threaten St Petersburg. But Germany might be able to exploit the mutual mistrust between Sweden and Russia. If Russia could be convinced of the danger of Swedish intervention in Finland and the likelihood that it would unleash a Finnish revolution, it would be obliged to detach considerable forces for the defence of St Petersburg. If Sweden could be persuaded that the Russian threat was a real one, it might join the Triple Alliance in time of war.

Schoen agreed with Moltke that it was to Germany's advantage to cultivate the mistrust between the two powers but did not favour an active policy. Germany, he thought, had time on its side. Pückler in Stockholm was much more pessimistic. He feared the growth of British influence in Sweden and thought that the combination of Gustav V as king, Lindman as prime minister and Taube as foreign minister offered Germany a situation which was as favourable as it was ever likely to have. Kaiser Wilhelm was impressed by Pückler's reasoning, noting on a despatch from Stockholm of 8 January 1910 that it was desirable to have a military convention between Germany and Sweden in the event of an attack from the east. In June 1910 Taube gave Pückler a very clear indication that he wanted closer relations between Sweden and Germany. Schoen remained cautious but his successor, the impetuous Kiderlen-Wächter, was much more forthcoming. As a result, probably, of a memorandum sent by Moltke to the Wilhelmstrasse earlier in the month, Kiderlen approached Trolle, the new Swedish minister in Berlin, on 26 August with a proposal that – without concluding a formal alliance between Germany and Sweden – the military leaders of the two countries should coordinate joint defence measures against a Russian attack. Kiderlen suggested that Moltke, who had family connections in Sweden, could travel to Stockholm without arousing undue attention. After lengthy discussions, in which the prime minister in particular expressed serious reservations, the Swedish government concluded in late October that it could not refuse the German invitation. It decided, however, to send the chief of the general staff, Knut Bildt, to Berlin since this would be less conspicuous than a visit by Moltke to Stockholm. Trolle was also ordered to make it clear to Kiderlen that Sweden did not wish its neutrality to be compromised by the military conversations. To this Kiderlen raised no objection. Like Moltke, however, he believed that a German–Russian war *would* activate military cooperation between Germany and Sweden even if Swedish neutrality was not directly threatened. As in the case of Denmark,

---

[113] Folke Lindberg, 'De svensk–tyska generalstabsförhandlingarna år 1910', *Historisk tidskrift* (Sweden) 77 (1957), pp. 1–28; Folke Lindberg, *Den svenska utrikespolitikens historia*, vol. III, part 4, *1872–1914* (Stockholm, 1958), pp. 249–56; W. M. Carlgren, *Neutralität oder Allianz. Deutschlands Beziehungen zu Schweden in den Anfangsjahren des Ersten Weltkrieges* (Stockholm, 1962), pp. 11–12.

formal political agreements were unnecessary if there was effective cooperation between the respective armed forces.

Bildt met Moltke in Berlin on 17 November 1910.[114] In outlining German operational plans against Russia, Moltke gave the Swedish general a completely false impression of Germany's real intentions. He postulated a war between the Central Powers and Russia alone rather than the two-front war embodied in the Schlieffen Plan. There was therefore no suggestion that the offensive against Russia would begin only after an offensive against France. On the contrary, German and Austrian armies would launch an assault in Poland, and the Germans would advance on St Petersburg from East Prussia, within fourteen days of the outbreak of war. Sweden would play its part by sending its entire army to Finland, preferably via the Åland Islands, to threaten the Russian capital more rapidly than could the German forces advancing from the south. According to this scenario Sweden would have a good chance of success. It was a prospect with which Moltke hoped to tempt the Swedes into cooperation with Germany. The reality, had they been persuaded, would have been very different. The bulk of Germany's forces would have been employed on the western front, not in tying down the Russians. Russia for its part would have had ample forces available to deal with a Swedish assault on its capital. In the last resort, however, the precise scenario was immaterial. Like Pückler, Moltke believed that Germany did not have time on its side and must bind Sweden politically to itself as quickly as possible. Military contacts were thus a means to a political goal.

Much remains unclear concerning the policy of the Swedish government after the meeting between Bildt and Moltke, but the views of the foreign minister and prime minister were certainly sharply opposed. Taube favoured military contacts as the means to a more general political understanding. For Taube the policy of passive neutrality was bankrupt. Sweden must obtain 'guarantees against all eventualities'; the German proposal meant a promise of support from 'the world's most powerful military state'. As a next step it should be supplemented by a similar but more far-reaching entente with Norway. Going along with Germany might also strengthen Sweden's position in the forthcoming German–Swedish trade negotiations, and win German backing for Sweden in the Åland question. Lindman, by contrast, feared that a closer alignment with Germany would alienate the Western powers, who might then feel justified in disclaiming any commitment to Sweden over the Åland Islands.[115] Yet despite his scepticism, Lindman did not wish to alienate the Germans by breaking off contact too abruptly. Nothing is known directly of the attitude of King Gustav V, or of the advice given by the chief of the general staff to the government. Lindberg suggests, however, that despite his pro-

---

[114] No German account of the meeting has survived. Bildt's report is printed in Folke Lindberg, 'De svensk–tyska generalstabsförhandlingarna', pp. 25–8.

[115] Gunnar Åselius, 'Storbritannien, Tyskland och den svenska neutraliteten 1880–1914: en omvärdering', *Historisk tidskrift* (Sweden) 114 (1994), pp. 228–66 (pp. 242–6).

German sympathies, Bildt was sceptical both about the practicalities of a Swedish invasion of Finland and the wider political implications of a departure from neutrality.[116] Certainly he told his son in 1912 that a military convention had been Moltke's aim and that he, Bildt, was glad that nothing had come of it, whilst Moltke for his part was later to disparage Bildt as 'a timid man, a man without vision'.[117]

The Swedes did not break off contact but neither did they take any initiative to prolong or broaden the discussions. There was no Swedish Lütken. If the Lindman government was non-committal, the Germans had still less to hope for from its Liberal successor, led by Karl Staaff, which came to power in 1911. There is indirect evidence that the Germans had hoped to take the talks further and that they were annoyed that no further progress had been made. In a letter of 5 September 1915 to Falkenhayn, Moltke's successor as chief of the general staff, Chancellor Bethmann Hollweg referred to unsuccessful attempts to bring about a closer political relationship between Germany and the Scandinavian countries: 'In the files of the General Staff Your Excellency will find negotiations on a military convention with Sweden which were dropped by the Swedish side.'[118] However, the position in Sweden after 1911 resembled that in Denmark after 1908: frustration after a promising start.

It was not the end of German attempts to draw Sweden into a closer relationship. Under Jagow, Kiderlen's successor after 1913, the Auswärtiges Amt reverted to the passive stance of Schoen. In July 1913 Jagow told the Swedish minister in Rome that he could not see the necessity of forcing Sweden to choose sides at the beginning of a German–Russian war, and that Sweden was less exposed to attack than any other power. Again, however, the activities of the legation in Stockholm were at variance with the cautious line pursued by the Wilhelmstrasse. Reichenau, minister to Sweden from 1911 to 1915, went even further than his predecessor Pückler in his pursuit of closer relations between Sweden and Germany. His idea that Sweden should become a German federal state found no support in the Foreign Office, but Reichenau was able to establish direct contact with the kaiser, speaking to him personally on the subject in January 1914.

The meeting was a great success. Reichenau informed the Foreign Office on 16 January that the kaiser wished for 'an alliance, or at least a military convention' with Sweden.[119] The idea was shelved by the Wilhelmstrasse, and Reichenau received a second reprimand for his interference in Swedish affairs. Carlgren is probably right to see both the Moltke–Bildt conversation and the activities of Reichenau and the kaiser as an aberration.[120] Caution had been the watchword of German policy towards Sweden ever since the time of Bismarck. Moltke himself was clearly unprepared to push through agreements on military cooperation in the face of manifest reluctance on the other side.

[116] Folke Lindberg, 'De svensk–tyska generalstabsförhandlingarna', pp. 20–1.
[117] Carlgren, Neutralität oder Allianz, pp. 15–16.   [118] Quoted ibid., p. 11.
[119] Quoted ibid., p. 22.   [120] Ibid., pp. 25–8.

Developments in Swedish domestic politics after 1911 did nothing to suggest that Sweden might become more forthcoming to German overtures. The Hammarskjöld government which took office in 1914 was conservative but insecure. As the international situation deteriorated Germany – rightly – devoted far more attention to the Balkans than it did to northern Europe.

By 1914 Germany was resigned to a largely passive naval strategy and had ruled out the possibility of diverting any part of its armed forces from the eastern and western fronts to the northern theatre. Its attempts to coordinate military preparations with Denmark had made only limited progress; with Sweden they had been wholly unsuccessful. It is true that German economic, political and cultural influence over Scandinavia was on the increase, but such influence could flourish only in peacetime. Great Britain might have been excluded from the Baltic but war, when it came, would reveal the latent strength of Britain's maritime position.

British planning for economic warfare against Germany

The survival of schemes for offensives in Denmark or the Baltic for so long was testimony to the power of wishful thinking at the Admiralty. So too was the persistent belief in the possibility of a close blockade of Germany. The abandonment of amphibious operations seemed to imply subordination to the army. In fact the role of the navy was to be transformed, not downgraded, by the abandonment of close blockade after 1912. The British government went to war in 1914 with a strategy of limited liability. Sending the BEF to France combined with economic pressure on Germany was, they believed, the only way of conducting the war without causing fundamental damage to the British economy and precipitating social breakdown.[121] The conduct of economic warfare was a task for the navy in the first instance. Among Cabinet ministers only Kitchener, the new secretary of state for war, anticipated a prolonged conflict and the need to raise the continental-scale army that this would entail.[122] Yet the architects of the strategy of economic warfare understood, even if their political masters did not, that it too implied a long war. They also knew that, if there could be no close blockade because of the danger of approaching Germany's coast, it had to be a blockade of Germany together with all those neutral countries with which Germany did business. Of these the most important were the 'adjacent neutrals' – the Netherlands, Belgium (until it was invaded by Germany), Denmark, Norway and Sweden – and the United States.

The development of economic blockade as an offensive weapon grew out of the insight that among Britain's potential enemies Germany, now heavily industrialised and reliant on overseas supplies, might be as vulnerable as Great

---

[121] Offer, *First World War*, pp. 308–10; David French, *British Economic and Strategic Planning 1905–1915* (London, 1982), pp. 85–97.

[122] French, *British Economic and Strategic Planning*, pp. 124–37.

Britain itself to economic pressure in time of war. Advocates of economic pressure like Hankey envisaged a war of limited liability in which, as in the Napoleonic era, Britain would not intervene on the European continent but wait for the enemy's economy to collapse. It was a strategy which appealed to ministers who wished as far as possible to conduct 'business as usual' in time of war, and was thus endorsed by the Military Needs of the Empire sub-committee of 1908–9. Since, however, a blockade would work too slowly to save France, the sub-committee also approved the General Staff's plan to send an expeditionary force across the Channel.[123]

Blockade had its critics. One was Admiral Wilson, who believed it would be ineffective because Germany would continue to obtain supplies from neighbouring neutrals, and disbanded the Trade Division when he became first sea lord in 1910.[124] Both the Foreign Office and the General Staff also disputed the Admiralty's assessment of the effects of economic pressure on Germany. Like Wilson, they assumed that Germany's neighbours would not be subject to the blockade. A memorandum produced for the army by the Board of Trade in 1909 acknowledged that Germany was dependent on overseas trade but concluded that the ports of Rotterdam and Antwerp would be able to handle enough tonnage to prevent the blockade from being effective. However Hankey, assistant secretary to the CID from 1908 and secretary from 1912, kept up the momentum of blockade, notably through the Trading with the Enemy inquiry of 1911–12. Owing in part to his efforts, Britain entered the war in 1914 still committed to the dual strategy of economic warfare and limited continental commitment which had been adopted in 1909.[125]

Clearly much depended on the way in which the neutrals were to be treated in time of war. The deliberations begun at the Admiralty and continued under Hankey at the CID implied a far-reaching interference with neutral trade. Even a close blockade would have this effect, while a more distant blockade entailed still tighter controls. The Admiralty had begun to recognise the impossibility of a close blockade as early as 1904, though it was resurrected by Admiral Wilson in 1911–12 and Churchill (despite his reservations prior to becoming first lord) still hankered after it in 1914.[126] In 1912 close blockade was replaced by an 'observational blockade' – a line of cruisers and destroyers patrolling between Newcastle upon Tyne and the coast of southern Norway, and southward towards the Dutch coast. This line was far too long and too close to Germany for safety, and it was replaced on the eve of war in July 1914 by a 'distant blockade' comprising two lines: one running between the Shetlands and the Norwegian coast, the other running south across the Channel from Dover.

[123] Offer, *First World War*, pp. 242–3.   [124] Ibid., pp. 285–6.
[125] Ibid., pp. 293–9.
[126] Marder, *Dreadnought to Scapa Flow* I, pp. 367–77. For Churchill's reservations about close blockade, see his letter to Grey of 30 August 1911, printed in Churchill, *World Crisis* I, p. 47.

There would still be gaps in the Royal Navy's cordon. One, of course, was the Baltic. Another was Norway. As the Ballard committee had noted in 1907, 'If Norway is neutral the line cannot be drawn right across to the Norwegian coast, but must end in Norwegian territorial waters.'[127] Despite the existence of these gaps and the absence of a formal blockade, it could still be hoped that a large proportion of Germany's seaborne supplies would come within the ambit of the British naval patrols. Only a small proportion of those supplies, however, would be carried in German merchant ships. Most would be carried in neutral ships to neutral destinations in Scandinavia and the Low Countries. How was this neutral traffic to be dealt with?

The question of neutral rights in wartime was the subject of intense international debate in the years before the First World War.[128] The nineteenth century had witnessed a growing convergence of opinion on maritime rights. At the close of the Napoleonic wars Britain, as the leading maritime power, had been largely alone in its insistence on the broadest possible interpretation of the belligerent rights of blockade, including the right to detain cargoes carried on neutral ships if it could be proved that the latter were destined ultimately for the enemy. But in the Declaration of Paris of 1856 Britain and France, now allies against Russia, eliminated their chief points of difference by confirming that a blockade must be 'effective' – that is, confined to the enemy's coasts and keeping a complete and continuous watch upon them – and that enemy goods carried in neutral ships could not be seized unless they constituted contraband of war – the latter being very narrowly defined. During the American civil war the United States came closer to the traditional British position in affirming that a blockade did not need to be total to be effective: blockade runners must be faced with the danger, but not necessarily the absolute certainty of capture. In addition, ships carrying contraband could be treated as blockade runners even if their first destination was a neutral port, as long as their goods were clearly intended to end up with the Confederacy.

Ultimately the doctrine of 'continuous voyage' was to have enormous implications for a war against a power like Germany which relied heavily on neutral shipping and the ports of adjacent neutrals in time of war. In the short term, however, Britain seemed to be the power which would lose most from a general acceptance of the doctrine of continuous voyage. No country was more dependent on imports of foodstuffs and raw material, much of it carried in

---

[127] Kemp, *Fisher Papers* II, p. 372.

[128] For discussions, see A. C. Bell, *A History of the Blockade of Germany and of the Countries Associated with Her in the Great War* (London, 1937; declassified 1961), pp. 1–32; Marion C. Siney, *The Allied Blockade of Germany 1914–1916* (Ann Arbor, Mich., 1954; repr. Westport, Conn., 1973), pp. 1–16; Clive Parry, 'Foreign Policy and International Law', in F. H. Hinsley (ed.), *British Foreign Policy Under Sir Edward Grey* (Cambridge, 1977), pp. 89–110; Arthur Marsden, 'The Blockade', in Hinsley, *British Foreign Policy*, pp. 488–515. Much the most lucid account is in John W. Coogan, *The End of Neutrality: The United States, Britain and Maritime Rights 1899–1915* (Ithaca, N. Y., and London, 1981).

neutral ships. In the late nineteenth century France was still regarded as Britain's most dangerous maritime enemy, well placed to attack British trade routes even if it was incapable of challenging its naval superiority in open combat. Britain was insistent above all that food and raw materials must never be treated as contraband.

By the first years of the twentieth century Britain was therefore moving towards a position where, as its foreign secretary privately assured President Theodore Roosevelt, it would 'be found on the side of neutral rather than of belligerent interests'.[129] Its inclination in this direction was strengthened by the experiences of two recent wars. In the Boer war it had been a belligerent, in the Russo-Japanese war a neutral, but both wars had seemed to confirm the strength of neutrals – or at least powerful ones like Germany in the first case and Britain and the United States in the second – in the face of belligerent attempts to impose a blockade. They had also confirmed that, whatever else might be defined as absolute contraband, food definitely was not. A further reason for favouring the weakening of belligerent rights was the assumption held in official circles around 1904–5 that economic pressure would not be effective against a modern continental power, and not worth the damage Britain would suffer by coming into conflict with neutrals such as the United States. As Coogan has pointed out, Britain was moving away from its traditional definition of belligerent rights at the very time when it was being drawn back into a continental commitment, and when changing technology was making it impossible to exercise an 'effective' blockade of the kind enshrined in the Declaration of Paris.[130]

British official opinion was thus very much in tune with the assumption, widespread at the turn of the century, that in view of the emergence of a large measure of international consensus, there was every reason to attempt to codify the laws of maritime warfare in a more liberal direction. It was reinforced by the coming to power of the Liberal Party, with a Radical wing committed to disarmament, in 1906. The movement reached fulfilment in the second Hague conference of 1907 and its sequel, the London naval conference of 1908–9. At The Hague, Great Britain was among those powers which successfully resisted the principal proposal put to the conference: that all private property should be immune from maritime capture. At the same time, however, British representatives pressed for the complete abolition of the doctrine of contraband. The Admiralty believed that a blockade could inflict serious damage on the German economy but that the stoppage of contraband would make little difference to Germany, as one of the leading arms manufacturers in the world. It was better to abandon the right to seize contraband than to risk antagonising powerful neutrals. Fortunately for the British, their proposal was rejected by the other powers. The main outcome of the conference was a decision to set up an international prize court. The law

[129] Lansdowne to Balfour, 18 January 1905 , quoted Coogan, *End of Neutrality*, p. 54.
[130] Ibid., pp. 74–5.

that it was to administer had to be codified. This was the task of the London conference.

The Declaration of London of 1909 marked a significant extension of neutral rights in wartime. Its most important provisions concerned the definition of contraband. 'Absolute contraband' remained confined to munitions and military supplies. 'Conditional contraband' was extended, at the insistence of the continental powers, to include food – but not food for civilian consumption – and other commodities which could be presumed to have a military destination either because they were consigned to the enemy authorities or a contractor who supplied them, or because they were destined for a fortified place 'or other place serving as a base for the armed forces of the enemy'. As a concession to neutrals, the doctrine of continuous voyage was not applied to conditional contraband. The main innovation was a 'free list' of goods which could never be declared contraband. It included such vital commodities as raw cotton, wool, silk, jute, flax and hemp, oilseeds, rubber, raw hides, fertilisers and metallic ores.

The Declaration excited enormous controversy. Most contemporary critics saw it as a craven abdication of the rights on which British naval supremacy rested. Others believed that it exposed Britain's import trade to maritime attack. Their combined objections were sufficient to ensure that it was never ratified by Parliament. Since the Admiralty was closely involved in the London negotiations it may be presumed that it was not wittingly signing away powers which it believed to be of vital importance. It may have regarded the Declaration of London as a compromise in which Britain signed away some of its rights as a belligerent – rights which seemed anachronistic to most experts – in return for greater safety for the merchant marine and for its food supply in time of war.[131] More plausibly, perhaps, Fisher may have 'allowed it to be negotiated with the deliberate intention of tearing it up in the event of war', while the view of McKenna, the first lord, was that 'the Germans are sure to infringe it in the early days of the war, then with much regret we tear it up – If they don't infringe it we must invent an infringement.'[132] Things were not quite so simple. As the first months of the war were to show, Britain was unable simply to tear up the Declaration of London. Although it had never been ratified, it remained a generally accepted statement of international law which Great Britain had helped to negotiate. Hankey, who alone in Whitehall had a clear conception of how economic warfare might be conducted in the future, was therefore justified in his fear that it would fatally hamper Britain's freedom of action.[133]

Some realisation of the implications of economic warfare for Britain's

[131] Offer, *First World War*, pp. 276–7.
[132] Grant Duff diary, February 1911, quoted ibid., p. 280.
[133] His criticisms were expressed in three papers written in 1911, one of which is quoted extensively in Bell, *Blockade*, pp. 20–2. See also Hankey, *Supreme Command* I, pp. 98–101; Offer, *First World War*, pp. 279–80.

relations with the smaller neutrals did begin to dawn on senior ministers and officials in the last pre-war years. The CID's sub-committee on Trading with the Enemy of 1911–12 acknowledged that the possibility of a more comprehensive blockade raised the question of Britain's relations with Holland and Belgium (if the latter was neutral), as well as with Denmark, Norway, Sweden and the United States.[134] In a memorandum written for the inquiry in February 1912 Lord Esher, a close associate of Hankey, wrote that in order to prevent a rapid German victory over France, it would be necessary to blockade not merely Germany but also the ports of Antwerp and Rotterdam 'whatever the political costs'.[135] The sub-committee's report endorsed this view but added 'the enigmatic comment that these were matters "which must be governed and modified by geographical considerations and commercial relations with particular states"'.[136]

When the CID considered the report in December 1912 its members were divided in their interpretation of this point. Lloyd George, the chancellor of the exchequer, was supported by Churchill in his insistence that the blockade must be applied to Holland and Belgium as well as to Germany. If they were accorded the rights laid down by the Declaration of London, 'we should be unable to bring any effective economic pressure upon Germany. It was essential that we should be able to do so.' Churchill assumed that they would both be overrun by Germany so that they 'could be blockaded on that ground alone'.[137] Asquith, however, was less certain that the Netherlands would be invaded and was worried about the danger of alienating neutrals not directly affected.[138] His doubts were shared by the Foreign Office. In the end the CID accepted the solution proposed by Lloyd George: that if the Low Countries remained neutral their imports should be rationed so that there was no surplus left for export to Germany. This was a pointer to the future, though none of those present at the meeting could have anticipated the extent to which rationing of neutrals would come to dominate British blockade policy following the outbreak of war in 1914.

---

[134] French, *British Economic and Strategic Planning*, pp. 29–30.
[135] Quoted in Offer, *First World War*, p. 298.
[136] Quoted in French, *British Economic and Strategic Planning*, p. 29.
[137] Quoted in Offer, *First World War*, p. 305.   [138] Coogan, *End of Neutrality*, p. 146.

4   Neutrality preserved: Scandinavia and the First World War

Denmark, Norway and Sweden were more fortunate than most European countries in that they were not directly involved in hostilities between 1914 and 1918. Both the Entente and the Central Powers were persuaded that they had more to gain from Scandinavian neutrality than from drawing the Scandinavian states into the war. Scandinavia proved marginal to the military and naval strategies of the belligerents to an extent unforeseen by pre-war planners. This was partly because the war lasted longer than most people had anticipated: much pre-war planning had been predicated on the assumption of a war of early engagements and rapid movement both on land and at sea – particularly in Scandinavian waters. It was also because attempts to break the deadlock on the western front by a flanking strategy were directed elsewhere: towards the eastern Mediterranean, not the Baltic. And because the war was prolonged, economic pressure became increasingly important to both sides. This heightened the significance of neutral Scandinavia as a transit route to Germany and Russia and as a source of supply to the Entente and the Central Powers.

In some respects their economic indispensability was advantageous to the Scandinavian states, or at least to the many individuals and firms who made large profits out of trading with the belligerents. However, most of the problems that confronted Scandinavian governments during the war resulted directly or indirectly from the attempts of the belligerents to conscript the Scandinavian economies into their respective war efforts. All three countries had to accept a drastic diminution of traditional neutral rights while establishing an unprecedented degree of government control and supervision over their domestic economies. Economic pressure from the West – in the form of coal and food embargoes – caused considerable hardship; pressure from Germany – in the form of unrestricted submarine warfare – led to the destruction of ships and the deaths of thousands of seamen. There were major political consequences as well. In Sweden, the war defeated the attempt by the king and Prime Minister Hammarskjöld to conduct affairs of state on 'patriotic' principles, without parliamentary interference, and helped to bring about the entry of the Social Democrats into government. In all three countries the war radicalised the working class.

The belligerents displayed only intermittent interest in enlisting the

Scandinavian states as active participants in the war, or in extending the theatre of operations into Scandinavian territory. Their main efforts were directed towards gaining control of Scandinavian resources and commerce and denying them to the enemy. Scandinavian leaders, for their part, conducted their affairs in such a way as to convince the belligerents that it was in their own best interests to avoid taking steps which might bring Scandinavia into the war. They also managed to persuade the two sides to be satisfied with a less than total control of Scandinavian trade. To this extent the war was a vindication of Scandinavian statesmanship. Yet the experiences of the three states differed widely. At the beginning of the war Denmark mined the Great Belt at Germany's behest but thereafter managed to maintain a remarkable equilibrium between British and German economic demands. Norway, who, in the words of Britain's wartime naval attaché in Scandinavia, 'was our best friend, and from whom there were no political consequences to be feared, received the worst treatment of the three Scandinavian States at the hands of the British Government'.[1] Whilst Britain imposed a coal embargo to force Norway to comply with its blockade measures, German submarine warfare took a heavy toll on Norwegian shipping and Norwegian lives. Sweden, conspicuously pro-German in its neutrality policy, was also subjected to severe British economic pressure in 1916–17. And, when it came round to a more even-handed policy, concluding a war trade agreement with the Allied and Associated Powers in May 1918, Sweden was faced with a new threat to its integrity in the form of the Baltic hegemony won by Germany as a result of its victory over tsarist Russia and its peace treaty with the Bolsheviks at Brest-Litovsk. However, this same victory, followed by Germany's defeat at the hands of the Western allies, permitted the emergence of Finland as a fourth sovereign state in northern Europe.

The contrasting experiences of the Scandinavian states were clearly due in large measure to differences in geographical position and resource endowment. But allowance must also be made for the nature of domestic politics in each of the three countries. In Denmark, and to a lesser extent in Norway, a large degree of consensus prevailed throughout the war. The minority Radical Liberal government which had ruled in Denmark since 1913 with Social Democratic support was broadened (though not turned into a 'national' government) in 1916 by the inclusion of 'supervisory' ministers without portfolio from the Liberal, Conservative and Social Democratic parties. The government of Gunnar Knudsen in Norway, and especially the foreign minister, Nils Claus Ihlen, came in for much criticism, but found a partial solution in the formation of a parliamentary foreign affairs committee early in 1917. Swedish politics were much more confrontational. The Hammarskjöld government was under pressure from both the right and the left: from the 'activists' who wished Sweden to intervene in the war on the side of the Central

[1] Rear-Admiral M. W. W. P. Consett, *The Triumph of Unarmed Forces (1914–1918)* (London, 1923), p. 106.

Powers and from the Liberals and Social Democrats who wished both to democratise the country and to pursue a more even-handed neutrality policy.

Much also depended on the personal qualities of Scandinavian leaders: on their assessment of the challenges and dangers posed by the war, and on their ability to manoeuvre to limit their consequences. Here too there were marked differences between the three countries. These resulted from the personalities of Scandinavian monarchs, prime ministers and foreign ministers, as well as from the relationships they managed to establish with the diplomatic representatives of the belligerents. Perhaps the most impressive achievement was that of Erik Scavenius, whose conduct of Danish foreign policy amounted to compliance with belligerent demands where this was unavoidable but going no further than was absolutely necessary. Although Scavenius kept his Cabinet colleagues in ignorance of some of his most important exchanges with belligerent governments, he was also in the habit of consulting the leaders of other political parties, while King Christian X gave support to the government at certain critical points. Scavenius was aided by his ability to inspire confidence in the diplomats of both sides. With successive British ministers – Sir Henry Lowther and, from 1916, Sir Ralph Paget – his relations were always correct and amicable; but the crucial relationship was with the German minister, Ulrich von Brockdorff-Rantzau. It was one of mutual respect and friendship in which the German minister, despite his abiding suspicion of the sympathies of the Danish population, consistently urged on the political and military authorities in Berlin the importance of respecting Danish neutrality.

Denmark's very vulnerability gave it a strength which Norway lacked. Ihlen was right when he told the Storting that Norway was the weakest of the three countries because it was not under threat of German invasion or likely to join the Central Powers, and was hence wholly exposed to British pressure.[2] Ihlen himself, in contrast to Scavenius, seemed secretive and dilatory in his dealings with foreign diplomats. He was subject to much criticism in the Storting and was frequently on bad terms with the British minister in Kristiania. This was not entirely Ihlen's fault, given Findlay's temperament. Findlay was, however, on reasonable terms with the Norwegian prime minister, Gunnar Knudsen, and enjoyed close relations with King Haakon.[3] The Norwegian naval authorities were also very forthcoming towards the British legation, and in particular towards Captain Consett, the British naval attaché to the Scandinavian countries. But failures of communication and misunderstandings – together with Norway's dependence on Britain – led to a drastic breach between the two countries over the blockade early in 1917. Germany had less scope for pressure or persuasion than Britain – apart from the brutal sanction of submarine warfare – but also had less effective diplomatic representation in Norway than in the other Scandinavian countries until 1917, when the

[2] Kåre Fasting, *Nils Claus Ihlen* (Oslo, 1955), p. 243.
[3] Tim Greve, *Haakon VII of Norway* (London, 1983), pp. 76–7.

colourless German minister Micahelles was replaced by the resourceful and ruthless Admiral von Hintze.

That Sweden was the most important of the Scandinavian countries was recognised by Britain, Germany and Russia in their choice of diplomatic representatives. At the outbreak of war the British had their man, Sir Esme Howard, firmly in place, while Nekludov, the able and civilised Russian ambassador, who had been in post since 1912, was to remain until 1917.[4] The Germans were not so fortunate. In January 1915 the Auswärtiges Amt responded promptly to a personal request from King Gustav V to the kaiser and replaced Reichenau, who had been intriguing blatantly with Swedish 'activists', with Hellmuth Lucius von Stoedten.[5] Lucius was at first a more effective operator, but later he too overplayed his hand. Nekludov described Lucius as 'quick, intelligent, shrewd and essentially cynical', but also as 'too excitable, too much of a *trickster*'.[6]

The Swedish side of the relationship with the belligerents was more troubled than that of Denmark or Norway. Whilst Scavenius and Ihlen were given a relatively free hand by their monarchs and government colleagues, the position of Sweden's first wartime foreign minister, the banker Knut Wallenberg, was more constrained. The prime minister, Hjalmar Hammarskjöld, was Sweden's leading expert on international law and played an active, often dominant role in the formulation and execution of Swedish policy until his fall in March 1917. He was frequently in conflict with the pragmatic Wallenberg, whose good relations with both the British and the German ministers in Stockholm did much to persuade both governments of his indispensability. Wallenberg had many strengths and his 'business connections as a financier with Great Britain, France and Russia' gave him, as Howard observed, 'a larger outlook than most of his fellow-countrymen possess'.[7] But he was a poor administrator who frequently failed to keep colleagues and subordinates informed of what he was doing. It was, for example, Wallenberg, not the ostensibly more pro-German Hammarskjöld, who – without consulting his colleagues – allowed Germany to use Swedish ciphers to communicate with its embassies and legations overseas – a practice which was to have damaging repercussions on Sweden's relations with the Allies as well as on Swedish domestic politics.

---

[4] A. Nekludoff, *Diplomatic Reminiscences Before and During the World War 1911–1917* (London, 1920).

[5] W. M. Carlgren, *Neutralität oder Allianz. Deutschlands Beziehungen zu Schweden in den Anfangsjahren des Ersten Weltkrieges* (Stockholm, 1962), pp. 73–5; Inger Schuberth, *Schweden und das Deutsche Reich im Ersten Weltkrieg. Die Aktivistenbewegung 1914–1918* (Bonn, 1981), pp. 21–7.

[6] Nekludoff, *Diplomatic Reminiscences*, pp. 340–1. His successor as German minister to Stockholm, Rudolf Nadolny, knew him as 'a dedicated cynic and skirt-chaser' [*rigoroser Spötter und Schürzenjäger*], who for this reason eventually became *persona non grata* even with the strongly pro-German queen: Rudolf Nadolny (ed. Günter Wollstein), *Mein Beitrag. Erinnerungen eines Botschafters des Deutschen Reiches* (Cologne, 1985), p. 145. For a balanced assessment, see Schuberth, *Schweden und das Deutsche Reich*, pp. 27–30.

[7] Howard to Grey, 17 August 1914, FO 371/2097, No. 41885.

Months before the fall of the Hammarskjöld ministry, Wallenberg had been marginalised by the prime minister's confrontational policy towards the Entente.

Arvid Lindman, his successor as foreign minister in the short-lived Conservative ministry of March–September 1917, lacked credibility with the Western powers owing to his pro-German reputation, while in terms of Swedish domestic politics the Swartz–Lindman government was all too evidently a stop-gap. Johannes Hellner, foreign minister in the Liberal–Social Democratic coalition which came to power after the elections of September 1917, was a more capable figure who had learned the difficulties of Sweden's position at first hand in war trade negotiations with the Allies. Like their predecessors, however, Hellner and his colleagues had to reckon with a further disruptive element in Swedish policy making. Whilst Christian X and Haakon VII gave their governments full support in their efforts to preserve neutrality, King Gustav V and his consort Queen Victoria intervened intermittently throughout the war to push Sweden in a more pro-German direction. At times they clearly hankered after military intervention on the side of the Central Powers, but the king lacked the will – and perhaps had a sufficiently realistic understanding of the temper of the Swedish people – to see his initiatives through to their logical conclusion.[8]

As small powers, the Scandinavian states were generally ordained to react, respond, adapt; there was little scope for policy initiatives, though all were to carry out important humanitarian work, especially among prisoners of war.[9] Norwegian leaders made no attempt to influence the attitudes or conduct of the belligerents, but Denmark and Sweden were less passive. In the first months of the war both King Christian X and, perhaps surprisingly, Scavenius gave strong support to the efforts of H. N. Andersen (head of the East Asiatic Company and a confidant of the king) to mediate between Britain, Germany and Russia.[10] Sweden was a stronger power with a tradition of active diplomacy. Sometimes it sought to influence the great powers in matters of high policy: Wallenberg's warning to Great Britain of 2 August 1914 is an example. Britain's behaviour, as well as that of France and Russia, *was* influenced to some degree, but much less than Wallenberg had hoped. Sweden also attempted to enhance its own position as a regional power. This was the purpose of the various initiatives over the Åland Islands emanating from the king of Sweden and other quarters in 1917–18, which ended in a humiliating and potentially damaging submission to Germany's terms in May 1918. A more promising arena for Swedish diplomatic activity was that of Scandinavian

---

[8] Wilhelm M. Carlgren, 'Gustaf V och utrikespolitiken', in *Studier i modern historia tillägnade Jarl Torbacke den 18 augusti 1990* (Stockholm, 1990), pp. 41–57.

[9] For an account of Danish efforts, see Bent Blüdnikow, 'Denmark During the First World War', *Journal of Contemporary History* 24 (1989), pp. 683–703.

[10] Wilhelm Ernst Winterhager, *Mission für den Frieden. Europäische Mächtepolitik und dänische Vermittlung im Ersten Weltkrieg. Vom August 1914 bis zum italienischen Kriegseintritt Mai 1915* (Stuttgart, 1984), p. 106.

cooperation. Swedish initiative lay behind the meetings of Scandinavian monarchs, prime ministers and foreign ministers which took place with increasing regularity from the autumn of 1914 onwards. If the practical consequences were limited, such meetings did much to dispel the mutual suspicions which existed among all three countries, but especially between Norway and Sweden after 1905, and laid the foundations for more extensive cooperation in the post-war period.

The outbreak of war

Even more than in the rest of Europe, the sudden deterioration of the European crisis in late July 1914 took Scandinavia by surprise. Some Scandinavians had been reassured, as relations between Austria and Serbia worsened, by the fact that Kaiser Wilhelm had not cut short his annual holiday in the Norwegian fjords. It was not until 25 July that he set out for home, accompanied by a number of ships of the High Seas Fleet.[11] On the same day President Poincaré and Prime Minister Viviani of France arrived in Stockholm on their return journey from St Petersburg. The news of Austria's rejection of the Serbian reply to its ultimatum sent the French visitors hurrying home without stopping, as scheduled, at Copenhagen and Kristiania. Once war had broken out on 1 August, there was still hope that Scandinavia might avoid direct involvement if the conflict remained confined to the European continent. The great danger was British intervention. The first consequence, so many believed, would be an Anglo-German naval clash in northern waters into which the Scandinavian countries would inescapably be drawn.

On 2 August the Swedish foreign minister sought to avert the danger by warning the British minister that Sweden might be forced to intervene on the side of the Central Powers if Britain, by declaring war on Germany, placed itself alongside Russia.[12] Such a statement could have had no influence on the deliberations of the British government, dominated as they were by Germany's violation of Belgian neutrality and Britain's moral commitments to France and Russia. Britain duly went to war on 4 August. For Howard, however, the presence of Wallenberg in the government was a guarantee against Swedish intervention, and he argued that it was imperative for Britain to 'do all we can to assist the minister for foreign affairs in his difficult task of maintaining Swedish neutrality'.[13] At Howard's suggestion, Britain gave an assurance to

[11] Findlay to FO, 26 and 27 July 1914, printed in *BD* XI, pp. 100, 119. On the significance of the kaiser's presence in Norwegian waters during this crucial period, see John C. G. Röhl, 'Germany', in Keith Wilson (ed.), *Decisions for War* (London, 1995), pp. 27–54 (p. 38).
[12] Howard to Grey, 2 August 1914, *BD* XI, p. 285; Torsten Gihl, *Den svenska utrikespolitikens historia*, vol. IV, *1914–1919* (Stockholm, 1951), pp. 34–5; W. M. Carlgren, *Ministären Hammarskjöld. Tillkomst, söndring, fall. Studier i svensk politik 1914–1917* (Stockholm, 1967), p. 50; Carlgren, *Neutralität oder Allianz*, pp. 40–1; Lord Howard of Penrith, *Theatre of Life* (2 vols., London, 1935–6), vol. II, pp. 221–3.
[13] Howard to Grey, 17 August 1914, FO 371/2097, No. 41885.

Sweden that it would not violate its neutrality and would come to its assistance in the event of aggression, and persuaded France and Russia to do the same.[14]

But in the first days there were widespread fears that the belligerents would seek to draw Scandinavia into the war. There were rumours that Britain might seize bases on the coast of Norway or Sweden in order to gain command of the entrances to the Baltic, or that Germany was putting pressure on Sweden to enter the war. King Gustav did not believe that Sweden could stay out of the war in the long run, while King Haakon told a Swedish representative on 6 August 1914 that he 'feared a breach of neutrality by England at any moment'.[15] Such anxieties were by no means groundless. Battle cruisers of the German High Seas Fleet had been off the Norwegian coast until 26 July. In April 1913 Grey had agreed with Churchill that Britain would be entitled to attack 'German ships found in Norwegian waters on the outbreak of war' since they 'would presumably have been put there for strategic reasons', although he had drawn the line at the seizure of a Norwegian harbour.[16] In early August, Admiral Jellicoe, the commander-in-chief of the Grand Fleet, sent a cruiser sweep along the Norwegian coast following a report from Kristiania that the German navy had established a base there.[17] The most alarming incident during these early days was one that remained unknown until after the war. On 9 August Admiral von Essen, the commander of the Russian Baltic Fleet, sailed for the island of Gotland where a Swedish naval force was assumed (wrongly) to be stationed in anticipation of a joint German–Swedish action against Russia.[18] Halfway to his destination he was recalled, the Russian authorities having come to the conclusion that Sweden had no immediate intention of entering the war.

There was, nevertheless, some discussion in Britain of the possibility of drawing Scandinavia and other European neutrals into an anti-German coalition. On 31 July Churchill, with a naval offensive in mind, sent Asquith a list of bases on Dutch, Danish, Norwegian and Swedish territory for possible capture without considering 'questions of violation of neutrality'.[19] The day before Britain declared war he wrote to Asquith and Grey advocating an alliance with Norway, the Netherlands and Belgium as a means of tightening the blockade.[20] On 4 August, before Germany's invasion of Belgium had

[14] Grey to Bertie (Paris), 4 August 1914, *BD* IX, p. 307; Grey to Howard, 4 August 1914, ibid., p. 330; Gihl, *Den svenska utrikespolitikens historia* IV, pp. 35–6. The British, Russian and French declarations were made on 4, 6 and 7 August respectively. However, Wallenberg refused to make them public: Bengt Holtze, 'Sverige i brittiska bedömningar under första världskriget', *Aktuellt och historiskt* 1971, pp. 113–80 (p. 113).

[15] Quoted in Carlgren, *Ministären Hammarskjöld*, p. 57 (n. 7).

[16] Grey to Churchill, 11 April 1913, *BD* X, p. 695; Olav Riste, *The Neutral Ally: Norway's Relations with Belligerent Powers in the First World War* (Oslo, 1965), pp. 33–6.

[17] Telegrams exchanged between Admiralty and Jellicoe, 6–7 August 1914, printed in A. Temple Patterson (ed.), *The Jellicoe Papers* (2 vols., London, 1966), vol. I, p. 48.

[18] Gihl, *Den svenska utrikespolitikens historia* IV, pp. 37–8.

[19] See ch. 3, pp. 91–2.

[20] David French, *British Strategy and War Aims 1914–1916* (London, 1986), pp. 28–9.

become known, the Foreign Office instructed Britain's representatives at Kristiania, The Hague and Brussels that Britain was prepared to join France and Russia in offering 'an alliance' (subsequently altered to 'common action') 'for the purpose of resisting use of force by Germany against them, and a guarantee to maintain their independence and integrity in future years'.[21] The instructions were cancelled following Germany's violation of Belgian neutrality but on 5 August Crowe minuted:

> It should be our endeavour to bring into a system of fighting alliance a ring of Powers surrounding the enemies. With Sweden, Norway and Holland neutral (at least neutral) we should, and I am convinced we could, bring into line with us Portugal and Spain, and I should not despair of winning over Italy, Greece and possibly Turkey.[22]

These countries, he continued, would have to be offered 'effective financial assistance and supplies of war material and guns'. Grey, too, identified the position of the smaller neutrals as being critical to the future of Britain as a great power. He told the American ambassador on 4 August:

> I had information that Germany was putting pressure on at least one of the smaller European States to join her in this war, and the issue for us was that, if Germany won, she would dominate France; the independence of Belgium, Holland, Denmark and perhaps of Norway and Sweden, would be a mere shadow: their separate existence as nations would really be a fiction; all their harbours would be at Germany's disposal; she would dominate the whole of Western Europe, and this would make our position quite impossible. We could not exist as a first-class State under such circumstances.[23]

However, although Grey described Crowe's proposal as 'timely', he did not pursue it.[24] Indeed, in early August Grey 'seemed stunned by the course of events and Nicolson as well as Crowe complained of the lethargic nature of his approach'.[25] It was nevertheless understandable that with its other preoccupations, the British government required nothing more than neutrality from the Scandinavian countries at this stage of the war.

Germany was equally satisfied with Scandinavian neutrality. Having adopted a defensive strategy, the German navy had no plans for action in Norwegian waters, and a neutral policy would preserve Norway from undue British influence especially if, as seemed likely, it was combined with a degree of alignment towards Sweden.[26] More surprisingly, perhaps, Germany made no move to draw Sweden into the war. There was no pressure for a military alliance from either the General Staff or the navy, and the Swedes themselves were able to convince Germany of the advantages of Swedish neutrality while leaving no doubt as to where their loyalties and sympathies ultimately lay. This was very much Wallenberg's achievement. In order to avert the danger of a German ultimatum – one which he, like others, overrated – he went even

[21] *BD* XI, p. 309; FO 371/2161, Nos. 35797, 35799.
[22] FO 371/2162, No. 36542.   [23] *BD* XI, p. 328.
[24] FO 371/2162, No. 36542; Sibyl Crowe and Edward Corp, *Our Ablest Public Servant: Sir Eyre Crowe GCB, GCMG, KCB, KCMG 1864–1925* (Braunton, 1993), pp. 274–5.
[25] Ibid., p. 274.   [26] Riste, *Neutral Ally*, p. 34.

further than the king in expressions of support: so far, in fact, that both the German minister, Reichenau, and Sweden's envoy in Berlin, Arvid Taube, believed for a time that intervention was imminent. Wallenberg's true intentions were revealed on 6 August when, strengthened by the neutrality declarations given by the Entente Powers, he requested a similar declaration from Berlin. Reichenau supported the idea, arguing that Sweden's military preparations were inadequate for immediate entry into the war and that such a declaration would reinforce confidence in Germany without prejudicing Swedish action in the future.[27] It was of some importance in this connection that the Swedish government had resisted the king's demand for immediate mobilisation.[28] The German assurance was duly given on 10 August but was made dependent on the maintenance of an attitude of 'benevolent neutrality' towards Germany.[29] This was very different from the 'strict neutrality' proclaimed in the Swedish neutrality declaration of 3 August, but was nevertheless something which had already been voluntarily conceded by the Swedes themselves.

The main thrust of German diplomacy was directed towards Denmark. In this case too, however, the motive was fundamentally defensive. On 5 August Denmark received a German request that it should lay mines in the Great Belt.[30] A brief but intense government crisis ended when the king intervened in support of compliance. The Danes announced that they would mine not only the Great Belt but also the Little Belt and the Drogden Channel on the Danish side of the Sound. Two consequences of the Danish decision are worth noting. First, Denmark's acquiescence did not imply that it would submit to further pressure. The German navy went on to seek information and preferential treatment for its ships from the Danish authorities; in September 1914 it requested that Denmark should lay mines in the Flint Channel in the Sound (which lay in both Danish and Swedish territorial waters) in order to prevent British submarines from entering the Baltic. All of these requests were refused by the Danish government. Its attitude was strongly supported by both Brockdorff-Rantzau and the Auswärtiges Amt, who argued that further demands would unleash a wave of anti-German feeling and make it difficult for the Danish king and government to maintain friendly relations with Germany.[31]

Secondly, Denmark managed to avoid antagonising the Entente. During the crisis of 5 August Danish ministers devoted little attention to the possible

[27] Jean-Pierre Mousson-Lestang, *Le parti social-démocrate et la politique étrangère de la Suède (1914–1918)* (Paris, 1988), p. 59.
[28] Carlgren, 'Gustaf V', p. 44.   [29] Text in Carlgren, *Neutralität oder Allianz*, p. 46.
[30] Viggo Sjøqvist, *Erik Scavenius. Danmarks udenrigsminister under to verdenskrige. Statsminister 1942–1945* (2 vols., Copenhagen, 1973), vol. I, *1877–1920*, pp. 116–23; Viggo Sjøqvist, *Peter Munch. Manden, politikeren, historikeren* (Copenhagen, 1976), pp. 95–8; Erik Arup (ed. Thyge Svenstrup), 'Den danske Regerings Forhandlinger og Beslutninger 5. August 1914', *Historisk tidsskrift* (Denmark) 91 (1991), pp. 402–27.
[31] Sjøqvist, *Scavenius* I, pp. 123–6, 132–4.

reactions of Britain and France. In fact Scavenius had reason to hope that Britain would show understanding for Denmark's position. When he had met Grey in London in May 1914 the latter had taken 'the opportunity of saying that we were aware of the delicate position of Denmark, that we should never be the first to violate her neutrality, and that we always desired to avoid placing her in an embarrassing position'.[32] The first response of the British minister proved reassuring. When told of the Danish government's decision to lay mines, Lowther declared that he found Denmark's action quite reasonable. As he put it later that month, Denmark could 'hardly be blamed if she be inclined to stretch a point to avoid giving offence to Germany at the present time'.[33] The British government, unable to defend Denmark and wishing to give Germany no excuse for an invasion, was quite willing to accept Lowther's judgement.

Although the three Scandinavian countries had reached agreement on joint neutrality regulations in 1912,[34] the most explicit expression of Scandinavian determination to remain outside the conflict was a declaration issued jointly by Sweden and Norway on 8 August 1914 in which the two countries affirmed their resolve to stay out of the war and 'to exclude the possibility that the state of war in Europe in any circumstances shall lead to one Kingdom taking hostile measures against the other'.[35] It derived from a much more ambitious Swedish proposal of 1 August for an offensive and defensive alliance between the two countries.[36] The initiative came from Wallenberg and was designed to serve a number of purposes. Like his warning to Howard of 2 August, it may have been intended to dissuade Britain from going to war by facing it with 'a neutral alliance of significant military strength' instead of an isolated, controllable Norway.[37] More realistically, Wallenberg's aim was to prevent Norway from being drawn into the war on the side of Britain and Russia, with the obvious danger that Sweden would be drawn in on the side of the Central Powers. An agreement with Norway would weaken the Swedish activists who were calling for intervention, while strengthening Wallenberg's own position within the government. In a longer perspective, a defensive alliance with Norway (a goal pursued by Wallenberg's two immediate predecessors as foreign minister, Taube and Ehrensvärd) would help put an end to the strained relations which had existed between the two countries since 1905.

In the light of Sweden's 'benevolent' neutrality towards Germany, and in the

---

[32] Grey to Kidston (Copenhagen), 11 May 1914, *BD* X, p. 743.
[33] Despatch of 25 August 1914, quoted in Tage Kaarsted, *Great Britain and Denmark 1914–1920* (Odense, 1979), p. 43.
[34] Gihl, *Den svenska utrikespolitikens historia* IV, p. 14.
[35] Text in Riste, *Neutral Ally*, p. 37.
[36] Olav Riste, 'Den svensk–norske nøytralitetsavtalen i august 1914', *Historisk tidsskrift* (Norway) 41 (1962), pp. 347–53; Carlgren, *Ministären Hammarskjöld*, pp. 43–71; Riste, *Neutral Ally*, pp. 37–41; Gihl, *Den svenska utrikespolitikens historia* IV, pp. 31–2; Fasting, *Ihlen*, pp. 138–9.
[37] Riste, *Neutral Ally*, p. 38.

context of those earlier proposals, it was understandable that some should have detected more sinister motives behind the project. Chevalley, the French minister in Kristiania, warned that an alliance between Norway and Sweden might serve as a prelude to a German–Scandinavian federation of the kind advocated by Taube a few years earlier.[38] Wallenberg was certainly looking beyond the immediate crisis, but his motives should perhaps be sought rather in his close personal associations with Norway: his wife was Norwegian and he had substantial business interests in the country. Wallenberg was to be disappointed in his larger goal. The Norwegian government responded cautiously; and both King Gustav and Wallenberg's government colleagues, who retained bitter memories of 1905, disavowed the alliance proposal. However, the joint neutrality declaration which emerged from the negotiations in Kristiania served at least part of the foreign minister's purpose. It undermined the position of the Swedish activists while reassuring the left that the government intended to pursue a policy of genuine neutrality. It was also greeted with satisfaction by both the British and Russian ministers in Kristiania as a guarantee against Swedish intervention.[39]

As a contribution to Scandinavian cooperation, the declaration of 8 August was a mixed blessing. While it helped to demonstrate that the divisions of 1905 between Norway and Sweden had been overcome, it left the Danes aggrieved at their exclusion.[40] Although subsequent Swedish initiatives took more account of Denmark, there remained a residue of suspicion on the part of both Denmark and Norway – not least because Scandinavian cooperation under Swedish tutelage seemed to carry the risk of confrontation with the Entente. Suspicion also greeted the invitation from King Gustav V to his fellow Scandinavian monarchs to demonstrate their mutual solidarity by meeting, together with their foreign ministers, at either Stockholm or Gothenburg, in December 1914. Both Christian X and Scavenius were initially inclined to return a polite refusal but eventually agreed on condition that the meeting was held at Malmö (for reasons of both geography and political symbolism).[41] Wallenberg, once again, was behind the Swedish invitation. His purpose was not only to show a solid Scandinavian front to the outside world, but also to strengthen Swedish neutrality at a time when Germany was beginning to take a tougher line towards Sweden and when Wallenberg himself was coming under attack from the right-wing Swedish press.[42]

The meeting at Malmö on 18–19 December gave the three foreign ministers the opportunity to meet and exchange information for the first time. It had few other positive consequences but was of some symbolic importance as an

[38] Despatches of 7 and 8 August 1914, cited in Mousson-Lestang, *Le parti social-démocrate*, p. 61.

[39] Karl Hildebrand, *Gustav V som människa och regent* (2 vols., Stockholm, 1948), vol. II, p. 168.

[40] Sjøqvist, *Scavenius* I, p. 142.   [41] Mousson-Lestang, *Le parti social-démocrate*, p. 106.

[42] Howard telegram to FO, 10 December 1914, FO 371/2097, No. 81268; Carlgren, *Ministären Hammarskjöld*, pp. 65–6; Carlgren, *Neutralität oder Allianz*, pp. 70–1.

expression of Scandinavian solidarity. Certainly it was taken seriously by the belligerents – more so than the actual results of the meeting warranted. The German government saw in it 'the nucleus of resistance against English pressure'.[43] British opinions were divided. Although he had approved the declaration of 8 August, Findlay in Kristiania was vehemently opposed to any closer Scandinavian cooperation under Sweden's aegis. He had written privately to Grey, in late November, warning that, whatever Wallenberg's own inclinations might be, he might become the prisoner of 'a pro-German Court clique' determined to bring Sweden into the war.[44] Findlay feared that at Malmö 'Norway by entering into any agreement will be escaping to a certain extent from our control and influence'.[45] Howard in Stockholm and Lowther in Copenhagen took a less alarmist view. Howard did not think that a closer association between the Scandinavian states of the kind foreshadowed by the declaration of 13 November would be disadvantageous to Britain.[46] Primed by Wallenberg, he correctly interpreted the Malmö meeting as a means of showing a common Scandinavian front and strengthening the foreign minister's domestic position.[47] The Foreign Office shared Howard's opinion: it was understandable that the Scandinavian countries should seek common means of mitigating belligerent pressure, and the Norwegians could be relied upon to avoid being drawn into the Swedish orbit.[48] Grey telegraphed that Britain could not oppose an understanding between the three countries: 'if it strengthens them to resist any forcible violations of their neutrality and leads to business-like arrangements between them in common for distinguishing between bona fide imports and those destined for Germany we have no reason to be other than favourable to such an understanding'.[49] No such arrangements were forthcoming. On the other hand, there was no evidence that any attempt had been made 'to form the Scandinavian countries into a pro-Teutonic bloc'.[50]

Economic warfare and the northern neutrals 1914–1918

1914–1915

As the British, French and German armies became deadlocked on the western front, both the Entente and the Central Powers were forced to contemplate the

[43] Bethmann Hollweg memorandum of 27 December 1914, quoted in Riste, *Neutral Ally*, p. 62.
[44] Findlay to Grey, 21 November 1914 (copy enclosed in Findlay to Grey, 21 October 1915, FO 371/2459, No. 159795).
[45] Findlay telegram to FO, 14 December 1914, FO 371/2097, No. 83078.
[46] Howard to Grey, 13 November 1914, FO 371/2097, No. 72533.
[47] Howard telegram to FO, 10 December 1914, FO 371/2097, No. 81268.
[48] Minute of 15 December 1914 on Findlay telegram to FO, 14 December 1914, FO 371/2097, No. 83078.
[49] Telegram to Findlay, 18 December 1914 (drafted by Grey), ibid.
[50] Howard to Grey, 31 January 1915, FO 371/2458, No. 2718.

prospect of a protracted war and turned increasing attention to means of exerting economic pressure on the enemy. The crisis of August 1914 had shown that none of the belligerents had any immediate interest in drawing the Scandinavian countries into the war. They now had to ensure that, as neutrals, the Scandinavian countries gave the greatest possible assistance to their own war effort and the least possible assistance to the enemy's. The 'adjacent neutrals' – the Netherlands, Denmark, Sweden and Norway – were important to both Britain and Germany as sources of supply, but to Germany and Russia alone as a transit route for goods from overseas. Technically, Britain never mounted an 'effective blockade' of Germany as defined by international law. The Royal Navy was unable to approach close enough to impose a close blockade of the German North Sea ports, though the few submarines that managed to work their way through the Sound and thereafter operated from Russian bases did significant damage to German trade in the Baltic.[51] It was capable, however, of mounting a 'distant blockade' since it controlled the sea routes by which commodities reached Germany through neighbouring neutral states. Britain's task was to ensure its own requirements, while at the same time cutting off the transit trade in contraband to Germany.

Britain had the capacity to exert enormous pressure on the neutrals. All were dependent to varying degrees – Sweden least, Norway most – on imports of food, fodder, raw materials and fuels: above all coal, of which Great Britain was by far the most important supplier. Britain also had much more immediate access than Germany to overseas sources from which to supply its own needs, thanks to the geographical location of the British Isles and the Royal Navy's command of the seas, as well as possession of a world-wide empire and financial resources sufficient – for a time at least – to fund extensive purchases in the United States. However, there were still powerful reasons to keep on good terms with the Scandinavian countries. Many Scandinavian products on which Britain relied could not be replaced easily from overseas sources, and shipping costs would increase if goods were taken from further afield.[52]

Britain also had to worry about Scandinavian political sympathies. The precarious balance between exerting the maximum pressure on Germany and conciliating neutral interests was highlighted by Grey when he spoke to officials of the new Contraband Department at the Foreign Office in November 1914. After emphasising 'the vital importance of our relations with America', Grey continued:

He said that our position with Sweden was particularly delicate since, with Archangel closed by ice, the only means of getting munitions to Russia was in transit across Sweden, the Russian government besides was very restive and apprehensive as to Swedish intentions, and we ourselves depended on Sweden, he was told by Mr

---

[51] Donald W. Mitchell, *A History of Russian and Soviet Sea Power* (New York, 1974), pp. 299–300.

[52] A. C. Bell, *A History of the Blockade of Germany and of the Countries Associated with Her in the Great War* (London, 1937; declassified 1961), p. 323.

Runciman [the president of the Board of Trade], for pit-props and iron-ore, and on Holland and Denmark for margarine and other supplies which had become very important. The object of our policy must of course be to cripple the enemy; but if, by a cast-iron insistence on our maximum claims, we exasperated those neutrals on whose goodwill we and our Allies were dependent we should simply lose the war. He wished the department to seek to oil the wheels of diplomacy in every possible way and to try to establish friendly relations with neutral traders themselves.[53]

Between 1914 and 1916 Britain's blockade measures were steadily intensified.[54] Although the first contraband lists, issued on 4 August 1914, corresponded closely to the provisions of the Declaration of London, an order in council of 20 August declared foodstuffs to be contraband and applied the doctrine of continuous voyage to conditional contraband. The latter could be seized, in other words, even if it was being carried in a neutral ship to a neutral port. By 29 October most of Germany's raw material requirements had been transferred from the conditional to the absolute contraband list. Britain also adopted new methods of inspection. When merchant vessels were intercepted they were not inspected in the open sea but were taken into a British harbour, where they could be detained indefinitely. On 2 November the Admiralty declared the whole of the North Sea a military area and required that all ships heading for Norway, the Baltic, Denmark and the Netherlands must not go to the north of Scotland but proceed through the Channel and along the east coast of England – where they would, of course, be much more readily subject to British naval controls.

In order to reduce friction with neutral states and to achieve a more systematic control of German trade, Britain moved in the autumn of 1914 towards the idea of negotiating war trade agreements with neutral governments. The most urgent priority was to reach agreement with the two neutrals which actually bordered on German territory – the Netherlands and Denmark – through which most of Germany's transit trade was conducted. In this context the agreement concluded between the British government and a group of Dutch merchants, the Netherlands Overseas Trust (NOT), on 26 December 1914 was of great significance.[55] The Dutch government, under intense German pressure, refused to compromise its neutrality by entering into an

[53] Memorandum by Alwyn Parker (head of Contraband Department), printed in G. M. Trevelyan, *Grey of Falloden* (London, 1937), pp. 305–7.
[54] The argument that, virtually from the outset, Britain was conducting economic warfare with blatant disregard for international law and with the tacit connivance of the United States is made in John W. Coogan, *The End of Neutrality: The United States, Britain and Maritime Rights 1899–1915* (Ithaca, N. Y., and London, 1981), chs. 8–10. On the whole this interpretation carries more conviction than the older view that Britain's conduct of economic warfare (and that of Grey in particular) 'was marked for two years by infirmity of purpose born of the fear of offending the neutrals' – particularly the United States: L. Guichard, *The Naval Blockade 1914–1918* (London, 1930), p. 310, quoted in Arthur Marsden, 'The Blockade', in F. H. Hinsley (ed.), *British Foreign Policy Under Sir Edward Grey* (Cambridge, 1977), pp. 488–515 (p. 490).
[55] For the negotiations, see Bell, *Blockade*, pp. 64–72; Marion C. Siney, *The Allied Blockade of Germany 1914–1916* (Ann Arbor, Mich., 1954; repr. Westport, Conn., 1973), pp. 34–44.

official agreement with Great Britain. It encouraged, however, the efforts of Dutch businessmen to establish an organisation which would both protect their commercial interests and provide Britain with a trustworthy guarantee against the re-export of contraband to Germany.[56]

Britain's negotiations with Denmark and Sweden were aimed at reaching agreements either with groups of merchants on the model of the NOT or with the governments themselves. In the course of 1915 the defects of this strategy became evident. Neutral governments could not be forced far along the path of collaboration with the British blockade before their neutrality was compromised irretrievably. Sweden was scarcely prepared to compromise at all. Britain thus came to adopt a policy of dealing directly with neutral traders and industrialists, with or without the tacit consent of the governments concerned. At first the difficulties were not so obvious. The fact that agreements could be reached both with Denmark (9 January 1915) and even with Sweden (8 December 1914) gave some hope that the pattern could be repeated.[57] Only with the intensified economic warfare inaugurated by Germany's declaration of unrestricted submarine warfare in February 1915 did the British authorities improvise a new approach.

Just as the German Admiralty Staff had conducted no systematic investigation in peacetime into the possibility of waging economic warfare against Great Britain,[58] so Germany's military authorities had made few economic preparations for a long war even though, according to Ludendorff, 'after the English naval manoeuvres of 1910–11, there were signs that England contemplated an extensive blockade'.[59] In August 1914, however, the implications of Britain's entry into the war for Germany's economic position were immediately grasped by the industrialists Wichard von Moellendorf and Walther Rathenau.[60] Appointed head of a new war raw materials department on 9 August, Rathenau devised a strategy for obtaining and conserving essential supplies, which included purchasing them from neutral countries. An exchange, or compensa-

For the NOT, see Amry Vandenbosch, *The Neutrality of the Netherlands During the World War* (Grand Rapids, Mich., 1927), pp. 205–13.

[56] Bell, *Blockade*, pp. 71–2.

[57] For the negotiations with Denmark, see Bell, *Blockade*, pp. 72–81; Siney, *Allied Blockade*, pp. 44–9; Kaarsted, *Great Britain and Denmark*, pp. 99–104; Eli F. Hecksher, Kurt Bergendal, Wilhelm Keilhau, Einar Cohn and Thorsteinn Thorsteinsson, *Sweden, Norway, Denmark and Iceland in the World War* (New Haven, Conn., 1930), pp. 419–20; Sjøqvist, *Scavenius* I, pp. 139–47. For the negotiations with Sweden, see Bell, *Blockade*, pp. 81–92; Siney, *Allied Blockade*, pp. 49–52; Hecksher et al., *Sweden*, pp. 60–1; Gihl, *Den svenska utrikespolitikens historia* IV, pp. 77–80.

[58] Bernd Stegemann, *Die deutsche Marinepolitik 1916–1918* (Berlin, 1970), pp. 20–2.

[59] Lothar Burchardt, *Friedenswirtschaft und Kriegsvorsorge. Deutschlands wirtschaftliche Rüstungsbestrebungen vor 1914* (Boppard am Rhein, 1968); Erich Ludendorff, *My War Memories 1914–1918* (2 vols., London, 1919), vol. I, p. 215.

[60] Count Harry Kessler, *Walther Rathenau: His Life and Work* (London, 1929), pp. 178–86; Gerald D. Feldman, *Army, Industry and Labor in Germany 1914–1918* (2nd edn, Oxford, 1992), pp. 45–52; Bell, *Blockade*, pp. 150–2.

tion, system was instituted by which German licences for export were issued only in return for an undertaking that goods required by Germany would be exported from the neutral country concerned. Together with the high prices paid by German buyers, the system constituted a significant breach in the Allied blockade and one about which the British authorities had great difficulty in obtaining accurate information.

Germany's early blockade measures were more restrained than those of Great Britain. In October 1914 German patrols began to seize neutral vessels in the Baltic and take them into German ports for search, but Germany's contraband lists were not enlarged to the same extent as Britain's.[61] Dependence on supplies from Denmark prevented the navy from attacking Denmark's trade with Britain as vigorously as it would have wished.[62] Sweden, however, was placed under pressure, despite its pro-German sympathies, partly in order to signal German displeasure with what was regarded as an unduly accommodating attitude towards the Entente in matters of war trade, partly in order to restrict the transit trade through Sweden to Russia.[63] Germany's main instrument of pressure was its treatment of Swedish timber exports as contraband, but by the beginning of 1915 the Germans had come to realise that this was an unwelcome burden on relations with Sweden at a sensitive time. In addition Germany was in desperate need of horses, of which Sweden was a major source of supply. In March 1915 an agreement was reached which allowed free passage of some timber to enemy countries in exchange for a large quota of Swedish horses for Germany.[64]

The spring of 1915 saw a drastic intensification of economic warfare on the part of both Germany and the Entente. Frustrated by the faltering progress of the German and Austro-Hungarian armies on the eastern and western fronts, by the constraints of a largely defensive naval strategy and by the growing effectiveness of British economic pressure, Germany proclaimed a policy of unrestricted submarine warfare on 4 February 1915. There were too few submarines to make the threat an effective deterrent to trade with the United Kingdom, and the policy was soon modified in response to neutral objections. Nevertheless, the German decision marked a new ruthlessness in the waging of war at sea. It also provided the British government with a pretext for going far beyond the measures adopted in the autumn.[65] The order in council of 11 March 1915 was aimed at cutting off Germany's entire overseas trade: exports as well as imports. It abolished the distinction between contraband and non-contraband goods and led to a far more rigorous policy of intercepting and

[61] Hecksher et al., *Sweden*, p. 57.
[62] Siney, *Allied Blockade*, p. 47; Sjøqvist, *Scavenius* I, pp. 136–8.
[63] Carlgren, *Neutralität oder Allianz*, pp. 68–72.
[64] Hecksher et al., *Sweden*, p. 64; Gihl, *Den svenska utrikespolitikens historia* IV, pp. 82–5; Carlgren, *Neutralität oder Allianz*, pp. 75–6.
[65] Lord Hankey, *The Supreme Command 1914–1918* (2 vols., London, 1961), vol. I, p. 353; minute by Churchill to the prime minister advocating repudiation of the Declarations of Paris and London, 25 February 1915, quoted ibid., pp. 366–7.

detaining neutral ships. This led to a radical reassessment of Britain's existing agreements with the adjacent neutrals. In effect Britain had to establish a rationing system by which the neutrals would be allowed to import as much as they needed for their own requirements, but which would leave no surplus to be exported to Germany. Rationing required some idea of what normal neutral imports were. If neutral governments were unable or unwilling to provide statistics, Britain would have to do the job itself: it was thus obliged in the course of 1915 to establish a comprehensive system of commercial intelligence in northern Europe.[66] Since neutral governments were naturally unwilling to enter into agreements which favoured one of the belligerents so blatantly, Britain also had to find organisations in neutral countries with which it could do business. The task of identifying and negotiating with such bodies occupied the British blockade authorities for much of 1915.

In the case of Denmark it was possible to negotiate with two groups of manufacturers and merchants, the industrial council (Industriråd) and the merchants' society (Grosserer Societet).[67] Although the British authorities had doubts about whether they could exert adequate controls over their members, they were reassured by the commercial attaché in Copenhagen that in such a small country as Denmark everyone knew everyone else's business. After protracted negotiations an agreement was signed on 19 November 1915 by which it was established that imports certified by the two organisations would be consumed in Denmark, while a certain number of specified articles could be re-exported to Norway and Sweden, and a much smaller number to Germany. By allowing the Industriråd and the Grosserer Societet to negotiate with foreign governments, the Danish government managed to maintain a position of balance between Britain and Germany and to avoid extensive interference in Denmark's economic life of the kind established by the British legation in Norway. But there were also disadvantages with this approach. As events in 1916 were to show, the state could not ultimately evade responsibility for agreements reached with foreign powers.

In the case of Norway, the British concentrated on reaching agreements with individual large firms or traders' organisations: first with the whale oil deal concluded between De Norske Fabriker and Lever Bros. in April 1915; later through the so-called Branch Agreements with groups of traders or manufacturers, beginning with the Norwegian Cotton Mills Association on 31 August 1915. By the end of the year practically the whole of the transit trade to Germany via Norway had been stopped.[68] Such agreements led to a degree of penetration of Norwegian economic life unequalled in Denmark, let alone

---

[66] British commercial espionage activities in Norway are described by the wartime head of the criminal investigation department in Kristiania in Joh. Søhr, *Spioner og bomber. Fra opdagelsespolitiets arbeidet under verdenskrigen* (Oslo, 1938), pp. 143–7, and in Tim Greve, *Spionjakt i Norge* (Oslo, 1982), pp. 25–99.

[67] Bell, *Blockade*, pp. 289–98; Siney, *Allied Blockade*, pp. 94–104.

[68] Riste, *Neutral Ally*, pp. 91–4; Paul G. Vigness, *The Neutrality of Norway in the World War* (Stanford, Calif., and London, 1932), pp. 47–50.

Sweden – a success due to Norway's greater dependence on Britain, the vigilance of the British legation and the acquiescence of the Norwegian government.

Unlike Denmark and Norway, Sweden chose openly to defy the validity of Britain's new blockade measures.[69] In the Anglo-Swedish negotiations which belatedly began in Stockholm in July 1915, the chief British negotiator, Robert Vansittart, was under pressure to avoid a breakdown of negotiations in order to keep the transit trade open and prevent Sweden siding still more openly with the Central Powers.[70] The draft agreement secured in early August 1915 was thus clearly favourable to Sweden. In view of the military situation and strong Russian representations that the negotiations should not be broken off, the Foreign Office felt unable to reject the draft agreement outright. But on 7 October the Swedes were presented with a new draft agreement containing more severe restrictions on Swedish trade. By the autumn the slowing of the German advance had made the military situation seem less alarming. More importantly, the British had come to realise that Sweden was more dependent on goods imported from overseas than either the British or the Swedish governments had hitherto appreciated. The Swedish bargaining position was strong, but not strong enough. Britain had the means to make life very difficult for Sweden if it chose.

1916–1917

The constraints which had hampered Britain's conduct of economic warfare in the first eighteen months of the war largely ceased to operate after the beginning of 1916. A new trading with the enemy act was passed in December 1915 to prevent British exports from reaching Germany. Partly in response to widespread criticism of the alleged leniency of the agreement with Denmark of November 1915, a Ministry of Blockade was established on 23 February 1916, with Lord Robert Cecil as the minister in charge and Sir Eyre Crowe as superintending under-secretary. In two orders in council of 30 March and 7 July 1916 the British government finally repudiated the limitations imposed by the Declaration of London. The battle of Jutland on 31 May 1916 provided further encouragement to those who wished to increase pressure on the northern neutrals, and the success of Brusilov's offensive in the east in June and July reduced the likelihood of Swedish intervention. On the other hand, the Allies failed to achieve a breakthrough at the battle of the Somme, while the intervention of Romania on the side of the Entente in August 1916 was

---

[69] Bell, *Blockade*, pp. 327–43; Gihl, *Den svenska utrikespolitikens historia* IV, pp. 145–59.
[70] On Vansittart's mission to Stockholm, see Lord Vansittart, *The Mist Procession* (London, 1958), pp. 145–53; B. J. C. McKercher, 'The Last Old Diplomat: Sir Robert Vansittart and British Foreign Policy', *Diplomacy and Statecraft* 6 (1995), pp. 1–38 (pp. 7–8). For Anglo-Swedish wartime economic relations, see also B. J. C. McKercher and Keith E. Neilson, '"The Triumph of Unarmed Forces": Sweden and the Allied Blockade of Germany 1914–1917', *Journal of Strategic Studies* 7 (1984), pp. 178–99.

followed in the autumn by a successful campaign by the Central Powers which brought Romania's rich supplies of agricultural produce and oil under their control.

Methods of limiting neutral trade with Germany which had emerged in the course of 1915 were extended and refined. One was the 'black list' of firms accused (not always justly) of trading with Germany – still, of course, a perfectly legitimate activity for the citizens of a neutral country.[71] In March 1916 control of neutral shipping was further refined with the introduction of the 'navicert' system which allowed shipments from the United States to Scandinavia with the minimum of interference to the firms concerned, while ensuring that the goods they carried were not destined for the enemy. Another key means of coercion was coal. The Admiralty took the lead by refusing bunker coal to ships engaged in the iron ore traffic from Narvik, and in July 1915 the system was extended to all ships carrying goods of enemy destination or origin. Control of coal for domestic consumption in the Scandinavian countries was more problematic. All were dependent on Britain as a supplier, but Norway was known to have large stockpiles, too much pressure on Denmark might drive it into the German orbit, and Germany itself proved capable of replacing Britain's supplies to Sweden when these were cut back.

The most decisive change in British policy in 1916 was the decision to restrict not merely the transit trade to Germany through Scandinavian ports, but also the domestic exports of the Scandinavian countries themselves. Exports to Britain of such products as fish, eggs, butter, meat and lard had fallen sharply, while exports to Germany had risen due to high prices and the workings of the compensation system. Of course Britain had no legal right to control neutral domestic produce; but legal constraints were clearly diminishing in force, while Britain unquestionably possessed, in its control of seaborne supplies to Scandinavia, the leverage necessary to enforce a reduction in exports to Germany.

In the course of 1916 the Danish government became more directly involved in negotiations with Great Britain and Germany when it became clear that the merchants' organisation was dangerously accommodating towards Britain's demands. Its promise to increase supplies to Britain could be fulfilled only at Germany's expense and entailed the danger of German reprisals. Scavenius was obliged to disavow an Anglo-Danish agreement reached in March and was then faced with the task of repairing relations with Great Britain.[72] It was fortunate for the Danes that in 1916 both Britain and Germany feared enemy action against Denmark (pp. 151–2). Influenced by rumours of German action, the Foreign Office rejected the option of coercing Denmark. When negotiations resumed in London in May 1916 the Danish negotiators eventually persuaded their British counterparts that exports to Britain could

---

[71] For an eloquent denunciation of this practice as applied to Norway, see Vigness, *Neutrality of Norway*, pp. 52–4.

[72] Sjøqvist, *Scavenius* I, p. 192.

not be restored to the pre-1914 level, but that through raising domestic consumption and a slight increase in bacon exports to Britain it would be possible to reduce the amount exported to Germany. The British, convinced that the Danes were acting in good faith and impressed by the sinking of a ship on the Esbjerg route in late July, decided not to insist on a written agreement. They were duly rewarded with an increase in Danish exports to Britain in the latter half of 1916. Denmark then had to appease Germany. The Germans wanted Danish horses, and Scavenius was able to secure Cecil's approval for an increased monthly quota. Denmark was thus much more successful in maintaining its balancing act between Britain and Germany than might have been expected at the beginning of 1916.[73] Neither Norway nor Sweden was to be so fortunate.

The Norwegian government became much more directly implicated than the Danish government in agreements to limit supplies of domestic products to Germany. It thus aroused German antagonism, while at the same time becoming entangled in disputes with Britain over the precise interpretation of those agreements. An agreement concluded in August 1916 secured 85 per cent of Norwegian fish exports for domestic consumption or for purchase by Great Britain at prices fixed until the end of the war, with only 15 per cent remaining available for export to Germany.[74] The Norwegian government, unlike that of Denmark, had engaged itself in a deal which discriminated explicitly against one of the belligerents. Unlike Scavenius, Ihlen did not keep Germany informed of the progress of the negotiations with Britain, and even hoped to keep the existence of the agreement secret.[75] But the Norwegians were exposed to the risk of German anger when the Germans came to hear of the agreement – as they soon did – and, by failing to consider whether Germany might be able to provide supplies for the fishing industry, deprived themselves of leverage in their negotiations with Britain.

A second agreement, aimed at cutting off Norway's exports of copper pyrites to Germany, was concluded on 30 August 1916. Its terms became the subject of misapprehensions which proved nearly catastrophic for Norway's relations with both belligerents. Germany required Norwegian pyrites not only for its copper content but also for its sulphur, which was used in the manufacture of ammunition. Through ambiguities of translation of some technical terms, the British and the Norwegians had different understandings of what categories of pyrites were subject to the export ban. Under pressure from Great Britain the Norwegian government placed an embargo on the export of all pyrites which came into effect on 30 October. Having gone so far to appease Britain, and

---

[73] Ibid., p. 195.
[74] Riste, *Neutral Ally*, pp. 96–107; Vigness, *Neutrality of Norway*, pp. 70–84; Hecksher et al., *Sweden*, pp. 317–24.
[75] For Ihlen's defence of his negotiating strategy, see his speech in a secret session of the Storting, 17 January 1917, quoted in Fasting, *Ihlen*, pp. 238–44.

especially in the light of the developing crisis with Germany on the submarine question (discussed p. 152), Ihlen then had to do something to meet Germany's requirements. In November 1916 he allowed exports of pyrites from the German-owned Stordø mines to start again. This produced a further complaint from Findlay, but this time Ihlen refused to give way. Norway's intransigence on the copper question, together with evidence of relatively large fish exports to Germany in the autumn of 1916, led Findlay to recommend on 9 December that an ultimatum should be presented to the Norwegian government threatening drastic action, 'which might include the demand for or even the seizure of a naval base', if Norway persevered in a policy prejudicial to British interests.[76]

As we shall see (pp. 152–4), Findlay's proposal came at a time when the British government had been actively debating for nearly two months the possibility that Norway might find itself at war with Germany. At one of its first meetings, on 12 December 1916, Lloyd George's new War Cabinet discussed the Norwegian situation.[77] Lord Robert Cecil opposed the idea of taking such extreme measures against a country which Britain was proposing to defend, while Admiral Jellicoe, the first sea lord, declared that it would be impracticable to occupy a port in the face of Norwegian opposition. The Cabinet decided instead to make a strong protest, followed if necessary by economic pressure in the form of embargoes on commodities such as copper, fishing supplies and coal. On 18 December Cecil presented the Norwegian minister with two memoranda detailing Norway's alleged violations of the fish and copper agreements.[78] On 22 December, when no reply had been received from the Norwegian government, Cecil ordered an embargo on coal exports to Norway.

The coal embargo came into operation at the beginning of January 1917, during an exceptionally cold winter, and led to widespread suffering throughout the country.[79] The Norwegian government endeavoured to meet Britain's demands on the two main questions at issue while not going so far as to endanger relations with Germany. On fish the British were prepared to accept Norwegian assurances that, although there had been certain irregularities, these would not be repeated. On pyrites, however, they would be satisfied with nothing less than a complete cessation of exports to Germany. This was more than Norway could afford to promise at first; but on 12 February 1917 Ihlen was able to convince the German minister that Norway had no choice but to comply with Britain's demands, while holding out the prospect of increased exports of hides and skins – and perhaps even fish – together with a loan of ten million kroner from the Bank of Norway. By now the German declaration of unrestricted submarine warfare had made a settlement of the dispute a matter of urgency to both Britain and Norway. On

---

[76] Quoted in Riste, *Neutral Ally*, p. 160.   [77] War Cabinet meeting 3, CAB 23/1.
[78] Riste, *Neutral Ally*, pp. 161–2.
[79] For a description of the effects, see Vigness, *Neutrality of Norway*, pp. 68–9.

14 February Ihlen informed the British government that Norway was prepared to ban all exports of pyrites to Germany; and on 17 February the coal embargo was lifted.

The embargo was probably the severest action undertaken by Britain against any neutral state during the First World War. It was the result, as Olav Riste has suggested, of a 'crisis of confidence' between Britain and Norway: 'a situation had been created in which each Government felt it was being deliberately misled by the other'.[80] The British feared that their 'grip over Norway was slipping under German pressure – a fear which the secretive attitude of the Norwegian Government did nothing to dispel'; the Norwegians resented being pushed into a confrontation with Germany as a result of favouring the Entente – a policy which, however, was evidently still not favourable enough in British eyes. The crisis could be resolved only when, on the one hand, Norway managed to achieve some kind of *modus vivendi* with Germany and, on the other, 'the British had achieved a more sober assessment of Norway's position'.[81]

After the failure to conclude a war trade agreement at the end of 1915, commercial relations between Britain and Sweden were conducted on a compensation basis which at first proved satisfactory to Sweden as far as imports from Britain were concerned, but did nothing to protect it from the rigours of the British blockade as applied to imports from overseas.[82] The Swedish government responded to the British-imposed privations with more acts of defiance but faced growing criticism from the Liberal and Social Democratic parties as well as from the business community, where the opposition was led by Marcus Wallenberg, Knut Wallenberg's half-brother.[83] Sweden's antagonistic policy towards Britain culminated in July 1916 with the mining of the Kogrund Channel.[84]

This narrow section of Swedish territorial waters was the means by which British submarines had been able to enter the Baltic. It was also the one remaining route by which British merchant ships trapped in the Baltic since the beginning of the war were able to make their escape. The British shipping shortage made their return a matter of urgency, and several ships got out through the channel in June 1916. Germany then put pressure on Sweden, threatening to halt its important export trade in timber to the United Kingdom unless the channel was closed.[85] The Swedes had refused earlier German requests, but this time they complied. Grohmann suggests that Sweden had begun to contemplate mining the channel because the increased British traffic,

---

[80] Riste, *Neutral Ally*, p. 166.   [81] Ibid., p. 167.

[82] Gihl, *Den svenska utrikespolitikens historia* IV, p. 159.

[83] Steven Koblik, *Sweden: The Neutral Victor. Sweden and the Western Powers 1917–1918* (Lund, 1972), p. 26.

[84] Gihl, *Den svenska utrikespolitikens historia* IV, pp. 211–21.

[85] Justus-Andreas Grohmann, *Die deutsch–schwedische Auseinandersetzung um die Fahrstrassen des Öresunds im Ersten Weltkrieg* (Boppard am Rhein, 1974).

combined with a growing number of violations of Swedish neutrality by German warships in pursuit of British ships, was placing an intolerable strain on the resources of the Swedish navy. A minefield, even though in contravention of international law and obviously favouring German interests, thus represented a genuine attempt to preserve Swedish neutrality.[86] There seems little doubt, however, that German pressure gave the decisive push to the closure of the Kogrund Channel, which was announced on 28 July. The Allies lodged a formal complaint and diplomatic exchanges continued until October, but it became clear that they did not wish to enter into a protracted debate on the legality of Sweden's action. The question had also lost some of its urgency since several more British ships had managed to leave the Baltic before the measure came into effect. But the incident served to reinforce Allied suspicion of Sweden and coloured their attitude towards the much more important conflicts over trade which developed in the autumn.[87]

During the summer of 1916 the full force of the British blockade was brought to bear upon Sweden for the first time. By late September the controls had become so severe, and the effects on living standards so far-reaching, that even Hammarskjöld was obliged to accept that negotiations should be begun with the Entente.[88] However, the Swedish delegation was unprepared for the scale of the British demands revealed when it arrived in London in November 1917.[89] In fact the British believed that their terms were quite generous. They had not demanded a halt to the iron ore trade with Germany or demanded Swedish tonnage, but they did want to prevent re-export to Germany and improved conditions for transit to Russia. Britain's resolve was strengthened by the coming to power of the Lloyd George coalition on 5 December 1916. In their reply to the British proposals, given on 7 December, the Swedish delegation went some way towards the British position, but when negotiations were resumed in January 1917 the British, far from moderating their position, constantly added new demands. Reports of the worsening economic position in Sweden – bread rationing had been introduced in December 1916 – and the growing political difficulties of the Hammarskjöld government reinforced Britain's conviction that toughness was the best policy.

The campaign of unrestricted submarine warfare launched by Germany on 1 February 1917 added a further element of compulsion. Britain detained all neutral ships in British ports and, with the breaking off of diplomatic relations between the United States and Germany on 2 February, the European neutrals were deprived of American support. On 2 February the Swedish delegation was presented with a draft agreement which offered no assurance of supplies of cereals or coal in the event of German reprisals and was couched in the form of

---

[86] Ibid., pp. 114–52, 169–70.
[87] Gihl, *Den svenska utrikespolitikens historia* IV, p. 220.
[88] Koblik, *Neutral Victor*, p. 28; Gihl, *Den svenska utrikespolitikens historia* IV, pp. 223–32; Carlgren, *Ministären Hammarskjöld*, pp. 150, 154.
[89] Koblik, *Neutral Victor*, p. 32.

an ultimatum: the draft must be accepted or rejected in its entirety. 'With those words Cecil precipitated a crisis in Sweden's foreign policy that ended only after sixteen months of severe economic hardship for Sweden and the collapse of two Swedish governments.'[90]

1917–1918

The German declaration of unrestricted submarine warfare was intended to starve Britain into surrender before the United States's entry into the war shifted the balance decisively in favour of the Entente. This effect was to be achieved by sinkings – which had already risen dramatically in the last months of 1916 – and by deterring neutral ship-owners and sailors from sailing in the service of the Allies. For Britain, the danger was real enough: in April 1917, 25 per cent of the ships leaving British ports failed to return. Together with the Russian revolution of February 1917, the failure of the Nivelle offensive in April and the meagre achievements of the British offensives that followed, the submarine campaign contributed to a growing sense, both within and outside government circles, that the war might prove unwinnable. Fears and frustration about the wider course of the war – compounded in the autumn by the Bolshevik revolution and Germany's victory in the east – were to influence Allied policy towards the northern neutrals throughout the year.

But the submarine campaign created difficulties for Germany too: not merely because it was a gamble that was bound to fail in the long run but, more immediately, because it led to conflict with neutral states on which the German war effort remained crucially dependent. Of course there was little need to worry about neutral sensibilities if, as the navy's expert advisers claimed, Britain would be forced to sue for peace by the summer. But how much reliance could be placed on their predictions? German doubts on this score, together with skilful neutral diplomacy, led to concessions which significantly weakened the effectiveness of the U-boat campaign. In the long run Britain's introduction of convoys was to prove decisive for the failure of the campaign. As long as the outcome remained undecided, however, the attitude of the neutrals was crucial. Could sufficient numbers of ship-owners and sailors be deterred from sailing in the service of the Allies? In the short term the measure was certainly effective. Neutral sailings to Great Britain came to a virtual standstill. But how long would the effect last, and how much damage might be inflicted on Germany's relations with the neutrals in the meantime?

The greatest degree of uncertainty surrounded Denmark. Sweden's pro-German sympathies were still relatively firm. Norway's attitude was clearly more suspect, but Norway was reckoned to be so dependent on imports that, as late as June 1917 (when the limitations of the campaign were already evident), the Admiralty Staff stated that it would not long survive their being

---

[90] Ibid., p. 15.

cut off.[91] It might be possible, however, to inflict significant damage on Denmark's trade with Britain. But the attempt to do so brought the Admiralty Staff into confrontation with all those elements in the German leadership who wished to maintain good relations with Denmark. They included the General Staff, the Copenhagen legation, the Wilhelmstrasse and the chancellor himself. The U-boat campaign threatened the tacit arrangements which allowed Denmark to maintain its trade with both belligerents. Germany's own supplies were therefore as much at risk as those of Great Britain. Once again, Scavenius employed his diplomatic skill to negotiate a breach in the total blockade of the British Isles which the naval leadership was attempting to impose.[92] By making judicious concessions, Scavenius secured German agreement to the passage of a small number of ships through the prohibited zone (*Sperrgebiet*) in the North Sea; then, in late February, the navy reluctantly agreed to allow Danish ships to use the shorter and safer route from Bergen rather than attempt the crossing direct. Admiral Holtzendorff tried to render the agreement ineffective by ordering that Danish ships should be torpedoed once they entered the prohibited zone.[93] But the first Danish sailings from Bergen, on 18 March, came through unscathed. By May it was becoming clear that the submarine campaign had not deterred neutral ship-owners and crews from sailing to Britain.

In these circumstances, and especially in view of the United States's entry into the war in April 1917, the German political leadership and high command, and even to some extent the Admiralty Staff as well, came to acknowledge that Germany must take a more conciliatory line towards the European neutrals. Holtzendorff ordered on 7 April that the Netherlands, Spain and Sweden should be treated 'more mildly' in order to avoid a breach which might do further damage to Germany's precarious economic position. The position of Denmark remained more complicated because in the spring of 1917 both the army high command and the naval leadership feared British action against Norway, to which Germany might have to respond by occupying the Jutland peninsula (pp. 154–6).[94] Moreover the navy's persistence in attempting to stop Danish exports to Britain led to a renewed crisis in late May. Scavenius's threat to resign as foreign minister on 22 May induced a state close to panic in Brockdorff-Rantzau. Under pressure from the Auswärtiges Amt, the navy gave way on 7 June.[95] By this time they must have realised that Germany lacked the means to make the submarine threat credible. At the beginning of June the commander-in-chief of the U-boat flotilla was informed that only two Danish ships had been sunk in the past two months. The Danes had reduced their stockpiles and were fulfilling their backlog of deliveries to Britain.[96] Scavenius, for his part, had demonstrated that there was a point beyond which he would not be moved, and that Germany must either take

---

[91] Stegemann, *Deutsche Marinepolitik*, p. 85.   [92] Sjøqvist, *Scavenius* I, pp. 220–7.
[93] Stegemann, *Deutsche Marinepolitik*, pp. 77–8.   [94] Ibid., pp. 82–4.
[95] Heckscher et al., *Sweden*, p. 466.   [96] Stegemann, *Deutsche Marinepolitik*, p. 85.

action which would allow him to remain in office, or face the unforeseeable consequences of his resignation.

The revolution of February 1917 in Russia and the entry of the United States into the war transformed relations between the Scandinavian countries and the Entente Powers. With the faltering of Russia's war effort, the Allies became less interested in the transit question. Sweden was thus deprived of one of its main bargaining counters in negotiations with the West at the same time as Germany was achieving a position of preponderance in the Baltic region. When the most powerful neutral in the world became a belligerent, the European neutrals lost the moral support they had derived from American opposition to British and German methods of waging economic warfare. Allied control over their import and export trades became almost total. The first embargo on American exports, proclaimed on 9 July 1917, confirmed neutral fears that the full weight of US economic power would be brought to bear upon their trade with Germany. By the summer the United States had served notice that it expected the neutrals to come up with proposals to serve as the basis for war trade negotiations.

Although the American embargo increased the pressure on the Scandinavian countries to negotiate, it also made them turn elsewhere for their essential supplies. One solution was to intensify the exchange of goods among the Scandinavian countries themselves.[97] More importantly, they turned to the Central Powers. Through a series of credit agreements negotiated with Germany and Austria-Hungary between August 1917 and the end of the war, Denmark obtained supplies of coal, salt, iron and shipbuilding materials in return for increased exports of pork and butter; similar arrangements, for coal in return for iron ore, cellulose and paper, were negotiated by Sweden in March 1918.[98] As Scavenius pointed out, the more goods Germany sold to Scandinavia, the more the former's influence would grow.[99] At a time when the military outlook still looked bleak for the Allies (with the Italian defeat at Caporetto, the military collapse of Russia and the Bolshevik revolution), there was thus pressure on both sides to reach agreements.

The negotiations between the Associated Powers and the northern neutrals were nevertheless protracted. Although a Norwegian mission led by Nansen arrived in Washington in July 1917, an agreement was not signed until 30 April 1918. The Swedish agreement was concluded a month later, on 29 May; the Danish agreement not until 18 September, within two months of the end of the war. All three agreements led to a further constriction of German imports of essential commodities, while in the case of Denmark and Sweden they also enabled the Entente to secure large quantities of shipping (an Anglo-

[97] Hecksher et al., *Sweden*, pp. 101–3, 470–1.
[98] Ibid., pp. 107–8, 469–70. An agreement between Norway and Germany was concluded on 27 September 1918, too late to have much effect: ibid., p. 371.
[99] Sjøqvist, *Scavenius* I, pp. 234–5.

Norwegian tonnage agreement had been signed in April 1917), of which it was in acute need. The delays were caused in part by prolonged disagreement, both within the American administration and between the United States and its allies, about the principles upon which the agreements were to be based. On the whole, the British had a better understanding than the Americans of the difficulties facing the neutrals – though this also made them less sentimental about any special virtues they might claim – while the American authorities charged with enforcing the blockade favoured the toughest possible line.

But the British also intervened on occasion to stiffen the American stance, while President Wilson repeatedly vetoed the more extreme demands of his advisers. This was partly because he was conscious of the discrepancy between the United States's former stance as a neutral and its present belligerency, partly because he believed some neutrals were more deserving than others. At an early stage he made it clear that Norway, presumably because of its shipping services to the Allies, was a special case, letting it be known on 17 July 1917 that 'he drew a distinction between shipments to Norway and other neutral countries of Europe'.[100] Responsibility for delay also lay with the Scandinavian governments. The Scandinavian countries still had reason to fear Germany and, while the outcome of the war remained uncertain, reason to expect that military setbacks might force the Associated Powers to moderate their demands. They also had to worry about the political repercussions if they were seen to take the initiative in negotiations which would result in further hardship for their own peoples. Norway in particular was reluctant to introduce rationing, even though the Americans made it clear at an early stage that it was a precondition for an agreement.[101]

The situation surrounding the negotiations with Sweden was the most complex of all. Sweden was more directly affected than Norway and Denmark by the changing fortunes of the war in the east.[102] Weakened at first by the February revolution in Russia, Sweden's bargaining position with the West was subsequently greatly strengthened by Germany's defeat of Russia at the end of 1917. At the same time, however, the elimination of the Russian counterweight made Sweden more dependent on Germany. Swedish domestic politics in 1917–18 were far more volatile than those of Denmark or Norway. Hammarskjöld's administration had fallen in March 1917. Its successor, the weak Swartz–Lindman government, was faced in April 1917 by food riots throughout Sweden and demonstrations in Stockholm in support of the Russian revolution. With a general election pending in September, Swedish politics were dominated by the determination of the left to push through

---

[100] Quoted in Thomas A. Bailey, *The Policy of the United States Toward the Neutrals 1917–1918* (Baltimore, Md., 1942), p. 117 (n. 36).

[101] Nansen to Ihlen, 30 August 1917, in Steinar Kjærheim (ed.), *Fridtjof Nansen. Brev* (4 vols., Oslo, 1961–6), vol. III, pp. 277–8.

[102] The fullest account of the negotiations is in Koblik, *Neutral Victor*, chs. 3–10. See also Bailey, *Policy of the United States*, ch. 5; Bell, *Blockade*, pp. 651–69; Hecksher et al., *Sweden*, part 1, ch. 8.

constitutional reform and the failure of the government to reach an agreement with Britain and the United States. Then, on 8 September, in the middle of the election campaign, the US government published the 'Luxburg telegrams' – despatches from the German minister in Buenos Aires which had been sent via Swedish diplomatic channels to Berlin and intercepted by British intelligence, recommending, among other things, that Argentine ships should be 'sunk without trace'.[103] As the British had hoped, the Luxburg affair discredited Sweden's Conservative government and contributed to their electoral defeat. On 19 October 1917 parliamentary government was finally established in Sweden with the formation of a Liberal–Social Democratic coalition, with Professor Nils Edén as prime minister, the socialist leader Hjalmar Branting as finance minister, and Johannes Hellner as foreign minister. Hellner, who stood for cooperation between business interests and the left, had led the negotiations with Britain in 1916–17 and was now looked on as the man who would bring about an agreement with the Western powers.

The Swedish–British negotiations had been left in suspense following the presentation of Lord Robert Cecil's 'ultimatum' on 2 February 1917, but Great Britain and the United States did not arrive at a coordinated negotiating position until 8 December 1917. Disagreement centred at first on whether it was possible to achieve a complete stoppage of Swedish iron ore exports to Germany, but by November the Allied shortage of tonnage, made more acute by the need to support Italy in the aftermath of Caporetto, meant that it had become imperative to obtain shipping from Sweden. However, by the time negotiations began in London on 13 December, the collapse of the eastern front, together with tempting German offers concerning the future of the Åland Islands, had made Sweden far less amenable to Western pressure.[104] For a number of reasons, including the realism of the new Swedish government, the urgency of the tonnage question and the ominous implications of German supremacy in the Baltic, all three parties worked for a speedy conclusion. A *modus vivendi* agreement was signed on 29 January 1918 but thereafter the negotiations ran into difficulties. The American authorities tightened their blockade policy with little regard for relations with Sweden. Meanwhile the conservative forces in Sweden became more assertive under the shelter of German military success, and the future of the Åland Islands became an increasingly contentious issue in Swedish politics. The British realised that the government needed a foreign policy success, and were instrumental in bringing about the conclusion of a draft agreement on 16 February which contained a generous figure for grain and fodder imports into Sweden in return for a reduction in ore exports of 2 million tons and 500,000 tons of shipping.

---

[103] Koblik, *Neutral Victor*, pp. 95–130. For details of British Admiralty interception and decryption of Swedish ciphers (including the more famous 'Zimmermann telegram'), see Christopher Andrew, *Secret Service: The Making of the British Intelligence Community* (London, 1985), pp. 107–14.

[104] See pp. 162–7 below.

The Swedish government moved cautiously, not wishing to accept the draft agreement until it had been cleared with Germany. In April 1918 Eric Trolle, a former minister to Germany, was sent to Berlin to obtain German approval. His mission was an outstanding success. First, the Germans made it clear that they could not meet Sweden's food requirements: Sweden thus had no alternative to reaching a deal with the West. Secondly they asked for alterations which placed no obstacle in the way of an agreement. They did so, in part, because Germany had sufficient stockpiles of Swedish ore to ensure that it would not be immediately affected by a reduction in exports. By this stage, too, the German authorities had probably 'lost heart about the submarine campaign, and were admitting among themselves that it had failed'.[105] The implications of the Swedish–German agreement of 16 April 1918 were nevertheless far-reaching. As Koblik puts it, 'by sending a delegation to Berlin, Sweden had indicated to Germany that it wished to alter formally its neutrality policy. The German acceptance of that change meant that Sweden would be free to shift its policy to a more even-handed neutrality.'[106] The general agreement of 29 May 1918 was thus 'a decisive victory for Swedish diplomacy'.[107] Sweden had been able to avoid American pressure of the kind that was exerted on Denmark and Norway. It had managed to adjust from a pro-German neutrality to one that was concerned 'solely with protecting the political interests of Sweden and the commercial ties Sweden had with both belligerent groups'. As we shall see, however, this new-found autonomy was immediately to be jeopardised by Sweden's entanglement in the question of the Åland Islands.

Scandinavian involvement in the war?

Sweden in 1915

Throughout the autumn of 1914, and in the first months of 1915, German diplomatic activity was focused principally on the Balkans. There was no indication that the General Staff looked to Sweden for a significant accretion of military strength to the Central Powers.[108] In the course of 1915, however, Sweden came to be seen as a possible means of putting pressure on Russia. At first Bethmann Hollweg hoped that the mediation efforts of H. N. Andersen might lead to a separate peace between Russia and the Central Powers. This hope was shaken and later dispelled by the negative results of Andersen's two

---

[105] Bell, *Blockade*, p. 662.   [106] Koblik, *Neutral Victor*, p. 201.

[107] Ibid., p. 212. B. J. C. McKercher, *Esme Howard: A Diplomatic Biography* (Cambridge, 1989), p. 183, describes the agreement as 'a stunning diplomatic triumph for the British and their allies'.

[108] Except where otherwise stated, this section is based on the definitive account in Carlgren, *Neutralität oder Allianz*.

missions to Petrograd in February and July 1915.[109] Attention shifted to
Sweden partly as a result of ill-considered Swedish diplomatic initiatives. In
February 1915 Gustav V wrote to the tsar offering his services as a
mediator;[110] in March he made an amateurish attempt to prevent Italian
intervention which soon became known to the Entente;[111] in May Hammarskjöld visited Berlin in order to sound the possibility of mediation (as well as to
clear up problems of Swedish–German trade). On each occasion Sweden
seemed to be less an impartial go-between than an agent of the Central
Powers. The growth of activist agitation in Sweden in the course of 1915
convinced many Germans that the tide of opinion was running strongly in
Germany's favour.[112] Even if Sweden did not intervene in the war, the threat
of intervention could be employed to demoralise Russia, and Swedish
diplomacy could be used to influence other wavering neutrals, notably
Romania. The prospect of Swedish intervention might also encourage Finnish
separatists to attempt an uprising against the Russian empire.[113] As an
incentive, Sweden could be offered a German promise of help at least in
achieving sovereignty over the Åland Islands, and possibly something much
grander: Swedish hegemony in northern Europe.

The first moves were made by Arthur Zimmermann, the under-secretary of
state at the Auswärtiges Amt and perhaps the one German official who took
Sweden seriously over a long period.[114] Hammarskjöld was not impressed
when Zimmermann held out the prospect of Swedish leadership of a future
Nordic bloc during his Berlin visit. However, Zimmermann found a receptive
intermediary in a high official of the Swedish court, Count Ludvig Douglas,
who conveyed the offer of an alliance to King Gustav on 8 June 1915. This
time the future Swedish empire was to encompass Finland and the Baltic
provinces of the Russian empire. Douglas sounded Hammarskjöld and
Wallenberg – to whom he held out the inducement of strengthening the
authority of crown and government – as well as the chief of the general staff
and leading conservative politicians. But in no case, apart from that of the
king, did he meet with a positive response.

Further approaches followed in June and July, but from early August
German efforts became more determined as Bethmann's Russian policy
underwent a decisive change from seeking a separate peace to securing a
military solution. On 11 August he sent the kaiser an optimistic assessment by
Taube, the inveterately pro-German Swedish minister in Berlin, of the

[109] Winterhager, *Mission für den Frieden*, ch. 8; Kaarsted, *Great Britain and Denmark*, pp.
87–91.
[110] Hildebrand, *Gustav V*, pp. 182–5.
[111] Gihl, *Den svenska utrikespolitikens historia* IV, pp. 128–31.
[112] Schuberth, *Schweden und das Deutsche Reich*, ch. 3; L. Torbjörn Norman, 'Right-Wing
Scandinavianism and the Russian Menace', in John Hiden and Aleksander Loit (eds.),
Contact or Isolation? Soviet–Western Relations in the Interwar Period (Stockholm, 1991), pp.
329–49.
[113] Schuberth, *Schweden und das Deutsche Reich*, pp. 39–44.
[114] Carlgren, *Neutralität oder Allianz*, pp. 108–9.

likelihood of Swedish entry into the war. It was accompanied by a proposal
from the German naval attaché in Stockholm, Fischer-Lossainen, for a
German landing in the Åland Islands aimed at provoking a Finnish uprising
against Russia and forcing Sweden into the war. The proposal was submitted
to Falkenhayn, the chief of the general staff, who decided that no action should
be taken until Sweden had made a firm decision to take Germany's side. It was
therefore necessary to keep up the political pressure on Sweden. More
dignitaries visited Stockholm in August and September, and German efforts
culminated on 15 November with the arrival in Stockholm of Prince Max of
Baden, a cousin of the queen, ostensibly to discuss prisoners of war on behalf
of the Red Cross.

Some confusion surrounded Prince Max's mission. Falkenhayn had already
ruled out an offensive against Petrograd through Finland, and in the autumn of
1915 the centre of military operations shifted to the Balkans with the attack on
Serbia by Germany, Austria–Hungary and Bulgaria. However, he favoured the
deployment of Swedish troops in the Baltic provinces, and believed Swedish
adherence to the Central Powers to be highly desirable for the effect it would
have 'on the other neutrals and on the morale of our opponents'.[115] For the
Wilhelmstrasse, too, there were still political advantages to be derived from a
Swedish alliance. It might add to the pressure on Great Britain to seek peace
(about which the German leadership remained surprisingly optimistic).
Sweden also figured in the ideas of *Mitteleuropa* which were being vigorously
debated in Germany and Austria at this time.[116] The General Staff wanted
closer economic, political and military cooperation with a number of European
countries, including Sweden, in order to combat Britain's economic pressure.
In the longer term, *Mitteleuropa* was a model for reorganising the European
economy under German leadership after the war. The Auswärtiges Amt
appears to have wanted Prince Max to win Sweden over to a close partnership
with Germany with a view to political and economic collaboration in the
future, not immediate military intervention. Both the General Staff and the
Auswärtiges Amt were therefore sceptical about the mission and appear to
have regarded it principally as a means of appeasing the Swedish activists.[117]
However, the instructions Prince Max received from the kaiser and Falkenhayn
still emphasised the goal of obtaining 'an alliance with Germany and a military
convention' with a view to joint operations against Petrograd.[118]

Prince Max therefore aimed at securing immediate Swedish intervention. In
exchange he offered Sweden German support during the war in the form of
troops, war material, coal and other economic requirements. After the war
Sweden would receive the Åland Islands, an adjustment of its frontier, an

[115] Conversation with Kapitän-zur-See Zenker (Naval Staff), 17 November 1915, quoted in
Bengt Holtze, 'Några militära bedömningar 1915 avseende Sverige', *Aktuellt och historiskt*
1969, pp. 95–116 (p. 99).
[116] See ch. 7, p. 245.   [117] Schuberth, *Schweden und das Deutsche Reich*, p. 68.
[118] Text printed in Carlgren, *Neutralität oder Allianz*, pp. 218–19.

autonomous or independent Finland as a buffer state and free access to the Russian market. If Germany entered into a customs union with other states, Sweden would have the right to become a member. Germany was also prepared to conclude an offensive and defensive alliance with Sweden.[119] It is hardly surprising that, faced with an alliance offer couched in such terms, the king and his ministers should have returned a negative answer. On 20 November 1915 King Gustav told Prince Max that Sweden could not go to war against Russia without some cause that would unite the whole country. Clearly Swedish hegemony in the north, however tempting to the king and his associates, was not something for which the majority of the Swedish population would be prepared to fight.

The Swedish government followed up its negative reply with gestures of goodwill to Germany, including a prohibition on belligerent submarines from using Swedish territorial waters – a measure designed to keep British submarines out of the Baltic. The Swedish refusal appears to have been accepted by Germany with remarkably little acrimony. Prince Max showed sympathy for Sweden's position. In view of the domestic situation, he told the kaiser, only an external threat could bring about Swedish entry into the war. The kaiser for his part merely sent a friendly telegram to King Gustav acknowledging the difficulties that stood in the way of the proposal but expressing confidence that Sweden would not 'miss its great opportunity'.[120] In fact the alliance project had been indefinitely shelved. The German leadership may have belatedly accepted Lucius's message that the activist party in Sweden was too small and isolated to carry a united country into the war.[121] Furthermore, the benefits of Swedish intervention were by no means self-evident, and there was much to support the view that Germany would gain more from Sweden as a benevolent neutral. Sweden's wartime relations with Germany had been friendly but remarkably self-assured: there was nothing to suggest that Sweden would be a comfortable alliance partner.

British anxiety about Swedish intentions, which surfaced periodically up to the beginning of 1916, was not based on any knowledge of Germany's overtures, but rather on the fear that events elsewhere in Europe or ill-judged action on the part of Russia might precipitate Swedish intervention. In order to reassure Sweden, the Allied ministers in Stockholm gave a second guarantee of Swedish independence and integrity in May 1915 to reinforce the one given at the outbreak of war.[122] But Britain also had to take account of Russian fears. Throughout 1915 the Russian military authorities were convinced that a Swedish attack was imminent.[123] Even if Sweden did not intervene, the transit

---

[119] Memorandum of 18 November 1915 in Prince Max's handwriting, on royal writing paper: text printed ibid., pp. 222–3.
[120] Quoted ibid., p. 229. [121] Schuberth, *Schweden und das Deutsche Reich*, pp. 61–2.
[122] Gihl, *Den svenska utrikespolitikens historia* IV, pp. 130–1. A similar declaration was given to Denmark on 4 June 1915: Kaarsted, *Great Britain and Denmark*, p. 53.
[123] Holtze, 'Sverige i brittiska bedömningar', pp. 122–3.

trade to Russia remained dependent on Swedish goodwill. The Russians thus repeatedly urged the British to moderate their war trade dealings with Sweden.[124] In response the British made a significant concession on the treatment of iron ore as contraband.[125] Finally, Britain had its own worries about the position of Norway. If Sweden entered the war, 'we should run the risk of seeing the Swedes establish a base for Germany on the western coast of Norway, which might turn our position in the North Sea, and would in any case threaten our communications with Russia via Archangel'.[126]

The most sustained debate on the question of Swedish intervention resulted from a series of misunderstandings which began when the Norwegian military authorities strengthened their defences in the Narvik region in the autumn of 1915. The Swedish General Staff linked this to reports from their military attaché in London that Britain planned a landing in Norway with the aim of establishing direct contact with Russia and, incidentally, depriving Germany of supplies of iron ore from northern Sweden.[127] The defensive measures undertaken by Sweden near the frontier with Norway were then interpreted by the French military attaché in Stockholm, Commandant Thomas, as pointing to the likelihood that, if Sweden went to war (which he doubted for the present), it would not move against Russia but would 'make a dash for Narvik', which could then be used as a base for German submarines.[128] Thomas suggested that the Allies should reach a prior arrangement with Norway to occupy Narvik as soon as Sweden entered the war. An approach to Norway was also proposed by Sazonov, the Russian foreign minister, towards the end of January 1916.[129] A promise of British military assistance, he suggested, might persuade Norway to oppose Sweden if the latter entered the war.

Although an approach to Norway was ultimately ruled out, the chief of the imperial general staff, Sir William Robertson, was asked to investigate the military implications of a Swedish declaration of war, and the question was discussed by the War Committee on 3 February 1916.[130] It was thought unlikely that Sweden would either attack Norway or go to war against Russia,

---

[124] They were backed by Lord Kitchener, the minister of war, who wrote on 23 June 1915 to Lord Crewe (deputising for Grey at the Foreign Office): 'If Russia had to find troops to meet an invasion of Finland by Sweden the situation in the Eastern theatre would become critical. The neutrality of Sweden is more important at the present time than preventing food and contraband reaching Germany' (FO 800/102).

[125] The case of the *Nike*, carrying iron ore from Luleå to Germany, which was captured by a British submarine in the Baltic in October 1915: correspondence in FO 372/720; Michael Wilson, *Baltic Assignment: British Submariners in Russia 1914–1919* (London, 1985), pp. 117–18.

[126] Walford Selby, 'Memorandum in Regard to the Attitude of Sweden', 1 April 1915, FO 371/2458, No. 38367.

[127] Holtze, 'Några militära bedömningar 1915'.

[128] Howard to Grey, 20 December 1915, FO 371/2459, No. 199926.

[129] Buchanan telegram, 30 January 1916, FO 371/2754, No. 18873.

[130] 'The Strategical Consequences of Swedish Intervention in the War on the Side of the Central Powers', 31 January 1916, CAB 42/7/18; meeting of War Committee, CAB 42/8/1.

but there remained the need to allay Russian anxiety about the danger of a renewed German offensive in the east. Moreover if Sweden did intervene it would be, in the words of the first sea lord, Sir Henry Jackson, 'absolutely impossible to force the Baltic' and thus bring British naval power directly to bear on Sweden.[131] By March 1916, however, it was evident that the Verdun offensive had transformed the situation by returning the centre of strategic attention to the western front and reducing Germany's capacity to undertake offensive operations in other theatres. Objectively there was thus little reason to expect fighting to break out in the far north of Scandinavia in the winter of 1915–16. Sweden had declined Germany's offer of an alliance in November 1915, and reports of aggressive intentions on the part of Sweden, Russia or Great Britain were mainly the products of the minds of over-imaginative military attachés.[132] With the new German offensive in the west, and in the light of the persistent reluctance of the British military and naval authorities to contemplate any kind of action in northern Europe, there was never any likelihood that either Sweden or Norway would become embroiled in the war at this stage.

Denmark and Norway in 1916–1917

The rumours about German or British military action against Denmark which were current in 1916 served to reinforce the caution of both belligerents. The reports received by the Foreign Office in April 1916 that Germany was planning to occupy Jutland seem to have originated in rumours deliberately spread by the News Department of the Foreign Office that Britain intended to send an expeditionary force to Schleswig.[133] After the battle of Jutland, and in particular after Romania's entry into the war, the Germans feared that Britain might seek to force an entry to the Baltic and that this might draw Denmark into the war on the Allied side. However, Brockdorff-Rantzau successfully reassured Ludendorff in September 1916 that there was no reason to doubt Denmark's determination to maintain its neutrality.[134] He also returned to Copenhagen with a personal message from the kaiser to King Christian explicitly acknowledging the correctness of Denmark's conduct.

On the British side, rumours of German action against Denmark appear to have been regarded mainly from the point of view of their effect on Danish morale. In April 1916, realising that German plans were based on the

---

[131] Meeting of War Committee, CAB 42/8/1.

[132] Vansittart minuted on 16 May 1916 on another 'alarmist' report from the French military attaché: 'Commandant Thomas has no long experience of Sweden – he only arrived in October if I remember right – and I would not call him a very good judge of a situation' (FO 371/2753, No. 91467).

[133] Goschen to Rumbold, 8 April 1916, FO 371/2754, No. 68561; FO telegram to Gurney (Copenhagen), 14 April 1916, and Gurney telegram to FO, 14 April 1916, FO 371/2754, No. 71840; Bell, *Blockade*, pp. 471–2.

[134] Sjøqvist, *Scavenius* I, p. 201.

assumption of a British landing, the Foreign Office wished to reassure Denmark about British intentions but also to promise that if it were attacked by Germany Britain would do all in its power 'to assist Denmark's resistance'.[135] But no such promise could be made in the light of the consensus of naval and military opinion, expressed authoritatively in a joint Admiralty–War Office memorandum of October 1916, that Britain was quite incapable of coming to Denmark's assistance.[136] The War Committee thus drew back from a secret proposal for military cooperation which seemed to have emanated indirectly from the Danish General Staff in September.[137] It also authorised the British minister to inform Scavenius that Britain would do nothing to bring Denmark or the other Scandinavian countries into hostilities with Germany.[138] Within a few weeks, therefore, Denmark had obtained reassurances from both sides.[139]

Norway's position was far more precarious. At the same time as it was embroiled in the dispute over the copper agreement with Great Britain (see pp. 137–9), it came under pressure from Germany on the question of submarine warfare. On 20 October 1916 Germany protested vehemently against a decree, introduced under Allied pressure, prohibiting the use of Norwegian territorial waters by submarines.[140] For Germany the key point at issue was the demand that neutrals should recognise submarine warfare as equal in principle to the methods of economic warfare employed by the Entente. Norway was therefore a test case for the future of German submarine warfare. In the light of the growing intensity of the German campaign against Norwegian merchant shipping, there was a widespread assumption in Norway that the country would soon be at war with Germany. It was a possibility that the British and French governments also had to take seriously.[141]

The French were particularly worried by the German note and asked the British government to 'do everything possible to encourage Norway' as well as to consider occupying bases on the Norwegian coast.[142] Their chief fear was that Germany might bomb the Norwegian nitrate factories on which the Allies, and France in particular, relied for the manufacture of explosives and ammunition.[143] The initial response of the British Cabinet, backed by the

---

[135] Grey minute (n.d.) on Gurney telegram to FO, 14 April 1916, and Admiralty to FO, 17 April 1916, FO 371/2754, No. 71840; Kaarsted, *Great Britain and Denmark*, pp. 61–2.

[136] 'The Military Situation in Denmark', CAB 42/22/8; War Committee meeting of 26 October 1916, ibid.

[137] The source was probably Captain Erik With, the strongly pro-British chief of military intelligence: Paget (Copenhagen) to Hardinge, 28 September 1916, FO 371/2754, No. 198788; Kaarsted, *Great Britain and Denmark*, pp. 65–9. Ole A. Hedegaard, *En general og hans samtid. General Erik With mellem Stauning og kaos* (Frederikssund, 1990), casts no direct light on the matter, though it documents the mutual mistrust of government ministers (especially Munch) and senior army officers (including With): pp. 50–6.

[138] Telegram to Paget, 27 October 1916, FO 371/2755, No. 215001.

[139] Sjøqvist, *Scavenius* I, p. 201.   [140] Riste, *Neutral Ally*, p. 141.

[141] Ibid., pp. 148–54; Holtze, 'Sverige i brittiska bedömningar', pp. 150–5.

[142] Granville (Paris) telegram to FO, 24 October 1916, FO 371/2755, No. 213288.

[143] Telegram to FO, 24 October 1916, ibid., No. 213376.

advice of the Admiralty, was that Britain had 'no desire whatever to encourage Norway to enter the war', but would 'come to her assistance to the utmost of our power in the event of an attack upon her by Germany'.[144] A very different perspective on the question was offered by a memorandum prepared by Crowe for the War Committee which argued that it would be to the advantage of the Allies if Norway was brought into the war.[145] The blockade would be strengthened first by the stoppage of all Norwegian exports to Germany; second by the diversion of the whole mercantile marine into the service of the Allies; and third by the opportunity to put greater pressure on Sweden, Denmark and the Netherlands. In addition Britain would obtain greater security for its own supplies from Norway, and the route to Archangel and Murmansk (when the railway to the latter port was completed) would be made safer. If, on the other hand, Norway gave in to German pressure, both the direct consequences and the indirect effects on other neutrals would be very great. There might be a chain reaction which, if it reached the United States, might force the Allies 'to abandon the blockade altogether'. For Crowe, as for the German naval authorities, Norway was a test case.

Crowe's memorandum swayed the War Committee in favour of a stronger line towards Norway. At its meeting on 31 October his views were strongly endorsed by McKenna (the chancellor of the exchequer) and Cecil, while Grey admitted that it would be 'disastrous' if Norway were allowed to 'cave in to Germany'.[146] At a further meeting on 2 November the members of the committee moved still further in favour of Norwegian involvement. As the prime minister summed up the debate, 'they were all agreed that they wanted Norway in. The only question was how to effect it – By assurances, or threats, or both?' It was left to Lloyd George to remind the War Committee of the limits of Allied capacity. 'We were', he said, 'suffering from the effect of not being able to support any ally who has come into the war with us.' Asquith agreed that 'it was a dangerous thing to offer to protect another small country unless we were able to do it'. The Committee nevertheless resolved to strengthen the diplomatic pressure it had authorised on 31 October. Grey was to reiterate the promise of support, but this time to add the warning that if Norway took any action to hamper trade with Great Britain, the consequence 'would be the cutting off of all overseas supplies for Norway'.[147]

While maintaining pressure on Norway, the British government had thus decided to do nothing which might precipitate Norwegian involvement in the war. Over the next two months the crisis between Norway and Germany remained in suspense and the Anglo-Norwegian copper dispute moved towards its climax, the imposition of the coal embargo on 22 December. It was against this background that the French again suggested that the Allies should consider the possibility that Norway might be forced into the war. On 11

---

[144] Telegram to Findlay, 27 October 1916, ibid., No. 215002.
[145] Crowe memorandum, 29 October 1916, ibid., No. 217609.
[146] CAB 42/22/13.   [147] CAB 42/23/3.

December 1916 the French commander-in-chief, Marshal Joffre, wrote to Robertson suggesting that the Allies should make preparations to meet a combined Swedish and German attack on Norway.[148] Although the likelihood of a Swedish attack was fanciful, the principal French fear remained a German attack on Norwegian nitrate plants. In the light of plans developed by Germany only a few months later, in the spring of 1917, this latter fear was by no means far-fetched. A second proposal came from Admiral Beatty, the commander-in-chief of the Grand Fleet. On 15 December he requested permission from the Admiralty to infringe Norway's territorial rights in order to intercept the traffic in contraband and prevent the passage of German raiders. If the result was to involve Norway in the war, Beatty wrote, 'I would point out that even with Norway as an enemy the situation would permit of the more effective use of our naval power, whilst with Norway as an ally the general strategic position would be immensely relieved.'[149]

The Admiralty's response was cautious. It accepted that if Norway was forced into the war by Germany it would be necessary for Britain to establish a base at Kristiansand, but found it 'difficult to see what advantage Germany would gain by hostilities with Norway'.[150] In a memorandum circulated to the War Cabinet on 30 December it accepted that there might be naval arguments in favour of involving Norway in the war but was worried about the political effect on other neutrals.[151] The War Cabinet too thought that Britain might lose its supplies from both Norway and Sweden, and asked Jellicoe to discuss with Beatty the possibility that other measures might be taken against German raiders.[152] The consensus at the beginning of 1917 was thus still against the idea of Norway's entering the war, or of seizing a naval base in the face of Norwegian opposition.[153] However, since rumours of impending British action continued to circulate in Stockholm, the Foreign Office asked the Admiralty for an authoritative statement of its views. On 3 March 1917 Howard was informed that the British government had 'definitely decided against the suggestion that they should seize a Naval base on the Norwegian Coast', and was authorised to make this statement known if he judged it appropriate.[154]

Denmark and Norway in 1917–1918

The intensification of submarine warfare from the summer of 1916 onwards, together with the debate on the resumption of an unrestricted U-boat

---

[148] ADM 137/1637.

[149] Beatty to Admiralty, 15 December 1916, ibid. See also Beatty to Balfour, 15 December 1916, quoted in Arthur J. Marder, *From the Dreadnought to Scapa Flow: The Royal Navy in the Fisher Era 1904–1919* (5 vols., London, 1961–70), vol. IV, p. 252.

[150] Admiralty to commander-in-chief of the Grand Fleet, 20 December 1916, ADM 137/1637.

[151] Ibid.   [152] War Cabinet meeting 23, 30 December 1916, CAB 23/1.

[153] Riste, *Neutral Ally*, p. 168.

[154] FO telegram to Howard, 3 March 1917, FO 371/3023, No. 48382.

campaign, led the German naval and military authorities for the first time to make detailed plans for operations against Denmark and Norway.[155] It was thought that the neutrals might be provoked into joining the Entente against Germany or, more plausibly, that Britain might seize the opportunity to launch a Baltic offensive or to establish a base on Norwegian territory. The Admiralty Staff had given serious consideration to the possibility of a British invasion of the Baltic as early as April 1916 but had decided that such action was improbable in view of the risks and the lack of plausible objectives.[156] Planning began in earnest in August 1916, when Romania's entry into the war prompted fears that Denmark, 'under the increasingly powerful influence of English propaganda', might take the same course.[157] Although the initiative came primarily from the navy, the General Staff was also worried about Danish sympathies.[158] The navy's plans, as they evolved in the autumn of 1916, rested on the premise that the army would have to occupy the Jutland peninsula and a number of the smaller islands. At first the General Staff was reluctant to spare any troops for such an operation, although Ludendorff ordered three cavalry regiments to be sent to North Schleswig to guard against a British landing as a precautionary measure in January 1917.[159] By April and May 1917, however, the high command had come to share the navy's fears.

German military intelligence indicated that Great Britain, supported by the United States, planned to establish a base at Kristiansand in southern Norway to combat the U-boat offensive. Ludendorff appears to have been particularly anxious at this prospect.[160] On 17 May 1917 the General Staff agreed to make sufficient troops available for an occupation of Jutland. The persistent distrust shown towards Denmark, especially by the German navy, created acute difficulties for German diplomacy. Brockdorff-Rantzau and the Auswärtiges Amt tried to reassure the navy of the Danish government's will to defend its neutrality and to persuade it of the political dangers of launching an unprovoked attack on Denmark. Brockdorff-Rantzau was particularly concerned that no irrevocable decision should be taken on the basis of reports from agents in Denmark and elsewhere, which were usually wholly without foundation. In order for his strategy to work, Brockdorff-Rantzau had to take Scavenius into his confidence; and Scavenius for his part had to provide the German minister with sufficient reassurance about Denmark's attitude to enable him to press his case with the highest authorities in Berlin.[161]

German nervousness was revealed in draft ultimatums sent to Brockdorff-Rantzau by the Reich Chancellery (Reichskanzlei) on 20 May 1917 for

[155] Walther Hubatsch, *Weserübung. Die deutsche Besetzung von Dänemark und Norwegen 1940* (Göttingen, 1960), pp. 11–12.
[156] Carl-Axel Gemzell, *Organization, Conflict and Innovation: A Study of German Naval Strategic Planning 1888–1940* (Lund, 1973), p. 163.
[157] Scheer to Holtzendorff, 30 August 1916, quoted ibid., p. 164 (n. 98).
[158] Sjøqvist, *Scavenius* I, pp. 237–55.
[159] Telegrams from Paget of 5, 9 and 22 February, FO 371/3078, Nos. 28664, 31086, 40788.
[160] Riste, *Neutral Ally*, p. 184.   [161] Sjøqvist, *Munch*, pp. 108–11.

presentation to the Danish government in the event of a British landing in Jutland or Norway. Brockdorff-Rantzau succeeded in modifying the tone of the draft notes, but it was only after further exchanges in July and August that the German military and naval authorities were convinced that the Danish government would in no circumstances make common cause with a power seeking to defeat Germany. On 25 September 1917 the new chancellor, Michaelis, told Brockdorff-Rantzau that it was no longer considered necessary to prepare an ultimatum to Denmark.

But if Denmark was relieved from diplomatic pressure, it was not out of danger. German naval planning for operations against Denmark continued at least until March 1918. And there was a growing emphasis on taking action unilaterally, irrespective of any British move against Denmark or Norway. Denmark was a major strategic objective in its own right, still more so in conjunction with Norway. For Prince Heinrich and for Admiral Scheer, the chief of the High Seas Fleet, northern Jutland was a potential base for the German fleet which would allow it to escape the confines of the Heligoland Bight. The occupation of Jutland was also the first stage in an operation aimed at controlling the northern Kattegat and the Skagerrak and thus dominating all the Scandinavian countries. It would, furthermore, 'create, here in the north, the necessary elbow-room, *the possibility of keeping the outlets to the ocean open in the future*'.[162] Here is the germ of the idea of acquiring bases in Scandinavia to enhance Germany's strategic position which was to play a prominent role in the debate on German naval strategy between the wars. It also reveals the intimate connection between Denmark and Norway in German naval thinking.[163]

Although the German navy had ruled out an invasion of Norway in December 1916, the Admiralty Staff was worried by the spring of 1917 that Britain might seek to establish bases on the south coast of the country. In an operational directive of 1 April 1917, Admiral von Holtzendorff stated that in order to counteract Britain's superior naval forces, Germany would have to occupy the Jutland peninsula, block the Kattegat with a large minefield, mine Norwegian harbours and shipping routes, and bomb Kristiania together with other ports and factories in southern Norway.[164] There was still no question of occupying Norwegian territory but there was serious cause for concern about the state of German–Norwegian relations. Negotiations for a major tonnage agreement between Britain and Norway had been in progress since February; and although the existence of the agreement, concluded in April 1917, remained 'Norway's best-kept war secret', the Norwegians knew that the Germans had their suspicions and feared reprisals if it came to their knowledge.[165] Tension between Norway and Germany increased in May with

[162] Prince Heinrich to Admiralty Staff, 30 April 1917, quoted in Gemzell, *Organization*, p. 171 (emphasis in original).
[163] Sjøqvist, *Scavenius I*, p. 254.   [164] Printed in Hubatsch, *Weserübung*, pp. 11–12.
[165] Riste, *Neutral Ally*, p. 178.

the German seizure, contrary to prize law, of the Norwegian ships *Thorunn* and *Harald Haarfagre*, and with the arrest in June of the German diplomatic courier Rautenfels (an adventurer of Finnish origin), with a large quantity of bombs which, it was assumed, were intended to be placed in merchant ships in Norwegian harbours.[166]

In the spring of 1917 the British authorities thus had every reason to take seriously the possibility of an outbreak of hostilities between Germany and Norway. In April the War Cabinet agreed that Norway should be supplied with anti-aircraft guns and aeroplanes to provide cover against the 'destruction of Norsk Hydro and other factories of military importance by airship attack'.[167] American intervention placed the question of Norwegian involvement in the war in a new light. As early as March 1917 Admiral Dawes, the outspokenly pro-Allied Norwegian commanding admiral, had spoken to Findlay about the possibility that the United States might occupy a base in Norway.[168] For Britain this would have the advantage that the United States would not be 'open to suspicion of desiring to keep a Gibraltar in the North'.[169] It would also enable the Royal Navy to economise on its overstretched resources. These considerations, together with its growing scepticism about the likelihood of Swedish intervention, led the Admiralty to look more favourably on the prospect of Norway's involvement in the war.[170] However, the War Office remained unconvinced, and it later emerged that the Admiralty was not 'proposing that any steps should be taken to encourage Norway to enter the war', but was merely 'concerned that all naval preparations should be made for that contingency should it present itself'.[171]

With the views of its military and naval advisers apparently opposed, the War Cabinet was understandably confused. After what one of its members, Lord Milner, described as a 'rather heated discussion' on Norway on 22 June 1917, the Cabinet could do no more than conclude that

it was desirable, on the one hand, to discourage Norway from entering the war, and on the other, not to convey the suggestion that the Allies were impotent to help her should she find herself forced to go to war. Our naval forces should at least be able to protect Norway from invasion by sea, and we could at least provide a certain amount of protection against Zeppelin raids.[172]

The War Cabinet decided, 'in view of . . . the serious factor which the

---

[166] Søhr, *Spioner og bomber*, pp. 72–98.
[167] Findlay telegram to FO, 7 April 1917, FO 371/3021, No. 81058; War Cabinet meeting 119, 16 April 1917, CAB 23/2.
[168] Bell, *Blockade*, p. 629.
[169] Findlay telegram to FO, 23 December 1917, FO 371/3025, No. 242594.
[170] Admiralty to FO, 7 May 1917, FO 371/3021, No. 93105.
[171] Director of military intelligence to FO, 11 June 1916, FO 371/3021, No. 116212; Admiralty to FO, 14 July 1917, ibid., No. 139784.
[172] War Cabinet meeting 168, CAB 23/3; Milner diary, 22 June 1917, quoted in Riste, *Neutral Ally*, p. 188.

Scandinavian countries may yet prove to be in determining the course of the war', to 'refer the whole question to the Cabinet Committee on War Policy for early consideration' and to ask the foreign secretary to consult the American ambassador on ways in which the United States 'would be prepared to co-operate in the event of Norway declaring war'. The Americans proved unresponsive.[173] However, the demand for clarity on the question of policy towards Norway and the other northern neutrals, voiced most vigorously by Cecil as minister of blockade, led to the establishment on 20 July of a 'Northern Neutrals Committee' under the chairmanship of Sir Edward Carson to investigate the position of the Scandinavian countries and the Netherlands.[174]

In their report of 27 August 1917 the majority of the Northern Neutrals Committee concluded that 'the intervention of these countries even on the side of the Allies would on the whole not be an advantage to the Allies'. They largely discounted the likelihood that Sweden would intervene on the side of the Central Powers and thought that Germany would invade Denmark only if it wished to launch an attack on Norway. The Allies could not, however, give any naval or military support to either Sweden or Denmark against Germany. The cases of the Netherlands and Norway were different, since Britain could do something to defend both countries against a German attack. The committee approved the Admiralty's contingency plans for establishing an advanced base at Kristiansand and urged that the situation regarding American cooperation should be clarified. The one dissenting voice was that of Lord Robert Cecil, who emphasised the 'important political and moral effect in Germany' of the entry into the war of any of the northern neutrals. It would convince the Germans of their increasing isolation and reinforce their fear of 'the economic effect of the loss of their markets after the war, and the destruction of the politico-commercial system that they have built up in various foreign countries'. They might indeed be so demoralised that they sued for peace. 'This consideration seems to counter-balance any strictly naval and military disadvantages that would attach to the declaration of war on Germany, at any rate by Norway.'[175]

The Admiralty had concurred in the committee's view that the entry of Norway into the war would be to the disadvantage of the Allies, thus apparently contradicting its earlier opinion. Findlay demanded an explanation of the Admiralty's change of view.[176] When the question was discussed by the War Cabinet on 7 September, Jellicoe stated that the Admiralty had been influenced by the heavy demands on both British and American naval resources necessitated by the introduction of convoys to combat the German submarine campaign.[177] The establishment of a base in Norway would impose further

---

[173] War Cabinet meeting 173, 2 July 1917, CAB 23/3; Riste, *Neutral Ally*, pp. 189–90.
[174] War Cabinet meeting 191, CAB 23/3.   [175] CAB 27/40.
[176] Telegram to FO, 4 September 1917, FO 371/3025, No. 173220.
[177] Admiralty memorandum, 'Reasons for Naval Staff's Change of Opinion Regarding Intervention of Norway', 6 September 1917, ADM 137/2711; War Cabinet meeting 225, CAB 23/4.

strains, although the Allies might be in a better position to help Norway by the spring. Findlay was therefore told that, while Norway's entry into the war was undesirable for the time being, he should encourage the Norwegians 'to take a firm line against German aggression'.[178]

The Admiralty's apparent vacillation over Norway was perhaps a by-product of the tremendous political pressure to which it was exposed as a result of the setbacks at sea during 1917. Lloyd George took the lead in pressing for a radical shake-up of its organisation and strategic thinking. The results included the introduction of convoys in the spring, a major reorganisation of the Admiralty's command structure and the dismissal first of Carson as first lord and then, in December 1917, of Jellicoe as first sea lord. The search for a more vigorous strategy led the Naval Staff in the autumn of 1917 to take a renewed interest in northern waters. The weakening position of the Russian Provisional Government prompted Jellicoe to ask Plans Division (established in July 1917) to consider the possibility of sending a fleet into the Baltic to relieve German naval pressure on Russia.[179] The conclusion, once again, was that no large-scale operation could be attempted 'without the previous destruction of the German fleet'.[180] Norway therefore remained the main focus of Admiralty interest, and the question was given a new dimension by the Allied decision, in September 1917, to adopt an American proposal to lay a mine barrage across the North Sea between the Orkneys and the Norwegian coast, in order to limit the operations of German submarines.[181]

The Northern Barrage

The Northern Barrage was a hugely ambitious project which was not begun until March 1918, but the British Naval Staff soon realised that if Norway entered the war on the Allied side, the mine barrier could be made far more effective – firstly because it could be extended into Norwegian territorial waters; secondly because a base on Norwegian territory would make it much easier to patrol the eastern end of the barrage. In October 1917 Plans Division argued strongly for establishing a base at Stavanger instead of Kristiansand. The former was a larger port and better placed for patrolling the barrage, and was less exposed to attack if Germany, either alone or in cooperation with Sweden, went to war against Norway.[182] The planners declared that

---

[178] Telegram to Findlay, 7 September 1917, FO 371/3025, No. 173220.

[179] Marder, *Dreadnought to Scapa Flow* IV, p. 243.

[180] Plans Division memorandum, 'Operations in the Baltic', 23 October 1917, ADM 137/2706.

[181] Rear-Admiral William Sowden Sims, *The Victory at Sea* (London, 1921), pp. 244–65; Bailey, *Policy of the United States*, pp. 410–12; Marder, *Dreadnought to Scapa Flow* V, p. 66; Riste, *Neutral Ally*, pp. 212–13.

[182] Plans Division memorandum, 'Norway and the Allies, Part I', 23 October 1917, ADM 137/2711.

The advantages that would accrue from the use of a base in Norway in connection with the future policy are so great that *it would seem advisable to establish a base here whether Norway has been previously forced into the war by Germany or not.*

There is reason to believe that Norway would not object to such action on our part, and might even welcome it as tending to bring the war to a more speedy conclusion.[183]

Their superiors at the Admiralty did not go so far. A Naval Staff memorandum of 6 December 1917 stressed the advantages to be gained by establishing a base at Stavanger but insisted that this must be secured only with Norwegian consent.[184] The Northern Neutrals Committee agreed that an attempt should be made to secure a base at Stavanger, with the assent of Norway, and that, 'provided Sweden remained neutral, it would be to our advantage for Norway to enter the war on our side'.[185] On 19 December the War Cabinet adopted the committee's recommendations that a diplomatic approach should be made to Norway and that the cooperation of the United States should be sought.[186]

Although Admiralty planning for the laying of the barrage proceeded officially 'on the assumption that no Norwegian base is likely to be available',[187] Beatty raised the idea of obtaining a port in Norway in January and February 1918, and the planners did not give up the idea of seizing a base by force.[188] In its detailed plans for establishing a base at Stavanger, drawn up in March 1918 shortly after mine-laying operations had begun, Plans Division wrote that 'Unless the political situation changes in such a manner as to render the Norwegian Government agreeable to our occupying a base in Norway, such occupation must be carried out as a *surprise, without previous notice,* and with adequate forces; the Norwegians can then plead "force majeure".'[189]

In early August 1918 the Anglo-American mine-laying operations reached the three-mile limit off the coast of Norway. The British and American governments had already begun to consider action to prevent German submarines from using Norwegian waters to evade the mine barrage, but they did not adopt the idea of seizing a base. Instead, Norway would be asked to lay mines in its own territorial waters to the east of the Northern Barrage.[190] On 7 August 1918, Findlay delivered a note demanding that Norway enforce its ban on the use of its waters by German submarines by laying a minefield, adding that this operation must be undertaken within four days.[191]

At a time when German–Norwegian relations were becoming more stable, with negotiations for a new trade agreement approaching their conclusion,

---

[183] Ibid. (emphasis in original).
[184] 'The Position of Norway', 6 December 1917, FO 371/3025, No. 242254.
[185] Memorandum of 14 December 1917, FO 371/3025, No. 238684.
[186] War Cabinet meeting 302, CAB 23/4.
[187] Operational directive quoted in Riste, *Neutral Ally*, p. 217.
[188] Marder, *Dreadnought to Scapa Flow* V, pp. 69–70.
[189] 'Establishment of a Base in the Stavanger Vicinity for a Detached Squadron', 29 March 1918, ADM 137/2711 (emphasis in original).
[190] Minutes of Imperial War Cabinet, 2 August 1918, quoted in Marder, *Dreadnought to Scapa Flow* V, p. 70.
[191] Riste, *Neutral Ally*, pp. 218–19.

Norway clearly wished to do nothing to antagonise Germany. On the other hand, it was assisted by the evident disparity between the attitude of Great Britain and that of its allies. The French and Italian representations in Kristiania were much milder than the British, while President Wilson declared that he was 'not in sympathy' with Britain's hard line towards Norway.[192] There were also divisions of opinion in Britain itself. On 12 August the Norwegian government returned a conciliatory note, rejecting the idea of laying mines but promising increased vigilance in the area concerned. This was regarded as insufficient, and Beatty was ordered to mine Norwegian waters without warning and in the face of probable Norwegian resistance. At this he drew the line, arguing that quite apart from numerous practical objections, notably the likelihood that the Norwegians would sweep the mines as soon as they had been laid, such action might do 'irreparable injury . . . to the good relations of two friendly navies and two friendly countries'.[193] To his own officers, Beatty spoke even more forcefully. It would, he said, 'be most repugnant to the officers and men in the Grand Fleet to steam in overwhelming strength into the waters of a small, but high-spirited people and coerce them'. If blood were shed, it 'would constitute a crime as bad as any the Germans had committed elsewhere'.[194]

The British therefore confined their efforts to persuasion. Realising, however, that compliance was unavoidable in the long run, Ihlen's subsequent diplomatic efforts were aimed at acceding with as little damage as possible to relations with Germany. He made it clear that the operation would be directed against all belligerent submarines and that legitimate merchant shipping would be unaffected. Two weeks after the signature of the German–Norwegian trade agreement of 14 September 1918, the Norwegian government announced its decision to lay a minefield for the purpose of enforcing its submarine decree. The German reaction was remarkably mild, probably because by the time the mine-laying operations were completed, in mid-October 1918, Germany had more pressing matters to worry about. Although Bailey points out that Norway had every right to lay mines in its own waters, a right already exercised by Sweden and Denmark, Riste concludes that the Norwegian operation was an act which went beyond Norway's obligations as a neutral.[195] It had been undertaken out of necessity because Britain had made it clear that it would take action if the Norwegians did not. Norway was lucky that it had taken place at such a late stage of the war: 'it is open to question whether Germany at a different time would have been satisfied with critical commentaries'.[196]

[192] Quoted ibid., p. 221.
[193] Memorandum by Balfour, 22 August 1918, quoted in Marder, *Dreadnought to Scapa Flow* V, p. 71.
[194] Paraphrased and quoted in Sir Henry Newbolt, *History of the Great War: Naval Operations*, vol. V (London, 1931), p. 349.
[195] Bailey, *Policy of the United States*, p. 419; Riste, *Neutral Ally*, pp. 223–4.
[196] Riste, *Neutral Ally*, p. 224.

The Åland question

If Norway's most conspicuously pro-Allied action went largely unremarked in the closing weeks of the war, Sweden was equally fortunate in being spared the consequences of a potentially far more dangerous dichotomy in its conduct towards the belligerents. In May 1918, at virtually the same time as the successful conclusion of a trade agreement with the Allied and Associated Powers, Sweden entered into an agreement with Germany over the Åland Islands which effectively acknowledged German hegemony – the 'German Monroe Doctrine' – in the Baltic region. By 1917–18 the future of the Åland Islands had become a contentious issue.[197] On the Swedish side, there was a desire for the permanent demilitarisation of the islands and, in conservative and activist circles, for annexation.[198] King Gustav V in particular remained preoccupied with the idea of Swedish sovereignty over the Ålands.[199] In Russia both the tsarist government (which had fortified the islands in January 1915) and its successor, the Provisional Government, aimed in the long term at the removal of the 'Åland servitude' of 1856.[200] Germany had used the offer of sovereignty over the islands as a bait to lure Sweden into an alliance in 1915, and did so again in an attempt to influence Swedish policy in 1917–18. In addition, some leading German industrialists advocated annexing the islands to Germany in order to prevent Britain from cutting off supplies of iron ore from Sweden in a future war.[201] Finally, the Åland Islands became an issue in the domestic politics of Finland (which declared its independence on 6 December 1917), as well as in relations between Finland, Germany and Sweden. The Swedish-speaking population of the islands expressed their desire to be rejoined to Sweden, while the Finnish government was determined not to relinquish its sovereignty over them.

German interest in the Åland Islands, largely dormant since the abortive overtures to Sweden of 1915, revived in 1917. The renewed German offensive against Petrograd in the summer heightened the importance of the islands as one of the outlying defences of the Russian capital. Ludendorff considered occupying the islands but was eventually persuaded that the operation was impracticable and that it would impede the forthcoming peace negotiations

---

[197] Göran Rystad, 'Die deutsche Monroedoktrin der Ostsee. Die Alandsfrage und die Entstehung des deutsch–schwedischen Geheimabkommens vom Mai 1918', in *Probleme deutscher Zeitgeschichte* (Stockholm, 1971), pp. 1–75; James Barros, *The Aland Islands Question: Its Settlement by the League of Nations* (New Haven, Conn., and London, 1968), chs. 1–3; Gihl, *Den svenska utrikespolitikens historia* IV, pp. 339–91.

[198] Schuberth, *Schweden und das Deutsche Reich*, pp. 127–34, 144–71.

[199] In February 1917 he took the opportunity of a visit to Copenhagen to ask King Christian to suggest to the tsar that he should cede the islands to Sweden at the end of the war. The king replied that Gustav might do the same for him in Berlin regarding Schleswig. The matter was not pursued: Carlgren, *Ministären Hammarskjöld*, pp. 276–9. For a discussion of Gustav's preoccupation with the Ålands, see Carlgren, 'Gustaf V', p. 47.

[200] Barros, *Aland Islands Question*, p. 59.

[201] Rystad, 'Die deutsche Monroedoktrin der Ostsee', pp. 27–8.

with the new Bolshevik regime in Russia (these opened at Brest-Litovsk in December 1917). The political leadership thought differently. Richard von Kühlmann, the new secretary of state at the Auswärtiges Amt, was attracted by the idea of occupying the islands as a means of strengthening Germany's hold over Sweden both in the short term and after the end of the war.[202] Since, however, Germany lacked the means to carry out the operation, Kühlmann fell back on the option that had been raised earlier in the war: a Swedish occupation of the Åland Islands under German auspices.

Aware of King Gustav V's personal interest in the Åland question, Kühlmann made two secret overtures to the king, on 11 November and 17 December 1917, behind the back of Sweden's new left-wing government. The first requested 'an unofficial but authentic reply' to the question of what the king's attitude would be if Germany captured Åland and then offered the islands for occupation by Swedish troops.[203] Following discussions with his ministers, the king returned a noncommittal reply which did not reject the German offer outright, but suggested that the question could best be discussed at a future peace conference. The second approach referred to the desire of the Åland islanders themselves for union with Sweden and promised to raise the issue in negotiations with Russia on certain conditions, including an increase in iron ore exports to Germany after the war. The king's reply was again cautious but the government clearly took this second German offer seriously. It sent a note on 23 December to Germany, Austria and Turkey (both of the latter powers being signatories of the Paris peace treaty of 1856) requesting that Sweden's interests in the Åland question should be safeguarded in the Brest-Litovsk negotiations. The note did not raise the question of sovereignty but asked that Russia should promise to dismantle the fortifications erected during the war, and proposed complete neutralisation as the best long-term solution to the status of the islands.

Unlike his French and Italian colleagues, Howard was not angered by the terms of the Swedish note. He advised the Foreign Office that Sweden was more likely than either Finland or Russia to keep the Ålands out of Germany's hands, and that Swedish possession of the islands was likely to set up a conflict of interests with Germany, the power striving for Baltic hegemony. Conversely, it would 'create an identity of interests between Sweden, with her control of the entrance to the Baltic, and ourselves in combating the powers having naval domination in that sea'.[204] On 2 January 1918 Kühlmann responded positively to the Swedish note. On 9 February, shortly before Trotsky dramatically broke off the negotiations at Brest-Litovsk, Kühlmann raised the prospect of neutralising the islands, but since this was of no advantage to Germany while

---

[202] Kühlmann's aim was to reach a peace settlement with Britain as quickly as possible; his philosophy, according to Fritz Fischer, was 'one of withdrawal in the west and security in the east and overseas': Fritz Fischer, *Germany's Aims in the First World War* (London, 1967), pp. 410–11.

[203] Rystad, 'Die deutsche Monroedoktrin der Ostsee', p. 16.

[204] Despatch of 11 January 1918, quoted in Barros, *Aland Islands Question*, p. 68.

the war lasted, the terms of the German–Russian treaty eventually concluded on 3 March merely stipulated that the Åland fortifications were 'to be removed as soon as possible', with their future status reserved for treatment by a 'special agreement' between Germany, Finland, Russia and Sweden, in consultation with 'other countries bordering upon the Baltic Sea'.[205]

As the Brest-Litovsk talks continued, however, the Åland question became increasingly intractable. On 4 January 1918 Sweden recognised Finnish independence without reservation, but the king still hankered after annexation, a solution which was being demanded with increasing urgency by the Ålanders themselves as the political situation in Finland deteriorated. Following the outbreak of the Finnish civil war at the end of January, the Finnish Whites appealed to both Germany and Sweden for assistance. Germany's foreign policy leadership did not wish to intervene while negotiations with the Bolsheviks were in progress, but tried to persuade the Swedes to do so. Prince Viktor von Wied visited Stockholm in February with the message that intervention offered the last and only chance for Sweden to acquire the Åland Islands. Even the king realised, however, that a military expedition to Finland was a political impossibility. Meanwhile, within the German military leadership and even in the Auswärtiges Amt, opinion was moving against the idea of Swedish possession of the islands. In the light of the trade negotiations in progress between Sweden and Great Britain, Ludendorff had now come round to the view that Finland was a more reliable ally than Sweden: moreover, the Finns had held out the prospect that they might cede the islands to Germany in return for military assistance.

On 13 February 1918 reports (greatly exaggerated) of atrocities committed by Russian soldiers on Åland led the Swedish government to decide to send an expedition to the islands – the 'first time troops had left Swedish territory in 110 years'.[206] Humanitarian motives were ostensibly uppermost, but there is little doubt that the king and queen, as well as the minister of marine, Erik Palmstierna, were thinking primarily in terms of annexation. A week later, however, the Germans themselves decided to occupy the islands. They did so in response to a new request for military support from the Finnish Whites (itself prompted by the German military high command following the breaking-off of the Brest-Litovsk negotiations by Trotsky). The Swedes were informed of the German decision on 21 February and ordered to remove their own forces from the islands, but were subsequently appeased by a decision that the islands should be divided between the occupying forces of the two countries.

After Brest-Litovsk, and in the light of the devastating success of Ludendorff's March offensive on the western front, an increasingly assertive note entered

[205] Article VI of Treaty of Brest-Litovsk, printed in John W. Wheeler-Bennett, *Brest-Litovsk: The Forgotten Peace March 1918* (London, 1938), pp. 406–7.
[206] The Swedish minister in Washington, quoted in Barros, *Aland Islands Question*, p. 80 (n. 49).

into German statements on Baltic questions in general and on the Ålands in particular.[207] They conveyed the message that the war had resulted in a wholly new situation in the Baltic. Germany had won the right to shape the future of the region and Russia was no longer a factor of any significance. Non-Baltic powers were to be excluded from a position of influence – the Baltic agreement of 1908 was cited as a model for future arrangements – and Sweden must face the fact that a settlement of the Åland question was impossible except on Germany's terms. Scandinavian cooperation was desirable as a means of excluding Western influence from the region and erecting a barrier against 'Slavdom and Bolshevism', and for this a close relationship between Sweden and Finland was vital. But however insistent German propaganda might be, the Swedes could not ignore more subtle reminders that the Entente still had a voice in Baltic affairs and the means to make its wishes felt. Howard took every opportunity to assure the Swedish foreign minister that Britain favoured Swedish sovereignty over the Ålands, but that this must be achieved through agreement with the Entente – Britain and France were, unlike Sweden or Germany, signatories of the 1856 treaty – and, if possible, by means of an understanding between Sweden and Finland. At a time when Sweden was negotiating for a trade agreement with the Western powers, these arguments were undoubtedly persuasive. Howard was able to observe with satisfaction the way in which Swedish conservatives were coming to regard Germany rather than Russia as the chief threat to Sweden.[208]

In the meantime, however, Sweden had to extricate itself from its Åland entanglements. The Swedish occupation of the islands had led to bitter recriminations with Finland; the German occupation had resulted in a severe loss of prestige for Sweden; the Western powers had indicated that no solution could be reached without their participation. On 25 April the government finally decided to remove Swedish troops from the islands. A few days later Sweden secured German agreement to the publication of a communiqué announcing that Sweden, Germany and Finland were prepared in principle to start negotiations for dismantling the Åland fortifications. The Swedish government appeared to have achieved its immediate objectives: Sweden had not retreated in the face of Finnish protests, and a solution to the fortifications question was in sight. It still held to the view that a definitive settlement of the status of the Åland Islands (entailing, so it hoped, a decision in favour of Swedish sovereignty) could be achieved only through the agreement of all the signatories of the Paris treaty of 1856.

The German government acted swiftly to disabuse the Swedes of the notion that Britain and France could have any say in Baltic affairs. The Swedish minister in Berlin was informed on 8 May of Germany's 'astonishment' that Sweden was still seeking to draw the Western powers into the question. Two

---

[207] Press and pamphlet literature (inspired by Auswärtiges Amt) summarised in Rystad, 'Die deutsche Monroedoktrin der Ostsee', pp. 36–43.
[208] McKercher, *Howard*, pp. 191–4.

days later the Swedish foreign minister was told that in Germany's opinion the Åland servitude had lapsed with Russia's fortification of the islands in 1915, and that the question would now be regulated exclusively by the treaty of Brest-Litovsk and the German–Finnish peace treaty of March 1918. The Western powers had no role to play in this or any other Baltic question. In this alarming situation the Swedish government decided to send Trolle to negotiate in Berlin for the second time within a month. On 17 May he achieved a compromise by which Sweden avoided a public acceptance of Germany's interpretation of the 1856 treaty, but secretly promised to enter into no negotiations with the Western powers on the Åland question without Germany's prior consent. When the Swedish government discussed the agreement on 21 May, both the prime minister and the foreign minister spoke in favour of acceptance. Sweden had no choice in view of Germany's dominant position in the Baltic, and the Western powers had, after all, stated that Sweden had no rights under the 1856 convention. After initial disagreements, the government decided to accept the agreement. Sweden's right to a say in the Åland question would henceforth depend on Germany, but at least Sweden would possess such a right – something which both Germany and the Western powers had hitherto denied.

Sweden had had to pay a very high price for Germany's concession on the dismantlement question.[209] The government had tried to avoid becoming dependent on Germany or antagonising the Entente. Now, however, a left-wing government had entered into an agreement which entailed precisely those dangers which it had striven so long to evade. Yet it seemed reasonable to assume, in the spring of 1918, that Germany would remain the dominant power in the Baltic, and that Sweden must adapt itself to that reality. No one could have anticipated the sudden collapse of German military power that occurred in the autumn. Even in the absence of a decisive German victory, therefore, Sweden would have to rely on Germany if it wished to achieve a satisfactory solution to the Åland question. Germany's defeat in November 1918 naturally led to the lapse of the agreement of 17 May. The Åland question now became one of the many to be dealt with by the peacemakers at Paris, and ultimately by the League of Nations. That Germany had not lost sight of its long-term goals is, however, made clear by a letter of 13 January 1919 to Lucius from Brockdorff-Rantzau, now German foreign minister.[210] It was no longer possible, he said, to exclude the Western powers from the Baltic; a Swedish–Finnish agreement on the demilitarisation of the Åland Islands was thus preferable to an international agreement from the German point of view. Agreements concluded by Baltic powers among themselves were still the best way to deny the Entente, especially Great Britain, a legal pretext to meddle in Baltic affairs. Demilitarisation of the Ålands was also in Germany's interest

---

[209] Rystad, 'Die deutsche Monroedoktrin der Ostsee', pp. 60–1.
[210] Cited (but with no indication of the source) ibid., pp. 64–5.

since it was the best means of keeping the Gulf of Bothnia open and securing German supplies of Swedish iron ore.

Scandinavian neutrality and the First World War

The longer the First World War lasted, the more it became an ideological war. To a much greater extent than the Central Powers, the Western Allies were able to appeal to universal principles in support of their war effort: these were enshrined most famously in Woodrow Wilson's Fourteen Points. The Scandinavian neutrals were thus exposed to the claim that since the West was fighting for values which they shared, they should make a more wholehearted commitment – either by being more accommodating in matters of war trade, or by actually entering the war on the Allied side. In practice, such claims were not made very often or very loudly or very explicitly. Though neutrals were expected to bend their neutrality, their right to remain neutral was not seriously challenged. The neutrals were able to retain at least a toehold on the moral high ground.

Allied representatives, it is true, were frequently exasperated by the prevarication of Scandinavian leaders and disgusted by the profiteering of Scandinavian businessmen and ship-owners. Howard wrote in his memoirs that the Swedes, like other neutrals (including Great Britain in other wars), were *tertii gaudentes*, because 'the one object of neutral Powers is to make all the money they can out of war by trading with belligerents and thus, intentionally or not, helping to prolong war to the latest hour possible'.[211] Sometimes this attitude came out into the open, as when Findlay asserted that the inflated price of Norwegian copper was 'the price of blood, – the blood of a friendly people to whom Norway would necessarily look for assistance in time of need'.[212] And the disdain is still palpable in one of the most arresting passages in Bell's official history of the blockade, completed in the 1930s, where Scandinavian responses to German submarine warfare are contrasted with their protests against British controls:

The seamen who thus lost their lives were, for the most part, poor, seafaring folk, who think of death at sea as a writ of destiny delivered and executed. No neutral government was embarrassed, and fashionable society in the northern capitals was not shocked by the death of a wealthy, influential citizen . . .

For the time being, therefore, the German system was better adjusted to general circumstances than the British: the German submarines had bereaved a few poor Scandinavian families . . . we had openly defied the most influential plutocracy in the world.[213]

However, morality also acted as a constraint on the belligerents, most strikingly with Beatty's repugnance at the thought of shedding of Norwegian blood – 'a crime as bad as any the Germans had committed elsewhere'.

[211] Howard, *Theatre of Life* II, p. 225; McKercher, *Howard*, p. 150.
[212] Quoted in Hecksher et al., *Sweden*, p. 335.   [213] Bell, *Blockade*, p. 422.

No doubt such scruples would have been overcome had the situation been judged sufficiently serious. But that moment never came and the Scandinavian states did not become directly involved in the war. Why not? Formal neutrality regulations had little relevance, as the fate of Hammarskjöld's attempts to uphold them made clear. Nor do the belligerents appear to have been influenced by their obligations under the Norwegian integrity treaty of 1907, to which the Norwegian government in any case made few references in its published pronouncements.[214] The actions of Scandinavian governments clearly played an important part, yet in the last resort Scandinavian statesmen had little influence on the decisions taken by the belligerents. Ihlen's diplomacy was frequently criticised, but nothing could have prevented Norwegian neutrality from being radically compromised in favour of the Allies in the last two years of the war. Sweden was perhaps 'the neutral victor', but it was saved from the consequences of German hegemony and its own Åland ambitions only by Allied victory at the end of 1918. Scavenius was an able diplomat but it has been suggested that Denmark's fate was 'determined by the interests of the great powers rather than by the technical skill of Danish diplomacy' – a judgement which Scavenius himself might have endorsed given his ruthless realism and his pre-war views on the relative unimportance of the Scandinavian theatre to the great powers.[215]

Scandinavian neutrality survived because it was useful to both sides, and because neither side achieved an absolute preponderance of power in northern Europe. The German submarine campaign could not destroy Allied superiority at sea, but on the other hand Germany's proximity to Denmark and its defeat of Russia helped to mitigate the Allied stranglehold over Scandinavian trade. In 1908 a British Admiralty planner had described the Scandinavian countries as 'hovering between the Sea Power and the Land Power' and had predicted that 'from their geographical position' they were 'almost certain to be drawn into the struggle in certain eventualities'.[216] That prediction had not been fulfilled. In consequence, it was possible to believe that neutrality had worked. Immediately after the war, admittedly, the Scandinavian countries were to relinquish neutrality in favour of membership of the new League of Nations. But there were always mental reservations, and neutrality again became their refuge when the international situation deteriorated in the late 1930s. By then, however, the conditions of their existence had been transformed. The ideological claims of the belligerents in the Second World War were more insistent, Scandinavian neutrality held fewer advantages and the balance of power in northern Europe had been destroyed.

---

[214] Patrick Salmon, *Foreign Policy and National Identity: The Norwegian Integrity Treaty 1907–1924* (Oslo, 1993), pp. 13–15.

[215] Carsten Due-Nielsen, 'Denmark and the First World War', *Scandinavian Journal of History* 10 (1985), pp. 1–18 (p. 12).

[216] ADM 116/1043B, part I.

5   The Nordic countries between the wars

Although they had made no direct contribution to the Allied victory, the Nordic countries were substantial net beneficiaries of the peace settlement. Their security had been enhanced by the destruction of Germany and Russia as great powers, apparently for the foreseeable future. The League of Nations, which derived in part from Scandinavian ideas and initiatives, offered a new approach to international security.[1] All four countries saw the end of the war as an opportunity for territorial expansion. For Denmark, of course, it was a matter of regaining territory lost in 1864. Following a plebiscite in 1920, the northern part of Slesvig was returned to Denmark, leaving a small Danish minority to the south of the new frontier and a rather larger German minority to the north.[2] Sweden laid claim to the Åland Islands. Having relied on German patronage in 1918, the Swedes turned in 1919 to the Paris peace conference, which then referred the question to the League of Nations.[3] In 1921 the League decided that the islands should remain in Finnish possession but with a large measure of self-determination, and that they should also be demilitarised. Sweden was thus the only Nordic country which did not gain territorially at the end of the war; but Swedish discomfiture, though vocal for a while, was relatively short-lived.[4]

Independent Finland sought to extend the historic frontiers of the Grand Duchy into East Karelia, the cradle of Finnish culture, and northward to the Arctic Ocean. The peacemakers gave Finland an Arctic port at Petsamo but refused to satisfy its designs on Karelia – a source of lasting resentment to Finnish nationalists.[5] Norway's ambitions extended into the Arctic region and

[1] S. Shepherd Jones, *The Scandinavian States and the League of Nations* (Princeton, N. J., 1939; repr. New York, 1969), chs. 3–4.

[2] H. W. V. Temperley (ed.) *A History of the Peace Conference of Paris* (6 vols., London, 1920–3), vol. II (London, 1920), pp. 197–206; Troels Fink, *Da Sønderjylland blev delt 1918–1920* (3 vols., Åbenrå, 1979).

[3] James Barros, *The Åland Islands Question: Its Settlement by the League of Nations* (New Haven, Conn., and London, 1968).

[4] Herbert Tingsten, *The Debate on the Foreign Policy of Sweden 1918–1939* (London, 1949), pp. 132–7.

[5] FO memorandum, 'Finland', October 1918, ADM 116/3235; Earl Curzon to Lord Acton (Helsinki), 18 February 1920, *DBFP*, 1, XI, pp. 222–3; Eino Lyytinen, *Finland in British Politics in the First World War* (Helsinki, 1980), pp. 146–51, 165–9; Juhani Paasivirta, *The Victors in World War I and Finland* (Helsinki, 1965), ch. 8.

still farther afield. They were fuelled by the conviction that Norway deserved some reward for its sacrifices in the Allied cause during the war.[6] Ideas that Norway should take over a German colony or lay claim to Russia's Murman coast were soon dismissed,[7] but the pre-war drive towards a 'greater Norway' in the far north was resumed with determination. Its greatest triumph came in 1920 when the peace conference recognised Norwegian sovereignty over the Svalbard (Spitsbergen) archipelago.[8] However, Norway continued to press its historic claims to East Greenland, while in 1921 Denmark extended its sovereignty, formerly confined to the west, over the whole island. Persistent friction between Norway and Denmark culminated in a major crisis when Norwegian adventurers laid claim to the territory in 1931. It was resolved only when the international court of justice at The Hague decided in favour of Denmark in April 1933. Finally, Iceland moved closer to independence. Under the act of union of December 1918 it became a sovereign state under the Danish crown, with a right to demand a revision of the act at any time after 1940.

Scandinavia and the post-war world

Between the wars Scandinavia came into its own. At meetings of the new League of Nations in Geneva, statesmen like Branting and Nansen lectured the great powers on their responsibilities and were listened to attentively. Scandinavia became a 'social laboratory'; its experiments in health, education and welfare – the 'Oslo breakfast' in Norwegian schools, the Danish folk high schools, Swedish consumer cooperatives and so on – were eagerly studied and reported, each country vying to be seen as a model of enlightened progress.[9] Sweden, above all, seemed to have achieved an almost miraculous 'middle way' between the excesses of unrestrained capitalism on the one hand and collectivisation on the other; or, put another way, between fascism and communism.[10] Where Shaw and the Webbs saw Soviet Russia as the archetype of the new civilisation, a younger generation of Anglo-Saxon socialists looked

---

[6] FO 'Memorandum on Norwegian and Danish Questions', 16 December 1918, ADM 116/ 2055.

[7] Reidar Omang, *Norsk utenrikstjeneste*, vol. II, *Stormfulle tider 1913–1928* (Oslo, 1959), pp. 260–77; F. Wedel Jarlsberg, *Reisen gjennem livet* (Oslo, 1932), pp. 366–72; Roald Berg, *Norsk utenrikspolitikks historie*, vol. II, *Norge på egen hånd 1905–1920* (Oslo, 1995), pp. 260–4.

[8] Trygve Mathisen, *Svalbard i internasjonal politikk 1871–1925* (Oslo, 1951); Roald Berg, 'Spitsbergen-saken 1905–1925', *Historisk tidsskrift* (Norway) 72 (1993), pp. 443–57; Berg, *Norsk utenrikspolitikks historie* II, pp. 272–87.

[9] See e.g. O. B. Grimley, *The New Norway: A People with the Spirit of Cooperation* (Oslo, 1939) (pp. 124–6 on the Oslo breakfast); Peter Manniche, *Denmark: A Social Laboratory* (Copenhagen, 1939); Sir E. D. Simon, *The Smaller Democracies* (London, 1939), a Left Book Club publication covering Switzerland, Sweden, Denmark, Norway and Finland.

[10] Marquis W. Childs, *Sweden: The Middle Way* (New Haven, Conn., 1936; revised and enlarged edn, 1938).

to Sweden.[11] Finland, independent since 1917, did not enjoy the same measure of international esteem. It was a much poorer society than its neighbours and, in the aftermath of civil war and revolution, it was politically divided and inward-looking. Its leaders concentrated on the construction of a Finnish national identity free from Swedish cultural dominance and based their claim to be an outpost of Western civilisation on their defeat of Bolshevism.[12] Yet the inter-war period also witnessed a growing sense of a common identity among the peoples of northern Europe – an identity which was increasingly termed 'Nordic' rather than 'Scandinavian' as Finland turned its back on the Russian borderlands and emphasised the cultural, political and social values that it shared with its Scandinavian neighbours.

There was nevertheless another side to Scandinavian life: the inconvenience of temperance and prohibition (in Norway 1921–7 and Finland 1919–32), the grinding poverty and monotony of rural life, a stifling bourgeois moralism and convention. Between the end of the war and the early 1930s public life was marred by political instability and pecuniary irresponsibility, the legacy of wartime profiteering exacerbated by lax financial controls. It was a febrile era which reached its apotheosis in the figure of the Swedish 'match king' Ivar Kreuger, who committed suicide in 1932 after the collapse of his multinational enterprises.

The striking juxtaposition of modernity and conservatism, of prosperity and egalitarianism, which characterised inter-war Scandinavia reflected the impact of rapid economic change on what were still in many respects traditional societies. For the inter-war period, despite its economic instability and chronic unemployment, was one of growth for all the Nordic economies. Between 1919 and 1939 annual growth rates averaged 2.7 per cent in Denmark, 3.0 per cent in Norway, 3.3 per cent in Sweden and as much as 5.3 per cent in Finland.[13] All four economies were still 'robust and in modern industrial terms relatively young',[14] with inherent tendencies to growth which asserted themselves even during the inter-war period: most vigorously in Finland, the most backward of the four economies, least in Denmark owing to its heavy reliance on agricultural exports. As in the early phase of industrialisation, technological innovation, capital investment, an increasingly well-qualified work force and the occupational shift from fishing, farming and forestry to manufacturing industry all played their part in the process of development and

---

[11] Margaret Cole and Charles Smith (eds.), *Democratic Sweden: A Volume of Studies Prepared by Members of the New Fabian Research Bureau* (London, 1938).

[12] Juhani Paasivirta, *Finland and Europe: The Early Years of Independence 1917–1939* (Helsinki, 1988), pp. 321–5.

[13] Hans Chr. Johansen et al., 'Hovedlinier in den økonomiske udvikling i de nordiske lande i mellemkrigstiden', in *Kriser och krispolitik i Norden i mellankrigstiden. Nordiska historikermötet in Uppsala 1974. Mötesrapport* (Uppsala, 1974), pp. 13–26 (p. 19).

[14] Karl-Gustaf Hildebrand, 'Economic Policy in Scandinavia During the Inter-War Period', *Scandinavian Economic History Review* 23 (1975), pp. 99–115 (p. 101) (a review of *Kriser och krispolitik*).

diversification – though not always rapidly enough to counteract high unemployment in the less dynamic sectors.

The small size and openness of the Nordic economies meant that they were directly affected by the fluctuations of the international economy. Whilst they imported a wide range of goods, both raw materials and finished products, their exports were still concentrated on a few major commodities: agricultural produce, iron ore, iron and steel products, timber and paper products, fish and shipping services. Primary products and semi-finished goods were the ones most directly affected by the endemic crisis of the inter-war period, and shipping also suffered from any downturn in the world economy. But, if dependence on foreign markets was a source of vulnerability, it was also a means by which the Nordic countries could share in the economic revival of larger economies. The building boom in Britain in the 1930s stimulated Scandinavian timber exports; rearmament in Germany, and later in Britain, led to a growing demand for Swedish iron ore. There was also, especially in the 1930s, a marked shift towards the domestic market. Protection for agriculture and the encouragement of new industries provided a surer basis for prosperity than uncertain markets overseas.

Finally, there were significant differences in economic policy on the part of Nordic governments and central banks. In the 1920s, policy amounted to little more than regaining and maintaining the gold standard; but the social and political impact of the great depression, together with the abandonment of the gold standard in 1931, made an independent economic policy both more necessary and more feasible. With the coming to power of social democratic parties in all four countries between 1929 and 1937, the scene was set for experiments in economic management. Some of these attracted wide attention as expressions of a new counter-cyclical philosophy which, in the guise of 'Keynesianism', was to be adopted throughout western Europe after the Second World War.[15]

At the end of the First World War there were manifestations of political upheaval in all three Scandinavian countries, while in Finland the achievement of independence was accompanied by an 'abortive revolution' and a bitter civil war between Reds and Whites.[16] The post-war years witnessed a conflict within Scandinavian socialist movements between reformism and the ideology of social revolution which was not to be resolved until the 1930s. At the same time there was a prolonged crisis of parliamentary politics, marked by a succession of minority governments led variously by conservatives, liberals and socialists. This too came to an end only with the great depression, which

[15] For a discussion of the extent to which there was a connection between Keynes and Swedish economists, see the review article by Bo Gustafsson, 'A Perennial of Doctrinal History: Keynes and "The Stockholm School"', *Economy and History* 16 (1973), pp. 114–28.

[16] The phrase comes from Risto Alapuro, *State and Revolution in Finland* (Berkeley, Los Angeles and London, 1988).

brought about a realignment based on a rapprochement between the political representatives of the two key interest groups in Scandinavian societies: farmers and workers. The relative ease with which such conflicts were resolved may reflect an innate spirit of compromise, but it also resulted from a process of hard political bargaining in which there were losers as well as winners. Nor did the 1930s see the end of political extremism. On the contrary, Norway, Denmark and Sweden all produced local variants of fascism or Nazism; and in the Lapua (or Lappo) movement Finland evolved its own home-grown version of right-wing extremism, a compound of religious fundamentalism, anti-communism and xenophobia.

The class antagonisms and political polarisation which characterised the immediate post-war period resulted in part from the privations of war and resentment against those who had profited from trading with the belligerents. They also reflected the influence of events in Russia. Contacts between Scandinavian socialists and the leaders of the Russian revolutionary movement were close. Scandinavia and Finland formed part of the 'northern underground',[17] one of the main routes by which revolutionaries travelled in and out of Russia both before and during the war, and the Socialist International met at Stockholm in June 1917. But class conflict was also an expression of long-term problems of adjustment to economic and political modernisation: the relatively late democratisation of Sweden and Denmark; rapid industrialisation and working-class isolation in Norway and Finland; the declining influence of liberalism and the rise of new parties representing the interests of the rural population.

In the early 1930s 'crisis agreements' between Agrarians and Socialists brought to Scandinavian politics the stability that had hitherto been lacking. The details varied from one country to another, but the essence was support for agriculture in exchange for a free hand to deal with the economic crisis and introduce measures of social reform. On 30 January 1933 (the day Hitler came into power), the Danish government concluded the 'Kanslergade agreement' with the Liberals. In Sweden, the minority Socialist government formed in 1932 reached a crisis agreement with the Agrarians in 1933 and the two parties became coalition partners in 1936. In Norway the Agrarians and the Labour Party made a pact which turned the minority Liberal government out of office and brought Labour to power in 1935. Finland followed a similar pattern, though somewhat later. In 1936 Agrarians and Socialists made an electoral agreement to contain the threat from the extreme right and to deal with the economic crisis which enabled them, together with the Liberals, to form a coalition government in 1937.

The agrarians had little to sacrifice in the way of ideology and gained much in terms of practical assistance. For the socialists, especially in Norway, compromise with other parties and with existing institutions required a greater

<hr />

[17] Michael Futrell, *Northern Underground: Episodes of Russian Revolutionary Transport and Communications Through Scandinavia and Finland 1863–1917* (London, 1963).

ideological adjustment. Economic crisis and the challenge of the extreme right provided the necessary impetus. The final compromise was with capitalism itself. In Norway and Sweden, the fact that socialist parties were in power with policies that were intended to save capitalism and not destroy it created a climate conducive to partnership between labour and business. The 'Main Agreement' of 1935 between the Norwegian trade union organisation and employers' federation was followed in 1938 by the more famous Saltsjöbaden Agreement between their Swedish counterparts. Socialist parties now appealed not merely to a class but to the nation. The 'People's Home' in Sweden; the portrayal of the Norwegian Labour Party as the 'People's Party'; the electoral slogan of the Danish Social Democrats, 'Stauning or chaos' – all were variations on this theme. In Scandinavia the left appropriated the rhetoric of national unity that was monopolised in other countries by the right.

Democracy and foreign policy

To what extent did the democratisation of Scandinavian societies influence the making of foreign policy? One very specific consequence was the elimination of the crown as an independent foreign policy actor. The Swedish and Danish monarchs undertook no further initiatives and made no foreign policy statements that were not authorised by their governments. The king of Norway had always been careful not to overstep the constitutional limits of his position (though he had played an important part in the diplomacy of the period 1905–7), but his role too diminished in importance after the First World War.[18] In Sweden there was a positive correlation between the breakthrough of parliamentarism and social democracy at the end of the war and the pursuit of an 'enlightened' foreign policy. The collapse of German power, together with constitutional reform, convinced Swedish conservatives that there was no hope of combining a German-oriented foreign policy with the restoration of monarchical power at home.[19] For the Liberal–Socialist coalition, conversely, foreign policy could be portrayed 'as an extension of the social philosophy guiding its internal politics'.[20]

The First World War heightened public interest in international affairs and brought about a major advance in parliamentary influence over the making of foreign policy. In Sweden the secret Riksdag foreign affairs committee established in January 1916 was reconstituted as the Utrikesnämnd (foreign affairs committee) in 1922.[21] From December 1914 onwards, closed sessions

---

[18] Tim Greve, *Haakon VII of Norway* (London, 1983), pp. 51–4, 97–9.
[19] Erik Lönnroth, *Den svenska utrikespolitikens historia*, vol. V, *1919–1939* (Stockholm, 1959), p. 9.
[20] Arne Ruth, 'The Second New Nation: The Mythology of Modern Sweden', in Stephen R. Graubard, (ed.), *Norden – The Passion for Equality* (Oslo, 1986), pp. 240–82 (p. 258).
[21] W. M. Carlgren, *Ministären Hammarskjöld. Tillkomst, söndring, fall. Studier i svensk politik 1914–1917* (Stockholm, 1967), pp. 97–117; Howard telegram to FO, 22 January 1916, FO 371/2754, No. 14169.

of the Danish Rigsdag were held to give the political parties more information on Denmark's position and members the opportunity to express views without their coming to the knowledge of the public.[22] A parliamentary committee, Det udenrigspolitiske Nævn, was founded in 1923, largely on the initiative of the former defence minister Peter Munch.[23] The Norwegian parliament's 'special committee for foreign affairs' was established early in 1917, following serious crises with both Germany and Britain. This was merged with the constitutional committee to become the Utenriks- og konstitutionskomité in December 1923.[24] In their (sometimes unwilling) search for consensus and for the broadest possible base of support for major decisions, the three Scandinavian governments were moving towards an increasingly 'co-optational' form of decision making, one based on 'continuous interaction between the executive, the bureaucracy, the parliamentary commissions and the relevant interest groups' which, Eisenstadt suggests, is characteristic of the conduct of foreign policy in small countries.[25]

In the 1920s, when minority government was the rule, the foreign affairs committees often enjoyed considerable influence. The Swedish committee drafted instructions for the Swedish representative at Geneva – usually the foreign minister – and parliamentary repercussions followed if he deviated from his brief.[26] In Norway a combination of weak governments and the chairmanship of the vigorous Conservative leader Carl J. Hambro at times left the impression that 'the conduct of important foreign affairs lay in the hands of M. Hambro rather than in those of the Ministry concerned'.[27]

In periods of greater stability, the committees developed into something rather different: an instrument by which governments built cross-party consensus in support of their policies. Co-opting leading parliamentarians on to the committees tended to enhance rather than limit governments' freedom of manoeuvre. As early as 1923 Norwegian critics of the system (who then included Hambro) condemned its excessive secrecy and pointed to the way in which complex issues were sprung on committee members who had not been able to prepare in advance, but who were then implicated in the government's decisions.[28] The pattern became more general in the 1930s. Munch, Danish foreign minister from 1929 to 1940, was adept at handling the committee in a

[22] Viggo Sjøqvist, *Erik Scavenius. Danmarks udenrigsminister under to verdenskrige. Statsminister 1942–1945* (2 vols., Copenhagen, 1973), vol. I, *1877–1920*, p. 145.

[23] Viggo Sjøqvist, *Peter Munch. Manden, politikeren, historikeren* (Copenhagen, 1976), p. 166.

[24] Erik Colban, *Stortinget og utenrikspolitikken* (Oslo, 1961), p. 31.

[25] S. N. Eisenstadt, 'Reflections on Centre–Periphery Relations and Small European States', in Risto Alapuro et al., *Small States in Comparative Perspective: Essays for Erik Allardt* (Oslo, 1985), pp. 41–9 (p. 47).

[26] L. Torbjörn Norman, '"A Foreign Policy Other than the Old Neutrality" – Aspects of Swedish Foreign Policy After the First World War', in John Hiden and Aleksander Loit (eds.), *The Baltic in International Relations Between the Two World Wars* (Stockholm, 1988), pp. 235–50 (pp. 239–40).

[27] F. O. Lindley, 'Notes on the Leading Personalities in Norway', 22 December 1926, FO 371/11758, N5743/5753/30.

[28] Hambro in secret session of the Storting, 9 June 1923, SA, Referater fra møter for lukkede

way that gave politicians the feeling that they were participating in the decision-making process. In Norway, the balance shifted in favour of the government with the appointment in 1935 of Norway's most effective foreign minister of the inter-war years, Halvdan Koht. Though the foreign affairs committee remained better informed than other members of parliament, and indeed than most members of the government, important issues were now decided in advance by the prime minister and foreign minister.[29]

Secret sessions of parliament, held only infrequently in Sweden (six times between 1921 and 1939) but more often in Norway, supplemented foreign affairs committees as a means by which a larger body of parliamentarians could be initiated into the policy-making process. Membership of the League of Nations offered a further opportunity to enhance the consensual approach to foreign policy without diminishing the power of government. Opposition politicians were regularly appointed to lead delegations to Geneva, transforming those who were initially sceptical of the League, like Hambro or the Swedish Conservative leader Ernst Trygger, into some of its strongest supporters.[30] On rare occasions delegates to the League were sufficiently prominent or strong-willed to defy instructions. Nansen, a non-party and world-renowned figure, acted virtually independently as Norway's delegate to the League Assembly in the 1920s, while Branting incurred the wrath of the foreign affairs committee when he ventured to use the League to censure French policy over the occupation of the Ruhr in 1923.[31]

In all three Scandinavian countries (though to a much lesser extent in Finland), there was a conscious effort to distance foreign policy from party politics. In contrast to their vigorous disagreement on domestic issues, politicians of all parties aimed at consensus: dissent was a luxury which they believed they could not afford. Hambro expressed this attitude well when he referred during the Second World War to 'the important fact that in Norway . . . foreign policy is considered a national affair as distinct from party politics. No small nation can afford to have its foreign relations made a matter of factitious controversy.'[32] In practice, the demand for unity and conformity contributed to the absence of vigorous parliamentary debates on foreign policy, though there were some notable exceptions such as the Swedish debate in 1920 on membership of the League of Nations.[33]

Policy making thus remained in the hands of an elite, though one defined more by ability – and in particular by academic achievement – than were the

---

dører i sesjonen 1923, Arkivnr 96, pp. 570–1; Swedish critics in 1932 and 1936 Riksdag debates, quoted in Lönnroth, *Den svenska utrikespolitikens historia* V, pp. 11–14.

[29] Trygve Lie, *Leve eller dø. Norge i krig* (Oslo, 1955), p. 57.

[30] Shepherd Jones, *Scandinavian States*, pp. 98–101; Erik Boheman, *På vakt* (2 vols., Stockholm, 1963–4), vol. I, *Från attaché til sändebud*, pp. 54–5; Frede Castberg, *Minner om politik og vitenskap fra årene 1900–1970* (Oslo, 1971), p. 27.

[31] Castberg, *Minner om politik*, pp. 26–7; Torbjörn Norman, ' "A Foreign Policy Other than the Old Neutrality" ', p. 242.

[32] Carl J. Hambro, *I Saw It Happen in Norway* (London, 1940), p. 83.

[33] Tingsten, *Foreign Policy of Sweden*, pp. 293–4.

predominantly aristocratic and bureaucratic elites of the pre-1914 period. Except in Finland, where eight of the eleven inter-war foreign ministers came from the foreign service, fewer career diplomats served as foreign minister than before the war.[34] But there remained a very large proportion of 'experts' among foreign ministers: international lawyers such as Erik Marks von Würtemberg and Östen Undén in Sweden and Arnold Ræstad in Norway; intellectuals like Branting, Rickard Sandler (Swedish foreign minister from 1932 to 1939); and the historians Munch and Koht. Having studied recent diplomatic history, the latter in particular regarded himself as an expert.[35] In the democratic era it was thus not run-of-the-mill parliamentarians who came to the fore but, especially in the 1930s, individuals with great self-confidence and strong views. Hambro's characterisation of Koht as 'the enlightened despot' was not far off the mark.[36]

Such forceful though isolated personalities were not always equipped to make the best use of the foreign ministries they headed. In Sweden, Denmark and Norway the First World War saw a massive expansion of personnel in both the bureaucracy at home and the foreign service: in Denmark, for example, the Foreign Ministry trebled in size while the foreign service doubled, its recruits now coming mainly from the middle classes rather than the aristocracy. Post-war reforms were aimed at building on and rationalising this growth. Foreign ministries were reorganised and new departments established. Among the innovations were press bureaux and legal divisions, and the appointment of special advisers in international law, reflecting the prominence of conciliation and arbitration at Geneva, as well as in the traditional Scandinavian approach to international affairs. Sometimes wartime lessons were taken too much to heart. The importance of wartime trade negotiations led to a reorganisation of the Swedish Foreign Ministry by which all such matters were handled by a new political-commercial division, with a separate trade division devoted to more routine matters of collecting and distributing commercial and economic information. Such an arrangement proved unnecessary in peacetime, and in 1928 responsibility for trade negotiations was handed over to the trade division, then headed by the future foreign minister Christian Günther.[37] The inter-war period also saw a deliberate broadening of Utrikesdepartementet's recruitment, bringing in a new generation of young men with new ideas who increasingly set their stamp on the administration.[38] Despite his distant and rather intimidating personality, Sandler proved an outstanding administrator, encouraging his officials to express themselves freely and often willing to take their advice.[39]

The reform of the Danish Foreign Ministry was aimed at enhancing its

[34] Jukka Nevakivi, 'The Finnish Foreign Service', in Zara Steiner (ed.), *The Times Survey of Foreign Ministries of the World* (London, 1982), pp. 185–99 (p. 188).

[35] Sigmund Skard, *Mennesket Halvdan Koht* (Oslo, 1982), p. 116.

[36] Lie, *Leve eller dø*, p. 68.

[37] Wilhelm Carlgren, 'Sweden: The Ministry for Foreign Affairs', in Steiner, *Times Survey of Foreign Ministries*, pp. 455–69 (p. 463); Boheman, *På vakt* I, pp. 127–8.

[38] Boheman, *På vakt* I, p. 128.   [39] Ibid., p. 58.

capacity to promote Denmark's economic interests. In 1921 the foreign service and Udenrigsministeriet were integrated but the economic climate of the 1920s was not conducive to expansion. The Rigsdag insisted on cutbacks and in 1927 a further reform divided the ministry into two main sections – an economic-political and a political-legal division. Only with the appointment of Peter Munch as foreign minister – 'the first real parliamentarian in the post' – did the Rigsdag's mistrust of the foreign service diminish.[40] Yet Munch failed to make the best use of the expertise at his disposal. He relied little on the advice of his officials and, in contrast to Erik Scavenius, held few meetings with them. Munch's coolness towards his advisers reflected his mistrust of experts, whether civilian or military. They should not, he believed, influence political decisions – that was a matter for the politicians alone. In the long run Munch's failure to consult officials weakened the ministry's effectiveness and, especially in the political field, deprived it of experience.[41]

The pattern was similar in Norway. The recommendations of a royal commission established in 1919 led to the merger of Utenriksdepartementet, the diplomatic service and the consular service in 1922.[42] Recruitment policies were also broadened, but public-spending cuts meant that the service was brought up to minimum strength only on the eve of the Second World War. Like Munch, Koht did much of the routine work of the Foreign Ministry himself and did not care for advice. His regime had many merits. The legations abroad were kept better informed, and Koht gave his staff a lecture on the international situation each Saturday morning.[43] But he remained a forbidding figure who set himself deliberately apart from his countrymen: 'M. Koht stated that Norwegians in general, including the press, knew nothing whatever about foreign affairs. He had found it quite useless to say anything to them because there was no bottom to their ignorance.'[44]

The making of foreign policy in Finland differed in important respects from that of the three Scandinavian countries. The stipulation in the constitution of 1919 that 'Finland's foreign relations are determined by the president' had real meaning. Even though no president of the inter-war period enjoyed the authority and independence of Finland's post-war presidents, all were in a position to exercise direct influence on the making of policy, not least through their right of nomination to all posts in the foreign service.[45] Presidential authority was enhanced by frequent changes of government, and the election of a new president could impart a different tone to Finnish foreign policy, if

---

[40] Klaus Kjølsen, 'Denmark: The Royal Danish Ministry of Foreign Affairs', in Steiner, *Times Survey of Foreign Ministries*, pp. 163–83 (p. 173).

[41] Sjøqvist, *Munch*, pp. 163–7.

[42] Erik-Wilhelm Norman, 'Norway: The Royal Norwegian Ministry of Foreign Affairs', in Steiner, *Times Survey of Foreign Ministries*, pp. 391–408 (p. 398); Omang, *Norsk utenrikstjeneste* II, pp. 368–74, 428–38.

[43] Skard, *Koht*, pp. 115–17.

[44] Sir Cecil Dormer to FO, 14 July 1939, FO 371/23656, N3481/64/63.

[45] Nevakivi, 'Finnish Foreign Service', p. 186.

not initiate a radical change of course. When Lauri Relander succeeded the first president of the Republic, K. J. Ståhlberg, in 1925, he inaugurated a period in which Finland was more confident and outgoing in its relations with its Scandinavian and Baltic neighbours than it had been under his more reserved predecessor. The identification of his two successors, P. E. Svinhufvud (1931–7) and Kyösti Kallio (1937–40), with, respectively, the right wing and the centre–left of Finnish politics also had implications for Finland's international position.

A Finnish foreign service had to be improvised following the achievement of independence in 1917.[46] Given the shortage of experienced personnel, Finland's first representatives abroad were predominantly university teachers, businessmen and journalists with a command of foreign languages. As in Norway after 1905, many Finns at first doubted whether the country needed a foreign service at all. However, the sceptics were persuaded by the success of Finnish diplomacy at Geneva in 1920–1, in the dispute with Sweden over the Åland Islands, and the Finnish parliament proved more willing than its Scandinavian counterparts to provide adequate funding. But establishing a foreign service from scratch entailed many difficulties. There was a persistent tension between the older, more experienced and more opinionated diplomats abroad and the younger officials in the ministry at home.[47]

The division was exacerbated by the language question: the first generation of Finnish diplomats came mainly from the Swedish–Finnish upper class, while the younger generation were predominantly Finnish speakers. Finnish inexperience in foreign affairs led to 'an underlying uncertainty and caution' and, in particular, to a reluctance to grapple with commercial issues at a time when other foreign services were becoming increasingly preoccupied with such questions.[48] The language question, the legacy of the civil war and the continuing polarisation of Finnish politics all helped to make Finnish foreign policy more politicised than that of the three Scandinavian countries. There was a strong 'activist' bias among the first recruits to the foreign service. Their influence was gradually counterbalanced by new appointments made by the pro-Entente foreign minister Rudolf Holsti in 1919–22, but when Holsti returned to office in 1936 he was faced with 'even more dangerous rivals belonging to a younger generation with radical right-wing views'.[49] These characteristically drew their support from the Agrarian Party, which was also the driving force behind the 'Finnicisation' of the bureaucracy. In the early years of independence in particular, consistency in foreign policy fell victim to domestic political conflict. A British diplomat commented on the 'intense personal jealousy and bitter party feeling' in Finland: 'Even foreign policy, which is so vital to a young community such as this, is recklessly subordinated to questions of a parish pump order.'[50]

---

[46] Ibid., pp. 186–9.   [47] Paasivirta, *Finland and Europe: Early Years*, pp. 285–9.
[48] Ibid., p. 289.   [49] Nevakivi, 'Finnish Foreign Service', p. 191.
[50] George Kidston to FO, 8 April 1921, FO 419/3, N4790/3051/56.

Problems of Nordic security and cooperation

The post-war settlement appeared to confirm Scandinavia's favoured position on the margin of Europe. Yet there were many indications of an underlying anxiety about the dangers posed by the outside world. Parts of the Baltic region, after all, remained highly unstable. The collapse of the Russian empire had not only led to the Bolshevik seizure of power but had also encouraged its subject nationalities – Poles, Finns, Estonians, Latvians and Lithuanians – to assert their claims to independence. Until the end of the civil war in 1921, Russia's future was obscure; thereafter the reality of Soviet power had to be confronted. Among the newly independent states of the region, Finland was the most stable but was on bad terms with the Soviets and – until the settlement of the Åland dispute in 1921 – with Sweden. The territories of the three small Baltic states – Estonia, Latvia and Lithuania – were fought over by Russian Whites and Reds, by the Germans, the British and the French, before achieving a precarious independence. Poland was located dangerously between Germany and Russia, yet threatened to destabilise the region with its own military and political ambitions.[51] Poland in turn was connected with French attempts to extend the *cordon sanitaire* against Bolshevik Russia into the Baltic region.[52] There was, finally, the threat of a German–Soviet combination which was given substance by the signature of the Rapallo treaty in April 1922.

Ideologically, too, Scandinavia was less remote than it seemed from international pressures. The Bolshevik revolution impinged directly, though to differing degrees, on the domestic politics of all four countries. The fight against communism was taken to its furthest extremes in Finland, but the Scandinavian countries were also vigilant against subversion and Nordic police forces and intelligence services worked closely with those of Great Britain and Germany.[53] The Scandinavian states followed the lead of Britain and France in breaking off diplomatic relations with the Soviets in November 1918 and did not recognise the Soviet Union until after Britain had done so in 1924.[54] For Norway in particular this attitude entailed a relatively high cost in terms of economic opportunities foregone and Arctic diplomatic issues left unresolved.

Scandinavian misgivings were expressed at an early stage in the debates on League membership in 1919–20. Neutrality appeared to have been vindicated by the outcome of the war. Should it now be jettisoned in favour of

---

[51] Kalervo Hovi, *Interessensphären im Baltikum. Finnland im Rahmen der Ostpolitik Polens 1919–1922* (Helsinki, 1984).

[52] Suzanne Champonnois, 'The Baltic States as an Aspect of Franco-Soviet Relations 1919–1934: A Policy or Several Policies?', in John Hiden and Aleksander Loit (eds.), *Contact or Isolation? Soviet–Western Relations in the Interwar Period* (Stockholm, 1991), pp. 405–13.

[53] C. G. McKay, 'Our Man in Reval', *Intelligence and National Security* 9 (1994), pp. 88–111; Patrick Salmon, 'British Security Interests in Scandinavia and the Baltic 1918–1939', in Hiden and Loit, *The Baltic in International Relations*, pp. 113–36 (pp. 119–20). See also pp. 225–7 in this volume.

[54] See pp. 223–5 in this volume.

membership of a League of Nations? Even though they had been excluded from the Paris peace conference, self-interest and shared democratic values placed the Scandinavian countries on the side of the victors. Yet the Allies – largely at France's instigation – had imposed a peace settlement on Germany that appeared manifestly unjust. Moreover, collective security imposed obligations in the form of economic and military sanctions which might involve the Scandinavian countries in war.

The Scandinavian states managed to prevent an obligation to participate in military sanctions from being written into the League Covenant, but only Denmark entered the League with any degree of enthusiasm.[55] Sweden was bitterly divided on the issue, while Norway's decision to join was taken in an overwhelmingly negative spirit: to avoid the isolation from the other Scandinavian countries and from Great Britain which would ensue if Norway was not numbered among the founding members.[56] Scandinavian attitudes quickly changed. Participation in the League offered an enhanced status and a forum for diplomatic activity on the part of the smaller states.[57] But both 'realists' and 'idealists' continued to have reservations, while on the left the League was for long regarded as a capitalist conspiracy against Soviet Russia.[58]

For much of the inter-war period, nevertheless, the threat of Scandinavian involvement in war could plausibly be regarded as remote. The existence of the League of Nations encouraged a faith in collective security (to which the Nordic countries expected to make only a minimal contribution) that endured until the *débâcle* over Abyssinia in 1935–6. With the rise of Nazism, however, the Nordic countries faced the prospect of a new European war. How they were affected would depend on who the belligerents were, and what kind of war they chose to fight. At least until 1937, the most likely scenario seemed to be a war between Germany and the Soviet Union. In these circumstances, the main focus would be on land and sea operations in the eastern Baltic, with the Åland Islands as a particular object of attention. A secondary theatre, but one much discussed at the time, would be the far north of Scandinavia, where the Soviet Union might launch a thrust through Finland to northern Sweden and Norway in order to deprive Germany of supplies of Swedish iron ore.

If war broke out between Germany and the Western powers (with or without Soviet participation), Scandinavia would face a contest for control of Scandinavian resources and the transit trade in goods from overseas resembling that of 1914–18. Since the belligerents could be expected to apply the lessons of the last war from the outset, they would probably attempt to control

[55] Shepherd Jones, *Scandinavian States*, pp. 61–2, 65–70.
[56] Ibid., pp. 70–80; Tingsten, *Foreign Policy of Sweden*, pp. 19–27; Nils Ørvik, *Sikkerhetspolitikken 1920–1939. Fra forhistorien til 9. april 1940* (2 vols., Oslo, 1960–1), vol. I, p. 36.
[57] See e.g. the comments of the former Swedish foreign minister Erik Palmstierna, quoted in Yngve Möller, *Östen Undén. En biografi* (Stockholm, 1986), pp. 94–5.
[58] Arne Bergsgård, 'Utrikspolitikk', in *Innstilling fra Undersøkelsekommisjonen av 1945. Bilag*, vol. I (Oslo, 1947), pp. 117–264 (pp. 122–3).

Scandinavian trade through a combination of naval power and war trade agreements. In these circumstances the Scandinavian countries might hope to escape direct involvement in hostilities. But both the development of military technology – particularly in the air – and the ruthless mentality of the leaders of Nazi Germany suggested that the tacit consensus which had kept Scandinavia out of the First World War might not materialise a second time. The one scenario not anticipated was the one that materialised in 1939, when Germany and the Soviet Union were effectively allies. Then northern Europe would lie within their joint sphere of influence, while Britain was excluded from the Baltic in a belated realisation of the German–Russian stratagems of the pre-1914 period.

As small states with barely adequate defences and populations whose preoccupations were overwhelmingly with their own internal affairs, what scope did the Nordic countries have for conducting coherent foreign and security policies? Could they, either singly or in combination, hope to influence the course of European politics in general, or at least carve out a sphere in northern Europe free from entanglement in great-power conflicts? To what extent were they capable even of protecting their own national interests? If they were of largely theoretical interest in the 1920s, such questions were to acquire increasing urgency following Hitler's accession to power. Until the early 1930s the security policies of the three Scandinavian countries (though not of Finland) broadly comprised as large a measure of disarmament as was compatible with membership of the League of Nations, combined with an avoidance of all commitments not specifically entailed in the League Covenant. They sought to preserve the essence of neutrality while paying lip-service to collective security, and disarmed to a greater degree than any would have dared to contemplate before the First World War. The contradiction between League membership and neutrality was to be exposed by the international crises of the 1930s. From the middle of the decade onward, under the impact of the Anglo-German naval agreement of 1935, which signalled Britain's renunciation of an active naval role in the Baltic, the Italian invasion of Abyssinia and the failure of the Western powers to resist the remilitarisation of the Rhineland, the Nordic states retreated into strict neutrality.

Foreshadowed as early as September 1934 by the Norwegian prime minister Mowinckel,[59] the retreat centred on Article 16, the sanctions clause of the League Covenant, and became precipitate following the collapse of sanctions against Italy in 1936. Without withdrawing from the League, the Nordic states, along with the Netherlands, Spain and Switzerland, declared in July 1936 'that, so long as the Covenant as a whole is applied so incompletely and inconsistently', they no longer felt obliged to participate in sanctions against an aggressor.[60] In May 1938 the Nordic countries reached agreement on joint

---

[59] Ørvik, *Sikkerhetspolitikken* I, pp. 219–26.
[60] Nils Ørvik, *The Decline of Neutrality 1914–1941* (2nd edn, London, 1971), pp. 177–9 (quotation from p. 178).

neutrality regulations in time of war. The process was completed in July 1938 when the Nordic foreign ministers, together with those of Belgium, the Netherlands and Luxemburg, stated explicitly that their governments regarded sanctions as being non-obligatory.[61] To this limited degree – in their shared desire to avoid entanglement in international conflict – the Nordic states were thus able to achieve a measure of political cooperation. More than that they were unable to accomplish. The strategic perceptions and defence priorities of the four countries remained divergent and ultimately irreconcilable.

Norway

Norwegian foreign policy appears to have lost momentum and direction after the remarkable fifteen-year period of 'internal consolidation and external expansion'[62] between the achievement of independence in 1905 and the acknowledgement of Norwegian sovereignty over Svalbard at the end of the war. Protection of Norway's extensive overseas economic interests had always been conceived as the primary peacetime function of Norwegian diplomacy. After the war it proved barely capable of fulfilling this task as Norway became embroiled in disputes with France, Spain and Portugal as a result of the adoption of prohibition in 1919, and with the Soviet Union over hunting and fishing rights in the Arctic. Once the Soviet Union had recognised Norway's claim to Svalbard in 1925, Norway lapsed into what Rolf Tamnes has termed a 'non-policy', making little effort to secure its sovereignty despite the Soviet Union's clear intention – evidently for security reasons – of consolidating its own mining interests in the archipelago.[63] This was partly because the expansionist thrust of Norwegian 'Arctic imperialism' had turned towards Greenland. But the history of the East Greenland dispute between 1931 and 1933 demonstrates the extent to which the close partnership between scientists, publicists and Foreign Ministry officials which had proved so successful in advancing Norway's claim to Svalbard had decayed, leaving a residue of chauvinism which the weak Agrarian government of the day was unable to restrain.

The principal irony of Norwegian foreign policy was the way in which it led to conflict with a country which was among its closest friends – Denmark – and with its chief protector, Great Britain. The protracted Anglo-Norwegian dispute over fisheries limits which had begun before the war reached a new pitch of intensity in the 1930s.[64] Norway's problems were partly the result of inexperience: the failure, for example, to anticipate the likely reaction of wine-producing countries to the introduction of prohibition. In the case of the

---

[61] Ibid., pp. 185–7.   [62] Berg, *Norsk utenrikspolitikks historie* II, p. 19.

[63] Rolf Tamnes, *Svalbard og stormaktene. Fra ingenmannsland til Kald Krig 1870–1953* (Oslo, 1991), pp. 10, 36–40.

[64] I have drawn in this paragraph on Odd-Bjørn Fure, *Norsk utenrikspolitikks historie*, vol. III, *Mellomkrigstid 1920–1940* (Oslo, 1996), part II, chs. 1–2.

fisheries dispute, they reflected the intrusion of modern technology and external economic pressures into one of the most politically and economically sensitive aspects of Norwegian life. Norway's attempt to enforce a four-mile limit was a response to the incursion into Norwegian waters of modern trawler fleets from countries such as Britain, Germany and France, which threatened the livelihood of the coastal population (Norway was the only major fishing nation which did not go over to trawling in the inter-war period). Preoccupied with disputes of such importance to the country's economic welfare and political identity, Norwegian foreign policy understandably lost sight of other issues, above all that of national security, for much of the inter-war period.

But as long as British naval supremacy remained unchallenged, Norway had little reason to fear involvement in war. There was thus little incentive to make commitments either to the League or to its own neighbours. Despite its having joined the League, the strongest impulse in Norwegian post-war policy was to return to the isolation the country had enjoyed before 1914. One of Norway's first actions after joining the League was to press for the abrogation of the integrity treaty of 1907 – an unwelcome symbol of great-power 'tutelage'.[65] The fact that the disappearance of the integrity treaty also removed a legal obstacle to the occupation of Norwegian territory in time of war made the Norwegian government's action, in the view of one British official, 'somewhat surprising. In fact, it would appear that they can hardly have realised the point.'[66] There was much truth in this observation. Norwegian politicians of all parties chose to believe that the improvement in inter-Scandinavian relations, the progress of international arbitration and gestures such as the Kellogg Pact had rendered war unthinkable; but that if the worst came to the worst, Norway could still rely on the implicit British guarantee.[67] Mowinckel, the chief architect of Norwegian disarmament, declared in 1929 that any threat from Sweden was now inconceivable, whilst, 'as regards sea strategy, we must remember that it is Britain which rules the northern seas, and that this will presumably be the case for a long time to come'.[68]

Norway's land defences could therefore be minimal, whilst at sea they could be confined to a 'neutrality guard'. The Norwegian armed forces were reduced in two main stages, in 1927 and 1933, with the main burden of the cuts falling on the army.[69] It was then to be the task of 'a far-sighted foreign policy leadership', as the defence bill of 1931 put it, 'to strengthen the defences if the situation becomes threatening'.[70] That task fell to the Labour government. Between 1934/5 and 1938/9 defence spending nearly doubled, and in 1939/40

---

[65] Patrick Salmon, *Foreign Policy and National Identity: The Norwegian Integrity Treaty 1907–1924* (Oslo, 1993).

[66] Minute by Esmond Ovey (Northern Department), 1 June 1922, quoted ibid., p. 33.

[67] For a comprehensive statement of this view, see memorandum by Mowinckel, 'PM ang. Norges forsvarspolitiske stilling', 20 February 1930, NUD, H 62 B 1/25, Bd 2.

[68] Quoted in T. K. Derry, *A History of Modern Norway 1814–1972* (Oxford, 1973), p. 348.

[69] Ørvik, *Sikkerhetspolitikken* I, pp. 63–88.

[70] Quoted in Bergsgård, 'Utrikspolitikk', p. 124.

it accounted for a third of total expenditure.[71] Norway's armed forces were nevertheless in a much weaker position than they had been in 1914. There was also a fatal ambiguity about their role in time of war which was expressed, for example, in the remark of a Labour parliamentarian that 'we should not go further than to mark our neutrality, "not to shoot". We should have a "guard", not a "defence".'[72]

Yet ambiguity was inherent in Norway's security predicament. Why should Norway arm against the only power considered capable of violating Norwegian neutrality if that power – Great Britain – was also the chief guarantor of Norwegian security? The possibility of German aggression was certainly considered: the Norwegian defence authorities were familiar with Vice-Admiral Wegener's argument about the need for bases on the Norwegian coast in a future naval war with Great Britain.[73] Indeed, the head of the navy declared in November 1936, in a memorandum seen by Koht, that there was 'every reason to fear that an attempt will be made to realise the idea of using the ports in southern Norway as a base for naval forces in a war against England'.[74] General Otto Ruge, the army chief, was also concerned in the late 1930s about the strategic implications of the development of Murmansk as a base for the Soviet navy and air force.[75] In neither case, however, was such awareness translated into policy decisions on the part of either the armed forces or the government. There was in fact a 'nearly complete lack of consultation and coordination of the country's foreign and defence or military policies' – a situation which has been attributed to 'the anti-military prejudice of both Koht, as foreign minister, and of Nygaardsvold as prime minister'.[76]

Attempts were of course made to pursue more 'enlightened' policies. Considerable importance was attached to the conclusion of arbitration treaties, such as those with Denmark, Finland and Sweden in 1927. Mowinckel was in favour of certain kinds of Nordic cooperation and it was on his initiative that the 'Oslo Group' of low-tariff states was formed in 1930 (see pp. 197–8). Like other Scandinavian statesmen in the 1920s, he was a believer in international cooperation and found the climate of Geneva congenial.[77] Between 1935 and 1939, Halvdan Koht – 'Norway's first foreign minister with a clearly

---

[71] On the shift in Labour's policy, see Rolf Danielsen, 'Forsvarsforliket 1937', in Ottar Dahl et al. (eds.), *Makt og motiv. Et festskrift til Jens Arup Seip* (Oslo, 1975), pp. 166–81.

[72] Magnus Nilssen, 30 March 1939, quoted in Halvdan Koht (ed. Steinar Kjærheim), *Rikspolitisk dagbok 1933–1940* (Oslo, 1985), p. 200.

[73] See pp. 326–7 in this volume.

[74] 'Sjøforsvarets gjenreisning. Kommanderende Admirals skrivelse av 16. november 1936', RAO, Koht Papers, 258/1.

[75] Ruge memorandum, 23 December 1937, NUD, 52 D 1 II. Ruge proposed asking the British authorities for intelligence on the situation in Murmansk; the Norwegian minister discussed the question with Captain Phillips, the head of Plans Division at the Admiralty: Erik Colban to NUD, 19 January 1938, ibid.

[76] Olav Riste, 'The Foreign Policy-Making Process in Norway: An Historical Perspective', in *Forsvarsstudier. Årbok for Forsvarshistorisk forskningssenter, Forsvarets høgskole 1982* (Oslo, 1983), pp. 232–45 (p. 239).

[77] Castberg, *Minner om politik*, p. 39.

formulated concept of the nation's foreign policy interests' – was still more active on the international stage. 'With an unusual mixture of nationalist and internationalist idealism', Koht 'believed that the smaller states of Europe, having no particular axes to grind, could and should play an active part in international diplomacy, as mediators working towards the peaceful settlement of disputes'.[78] In his pursuit of an 'active peace policy', Koht visited thirteen foreign capitals (but not Berlin or Rome), though his main emphasis was on the League of Nations. He appears to have worked with diminishing hope of success, but out of a sense of duty both to his own conscience and to the world. After the autumn 1938 session in Geneva he wrote: 'I shall never abandon the struggle for a better world, for that would be to abandon my soul.'[79]

Denmark

Danish leaders after the First World War were fully aware of their country's strategic vulnerability despite Germany's temporary weakness. Their response was 'to remove every pretext for Germany to invade Denmark' and to repudiate any suggestion of active Danish participation in collective security.[80] The corollary of this attitude, in terms of defence policy, was almost total disarmament, achieved in successive reductions between 1922 and 1932.[81] The drive to economise was a powerful motive behind Danish policy, especially after 1929, but it also reflected the convictions of those who believed that, as Peter Munch, then defence minister, declared in November 1919, 'it was simply impossible to create an effective defence system in Denmark'.[82] The implicit assumption, broadly shared by the parties of the left, was that Denmark neither could nor should offer resistance against an overwhelming show of force by Germany.[83] This view was contested by conservatives and by the king, as well as by the robustly pro-British General With, whose appointment in 1931 as commander-in-chief infuriated Munch, now foreign minister.[84] However, inter-service rivalries undermined the efforts of army and navy to persuade reluctant politicians of the importance of rearmament.[85] On the eve of the Second World War there was little doubt that, as a British official

[78] Riste, 'Foreign Policy-Making Process in Norway', p. 238.
[79] Quoted in Skard, *Koht*, p. 119.
[80] H. A. Grant Watson to FO, 12 December 1919, *DBFP*, 1, V, pp. 915–16.
[81] Viggo Sjøqvist, *Danmarks udenrigspolitik 1933–1940* (Copenhagen, 1966), pp. 22–30.
[82] Sjøqvist, *Munch*, pp. 111–12. On the evolution of Munch's ideas on defence, see Wilhelm Christmas-Møller, 'Forsvarsminister P. Munchs opfattelse af Danmarks stilling som militærmakt – belyst ved hans forvaltning af sit ressort 1913–1920', in Bertel Heurlin and Christian Thune (eds.), *Danmark og det internationale system. Festskrift til Ole Karup Pedersen* (Copenhagen, 1989), pp. 205–22.
[83] Sjøqvist, *Danmarks udenrigspolitik*, p. 29.
[84] Ole A. Hedegaard, *En general og hans samtid. General Erik With mellem Stauning og kaos* (Frederikssund, 1990), pp. 104–6. For the views of King Christian, see e.g. Granville to FO, 12 January 1925, FO 419/13, N353/353/15; Hohler to Sir Frederick Ponsonby (private secretary to King George V), 11 May 1929, Hohler Papers, vol. 1929.
[85] Sjøqvist, *Danmarks udenrigspolitik*, p. 356.

put it, 'the Danes will allow their country to be over-run without offering resistance: General With would like to take a more courageous line, but he has been over-ruled'.[86]

Even advocates of a strong defence were conservative in their assessment of Denmark's strategic situation. In two studies written in May 1936, Lieutenant E. Gøtke-Hansen concluded, on the basis of a study of German policy between 1914 and 1918, that Germany was likely to occupy Danish territory immediately upon the outbreak of war in order to secure naval and air supremacy over the Kattegat and Skagerrak.[87] Denmark's armed forces must therefore be prepared not merely to mount a 'neutrality guard', but to fight for the country's existence; and for this purpose they should be concentrated in Jutland and Fyn, whilst ensuring that Copenhagen had sufficient defences to resist an intimidatory air attack. Even General With deemed this blunt message too unpalatable to be passed on to the government.[88] Percipient in his assessment of the importance of air power, Gøtke-Hansen was nevertheless slow to consider the possibility that Denmark and the Kattegat might be merely stepping stones to wider strategic objectives. But in an 'afterthought' dated 18 January 1939 he noted that 'German supremacy over Kattegat and Skagerrak means possibility of German offensive against Norway, in order to establish U-boat bases with access to the ocean on the Norwegian west coast'.[89] Control of Norway, he went on, would also secure Swedish iron ore supplies against British interference. Although other officers had arrived at the same view, no operational or logistical decisions resulted from this insight, let alone any effective military collaboration with Denmark's Scandinavian neighbours.

Denmark's more exposed geographical position, together with the existence of a potential source of friction with Germany in North Slesvig, made Danish foreign policy more circumspect than that of the other Nordic states. But there remained differences of emphasis between the Social Democratic and Radical Liberal members of the coalition governments of the 1930s. Stauning was readier than Munch to employ the rhetoric of Nordic unity, as in his statement in a speech of 17 October 1933 that Denmark's southern frontier was 'the frontier of the North' and that an attack there would be a matter for Scandinavia as a whole.[90] He soon made it clear, however, that he had not been thinking of a defensive alliance but merely of 'sympathy and moral support'.[91] The anxiety which lay behind his speech (prompted by Rosenberg's

---

[86] Minute by D. W. Lascelles (Northern Department), 29 August 1939, FO 371/23657, N3981/64/63.

[87] E. Gøtke, *Forudsætningerne for 9. april 1940. Danmarks strategiske situation før 2. verdenskrig belyst ved to studier udarbejdet 1936 af adjutanten ved Sjællandske Division* (Copenhagen, 1979).

[88] Letter of 20 November 1937, printed ibid., p. 30.   [89] Ibid., p. 26.

[90] Sjøqvist, *Danmarks udenrigspolitik*, p. 58.

[91] Quoted in Anthony Upton, 'The Crisis of Scandinavia and the Collapse of Interwar Ideals 1938–1940', in Peter M. R. Stirk (ed.), *European Unity in Context: The Interwar Period* (London and New York, 1989), pp. 170–87 (p. 173).

hint in the German frontier town of Flensburg on 11 October that the border question might be a matter for revision, and by Hitler's announcement shortly afterwards of Germany's withdrawal from the League of Nations) also made Stauning more prepared than Munch to consider reversing Denmark's policy of disarmament. In 1935, too, he proved susceptible to the influence of General With – until Munch made clear that the choice lay between strengthening Denmark's defences and the departure of the Radical Liberals from the coalition.[92]

Stauning was, on the other hand, ready to consider a direct bilateral deal with Germany: his pragmatism and his knowledge of the country through a lifetime's contact with German social democracy appear to have outweighed his repugnance for the Nazi regime. Munch's apparent passivity in the face of the increasing German threat thus led Stauning to attempt a foreign policy initiative of his own. His visit to London in April 1937 was undertaken in part to sound out the British government on the possibility of military support for Denmark; but more importantly to establish contact with the German ambassador Ribbentrop, with a view to the conclusion of a non-aggression pact. The approach came to nothing when rumours leaked to the press, but seems to have soured relations between prime minister and foreign minister.[93]

Munch remained the principal shaper of Danish foreign policy until the catastrophe of 1940. He had no faith in defence or in Scandinavian military cooperation. But until the Western powers had taken the lead in dismantling collective security, as they did in the aftermath of Abyssinia, he was not prepared to initiate a return to strict neutrality. For Munch, Denmark remained dependent on the support of the League in the event of a German move against the Slesvig frontier. As long as any hope remained, Denmark would not withdraw its allegiance. This was also a matter of principle. Munch 'regarded it as impossible to achieve any form of security either through rearmament or through help from the Nordic countries. He could see only one possibility: to stick to the League of Nations, weak though it might be.'[94] In his public statements, Munch permitted himself some optimism since he believed that it was necessary at least to act on the assumption that peace could be rescued. Privately he had no illusions and expected the dictator states to go to war as soon as they were ready.[95]

The logic of Denmark's position was a growing divergence from Scandinavia both economically and politically. Just as its greater dependence on British and German markets entailed an economic reorientation (see pp. 198, 271–3), so Denmark drew the appropriate conclusion from Britain's declaration of disinterest in 1937, making overtures for a non-aggression pact with Germany in 1937–8 and ultimately becoming the only Nordic country to accept Hitler's offer of such a pact in May 1939. Yet Munch fought against isolation and was

[92] Sjøqvist, *Munch*, pp. 206–8.
[93] Sjøqvist, *Danmarks udenrigspolitik*, pp. 193–8; Sjøqvist, *Munch*, pp. 210–12.
[94] Sjøqvist, *Munch*, p. 207.   [95] Ibid., p. 225.

deeply disappointed when none of Denmark's neighbours followed the same path.[96] Denmark needed the moral backing of the other Scandinavian countries even if military support was neither expected nor desired.

Sweden

Sweden's pretensions to a leading role in European politics, hitherto the preserve of the right, were embraced after the war by the centre–left and displaced to Geneva. Here Sweden could carry some weight through the influence of leading personalities such as Branting and the strength of its commitment to international reconciliation. In 1923–6 Swedish influence was further enhanced by its occupation of one of the non-permanent seats on the League Council. Sweden's voluntary renunciation of that seat, enabling Germany to become a permanent member of the Council, was regarded a major contribution to the peaceful stabilisation of Europe in the aftermath of the Locarno treaties.[97] From the outset there were differences of emphasis among Swedish supporters of the League. Branting saw it as an indirect means of restoring the unity of international socialism that had been destroyed by the war and, more immediately, of strengthening the democratic and socialist forces in Weimar Germany.[98] Hence his opposition to France's hard line over the Ruhr in 1923.[99] The former foreign minister Erik Palmstierna, now minister in London, sought, more eccentrically, to bring about an open alignment between Sweden and Great Britain – an 'Anglo-Swedish entente' – in which the two states would exercise joint naval hegemony in the Baltic region. The idea was ventilated in the *Daily Telegraph* in August 1923 and subsequently taken up in the conservative Swedish press, but vigorously disclaimed by the Swedish government.[100]

Both supporters of the League and adherents of the traditional policy of neutrality were generally reluctant to contemplate a more active role in the Baltic. Individuals like Palmstierna or the Conservative foreign minister Carl Hederstierna, whose advocacy of an alliance with Finland led to his fall from office in 1923, were in a small minority. Within the Swedish foreign policy establishment there remained a vein of conservative scepticism represented by such influential figures as Torvald Höjer, head of the Political Department of

[96] Ibid., p. 213.
[97] The role of the Swedish foreign minister Östen Undén on this issue remains controversial: see Erik Lönnroth, 'Sweden: The Diplomacy of Östen Undén', in Gordon A. Craig and Felix Gilbert (eds.), *The Diplomats 1919–1939* (Princeton, N. J., 1953), pp. 86–99; Lönnroth, *Den svenska utrikespolitikens historia* V, pp. 77–104; Möller, *Undén*, pp. 117–30.
[98] Torbjörn Norman, '"A Foreign Policy Other than the Old Neutrality"', pp. 240–2.
[99] Rudolf Nadolny (ed. Günter Wollstein), *Mein Beitrag. Erinnerungen eines Botschafters des Deutschen Reiches* (Cologne, 1985), pp. 145–6.
[100] Nadolny (Stockholm) to AA, 6 and 27 July 1923, PA, AA Pol. Abt. IV, Schweden, Politik 3 – England; Barclay (Stockholm) to FO, 1 August 1923, FO 371/9380, N6741/6741/42; Torbjörn Norman, '"A Foreign Policy Other than the Old Neutrality"', pp. 242–6.

the Foreign Ministry from 1919 to 1923 and subsequently minister to Norway, who 'embodied the traditions of strict Swedish neutrality as a pragmatic principle'.[101] Mistrustful of commitments to Sweden's Baltic neighbours and of any attempt to assert leadership in the Baltic region, Höjer also warned that Sweden should not appear as the 'knight errant of international law'. Given that Sweden had chosen to disarm, it had no choice, in his view, but to renounce an active role in power politics. The worsening international situation in the 1930s led to a convergence between the sceptics and the idealists. The change was personified by Undén, who declared in a speech at Uppsala in August 1935 that Sweden might be forced to resume its former policy of neutrality.[102] However, Undén's spirit of resignation was not shared by his party colleague and successor as foreign minister, Rickard Sandler. As we shall see, Sandler was to draw a different conclusion from the failure of the League and was to strike out on a new path of Nordic defence cooperation.

After the First World War, Sweden's strategic position had been greatly enhanced by the destruction of the German navy and the emergence of independent Finland as a buffer to the east. For a short time in 1920–1 Branting was perturbed by the prospect of British naval hegemony in the Baltic – it was for this reason that he opposed the destruction of the Soviet fleet when the idea was raised by Palmstierna – but Britain's reluctance to play an active role in Baltic affairs was soon evident.[103] Sweden disarmed to a considerable extent in 1925, and the appointment of a new Defence Commission in 1930 was expected to lead to further reductions.[104] By the time it reported in 1935, however, the international situation had deteriorated and the reorganisation of 1936 was aimed at restoring Sweden's defence capability.[105] Both the navy and the army were modernised, but the main priority was given to the development of air power: the origins of the modern Swedish aircraft industry date from the late 1930s.[106] By 1939 Sweden was again becoming a power to be reckoned with in the northern European strategic equation.

The Swedish defence debate was characterised by a strong and articulate opposition to disarmament on the part of leading army officers. It was expressed in Captain Axel Rappe's pamphlet *Sveriges läge* of 1923; in the comments of the Commission of Generals on the report of the 1919 Defence

---

[101] Torbjörn Norman, '"A Foreign Policy Other than the Old Neutrality"', p. 247.
[102] Though the draft of Undén's speech reveals that privately his views had not changed: ibid., p. 249.
[103] Lönnroth, *Den svenska utrikespolitikens historia* V, p. 59; Jorma Kalela, *Grannar på skilda vägar. Den finländsk–svenska samarbetet i den finländska och svenska utrikespolitiken 1921–1923* (Helsinki, 1971), p. 42; Ramsay to FO, 3 August 1921, FO 419/8, N9103/3808/63.
[104] Tingsten, *Foreign Policy of Sweden*, pp. 155–72, 277–82.
[105] Arvid Cronenberg, 'Kapplöpning med tiden. Svensk krigsorganisation och krigsplanering', in Bo Hugemark (ed.), *Stormvarning. Sverige inför andra världskriget* (Stockholm, 1989), pp. 91–122.
[106] Klaus-Richard Böhme, 'Huvuddragen i svensk försvarspolitik 1925–1945', in Bo Hugemark (ed.), *Neutralitet och försvar. Perspektiv på svensk säkerhetspolitik 1809–1985* (Stockholm, 1986), pp. 166–84.

Commission in the same year; and in the substantial study of Sweden's strategic position, *Antingen – eller*, edited in 1930 by Major Helge Jung (later, like Rappe, to become chief of the general staff).[107] Apart from the need to maintain a strong defence, these works shared an assumption that the chief threat to Swedish security came from the Soviet Union and that the best way to meet it lay in military cooperation with Finland.[108] By the late 1930s such views had come to coincide, at least in some measure, with the priorities of Sweden's foreign policy leadership.

Finland

The circumstances in which Finland achieved independence, together with the close proximity of the Soviet Union, ensured that there was a much greater consensus in favour of a strong national defence than in the other Nordic countries.[109] It was a concern which was also directed inward. The voluntary Civic Guard, 100,000 strong, acted as a reserve for the regular armed forces in time of war but was also vigilant in its scrutiny of the internal enemy on the left. In the 1920s the development of an effective defence force was hampered by budgetary constraints, but spending increased after Mannerheim became chairman of the Defence Council in 1931. There were also divisions within the officer corps between German-trained Jägers and officers who had served in the imperial Russian army. These rivalries delayed the adoption of a coherent defensive strategy, with the ex-Russian artillery experts favouring a coastal defence and wishing 'to mount every gun left behind by the Russians',[110] while the Jägers advocated a mobile defence on the frontier. A British advisory mission led by General Walter Kirke in 1924–5 helped to shift the balance in favour of the latter. As General Kirke later recalled,

the senior Finnish Generals who had served with the Russians were, with the exception of Mannerheim, firm believers in the Russian doctrine of bricks and mortar, – what we now call 'Magenitis', from the Maginot Line mentality, – which was anathema to me, as to the younger officers who had served with the German army. They wanted the support of my authority to prevent a slip back into a passive defence mentality.[111]

The Finns expected the Karelian Isthmus to be the main target of any Soviet offensive: the terrain of the long eastern frontier was reckoned to be so inhospitable as to rule out any large-scale attack except in the far north at Petsamo. But a combination of natural and man-made obstacles offered a

---

[107] Arvid Cronenberg, *Militär intressegrupp-politik. Kretsen kring Ny Militär Tidskrift och dess väg till inflytande i 1930 års forsvarskommission* (Stockholm, 1977).

[108] Tingsten, *Foreign Policy of Sweden*, pp. 150–2.

[109] Kari Selén, 'The Main Lines of Finnish Security Policy Between the World Wars', *Revue internationale d'histoire militaire* 62 (1985), pp. 15–35; H. M. Tillotson, *Finland at Peace and War 1918–1993* (Norwich, 1993), chs. 6–8.

[110] General Sir Walter Kirke, 'Autobiographical Notes', IWM, WMK 13 (Kirke Papers, vol. VII), p. 9.

[111] Ibid., p. 11.

reasonable chance of halting the Red Army on the Isthmus. The defensive installations, planned by a French engineer in 1919 (and already regarded by a visiting British intelligence officer in 1924 as 'practically impregnable'),[112] were strengthened from the late 1920s and reinforced further in the summer of 1939. Observing the Finnish army manoeuvres which took place in early August 1939, the British military attaché was struck by the powers of endurance of the ordinary Finnish soldier and by his 'definite determination of defending his country' but was otherwise unimpressed: 'The training and experience of the Higher Commanders appears to leave much to be desired; the equipment and armament of units is in a very bad condition and the only hopeful feature appears to be the natural difficulties of the country.'[113]

Finnish foreign policy was dominated by the fear of Soviet aggression and by the conviction that Finland could not withstand a Soviet attack without external support. For much of the inter-war period this entailed a search for allies: only in 1935 did Finnish policy officially become one of neutrality and alignment with the Scandinavian states. The search began before the end of the First World War, when calculations about the likely outcome of the war were instrumental in bringing about an orientation towards Germany. Finnish leaders expected the Germans to remain dominant in the east even if they did not win the war, while the Western powers were regarded as being too remote and as having too little interest in helping Finland against Bolshevism.[114] Under German influence and in pursuit of their own territorial aspirations at Petsamo and in Karelia, the Finns came close in 1918 to open conflict with Great Britain. But some Finnish leaders, notably the future foreign minister Rudolf Holsti and the victorious White commander Mannerheim, believed that Finland's future lay in an orientation towards the Entente.[115] Even pro-Germans like Professor Edvard Hjelt, Finnish representative in Berlin, were wary of placing unlimited faith in Germany and were already looking to Sweden and the other Scandinavian states as a means of counterbalancing German influence.[116]

In the immediate post-war period, however, with the Swedish option foreclosed by the dispute over the Åland Islands, the main thrust of Finland's alliance policy was towards the Baltic states and Poland. First mooted in 1919, the border-states orientation was pursued most seriously in 1921–2, in the

---

[112] Report on a visit to the Baltic states, Finland, Sweden and Norway, May–June 1924, by Lt-Col. F. P. Nosworthy, WO 106/1573.

[113] Report on manoeuvres of 7–12 August 1939 by Col. C. S. Vale, FO 371/23648, N4234/1284/56. See also Vale's 'General Notes on the Soviet–Finnish Frontier and Its Defensive Possibilities', 30 August 1939, FO 371/23692, N4235/991/38.

[114] Lyytinen, *Finland in British Politics*, p. 117.

[115] On Holsti's Anglophilism and general political philosophy, see Ilmari Susiluoto, 'The Origins and Development of Political Formations: The Political Science Practiced by Rudolf Holsti', in Jukka Kanerva and Kari Palonen (eds.), *Transformation of Ideas on a Periphery: Political Studies in Finnish History* (Helsinki, 1987), pp. 76–97.

[116] Torbjörn Norman, 'Right-Wing Scandinavianism and the Russian Menace', in Hiden and Loit, *Contact or Isolation?*, pp. 329–49 (p. 334).

wake of the crisis with the Soviet Union provoked when Finnish volunteers attempted to intervene in support of a peasant uprising in East Karelia in November 1921.[117] It was a policy identified particularly closely with Holsti, who appears to have pursued it partly in order to avoid isolation but also because he believed that a border-states alliance would receive the support of the Western powers. But the border states were a quarrelsome group and among them only Poland was a significant military power. Mannerheim, out of politics but still an influential figure on the right, was in favour of an alliance with Poland but not with Estonia, Latvia or Lithuania.[118] The chief of the general staff, Oskar Enckell, thought that a military alliance would be of use only if all members had concluded peace with the Soviet Union: if not, the danger of conflict would be too great.[119] There was, however, 'somewhat fragmented, but nevertheless relatively extensive support' for Holsti when he took part in the negotiations between Finnish, Estonian, Latvian and Polish delegates at Warsaw in March 1922, which represented the high point of border-states cooperation.[120]

The Warsaw agreement of 17 March 1922 fell far short of a full military alliance, yet Finnish commitment of any kind soon came to appear inadvisable, especially in the light of the Rapallo treaty of April 1922. If Poland and the Baltic states were to become the object of German and Soviet attention, it was better that Finland should not become involved. Domestic opposition to the agreement was fuelled by personal and political rivalries[121] and reinforced by Swedish and German advice. Rudolf Nadolny, German minister in Stockholm, warned the Finns against becoming involved with Polish adventurism and suggested that they should not underestimate the advantages of a Scandinavian orientation.[122] The Finnish Diet's refusal, in May 1922, to ratify the Warsaw treaty brought about the fall of Holsti. It also signalled the end of Finland's attempt to enhance its security through an alliance with the Baltic states and Poland.[123]

In view of Britain's withdrawal from the eastern Baltic after 1921, Sweden came to appear Finland's only remaining hope.[124] Werner Söderhjelm, Finnish minister in Stockholm, favoured a Scandinavian orientation as a means of getting closer to the great powers that were 'really anti-Bolshevik' – France and the United States.[125] Others, especially in the armed forces, saw Sweden as a possible military ally in its own right. The inclination to look to Sweden was naturally strong among the Swedish minority (though Hjalmar Procopé, a

---

[117] Paasivirta, *Finland and Europe: Early Years*, pp. 299–306.   [118] Ibid., p. 302.

[119] Martti Turtola, *Från Torne älv till Systerbäck. Hemligt försvarssamarbete mellan Finland och Sverige 1923–1940* (Stockholm, 1987), p. 19.

[120] Paasivirta, *Finland and Europe: Early Years*, pp. 302–3.

[121] Rennie (Helsinki) to FO, 25 March 1922, *DBFP*, 1, XXIII, pp. 438–40.

[122] Magnus Lemberg, *Hjalmar J. Procopé som aktivist, utrikesminister och svensk partiman. Procopés politiska verksamhet till år 1926* (Helsinki, 1985), p. 151.

[123] Kalervo Hovi, *Interessensphären im Baltikum.*   [124] Kalela, *Grannar på skilda vägar.*

[125] Quoted in Lemberg, *Procopé*, p. 160.

leading member of the Swedish Party and a future foreign minister, was reluctant to give up the idea of a Polish alliance) and, conversely, opposed by ultra-nationalists. The unlikelihood of overt Swedish support was made clear by the hostile public response to Hederstierna's speech in October 1923. But the fact that Finnish fears of Soviet Russia were shared by the Swedish military establishment created the basis for covert military collaboration between the two states. Although Hederstierna was forced to resign, secret cooperation between the Swedish and Finnish armed forces began soon afterwards. By the late 1930s the Swedish General Staff had developed extensive plans for intervention in Finland in the event of war. It has been suggested by Martti Turtola that the existence of such plans may have contributed to Finland's uncompromising stance in the autumn of 1939 in its negotiations with the Soviet Union – the breakdown of which led to the Soviet invasion of Finland on 30 November.[126]

The end of the 'alliance phase' of Finnish security policy, coinciding with the more stable international situation of the late 1920s, led Finland to adopt a more active role in the League of Nations. Leading politicians expressed the view that membership of the League was, in itself, a sufficient guarantee of Finnish security.[127] But this optimism was combined with a continuing reserve towards the Soviet Union which led, for example, to the collapse of negotiations for a non-aggression treaty in 1926.[128] Finland's isolation became a matter for concern in the early 1930s, when relations with the USSR deteriorated as a result of the rightward swing in Finnish politics, together with the Soviet government's forcible relocation of the Ingrian population of the Leningrad region.[129] Both governments, however, had an interest in normal-ising bilateral relations: the Soviet Union in particular was keen, as the Japanese threat grew in the Far East, to build up a network of non-aggression treaties with its European neighbours. A Finnish–Soviet non-aggression treaty was ultimately concluded in January 1932.[130]

If few members of the Finnish political establishment regarded the treaty as offering any long-term security, there was little inclination after 1933 to seek salvation in an alignment with Nazi Germany. With Germany's departure from the League in 1933, the entry of the Soviet Union the following year and the growing ineffectiveness of the League itself, the advantages of seeking shelter from great-power conflict in a Scandinavian orientation became more widely recognised.[131] Mannerheim used his influence as chairman of the Defence

---

[126] Turtola, *Från Torne älv till Systerbäck*, pp. 13–14, 207–13. For a rejoinder, see Krister Wahlbäck, 'Svek Sverige Finland hösten 1939?', *Historisk tidskrift för Finland* 74 (1989), pp. 245–76.

[127] E.g. Foreign Minister Väinö Voionmaa (October 1927), quoted in W. M. Carlgren, *Varken – eller. Reflexioner kring Sveriges Ålandpolitik 1938–1939* (Stockholm, 1977), pp. 28–9.

[128] Paasivirta, *Finland and Europe: Early Years*, pp. 309–12.

[129] The Ingrians were ethnically related to the Finns.

[130] Paasivirta, *Finland and Europe: Early Years*, pp. 396–400.   [131] Ibid., pp. 401–4.

Council to develop Finland's relations with Scandinavia in general and Sweden in particular. Holsti, who returned as foreign minister in the autumn of 1936, wished to link this new approach with the one he had long favoured – an orientation towards the Western powers – but also sought to normalise relations with the Soviet Union.[132] His visit to Moscow in February 1937, together with the election of President Kallio and the formation of the centre–left Cajander government (in which Holsti continued to serve as foreign minister), appears to have reassured the Soviet Union about Finland's determination to remain neutral in the event of war.[133]

The need for reassurance was self-evident in the light of the threatening speech of the Leningrad Party chief Andrei Zhdanov in November 1936, which warned Finland and the other border states against allowing their territories to be used as a base for aggression against the Soviet Union. But the Soviets were receiving conflicting signals. On the one hand the conciliatory attitude of the Finnish government may have led to over-optimism about the likelihood of Finland's entering into a bilateral security arrangement with the Soviet Union: hence the secret overtures to Holsti and other members of the government that were initiated in April 1938 (see ch. 9, pp. 350–3).[134] On the other hand, there were many indications of pro-German sympathies within right-wing and military circles, together with increasingly ostentatious demonstrations of interest in Finland on the part of the German military and Nazi Party leadership. Combined with the characteristic Finnish habit of totally mistrusting Soviet intentions, failing to appreciate Soviet anxieties and yet underrating the USSR's military capacity, it becomes possible to understand the mutual incomprehension that led to the Soviet–Finnish 'Winter War' which broke out in November 1939. Even before the war, however, miscalculations about Soviet attitudes were to contribute to the failure of the most ambitious attempt at Nordic security cooperation in the inter-war period: the Swedish–Finnish initiative of 1938–9 for the refortification of the Åland Islands.

Nordic cooperation

During the First World War Scandinavian economic cooperation had made significant progress; there had also been notable demonstrations of political unity at the meetings of the Scandinavian monarchs at Malmö in 1914 and Kristiania in 1917. Much of the suspicion and resentment of the years surrounding 1905 had dissipated under the influence of shared wartime experiences. It was therefore not surprising that at the end of the war there were many proposals for more permanent and more far-reaching expressions of Scandinavian solidarity.[135] Some private initiatives proved successful.

[132] Ibid., pp. 456–66.   [133] Ibid., pp. 458–9.
[134] Max Jakobson, *The Diplomacy of the Winter War* (Cambridge, Mass., 1961), pp. 11–50.
[135] Raymond E. Lindgren, *Norway–Sweden: Union, Disunion and Scandinavian Integration* (Princeton, N. J., 1959), ch. 14.

Foreningen Norden (The Nordic Society), founded in 1918–19 on the initiative of prominent academics, businessmen and politicians in Denmark, Sweden and Norway, aimed to promote awareness of a common Nordic identity, at first mainly in the cultural but later also in the economic field.[136] Even so, the Norwegians were keen to stress that the new organisation had nothing to do with politics.[137] Norwegian and Danish reluctance to contemplate more far-reaching cooperation doomed attempts to enlarge on wartime achievements at an official level. The fact that the initiative to continue the wartime meetings of foreign ministers, heads of government and economic experts came from Sweden, as it had done throughout the war, aroused Norwegian suspicions – in part justified – that the Swedes wished to use cooperation as a means of asserting their leadership role in Scandinavia.

From the start, attempts to promote greater solidarity among the Nordic states were confronted with the perennial problems. Which states were to be included? In which areas was cooperation to take place? At what levels was it to be conducted? The potential framework had been widened, but also complicated, by Finnish independence. Even though economic development and political democratisation made it easier for Scandinavian – and to an increasing extent Finnish – politicians to speak to one another, the barriers to political and military cooperation remained. Certainly as far as Norway and Denmark were concerned, the geopolitical situations of the Nordic countries remained so divergent that few could imagine circumstances in which cooperation was more advantageous than isolation. Rather than reducing the risks of involvement in war, cooperation seemed likely to increase them.

The situation for Sweden and Finland was different. Munch explained the difference candidly when he told the Rigsdag's foreign affairs committee in February 1939 that Sweden and Finland were prepared to fight a 'long-term struggle for existence', while Denmark and Norway would merely mount a 'neutrality guard'.[138] Finland, as we have seen, felt a pressing practical need for military cooperation with Sweden. Swedish political and military leaders, for their part, 'tended to regard the North as a strategic unity, with Sweden as its leading state and natural centre; politically, militarily and economically'.[139] For Sweden, all of its neighbours were potential buffer zones. Sweden thus had an interest in ensuring that Norway, Denmark and Finland were capable of defending themselves, and was prepared to initiate discussions on how this might be achieved, by either bilateral or multilateral cooperation. But the central dilemma remained. In periods of low tension, cooperation was unnecessary; in periods of high tension it was too risky. A fundamental divergence of interests, rather than opposition from the European great

[136] Henning Nielsen, *Nordens enhed gennem tiderne* (3 vols., Copenhagen, 1938), vol. III, pp. 195–9, 379–82.
[137] Berg, *Norsk utenrikspolitikks historie* II, pp. 322–3.
[138] Meeting of 10 February 1939, quoted in Sjøqvist, *Munch*, pp. 228–9.
[139] Sven G. Holtsmark and Tom Kristiansen, *En nordisk illusion? Norge og militært samarbeid i Nord 1918–1940* (Oslo, 1991), p. 8.

powers, thus lay at the heart of the Scandinavian failure to achieve a greater measure of political and strategic unity between the wars.[140]

The deterioration of the international economic and political situation after 1929 helped to revive the momentum of Scandinavian cooperation but also defined the limits of what it could achieve. Substantial progress was made in the economic field, much less in that of foreign policy (except in the sense that the Nordic states were able to coordinate their retreat from collective security) and less still in that of defence. The most substantial expression of inter-war economic cooperation was the Oslo Convention, which came into existence in 1930 on the initiative of the Norwegian prime minister Johan Mowinckel. The Convention, whose original signatories comprised Norway, Sweden and Denmark together with Belgium, the Netherlands and Luxemburg (Finland joined in 1933), represented a grouping of low-tariff countries formed in the aftermath of the breakdown of the Geneva tariff conference of 1930.[141] It had some symbolic significance as an attempt to resist the world-wide drift towards protectionism but was of little practical value: its members merely agreed to notify one another in advance of any tariff changes they proposed to make. Like the more ambitious Ouchy Convention of June 1932, the Oslo arrangement was sabotaged by the refusal of Great Britain and Germany either to participate or to waive their most-favoured-nation rights. Indeed, the mere fact of British and German opposition was sufficient to deter the Scandinavian countries from joining the Ouchy Convention.

For Mowinckel, however, Oslo represented a means by which the Scandinavian states could set an example, win the support of like-minded countries, and ultimately form a nucleus for the revival of free trade throughout the world.[142] That such hopes were not wholly unrealistic is indicated by the continuing ambivalence of Great Britain on the issue of protection versus free trade even after the adoption of tariffs in 1932 (see ch. 7, pp. 258–60). The Swedish–Belgian–Dutch initiative of 1937 for the 'revival' of the Oslo Convention, by transforming it into a free trade bloc with the participation of one or more major powers, also suggested that the cause of trade liberalisation could still win support, not least because it was one to which the United States had by then become a convert. Among the Nordic countries themselves, there was increasing coordination of government activity at an administrative level – for example in customs and communications – as well as cooperation between employers' organisations and trade unions, and between many branches of industry and commerce. But the Nordic countries remained distinct economic

---

[140] Ibid., p. 29.
[141] Ger van Roon, *Small States in Years of Depression: The Oslo Alliance 1930–1940* (Assen and Maastricht, 1989), ch. 1.
[142] Speech to the Northern Interparliamentary Union, reported in Wingfield (Oslo) to FO, 28 June 1932, FO 433/1, W7703/6995/50.

entities, whose structural similarities tended to make their interests competitive with one another rather than complementary.

Nevertheless, increased cooperation, both informally and at an institutional level, gave the Nordic countries greater self-confidence in asserting their economic interests in the face of bilateralist pressure from Great Britain and Germany. For the British, both the existence of the Oslo Convention, and the fact that it had been initiated by a man regarded as the most inveterate opponent of the British blockade in Norway, recalled the cooperation which had helped to strengthen Scandinavian resistance to British economic pressure during the First World War.[143] In 1932 the British minister in Oslo echoed Findlay's objections of a decade earlier to a Scandinavian combination which would be dominated by Sweden and which 'might result in utilising Norway, with all her importance as a strategic factor, to subserve ends which are not Norwegian ones and may be to the detriment of the United Kingdom'.[144] There was some substance to such fears. Early in 1937 Swedish politicians and economists were openly critical of the way in which British commercial pressure had transformed Denmark into a closed economic system, increasingly isolated from the other Nordic countries. 'The blame for Denmark's ills is all laid at the United Kingdom's door', a Bank of England official noted.[145] The 'revival' of the Oslo Convention in 1937 was a clear challenge to the protectionist trading system built up by Great Britain since 1931.[146] It was repulsed without difficulty but was nevertheless a disquieting indication of the growing self-assurance of the smaller European states.

The revival of political cooperation began when the meetings of the three Scandinavian foreign ministers were resumed in Copenhagen in 1932 after ten years of 'hibernation'.[147] Owing to the antagonism between Norway and Denmark over the East Greenland question they did not meet again until September 1934, when they were joined, at Sandler's invitation, by the Finnish foreign minister. Finland's increasing participation in Nordic economic and political collaboration represented in one sense a fulfilment of the hopes expressed by a British official in the early 1920s: that Finland would gravitate into 'the orbit of the civilized, unbellicose and let us hope permanently neutral Scandinavian bloc – neutral herself and no cause of war to others'.[148] However Finland's relationship with the Scandinavian countries remained problema-

---

[143] See e.g. Findlay's characterisation of Mowinckel, 'whose constitutionally Germanic tendencies are perhaps due to the Hanseatic origin of his family, and who throughout the War, in spite of many professions of sympathy, was the most dangerous opponent of all our blockade measures in Norway': despatch of 29 June 1922, FO 371/8106, N6414/3904/63.

[144] Charles Wingfield to FO, 28 June 1932, FO 433/1, W7703/6995/50.

[145] Memorandum by Cameron Cobbold, 5 February 1937, BEA, OV 27/5.

[146] Bengt Nilson, *Handelspolitik under skärpt konkurrens. England och Sverige 1929–1939* (Lund, 1983), pp. 76–81.

[147] Yngve Möller, *Rickard Sandler. Folkbildare. Utrikesminister* (Stockholm, 1990), p. 252.

[148] Minute by Esmond Ovey, 26 January 1922, FO 371/8104, N762/82/63.

tical. If, from the Scandinavian point of view, Finnish participation helped to strengthen Finnish democracy and consolidate a buffer against Soviet aggression, it also heightened the risk of Scandinavian involvement in a German–Soviet war. For Munch in particular, Finnish participation threatened to disturb the non-provocative character of Scandinavian cooperation.[149] And it was true that Finland had not abandoned, merely sublimated, its search for an alliance partner. Through the ambiguity of Finland's principal Scandinavian interlocutor, Rickard Sandler, the Finns were led to expect more in the way of support than any of the Scandinavian countries, including Sweden, were prepared to offer.

Nordic defence cooperation first became a serious issue in the aftermath of the breakdown of collective security over Abyssinia in 1935–6.[150] By the time their foreign ministers met in Copenhagen in August 1936, the Nordic countries had already followed the British lead and repudiated their sanctions obligations under Article 16 of the League Covenant. At the Copenhagen meeting the possibility of a Nordic regional pact under the auspices of the League was formally raised for the first time.[151] It received little support. On the one hand, Sweden (represented by K. G. Westman, foreign minister in the short-lived bourgeois government of 1936) was not prepared to commit itself unconditionally to the defence of Denmark or any other Nordic country. On the other, Denmark and Norway could contemplate a regional pact only if Great Britain was also a member. Yet, Munch asserted, Britain had abandoned the Baltic and was not interested in Denmark's maritime position.

Only Finland was unreservedly in favour of pursuing the military implications of Nordic cooperation. Mannerheim in particular sought to use the League's endorsement of regional groupings as a means of enhancing Finnish security. He was encouraged by a conversation with the British foreign secretary Anthony Eden in January 1936 in which the latter appeared to favour a regional pact among the Nordic states, though he gave no promise of British support.[152] Like Munch, but in a positive rather than a negative sense, the Finns regarded Britain's attitude as being decisive for any Nordic security arrangement. According to a memorandum prepared in advance of the Copenhagen meeting by the Finnish foreign policy expert Rafael Erich, Britain perceived 'perhaps more clearly than the other powers the importance of these countries, their need for security and also their desire to stay outside great-

[149] Sjøqvist, *Danmarks udenrigspolitik*, pp. 99–100.
[150] Nils Ørvik, 'From Collective Security to Neutrality: The Nordic Powers, the League of Nations, Britain and the Approach of War 1935–1939', in K. Bourne and D. C. Watt (eds.), *Studies in International History: Essays Presented to W. Norton Medlicott* (London, 1967), pp. 385–401.
[151] Sjøqvist, *Danmarks udenrigspolitik*, pp. 157–8; Lönnroth, *Den svenska utrikespolitikens historia* V, pp. 187–8.
[152] Eden to Grant-Watson (Helsinki), 31 January 1936, FO 371/20330, N623/623/56; Baron C. G. E. Mannerheim, *The Memoirs of Marshal Mannerheim* (London, 1953), pp. 285–8; Turtola, *Från Torne älv till Systerbäck*, pp. 173–5.

power complications'.[153] The task was now to discover whether the prospect of British support was quite as hopeless as Munch believed. The omens were not promising. The signature of the Anglo-German naval agreement in June 1935 had shown that Britain's relations with the countries of northern Europe were subject to wider and more pressing policy considerations.[154] Viewed in a more optimistic light, however, the period 1936–7 was one in which, although collective security had been discredited, Great Britain had not yet been wholly written off as a source of support. Hence the series of visits paid by Nordic leaders to London in these years aimed, in part at least, at clarifying Britain's position: first Mannerheim in January 1936; then, in March and April 1937 respectively, Sandler and Stauning.

If Mannerheim stood at one extreme on the issue of Nordic defence cooperation, Stauning stood at the other. In a contentious speech in the Swedish university city of Lund on 8 March 1937, Stauning characterised a Nordic defence alliance as 'utopian' – not the first or the last occasion on which he used that term.[155] Denmark could not, he declared, act as a 'watchdog' for the North. Having been given no support by Sweden in 1864, it could not now be expected to defend its southern frontier in order to enhance the security of the other Nordic states. It was the calculated bluntness of Stauning's language rather than the content of his speech which aroused controversy. Knowing that Swedish ministers had made no commitment to coordinate their defence policies with those of Denmark, Stauning wished to remind the Swedish public that little of substance lay behind the rhetoric of Nordic cooperation.[156] Stauning was also preoccupied in early 1937 with his initiative for a bilateral agreement with Germany and probably wished to reassure the Germans that there was no chance of Denmark's aligning itself with a Nordic defence arrangement which would be, implicitly at least, anti-German.[157] His intention may also have been to deflect German criticism before his visit to London.[158] It has been suggested, finally, that Stauning aimed to prevent the formation of a regional defence arrangement among the other three Nordic states, which would serve further to heighten Denmark's isolation.[159]

Stauning's conversation with Eden on 8 April 1937 confirmed that, apart from its commitments to France and Belgium under the Locarno treaties, Britain had no obligations in Europe beyond those contained in the League Covenant.[160] If Denmark were attacked by Germany, which seemed improb-

---

[153] Quoted in Turtola, *Från Torne älv till Systerbäck*, p. 182.

[154] See chs. 8 and 9, pp. 298–300 and 335.

[155] Speech at Social Democratic conference in Copenhagen, reported in Ramsay to FO, 18 November 1936, FO 371/20332, N5805/1923/63; conversation with Eden, 8 April 1937, FO 371/21075, N1937/1380/15.

[156] Sjøqvist, *Danmarks udenrigspolitik*, pp. 182–3.

[157] Ibid., p. 180. For his success in this respect, see Duckwitz (Copenhagen) to Grundherr, 15 March 1937, PA, AA Abt. Pol. VI Po. 2, Dänemark, Bd 1.

[158] Lönnroth, *Den svenska utrikespolitikens historia* V, pp. 188–9.

[159] Ørvik, 'From Collective Security to Neutrality', pp. 392–3.

[160] FO 371/21075, N1937/1380/15.

able, Britain would offer diplomatic support, but that was all.[161] This information came as neither a surprise nor a disappointment to Stauning who was, moreover, encouraged by the warm endorsement by Neville Chamberlain, soon to become prime minister, of his suggestion that the only hope for world peace lay in a rapprochement between Britain and Germany.[162]

When the Swedish foreign minister Sandler visited London a few weeks before Stauning, in mid-March 1937, he received a very similar message from Eden but chose to interpret it more positively. Sandler may already have had in mind some kind of Nordic defence arrangement, for which British support would be a prerequisite. He had been encouraged by the start of the British rearmament programme in 1936 and now wished to sound out Britain's attitude towards the most exposed part of the Nordic region: the Danish–German frontier.[163] In conversation with Sandler on 15 March, Eden cited a speech he had delivered at Leamington in November 1936 in which, while disclaiming any specific European obligations beyond Locarno, he had indicated that British arms might be used to assist any victim of unprovoked aggression. He could, however, make no promises concerning Denmark, while Sandler, when challenged, had to admit that Sweden too would be unable 'to offer any effective resistance' in the event of a German demand upon Denmark.[164]

Sandler nevertheless felt able to inform the Nordic foreign ministers, at their meeting in Helsinki in April, that Eden's Leamington speech held out a real possibility that Britain '*might* yet', in Ørvik's words, 'come to the rescue of a League member who had fallen prey to aggression. Therefore, one might still hope for British support for a regional defence arrangement of the Nordic states.'[165] He cited Eden's words again in a radio speech on 28 April, though he did not venture to mention the possibility of a Nordic defence alliance.[166] Sandler's private thoughts appear to have been less sanguine than his public utterances. His reference to the Anglo-German naval agreement in a statement to the Riksdag's foreign affairs committee shortly before his London visit indicated that he was as aware as anyone that it signified a diminished British naval interest in the Baltic, and he said as much again to Eden.[167] Moreover

---

[161] 'Powerful' support, according to Stauning's account to Det udenrigspolitiske Nævn, the parliamentary committee on foreign affairs, 4 May 1937, RA, UM 64 Dan. 73a, Bd XXV.

[162] Sjøqvist, *Danmarks udenrigspolitik*, p. 193.

[163] Lönnroth, *Den svenska utrikespolitikens historia* V, pp. 189–90, states that Sandler also wished to discuss the position of Finland, but this subject was not raised during his conversation with Eden.

[164] Eden to Palairet (Stockholm), 15 March 1937, FO 371/21072, N1499/26/15.

[165] Ørvik, 'From Collective Security to Neutrality', p. 391.

[166] Lönnroth, *Den svenska utrikespolitikens historia* V, p. 192.

[167] Möller, *Sandler*, p. 319. This part of the conversation does not appear in the official British record but is confirmed by the memoirs of a Swedish diplomat who accompanied Sandler to London: Gunnar Hägglöf, *Möte med Europa. Paris–London–Moskva–Genève–Berlin* (Stockholm, 1971), p. 174.

Sandler's own record of that conversation was less positive than the version he gave to his Nordic ministerial colleagues.[168]

In promoting the idea of Nordic defence cooperation, Sandler was rarely explicit about what it would entail. That 'his public utterances were rarely models of clarity' was deliberate.[169] Sandler could not have forgotten Hederstierna's fate in 1923. He disclaimed any attempt to construct a full-scale military alliance; yet, carried to its logical conclusion, a common endeavour to preserve Scandinavian neutrality would have required each country to take some responsibility for the defence of its neighbours: 'in some critical situations it will be possible to say that a neutrality that has become Nordic is no longer neutrality, because thereby Sweden does not take a neutral stance towards a brother country'.[170]

Sandler's basic idea appears to have been that the Nordic countries should form a neutral bloc and coordinate military and economic measures in certain limited fields. This would enhance their capacity to stand apart from conflicts between the great powers and permit them to be written out of their strategic calculations, but it would also enable them to assist one another if the worst came to the worst.[171] If they could reach agreement on limited measures it might be possible, he believed, to make progress towards 'larger projects and solutions'.[172] At its most extensive, as outlined at the meeting of Nordic foreign ministers in Oslo in April 1938, Sandler's conception included collaboration in the defence of the Åland Islands, Lapland and the Sound, the stockpiling of strategic goods and the joint production of war materials. However, the Åland option was clearly the one closest to Sandler's heart. He may thus have intended to make it acceptable by merging it in the broader context of Nordic solidarity.[173]

In certain very limited respects, military cooperation of the kind advocated by Sandler did make some progress in the years 1938–9.[174] The Swedish and Norwegian air forces exchanged information on air defences; their naval counterparts agreed to keep each other informed of the movements of foreign warships in Scandinavian waters; blackout arrangements for cities bordering the Sound were discussed by the Swedish and Danish authorities; Sweden, Norway and Finland discussed communications in the far north. In each case the initiative came from the Swedish side. There were also discussions on economic cooperation in wartime both among the Nordic states and – very belatedly – within the wider context of the Oslo group.[175] But, as Holtsmark and Kristiansen have suggested, such measures were adopted precisely because

---

[168] Lönnroth, *Den svenska utrikespolitikens historia* V, p. 190.
[169] Upton, 'Crisis of Scandinavia', p. 173.
[170] Radio address of 4 April 1938, quoted in Upton, 'Crisis of Scandinavia', p. 174.
[171] Möller, *Sandler*, pp. 336–7, 343–4, 354–5; Upton, 'Crisis of Scandinavia', p. 172.
[172] Hägglöf, *Möte med Europa*, p. 174.   [173] Upton, 'Crisis of Scandinavia', p. 174.
[174] Holtsmark and Kristiansen, *En nordisk illusion?*, pp. 68–76; Turtola, *Från Torne älv till Systerbäck*, pp. 191–2.
[175] Roon, *Small States*, pp. 262–3, 290, 298–307.

they were not regarded as the prelude to a military alliance.[176] Even Koht, normally vigilant, was content to treat cooperation at this level as a technical matter, to be dealt with by the armed forces rather than by foreign ministries.

In the light of Britain's refusal to make any gesture of support and the refusal of Denmark and Norway to contemplate more far-reaching cooperation, Sandler fell back on the Swedish–Finnish axis as the only one based on a real community of interest and a shared perception of threat. The Anschluss crisis of March 1938 appears to have been decisive for Sandler's adoption of a proposal which had been under consideration for some time by Swedish and Finnish military leaders, for the refortification of the Åland Islands.[177] With the increasing likelihood of war between Germany and the Soviet Union, the Åland convention of 1921 had come to be regarded as an insufficient guarantee against the seizure of the islands by one or other of the belligerents. The strategic importance of the Åland Islands derived from their position at the entrance to the Gulf of Bothnia, controlling the German iron ore route from Luleå but also representing, in the hands of a hostile power, a direct threat to the security of Stockholm and central Sweden. Politically, Sandler believed, an agreement for the joint fortification of the Ålands would reinforce Finland's Scandinavian orientation and prevent it from looking to Germany for support. And the more Finland was associated with Sweden and Scandinavia, the less it would be regarded by the Soviet Union as a security threat.

The need to reassure the USSR explained the complex nature of the 'Stockholm plan' agreed by the Finnish and Swedish governments in July 1938 and presented to the signatories of the Åland convention (Britain, France, Germany and Italy), together with the Soviet Union, in January 1939.[178] Part of the plan entailed a revision of the Åland convention, for which the consent of the signatories was required, but another part was made dependent on a decision by the Council of the League of Nations. The Soviet Union had not signed the convention, but was a member of the League Council. It could thus be given an opportunity to make its views known and, so it was hoped, give its approval when the Council met in May 1939.

There was clearly something wrong with a plan which was intended to prevent the great powers from attacking the Ålands but which could not be put into effect without their consent.[179] The Germans had decided that the refortification of the islands was in their interest but linked their approval, eventually given on 2 May, to an assurance that Sweden would continue to

[176] Holtsmark and Kristiansen, *En nordisk illusion?*, pp. 68, 76, 90.
[177] For the Finnish military background, see Turtola, *Från Torne älv till Systerbäck*, pp. 150–3; for the Swedish, see Carlgren, *Varken – eller*, pp. 9–25, 74–83.
[178] The most authoritative accounts of the origins and development of the Swedish–Finnish plan are in Krister Wahlbäck, *Finlandsfrågan i svensk politik 1937–1940* (Stockholm, 1964), and Carlgren, *Varken – eller*. For a concise account based on Swedish and Finnish sources, see Upton, 'Crisis of Scandinavia'.
[179] Carlgren, *Varken – eller*, p. 215.

supply normal quantities of iron ore in time of war.[180] The British, whose interests were affected less directly, had given their approval in February but remained ambivalent about the merits of the plan and were increasingly anxious not to antagonise the USSR at a time when negotiations for a British–French–Soviet alliance were in progress.[181] The attitude of the Soviet Union was therefore crucial.

The Soviet response has to be seen in the context of its secret overtures to Finland, initiated in the spring of 1938, aimed at reaching some kind of security arrangement which would prevent Finnish territory from being used in a German attack on the USSR.[182] Although Litvinov's initial comments on the possibility of Finland's refortifying the islands were decidedly negative, Sandler felt that the Soviets were more positive towards both Sweden and the idea of Swedish–Finnish cooperation.[183] Indeed, early in 1939 they indicated that they might approve the plan on condition that the fortifications would never be handed over to Germany. Their approval was also linked to a proposal made in March 1939 that a group of islands in the Gulf of Finland which were important to the security of Leningrad should be leased to the Soviet Union for thirty years.[184] The Finnish refusal to accept this proposal led to the lapse of the secret contacts between the two countries early in April. Shortly afterwards Litvinov was replaced by Molotov as commissar for foreign affairs. There was now no hope of Soviet approval. When the League Council met in May, Molotov insisted that a decision on the plan must be postponed. In the face of this effective veto, the Swedish government withdrew its support for the plan. The signature of the Nazi–Soviet pact at the end of August 1939 transformed the balance of power in the Baltic and made the Åland plan redundant.

The Soviet veto was clearly decisive, yet there can be no doubt that the Åland plan had weaknesses which were inherent from the outset: in the relationship between Sweden and Finland, in relations between the armed forces and civilian politicians, and within the Swedish government itself. Swedish and Finnish priorities were fundamentally different. The Finns were preparing for war, the Swedes seeking to avoid it. Yet Sweden was still contemplating a fundamental change in its neutrality policy. In order to preserve its neutrality, Sweden would be taking on security obligations beyond its frontiers. This was an issue of critical importance on which the decisive challenge came not from parliament or public opinion but from within the Cabinet. The attitude of the prime minister, Per Albin Hansson, was at best ambivalent. Ostensibly a supporter of the plan, he assured one critic that

---

[180] Gerd R. Ueberschär, *Hitler und Finnland. Die deutsch–finnischen Beziehungen während des Hitler–Stalin-Paktes* (Wiesbaden, 1978), pp. 45–9. See also pp. 325–6 in this volume.

[181] Thomas Munch-Petersen, 'Great Britain and the Revision of the Åland Convention', *Scandia* 41 (1975), pp. 67–86.

[182] See pp. 350–3 in this volume.   [183] Carlgren, *Varken – eller*, pp. 98–101, 139–44.

[184] Soviet records of Soviet–Finnish exchanges, 5–11 March 1939, printed in 'The Winter War (Documents on Soviet–Finnish Relations in 1939–1940)', *International Affairs* (Moscow) 1989, No. 9, pp. 49–71 (pp. 53–7).

'nothing will come of it, and I shall not be the one to grieve over it'.[185] However, Ernst Wigforss, the minister of finance and one of the strongest figures in the government, was hostile to both Sandler and the Åland plan, and was instrumental in securing its rejection by the Cabinet in June 1939. The government's stance, and Sandler's isolation, were to be confirmed in December 1939 when, following the Soviet attack, Finland asked Sweden to implement the Stockholm plan. The government refused to do so and Sandler had no option but to resign.

[185] Quoted in Upton, 'Crisis of Scandinavia', p. 178.

6 Confrontation and co-existence: Scandinavia and the great powers after the First World War

Before 1914 Scandinavia had felt the repercussions of confrontation between the great powers without being the principal focus of their attention. The Nordic states were affected in a similarly indirect way by the changing international climate of the post-war period: first the transition from war to peace under the auspices of the treaty of Versailles; then, in the Locarno era after 1925, the emergence of a more equitable international order; finally, the onset of the great depression. But although the European powers rarely took a direct interest in Scandinavian affairs, their attention was drawn to northern Europe, especially in the early 1920s, by the persistent instability of the eastern Baltic.

After a period of active involvement with the newly independent states of Finland, Estonia and Latvia, Great Britain withdrew its naval presence from the eastern Baltic in 1921 but retained an interest in reducing friction among the states of the region – for example, between Poland and Lithuania over the disputed Vilnius territory – in the interests of European peace in general and as a bulwark against Bolshevik Russia.[1] France was concerned much more overtly with the construction of a *cordon sanitaire* against Bolshevism centred on Poland and the countries of the 'Little Entente', which also had Baltic ramifications. Russia and Germany, at whose expense the new order in eastern Europe had been constructed, had a shared interest in the demise of Poland, the largest of the new states, but were able to find a basis for co-existence with Estonia, Latvia and Lithuania. Nevertheless, the long-term existence of these three small states was precarious and it was widely assumed that they must ultimately be reabsorbed by Russia. The one new state whose survival seemed assured was Finland. Even the Soviets, in concluding a peace treaty with Finland at Tartu (Dorpat) in 1920, seem to have acknowledged that it was in a different category from the three Baltic states. Finland constituted a bridge between the eastern Baltic and Scandinavia. For Sweden above all it was a potential barrier to Soviet incursions, but at the same time a source of danger if it allowed its fate to be identified too closely with that of Poland and the three Baltic states. Finland also became part of the front line in the ideological

[1] For a German perspective on Britain's Baltic policy, see John Hiden, *The Baltic States and Weimar* Ostpolitik (Cambridge, 1987), pp. 145–7.

confrontation between Soviet Russia and the West in general, and Great Britain in particular.

Britain's preoccupation with the European balance of power made it vigilant towards supposed hegemonic aspirations on the part of other powers: Germany, France and Russia. To this traditional concern was added the new challenge of Soviet communism. In the early 1920s the Scandinavian states were conscripted with varying degrees of reluctance into Britain's diplomatic campaign against the Bolshevik regime. Finland, Estonia and Latvia had fewer qualms about becoming tacit partners in Western surveillance of their formidable neighbour. The Soviet Union for its part was preoccupied with the danger of 'encirclement' by the capitalist powers, led by Great Britain and possibly embracing several of the smaller states of the region. With the memory of Western intervention in the Russian civil war still fresh, there were also fears of a British-led military attack. Diplomatically, the Soviet Union sought to neutralise this threat by concluding non-aggression pacts with neighbouring states; militarily it could do little more than adopt a defensive strategy, relying on diplomacy to supplement its meagre naval forces in the Baltic Sea and the Arctic Ocean. At the same time, the activities of the Communist International in Scandinavia indicated that the Soviet Union had not abandoned its revolutionary aspirations in the region.

Institutions and ideologies: great-power relations with the Nordic states

The modernisation of Nordic societies between the wars continued to be accompanied by a high degree of exposure to external influences – cultural, technological and political. German influence remained strong in Finland and in academic circles more generally.[2] The class conflicts which characterised Nordic societies at least up to the mid-1930s led both the left and the right to look abroad for support and inspiration. In the most divided societies, Finland and Norway, the Soviet Union was the obvious model for the left, while on the right Italian fascism exercised a strong appeal until it was supplanted by the more vigorous German variant. However, the Anglo-Saxon countries came increasingly to be regarded as the chief models of progress. The Swedish political commentator Herbert Tingsten saw the 1920s as a period in which 'culturally and ideologically British influence grew stronger and stronger', and the one during which 'Britain stepped into Germany's old place in the Swedish cultural world'.[3] In Finland, a British minister discerned the rise of a new generation of politicians, 'enthusiastic, ambitious and hard-bitten', for whom

---

[2] Juhani Paasivirta, *Finland and Europe: The Early Years of Independence 1917–1939* (Helsinki, 1988), pp. 321–47, 482–500.

[3] Herbert Tingsten, *The Debate on the Foreign Policy of Sweden 1918–1939* (London, 1949), p. 28.

the confines of the Baltic and even of Scandinavia were too narrow. 'Nowadays', said one, 'we leap over Scandinavia to England.'[4]

English replaced German as the first foreign language spoken in Scandinavia. But in learning English many looked beyond Great Britain to the USA. The chief source of technical instruction, formerly Germany, was now the United States. It had also grown enormously in wealth and prestige. Even in Norway, where British influence had formerly been 'paramount', Britain's standing had already declined significantly by 1929: 'London is no longer regarded as the real financial centre of the world, and, though Norwegians much prefer their old business friends to the Americans, it is impossible for them to avoid looking more and more to New York.'[5] Admiration for the United States was perhaps strongest in Sweden. This was, one British diplomat condescendingly suggested, 'partly because of her predominant wealth and power, partly because of the large number of Swedes settled there, and partly because the United States also is undeveloped intellectually and the Swede finds in her material, scientific and mechanical civilisation something which he really can understand'.[6] In such a climate it was not surprising that, after 1933, clumsy expressions of Nazi admiration for the inhabitants of Scandinavia on the grounds of their Nordic racial identity merely intensified the eclipse of German cultural influence.[7] 'At the moment we are not *modern* in Scandinavia', lamented a German academic in 1935.[8] According to a German racial expert who visited the Nordic countries in the summer of 1936, Scandinavians lived 'too well, too materialistically and too undisturbed' to be receptive to National Socialist doctrines.[9]

In Great Britain, Germany and Soviet Russia the task of conducting relations with the Nordic countries fell to foreign ministries and diplomatic services which had been radically affected, in both organisation and influence, by the First World War and its aftermath. The changes were of course most extreme in the case of Bolshevik Russia, a revolutionary state which was nevertheless obliged to reach a *modus vivendi* with the outside world.[10] Two institutions

---

[4] Ernest Rennie to FO, 27 February 1929, FO 419/20, N1676/233/56. This impression is supported by the observations on Finnish interest in Britain and the English language in E. W. Polson Newman, *Britain and the Baltic* (London, 1930), pp. 219–23.

[5] Sir F. Lindley to FO, 2 September 1929, FO 419/21, N4026/443/30.

[6] Sir Tudor Vaughan, 'Sweden. Annual Report, 1928', 8 March 1929, FO 371/14055, N1989/1989/42.

[7] Hans-Jürgen Lutzhöft, *Der Nordische Gedanke in Deutschland 1920–1940* (Stuttgart, 1971).

[8] Memorandum by Dr Kappner (Stockholm representative of the Akademisches Austauschdienst), 'Schweden als baltisches Kulturzentrum', 18 June 1935, enclosure in Wied to AA, 24 July 1935, PA, AA Pol. Abt. IV Nd, Schweden, Politik, Bd 1.

[9] Report on tour of Scandinavia by SS Unterstrumführer Dr Alfred Thoss, 21 August 1936, BA, Nachlass Darré 42.

[10] Teddy J. Uldricks, *Diplomacy and Ideology: The Origins of Soviet Foreign Relations 1917–1930* (London and Beverly Hills, 1979); Theodore H. von Laue, 'Soviet Diplomacy: G. V. Chicherin, People's Commissar for Foreign Affairs 1918–1930', in Gordon A. Craig and Felix Gilbert (eds.), *The Diplomats 1919–1939* (Princeton, N. J., 1953), pp. 234–81.

embodied this dichotomy. One was the Commissariat for Foreign Affairs (Narkomindel), which had inherited some of the diplomats of the old regime and all of its great-power pretensions. Narkomindel insisted (despite Trotsky's repudiation of imperialist treaties) on the maintenance of Russia's legal rights in issues affecting the Nordic countries such as the international status of the Åland Islands or of Svalbard.[11] The other was the Communist International, which represented the continuing commitment to world revolution and took a particular interest in the countries of northern Europe. Finnish Communists such as Arvo Tuominen and Otto Kuusinen were prominent within the leadership, and the Comintern maintained a network of agents in Scandinavia.[12] According to the testimony of the German Communist Richard Krebs, Comintern agents were particularly active in northern Norway in the 1930s.[13]

Chicherin, head of Narkomindel from 1918 to 1930, insisted that a strict distinction must be observed between the actions of the Soviet state and those of the Comintern.[14] But it would be misleading to draw too sharp a contrast between a pragmatic Narkomindel and an ideologically driven Comintern. Chicherin was steeped in the history of tsarist diplomacy but there is nothing to suggest that he or his successor Litvinov were not convinced revolutionaries, or that revolutionaries could not make good diplomats.[15] Soviet Russia's first officially accredited diplomatic representative in Norway, Aleksandra Kollontai, knew Scandinavia well as a result of her clandestine travels.[16] She was able to exploit her contacts on the left of Norwegian politics, while establishing excellent working relationships with bourgeois ministers.[17] Indeed, her

[11] Patrick Salmon, 'Perceptions and Misperceptions: Great Britain and the Soviet Union in Scandinavia and the Baltic Region 1918–1939', in John Hiden and Aleksander Loit (eds.), *Contact or Isolation? Soviet–Western Relations in the Interwar Period* (Stockholm, 1991), pp. 415–29 (p. 418).

[12] Arvo Tuominen, *The Bells of the Kremlin: An Experience in Communism* (Hanover and London, 1983); Aino Kuusinen, *Before and After Stalin* (London, 1974).

[13] Jan Valtin (pseud. of Richard Krebs), *Out of the Night* (London, 1941; repr. London, 1988), pp. 322, 388–9.

[14] Chicherin to Mikhailov (Kristiania), 18 November 1921, in Sven Holtsmark (ed.), *Norge og Sovjetunionen 1917–1955. En utenrikspolitisk dokumentasjon* (Oslo, 1995), pp. 72–3.

[15] Timothy Edward O'Connor, *Diplomacy and Revolution: G. V. Chicherin and Soviet Foreign Affairs 1918–1930* (Ames, Iowa, 1988), pp. 9–10. Chicherin had made a study of the nineteenth-century Russian foreign minister Gorchakov. He was also familiar with Isvolsky's diplomacy at the time of the negotiations for the Norwegian integrity treaty in 1907: see Patrick Salmon, *Foreign Policy and National Identity: The Norwegian Integrity Treaty 1907–1924* (Oslo, 1993), p. 39.

[16] Kollontai's diaries for this period have been published in the Moscow periodical *International Affairs* 1988, No. 10, pp. 117–27, No. 11, pp. 127–36, No. 12, pp. 107–18; 1989, No. 1, pp. 106–22, though their historical value is reduced by Kollontai's own 'editing' in the 1940s and by subsequent cuts in the text. See Sven Holtsmark, *A Soviet Grab for the High North? USSR, Svalbard and Northern Norway 1920–1953* (Oslo, 1993), p. 21 (n. 21).

[17] Though Chicherin criticised her for going too far in interfering in domestic Norwegian politics: Chicherin to Kollontai, 4 November 1922, in Holtsmark, *Norge og Sovjetunionen*, p. 86. Kollontai to Litvinov, 12 February 1923, refers to information given to her by Communist members of the Storting's foreign affairs committee: ibid., pp. 94–6.

successor was advised by Litvinov that, in a country with such strong democratic traditions as Norway, it was necessary to win friends in all sections of Norwegian society since it was not only the party which happened to be in government that made policy.[18] Kollontai's diplomatic skills and Scandinavian contacts were later to be put to use when, as minister to Sweden, she served as a key intermediary between Finland and the Soviet Union during the Second World War.[19] To an increasing extent, however, Soviet diplomats acted as the instruments of Stalin's will: bringing pressure on the Norwegian government to secure the expulsion of Trotsky from Norway in 1936; or, in the late 1930s, laying the diplomatic groundwork for the extension of the Soviet defensive sphere westwards to meet the anticipated German attack.

The reform of the German Foreign Office undertaken in the first years of the Weimar Republic was aimed at making it more competent in economic matters, more open in its recruitment procedures and, for the first time, democratically accountable.[20] None of these objectives was fully realised. One important innovation was the reorganisation of the Auswärtiges Amt's departments on a regional basis – at first six, but reduced in 1921 to three – in order to overcome what Schüler, the chief architect of the reforms, described as 'one of the basic errors of the old Foreign Office': the separation of politics and economics.[21] After 1921 Scandinavian affairs, along with those of eastern Europe and the Far East, were the responsibility of Abteilung (Department) IV. The reforms also led to the establishment of a special department for foreign trade, Abteilung X, as a means of collecting commercial intelligence and enhancing the Wilhelmstrasse's traditional pre-eminence in the making of commercial policy.

Rivalry over the control of foreign trade policy between the Auswärtiges Amt and the newly established Economics Ministry led to administrative confusion, and Abteilung X was dissolved in October 1921.[22] The Foreign Office's

[18] Litvinov to A. M. Makar, 18 May 1926, ibid., pp. 146–8.

[19] Kaare Hauge, *Alexandra Mikhailovna Kollontai: The Scandinavian Period 1922–1945* (Ph.D thesis, University of Minnesota, 1971; published Ann Arbor, Mich., 1986); Ingemar Lindedahl, 'Alexandra Kollontaj och Norden', in Mats Bergquist, Alf W. Johansson and Krister Wahlbäck (eds.), *Utrikespolitik och historia. Studier tillägnade Wilhelm M. Carlgren den 6 maj 1987* (Stockholm, 1987), pp. 145–62.

[20] Peter Krüger, *Die Aussenpolitik der Republik von Weimar* (Darmstadt, 1985), pp. 23–30; Kurt Doss, *Das deutsche Auswärtige Amt im Übergang vom Kaiserreich zur Weimarer Republik. Die Schülersche Reform* (Düsseldorf, 1977); Hans-Jürgen Döscher, *Das Auswärtige Amt im Dritten Reich. Diplomatie im Schatten der 'Endlösung'* (Berlin, 1987); Hans-Adolf Jacobsen, *Nationalsozialistische Aussenpolitik 1933–1938* (Frankfurt am Main and Berlin, 1968), pp. 20–2.

[21] Quoted in Döscher, *Das Auswärtige Amt im Dritten Reich*, p. 22.

[22] Friedrich Facius, *Wirtschaft und Staat. Die Entwicklung der staatlichen Wirtschaftsverwaltung in Deutschland vom 17. Jahrhundert bis 1945* (Boppard am Rhein, 1959), p. 109; Hans-Jürgen Schröder, 'Zur politischen Bedeutung der deutschen Handelspolitik nach dem Ersten Weltkrieg', in Gerald D. Feldman, Carl-Ludwig Holtfrerich, Gerhard A. Ritter and Peter-Christian Witt (eds.), *Die deutsche Inflation. Eine Zwischenbilanz* (Berlin and New York, 1982), pp. 235–51.

leading role in international economic relations was, however, reasserted with the establishment of a department for reparations questions and economic affairs (Sonderreferat Wirtschaft) under Karl Ritter, a former economic journalist and colonial administrator who, in his capacity as controller of food and raw material supplies at the Ministry of the Interior, had worked closely with Rathenau during the war.[23] Its pre-eminence was reinforced by the establishment in 1925 of the semi-secret Handelspolitischer Ausschuss (trade policy committee). Chaired by Ritter, the HPA also included representatives of the Ministries of Economics, Finance and Agriculture. Its members possessed unrivalled expertise in international economic negotiations and had close personal contacts with business leaders.[24] But it was never possible fully to resolve the conflicting interests of the various ministries claiming a voice in the making of foreign economic policy. The struggle was largely suppressed between 1925 and 1929, but broke out with new intensity under the impact of the great depression.[25] Even the HPA was not immune from such pressures, with the representative of the Agriculture Ministry frequently finding himself at loggerheads with the other members.[26]

In terms of recruitment, the 'Schüler' reforms were soon undermined in favour of the traditional career diplomats, but the administrative structure survived largely unaltered until 1936 when, under Constantin von Neurath as foreign minister and Bernhard von Bülow as state secretary, the essentials of the pre-1918 system were restored.[27] Political and economic affairs were separated once more. Relations with the Scandinavian and Baltic states were now the responsibility of the sixth section of the Political Department (Pol VI), headed by Werner von Grundherr, while Ritter presided over an enlarged Economic Policy Department (Abteilung W).

Like other aspects of public life in the Third Reich, foreign policy became a focus of interest for members of the new National Socialist hierarchy as they attempted to carve out spheres of influence in competition both among themselves and with the old ministerial bureaucracy. Scandinavia occupied a special place in National Socialist ideology as the place where the purest

---

[23] Dörte Doering, 'Deutsche Aussenwirtschaftspolitik 1933–1935. Die Gleichschaltung der Aussenwirtschaft in der Frühphase des nationalsozialistischen Regimes' (Doctoral dissertation, Free University of Berlin, 1969), pp. 100–5.

[24] Dirk Stegmann, '"Mitteleuropa" 1925–1934. Zum Problem der Kontinuität deutscher Handelspolitik von Stresemann bis Hitler', in Stegmann, Bernd-Jürgen Wendt and Peter-Christian Witt (eds.), Industrielle Gesellschaft und politisches System (Bonn, 1978), pp. 203–21; Karl Heinrich Pohl, Weimars Wirtschaft und die Aussenpolitik der Republik 1924–1926 (Düsseldorf, 1979), pp. 76–8.

[25] Hajo Holborn, 'Diplomats and Diplomacy in the Early Weimar Republic', in Craig and Gilbert, The Diplomats 1919–1939, pp. 123–71 (p. 150).

[26] Harm Schröter, Aussenpolitik und Wirtschaftsinteresse. Skandinavien im aussenwirtschaftlichen Kalkül Deutschlands und Grossbritanniens 1918–1939 (Frankfurt am Main, Berne and New York, 1983), pp. 39–40.

[27] Döscher, Das Auswärtige Amt im Dritten Reich, p. 24; Jacobsen, Nationalsozialistische Aussenpolitik, p. 22.

specimens of the Nordic race were supposed to live.[28] Each of the two leading exponents of Nordic racism, Alfred Rosenberg and R. Walther Darré (the Party's agricultural expert), sought to circumvent established diplomatic channels and construct direct cultural, political and economic links with the Scandinavian countries.[29] Rosenberg worked through his 'Foreign Policy Office' (Aussenpolitisches Amt); Darré through the 'Nordic Peasant Office' (Nordisches Bauernkontor) attached to his 'Reich Peasant Office' in the ancient city of Goslar. The connecting link between the two, and the chief instrument of Nazi cultural propaganda in Scandinavia, was the 'Nordic Society' (Nordische Gesellschaft), founded in Lübeck in 1921 as a means of re-establishing the contacts between Germany and Scandinavia lost during the war, and by 1933 an enthusiastic candidate for *Gleichschaltung* ('coordination') along National Socialist lines.[30] By 1938 another Nordic enthusiast, Heinrich Himmler, had already raised the prospect of recruiting 'Germanic blood' from northern Europe to serve as SS auxiliary troops.[31] During the war Himmler was to develop further links with Scandinavia in his capacity as Reichs-kommissar für die Festigung des Deutschen Volkstums (Reich commissar for the strengthening of Germandom).

The Auswärtiges Amt and the German legations in the Scandinavian capitals managed to fend off direct assaults on their position. The economic expertise of Ritter and his colleagues made them indispensable, as German foreign trade was restructured on a bilateral basis. Indeed, Ritter in his post-war interrogation was to contrast the Hitler regime, which had left him 'pretty much to his own devices', with the constant interference of Weimar parliamentarians.[32] The Wilhelmstrasse also conducted a sustained and successful campaign against the interference of the Nordische Gesellschaft.[33] But German diplomacy was compromised in more subtle ways. One example was the appointment as minister to Sweden in 1933 of Viktor Prinz zu Wied, who had served briefly in Stockholm in the early 1920s before being dismissed

---

[28] Lutzhöft, *Nordische Gedanke*; Geoffrey Field, 'Nordic Racism', *Journal of the History of Ideas* 38 (1977), pp. 523–40.

[29] On Rosenberg, see Jacobsen, *Nationalsozialistische Aussenpolitik*, pp. 45–89; Hans-Dietrich Loock, *Quisling, Rosenberg und Terboven. Zur Vorgeschichte und Geschichte der nationalsozialistischen Revolution in Norwegen* (Stuttgart, 1970), pp. 158–204; Seppo Kuusisto, *Alfred Rosenberg in der nationalsozialistischen Aussenpolitik 1933–1939* (Helsinki, 1984). On Darré, see Anna Bramwell, *Blood and Soil: Walther Darré and Hitler's 'Green Party'* (Bourne End, 1985).

[30] Jacobsen, *Nationalsozialistische Aussenpolitik*, pp. 483–95; Kuusisto, *Rosenberg*, pp. 299–304; Loock, *Quisling*, pp. 165–71. For a notably comprehensive statement of National Socialist interest in Scandinavia, see the draft of a lecture by SS Unterstumführer Dr Alfred Thoss (Nordische Bauernkontor, Goslar), 'Deutschland und der Norden', 29 January 1936, BA, Nachlass Darré 42.

[31] Hans-Dietrich Loock, 'Nordeuropa zwischen Aussenpolitik und "grossgermanischer" Innenpolitik', in Manfred Funke (ed.), *Hitler, Deutschland und die Mächte. Materialen zur Aussenpolitik des Dritten Reiches* (Düsseldorf, 1978), pp. 684–706 (pp. 691–2).

[32] Paul Seabury, *The Wilhelmstrasse: A Study of German Diplomats Under the Nazi Regime* (Berkeley and Los Angeles, 1954), p. 29.

[33] Documented in *DGFP*, D, V, pp. 556–74.

from the diplomatic service on grounds of incompetence. Wied had then 'thrown himself into the arms of Hermann Göring' (living in Sweden following the failure of the Munich putsch of 1923), had joined the Nazi Party in 1931 and had served as a useful channel of communication between Neurath and Hitler.[34] Another compromise was the use of commercial negotiations to enforce the 'Aryanisation' of business relationships between German and Scandinavian firms.[35] 'Political' appointments did not invariably imply a loss of diplomatic autonomy. Dr Sahm, a former mayor of Berlin appointed to Oslo in 1936 after falling out with Goebbels, was regarded as 'a moderate Party man' of notable integrity.[36] But as German diplomacy became more assertive in the late 1930s, the distinction between the interests of Party and state became increasingly blurred.[37]

For Germany after the First World War, the Scandinavian ex-neutrals were among the few countries where it was still possible to maintain foreign missions, and where German criticisms of the Versailles treaty might obtain a sympathetic hearing. Scandinavian markets were also the object of particular attention in the post-war German export drive. The appointment in 1920 of Wallroth, formerly president of the Lübeck chamber of commerce, as chargé d'affaires in Helsinki indicated, in the view of the British minister, 'that the Germans intend now to concentrate upon pushing their trade with this country'.[38] As was the case with Britain, able diplomats might spend a few years in the Scandinavian capitals before moving on to more important postings. Rudolf Nadolny, ambassador to Moscow at the time of the Nazi 'seizure of power', had served as minister to Stockholm in the early 1920s; Ernst von Weizsäcker, the future state secretary, served as counsellor in Copenhagen and later, in the early 1930s, as first secretary in Oslo.[39] Copenhagen remained the key diplomatic posting. It was still a major centre of communications and was the capital of a country which the conventional wisdom of German diplomacy regarded as the 'bridge', 'door' or 'key' to Scandinavia.[40] In particular the question of the frontier between Germany and

34 Rudolf Nadolny (ed. Günter Wollstein), *Mein Beitrag. Erinnerungen eines Botschafters des Deutschen Reiches* (Cologne, 1985), pp. 154–5; Döscher, *Das Auswärtige Amt im Dritten Reich*, pp. 59–61. According to Otto Wagener, Wied's appointment was made at Göring's request: Otto Wagener (ed. Henry Ashby Turner Jr), *Hitler aus nächster Nähe. Aufzeichnungen eines Vertrauten 1929–1932* (Frankfurt am Main, Berlin and Vienna, 1978), p. 315.

35 See ch. 8, p. 312.

36 Scheel (Berlin) to Oslo, 5 March 1936, NUD, H 62 C, Bd 3; Jacobsen, *Nationalsozialistische Aussenpolitik*, p. 27.

37 Döscher, *Das Auswärtige Amt im Dritten Reich*, argues that the Wilhelmstrasse was penetrated by Nazism, and in particular by the SS, to a far greater extent than historians have hitherto acknowledged.

38 George Kidston, 'Finland. Annual Report, 1920', 24 January 1921, FO 371/6768, N1702/1702/56.

39 Nadolny, *Mein Beitrag*, pp. 145–63; Leonidas E. Hill (ed.), *Die Weizsäcker-Papiere: 1900–1932* (Berlin, 1982), pp. 366–78; Hill (ed.), *Die Weizsäcker-Papiere: 1933–1950* (Berlin, 1974), pp. 59–74; Ernst von Weizsäcker, *Erinnerungen* (Munich, 1950), pp. 68–73, 97–108.

40 Holborn, 'Diplomats and Diplomacy', p. 132; Mutius (Copenhagen) to AA, 4 November

Denmark in Schleswig – part of which had been returned to Denmark in 1920, and the only point at which the Versailles settlement affected Scandinavia directly – could be used to demonstrate that Germany must be taken seriously. Copenhagen's importance was indicated by the number of weighty figures who were appointed to head the German legation there: Neurath, who replaced Brockdorff-Rantzau when the latter became foreign minister in 1919; Ulrich von Hassell in 1926; then Herbert von Richthofen, followed in 1936 by the more pliable Cecil von Renthe-Fink, who had risen rapidly through the diplomatic service and was to end his career as special representative to the French puppet government at Vichy.[41]

The reform of the British Foreign Office at the end of the First World War paralleled that of the Auswärtiges Amt, with a merger of the Foreign Office and the diplomatic and consular services, and a reorganisation of departmental responsibilities which placed Scandinavian affairs, along with those of Finland and the Baltic states, Poland, the Soviet Union and Afghanistan, in the hands of a new Northern Department.[42] Two men dominated the Northern Department in the inter-war period: its first head, J. D. Gregory (dismissed in 1927 for speculating in French francs) and Laurence Collier, who headed the department from 1932 to 1941.[43] Both forceful personalities, they held views in many respects diametrically opposed. Gregory was one of the Foreign Office's fiercest opponents of Bolshevism, both on ideological grounds and because a revived Russia 'must in the long run become once again a standing menace to our Eastern interests'.[44] However, he was also a pragmatist who did not favour the kind of anti-communist crusade favoured by other members of the Foreign Office, as well as by many Conservatives, in the 1920s.[45] Collier's attitude, shaped by the rising menace of Nazi Germany, was much less hostile to Soviet Russia. One of the leading opponents within the Foreign Office of the policy of appeasement, Collier trenchantly contested 'the idea that communism is a greater danger at present than the ambitions of Hitler and Mussolini'.[46] Yet the standing of the Northern Department itself was subtly diminished in the course of the inter-war period. Although there was a

---

1925, PA, AA Nachlass von Renthe-Fink, Paket 1/1; Richthofen to AA, 23 June 1931, PA, AA Abt. IV Nd, Pol. 2, Dänemark, Bd 9.

[41] John L. Heineman, *Hitler's First Foreign Minister: Constantin Freiherr von Neurath* (Berkeley, New York and London, 1980), pp. 20–3; Gregor Schöllgen, *A Conservative Against Hitler. Ulrich von Hassell: Diplomat in Imperial Germany, the Weimar Republic and the Third Reich 1881–1944* (London, 1991), pp. 35–43. For Renthe-Fink, see Döscher, *Das Auswärtige Amt im Dritten Reich*, p. 46.

[42] Ephraim Maisel, *The Foreign Office and Foreign Policy 1919–1926* (Brighton, 1994), ch. 1.

[43] J. D. Gregory, *On the Edge of Diplomacy: Rambles and Reflections 1902–1928* (London, 1928), ch. 4.

[44] Quoted in Stephen White, *Britain and the Bolshevik Revolution* (London, 1979), p. 195.

[45] Gabriel Gorodetsky, *The Precarious Truce: Anglo-Soviet Relations 1924–1927* (Cambridge, 1977), p. 188.

[46] Minute of 21 July 1938, FO 371/22304, N3587/2700/42; Donald Lammers, 'Fascism, Communism and the Foreign Office 1937–1939', *Journal of Contemporary History* 6, 3 (1971), pp. 66–86.

considerable reserve of talent in the Northern Department in the years immediately following the First World War and the Bolshevik revolution, by the 1930s the brightest and best of the Foreign Office's new recruits were tending to enter the Central Department which dealt with German affairs. Responsibility for Poland was also transferred from the Northern to the Central Department. Nor was either Gregory or Collier quite in the mainstream of Foreign Office opinion: the latter certainly alienated some colleagues by the vigour with which he expressed his views.

In one important respect, reform left the Foreign Office weaker than it had been before the war. During the war there was strong pressure from members of the Foreign Office such as Eyre Crowe and Victor Wellesley, as well as from businessmen, for the creation of a commercial intelligence department which would enable British diplomacy to give British exporters the kind of support enjoyed by their German competitors.[47] It led to the establishment in 1917 of the Department of Overseas Trade. Through a compromise which satisfied no one, the DOT was placed under the joint control of the Foreign Office and the Board of Trade.[48] The result was confusion and duplication of activity, preventing the development of a coherent and coordinated export strategy. The Board of Trade, having lost many of its responsibilities for the domestic economy, became more exclusively concerned with international trade and thus saw little need for the DOT, while the Foreign Office, deprived of information when its Commercial Section was wound up, found itself increasingly excluded from the decision-making process.[49] It was only with the formation of the Economic Relations Section under Frank Ashton Gwatkin in 1930 (a move fiercely opposed by Sir Warren Fisher, head of the Treasury and of the Civil Service) that the marginalisation of the Foreign Office from international economic relations began to be overcome.[50]

Scandinavia was not on the main route to advancement in the British diplomatic service. During the First World War Britain had been represented in the Scandinavian capitals by such proconsular figures as Sir Mansfeldt Findlay and Sir Esme Howard. By the mid-1920s Scandinavia was something of a diplomatic backwater. With the exception of Helsinki, and in contrast to the otherwise less important Baltic states, the Nordic capitals did not serve as

---

[47] R. P. T. Davenport-Hines, *Dudley Docker: The Life and Times of a Trade Warrior* (Cambridge, 1984), pp. 133–7.

[48] Ephraim Maisel, 'The Formation of the Department of Overseas Trade 1919–1926', *Journal of Contemporary History* 24 (1989), pp. 169–90 (also printed as Appendix 1 of Maisel, *Foreign Office and Foreign Policy*, pp. 189–203).

[49] Robert W. D. Boyce, *British Capitalism at the Crossroads 1919–1932: A Study in Politics, Economics and International Relations* (Cambridge, 1987), pp. 29–30. On the 'marginalisation' of the Foreign Office, see also Boyce, 'British Capitalism and the Idea of European Unity Between the Wars', in Peter M. R. Stirk (ed.), *European Unity in Context: The Interwar Period* (London and New York, 1989), pp. 65–83 (pp. 67–8).

[50] D. G. Boadle, 'The Formation of the Foreign Office Economic Relations Section 1930–1937', *Historical Journal* 20 (1977), pp. 919–36.

listening posts for the Soviet Union.[51] Germany posed a threat only in the field of commerce. Hence, perhaps, the rather uneven quality of Britain's diplomatic representation in northern Europe. A few diplomats were eccentric or worse. Sir Patrick Ramsay, minister to Denmark in the late 1930s, was (though competent in most respects) notable for his prejudices against Jews and journalists and, most of all, Jewish journalists. On the eve of the Second World War the Foreign Office was obliged to bow to his refusal to allow the appointment of a press attaché to the Copenhagen legation.[52] But against such conspicuous cases must be set the much larger number of effective diplomats who worked, often unobtrusively, to foster relations between Britain and the Nordic countries: for example, Sir Ernest Rennie, minister in Helsinki in the first decade of Finnish independence; or Sir Thomas Hohler, in Copenhagen in the early 1930s, who confuted the notion that British diplomats were indifferent to trade by his vigorous promotion of British exports.[53]

Before 1914 the diplomats of both the Scandinavian countries and the European great powers had been drawn from broadly similar social backgrounds and had many values in common. This homogeneous diplomatic culture became fragmented in the inter-war period. Relationships between diplomats and the governments to which they were accredited became more difficult when each represented widely different political systems, whether Soviet or National Socialist or the varying brands of democracy represented by Great Britain, Weimar Germany and the Nordic countries themselves. The Soviet and, after 1933, German legations in the Nordic capitals came to be peopled by individuals of apparently lowly or indeterminate status who might nevertheless have special lines of communication with the Party or the regime, bypassing conventional diplomatic channels. Boris Yartsev, who initiated secret Soviet–Finnish discussions on security questions in 1938, belonged to this category; so too did officials of the Nazi Party's Auslands-Organisation (AO) or the 'police attachés' whose true status was usually unknown even to the ministers who headed the German legations.[54] Both the SS and the SD maintained networks of informers, sometimes German, sometimes native, who reported on the activities of 'Marxist' parties and German émigrés. In one case, that of Renthe-Fink in Denmark, a career diplomat ended up as Reich Plenipotentiary in a German-occupied country.

At the same time, however, diplomats and officials often managed to

---

[51] See pp. 225–7.

[52] It was on this occasion that Vansittart described Ramsay as 'one of the worst ministers in the Service': minute of 21 January 1939, FO 371/22262, N6276/253/15.

[53] See e.g. the tribute to Rennie in Collier minute, 6 June 1930, FO 371/14809, N3748/243/56. For Hohler, see also ch. 7, pp. 252–3.

[54] On the AO, see Donald M. McKale, The Swastika Outside Germany (Kent, Ohio, 1977), esp. ch. 4; on 'police attachés', see Loock, 'Nordeuropa', p. 691. See also Renthe-Fink's obsequious letter of 30 November 1937 to Hensel, the newly appointed AO representative in Copenhagen: PA, AA Nachlass von Renthe-Fink, Paket 1/7.

maintain efficient and even amicable working relationships irrespective of the political differences between their respective regimes. On the whole, friendlier and more intimate relationships appear to have been established by German officials with their Scandinavian counterparts than by the British. Men like Ritter, Wiehl and Clodius of the Foreign Office or Alex Walter, a member of the Agriculture Ministry and long-standing chairman of the German–Scandinavian inter-governmental trade committees, were frequently brutal and overbearing. Culturally, however, they stood closer to Scandinavia than the aloof and insular British. There is much evidence, conversely, of the high regard in which many Scandinavian officials were held within the ministerial bureaucracy in Berlin.[55] In the early 1920s members of the new Soviet regime were often notably open towards Scandinavian diplomats. In part this was because the Scandinavian countries represented a weak link in the Western diplomatic 'encirclement' of the Soviet Union: there was thus an incentive to encourage them to break ranks. But Chicherin in particular was prepared to take the Norwegian representative in Moscow into his confidence in a way that his British counterpart Lord Curzon would never have deigned to do.[56] Scandinavian diplomats remained *persona grata* in Moscow when Britain broke off diplomatic relations in 1927. Indeed the Norwegian minister took charge of British interests, and both the Norwegian and Danish legations remained useful sources of information on the Soviet Union even after diplomatic relations were restored.[57]

Paradoxically, perhaps, the democratisation of the Nordic countries between the wars led to a subtle divergence between Britain and Scandinavia. A new generation of politicians came to the fore in the 1930s, often with working-class or academic backgrounds, who had little in common with Great Britain even though they had no sympathy for Nazi Germany, and little or none for the Soviet Union. The tendency was most noticeable in Norway and Finland, the newest independent states in Scandinavia, and the most self-consciously assertive. The British minister to Norway noted with regret in 1929 that 'The growth of a rather narrow and self-sufficient spirit of nationalism has been a feature of the last few years, and the younger generation appears less cultivated than the older.'[58] His successor in the late 1930s, Sir Cecil Dormer, had no social contacts with members of the Labour government. A Norwegian historian who interviewed Dormer after the war found that 'all he could remember was dinners at the palace'.[59] The divergence was epitomised by the

---

[55] E.g. Scherpenberg memorandum, 17 March 1938, proposing decorations for a number of Swedish officials, but in particular for Richert, the minister in Berlin, in recognition of his tireless efforts in the service of German–Swedish trade (especially exports of iron ore): PA, AA HaPol. VI, Schweden, Handel 13A.

[56] Salmon, *Foreign Policy and National Identity*, pp. 38–40.

[57] Salmon, 'Perceptions and Misperceptions', pp. 422–3.

[58] Sir F. Lindley to FO, 2 September 1929, FO 419/21, N4026/443/30.

[59] Olav Riste, quoted in Patrick Salmon (ed.), *Britain and Norway in the Second World War* (London, 1995), p. 37.

figure of the Norwegian foreign minister, 'the pedantic and narrow-minded historian M. Koht', as he was described (unfairly) by the British historian and Norwegian expert G. M. Gathorne-Hardy.[60] Koht was aware that the Royal Navy remained Norway's ultimate line of defence but believed that, for this very reason, Norway must keep its distance from Great Britain. Allied to this belief was a deep-seated mistrust of great-power politics which was, however, by no means confined to politicians of the left. Indeed the views of the Liberal Mowinckel and the Conservative Hambro were identical with those of Koht in this respect; and both politicians were even more unpopular than Koht with Foreign Office officials.

A similar development took place in Denmark, where the rise of the Social Democrats in domestic politics was accompanied by the return of all that the British most disliked in pacifism and small-state dogmatism, in the person of the Radical Liberal foreign minister Peter Munch. The situation in Sweden was ostensibly more encouraging. By the 1930s there were few traces of the old pro-Germanism which, from the British point of view, had disfigured Swedish foreign policy. However, the continuing strength of Swedish neutralism was masked by the affinity which developed in the early 1930s between the Social Democratic foreign minister Sandler and Anthony Eden, Britain's minister for League of Nations affairs. Sandler was a more isolated figure in the Swedish government than the British realised, allowed to go his own way only as long as his personal predilections did not jeopardise Sweden's neutral status and disavowed (in December 1939) when they seemed in danger of doing so.

Great Britain, the Paris peace conference and the problem of Soviet Russia

At the end of the First World War Great Britain enjoyed a position of unprecedented prestige and authority in northern Europe. The Royal Navy, excluded from the Baltic for four years, now operated there with impunity. British squadrons enforced the blockade of Germany (extended into the Baltic for the first time after the armistice, and maintained until the signature of the Versailles treaty in June 1919), attacked the Red Fleet in the Gulf of Finland and contributed decisively to the independence of Estonia and Latvia.[61] British commerce was (briefly) in the ascendant. Yet there was a curious absent-mindedness about Britain's treatment of Scandinavian and Baltic issues at the Paris peace conference which reflected the relatively low priority attached to the region by British policy makers. The Admiralty was reluctant to let its ships endure the rigours of too many Baltic winters, whilst ministers and officials

---

[60] G. M. Gathorne-Hardy (FO Political Intelligence Department), 'Memorandum Respecting Scandinavia and the War', 20 March 1940, FO 371/24815, N3621/2/63.

[61] For these operations, see Geoffrey Bennett, *Cowan's War: The Story of British Naval Operations in the Baltic 1918–1920* (London, 1964); Augustus Agar, *Baltic Episode* (London, 1963); Edgar Anderson, 'An Undeclared Naval War', *Journal of Central European Affairs* 22 (1962), pp. 43–78.

had few illusions about Britain's ability to influence events in the Baltic area in the long term.[62] This almost fatalistic attitude, combined with a desire to revert to isolation and avoid continental commitments, helps to explain Britain's relative passivity, which stood in sharp contrast to its aggressive commercial policy towards the Scandinavian countries during the immediate post-war years.[63] British leaders were also, of course, preoccupied with more pressing issues, among which the problems of defending a world-wide empire (and consolidating its post-war gains) were paramount.

If any guiding principles can be discerned in the British approach to Scandinavian and Baltic questions at the peace conference, they were to avoid antagonisms between the states of the region which might lead to conflict in the future, and to deny any one great power – Germany, Russia or France – the opportunity to exercise hegemonic power in northern Europe. British influence at the peace conference was thus exerted in order to limit territorial claims that might cause friction between governments and nationalities. Finland, for example, was to gain an outlet on the Arctic Ocean at Russia's expense but not the much larger territory of Eastern Karelia.[64] The question of the Slesvig frontier was resolved by means of a compromise designed to cause the least possible offence to either Danish or German opinion.[65] On the dispute over the sovereignty of the Åland Islands, British views shifted pragmatically, first favouring Sweden as the stronger Baltic power, but later supporting the League solution of Finnish sovereignty combined with neutralisation when this appeared more in accordance with what Curzon termed the 'broad principles and considerations' which decided 'the destinies of nations'.[66]

It was taken for granted that German power would – and indeed must – revive in some form. In these circumstances Britain concentrated on certain specific objectives which would limit Germany's ability to threaten British interests, while leaving it intact as an important element in the European balance of power: a barrier both to French hegemonic pretensions and to Bolshevism. From the naval point of view, the key desiderata were the destruction of German naval power and a guarantee of free access to the Baltic for British ships in time of war.[67] Yet there was no mention of the Baltic in the armistice proposals drafted by the Admiralty in October 1918. It was left to the

---

[62] See Merja-Liisa Hinkkanen-Lievonen, *British Trade and Enterprise in the Baltic States 1919–1925* (Helsinki, 1984), pp. 91–3, for arguments between the Admiralty and the Foreign Office on the question of a British naval presence in the eastern Baltic.

[63] See ch. 7, pp. 236–41.

[64] FO to Lord Acton (Helsinki), 18 February 1920, *DBFP*, 1, XI, pp. 222–3.

[65] H. W. V. Temperley (ed.), *A History of the Peace Conference of Paris* (6 vols., London, 1920–3), vol. II, pp. 197–206; Olavi Hovi, *The Baltic Area in British Policy 1918–1921*, vol. I, *From the Compiègne Armistice to the Implementation of the Versailles Treaty, 11.11.1918–20.1.1920* (Helsinki, 1980), pp. 121–2.

[66] Conversation with the Swedish minister (Palmstierna), 11 May 1921, FO 371/6948, N5663/85/42.

[67] These had been anticipated in an Admiralty 'Note on the Possible Terms of Peace' of 12 October 1916, CAB 42/21/8.

commander of the Grand Fleet, Admiral Beatty, to insist that the principle of free access to the Baltic, 'for which Nelson fought at Copenhagen', should be included among its terms.[68]

Britain's experts subsequently proved unable to devise more permanent solutions to the dual problem of keeping the Danish Straits open in wartime and denying Germany the strategic advantage of the Kiel Canal. In view of Denmark's clear inability to keep the Straits open during the war, the Foreign Office favoured an international agreement to give the Straits the same status as the Dardanelles and Bosphorus, with their defence being guaranteed by an international force.[69] The Admiralty agreed that the Belts and Sound should be internationalised, and that German fortifications in the area should be dismantled, but evidently did not believe that German naval command could be disputed in time of war.[70] The options of destroying the Kiel Canal, neutralising it and handing it over to Denmark were all considered and rejected as impracticable; the only alternative therefore was to leave it in German hands while 'rendering it as difficult as possible for Germany to resurrect that navy, the greater part of which she will be deprived of at the Peace Conference'.[71] This was the solution eventually adopted,[72] though it was to be rendered ineffective by the revival of German naval power in the 1930s.

The status of the Danish Straits was one of many issues left unresolved at the time of the signature of the Versailles treaty in June 1919, to be considered subsequently by the Baltic Commission and the Council of Foreign Ministers. Although the British proposed an international agreement at the meeting of the commission in September 1919, they received little support from France, and the British themselves soon showed less interest in a question which had lost much of its urgency following the destruction of German naval power and the success of the Royal Navy against the Bolsheviks in the summer of 1919.[73] But Great Britain continued to insist on the principle of an open Baltic. Neutralisation of the Baltic, proposed at various times by Finland, the Baltic states and the Soviet Union in the early 1920s, was consistently resisted by the Admiralty.[74] 'We have always opposed seas being neutralised: such neutralisation enhances military power at the expense of sea power.'[75] Until the early

---

[68] Naval Terms of Armistice, 23 October 1918, quoted in Olavi Hovi, *Baltic Area* I, p. 43.
[69] 'Memorandum on Norwegian and Danish Questions', 16 December 1918, ADM 116/2055.
[70] 'Notes on Matters Affecting Naval Interests Connected with the Peace Settlement', December 1918, ADM 116/1861; Admiralty to FO, 13 January 1919, ADM 116/2055.
[71] Memorandum by first sea lord (Admiral Wemyss), 18 December 1918, ADM 116/1861.
[72] Arthur J. Marder, *From the Dreadnought to Scapa Flow: The Royal Navy in the Fisher Era 1904–1919* (5 vols., London, 1961–70), vol. V, *Victory and Aftermath (January 1918–June 1919)*, pp. 251–3; Olavi Hovi, *Baltic Area* I, pp. 118–21.
[73] Olavi Hovi, *Baltic Area* I, pp. 171–4.
[74] For a discussion of the Finnish and Baltic proposals, see Erik Lönnroth, *Den svenska utrikespolitikens historia*, vol. V, *1919–1939* (Stockholm, 1959), pp. 57–9. For Soviet views, see p. 230 below.
[75] Vice-Admiral Sir William Fisher (DCNS) to Sir Thomas Hohler, 30 July 1928, Hohler Papers, vol. 1928.

1930s British politicians and admirals lectured the Danes on the need to retain sufficient defences to keep the Danish Straits open in time of war.[76] The war they had principally in mind was one between Germany and the USSR.[77] Thereafter, with the increasing likelihood of a British–German war, declarations of British interest in the entrances to the Baltic became more infrequent.

For a short time after the end of the war, it appeared that Britain might have to confront a large-scale re-ordering of relations among the smaller states of Scandinavia and the Baltic region. There was widespread discussion in 1918–19 not only of closer collaboration between the three Scandinavian states, but also of much more ambitious schemes, including the possibility of a Baltic league or entente comprising Scandinavia, Finland, the Baltic states and, in some variants, Poland as well.[78] These latter ideas emanated from Baltic nationalists as well as from right-wing Swedish and Finnish circles seeking to maintain the wartime vision of Swedish hegemony in northern Europe: 'the dream of Fennoscandia'.[79] British reactions to such ideas ranged from mild scepticism to deep hostility. The Whitehall debate was thus largely a rehearsal of positions which had become entrenched during the war.

Howard was the most articulate champion, both at Stockholm and in his subsequent role as chairman of the Baltic Commission at the Paris peace conference, of the idea of Swedish leadership of a group of Scandinavian or Baltic states. He believed that Swedish pro-Germanism was in decline and that Sweden shared Britain's interest in an open Baltic.[80] It is clear, however, that Howard envisaged only a very loose grouping of northern European states which would have no military power in itself, but would merely enable them to speak 'with one voice at any future Conference on Baltic questions'.[81] He added that such a league would be of no interest to Norway and that the Danes, too, might be too timid to commit themselves to anything likely to bring them into dispute with Germany. A Baltic league would therefore make a Scandinavian union less likely. This argument seems to have carried some

[76] William Bridgeman and Austen Chamberlain, quoted in Richthofen (Copenhagen) to AA, 9 March 1931, PA, AA Nachlass von Renthe-Fink 1/1; interview between Admiral Chatfield and king of Denmark, 15 December 1933, ADM 116/2970.

[77] Field-Marshal Sir George Milne (CIGS) to Hohler, 22 December 1931, Hohler Papers, vol. 1931; Admiralty to FO, 30 December 1931, FO 371/15555, N8300/115/15.

[78] Political Intelligence Department (PID), 'Memorandum on Scandinavian Cooperation', 1 August 1918, FO 371/3359, No. 138945; Olavi Hovi, Baltic Area I, pp. 55–7.

[79] Torbjörn Norman, 'Drömmen om Fennoskandia. Alexis Gripenberg och det fria Finlands utrikespolitiska orientering', in Studier i modern historia tillägnade Jarl Torbacke den 18 augusti 1990 (Stockholm, 1990), pp. 169–89.

[80] Howard to FO, 29 July 1918 (commenting on a memorandum of 15 March 1918 by Col. Wade, military attaché at Copenhagen, on 'Prospects of a Scandinavian League'), FO 371/3358, No. 136210; Howard memorandum, 'Baltic League', 28 November 1918, FO 371/3349, No. 199232.

[81] FO 371/3349, No. 199232. Balfour commented: 'Most leagues have been established for purposes of defence. This League apparently is to start with the admission that other people must do all the fighting required to keep open the Baltic.'

weight with both Balfour, the foreign secretary, and Lord Robert Cecil, though the likelihood that any Baltic league would come into existence already appeared remote at the beginning of 1919.[82] It was also designed to deflect criticism from Sir Mansfeldt Findlay in Kristiania, who remained predictably hostile to any arrangement which threatened to reward Sweden for its pro-German record in wartime, and to bring about a Scandinavian combination which must inevitably be detrimental to British interests.[83]

Abetted by George Fullerton-Carnegie of the Political Intelligence Department, Findlay deployed both familiar and novel arguments in support of his case.[84] The two men contended that the German menace had by no means disappeared with the overthrow of the old imperial order. Indeed the fact that socialists were now in power in Berlin opened up new opportunities:

> If a stable Government is established in Germany the Moderate Socialists will in it play the principal role. Both in Denmark and in Sweden the Moderate Socialists occupy a very important and influential position . . . What more natural than that in both countries these Socialists should look to Germany for light and leading in the future as they did in pre-war times? . . . There is, therefore, I submit, a probability of German political influence – exercised in the future without the 'mailed fist' concomitant – becoming very powerful in Northern Europe in the comparatively near future.[85]

The one country which remained susceptible to British influence at all times was Norway. As Findlay put it, 'as long as our sea power is maintained, it will be both the interest and the natural inclination of Norway to be on the best terms with us. In case of necessity they could almost be compelled to be so.'[86] It was thus vital that Norway should not form part of a Scandinavian bloc. Fortunately, from the British point of view, Norwegian and Danish resistance to Scandinavian political cooperation soon became evident.[87] Nor did the 'cautious and unenterprising foreign policy' of Sweden's Liberal and Social Democratic administrations portend any immediate revival of Swedish hegemonic ambitions.[88] Howard's successor in Stockholm, Colville Barclay, predicted accurately that the Scandinavian countries would probably be able to work together on uncontroversial matters, 'especially at Geneva, where the main responsibility of the decisions of the League of Nations will fall on broader shoulders', but that on larger issues their interests would prove as irreconcilable as they had been in the past: 'Norway and Sweden will remain back to back geographically with divergent political and commercial interests,

---

[82] Minute by G. Fullerton-Carnegie (PID File 83), 1 March 1919, FO 371/4375.
[83] Findlay memorandum, 'The Position of the Scandinavian States and Finland', 12 November 1918, ibid.
[84] Findlay to FO, 12 February 1919, ibid.
[85] Fullerton-Carnegie minute, 1 March 1919, ibid.
[86] Findlay to FO, 29 June 1922, FO 371/8106, N6414/3904/63.
[87] See e.g. the views of the Danish foreign minister Harald Scavenius, reported in Marling to FO, 16 November 1920, FO 371/5386, N2999/2996/15.
[88] Barclay (Stockholm) to FO, 20 December 1920, FO 371/5454, N4857/2796/42.

and Denmark will still have an overwhelming neighbour in Germany, with a new source of anxiety in Schleswig.'[89]

But as the prospect of effective cooperation receded, Nordic solidarity of a vaguer sort came to be favoured precisely because it had no military and few political implications. Between 1921 and 1923 Esmond Ovey of the Northern Department (who had served as first secretary in Kristiania during the war) urged repeatedly that Finland should be encouraged to orient its foreign policy towards Scandinavia rather than throw in its lot with Poland and the Baltic states.[90] 'The Scandinavian states are pacific and timorous', he wrote. 'These qualities saved them from the recent great war . . . Finland should steer clear of any entangling military alliances and cultivate a moral, social and economic solidarity with Norway, Sweden and Denmark.'[91] In the early 1920s such ideas were premature, though ten years later Finland was well on the way to establishing a credible Nordic identity. As we have seen, however, Finland's Scandinavian alignment was to bring problems of its own.

As long as Germany remained disarmed, Britain's chief strategic and political concerns in northern Europe were with the intentions of the Soviet Union and France. Until the mid-1920s French ambitions were regarded as the most immediate threat to the stability of the Baltic. Here as elsewhere the French had pressed for a punitive peace settlement rather than one reflecting what the British saw as the underlying realities of power in the region.[92] Greatly overestimating French strength, the British opposed the policy of the *cordon sanitaire*. They deprecated the proliferation of French military advisers in eastern Europe and the Baltic and resisted the inclusion of the Baltic states in the Franco-Polish alliance.[93] 'It is devoutly to be hoped', wrote one Foreign Office official, 'that the Baltic states and Finland will not be sucked into the maelstrom of pan-gallic imperialism.'[94] According to the German minister in Helsinki, members of General Kirke's military mission to Finland in 1924 'made no secret of their great aversion to the French' and even advised the Finns to orient their foreign policy towards Germany.[95]

Britain's principal interest, however, was in the containment of the Soviet Union. Between 1917 and 1924 British policy towards the new Soviet regime underwent many changes, each of which had implications for the smaller states of northern Europe. Britain's first response was to attempt to destroy the

---

[89] Ibid.

[90] E.g. memorandum of 25 August 1921, 'Finland and Its Future Foreign Policy', FO 371/6776, N10844/10844/56; minute of 26 January 1922, FO 371/8104, N762/82/63.

[91] Minute of 27 September 1923, FO 371/9297, N7753/484/56.

[92] Olavi Hovi, *Baltic Area* I, p. 122.

[93] Kalervo Hovi, *Cordon Sanitaire or Barrière de l'Est? The Emergence of the New French Eastern Alliance Policy 1917–1919* (Turku, 1975); Hinkkanen-Lievonen, *British Trade and Enterprise*, pp. 102–3, 110–12; Kidston (Helsinki) to FO, 29 June 1920, *DBFP*, 1, XI, pp. 364–6.

[94] Minute by P. M. Roberts, 27 March 1922, FO 371/8105, N2869/82/63.

[95] Zech to AA, 6 September 1924, PA, AA Pol. Abt. III England, Politik 3 – Finnland.

Bolshevik regime – through military intervention in the civil war, and through support for Estonia and Latvia in their efforts to free their territories from Soviet and Soviet-backed forces. Cooperation between the British armed forces and those of the Baltic states and Finland produced a legacy of friendship with Britain and suspicion on the part of the Soviet Union which was to have ominous consequences in 1939, when the Soviets proved to have longer memories than the British. Intervention having failed, Britain then tried to isolate the Bolsheviks, exerting pressure on the Scandinavian states to break off diplomatic relations late in 1918 and remaining alert to any signs of normalisation thereafter.[96]

The attention paid to Sweden, Denmark and Norway in these years by both the British and Soviet governments was a tribute to their importance as intermediaries between Russia and the outside world. At the end of 1918 they were the only three countries with diplomatic representation in Russia; between November 1918 and its closure in January 1919, the Soviet mission in Stockholm was the Soviet government's only representation abroad. Scandinavia was a weak link in the Western economic blockade of Russia: Sweden in particular helped to circumvent British and American restrictions on the use of Russian gold, with vast quantities being reprocessed by the Swedish mint in 1920–1.[97] Sweden was Soviet Russia's most important trading partner in 1918 and again in 1920. Scandinavian reluctance to participate in the Western ideological crusade did not reflect sympathy for the Bolsheviks, merely the hope that Scandinavian economic interests in Russia could be preserved during the short period which was expected to elapse before the regime collapsed.

Having led the campaign for isolation, Britain became the first of the Western powers to acknowledge the need for co-existence. The tortuous route to diplomatic recognition was intimately linked with the question of Anglo-Soviet economic relations. The first stage began under the Lloyd George coalition with the O'Grady trade mission to Moscow early in 1920 and was completed with the signature of a trade agreement in March 1921 which marked Britain's *de facto* recognition of the Soviet government. A phase of confrontation under the Conservatives, with the 'Curzon note' of May 1923, was succeeded by the final granting of *de jure* recognition by Ramsay MacDonald's Labour government in February 1924. At each twist of the path the Scandinavian states were subjected to diplomatic pressure from both Great Britain and the Soviet regime.

Norway in particular felt a pressing need to normalise relations with Soviet Russia out of concern for the economic interests of the fishermen and hunters

---

[96] Sune Jungar, 'Bolsjevikmissionen lämnar Stockholm. Sveriges brytning med sovjetregeringen 1918', in *Studier i modern historia*, pp. 151–67; Egil Danielsen, *Norge–Sovjetunionen. Norsk utenrikspolitikk overfor Sovjetunionen 1917–1940* (Oslo, 1964), pp. 66–9.

[97] Christine White, '"Riches Have Wings": The Use of Russian Gold in Soviet Foreign Trade 1918–1922', in Hiden and Loit, *Contact or Isolation?*, pp. 117–36.

of northern Norway, as well as to secure the new regime's acknowledgement of its sovereignty over Svalbard.[98] It therefore became the first Scandinavian state to follow the British lead, concluding a trade agreement in September 1921 in which it became the first country in the world to recognise the Soviet government's foreign trade monopoly. But Norway then fell foul of the deterioration in Anglo-Soviet relations. Whilst the Soviets exploited Norwegian anxieties in an effort to persuade Norway to break ranks and grant *de jure* recognition in advance of Great Britain and other Western powers, the British hinted at the consequences for Norway's currency and credit position if it went ahead alone.[99] Ultimately Norway's ties with the West proved the stronger and Norwegian recognition of the Soviet Union followed two weeks after that of Great Britain. Denmark for its part tried for a short time to organise a common front among the smaller powers to *prevent* British recognition, before it too was eventually obliged to fall into line.[100]

Relations between Britain and the Soviet Union in the latter half of the 1920s were marked by mutual mistrust and by a breach of diplomatic relations which lasted from 1927 to 1929. The 1928 Review of Imperial Defence identified the Soviet Union as the main threat to British security – an assessment which was not formally superseded until November 1933, when the USSR was replaced by Germany and Japan.[101] In considering the scenario of a war provoked by a Soviet occupation of Afghanistan, the Admiralty suggested in 1932 that 'an early and vigorous Naval offensive' in Baltic and Arctic waters would produce an important diversionary effect. For this purpose 'the establishment of a secure advanced base in *Finland* or possibly *Esthonia*' was 'almost essential'.[102]

If they remained sceptical about the military capacity of Estonia and Latvia, the British authorities took a consistent interest in Finland's defence potential. The Finnish request in 1924 for a mission to advise on matters of military organisation and frontier defence was welcomed by the Foreign Office since it indicated that British military expertise was now rated more highly than that of either France or Germany, and signified an increasingly pro-British foreign policy on Finland's part.[103] The businesslike approach to Finland's defence problems adopted by General Kirke's advisory mission in 1924–5 greatly enhanced British prestige and led to requests for naval and air advisers.[104] The Foreign Office was keen to respond positively to such requests, partly as a

[98] Salmon, *Foreign Policy and National Identity*, pp. 47–53.
[99] Benjamin Vogt (London) to Foreign Minister Michelet, 13 October 1923, NUD, P 10 A 3/17, Bd III.
[100] Bent Jensen, 'Denmark and the Russian Question 1917–1924: Private Interests, Official Policy and Great Power Pressure', in Hiden and Loit, *Contact or Isolation?*, pp. 43–55 (p. 53).
[101] CAB 53/16, COS Paper No. 165; Norman Gibbs, *Grand Strategy*, vol. I (London, 1976), p. 94.
[102] 'War with Russia: Naval Appreciation, August 1932', ADM 116/3480.
[103] Rennie to FO, 24 March 1924, and FO minutes, FO 371/10421, N3048/40/56.
[104] Kirke report on mission, 2 April 1925, FO 371/10990, N1954/235/56; Rennie to FO, 22

means of countering German influence, but also in order to influence the purchasing policies of the Finnish armed forces. An air adviser was appointed in 1925 for a period of two years, and in 1929 a retired officer took on the post of naval adviser.[105] This latter post became a permanent one, renewed under successive officers until the outbreak of war.

Another consequence of British concern with the security threat posed by the Soviet Union was the development of unusually close relations between the British armed forces and intelligence services and their counterparts in Finland and, to a lesser extent, the Baltic states. The contacts between Finnish and British officers established during the intervention period of 1918–20 were reinforced by the Kirke mission and by Mannerheim's frequent visits to Britain. Intelligence cooperation was very close. Helsinki, along with Tallinn and Riga, was among the most important listening posts for Western intelligence services.[106] Harry Carr, the SIS head of station in Helsinki from 1925 to 1941, 'built up a particularly close connection with Finnish intelligence, whose officers regularly visited both SIS and MI5 headquarters in London'.[107] His activities were not confined to surveillance: when Anglo-Soviet relations worsened in 1927, Carr helped to organise guerrilla raids across the border from Finland into Russia.[108]

Such matters were far beyond the purview of government ministers, and even questions of advice and arms sales to the Finnish armed forces were dealt with by officials of the Foreign Office, the Treasury and the service ministries without ministerial interference. Yet the cumulative effect of such actions – whether covert or merely bureaucratic – was, implicitly at least, to identify British interests with those of a state whose virtual *raison d'être* was hostility to Soviet Russia. There appears to have been only one occasion on which a government minister registered a protest against this tendency. In June 1924 Charles Trevelyan, president of the Board of Education in the Labour government and a passionate internationalist, alerted the Cabinet to the decision to send a military mission to Finland.[109] This, he said, would be regarded by the Soviets as an affront and was 'incompatible with our new world attitude towards foreign nations'.[110] Ramsay MacDonald, as prime minister and foreign secretary, was clearly discomfited by the fact that his

December 1924, ibid., N235/235/56; Rennie to Orde (FO), 23 March 1926, FO 371/11752, N1664/401/56.

[105] Correspondence in FO 371/10990, N235; FO 371/11752, N401.

[106] Nigel West (pseud. of Rupert Allason), *MI6* (London, 1983), pp. 60–1, 64–5, 80–3; Tom Bower, *The Red Web: MI6 and the KGB Master Coup* (London, 1989), ch. 1; Jukka Rislakki, 'Finland som objekt och arena för underrättelseverksamhet', *Historisk tidskrift för Finland* 77 (1992), pp. 595–608.

[107] Christopher Andrew, *Secret Service: The Making of the British Intelligence Community* (London, 1985), p. 350. Bower, *Red Web*, deals with Carr's entire career in British intelligence. For Helsinki, see ch. 1, esp. p. 29.

[108] Bower, *Red Web*, pp. 26–7.   [109] Cabinet meeting, 18 June 1924, CAB 23/48.

[110] 'Military Mission to Finland. Note by the President of the Board of Education', 17 June 1924, CAB 24/167.

officials had not seen fit to consult him, but was persuaded that 'it would be fatal both to our prestige and to our growing commercial interest in the Baltic' if the mission were not allowed to go ahead.[111]

Throughout the inter-war period there was a persistent suspicion on the left of British politics that Finland was a willing agent of Britain's anti-Soviet designs. It culminated in the characterisation of Finland as 'A British Client State' in *Must the War Spread?*, D. N. Pritt's polemic against British support for Finland during the Winter War, published in January 1940. Pritt, who had been a foreign observer at the trial of the Finnish Communist Toivo Antikainen in 1934, an international *cause célèbre*, cited the existence of a British adviser to the Finnish navy in support of his allegation. The only other country with such an adviser, he said, was Greece, whose credentials as a British client state were not in doubt.[112] Stalin shared the suspicion of the Anglo-Finnish connection. During the negotiations in the autumn of 1939 which preceded the Soviet invasion of Finland, he recalled the days of the civil war when the British had used Finnish territory to launch torpedo-boat attacks on Kronstadt and had sent troops to Murmansk.[113]

The Soviet Union and the Nordic countries

Soviet attitudes and policies towards the Nordic countries were marked by 'the inherent and ineradicable duality of Soviet relations with the outside world':[114] the conflict between, on the one hand, the revolutionary impulse associated with the Communist International and, on the other, Narkomindel's acknowledgement of the necessity of co-existence.[115] This 'realist' strand of Soviet policy making encompassed, among other aspects, the insistence on Russia's traditional rights as a great power; the desire for international recognition; and, above all, a fear of Western military intervention led by either Great Britain (in the 1920s) or Germany (in the 1930s) which persisted throughout the inter-war period. But until the ascendancy of Stalin and the doctrine of 'socialism in one country' were assured, Comintern represented a formidable alternative to Narkomindel's pragmatism. A useful starting point for considering the role of the Nordic countries in Comintern strategy is the distinction drawn by Arvo Tuominen, the organisation's 'Adviser on Scandinavia' from 1924 to 1930, between the three Scandinavian countries on the one hand and Finland, the Baltic states and Poland on the other. In all of the latter countries the

---

[111] Minutes by E. H. Carr and Ramsay MacDonald, 19 and 21 June 1924, FO 371/10421, N5220/40/56.

[112] D. N. Pritt, *Must the War Spread?* (London, 1940), pp. 96–136.

[113] Max Jakobson, *The Diplomacy of the Winter War* (Cambridge, Mass., 1961), pp. 117, 124. See also ch. 9, p. 355.

[114] E. H. Carr, *A History of Soviet Russia*, vol. IV, *The Interregnum 1923–1924* (London, 1954), p. 214.

[115] For an elaboration of this point, see Sven Holtsmark, *Enemy Springboard or Benevolent Buffer? Soviet Attitudes to Nordic Cooperation 1920–1955* (Oslo, 1992), pp. 7–8. See also pp. 208–10 above.

Communist Party was illegal and was therefore forced to operate clandestinely.[116] In Scandinavia, communist parties were legal but weak. As Kuusinen admitted to the fourth world congress of the Comintern in 1922, the problem of communism in Scandinavia was that it faced strongly organised social democratic parties which had captured and retained the allegiances of the working class and dominated the trade union movement.[117]

Finnish communism was a much more formidable force. Its exiled leaders were prominent in the founding of the Comintern in March 1919 and remained active in its organisation. One of them, Otto Kuusinen, became one of the great survivors of Soviet politics and retained a position of considerable influence in both Comintern and Soviet affairs.[118] Communist activities in Finland were assisted by the permeability of the Finnish–Soviet frontier and the Finnish coastline, but hampered by the effectiveness of the Finnish government's security and intelligence services.[119]

However, communism did hold a persistent appeal for many of the inhabitants of the sparsely populated far north of Scandinavia: small farmers, fishermen, forestry workers and miners. Frequently, moreover, Russia seemed closer both geographically and psychologically than capital cities and more prosperous regions many hundreds of miles to the south. Both Finnish communists and the Kremlin appear to have given serious thought to the possibility of establishing a Soviet republic in this remote and inhospitable region. Around 1920 the Finnish Communist Edvard Gylling (later prime minister of the ill-fated Karelian Autonomous Soviet Socialist Republic)[120] developed a plan by which the northern districts of Finland, Sweden and Norway would, at some opportune time, be forcibly incorporated into Soviet Karelia, which would thus be expanded into the 'Soviet Republic of the North'.[121] Whether the use of force was seriously considered is unclear. The Soviet government was well aware that there was widespread agitation in northern Norway in 1920 aimed at secession and joining the Soviet state.[122] It may thus have believed that such an objective could be achieved by voluntary means – though the fate of the communist uprisings in Germany in 1923 and the abortive Estonian coup in 1924 soon made it aware of the limitations of revolutionary activity unaided by Soviet military intervention.

The Soviet leadership responded to these setbacks by 'trying to carry through a diplomatic holding action in Western Europe while pursuing

---

[116] Tuominen, *Bells of the Kremlin*, p. 68.
[117] A. F. Upton, *The Communist Parties of Scandinavia and Finland* (London, 1973), pp. 7–8.
[118] John H. Hodgson, *Den röda eminensen. O. W. Kuusinens politiska biografi* (Helsinki, 1974).
[119] Upton, *Communist Parties*, pp. 121–3.
[120] For Soviet Karelia, see John H. Hodgson, *Communism in Finland: A History and Interpretation* (Princeton, N. J., 1966), ch. 6.
[121] Tuominen, *Bells of the Kremlin*, pp. 45–6; Upton, *Communist Parties*, p. 144.
[122] Sune Jungar, 'The XXth-Century Varangians: The Russian Policy of Sweden, Norway and Denmark After the Revolution. Some Comparative Observations', in Hiden and Loit, *Contact or Isolation?*, pp. 161–74 (p. 167).

anticolonialist and revolutionary goals in Asia'.[123] But the Comintern remained active in northern Norway, as well as in the rest of Scandinavia, throughout the 1920s and 1930s. After Hitler came to power, Copenhagen replaced Berlin as the main centre for Comintern activities in western Europe.[124] Though its activities came to be directed towards reducing the potential contribution of Scandinavia to Germany in the event of a German–Soviet war – for example by fomenting strike activity among the railwaymen and dockers of the northern Swedish iron ore fields and the port of Narvik[125] – revolutionary hopes had not been abandoned. Indeed, Kuusinen apparently once told his wife that 'he dreamed of controlling Finland and, eventually, being "proconsul" for the whole of Scandinavia; then, after the rest of Europe had surrendered to communism, he would return to Moscow and be the *éminence grise* of the Soviet empire'.[126] In the light of Kuusinen's role in the establishment of the puppet 'People's Government of Finland' following the Soviet invasion of November 1939, such fantasies may not have been without influence on Soviet policy.

If revolutionary ambitions formed one aspect of Soviet relations with the outside world, defensive motives were uppermost in the Soviet obsession with a British-led intervention which was fuelled by the return to power of the Conservatives in Great Britain at the end of 1924 and culminated in the war scare of 1927.[127] There was persistent concern with the uses to which the border states might be put by hostile great powers. Chicherin repeatedly warned the Baltic states against functioning as the vanguard of an anti-Soviet coalition.[128] In 1925 he described the visit of a British naval squadron to Baltic ports as 'sinister machinations destined to convert the Baltic Sea into a British lake'.[129] The Voldemaras coup of 1926 in Lithuania was regarded as evidence of Western encirclement, while Chicherin told the Estonians (not implausibly in the light of the Admiralty assessment noted earlier) that the British regarded their country 'as the "advance post" in the defence of India'.[130] During the 1927 war scare a member of Narkomindel sketched 'an imminent situation in which Britain would blockade the USSR by sea and urge Poland on to a land attack that would be joined by Rumania in the south and by Finland in the north'.[131] In March 1927 the central committee of the

[123] Harvey L. Dyck, 'German–Soviet Relations and the Anglo-Soviet Break 1927', *Slavic Review* 25 (1966), pp. 67–83 (p. 68).
[124] Valtin, *Out of the Night*, p. 377.   [125] Ibid., pp. 388–9.
[126] Kuusinen, *Before and After Stalin*, p. 231.
[127] Teddy J. Uldricks, 'Russia and Europe: Diplomacy, Revolution and Economic Development in the 1920s', *International History Review* 1 (1979), pp. 55–83 (pp. 75–8); John P. Sontag, 'The Soviet War Scare of 1926–1927', *Russian Review* 34 (1975), pp. 66–77.
[128] O'Connor, *Diplomacy and Revolution*, p. 131.
[129] Gorodetsky, *Precarious Truce*, p. 72.
[130] O'Connor, *Diplomacy and Revolution*, p. 132.
[131] As reported by the German ambassador, Brockdorff-Rantzau, on 5 September 1927: Dyck, 'German–Soviet Relations', p. 80.

Communist Party went as far as to discuss the possibility of a pre-emptive strike against Finland.[132] On the whole, the Scandinavian states were viewed with less anxiety. However, the Soviets had been worried about the stationing of a British warship at the port of Vardø in north Norway in 1922–3, with the ostensible purpose of protecting British trawlers against arrest within the twelve-mile limit claimed by the Soviets, at a time when the dispute provoked by the 'Curzon note' was at its height.[133]

The Soviets were rightly preoccupied with their strategic weakness in the Baltic Sea. During the civil war Russian territory had been the object of attack by the Royal Navy, in close collaboration with Finnish, Estonian and Latvian forces. The imperial Russian navy had been decimated; the Soviet Union's Baltic coastline had been reduced to a few kilometres in the vicinity of Leningrad; the new Soviet navy was under a cloud following the Kronstadt uprising of March 1921. Naval reconstruction was not seriously attempted until the inauguration of the first five-year plan in 1928. It was backed at first by a strategic doctrine which accepted that the navy's role would be primarily defensive and closely coordinated with the Red Army, and which was aimed at preventing the enemy (assumed at this time to be Great Britain) from gaining a foothold on Soviet territory through the use of mines, submarines, torpedo boats and aircraft.[134] Later, under Stalin, the navy adopted a 'big-ship' strategy which was far less appropriate to Baltic defence, though it did lead to the development of bases on the Arctic Ocean (to which the Baltic was linked following the completion of the White Sea Canal in 1933).

Diplomacy offered another line of defence. At the Lausanne conference in 1922 and again at the Rome conference on naval disarmament in 1924, the Soviet representative proposed closing the Baltic to the warships of all non-riparian states, thus espousing the doctrine of the Baltic as a closed sea more explicitly than the tsarist government had ever done.[135] The Soviet Union was also concerned with the status of the Danish Straits. Chicherin argued that they should be closed by Denmark to prevent the British from attacking the Soviet Union via the Baltic, and Soviet diplomacy repeatedly criticised Danish and Swedish plans to dredge channels in the Sound in order, so it was alleged, to permit the passage of British warships.[136]

But the main thrust of Soviet diplomacy from 1925 onwards was the attempt to construct a system of non-aggression treaties with the USSR's

[132] Upton, *Communist Parties*, pp. 173–4.
[133] Salmon, *Foreign Policy and National Identity*, pp. 47–9.
[134] Donald W. Mitchell, *A History of Russian and Soviet Sea Power* (New York, 1974), pp. 355–76; Jürgen Rohwer, 'Alternating Russian and Soviet Naval Strategies', in Philip S. Gillette and Willard C. Frank Jr (eds.), *The Sources of Soviet Naval Conduct* (Lexington, Mass., 1990), pp. 95–120.
[135] K. Grzybowski, 'The Soviet Doctrine of Mare Clausum and Policies in Black and Baltic Seas', *Journal of Central European Affairs* 14 (1954–5), pp. 339–53.
[136] Holtsmark, *Enemy Springboard*, pp. 24–7; W. M. Carlgren, *Varken – eller. Reflexioner kring Sveriges Ålandpolitik 1938–1939* (Stockholm, 1977), pp. 32–3.

western neighbours.[137] Finland, the Baltic states and Poland were the principal objects of attention, but overtures were also made to the three Scandinavian states. Negotiations with the border states were protracted. An agreement was signed with Lithuania in 1926 but pacts with Poland, Estonia, Latvia and Finland followed only in 1932.[138] Negotiations with the Scandinavian states were more fitful and were ultimately without result.[139] In each case the stumbling block was the conflict between, on the one hand, the Soviet desire for declarations of neutrality and non-aggression as part of a larger network of non-aggression treaties and, on the other hand, the Scandinavian aim to establish formal procedures for conflict resolution in the form of mediation or arbitration. The Soviets resisted all proposals for arbitration, insisting that disputes must be settled directly by the parties concerned without the intervention of third parties. Discussions between the Soviet Union and Sweden, initiated in 1926, reached deadlock on this point as early as 1927 and were pursued no further. Denmark was sounded on the question of a non-aggression pact in 1930. Stauning was favourably disposed 'in principle' but, characteristically, wanted pacts to be concluded simultaneously with the Soviet Union, Great Britain and Germany. The discussions which began in the summer of 1930 encountered the usual obstacles and petered out during the following spring.

As usual, the Norwegians proved more receptive to Soviet proposals while the Soviets, for their part, were prepared to go further to meet Norway's wishes than those of the other Scandinavian states. The idea of a Soviet–Norwegian non-aggression treaty, raised tentatively by Litvinov in 1926, was still being pursued seriously by both sides as late as 1933, but again ultimately without result. As Litvinov pointed out, Norway was of greater interest to the Soviet Union than its small size might have suggested.[140] When (*when*, not if) the West attacked the USSR, Norwegian territory might be used as a base for foreign intervention.[141] Norway, like other small states, would also come under pressure, as in the last war, to favour one or other of the belligerents. The pressure traditionally exerted by Britain would be made still more effective in any future conflict by the existence of the League of Nations. However, cooperation with great powers such as Britain had often been contrary to Norwegian interests in the past. Of the three Scandinavian states, Norway had been the least hostile towards the new Russia and the most reserved towards Nordic cooperation. These

---

[137] J. A. Large, 'The Origins of Soviet Collective Security Policy 1930–1932', *Soviet Studies* 30 (1976), pp. 212–36.

[138] Ibid., pp. 221–7.

[139] This section relies principally on an unpublished manuscript by Sven Holtsmark based on Soviet documents, 'Spørsmålet om sovjetiske ikke-angrepsavtaler med de skandinaviske land', and on Holtsmark, *Norge og Sovjetunionen*.

[140] Litvinov to Makar (Oslo), 18 May 1926, in Holtsmark, *Norge og Sovjetunionen*, pp. 146–8.

[141] Litvinov to Surits (Kristiania), 3 February 1923, ibid., pp. 92–4; Salmon, *Foreign Policy and National Identity*, p. 41.

divergences might be exploited by a skilful diplomacy which demonstrated to Norway and other small countries that the Soviet Union, unlike tsarist Russia, was interested in consolidating the independence of the Scandinavian states and increasing their capacity for resistance to the demands of the great powers.

Mowinckel was strongly attracted to the idea of a non-aggression pact when it was first proposed by Kollontai (serving for a second term as minister to Norway) in February 1928, and remained committed to it thereafter as 'confirmation of our sincerity in the struggle for peace'.[142] However, the Norwegian–Soviet negotiations in 1928–30 revealed that there was an unbridgeable divide between, on the one hand, Norway's desire that the pact should be linked to an arbitration treaty and, on the other, the Soviet insistence on a declaration of Norwegian neutrality. On the Norwegian side there were strong objections to any dilution of Norway's obligations under the League Covenant,[143] as well as suspicion of Soviet motives. Urbye, the minister in Moscow, regarded the strategy of concluding non-aggression treaties as a device for playing one state off against another and meddling in the foreign policies of smaller powers.[144] Litvinov for his part was scathing about Mowinckel's failure to appreciate what the Soviet Union was trying to achieve.[145] The matter lapsed under the Agrarian-led government of 1931–3 (with Quisling as minister of defence, relations between Norway and the Soviet Union reached an all-time low),[146] but the return of Mowinckel to office in 1933 was greeted by the Soviets as an opportunity to revive the idea of a non-aggression pact. Although they were careful not to demonstrate their interest too openly, the conclusion of a pact with a sympathetic capitalist state such as Norway, at a time of growing international instability and shortly after Hitler's accession to power, was regarded as a matter of 'considerable importance' to the Soviet Union.[147] Mowinckel for his part remained enthusiastic.[148] However, Norwegian and Soviet priorities still remained far apart, with the former wanting an arbitration treaty and the latter refusing to contemplate this unless it was attached to a non-aggression pact. The proposal was thus allowed once again to lapse.

After 1933 the Soviet Union dropped non-aggression pacts in favour of more direct means of containing a threat which it now perceived as coming from Germany rather than the capitalist world as a whole. There were also signs of a cooling of relations with the Mowinckel government. The prime minister's comments at Geneva on the famine in Ukraine were regarded as

[142] Kollontai telegram to Narkomindel, 23 February 1928, in Holtsmark, *Norge og Sovjetunionen*, p. 153; Kollontai to Litvinov, 5 September 1928, ibid., pp. 161–2.

[143] Memorandum on Soviet draft by Frede Castberg, 11 December 1928, ibid., pp. 164–5.

[144] Urbye to NUD, 10 June 1929, ibid., pp. 171–3.

[145] Litvinov to Kollontai, 18 December 1928, ibid., pp. 166–8.

[146] Stomoniakov (Narkomindel) to Bekzadian (Oslo), 3 March 1932, ibid., pp. 188–9.

[147] Stomoniakov to Bekzadian, 27 March and 13 April 1933, ibid., pp. 202–5.

[148] Bekzadian to Stomoniakov, 12 July 1933, ibid., pp. 205–6.

unfriendly, while Norway was judged to be coming increasingly under British economic and political influence.[149] The Soviets also detected suspicious evidence of a revival of Scandinavian cooperation, especially in the military sphere.[150] Mowinckel did not give up so quickly. In April 1934 he proposed to Munch and Sandler a joint Scandinavian initiative to conclude non-aggression treaties with the USSR and thus demonstrate 'our active interest in peace'.[151] At first Munch was positively disposed and, whilst Sandler preferred to work within the framework of the disarmament conference, there was agreement that the three Scandinavian states should consult together on the question. However, his colleagues proved much less receptive when Mowinckel raised it again at the foreign ministers' meeting in Stockholm in September 1934. Once again the question was allowed to lapse.

The progress of Nordic cooperation continued to be scrutinised more closely, and taken more seriously, by the Soviet Union than by the other great powers. As Sven Holtsmark has shown, this concern was expressed in contradictory terms. The basic Soviet position was one of opposition, based on the assumption that 'a Scandinavian or Nordic regional group would extend the influence of the Western great powers right up to the very borders of the Soviet Union'.[152] The Soviet Union thus perpetuated the traditional tsarist suspicion of a united Scandinavia, as well as its preference for 'divide and rule' tactics. But there occasionally surfaced an alternative, more positive approach which chose to regard Nordic cooperation as a potential barrier to foreign intervention. It was represented in the mid-1920s by Chicherin. An increasingly isolated figure within the Soviet policy-making establishment, Chicherin had nevertheless developed a coherent, if idiosyncratic view of the role of small states in international affairs. He regretted the fact that 'the close Scandinavian cooperation which had developed during the First World War had faded when hostilities ended'. Cooperation between the states of northern Europe, linked if possible to the smaller states of 'Central Europe', would, in his view, enable these states to 'play a useful role as strong buffers between the Soviet Union and the hostile Western great powers'.[153] Chicherin was evidently prepared to credit the smaller European states with a far greater capacity for independent action than were his colleagues. By the late 1930s, however, such stray hints had apparently, in a striking reversal, become official policy. With the identification of Hitler's Germany as the main threat to Soviet security, and with the new emphasis on collective security from 1935 onwards, statements in the Soviet press, as well as by Scandinavian communist parties, propagated the

[149] Stomoniakov to Ananov (Oslo), 17 October 1933, and to Bekzadian, 16 June 1934, ibid., pp. 206–7, 208–9.
[150] Urbye to NUD, 22 November 1934; Ananov to Beriosov (Narkomindel), 24 December 1934, ibid., pp. 209–11.
[151] Quoted in Holtsmark, 'Spørsmålet'.   [152] Holtsmark, *Enemy Springboard*, p. 6.
[153] Ibid., pp. 23–4.

view that Nordic military cooperation could act as a barrier to German aggression.[154] It is nevertheless worth recalling that in 1939 the Soviet Union blocked the Åland plan, the one occasion on which such cooperation had any prospect of taking concrete form.

[154] Ibid., pp. 36–58.

7 Britain, Germany and the Nordic economies 1916–1936

The First World War demonstrated that economic and political power were inseparable. Just as economic resources were crucial to the military effort, so war could be used to advance the economic interests of the belligerents.[1] In Britain, the immediate problem of enforcing the blockade of the Central Powers became overlaid with that of meeting the long-term challenge of German industry. From 1916 onwards, attempts were made to supplant German trade in markets where it had traditionally been dominant. Remarkable and sometimes ruthless efforts were made in the years 1918–21 to convert Britain's temporary commercial predominance, the result of abnormal postwar conditions, into something more permanent. The Nordic countries were a particular object of British interest as traditional German markets which had a strong growth potential in their own right, but they were also regarded as a transit route to the much larger market opportunities that were expected to materialise in post-revolutionary Russia.[2]

By 1921 the impetus had waned and the British economy had relapsed into stagnation. But this early post-war phase foreshadowed the radical shift of policy which followed the abandonment of the gold standard and the adoption of tariff protection in 1931–2. This time there was a far more systematic employment of state power, through tariffs and trade bargaining, but again the Nordic countries were among the principal objects of attention. The depreciation of sterling, together with the bilateral trade agreements concluded in 1933 with Denmark, Norway, Sweden and Finland, helped to make Scandinavia one of Britain's most important export markets by the mid-1930s. Achieved at a time of German weakness, this success was, however, to be undermined by the revival of German competition after 1933.

In Germany, the task of withstanding Allied economic pressure during the First World War became merged into the larger goal of the economic and political reorganisation of continental Europe under German leadership. Scandinavia was integral to German aspirations. At first the Nordic countries were intended to serve Germany's needs as a component of *Mitteleuropa*, the

---

[1] Georges-Henri Soutou, *L'or et le sang. Les buts de guerre économiques de la Première Guerre mondiale* (Paris, 1989).

[2] On the Russian 'Eldorado', see Merja-Liisa Hinkkanen-Lievonen, *British Trade and Enterprise in the Baltic States 1919–1925* (Helsinki, 1984), pp. 113–24.

German-dominated economic sphere. Germany's sudden military collapse in 1918 pushed *Mitteleuropa* off the agenda, to be replaced by the more immediate demands of economic survival and political revisionism, but relations with Scandinavia remained important as contributing to the fulfilment of those goals. Finally, following the onset of the great depression, economic relations with Scandinavia fell victim to the competing demands of German economic interest groups, among which those calling for agricultural protection and autarky increasingly gained the upper hand. But this period also saw the revival of the idea of a special economic relationship between Germany and Scandinavia which foreshadowed, albeit in a less crudely exploitative form, the Nazi *Grosswirtschaftsraum*. The coming to power of Nazism in 1933 suppressed Germany's internal conflicts and made possible a new and more constructive commercial policy towards the Nordic countries. German recovery, combined with Britain's enhanced commercial position in the region, exposed the Nordic countries to an unprecedented degree of bilateralist pressure. It also under-pinned the Nazi regime's heightened ideological and strategic interest in Scandinavia.

The British challenge to German trade 1916–1921

The latter half of the First World War and the immediate post-war period revealed a new readiness to use the power of the state to promote British economic interests. The effort also had a political dimension. There was a widespread conviction that 'British trade and British foreign policy must be more intimately connected than in the past.'[3] Scandinavia and the Baltic attracted attention as an area of opportunity. The freedom with which the Royal Navy roamed Baltic waters was only the most visible expression of the unprecedented prestige enjoyed by Britain in northern Europe at the end of the First World War. It was natural to assume that trade would follow the flag and that, in turn, political influence would follow where British businessmen led. Conversely, an increase in German exports was, in the words of the British minister to Finland in 1921, 'more than merely a matter of interest from the point of view of trade. It is also significant of the expansion of Germany in the Baltic regions.'[4]

The Paris Economic Conference of June 1916 was the chief expression of Allied attempts to restrain Germany's economic dynamism.[5] It reflected French fears of German economic dominance combined with the desire of British tariff reformers to weaken German trade.[6] The resolutions adopted by

[3] Memorandum by Allan Graham (British commercial secretary, Copenhagen), 6 March 1918, FO 382/1942, No. 69337.
[4] Ernest Rennie to FO, 8 July 1921, *DBFP*, 1, XXIII, pp. 119–20.
[5] Soutou, *L'or et le sang*, chs. 7–8.
[6] Heide-Irene Schmidt, 'Wirtschaftliche Kriegsziele Englands und interalliierte Kooperation. Die Pariser Wirtschaftskonferenz 1916', *Militärgeschichtliche Mitteilungen* 29 (1981), pp. 37–54; John Turner, *British Politics and the Great War: Coalition and Conflict 1915–1918*

the conference for the post-war 'reconstruction period' included preferential access to raw materials for countries which had suffered from German 'spoliation' and – most importantly from the British point of view – denying Germany most-favoured-nation treatment for an unspecified period after the end of the war.[7]

For the Scandinavian countries, the Paris resolutions indicated that the Allies had no immediate desire to restore freedom of trade after the war, but rather saw the post-war period as one of continued economic warfare between a small number of large trading blocs. This was a disturbing prospect for small neutrals wholly dependent on unfettered access to foreign markets.[8] In fact the Paris resolutions were to be largely superseded by reparations as a means of limiting German economic power. But Articles 264–7 of the Versailles treaty required Germany to grant most-favoured-nation treatment to the Allied Powers until 10 January 1925.[9] This placed severe restraints on German commercial policy for five years (with the possibility, under Article 280, of extending the period indefinitely), since any concessions won through negotiations with another country would automatically be shared by Germany's former enemies – unless they could be kept secret (as was, for example, the German–Swedish treaty of March 1920).

The wartime campaign against German trade became part of a wider effort to restore British power in relation not only to Germany but also to the United States.[10] However, it proved difficult to weaken one competitor without strengthening the other. In Scandinavia in particular, energetic American competition was aided by the fact that Britain had to 'bear the odium of the Blockade policy . . . we have devoted ourselves so much to the prevention of goods reaching Germany via Sweden that this has naturally prevented us from doing much to push British trade in Sweden'.[11] British efforts were also hampered by institutional weakness of which, as we have seen, the establishment of the new Department of Overseas Trade in 1917 was symptomatic. Yet

(New Haven, Conn., 1991), pp. 83–6; Peter Cline, 'Winding Down the War Economy: British Plans for Peacetime Recovery 1916–1919', in Kathleen Burk (ed.), *War and the State: The Transformation of British Government 1914–1919* (London, 1982), pp. 157–81.

[7] Robert E. Bunselmayer, *The Cost of the War: British Economic War Aims and the Origins of Reparations* (Hamden, Conn., 1975), pp. 39–40; Heide-Irene Schmidt, 'Wirtschaftliche Kriegsziele', pp. 43–4.

[8] Olof Åhlander, *Staat, Wirtschaft und Handelspolitik. Schweden und Deutschland 1918–1921* (Lund, 1983), p. 27.

[9] Georges-Henri Soutou, 'German Economic War Aims Reconsidered', in Hans-Jürgen Schröder (ed.), *Confrontation and Cooperation: Germany and the United States in the Era of World War I 1900–1924* (Providence, R. I., and Oxford, 1993), pp. 315–21; Elisabeth Glaser-Schmidt, 'German and American Concepts to Restore a Liberal World Trading System After World War I', in Schröder, *Confrontation and Cooperation*, pp. 353–76.

[10] Esa Sundbäck, ' "A Convenient Buffer Between Scandinavia and Russia": Great Britain, Scandinavia and the Birth of Finland After the First World War', *Jahrbücher für Geschichte Osteuropas* 42 (1994), pp. 355–75; Heide-Irene Schmidt, 'Wirtschaftliche Kriegsziele', p. 47.

[11] Memorandum by O. S. Philpotts (Stockholm legation), 10 July 1918, FO 368/1992, No. 12630.

there was a remarkable degree of consensus in business and official circles on the need to conquer markets where Germany had traditionally been dominant. The Federation of British Industries (FBI), founded in 1916 by the energetic Birmingham industrialist Dudley Docker (inspired in part by Marcus Wallenberg's description of the influential position enjoyed by the Swedish employers' organisation), agitated for government support and worked closely with the DOT under its first head, Arthur Steel-Maitland.[12] After the armistice it appointed its own trade commissioners to represent British manufacturing interests in markets formerly dominated by German commerce. The first areas selected were Spain, Greece, the East Indies and Scandinavia.[13] The British authorities were alert to the danger that Germany might cloak its activities in neutral markets either by direct investment or by working through neutral intermediaries.[14] They also feared the growth of competition in Scandinavia not only from Germany, but also from France, the United States and the Scandinavian countries themselves. Reports that Swedish companies were being formed to capture trade formerly in the hands of the belligerents led the authorities to take considerable interest in a proposal to establish a British-owned 'syndicate' to ensure that the profit of some of Sweden's overseas trade should come into British hands, even when goods were imported direct into Sweden from overseas.[15]

The arguments in favour of an active commercial policy in northern Europe were set out with exceptional clarity by Allan Graham, commercial adviser to the Copenhagen legation, in a memorandum of March 1918.[16] The occasion was a proposal by the Danish ship-owner H. N. Andersen that Copenhagen should replace Hamburg as the chief *entrepôt* for Scandinavian trade 'and thus weaken Germany's economic control over Scandinavia and the Baltic'; and that Britain should ultimately acquire a controlling interest in the free port at Copenhagen, 'the key of the Baltic', so as to be able to exercise commercial and political influence over the entire region.[17] Graham was attracted by the scheme as a means of undermining Germany's traditional commercial dominance in northern Europe. He argued that 'If the unthinkable happens and Germany retains her grip on Russia and the Baltic there will be little hope

[12] Richard Davenport-Hines, *Dudley Docker: The Life and Times of a Trade Warrior* (Cambridge, 1984), pp. 108–9.
[13] Ibid., pp. 112–13.
[14] Howard to FO, 3 August 1918, FO 368/1993, reporting the intention of the Swedish subsidiary of AEG to establish a factory in Malmö; Consul Churchill (Stockholm) to FO, 23 August 1918, ibid., No. 151318, reporting German approach to the Swedish General Export Association; DOT to Ministry of Blockade and War Trade Department, 7 October 1918, ibid., No. 168820, asking for information on this and any future developments.
[15] Howard to FO, 2 March 1918, FO 368/1992, No. 62849, and subsequent correspondence. In 1919 the firm 'AB Svensk–Engelska Oceankompaniet' was founded with a number of Swedish directors, including Axel Bildt: Åhlander, *Staat, Wirtschaft und Handelspolitik*, p. 372 (n. 10).
[16] Memorandum of 6 March 1918, FO 382/1942, No. 69337.
[17] 'Memorandum of Interview Between Mr Andersen and Mr Graham March 5th 1918', ibid.

for Great Britain's trade or influence in the Baltic unless she can obtain Scandinavian help as suggested by the scheme.' Even if Germany lost the war, 'she [would] undoubtedly make desperate efforts to revive her trade connections by making use of neutral countries as covers for her manufactures'. There were further arguments. Norway and Sweden would probably 'become more important from a Trade point of view than they were before the war, owing to their great natural resources of raw materials'. Scandinavia was also a link with Russia, 'and though the possibilities of trade with Scandinavia may be limited, there is practically no limit to the possibilities of trade with Russia'. Finally, having lived for two months with the American commercial attaché, Graham knew that 'the Americans are going to make big efforts to extend their connections with Scandinavia'.[18]

There were many indications in 1918–19 that officials in the Foreign Office, the Board of Trade and the DOT accepted these arguments. Repeatedly, however, proposals for encouraging British–Scandinavian trade proved impracticable, received insufficient government and business support, or were judged less urgent than other priorities. Andersen's scheme for a British presence at Copenhagen, pursued in various guises at least until 1923, was attractive at first sight but proved to be another of those 'largely nebulous plans' with which Andersen had made senior British officials all too familiar during the war.[19] The first meeting of the Advisory Committee to the DOT, in April 1918, discussed a proposed commercial mission either to Morocco or to Scandinavia 'to study especially the preparations which Germany is making to develop her trade both now and after the war and also the industrial changes caused by the war in Scandinavia and their probable consequences for our trade with Northern Europe'.[20] Despite the strong backing of Sir Ralph Paget, the minister in Copenhagen, the committee accepted the department's advice 'that, if only one mission can be sent, a Mission to Morocco would be likely to be of greater value to British trade'. A year later, in May 1919, the Advisory Committee received a proposal to support a visit of Scandinavian businessmen to Great Britain. The purpose was to counteract a vigorous American commercial drive and to dispel 'the impression that traders in this country are lethargic and cannot supply what they [the Scandinavians] want', at a time when 'the German manufacturers are still out of the Scandinavian market'.[21] But the Federation of British Industries (FBI) had already 'decided not to take any steps in this matter', and although the Advisory Committee considered the visit desirable, it decided that it should be postponed until the many

---

18 Memorandum of 6 March 1918, ibid.
19 Minute by Sir Eyre Crowe, 29 March 1923, FO 371/9294, N2842/807/15.
20 BT memorandum, 'Proposed Commercial Mission Either (1) to Morocco or (2) to Scandinavia', BT 90/14; minutes of meeting of Advisory Committee, 17 April 1918, BT 90/1.
21 BT memorandum, 'Proposed Visit of Scandinavian Business Men to the United Kingdom', BT 90/15.

restrictions and controls on British trade had been removed.[22] There is no indication that the visit ever took place. The FBI's attitude was symptomatic of the loss of momentum suffered by the organisation with the end of the wartime ascendancy of the 'productioneers'.[23]

A final example is provided by the Swedish proposal to establish a fast train–ferry service between Gothenburg and an English port. This was welcomed in 1918 by the Foreign Office and the Board of Trade, and particularly by Sir Esme Howard, as a means of reducing German political influence, making British exports more competitive and developing the transit trade to Russia.[24] However, the service would have to be subsidised by both the Swedish and the British governments, and in July 1919 the Board decided that such a subsidy could not be justified 'at a time when so many calls are being made upon public funds'.[25] The scheme was eventually shelved in 1921.[26]

Other measures proved more effective. The blockade of Germany, extended into the Baltic and maintained until the signature of the Versailles treaty in June 1919, cut the Scandinavian countries off from Germany more completely than they had been during the war. A blockade was threatened again at the time of the reparations crisis in the spring of 1921. British ships also prevented Scandinavian merchantmen from reaching Russian ports several months before a blockade of the Bolsheviks was officially declared in the autumn of 1919.[27] The continuing presence of the Royal Navy in Baltic waters was intended to secure neutral markets. As J. D. Gregory put it in September 1921: 'the two motives which underlie naval cruises in the Baltic are to support the policy of the Allies and the League of Nations at Danzig, Memel and in the newly formed States, and to improve relations between the United Kingdom, Scandinavia and the Baltic States, more especially with a view to increasing trade'.[28]

Britain also exploited its monopoly position as a coal supplier to Scandinavian markets. It was able to do so because the coal industry, normally highly fragmented both regionally and in terms of ownership, was under state control between 1917 and 1921, and because of the temporary eclipse of competitors such as Germany.[29] But British economic pressure on Scandinavia slackened abruptly in 1921. The immediate causes were the end of the post-war boom,

[22] Minutes of meeting of Advisory Committee, 7 May 1919, BT 90/2.

[23] Davenport-Hines, *Dudley Docker*, p. 113.

[24] Howard memorandum, 18 November 1918, FO 368/1992, No. 175372; report of meeting at Board of Trade (attended by Howard), 11 December 1918; Howard 'Memorandum on Political Advantages of the Proposed Improved Steamer Service Between Great Britain and Sweden', 7 December 1918, BT 198/4.

[25] Minutes of meeting of Board of Trade, 11 July 1919, ibid.

[26] Sir Colville Barclay, 'Sweden. Annual Report, 1921' (p. 30), 28 June 1922, FO 371/8234, N6407/6407/42.

[27] Åhlander, *Staat, Wirtschaft und Handelspolitik*, p. 74.

[28] Letter to Ramsay (Stockholm), 12 September 1921, quoted ibid., p. 334.

[29] Barry Supple, *The History of the British Coal Industry*, vol. IV, *1913–1946: The Political Economy of Decline* (Oxford, 1987), chs. 3–4 (esp. pp. 114–15); Åhlander, *Staat, Wirtschaft und Handelspolitik*, ch. 2.

the dismantlement of wartime controls and the reversion of British business to its traditional free-trade preferences. Much of the impetus for a vigorous, state-supported export drive had arisen from the fear of a strong Germany and an inconclusive end to the war; Germany's defeat removed the sense of urgency from both government and industry.[30] In the case of coal, pressure was eased by an American export offensive in the summer of 1920 followed by the British coal strike in April 1921.[31] Above all, however, the loss of momentum was due to the recovery of German trade.

By the middle of 1921 British officials were becoming alarmed by the vigorous revival of German exports to Scandinavia at a time when British trade remained depressed, with little prospect of an industrial revival.[32]

Germany overtook Great Britain as the leading exporter to Denmark, Finland and Sweden in 1921, and to Norway in 1923, and maintained its advantage (with the exception of Norway in 1924–5 and 1927) with a widening margin until the great depression. The most dramatic reversal was in Finland.[33] Part of the blame lay with British exporters who failed to advertise because they were 'labouring under the impression that, as in the past, the bulk of the imports into Finland will continue to come from the United Kingdom'.[34] A more significant factor was currency depreciation, which allowed Germany to sell at around half the price of British goods. The Finns, it was reported, felt obliged to buy cotton spinning and weaving machines at those prices, 'hoping in a year or so when they become useless and have to be thrown out they will be able to replace them by British-made machines at less expense'.[35] The new British minister in Helsinki, Ernest Rennie, identified more deep-seated reasons for Germany's success, including the proximity of the German Baltic ports, 'the very wide-spread knowledge of the German language, not only in business circles but in conventional and literary circles and in a very general way all over the country' and the legacy of German military support for the Whites in 1918.[36] Trade with Britain, by contrast, was 'almost stationary'. If it declined further, 'British influence in general must suffer a corresponding set-back'.[37]

The worst fears of 1921 were not realised. Finland was such a buoyant market in the 1920s that there was room for both British and German exports. The annual report for 1922 noted that 'except as regards certain specialised imports, e.g. electrical machinery, British manufacturers and products are

[30] Cline, 'Winding Down the War Economy', pp. 174–8.
[31] Supple, British Coal Industry IV, pp. 153–4.
[32] Sir Charles Marling (Copenhagen) to FO, 6 July 1921 (commenting on recent meeting in Stockholm of the three British commercial secretaries in Scandinavia), FO 371/6781, N8013/8013/63.
[33] William R. Mead, 'Anglo-Finnish Commercial Relations Since 1918', Baltic and Scandinavian Countries 5 (1939), pp. 117–25 (pp. 120–1).
[34] Consul H. Mackie (Helsinki) to DOT, 11 June 1921, FO 371/6773, N7764/7700/56.
[35] Mackie to DOT, 2 July 1921, ibid., N8277/7700/56.
[36] Ernest Rennie to FO, 8 July 1921, DBFP, 1, XXIII, pp. 119–20.
[37] See also minute by F. Maxse, 20 July 1921, N8224/8138/56, FO 371/6776.

Table 6 *British and German exports as a percentage of the total imports of the Nordic countries 1919–1929*

	Denmark		Finland		Norway		Sweden		Total	
	Germany	UK	Germany	UK	Germany	UK	Germany	UK	Germany	UK
1919	12.9	31.2	6.3	26.9	6.0	30.2	10.6	26.4	9.0	28.7
1920	16.4	27.4	16.8	27.7	10.6	32.8	15.1	27.6	14.7	28.9
1921	27.2	18.0	33.6	19.8	18.5	25.8	25.8	17.3	26.3	20.2
1922	30.7	22.0	33.1	21.8	21.5	22.4	28.2	24.1	28.4	22.6
1923	32.1	20.0	34.0	18.4	22.9	21.9	26.4	21.9	28.9	20.6
1924	27.4	18.9	29.9	18.7	20.3	23.8	24.8	21.6	25.6	20.8
1925	28.0	14.7	31.9	17.0	20.3	22.6	26.1	20.1	26.6	18.6
1926	31.1	11.5	34.8	12.8	20.4	19.4	30.9	14.8	29.3	14.6
1927	30.6	13.1	32.5	14.5	20.2	20.4	30.6	16.7	28.5	16.2
1928	32.7	13.8	37.0	12.4	21.2	19.3	31.1	16.1	30.5	15.4
1929	32.9	14.7	38.3	13.0	24.3	20.7	30.7	17.3	31.6	16.4

Source: Based on B. R. Mitchell, *International Historical Statistics: Europe 1750–1988* (New York, 1992), table E2.

steadily ousting the German in the public estimation'.[38] But the deficiencies of British salesmanship remained all too evident. In 1926 the British minister complained that 'the statistics for the last year do not show the expansion of British imports into this country which a couple of years ago there seemed to be good reason to expect'. Probably ten times as many German commercial travellers visited Finland as British, and British firms were in the habit of leaving 'the agencies for their business in the hands of natives, and even in many cases, foreign agents'.[39]

Complaints about British salesmanship were not confined to Finland. The annual report for Sweden in 1922 noted that there had 'rarely been such a favourable opportunity to expand British trade', but that there was 'still much headway to be made':

Traders are still much too prone to stop short at Christiania and Copenhagen and leave Sweden to be settled either by correspondence or by agents in one or other of those capitals; thus virtually making a commercial present of Sweden to Germany, which is under no delusion as to the value of the Swedish market.[40]

Such criticisms reflected the habitual irritation of diplomats and commercial experts who felt that their best efforts on behalf of British trade were being obstructed by an obtuse and ungrateful business community. But the frequency with which they were expressed supports the view that there was something about the nature of the British export economy which made it peculiarly incapable of responding to the challenges of the inter-war period.[41]

Part of the explanation was clearly structural. British exports were concentrated in branches such as coal and textiles for which demand was declining, and not enough in newer products such as automobiles and consumer goods. They were oriented primarily towards less developed markets overseas, while Germany sold high-quality goods in the more developed European markets. The relatively high price of British exports was exacerbated by the overvaluation of sterling between 1925 and 1931. Britain's uncompetitiveness also derived from the structure of British industry, which was characterised by a large number of small- to medium-sized firms, competing with one another at home and in foreign markets, in contrast to the large integrated works typical of German industry. There were few industry-wide trade associations at home or selling organisations abroad. British manufacturers thus remained dependent on merchants as intermediaries between themselves and foreign customers.[42] Whilst British producers often seemed to be more interested in making goods than selling them, the merchants tended to

[38] 'Annual Report for Finland, 1922' (p. 2), 20 January 1923, FO 371/9267, N996/996/56.
[39] Rennie to FO, 10 February 1926, FO 371/11752, N1109/1109/56.
[40] Sir Colville Barclay, 'Annual Report for Sweden, 1922', 31 March 1923, FO 371/9380, N3209/3209/42.
[41] Clemens A. Wurm, 'Der Exporthandel und die britische Wirtschaft 1919–1939', Vierteljahrsschrift für Sozial- und Wirtschaftsgeschichte 68 (1981), pp. 191–224.
[42] PEP, Report on International Trade (London, 1937), esp. ch. 5.

expect customers to come to them rather than going out to look for them. They were 'order takers' rather than 'order getters'.[43]

It was symptomatic of the British approach that the export to Scandinavia with which industry and government were most consistently preoccupied during the inter-war period was coal – the product of a declining industry, and one in which Britain's chief competitor after 1926 was not Germany but Poland.[44] Yet Britain's passivity also reflected a basic satisfaction with the system of multilateral trade which had developed by the late 1920s. The pre-war 'triangular' pattern of British–Scandinavian–German trade had been restored, and in this context Germany was not so much a competitor as a partner. Their sales to Great Britain provided the Nordic countries with earnings which they used to purchase goods from Germany, including the capital goods which helped further to diversify their economies. The deficits in Britain's trade with Scandinavia were balanced by surpluses in trade with overseas markets, and by the invisible earnings of the City of London. It was an international division of labour from which all parties could benefit. All of these assumptions were to be destroyed by the depression. The challenge to free trade and to multilateralism, largely suppressed after the defeat of the Baldwin government on the tariff issue in 1923, was to resurface and to be directed with special intensity towards Scandinavia.

But in one important respect the attempt to return to pre-war conditions and values enhanced Britain's presence in Scandinavia. Like other European central banks, those of the Nordic countries were targeted by Montagu Norman, the governor of the Bank of England, as part of his campaign to promote central bank cooperation and restore the gold standard.[45] Norman told Nicolai Rygg, governor of Norges Bank, that he had 'long felt that for the purpose of the economic rehabilitation of Europe – and indeed of the World – no practical measures would be more helpful than whole-hearted and continuous co-operation between the various Central Banks'.[46] The Bank of England gave both moral and financial support (in the form of sterling credits) to the efforts of Norway, Denmark and Finland to restore the gold standard (Sweden had returned to gold in 1922). It also built up a large body of information on the workings of the banking systems and on economic conditions in the Nordic countries. Bank officials visited the Nordic countries periodically, while promising Scandinavians were given intensive training in

---

[43] Report of the British Economic Mission to the Far East, 1931, quoted in C. A. Wurm, 'Britische Aussenwirtschaft 1919–1939. Exportverfall, Aussenhandelsorganisation und Unternehmerverhalten', *Scripta Mercuriae* 17 (1983), pp. 1–40 (p. 16).

[44] Patrick Salmon, 'Polish–British Competition in the Coal Markets of Northern Europe 1927–1934', *Scripta historiae oeconomicae* 16 (1981), pp. 217–43.

[45] On Norman's personality and mission, see Andrew Boyle, *Montagu Norman* (London, 1967), esp. chs. 6–9. On the Bank's international role, see P. L. Cottrell, 'The Bank of England in Its International Setting 1918–1972', in Richard Roberts and David Kynaston (eds.), *The Bank of England: Money, Power and Influence 1694–1994* (Oxford, 1995), pp. 83–139.

[46] Norman to Rygg, 17 May 1923, BEA, OV 26/22.

the Bank of England's methods. Ironically, however, a genuine Anglo-Scandinavian 'special relationship' in the banking sphere emerged only after – and in part because of – the wreckage of Norman's vision in the financial crisis of 1931.[47]

Germany from *Mitteleuropa* to revisionism 1916–1932

For Germany, like Britain, there was a continuum between wartime and peacetime efforts to develop economic relations with northern Europe. The wartime debate on *Mitteleuropa* was given impetus first by the resolutions of the Paris Economic Conference, which indicated that the Entente Powers were intent upon establishing an economic bloc directed against Germany, and secondly by the decisions of the Imperial War Conference in 1917, which threatened to turn the British empire, with its enormous supplies of raw materials, into a closed economic system.[48] In order to meet this post-war challenge, it was felt that Germany must establish an economic sphere comprising much of continental Europe, including the states of 'north-eastern Europe'.[49] In August 1917 the German chancellor Michaelis told two Swedish visitors that Germany needed to abandon its old alliance policies in favour of 'economic associations': 'Germany and its allies intended to establish a great purchasing trust for the purchase and distribution of raw materials after the war . . . It would perhaps be advantageous for Sweden to join in.'[50] Germany's concern with Swedish ore supplies was evident in its Åland diplomacy in 1918 (ch. 4, pp. 162–7), when it offered Sweden sovereignty over the islands in exchange for an agreement to increase ore exports after the end of the war. In February 1918 the industrialist August Thyssen wrote to Chancellor Hertling emphasising the crucial importance of Swedish iron ore for the production of high-grade steel, and arguing that, in view of Britain's great influence over Norway (which might even result in the establishment of a naval base at Narvik), it was all the more important for Germany to secure the Baltic export route by consolidating its position in Finland.[51]

Finland was the 'cornerstone' of Germany's position in north-eastern

[47] See ch. 8, pp. 280–2.

[48] On the development of *Mitteleuropa* ideas before and during the war, see Henry Cord Meyer, *'Mitteleuropa' in German Thought and Action 1815–1945* (The Hague, 1955); Peter Theiner, '"Mitteleuropa"-Pläne im Wilhelminischen Deutschland', in Helmut Berding (ed.), *Wirtschaftliche und politische Integration in Europa im 19. und 20. Jahrhundert* (Göttingen, 1984), pp. 128–48; Soutou, *L'or et le sang*, chs. 1–3, 9, 14–15. On the possibility of including the Scandinavian countries in *Mitteleuropa*, see Fritz Fischer, *Griff nach der Weltmacht. Die Kriegszielpolitik des kaiserlichen Deutschland 1914–1918* (revised edn, Düsseldorf, 1977), pp. 208–15.

[49] Memorandum by Schoenebek (Reichsamt des Innern), quoted in Åhlander, *Staat, Wirtschaft und Handelspolitik*, pp. 40–1.

[50] Conversation with C. G. Westman and Eric Trolle (Swedish minister in Berlin), recorded in K. G. Westman (ed. W. M. Carlgren), *Politiska anteckningar april 1917–augusti 1939* (Stockholm, 1987), p. 11 (entry for 8 August 1917).

[51] Åhlander, *Staat, Wirtschaft und Handelspolitik*, p. 43.

Europe in 1918.[52] A meeting of industrialists at the Stahlhof in Düsseldorf in May 1918 demanded 'the permanent military occupation of the European supply routes to northern Russia', including the Murman coast, Finland and the Åland Islands.[53] In the event, Swedish or Finnish control of a demilitarised Åland, together with the long-term agreement concluded with Sweden in May 1918, were judged a sufficient guarantee of German iron ore supplies. But Germany's political and military leadership were fully aware of Finland's importance. The German–Finnish treaties of 7 March 1918 signalled the fact that the country was firmly within the German orbit, a month before von der Goltz's troops landed at Hanko. The terms of the trade treaty made it clear that Finland was to be merely an economic satellite, its trade oriented almost exclusively towards Germany and German-controlled territories in the east.[54]

The prospect of defeat curbed German ambitions. The economic priorities now were to maintain raw material imports for the iron and steel industry, to preserve export markets and to prevent the seizure of German assets abroad. At a meeting on 3 September 1918 between officials and representatives of heavy industry at the Reichswirtschaftsamt (Reich Economic Office), attention quickly turned to the neutral countries, and in particular to Sweden, as a means of achieving these goals.[55] Swedish iron ore posed a particular problem. Although the supply of phosphoric ore from northern Sweden was guaranteed by long-term agreements, no such security existed for the smaller quantities of low-phosphorus ore from central Sweden which were essential for the production of high-grade steel. Foreign purchases of iron ore mines, which had taken place on a large scale in the immediate pre-war years as a means of circumventing Swedish export controls, had been blocked by the Swedish 'restriction law' of 1916.[56] Moreover, some German-owned mines had already passed into Swedish control during the war. The industrialists argued against Sweden's restrictions on foreign capital, asserting that German citizens should be granted the same rights in Sweden as Swedish citizens in Germany. They also deplored the way in which the war, by preventing neighbouring countries such as Sweden from buying German goods, had encouraged them to build up their own industries. In export markets such as the Netherlands, indeed, Swedish industry had become a dangerous competitor. They concluded by affirming the necessity of promoting German exports to neutral countries by all possible means.

Like other former neutrals such as Switzerland and the Netherlands, the

[52] Fischer, Griff nach der Weltmacht, pp. 449–54.   [53] Quoted ibid., p. 498.

[54] C. Jay Smith Jr, Finland and the Russian Revolution 1917–1922 (Athens, Ga., 1958), pp. 61–3; Fischer, Griff nach der Weltmacht, pp. 451–2; Juhani Paasivirta, Finland and Europe: The Early Years of Independence 1917–1939 (Helsinki, 1988), pp. 151–2; Soutou, L'or et le sang, pp. 666–8. For a contrary view, see Walther Hubatsch, 'Finnland in der deutschen Ostseepolitik 1914–1918', in Hubatsch, Unruhe des Nordens. Studien zur deutsch–skandinavischen Geschichte (Göttingen, Berlin and Frankfurt am Main, 1956), pp. 106–49.

[55] Åhlander, Staat, Wirtschaft und Handelspolitik, pp. 44–8.

[56] Sven Nordlund, Upptäckten av Sverige. Utländska direktinvestingar i Sverige 1895–1945 (Umeå, 1989), pp. 52–5.

Scandinavian countries were rich in capital, had a strong import capacity, and were still prepared to do business with Germany.[57] They had traded profitably with Germany throughout the war and many traditional commercial and cultural links had survived. Although German exports to Scandinavia declined in the chaotic economic conditions of 1919, they recovered dramatically in 1920–1. The vigorous efforts of German salesmanship in Scandinavia were aided by the rapid demobilisation of industry and, most of all, by the competitive advantage afforded by a depreciated currency. Inflation kept the German economy buoyant during the world economic crisis of 1920–1. The strong demand for foreign imports made Germany an attractive market for neighbouring countries. Some, like Sweden, also wished to diversify their trade in order to avoid undue dependence on the Western powers. State control of foreign trade enabled Germany to circumvent the most-favoured-nation provisions of the Versailles treaty. Sweden received generous import quotas in the Swedish–German agreement of March 1920, but because the agreement was kept secret and unofficial, these concessions did not have to be passed on to the Allies. In return, the position of German industry in the Swedish market was secured and – most importantly – supplies of Swedish iron ore were guaranteed.[58]

German officials and politicians were fully aware of the political implications of foreign trade at a time when Germany's military defeat and disarmament had made German economic power 'the only thing', as Stresemann later put it, 'with which we can still make foreign policy'.[59] Sometimes economic pressure was directly employed as a means of extracting political concessions. The threat to cut off essential coal deliveries was used in 1920 to force Denmark to enter into bilateral discussions on the Slesvig question without the interference of the Allied Powers.[60] The strategy of using 'Denmark's distress as a means of economic and political pressure and thus making it unmistakably clear that they are dependent on us'[61] was rewarded with success in May 1921 when Denmark agreed to open bilateral talks on Slesvig – Germany's first direct contact with a foreign nation on a matter related to the Versailles treaty.[62] The provisional trade agreements of 1920–1 also served the cause of revisionism either directly, like the agreement with Czechoslovakia of June 1920, which

[57] Harm Schröter, *Aussenpolitik und Wirtschaftsinteresse. Skandinavien im aussenwirtschaftlichen Kalkül Deutschlands und Grossbritanniens 1918–1939* (Frankfurt am Main, Berne and New York, 1983), p. 24.

[58] Åhlander, *Staat, Wirtschaft und Handelspolitik*, pp. 131–53.

[59] Speech of 22 November 1925, quoted in Hans-Jürgen Schröder, 'Zur politischen Bedeutung der deutschen Handelspolitik nach dem Ersten Weltkrieg', in Gerald D. Feldman, Carl-Ludwig Holtfrerich, Gerhard A. Ritter and Peter-Christian Witt (eds.), *Die deutsche Inflation. Eine Zwischenbilanz* (Berlin and New York, 1982), pp. 235–51 (p. 249).

[60] Correspondence in ZSta., AA 64078, summarised in memorandum by Jena, 3 August 1920.

[61] Memorandum, Jena, 1 July 1920, ZSta., AA 66019.

[62] John L. Heineman, *Hitler's First Foreign Minister: Constantin Freiherr von Neurath* (Berkeley, New York and London, 1980), p. 22.

undermined the French security sphere in eastern Europe, or implicitly by the mere fact of their existence.

The recovery of Germany's autonomy in foreign trade, with the expiry of the Versailles provisions at the beginning of 1925, both eased and rendered more complicated the task of German policy makers. Germany was now free to conclude commercial agreements in accordance with the liberal ethos which prevailed in a period when both Germany and the world economy as a whole had regained something of their pre-war stability and prosperity. The moderate protective tariffs for agriculture and heavy industry contained in the 'small tariff revision' of August 1925 indicated that Germany would not revert to the protectionism of the pre-war period, but would use tariffs as a bargaining counter to obtain most-favoured-nation treatment for its exports in world markets.[63] In contrast to the fragmented conditions of the immediate post-war years, Germany also acquired an effective body for the formulation and conduct of foreign trade policy, with the establishment of the Handelspolitischer Ausschuss in 1925 (ch. 5, p. 211).[64]

But the 'qualified victory for German export industries'[65] (with which the German foreign minister, Gustav Stresemann, was closely identified) represented by the tariff of 1925 also entailed the politicisation of tariff policy. This was, of course, nothing new. Tariffs had been a contentious political issue in imperial Germany, and the conflicts between interest groups and political parties representing agriculture, heavy industry and the export industries which preceded the adoption of the new tariff were merely the continuation of an old struggle. In one respect, indeed, the farmers were able to win more protection than they had enjoyed under the 1902 Bülow tariff. A duty was imposed for the first time on imports of live cattle for slaughter – a concession which was later to have serious consequences for Danish agriculture. There remained a fundamental dichotomy between the agrarian view of tariffs as an instrument of protection, and that of industrialists and officials, who regarded them as negotiating tools.

The new German commercial treaty system, of which the agreement with France in 1927 became the cornerstone, represented one aspect of the rehabilitation of Germany in the mid-1920s. Together with the Dawes Plan of 1924 and the formation of the International Steel Cartel in 1925, it constituted an economic counterpart of the Locarno treaties of 1925.[66] The Nordic countries had their part to play in this process. Most-favoured-nation treaties

[63] Dirk Stegmann, 'Deutsche Zoll- und Handelspolitik 1924/5–1929 unter besonderer Berücksichtigung agrarischer und industrieller Interessen', in Hans Mommsen, Dietmar Petzina and Bernd Weisbrod (eds.), *Industrielles System und politische Entwicklung in der Weimarer Republik* (Düsseldorf, 1974), pp. 499–513.

[64] But for a more critical view of the HPA, see Joachim Radkau, 'Entscheidungsprozesse und Entscheidungsdefizite in der deutschen Aussenwirtschaftspolitik 1933–1940', *Geschichte und Gesellschaft* 2 (1976), pp. 33–65.

[65] John Hiden, *The Baltic States and Weimar* Ostpolitik (Cambridge, 1987), p. 172.

[66] Clemens Wurm, *Business, Politics and International Relations: Steel, Cotton and International Cartels in British Politics 1924–1939* (Cambridge, 1993), pp. 16–17; Robert Boyce, *British*

with Denmark and Norway were already in force, but in 1926 a supplementary agreement was signed with Denmark and new treaties were concluded with Sweden and Finland.[67] Since they were already low-tariff countries, the concessions made by Sweden and Denmark were mainly symbolic; but Denmark reduced its visa restrictions and fees for German commercial travellers (a form of disguised protectionism practised by all the Nordic countries), while Sweden agreed that no export duty or other restrictions should be placed on the export of iron ore.[68] In return, Germany reduced the duty on a number of imports from Denmark and Sweden, including Danish exports of horses and cheese, on which the Danes had felt disadvantaged in comparison with other exporting countries.[69] The negotiations with Finland were more difficult since both sides wanted, and ultimately obtained, more substantial tariff reductions. The German concessions on Finnish butter and cheese exports were later to be of considerable significance since they benefited more important producing countries via the most-favoured-nation clause.[70]

In justifying the agreements to other ministries, the Reichstag and the governments of the federal states, the Auswärtiges Amt drew attention (not without an element of special pleading) to their wider economic and political significance.[71] The treaties demonstrated that the new German tariff was an effective negotiating instrument; and the Danish agreement had headed off the danger that Denmark might introduce a negotiating tariff on the German model. Politically, the agreements would contribute to improved relations with the Nordic countries, especially in the context of the League of Nations. Germany's impending entry into the League would be welcomed by the smaller ex-neutrals as offering a counterweight to the overbearing influence of Britain and France, and they might back Germany on issues such as disarmament, minorities and reparations, which were crucial to its rehabilitation as a great power. While it remained true that Germany 'should not give economic gifts purely for political reasons',[72] German tariff policy had, the Wilhelmstrasse argued, proved its worth by contributing to a climate favourable to German revisionism. In this context, however, the sheer size of the German economy constituted both a political asset and a restraint:

The strongest factor in reviving our reputation and influence abroad is the consumer potential of a population of 60 million. We are the second greatest consumer in the

[67] Schröter, *Aussenpolitik und Wirtschaftsinteresse*, pp. 40–4.
[68] Undated AA memoranda on treaties with Denmark (c. 15 April 1926) and Sweden (c. 25 June 1926), *ADAP*, B, III, pp. 247–50, 312–14; draft memorandum for Foreign Minister Stresemann, 5 May 1926, PA, AA Abt. IV Nd, Handel 13 Dänemark, Bd 2.
[69] Meeting of the Rigsdag's economic committee (Erhvervsudvalg), 12 January 1926, RA, UM, 72 Tys. 1, Bd 8.
[70] Schröter, *Aussenpolitik und Wirtschaftsinteresse*, pp. 43–4.
[71] See, in addition to documents cited in n. 68, Stresemann to Länderregierungen, 20 April 1926, PA, AA Handakten Eisenlohr, Dänemark, Bd 1.
[72] Undated AA memorandum on treaty with Sweden (c. 25 June 1926), *ADAP*, B, III, pp. 312–14.

world after the United States. Therein lies a power factor which is perhaps not yet sufficiently appreciated. But conversely we also have a special obligation to those countries bordering on Germany which, owing to their proximity and economic structure, are vitally dependent on the German market.[73]

After 1929 this caveat was to be all too frequently ignored or forgotten.

The performance of German industry in Scandinavian export markets was not merely the mirror image of Great Britain's. German industry had its own preoccupations and its own problems: in particular, a chronic shortage of capital. Harm Schröter has suggested that, especially in the light of the catastrophic experiences of the First World War and the crisis-ridden economic conditions of much of the inter-war period, German companies 'had one overriding goal: security'.[74] They were interested in Scandinavia not simply as a profitable area of economic activity, but because it was close to home and because its economic, political and cultural conditions were familiar. Often the priorities of German business coincided with those of the state: both, for example, were concerned with long-term security in the supply of raw materials. Government tariff policy was also clearly intended to serve the interests of German exporters, who had ample opportunity to make their wishes known. But private industry operated independently of the state and often used methods of which government was, or chose to be, unaware. Shortage of capital and Scandinavian legislation made it difficult for German firms to invest directly, but a certain amount of direct investment, often concealed by the use of 'dummy' companies, was carried out, especially by the steel and chemical industries, as well as by firms seeking to evade the disarmament provisions of the treaty of Versailles.[75] International cartel agreements were used as a means of reserving Scandinavian markets for German producers and (through secret collaboration with, for example, the British and Belgian industries) of preventing the Nordic countries from establishing their own chemical works.[76]

The imbalance between German exports to the Nordic countries and its imports from them posed no fundamental difficulties until the latter were threatened by the rise of German agricultural protectionism after 1929. The endemic structural crisis of German agriculture was exacerbated by the world-wide agricultural depression in 1927–8. The crisis hit the dairy industry first and led to the radicalisation of the small farmers of Schleswig-Holstein, in the *Landvolkbewegung* of 1928. In February 1929 the major agrarian pressure groups formed the 'Green Front' with a programme which included protection against foreign imports, for which the denunciation of the most-favoured-nation agreements with such countries as Sweden and Finland was a

---

[73] Undated AA memorandum on treaty with Denmark (c. 15 April 1926), ibid., pp. 247–50.
[74] Harm Schröter, 'Risk and Control in Multinational Enterprise: German Businesses in Scandinavia 1918–1939', *Business History Review* 62 (1988), pp. 420–43 (p. 421).
[75] Nordlund, *Upptäckten av Sverige*, pp. 161–78.   [76] See ch. 8, pp. 294–5.

prerequisite.[77] The government, a left–centre coalition led by the Social Democrat Hermann Müller, responded in May 1929 with an emergency programme which envisaged restrictions on imports of cattle, pigs, meat and dairy products.

The proposals were sharply criticised by the Auswärtiges Amt, which warned that they would seriously damage Germany's relations with the Netherlands, the Scandinavian countries and the Baltic states. If their exports of agricultural produce were reduced, these countries would retaliate by switching their imports from Germany to Great Britain. They would react strongly if existing trade agreements were denounced. Denmark, Sweden and Finland were 'among the few neutral countries in the world with whom our relations have generally developed without friction, and often in a positively friendly manner, and whose support for our international efforts – for example, in the League of Nations – we have frequently called upon'. With Denmark in particular there had been a noticeable improvement in recent years: there was now a chance of reaching a settlement on the border question and 'detaching Denmark from the formerly strong French influence'. Most importantly, the German minority in North Slesvig, already suffering economic hardship, would be virtually ruined if the new measures came into effect: 'All that we have done for years to sustain the German minority in Denmark would have been for nothing.'[78]

To an even greater extent than the other Nordic countries, Denmark was to feel the impact of German protectionism. At the same time, through its dependence on the British market, Denmark was exposed to the growth of protectionist agitation in Great Britain. Although the bulk of Danish agricultural exports went to Britain, Denmark relied on the German market for sales of horses, butter and eggs. Germany was also the only outlet for live cattle which had reached the end of their milk-producing lives. By the late 1920s this trade amounted to 250,000 head of cattle a year. When the German–Swedish trade agreement was renegotiated in November 1930, the tariff on cattle was increased and Sweden was compensated by being allowed a quota at the old level corresponding to its normal export of 5,000 head of cattle a year. But Denmark's far larger export would be decimated by the new tariff.[79] The Danes realised that they were the main target and regarded the new agreement as a transparent evasion of Germany's most-favoured-nation obligations. A further blow to Danish exports was struck when a new agreement with Finland, in July 1930, enabled the most-favoured-nation provisions on butter (which had shielded Denmark and the Netherlands from the increases

[77] Dieter Gessner, 'The Dilemma of German Agriculture During the Weimar Republic', in Richard Bessel and E. J. Feuchtwanger (eds.), *Social Change and Political Development in Weimar Germany* (London, 1981), pp. 134–54; Gessner, 'Agrarian Protectionism in the Weimar Republic', *Journal of Contemporary History* 12 (1977), pp. 759–78.
[78] Memorandum by Abteilung IV, 30 May 1929, PA, AA Abt. IV Nd, Handel 13, Dänemark, Bd 2.
[79] Ministerial discussion, 18 October 1929, PA, AA Handakten Eisenlohr, Dänemark, Bd 2.

introduced in 1929) to be bypassed in the same way as the agreement with Sweden had affected cattle.

Each of these measures intensified the Danish propaganda campaign against German goods, and in favour of purchases from Great Britain, which had assumed major dimensions by the beginning of 1930. The German minister in Copenhagen, Ulrich von Hassell, warned that the Swedish–German treaty had given fresh impetus to a movement which might have political as well as economic consequences. Hassell urged that some form of concession should be made to Denmark; but the Danish representations on the cattle question were categorically rejected.[80] By the beginning of 1930 British commercial propaganda and Danish propaganda for British goods were being conducted so vigorously – with talk of the foundation of an Anglo-Danish chamber of commerce and plans for a British exhibition in Copenhagen in 1932 – that the Auswärtiges Amt was contemplating a concerted counter-propaganda campaign. A meeting at the Wilhelmstrasse in March 1930 agreed that strident propaganda should be avoided, and that a more subtle influence should be brought to bear on both the German and the Danish press. A similarly low-key approach was recommended by a meeting in April between representatives of the Economics Ministry and business interest groups.[81]

There was indeed evidence that the intensity of the campaign in favour of British goods, and in particular the prominent role played by the British legation and the minister, Sir Thomas Hohler, were becoming counter-productive.[82] Appointed to Copenhagen in 1928, Hohler was firmly convinced of the primacy of economic factors in international relations,[83] and was unusual among British diplomats for his close and friendly relations with the DOT.[84] As a country enjoying a particularly large active trade balance with the United Kingdom, Denmark had long been the target of British critics of free trade and had been making efforts to reorient its purchases to Great Britain since as early as 1926.[85] In 1927 the Labour MP Frank Hodges warned the Danes that Britain could not be expected to continue to buy large quantities of

[80] Meeting of HPA, 23 December 1929, ibid.; RIIA, *World Agriculture: An International Survey* (London, 1932), pp. 188–9; Peter Munch, *Erindringer 1924–1933. Afrustningsfor-handlinger og verdenskrise* (Copenhagen, 1964), p. 218.

[81] Aufzeichnung Meynen (AA) 17 March 1930, PA, AA Abt. IV Nd, Handel 11, Dänemark, Bd 2; Vermerk Posse (RWM), 14 April 1930, ibid.

[82] Hassell to AA, 25 March 1930, PA, AA Abt. IV Nd, Handel 12, Dänemark – England, Bd 1.

[83] See especially Hohler to Vansittart, 28 May 1931, Hohler Papers, vol. 1931. Interestingly, however, he opposed the proposal by Sir Victor Wellesley that a special politico-economic department should be established within the FO: Hohler to Wellesley, 23 December 1930, Hohler Papers, vol. 1930.

[84] Sir Edward Crowe (DOT) to Hohler, 27 July 1928; Hohler to Crowe, 31 July 1928, Hohler Papers, vol. 1928. The DOT for their part were 'lost in admiration' for what Hohler had done for British trade: 'You have furnished a fine example of what can be done by an energetic man with imagination' (J. Picton Bagge to Hohler, 7 February 1930, Hohler Papers, vol. 1930).

Danish products unless Denmark bought more from Britain, in particular coal; a similar message was conveyed the following year by Sir Philip Cunliffe-Lister, the president of the Board of Trade.[86] Lord Beaverbrook's Empire Free Trade campaign, launched in 1929, was particularly hostile to Denmark as a country in direct competition with empire agricultural producers such as Canada, Australia and New Zealand.[87]

It was thus virtually a reflex action for Denmark to respond to German protectionism by threatening a shift of purchases from Germany to Great Britain.[88] The obstacles to such a shift, however, were familiar ones: the high price of British goods, the unsuitability of many British products to Danish market requirements and lack of interest in the Danish market on the part of British manufacturers. By the spring of 1930 there were signs that the boycott movement was abating, but German protectionism once again destroyed hopes of an improvement in commercial relations between the two countries. The new trade agreement with Finland in July 1930 was primarily aimed, as we have seen, at the most-favoured-nation rights of larger butter producers such as Denmark, the Netherlands and Estonia. Anti-German feeling was strengthened by news of parallel movements in the Netherlands and Estonia and by the growth of the empire preference idea in Great Britain.

By the autumn of 1930 Denmark was itself beginning to be hit by the agricultural crisis. Danish farmers had taken advantage of the falling cost of feeding-stuffs to increase pig production for the British market. When their competitors did the same, bacon prices fell; butter prices fell too, though less dramatically. One consequence was the political radicalisation of the farmers, and especially smallholders, with the formation of the right-wing movement Landbrugernes Sammenslutning. In attempting to maintain the market for Danish products abroad, the Danish government could exert virtually no influence on German or British policy but could only try to alleviate the situation through negotiation, seeking other markets and 'supporting Britain's international efforts in favour of free trade, in order thereby to diminish the risk that Britain might go over to a protectionist policy'.[89] It was precisely at this time, of course, that the protectionist campaign in Britain was gaining momentum. Once tariffs had been adopted, following the sterling crisis of 1931, Britain was in possession of the weapon it had hitherto lacked. As we

---

[85] Sir Milne Cheetham, 'Annual Report on Denmark, 1926' (p. 2), 11 January 1927, FO 371/12561, N221/221/15.

[86] Hassell to AA, 9 November 1927 and 10 April 1928, PA, AA Abt. IV Nd, Handel 12 Dänemark – England, Bd 1. Hodges described himself as a 'free trade man'; he was in fact one of four Labour MPs who were 'in active but secret negotiations with the Empire Industries Association': Tim Rooth, *British Protectionism and the International Economy: Overseas Commercial Policy in the 1930s* (Cambridge, 1992), p. 43.

[87] Hohler, 'Annual Report on Denmark, 1930' (p. 3), 14 February 1931, FO 371/15358, N1484/1484/15.

[88] Hassell to AA, 12 July 1929, PA, AA Abt. IV Nd, Handel 11 Dänemark, Bd 2.

[89] Munch, *Erindringer 1924–1933*, p. 221.

shall see, it was now in a position to bring real pressure to bear on countries, such as Denmark, which were heavily dependent on the British market.

Increasingly subject to the cross-currents of British and German commercial pressure, Danish–German political relations nevertheless developed positively up to the early 1930s. North Slesvig was the key to the relationship.[90] In 1925 the German minister, Mutius, summarised Danish foreign policy as comprising three components: avoiding international entanglements, maintaining good relations with Britain and holding on to the territorial gains of 1920. In this latter respect Denmark was 'a kind of spiritual member of the Entente'.[91] At the same time, however, the Danes recognised the importance of good relations with Germany. Whilst the settlement of 1920 was too closely identified with the 'injustice' of Versailles to permit a formal German acknowledgement of the new frontier, it was vital to dispel Danish fears of an attempt to change the frontier by force. Both the Auswärtiges Amt and the Copenhagen legation continued to emphasise that a normalisation of relations in the frontier districts would pay dividends by making Denmark more amenable and by fostering relations with Scandinavia as a whole. For if North Slesvig was the key to German–Danish relations, Denmark was, as Mutius put it, the 'threshold' to Scandinavia.[92] Hence the dual strategy of maintaining the economic position of the German minority in North Slesvig (for example through support for the Vogelgesang organisation, founded in 1926 to subsidise German farmers)[93] while at the same time adopting a conciliatory attitude towards Denmark on border issues.

This approach was inevitably damaged by the deterioration in commercial relations between the two countries. Nevertheless, the Danish and German governments were able in June 1931 to conclude an agreement facilitating local transactions across the frontier.[94] Shortly afterwards, the German minister, Richthofen, reported 'a new spirit' in the border districts, one of mutual respect and of a desire to pursue Danish and German interests not through force or pressure but by 'peaceful cultural means'. This must in the

---

[90] The Weimar period is discussed briefly in Sven Tägil, *Deutschland und die deutsche Minderheit in Nordschleswig. Eine Studie zur deutschen Grenzpolitik 1933–1939* (Lund, 1970), pp. 5–17.

[91] Mutius to AA, 4 November 1925, PA, AA Nachlass von Renthe-Fink, Paket 1/1. See also Ernst von Weizsäcker's much less restrained comments on Denmark's 'accursed marriage with the treaty of Versailles and with French policy': diary entry for 18 January 1925, in Leonidas E. Hill (ed.), *Die Weizsäcker-Papiere: 1900–1932* (Berlin, 1982), p. 367.

[92] Mutius to AA, 4 November 1925, PA, AA Nachlass von Renthe-Fink, Paket 1/1.

[93] For a statement of financial subsidies to German minorities in North Slesvig and elsewhere, see *ADAP*, B, V, doc. 263 (28 June 1927) (with map). For the Kreditanstalt Vogelgesang, see Hassell to AA, 22 February 1927, *ADAP*, B, IV, pp. 387–90; Tägil, *Deutschland und die deutsche Minderheit*, pp. 12–14; and (for a highly critical account) Joachim Joesten, *Denmark's Day of Doom* (London, 1939), pp. 194–7.

[94] 'Abkommen über Erleichterung im kleinen Grenzverkehr', 3 June 1931, PA, AA Handakten Eisenlohr, Dänemark, Bd 2.

long run lead to a significant improvement in German–Danish relations – cultural, economic and political:

And this seems to me of greater general political significance than is usually recognised even today in Germany where, owing to the pressure of circumstances, attention is all too often directed solely towards the west or the east . . . today the bridge from Germany to the Scandinavian countries still leads over Denmark.[95]

The most articulate exponent of the policy of developing relations with Denmark as a bridge to Scandinavia was Ulrich von Hassell, German minister in Copenhagen from 1926 to 1930.[96] Hassell's ideas were not confined to Scandinavia: with his appointment to Belgrade in 1930, he added the Balkans to the Baltic region as one of the chief areas of potential German activity. Both regions formed part of his scheme for the reorganisation of Europe under German leadership. Hassell, Tirpitz's son-in-law and a founder member of the German National People's Party (DNVP), emphasised the development of economic relations, as well as the alleged racial affinities between the Scandinavian and German peoples. He thus represents a link between the old conception of *Mitteleuropa* and the Nordic racism of the National Socialists. It should be stressed, however, that notions of racial affinity were a commonplace of the era. Indeed, in Hassell's first encounter with the new Danish foreign minister Laust Moltesen in January 1927, it was the latter who declared that Scandinavia was 'racially related' to Germany.[97] Moltesen suggested that the five Nordic countries should cooperate more closely and that Scandinavianism should ultimately become a kind of 'Teutonism' through the inclusion of Germany.

Hassell propagated the idea of 'a future customs union between Germany, Holland and the Nordic states'.[98] He saw both a danger and an opportunity in the increasing pressure on Denmark to buy more British goods. The danger was the obvious one that British success would be purchased primarily at Germany's expense, and that in the long term an increased familiarity with Great Britain and the English language would lead to a decline in German influence. The opportunity lay in the growth of the idea of European economic cooperation in response to Europe's dwindling political and economic role in the world. In this context Germany would naturally look first to its neighbours. 'Here Denmark belongs to the first rank, not only as a Germanically closely neighbouring country but also owing to its geographical key- or bridge-like position.'[99]

The obstacles to the development of a closer relationship were the border

---

[95] Richthofen to AA, 23 June 1931, PA, AA Abt. IV Nd, Pol. 2 Dänemark, Bd 9.
[96] Gregor Schöllgen, *A Conservative Against Hitler. Ulrich von Hassell: Diplomat in Imperial Germany, the Weimar Republic and the Third Reich 1881–1944* (London, 1991), ch. 4.
[97] Hassell to AA, 4 January 1927, *ADAP*, B, IV, pp. 10–13; Schöllgen, *Conservative Against Hitler*, pp. 37–8.
[98] 'Gesandtmodtagelse. Den tyske Minister von Hassell', 29 April 1927, RA, UM 72 Tys. 1, Bd 8.
[99] Hassell to AA, 28 April 1927, PA, AA Abt. IV Nd, Handel 11 Dänemark, Bd 1.

question and Denmark's fear of its stronger neighbour. However, the decisive factor would be the market opportunities for Danish exports: 'If the British Empire idea develops practically in such a way as drastically to restrict the English market for Danish products, Denmark will necessarily be thrown back upon Germany. No other market of equal importance is available.' Hassell repeatedly drew attention to the ramifications of the North Slesvig question and its importance for German–Danish relations. Insisting too vehemently on a revision of the border would be counterproductive. So too would any attempt to restrict the German market for Danish agricultural products, since this would do disproportionate damage to the economic interests of both the Danish and the German populations of North Slesvig. Nor, as some nationalist circles were demanding, should economic pressure be used to force Denmark to return the province to Germany. Rather than demanding an 'economic *Anschluss*' between North Slesvig and Germany, there should be an economic *Anschluss* with Denmark as a whole, 'in the sense of a systematic development, for political and economic reasons, of a closer economic cooperation and connection between Germany and Denmark'.[100]

The most sustained expression of Hassell's views on Scandinavia was a lengthy memorandum of July 1928 on 'The Nordic Idea' (*Der Nordische Gedanke*).[101] Hassell posed the question of whether the Danish version of the Nordic idea – Nordic solidarity in support of the frontier of 1920 – was objectionable from Germany's point of view. He argued that it was not. Denmark was still the 'bridge' to Scandinavia. As yet Scandinavian political and economic cooperation were of limited importance: the Nordic idea had substance only in the cultural sphere. And this, Hassell argued, was no threat to Germany. On the contrary, greater solidarity with their Scandinavian neighbours would give the Danes confidence and keep them away from malign influences (in other words, the French). The Nordic idea, moreover, was still only at an early stage of development. As an expression of the revival of traditional European cultures in the face of the American challenge, cooperation between the Nordic nations, 'so closely related to ourselves', was something which Germany could only welcome.

Hassell was aware of the need to avoid alienating Germany's northern neighbours, or antagonising the Western powers, by asserting Germany's leadership aspirations too openly. Germany should adopt a low profile and avoid slogans such as 'Germanic solidarity with Scandinavia'.[102] Although 'the construction of a syndicate of states bordering on the Baltic' was an attractive prospect, the time for this was 'not yet ripe'.[103] A similar caution characterised his comments, in August 1929, on suggestions that Estonia and Latvia should

---

[100] Hassell to AA, 3 June 1927, *ADAP*, B, V, pp. 458–61.

[101] 'Der Nordische Gedanke, insbesondere unter dem Gesichtspunkte der deutsch–dänischen Beziehungen', 17 July 1928, PA, AA Nachlass von Renthe-Fink, Paket 1/1.

[102] Memorandum of 30 November 1928, PA, AA Gesandtschaft Kopenhagen – Das Ostseeproblem.

[103] Ibid.; Schöllgen, *Conservative Against Hitler*, p. 38.

be encouraged to develop closer links with Scandinavia. Such a development would have the welcome effect of 'detaching these two countries from south-eastern connections', but at present the practical obstacles were simply too great.[104] Hassell's assessments appear to have been shared by his colleagues in the Auswärtiges Amt. His influence can be traced in the Foreign Office's warnings about the dangers of German agrarian protectionism.[105] In stressing the need for a low profile he merely echoed the warning of his predecessor Mutius: 'the less said on our side about a common Germanic culture, the better'.[106]

The onset of the depression condemned Hassell's German–Scandinavian partnership to oblivion, though a travesty was to reappear after 1933 in the form of the 'Nordic community of fate' (*Nordische Schicksalsgemeinschaft*) proclaimed by Alfred Rosenberg. Hassell's biographer notes, however, that his years in Copenhagen were to have an important influence on his wartime thinking.[107] As he moved towards a position of opposition to the Nazi regime, Hassell's ideas for a post-Hitler Europe returned to the Baltic region. In his essay 'Dominium maris baltici', published in 1943, Hassell declared that 'the organisation of the Baltic Sea region had now become a German task'.[108] Interestingly, his plans for the region now entailed, among other things, the reincorporation of North Slesvig into the Reich.

Germany's relations with Denmark and, to an increasing extent, with the other Scandinavian countries, deteriorated rapidly after Hassell's departure from Copenhagen. His successor Richthofen was, as we have seen, still optimistic in June 1931. By October 1932 he was warning that if German imports of Danish cattle were to be restricted still further, 'a gulf will open up between ourselves and the North that will not be bridged for decades'.[109] At the same time, the Nordische Gesellschaft wrote to Admiral Raeder, the commander-in-chief of the German navy, predicting that Scandinavia's growing economic orientation towards Great Britain would make the region 'politically an appendage [*Anhängsel*] of the empire', and that militarily the Baltic would become 'an appendage of the Ocean'.[110] Meanwhile the German chamber of commerce in Helsinki reminded the advocates of autarky that the Scandinavian countries had constituted a major gap in the Allied blockade

---

[104] Hassell to AA, 7 August 1929, PA, AA Nachlass von Renthe-Fink, Paket 1/1.
[105] E.g. the memorandum by Abteilung IV, 30 May 1929, PA, AA Abt. IV Nd, Handel 13, Dänemark, Bd 2.
[106] Mutius to AA, 4 November 1925, PA, AA Nachlass von Renthe-Fink, Paket 1/1.
[107] For Hassell's wartime ideas, see also Hermann Graml, 'Resistance Thinking on Foreign Policy', in Graml, Hans Mommsen, Hans-Joachim Reichhardt and Ernst Wolf, *The German Resistance to Hitler* (London, 1970), pp. 1–54.
[108] Quoted from Ulrich von Hassell, *Europäische Lebensfragen im Lichte der Gegenwart* (Berlin, n.d. [1943]), in Schöllgen, *Conservative Against Hitler*, p. 101.
[109] Richthofen to AA, 31 October 1932, PA, AA Handakten Clodius, Dänemark, Bd 3.
[110] Dr Ernst Timm (Leiter des Stabes der Nordischen Gesellschaft) to Raeder, 3 October 1932, BA, Sammlung Jacobsen, ZSg 133/50.

during the last war: 'they might therefore be more valuable in case of war than a German agriculture developed at their expense'.[111]

The British commercial offensive 1931–1935

The revolution in British economic policy of 1931–2 resulting from the sterling crisis of August 1931 had a direct impact on the countries of northern Europe. The abandonment of the gold standard in September 1931 went a long way towards eliminating the overpricing that had been one of the chief handicaps to the sale of British goods. It also led to the creation of a loose 'sterling area' comprising much of the empire together with countries dependent on the British market which had followed Britain off gold, including the four Nordic countries.[112] The introduction of tariff protection in two stages, in November 1931 and February 1932, was followed by the establishment of a new imperial economic system at the Ottawa conference in August 1932.[113] Ottawa was followed in turn by the conclusion of a series of bilateral trade agreements with foreign countries.[114] The first, in the spring of 1933, were with Denmark, Norway, Sweden and Argentina. Finland followed in September 1933, and the three Baltic states in July 1934.

The revolution of 1931–2 was the outcome of developments which had begun long before.[115] It was also incomplete. Much of the new 'national' government's programme derived from the attack on free trade that had begun in the late nineteenth century, and more immediately from the detailed planning of the Conservative Party after its election defeat in 1929.[116] Demands for protection on the part of key industries such as steel and textiles had been growing since the mid-1920s.[117] They were joined by agriculture when food prices collapsed at the end of the decade: Denmark, as we have seen, was one of the chief targets. Protection was not, however, the most obvious source of relief for Britain's export industries. The protectionists were unable to demonstrate why a country like Britain, so uniquely dependent on foreign markets to pay for its imports of vital commodities, should deliberately isolate itself from the world economy. Ramsay MacDonald grasped the

---

[111] Deutsche Handelskammer in Finnland, 'Wirtschaftsbericht III. Viertel 1932', 14 October 1932, BA, R 43 I/1177.

[112] Ian M. Drummond, *The Floating Pound and the Sterling Area 1931–1939* (Cambridge, 1981).

[113] Ian M. Drummond, *Imperial Economic Policy 1917–1939: Studies in Expansion and Protection* (London, 1974).

[114] For a detailed discussion, see Rooth, *British Protectionism*, chs. 2–4.

[115] The most comprehensive account of the background to these changes is in Boyce, *British Capitalism at the Crossroads*. For the domestic political context, see Philip Williamson, *National Crisis and National Government: British Politics, the Economy and Empire 1926–1932* (Cambridge, 1992).

[116] John Ramsden, *A History of the Conservative Party: The Age of Balfour and Baldwin 1902–1940* (London, 1978), pp. 296–324.

[117] Rooth, *British Protectionism*, pp. 41–63; Wurm, *Business, Politics and International Relations*, pp. 30–42, 203–5.

essential point when he wrote: 'I dread tariff wars. Of all big countries in the world we are in perhaps the weakest position to engage in such conflicts.'[118]

Nor was protection the only function of the tariff. A revenue tariff had been advocated by a number of leading economists (including Keynes) and had been taken seriously by the Labour government as a means of balancing the budget.[119] Chamberlain, introducing the Import Duties Bill in February 1932, still put revenue and the balance of payments at the top of his list of priorities.[120] Yet a tariff designed to produce revenue by taxing imports directly contradicted the purpose of protecting British industry by keeping imports out. And both functions were difficult to reconcile with the use of the tariff as a negotiating instrument aimed at winning concessions for British trade from foreign governments. The conflict between protection and free trade, as well as ambiguity about the function of the tariff, pervaded government policy and vitally affected Britain's negotiations with the Nordic countries.

Tacitly, the government admitted that the tariff could do little to improve Britain's export prospects. The main thrust of its policy was towards strengthening the domestic economy. Empire trade came second and trade with foreign countries a poor third. But the government was obliged to show that it was doing something for Britain's depressed export industries: iron and steel, textiles and, above all, coal. Even within this limited perspective, tariff bargaining came low on the scale of priorities. The Cabinet Committee on the Balance of Trade, reporting in January 1932, anticipated that the main source of export growth would be the depreciation of sterling, followed by the protective effect of the tariff accompanied by industrial rationalisation, and only in third place by negotiations for tariff reductions with foreign countries.[121]

There were, however, further arguments in favour of negotiations. Some were of a short-term political nature; others reflected broader considerations. The government wished first to disprove the charge that tariffs and imperial preference had tied Britain's hands in its commercial relations with foreign countries. This was a matter of urgency in the aftermath of Ottawa, which had been followed by the resignation of a number of free-trading ministers, including the Labour ex-chancellor Philip Snowden and the National Liberal leader Sir Herbert Samuel. 'If we can only show, before Parliament meets, that negotiations with foreign countries *are* proceeding usefully, Samuel will "miss the bus"', his former National Liberal colleague Sir John Simon, the foreign

---

[118] MacDonald to Walter Runciman (president of the Board of Trade), 28 December 1931, RL, Runciman Papers, WR 245.

[119] Williamson, *National Crisis*, pp. 97–8, 197; Susan Howson and Donald Winch, *The Economic Advisory Council 1930–1939: A Study in Economic Advice During Depression and Recovery* (Cambridge, 1977), pp. 72, 76, 81.

[120] Barry Eichengreen, 'Sterling and the Tariff 1929–1932', in Eichengreen, *Elusive Stability: Essays in the History of International Finance 1919–1939* (Cambridge, 1990), pp. 180–214, interprets the decision as 'an attempt to strengthen the trade balance and prevent the exchange rate from depreciating excessively' (p. 181).

[121] CAB 24/227, 19 January 1932.

secretary, urged in October 1932.[122] But to show rapid progress it was necessary to negotiate first with those countries with whom Britain's bargaining position was strongest: those with which it had the largest adverse trade balances. Hence the priority attached to reaching agreements with the Scandinavian states and Argentina.

In a broader perspective, trade negotiations would signal to foreign governments the fact that Britain had no intention of severing its links with the international economy despite the increased emphasis on national and imperial self-sufficiency. This was a matter of particular concern to the Board of Trade which was, under the presidency of the Liberal ex-free trader Walter Runciman, the chief bastion of multilateralism in Whitehall in the 1930s.[123] The Foreign Office shared this view, having already voiced its anxiety over the political implications of Britain's new economic policies with the warning that 'a high protective tariff, combined with empire preference, implies a measure of dissociation from Europe [and] a corresponding diminution of our influence over European affairs'.[124] The question was also of urgent interest to those foreign countries most dependent on the British market for their livelihood. Anxious to accommodate themselves to the probable change in British policy, the Scandinavian countries had stepped up their purchases of British goods since 1930 (in the case of Denmark even earlier) and had canvassed the idea of trade negotiations since the end of 1931.[125] Their willingness to negotiate was another reason for dealing with them first.

The practical benefit of trade negotiations depended, however, on what Britain could offer the Scandinavian countries and what they could offer in return. The latter already had low tariffs and imposed no duty at all on coal, the product in which Britain was most interested. Moreover, any tariff concessions made to Britain would be passed on automatically to competitors such as Germany through the operation of the most-favoured-nation clause. The scope for British concessions was limited by the privileged access to the British market won by Dominion farmers at Ottawa, together with the government's commitment to increased domestic agricultural production. Both of these constraints affected Denmark in the first instance, while Norway and Sweden were affected by the resistance of some sections of British manufacturing industry, such as paper and iron and steel, to bargaining away the tariff protection they had so recently won.[126] In the course of 1932 Board

[122] Simon to MacDonald, 6 October 1932, FO 800/287.

[123] John S. Eyers, 'Government Direction of Britain's Overseas Trade Policy 1932–1937' (DPhil. thesis, University of Oxford, 1977), pp. 33–40.

[124] FO memorandum, 'Changing Conditions in British Foreign Policy . . .' (p. 4), 26 November 1931, CAB 24/225.

[125] Sir M. Cheetham, 'Annual Report on Denmark for 1926', 11 January 1927, FO 371/ 12561, N221/221/15; Danish efforts summarised in Foreign Ministry memorandum, 'Hvad der fra privat Side gøres for at forbedre Danmarks Handelsbalance i Forhold til England', May 1932, RA, UM 64 Dan. 73a, Bd 3; The Times, 'The Future of Sterling As Scandinavia Sees It. Hopes of a Common Policy', 4 November 1931.

[126] Runciman memorandum, 'The Ottawa Agreements and Impending Tariff Negotiations

of Trade officials attempted to construct a negotiating strategy that would reconcile the government's conflicting objectives. By the autumn they had arrived at the conclusion reached much earlier by the Scandinavian governments: that significant advantages for British exports could be obtained only by contravening the spirit, if not the letter, of the most-favoured-nation clause.[127]

Pressures from domestic and Dominion producers made the negotiations with the Scandinavian countries less straightforward than might have been expected in the light of Britain's ostensibly strong bargaining position.[128] In February and March 1933 they ran into serious difficulties with Denmark over butter, and with Sweden over iron and steel. Meanwhile 'the "canny" Norwegians, of course, discovered fairly soon Mr Runciman's anxiety to make any sort of agreement to show to Parliament as a result of Ottawa', and turned it to their advantage.[129] Indeed the Danish minister in Oslo reported that the British were requesting tariff reductions which were bound to benefit their competitors more than themselves, simply in order to achieve visible results.[130] On the whole, however, they sought little in the way of tariff reductions and could offer little in return. In the Anglo-Scandinavian agreements of 1933 Britain obtained the stabilisation of existing rates of duty and, in a few cases, actual reductions, together with a number of specific concessions such as the abolition of licences for commercial travellers.[131]

In return, Britain made limited tariff concessions on industrial products such as pulp, paper and iron and steel. For bacon, butter and eggs, which were of vital concern to Denmark, the British merely gave an undertaking that existing rates of duty would not be increased and that, in the event of quota restrictions being imposed, each exporting country would receive a guaranteed percentage

with Foreign Countries', 6 October 1932, CAB 24/233; memorandum by Walter Elliot (minister of agriculture), 'Impending Tariff Negotiations with Foreign Countries. Position of Home Agriculture', 21 October 1932, CAB 27/489; minute by W. J. Glenny (commercial secretary, Stockholm), 11 November 1932, BT 11/132.

[127] Cabinet meeting, 23 November 1932, CAB 23/73; Danish Foreign Ministry memorandum, 29 December 1931, RA, UM 72 Stb., Bd 1; Foreign Ministry 'Memorandum vedrørende det handelspolitiske Forhold til Storbritannien', June 1932, RA, UM 64 Dan. 73a, Bd 3.

[128] For details of the negotiations, see Rooth, *British Protectionism*, chs. 4–6. For the negotiations with Sweden, see also Bengt Nilson, *Handelspolitik under skärpt konkurrens. England och Sverige 1929–1939* (Lund, 1983), ch. 4. For Denmark, see Susan Seymour, *Anglo-Danish Relations and Germany 1933–1945* (Odense, 1982), pp. 21–5. For an account which concentrates mainly on the Baltic states but is also informative on the general background of British policy, see David E. Kaiser, *Economic Diplomacy and the Origins of the Second World War: Germany, Britain, France and Eastern Europe 1930–1939* (Princeton, N. J., 1980), ch. 4.

[129] Minute by Laurence Collier (Northern Department), 14 January 1933, FO 371/17212, N242/1/63.

[130] Kauffman to UM, 1 February 1933, RA, UM 64 Dan. 73a, Bd 10.

[131] This of course benefited Germany more than Britain except in Sweden, where the lapse of the German–Swedish commercial treaty in 1933 meant that Germany did not, in this respect, enjoy most-favoured-nation rights until 1937: 'Memorandum by the Head of Division V of the Economic Policy Department' (Hilger van Scherpenberg), 20 May 1937, *DGFP*, C, VI, pp. 770–1.

of total British imports from foreign countries – but with no guarantee as to the actual amount. Stabilisation of their existing market share, together with security against further tariff increases, were therefore the main benefits won by the Scandinavian countries. At a time of extreme uncertainty in world trade these were not insignificant gains. Furthermore, only one product, bacon, was actually subjected to quota restrictions; and Danish farmers found that a reduction in volume was compensated for by a rise in prices.[132]

Britain benefited much less from tariff reductions than from a number of non-tariff arrangements which gave preferential treatment without technically violating the most-favoured-nation clause. They comprised three major innovations. The first concerned coal, Britain's chief preoccupation. Each Nordic government gave a direct undertaking that a fixed proportion of its country's annual coal import would come from Britain. The percentages arrived at – 47 per cent for Sweden, 70 per cent for Norway, 75 per cent for Finland and 80 per cent for Denmark – were a clear reflection of the relative negotiating strengths of the countries concerned. Numerous other products were covered by a second device, the ostensibly private 'purchase agreements' concluded between British suppliers and Nordic importers that were appended to the official agreements. Applying only to Denmark and Finland, the agreements covered products including iron and steel, salt, jute (for wrapping bacon and hams), flour and commercial vehicles. 'These purchase agreements constituted a novel departure in British commercial practice in that they put the Board of Trade and the Foreign Office in the novel role of diplomatic bag-men acting on behalf of United Kingdom traders and industrialists.'[133]

Finally the Danish and Finnish governments – again those in the weakest bargaining positions – undertook less precise but more far-reaching obligations. A clause in the Anglo-Danish agreement recorded the Danish government's promise to 'keep in view the balance of trade between the two countries' – a tacit understanding that the Danish import licensing system, the Valutacentral (also known as the Valutakontor) established at the beginning of 1932, would continue to discriminate in favour of British goods. The Anglo-Finnish agreement was more explicit: 'The Finnish Government have declared their intention, in view of the favourable balance of trade which they enjoy, of encouraging and promoting imports by all means at their disposal.' This meant, among other things, orders from government departments and state-owned bodies such as the railways. It was in such clauses that what an American critic termed the 'distinctly bilateral flavour' of the Anglo-Scandinavian agreements was most evident.[134] They were also the aspects to which the Germans took most exception.

British trade with Scandinavia prospered in the 1930s. Exports rose from a

---

[132] Seymour, *Anglo-Danish Relations*, pp. 26–7.

[133] E. V. Francis, *Britain's Economic Strategy* (London, 1939), p. 270.

[134] Henry J. Tasca, *World Trading Systems: A Study of American and British Commercial Policies* (Paris, 1939), p. 54.

low point of £26.6 million in 1932 to £47.3 million in the boom year of 1937. In contrast, British imports from the Nordic countries fell from £84.3 million in 1931 to £71.1 million in 1933. They then rose again but exceeded the 1931 figure for the first time only in 1937 (£94 million). The trade balance was therefore much less disadvantageous to Britain – a useful debating point as far as the government was concerned. Elaborate calculations were made of the number of extra miners who would find work as a result of the Anglo-Scandinavian agreements, and the Cabinet arranged that the announcement of their successful conclusion 'should be made at an opportune time during the debate on the vote of censure on unemployment'.[135] It remains difficult to quantify the overall contribution of the trade agreements to the growth of British exports. Tim Rooth's analysis suggests that they did limit the growth of Scandinavian protection and that some tariff reductions, particularly those on textiles secured in the negotiations with Denmark and Finland, were of value.[136] The non-tariff arrangements on coal and other commodities, together with the trade diversion practised by the Danish Valutacentral were of much greater significance. But more important still was the fact that the Nordic economies were growing rapidly, with a particularly strong demand for imports of machinery.

Given such buoyancy, it is hardly surprising that Britain was able to meet some of this demand; it is nevertheless noteworthy that machinery exports to Sweden virtually doubled, and that in 1935 Britain overtook Sweden to become the second largest supplier of machinery to Finland. A number of other factors favoured British trade in the early 1930s. German–Scandinavian relations had continued to deteriorate, reaching their nadir in the early weeks of the Hitler regime with the denunciation of the German–Swedish trade agreement and a drastic reduction in German imports of butter from Denmark.[137] As we have seen, bilateralist pressure to buy more British goods had been exerted long before the conclusion of the trade agreements, by both official and unofficial means. Denmark and, to a lesser extent, Finland had been the main targets.[138] The propaganda campaign in favour of British goods launched by Danish importers' organisations in 1930 culminated in the British Exhibition held in Copenhagen in October 1932 under the patronage of the Prince of Wales.[139] A 'British Week' followed in Helsinki a year later.[140]

[135] FO 'Memorandum Respecting Trade Agreements', 11 July 1933, FO 433/1, W8174/285/50; Cabinet meeting, 12 April 1933, CAB 23/75.

[136] Rooth, *British Protectionism*, pp. 240–6.

[137] Nilson, *Handelspolitik*, pp. 49–53; Rooth, *British Protectionism*, pp. 126–8; Klaus Wittmann, *Schwedens Wirtschaftsbeziehungen zum Dritten Reich 1933–1945* (Munich and Vienna, 1978), pp. 34–48; Hohler to FO, 10 February 1933, FO 371/17201, N973/210/15.

[138] Eduard Reventlow, *I dansk tjeneste* (Copenhagen, 1956), pp. 86–8.

[139] Hohler to FO, 29 September 1932, FO 419/26, N5667/60/15, and 10 October 1932, ibid., N5928/60/15.

[140] R. Keith Jopson (commercial secretary, Helsinki), 'Memorandum on the Commercial Aspects of "British Week" in Finland', 28 October 1933, FO 419/28, N7936/686/56.

The recovery of Germany 1933–1936

German–Scandinavian trade revived after 1933 under the auspices of economic policies designed in the short term for war-readiness and in the long term for the economic and political reorganisation of much of continental Europe – including Scandinavia – under German leadership.[141] The reactivation of Germany's long-standing assets in Scandinavian trade came about through a revival of demand in both Germany and the Scandinavian countries, and through German skill in developing the techniques of bilateral trade. These two areas – the degree of market opportunity offered to Scandinavian exports, and the mechanism of commercial policy – were the ones in which Britain's relative weakness was most clearly revealed. It was not, however, simply a story of German success and British failure. Bilateralism placed its own constraints on German–Scandinavian trade which became increasingly evident as the demands of a war-oriented economy grew.

By 1933 German–Scandinavian trade had fallen to a third of its 1929 level and there were strong incentives on both sides for a revival. For the Scandinavian countries the experience of tariff bargaining and the continuing restriction of British agricultural imports confirmed that it was not in their interest to have too one-sided an economic orientation towards Great Britain. Germany remained their second largest customer, and for some products virtually the only market. Swedish iron ore was the most obvious example, but here the dependence was mutual. The case of Danish live cattle, on the other hand, shows how a commodity of relatively minor importance to Germany might be of vital interest to its trading partner, thus constituting a valuable bargaining counter. By 1933 the export of cattle to Germany had been cut to 17,000 head per annum. It was a question of political as well as economic importance to the Danish government, since it concerned the wellbeing of the potentially disaffected population of North Slesvig, only recently recovered from Germany.

In Germany, as we have seen, it was acknowledged that the deterioration in German–Scandinavian commercial relations had political and strategic implications. Anxiety about Germany's position in northern Europe formed one element in the re-evaluation of German commercial policy that took place in official circles under the impact of the depression. As in Britain, there was widespread disillusionment with free trade and growing support for ideas of economic self-sufficiency and bloc-building. German attention was directed

---

[141] For Scandinavian aspects of German *Grossraum* thinking, see Schröter, *Aussenpolitik und Wirtschaftsinteresse*, pp. 81–2, 114–15; Wittmann, *Schwedens Wirtschaftsbeziehungen*, pp. 200–40; Dietrich Eichholz, 'Expansionsrichtung Nordeuropa', *Zeitschrift für Geschichtswissenschaft* 27 (1979), pp. 17–31; Alan S. Milward, *The Fascist Economy in Norway* (Oxford, 1972), pp. 3–9, 287–300; and Wolfgang Wilhelmus, 'Das schwedische Echo auf die faschistischen "Neuordnungspläne" im Zweiten Weltkrieg', *Jahrbuch für Wirtschaftsgeschichte* 1975, 1, pp. 35–46. For a contemporary view, see Ernst Timm, 'Warum Skandinavien?', *Ruhr und Rhein* 14 (1933), pp. 666–7.

towards neighbouring agrarian and primary-producing countries, especially in central and south-eastern Europe but also in the north.[142]

Less than two months after Stresemann's death in October 1929, his party colleague Dietrich, the minister of agriculture, told the Danish minister in Berlin that Stresemann's policy had been directed too much towards the west and had taken too little account of Germany's relations with the countries bordering it to the north and east.[143] One of the most articulate advocates of a new departure was Hans Ernst Posse, head of the trade division and later state secretary at the Ministry of Economics, who favoured the abandonment of the most-favoured-nation principle and the construction of a German-dominated European trading bloc based on preferential agreements, for which the empire bloc created at Ottawa offered a convenient precedent.[144] With the advent to power of the Nazi regime, Posse's views gained a receptive audience.[145] A memorandum based on his ideas which was submitted to Hitler in May 1933 envisaged a European *Wirtschaftsraum* in which, through its 'technology, business spirit and organisational talent, Germany could play a leading role'.[146] The aim would be to 'draw a line through Europe from the north and north-west to the south-east', taking in Scandinavia, Belgium and the Netherlands on the one hand, and Austria, Hungary, Yugoslavia, Bulgaria and Romania on the other.

As far as the Nordic countries were concerned, Germany's interest lay first and foremost in the maintenance of its export surpluses – an important source of scarce foreign exchange – and in regaining the market share lost to Great Britain. German officials chose to lay the blame for Germany's losses on the Anglo-Scandinavian trade agreements, and on the measures adopted by the Nordic governments, such as the Danish exchange control system, to give preference to British goods.[147] Ritter delegated to one of his junior colleagues, Hans Kroll, the task of 'opening the eyes' of the Scandinavians to the

---

[142] On German policy towards south-eastern Europe, see Kaiser, *Economic Diplomacy*, ch. 2; Hans-Jürgen Schröder, 'Deutsche Südosteuropapolitik 1926–1936. Zur Kontinuität deutscher Aussenpolitik in der Weltwirtschaftskrise', *Geschichte und Gesellschaft* 2 (1976), pp. 5–32. For a contemporary discussion, which places Scandinavia, Finland and the Baltic states (along with Czechoslovakia and Yugoslavia) in the 'third zone' of the future German economic sphere, see Karl Krüger, *Deutsche Grossraumwirtschaft* (Hamburg, 1932), pp. 191–8.

[143] Zahle to UM, 26 November 1929, RA, UM 64 Dan. 80a, Bd 14.

[144] Posse memorandum, 'Die deutsche Handelspolitik des Jahres 1931', 4 February 1932, BA, R 43 I/1078; Hans Ernst Posse, 'Die Hauptlinien der deutschen Handelspolitik', in Deutsches Institut für Bankwissenschaft und Bankwesen (ed.), *Probleme des deutschen Wirtschaftslebens. Erstrebtes und Erreichtes* (Leipzig, 1937), pp. 481–513 (pp. 498–9). See also Eckart Teichert, *Autarkie und Grossraumwirtschaft in Deutschland 1930–1939* (Munich, 1984), pp. 105–28.

[145] For Nazi views on foreign trade before coming to power, see Hans-Erich Volkmann, 'Das aussenwirtschaftliche Programm der NSDAP 1930–1933', *Archiv für Sozialgeschichte* 17 (1977), pp. 251–74.

[146] Memorandum by Willuhn (Reichskanzlei), 27 May 1933, BA, R 43 II/329.

[147] German–Danish trade talks, 10–11 May 1933, PA, AA Sonderreferat Wirtschaft (W), Handel 12, Bd 3; RA, UM 64 Dan. 80a, Bd 22; L. Bolt-Jørgensen to UM, reporting

'foolishness and shortsightedness' of their agreements with Britain.[148] Privately, German officials were sometimes prepared to admit that German policy bore much of the responsibility, and indeed that the situation had worsened with the appointment of the Nazis' coalition partner Alfred Hugenberg, the leader of the DNVP, as minister of agriculture in January 1933.[149]

The five months during which Hugenberg headed the Ministries of Agriculture and Economics, deluding himself that he had become 'economic dictator' of Germany, marked the high point of German agrarian protectionism.[150] His replacement as minister of agriculture by the 'Reich Peasant Leader' Darré at the end of June 1933 was the first stage in a process which, by the autumn, had brought an end to the paralysis of German commercial policy.[151] The end of agrarian protectionism was a by-product of the reforms introduced by Darré in order to restore the prosperity and self-esteem of German farmers. It was ironic that a regime for which the rural vote had been crucial in its rise to power, and which remained steeped in agrarian ideology, should have ended the farmers' veto over German commercial policy – and that this should have been achieved by a technicality. For the establishment of monopoly control over the markets for a succession of agricultural commodities, which gave farmers guaranteed prices, at the same time offered a convenient means of circumventing the most-favoured-nation clause, from which state monopolies were exempt by international convention. Foreign countries could now be granted fixed import quotas which would not depress prices, and which did not have to be extended automatically to third parties. These changes were accompanied by the German government's formal abandonment of multilateralism. In October 1933 the Cabinet approved Posse's proposal for 'a more active commercial policy based on the principle of reciprocity', directed in the first instance towards 'markets dominated by German businessmen . . . especially south-east Europe and the countries of

conversation with Ritter, 19 July 1933, ibid.; AA telegram to Copenhagen, 14 November 1933, PA, AA Abt. IV Nd, Dänemark, Handel 11, Bd 4.

[148] Bolt-Jørgensen to Mohr, 16 December 1933, RA, UM 64 Dan. 80a, Bd 23; Kroll to Statistisches Reichsamt, 18 August 1933, PA, AA Sonderreferat W, Handel 11, Bd 3. See Hans Kroll, *Lebenserinnerungen eines Botschafters* (Cologne and Berlin, 1967), pp. 68–9, for the period when the author served in the economic division as Ritter's 'right-hand man'.

[149] Bolt-Jørgensen to UM, 10 February 1933, RA, UM 72 Tys., Bd 21; Bolt-Jørgensen to Mohr, 7 April 1933, RA, UM 64 Dan 80a, Bd 22; Bülow (state secretary) to propaganda ministry and other ministries, 31 July 1933, PA, AA Abt. IV Nd, Pol. 2, Dänemark, Bd 10. On Hugenberg, see John A. Leopold, *Alfred Hugenberg: The Radical National Campaign Against the Weimar Republic* (New Haven, Conn., and London, 1977), ch. 6.

[150] The Cabinet meeting of 16 February 1933 gives a good indication of the depth of disagreement between the foreign minister (Neurath) and Hugenberg on the consequences of German tariff increases: BA, R 43 II/800.

[151] J. E. Farquarson, *The Plough and the Swastika: The NSDAP and Agriculture in Germany 1928–1945* (London and Beverly Hills, 1976), ch. 4; Gustavo Corni, *Hitler and the Peasants: Agrarian Policy of the Third Reich 1930–1939* (New York, Oxford and Munich, 1990), chs. 4–6.

north and north-west Europe'.[152] It also authorised the establishment of a new commercial intelligence bureau, the Reichsstelle für den Aussenhandel (RfdA), to replace the Zentralstelle für den Aussenhandel.[153]

These decisions did not bring an immediate end to the confusion of official trade policy. In the absence of a clear lead from government, German industry had already taken steps to restore trade links with Scandinavia. As early as October 1932 the German employers' organisation, the Reichsverband der Deutschen Industrie (RDI), was planning a propaganda campaign centred on Sweden, Germany's most important Scandinavian market; and in the summer of 1933 two leading directors of the chemical combine IG Farben visited the region to investigate German export prospects.[154] Commercial policy was not immune from the encroachments of Nazi functionaries. Alfred Rosenberg, thwarted in his direct assault on the Foreign Office, tried to infiltrate the bureaucratic machine dominated by Ritter, Posse and their colleagues in the HPA. Werner Daitz, head of the trade division of Rosenberg's Aussenpolitisches Amt and a noted *Grossraum* theorist, came up towards the end of 1933 with schemes for importing Danish cattle and pigs through his home city of Lübeck, the latter to be utilised in Germany's strategic fats plan. Such a policy would also, he claimed, reinforce Germany's naval position by improving relations with Denmark, 'the naval bridge to Sweden'.[155] The intrusion was repulsed without difficulty by Ritter, but another episode from the same period illustrates the way in which commercial relations between Germany and Scandinavia were beginning to be distorted by bilateralism and permeated by Nazi racism.

Towards the end of 1933 the Berlin-based Deutsch–Dänische Wirtschaftsvereinigung (DDWV, or German–Danish Economic Association) was found to be acting contrary to the aims of the German authorities (the RfdA, the

---

[152] Cabinet meeting, 4 October 1933, BA, R 43 II/301a; Kaiser, *Economic Diplomacy*, pp. 73–4.

[153] 'Entwurf eines Gesetzes über das wirtschaftliche Nachrichten- und Auskunftwesen', 12 September 1933, BA, R 43 II/329.

[154] Schröter, *Aussenpolitik und Wirtschaftsinteresse*, pp. 78, 82–4, 286. On IG Farben's foreign activities in this period, see Peter Hayes, *Industry and Ideology: IG Farben in the Nazi Era* (Cambridge, 1987), pp. 105–6.

[155] HPA meeting, 9 November 1933; Ritter minute, 14 November 1933; AA telegram to Copenhagen, 14 November 1933: all in PA, AA Abt. IV Nd, Dänemark, Handel 11, Bd 4; two minutes by Ritter, recording conversations with Daitz, 1 December 1933, PA, AA Handakten Clodius, Bd 4; A. P. Jacobsen (agricultural attaché, Berlin) to Danish Ministry of Agriculture, 11 December 1933, RA, UM 64 Dan. 80a, Bd 23. On the APA and foreign trade policy, see Seppo Kuusisto, *Alfred Rosenberg in der nationalsozialistischen Aussenpolitik 1933–1939* (Helsinki, 1984), pp. 56–60. On Daitz, see Franz L. Neumann, *Behemoth: The Structure and Practice of National Socialism 1933–1944* (London, 1944; repr. New York, 1966), pp. 171–3; Peter M. R. Stirk, 'Authoritarian and National Socialist Conceptions of Nation, State and Europe', in Stirk (ed.), *European Unity in Context: The Interwar Period* (London and New York, 1989), pp. 125–48 (pp. 142–6); Wittmann, *Schwedens Wirtschaftsbeziehungen*, pp. 213–19; Jean Freymond, *Le IIIe Reich et la réorganisation économique de l'Europe 1940–1942. Origines et projets* (Leiden, 1974), pp. 55, 61–2; and Hans-Adolf Jacobsen, *Nationalsozialistische Aussenpolitik 1933–1938* (Frankfurt am Main and Berlin, 1968), pp. 61–2.

economic division of the Foreign Office and the Copenhagen legation).[156] The DDWV was passing on confidential information to its members, and in particular revealing details of a practice by which German goods were sent to Britain, stamped with British marks of origin, and then sent to Denmark in order to circumvent the controls of the Valutacentral – although the latter was well aware of what was going on. The matter was complicated by the fact that the business was conducted by two Jewish brothers, one in Berlin, the other in Copenhagen. Their activities were being attacked in Julius Streicher's organ *Der Stürmer*, and the Copenhagen brother feared arrest if he visited Germany.[157] The problem was resolved in January 1934, first by the RfdA, which sent a sharp warning to the Ministry of Propaganda to curb the comments of the Nazi press; and then by Ritter, who wrote to the two Jewish businessmen to calm their fears and assure them that their deceptions were entirely satisfactory from the point of view of German economic interests.[158]

Germany's new commercial strategy bore its first fruits in the trade agreements concluded with the Netherlands in December 1933, and with Denmark, Finland, Hungary and Yugoslavia in the spring of 1934.[159] All contained significant, if not over-generous, concessions on agricultural products in which the debt to Germany's new agricultural regime was explicitly acknowledged. In the negotiations with Denmark, for example, there was deadlock until cattle were brought into the German state monopoly on 26 February 1934. The agreement was signed on 1 March. 'Only the decision to regulate the German cattle market', reported the chief German negotiator (an official from the Ministry of Agriculture), 'created the basis for an arrangement with Denmark which would on the one hand take sufficient account of Denmark's economic and political requirements, and on the other demand no intolerable sacrifice on the part of German agriculture.'[160]

Such agreements were not reached without hard bargaining; nor, in the case of Finland, was Germany able to achieve full equality of treatment even after a three-month tariff war. The German negotiators appear to have modified their initially tough line towards Finland in response to an appeal from the foreign minister to be more conciliatory in view of Finland's pro-German attitude on

---

[156] Krüger (commercial attaché, Copenhagen) to AA, 13 November 1933; Ritter to Krüger, 4 January 1934, all in PA, AA Sonderreferat W, Finanzwesen 16, Dänemark, Bd 2.

[157] Gustav Loeb to Rudolf Loeb, 19 November 1933 (copy enclosed in Ritter to Krüger, 4 January 1934), ibid.

[158] RfdA to Reichsministerium für Volksaufklärung, 5 January 1934; Ritter to Gustav Loeb, 27 January 1934, both ibid. On the efforts of Posse at the Ministry of Economics to minimise the damaging effects on German foreign trade of attacks on Jewish businesses, see Friedrich Facius, *Wirtschaft und Staat. Die Entwicklung der staatlichen Wirtschaftsverwaltung in Deutschland vom 17. Jahrhundert bis 1945* (Boppard am Rhein, 1959), p. 147.

[159] Otto Sarnow, 'Handelspolitische Aktivität in Europa', *Volk und Reich* 5 (1934), pp. 321–30; Kaiser, *Economic Diplomacy*, pp. 75–7.

[160] Report by Koehler, 21 March 1934, PA, Abt. IV Nd, Handel 13, Dänemark, Bd 3.

questions of 'eastern and Baltic policy' at a time when Germany had just signed a non-aggression pact with Poland and relations with the Soviet Union were deteriorating.[161] In cases where Germany's bargaining position was stronger, however, the outcome was much more advantageous.

In the treaty with Denmark of 1 March 1934, the Danes gave a number of far-reaching undertakings in return for an increased export quota of 50,000 head of cattle annually.[162] They agreed to take note of German wishes regarding particular export interests and to ensure that established business connections were not lost by German firms to foreign competitors. They also gave secret undertakings to increase purchases of German coal and salt. Even then, the Danes were expected to subsidise the sale of the meat from the cattle at specially low prices (mainly to SA units). If the German–Danish treaty thus bore a strong resemblance to the Anglo-Danish agreement of the previous year, it differed in two important respects. First, the Danes undertook to issue import licences sufficient to maintain a trade ratio of 2:1 in Germany's favour. Second, like the other agreements concluded at this time, the German–Danish treaty provided for the establishment of an inter-governmental committee to supervise bilateral trade.[163] There was to be no comparable Anglo-Danish committee until 1936, and the British never succeeded in establishing a fixed ratio on the German model.

For Germany, the implications of the German–Danish treaty were not confined to Denmark, nor were they exclusively economic. Koehler, the leader of the German delegation, described Germany's objectives as being in the first instance political: to create better feeling towards Germany in Denmark and to cut the ground from under anti-German propaganda. Only in second place came the 'purely economic' goal of increasing German exports.[164] And, Koehler concluded,

The political significance of the new agreement is not confined to Denmark alone. Denmark should rather be seen as a bridge to the northern countries as a whole, which Germany has successfully crossed with this agreement. It is to be hoped that the effects of the Danish treaty will soon spread to Sweden and Norway, and lead to the shattering of the ring set around these countries by England [zur Sprengung des von England um diese Länder gelegten Ringes].[165]

As in the case of Britain, however, it is difficult to detect any marked improvement in political relations resulting from Germany's alleged generosity:

---

[161] Neurath to Schmitt (minister of economics), 19 February 1934, ZSta., AA 63850.

[162] An account of the negotiations is given in Martin Dyrbye, 'Dansk–tyske handelsforbindelser 1933–1934, med særligt henblik på afslutningen af den dansk–tyske overenskomst vedrørende den gensidige vareudveksling af 1. marts 1934' (Specialeafhandling i historie, University of Copenhagen, 1984).

[163] On the significance of these committees as 'instruments of bilateralism', see Wittmann, Schwedens Wirtschaftsbeziehungen, pp. 93–7.

[164] Report by Koehler, 21 March 1934, PA, Abt. IV Nd, Handel 13, Dänemark, Bd 3.

[165] See the very similar expression in an AA memorandum of 21 March 1934, quoted in Viggo Sjøqvist, Danmarks udenrigspolitik 1933–1940 (Copenhagen, 1966), p. 75.

some growth in pro-German feeling among Danish farmers, perhaps, but nothing corresponding to Koehler's inflated aspirations. To the Danish government, which had purchased a minor alleviation of the condition of Jutland farmers at the expense of the two main beneficiaries of exchange control, British exporters and new Danish manufacturing industries, the agreement represented yet another adaptation to the bilateralist demands of a great power.

If the coming to power of the Nazi regime permitted the resumption of an active trade policy, it also plunged Germany into new problems through its chosen methods of economic recovery.[166] The new economic policies, with their emphasis on public investment at the expense of private consumption, stimulated the demand for imported raw materials and semi-finished goods while reducing Germany's capacity to export the industrial products necessary to pay for them. The result was a foreign exchange crisis in the summer of 1934 which brought about further major changes in the structure of German foreign trade. The 'New Plan' of September 1934, credited to the minister of economics Hjalmar Schacht but largely devised by the HPA, extended and formalised the *ad hoc* arrangements for exchange clearing which had existed between Germany and a number of countries since 1932.[167]

The effect of the New Plan was to intensify Germany's economic relations with countries which themselves lacked foreign exchange or were judged politically and strategically important or both. As Ritter put it: 'Away from Africa and the Commonwealth, towards South America, the Balkans and the Far East.'[168] German financial weakness and the commercial strategy pursued by the HPA under the New Plan thus combined to loosen Germany's links with traditionally important trading partners such as Great Britain and the United States, and to strengthen them with others selected on new criteria. To some extent Germany's choice of trading partners was a matter of expediency,[169] but the intensification of trade with south-eastern Europe was intended both to serve immediate political purposes (undermining the French alliance system in eastern Europe) and, in the longer term, to make Germany less vulnerable to economic blockade in time of war.[170]

The Nordic countries occupied an intermediate position in this scheme. On

---

[166] R. J. Overy, *The Nazi Economic Recovery 1932–1938* (London, 1982), chs. 3–4; Harold James, *The German Slump: Politics and Economics 1924–1936* (Oxford, 1986), ch. 10.

[167] Gerhard Kroll, *Von der Weltwirtschaftskrise zur Staatskonjunktur* (Berlin, 1958), ch. 14; Avraham Barkai, *Nazi Economics: Ideology, Theory and Policy* (Oxford, New York and Munich, 1990), pp. 172–83.

[168] Hans Kroll, *Lebenserinnerungen*, p. 83.

[169] See e.g. 'Richtlinien für die Deutsche Handelsdelegation für Südamerika', approved by the HPA on 27 June 1934, in which the primary goal was defined as being to obtain raw materials without the use of foreign exchange: ZSta., AA 65155.

[170] For the anti-French thrust of German policy, see Nicole Jordan, *The Popular Front and Central Europe: The Dilemmas of French Impotence 1918–1940* (Cambridge, 1992), ch. 3; Kaiser, *Economic Diplomacy*, ch. 5.

the one hand they fitted in with the German trend towards increased trade with neighbouring primary-producing countries. On the other hand their economies, with the partial exception of Denmark, were more diversified than those of south-eastern Europe, and their populations enjoyed much higher living standards. They were also in a stronger financial position. Sweden was one of Germany's leading creditors, and all four earned large quantities of foreign exchange from their export surpluses with Great Britain. The British presence denied Germany the monopolistic position that it enjoyed in the trade of most of the Balkan countries.[171] This fact, together with the general absence in Scandinavia of exchange and import controls – Denmark was again the exception – gave Germany less scope to employ the techniques of bilateral trade as instruments of economic penetration than in south-eastern Europe. At the same time, Germany benefited from the British presence since Germany's export surpluses with the Nordic countries enabled it to tap the proceeds of their trade with Britain. This helps to explain why German officials resisted the inbuilt tendency of bilateral trade towards equalisation, and showed no interest in allowing adverse trade balances to build up – resulting in the notorious 'blocked mark accounts' at the Reichsbank – as frequently occurred with the countries of south-east Europe.[172]

Exchange clearing and payments agreements with the Nordic countries thus supplemented the trade agreements of 1934 and ultimately became the principal instrument of German commercial policy. Although they were not employed in precisely the same manner as in Germany's relations with the Danubian and Balkan states, similar patterns began to emerge. The clearest example was Denmark, which differed from its Scandinavian neighbours, and resembled the countries of south-eastern Europe, in two key respects: its dependence on agricultural exports and its system of exchange control. The distortion of traditional trading patterns by the conflicting economic policies of the Nazi regime was evident as early as the autumn of 1934, when Darré's policy of strategic stockpiling led to a sharp increase in German imports from Denmark – not merely of dairy products, but of the grain and fodder which the

---

[171] Albert O. Hirschman, *National Power and the Structure of Foreign Trade* (Berkeley and Los Angeles, 1945), pp. 109–14.

[172] For contemporary interpretations of clearings as instruments of German economic penetration and political hegemony, see e.g. Antonin Basch, *The Danube Basin and the German Economic Sphere* (New York, 1943); Paul Einzig, *Bloodless Invasion: German Economic Penetration into the Danubian States and the Balkans* (London, 1938). Modern studies with a similar emphasis include Jordan, *Popular Front*, ch. 3; Kaiser, *Economic Diplomacy*, pp. 130–2; Hans-Jürgen Schröder, 'Südosteuropa als "Informal Empire" Deutschlands 1933–1939. Das Beispiel Jugoslawien', *Jahrbücher für Geschichte Osteuropas* 23 (1975), pp. 70–96; Bernd-Jürgen Wendt, 'Südosteuropa in der nationalsozialistischen Grossraumwirtschaft', in Gerhard Hirschfeld and Lothar Kettenacker (eds.), *Der 'Führerstaat'. Mythos und Realität* (Stuttgart, 1981), pp. 414–55. Interpretations stressing economic necessity include Larry Neal, 'The Economics and Finance of Bilateral Exchange Clearing: Germany 1934–1938', *Economic History Review* 32 (1979), pp. 391–404; and Alan S. Milward, 'The Reichsmark Bloc and the International Economy', in Hirschfeld and Kettenacker, *Der 'Führerstaat'*, pp. 377–413.

Danes themselves required and were obliged to replace by purchases from abroad, paid for in sterling.[173] Denmark was then under pressure to buy more German goods in order to maintain the 2:1 ratio fixed in the 1934 trade agreement. Although this proved impossible to achieve in practice, the proportion of about 1.2:1 to which the ratio had fallen by 1936 still left a significant margin by which Danish imports had to be increased in order to prevent an accumulation of blocked marks in the Danish clearing account at the Reichsbank.[174] 'The tendency', noted the British legation, 'has some resemblance to the commercial penetration which Germany has so successfully pursued in South-Eastern Europe.'[175]

It was, however, in the interest of neither party to allow such blocked mark accounts to develop. Responsibility for the problem lay on both sides. On the one hand, Denmark was neither able nor willing to buy sufficient quantities of German goods, for which German officials blamed 'the devious policy of the Valutacentral', while on the other hand Germany was unable, owing to raw material shortages, to supply the goods that the Danes did wish to buy.[176] But the weaker party had to go more than halfway to find a solution. A deal reached in September 1936 indicates the lengths to which the Danish government went in order to secure increased export outlets for its farmers. In return for supplementary export quotas to the value of RM 6 million, Denmark agreed to purchase German coal to an equivalent value. A total of 600,000 tons was to be imported over a ten-year period so as not to contravene the Anglo-Danish agreement of 1933, and the Danish government was to pay not only for the entire quantity in advance, but also for the cost of storage in Germany of the portion not yet delivered.[177]

The Germans for their part started to exploit their superior bargaining position in order to acquire foreign exchange. From 1935 onwards the Danes were required to pay for a proportion of their imports from Germany in foreign exchange – the so-called *Devisenspitze*, fixed in 1936 at RM 12 million annually – rather than through clearing.[178] The clearing system itself was revised at the end of 1936 to make it more responsive to German requirements. By basing German imports from Denmark on the amount imported by Denmark from Germany in the previous quarter, the onus was shifted on to the Danes: what

[173] Richthofen to AA, 30 October 1934, PA, AA Sonderreferat W, Finanzwesen 16, Dänemark, Bd 3.
[174] German–Danish discussions, 19–20 June 1936, PA, AA Handakten Clodius, Dänemark, Bd 4; 'Survey of the Economic and Financial Situation in Denmark, January–July 1936', FO 371/20323, N4401/119/15.
[175] Sir Patrick Ramsay to FO, 2 July 1936, ibid., N3841/110/15.
[176] Memorandum by Scherpenberg, 12 August 1936, PA, AA Handakten Wiehl, Dänemark, Bd 3.
[177] Alex Walter (chairman of German delegation) to AA, 14 September 1936, ZSta., AA 67770; A. W. G. Randall (Copenhagen) to FO, 23 September 1936, FO 371/20323, N4850/110/15. The episode was cited as an instance of Denmark's subservience to Germany in Joesten, *Denmark's Day of Doom*, p. 48.
[178] Sjøqvist, *Danmarks udenrigspolitik*, pp. 203–6. As a special concession the sum was reduced to RM 8.5 million for 1937 only.

they were able to sell now depended solely on what they were prepared to buy.[179] In addition, the Danish government was obliged to take over from the National Bank the responsibility for ensuring that the *Devisenspitze* was paid. It was not surprising that such developments, to the extent that they became publicly known, contributed to allegations in 1937 that Denmark was becoming increasingly isolated from its Scandinavian neighbours and was gravitating into the German orbit in the manner of south-eastern Europe.[180]

[179] Memorandum by Scherpenberg, 10 January 1937, PA, AA Handakten Wiehl, Dänemark, Bd 3.

[180] These claims were made in Norway chiefly by the journalist Johan Vogt: see Ramsay to FO, 30 June 1937, FO 419/31, N3842/230/63; Randall to FO, 19 August 1937, FO 371/21072, N4298/26/15. Vogt republished his articles in *Den tyske Indflydelse i Danmark* (Copenhagen, 1937). His autobiography, *Om fred og strid mellom hjerte og hode* (Oslo, 1975), provides information on their origin. Joesten, *Denmark's Day of Doom*, elaborates similar themes, esp. in ch. 2.

8 Power, ideology and markets: Great Britain, Germany and Scandinavia 1933–1939

Scandinavia was one of the few regions in the world whose economic importance to both Great Britain and Germany grew in the course of the 1930s. This change had political implications at a time in which Germany was mounting an increasingly effective challenge to the Versailles system of which Britain was one of the chief props. Although it was never at the forefront of either British or German attention, Scandinavia became a stage on which Anglo-German rivalries were played out. As political relations between the two powers deteriorated in the late 1930s, commercial competition became transformed into a contest for economic and political influence over a region whose geographical position and natural resources ensured that it would be of even greater strategic significance in a future war than it had been in 1914–18.

The most obvious indicator of Scandinavia's heightened importance is British and German export performance. Britain's exports to the Nordic countries increased dramatically after 1931, but the degree of improvement varies according to the criteria by which they are measured. The statistics published by the Nordic countries give the most favourable impression of Britain's performance – but also overstate the improvement since they are based on country of purchase rather than country of origin.[1]

On this reckoning, Britain overtook Germany as the leading supplier to Denmark in 1933 and retained that lead until 1939. British exports to Finland exceeded Germany's for the first time in 1934 but Germany regained the lead in 1939. Germany never lost its leading position in Sweden's import trade, but Britain narrowed the gap significantly between 1934 and 1937. In Norway the two countries were more evenly matched. Britain took the lead in 1930, lost it again in 1931, then held it by a narrow margin from 1932 to 1937. Harm Schröter's conversion of the British and German figures to US dollars suggests that the value of German exports to Scandinavia always exceeded that of British exports, and that, although Britain had significantly narrowed the gap by the mid-1930s, German trade had recovered markedly by the outbreak of war (table 8).

Scandinavian export markets were also of greater relative importance to both Britain and Germany than they had been before the depression. While

---

[1] See p. 44 (n. 91) above.

Table 7 *British and German exports as a percentage of the total imports of the Nordic countries 1929–1939*

	Denmark		Finland		Norway		Sweden		Total	
	Germany	UK	Germany	UK	Germany	UK	Germany	UK	Germany	UK
1929	32.9	14.7	38.3	13.0	24.3	20.7	30.7	17.3	31.6	16.4
1930	34.2	14.5	37.1	13.7	21.5	25.7	32.1	15.8	31.2	17.4
1931	33.5	14.9	35.0	12.6	23.0	20.2	33.1	14.1	31.2	15.5
1932	25.9	22.3	28.6	18.3	21.3	21.6	29.4	16.8	26.3	19.8
1933	22.7	28.1	27.5	20.6	20.9	22.9	29.2	18.0	25.1	22.4
1934	21.3	30.1	20.7	22.8	19.1	22.9	26.8	19.5	22.0	23.8
1935	22.0	36.0	20.4	24.2	17.0	17.8	24.3	19.3	20.9	24.3
1936	25.3	36.5	19.3	24.2	17.6	17.8	24.4	19.2	21.7	24.4
1937	23.9	37.7	19.7	22.5	16.9	18.3	22.8	19.0	20.8	24.4
1938	24.0	33.8	20.3	21.9	18.4	16.2	24.0	18.3	21.7	22.6
1939	26.4	32.2	22.0	19.1	19.0	16.8	26.1	18.1	23.4	21.6

Source: Based on B. R. Mitchell, *International Historical Statistics: Europe, 1750–1988* (New York, 1992), table E2.

Table 8 *British and German trade with the Nordic countries expressed in terms of value (US $m) and as a percentage of each other's trade*

	1913		1925		1929		1932		1936		1939	
	UK	Germany	UK	Germany	UK	Germany	UK	Germany	UK	Germany	UK	Germany
Exports (US $m)	108	184	189	230	182	327	83	128	193	225	212	343
British as % of German	58.7		82.2		55.7		72.7		85.8		61.8	
Imports (US $m)	219	131	464	133	539	237	259	70	403	194	395	266
German as % of British	59.8		28.7		44.0		27.0		48.1		67.3	

Source: Harm Schröter, *Aussenpolitik und Wirtschaftsinteresse. Skandinavien im aussenwirtschaftlichen Kalkül Deutschlands und Grossbritanniens 1918–1939* (Frankfurt am Main, Berne and New York, 1983), pp. 17–18.

British exports as a whole fell in value by 35 per cent between 1929 and 1938, those to the Nordic countries rose by nearly 18 per cent and represented 9.1 per cent of total British exports against only 5.1 per cent in 1929. It was an improvement bettered only by the performance of Britain's trade with the countries of the British empire.[2] For Germany, Scandinavia accounted for 12.9 per cent of exports in 1938 against 10.2 per cent in 1929.[3] Britain continued to import much more than Germany from Scandinavia, but from the point of view of Scandinavian perceptions of opportunity it was significant that the Scandinavian share of the German import market grew from 7.4 to 11.4 per cent between 1929 and 1938, while its share of the British market remained largely static, rising only from 9.1 to 10.1 per cent over the same period. These figures reflect in part the squeezing out of commercial competitors with less leverage, such as the United States and Poland. But they also indicate a degree of Anglo-German competition which was unprecedented apart from the short post-war period between 1918 and 1921.

As we have seen, Britain's new position of strength in Scandinavian markets was to a large degree artificial – the product not of effective salesmanship, but of temporary German weakness combined with government leverage against countries whose dependence on exports to Britain placed them in a disadvantageous bargaining position. Germany had underlying economic assets which were brought to bear once again from the mid-1930s onwards. By this time the Nazi regime had resolved – by one means or other – much of the policy disarray of the last years of the Weimar Republic. But Schröter suggests that 'The most important reasons for Germany's success lay not in the policy of Berlin, but in the structure of the German economy.'[4] Germany's export interests were still concentrated to a greater extent than Britain's in the more dynamic industrial sectors such as chemicals, engineering and electronics. German industry's high degree of organisation and the commanding position in European markets secured by international cartel agreements and direct, though often concealed, investment represented strengths only imperfectly perceived or understood by foreign competitors and, Schröter argues, rendered industry in large measure immune even from the interference of the German government.

The intensity of Anglo-German competition in Scandinavia was in part a paradoxical consequence of the fact that foreign trade was of less importance to either Britain or Germany than it had been before the depression. Both sought economic recovery in the revival of domestic demand either through stimulating private consumption, as with the British 'building boom', or through government-directed investment in infrastructure and armaments, as

---

[2] Alfred E. Kahn, *Great Britain and the World Economy* (London, 1946), pp. 208–14.

[3] René Erbe, *Die nationalsozialistische Wirtschaftspolitik 1933–1939 im Lichte der modernen Theorie* (Zurich, 1958), p. 76.

[4] Harm Schröter, *Aussenpolitik und Wirtschaftsinteresse. Skandinavien im aussenwirtschaftlichen Kalkül Deutschlands und Grossbritanniens 1918–1939* (Frankfurt am Main, Berne and New York, 1983), p. 390.

in Germany. Neither could afford to dispense with foreign trade entirely, but both tried to construct their own trading blocs on principles that were avowedly politico-strategic as well as economic. In each case a core industrial state aimed to exercise hegemonic power over an array of dependent or 'complementary' primary-producing areas: Britain with the countries of the empire, Germany with the agrarian states of south-eastern Europe.[5] Such was the theory. In practice self-contained economic blocs proved impossible to establish, and in any case could have supplied only a limited proportion of the imports and the export outlets required by an advanced industrial state. The future, as the post-war period was to show, lay in trading with other advanced economies.[6]

In this context the importance of the Nordic countries lay in the fact that they were both primary-producers and rapidly developing economies. Their exports included a number of products for which substitutes could not easily be found. British and Dominion producers had difficulty in producing an alternative to Danish bacon that was acceptable to British consumers; Scandinavian timber helped to build British houses; the German steel industry remained dependent on Swedish iron ore despite Göring's attempt in the late 1930s to exploit domestic sources of low-grade ore.[7] Northern Europe was also a profitable export market, dependent on the import of a number of key commodities such as coal, petroleum and fertilisers and, with its high standard of living (very different from the depressed agrarian economies of south-eastern Europe), capable of absorbing a wide range of modern industrial and consumer goods. Scandinavia was thus one of the few points on the redrawn map of world trade where the British and German economic spheres intersected. It is therefore not surprising that there were those who thought that the region could be accommodated either in a stretched version of the British empire or in a German-dominated *Grossraumwirtschaft*.

For the Nordic countries, the economic consequences of this enhanced interest on the part of Britain and Germany were not wholly disadvantageous. The increased demand for many of their products enabled them to share in varying degrees (Sweden most, Denmark least) in the economic recovery of their two major customers. But their bilateral economic commitments to Britain and Germany placed the Nordic countries in an increasingly exposed position as political relations between the two powers deteriorated. Both

---

[5] Stephen D. Krasner, 'State Power and the Structure of International Trade', *World Politics* 28 (1976), pp. 317–47; Alan S. Milward, *The New Order and the French Economy* (Oxford, 1970), chs. 1–2; Jean Freymond, *Le IIIe Reich et la réorganisation économique de l'Europe 1940–1942. Origines et projets* (Leiden, 1974); Peter M. R. Stirk, 'Authoritarian and National Socialist Conceptions of Nation, State and Europe', in Stirk (ed.), *European Unity in Context: The Interwar Period* (London and New York, 1989), pp. 125–48; Eckart Teichert, *Autarkie und Grossraumwirtschaft in Deutschland 1930–1939* (Munich, 1984).

[6] Alan Milward, 'Der deutsche Handel und der Welthandel 1925–1939', in Hans Mommsen, Dietmar Petzina and Bernd Weisbrod (eds.), *Industrielles System und politische Entwicklung in der Weimarer Republik* (Düsseldorf, 1974), pp. 472–84.

[7] Dietmar Petzina, *Autarkiepolitik im Dritten Reich. Der nationalsozialistische Vierjahresplan* (Stuttgart, 1968).

powers made moral and political demands on Scandinavian allegiances, each emphasising the points at which their respective traditions, interests or racial identities allegedly coincided with those of Scandinavia. On the whole, National Socialist doctrines found little resonance in the Nordic countries. Germany's strength lay rather in the realities of power. Germany was growing in military strength and was close to Scandinavia; Britain came to seem both geographically and psychologically remote at a time when the Western democracies were mounting an increasingly ineffective defence against the combined challenge of Germany, Italy and Japan.

Scandinavia as a British sphere of influence?

The economic convergence between Great Britain and Scandinavia in the early 1930s gave rise to suggestions on both sides that the relationship should be placed on a more formal basis. At the beginning of 1932, when the future outline of British tariff policy was still unclear, a number of Scandinavians, including the distinguished Swedish economist Bertil Ohlin, suggested linking the Scandinavian countries to Britain within a free-trade or low-tariff area, or even establishing a formal relationship with the British empire.[8] A British junior minister, William Ormsby-Gore, appeared to favour the idea in an interview with the Copenhagen newspaper *Politiken*,[9] while Chamberlain referred privately to the possibility of joining with other European low-tariff countries in 'an association which, with the aid of a common policy on currency, may presently give the United Kingdom a preponderating influence in directing Europe as a whole back to sounder methods'.[10] Ormsby-Gore's interview was swiftly retracted, and ministers repudiated the idea of a closer association with Scandinavia when it threatened to complicate the forthcoming Ottawa negotiations.[11]

However, Scandinavian membership of the British empire continued to be canvassed in a number of quarters. It was advocated in a speech to the Norwegian chamber of commerce in London by the Anglo-Norwegian businessman and publicist Sir Karl Knudsen, who was later to declare that he 'had always believed that the Northern countries belonged spiritually to the

---

[8] A. Clark Kerr (Stockholm) to FO, 19 January 1932, FO 371/16385, W849/63/50; Ohlin article in *Stockholms-Tidningen*, 29 January 1932 (translation in FO 371/13686, W1280/63/50). See also the sympathetic comments of the *Economist*, 9 January 1932, p. 64, and 23 January 1932, p. 160.

[9] The interview, on 25 January 1932, attracted wide attention: see reports in the *Daily Herald, Manchester Guardian* and *Evening Standard* of 26 January; Ahlefeldt-Laurvig (Danish minister in London) to UM, reporting Runciman's annoyance with the interview, 26 January 1932, RA, UM 72 Stb. 1; Richthofen telegram to AA, 26 January 1932, BA, R 43 1/1090.

[10] Chamberlain to Snowden, 15 January 1932, printed in Keith Feiling, *The Life of Neville Chamberlain* (London, 1946), p. 203. It should be noted, however, that Chamberlain was writing to a notorious free-trader on the eve of the Cabinet's decision to adopt protection.

[11] Ormsby-Gore to Runciman, 25 January 1932, RL, Runciman Papers, WR 254; leading article in *The Times*, 22 March 1932.

British Commonwealth as much as any Dominion'.[12] A Bank of England official, Francis Rodd, reflected after a visit to Copenhagen:

I think if London allows we can link this country as closely to us as any dominion. Who knows indeed whether in the ultimate development of the curious association called the British empire, Denmark may not find her permanent place, and a more welcome one than Ireland is so uncomfortably occupying.[13]

Even the arch-imperialist Leo Amery advised Scandinavians, during a tour of the region in May 1932, that they had to choose between joining either an economic bloc based on Britain, with whom there existed 'shared cultural values', or one based on 'Central Europe'.[14] There is, finally, an intriguing recollection recorded in 1939 by Thomas Jones, Stanley Baldwin's confidant, that he 'used to urge S.B. to begin a policy which would bring in Denmark, Norway and Sweden into a new sort of British Commonwealth but he disliked all "foreigners" and would do nothing'.[15]

Such ideas barely survived the impact of Ottawa and of Anglo-Scandinavian tariff bargaining, but another opportunity for leadership was offered by the existence of the sterling area. Senior Treasury officials saw it as a means of developing mutual trade among its members, and of providing a new role and restored prestige for sterling itself. 'The natural leading components of such a sterling block are first of all the various parts of the empire and secondly the Scandinavian countries.'[16] At the Bank of England, too, officials acknowledged that a new Anglo-Scandinavian relationship had come into existence since 1931:

Our sudden departure from the gold standard threw the currency authorities of Scandinavia (particularly the Danish) into our arms. We folded them to us because we recognised the consequences to them of the step we had taken and we advised them when we could. But they have since brought their luggage with the Trade Agreements, shewing that they intend to stay, and if we have allowed them to unpack the mass of problems arising from these Agreements we can hardly escape future responsibility.[17]

---

[12] *The Times*, 29 April 1932; Knudsen's contribution to a discussion at Chatham House following an address by George Soloveytchik, printed as Soloveytchik, 'Fears and Realities in Scandinavia', *International Affairs* 16 (1937), pp. 894–919 (p. 914).

[13] Rodd to Hohler, 18 April 1932, Hohler Papers, vol. 1932. Rodd told the Danish foreign minister that after Ottawa Britain wished 'to create a sterling family in terms of both monetary and commercial policy': Peter Munch, *Erindringer 1924–1933. Afrustningsforhandlinger og verdenskrise* (Copenhagen, 1964), p. 277.

[14] Interview in *Svenska Dagbladet*, reported in Meynen (Stockholm) to AA, 20 May 1932, PA, AA Handakten Wiehl, Bd 3. See also the report of Amery's statements in Oslo in *The Times*, 25 May 1932, and the account in L. S. Amery, *My Political Life* (3 vols., London, 1953–5), vol. III, *The Unforgiving Years 1929–1940*, pp. 116–18, which shows, incidentally, that well after the Second World War Amery still thought that there was 'much to commend the accession of all the Scandinavian countries, including Iceland and Greenland, to the Britannic system'.

[15] Thomas Jones, *A Diary with Letters 1931–1950* (London, 1954), p. 430.

[16] Quoted in Ian M. Drummond, *The Floating Pound and the Sterling Area 1931–1939* (Cambridge, 1981), p. 10.

[17] Memorandum by N. P. Biggs, 'Scandinavia in the Sterling Area', 21 February 1934, BEA, OV 26/2.

There was a promising start when a loan of £1 million was made to Denmark in April 1933 for the construction of the Storstrøm Bridge (between the islands of Zealand and Falster), the first significant breach in the embargo on foreign loans imposed by the government at the time of the sterling crisis.[18]

But the sterling area failed to develop into a cohesive economic bloc. Capital issues for foreign countries on the London market remained far smaller than those for the United Kingdom itself or for the empire; and, as was pointed out in 1936, 'an increase in foreign lending would require willingness of the Government to adopt a commercial policy sufficiently liberal that borrowers could increase their exports to Great Britain for the purpose of making interest payments and ultimately of repaying their loans'.[19] The Bank of England chafed at these constraints. Bank officials argued repeatedly that the rules should be relaxed in favour of Norway, Iceland or Denmark.[20] The question of a loan to Denmark was debated at length in 1934–5 but was ultimately vetoed by the Treasury.[21] When the City of Oslo raised a loan in Amsterdam in 1937 (against the advice of the Bank of Norway), a Bank official asked, rhetorically, if the Norwegian authorities could not prevent municipalities from borrowing abroad, 'are we justified and, if so, on what grounds, in penalising our own market?'[22] The Bank of England's frustration reflected the extent to which its influence, and that of economic 'internationalism', had declined since 1931. With its new emphasis on the domestic economy and the empire, the government was unwilling to take on responsibilities for other sterling area countries – despite the admonition by the *Midland Bank Monthly Review* that, in the case of the Scandinavian countries, 'The welfare of sixteen million people very similar to ourselves cannot but be a matter of serious and continuous concern to the Government of this country.'[23]

It is true that relations between the Bank of England and the Nordic central banks were deepened and strengthened after 1931. After the collapse of sterling Montagu Norman was never able to re-establish his authority as arch-priest of the gold standard and mentor of aspiring European central bankers. But with the support of a number of able and articulate advisers, notably Harry Siepmann, Francis Rodd (before his departure for Morgan Grenfell) and Cameron Cobbold (a future governor of the Bank of England), he

[18] Tim Rooth, *British Protectionism and the International Economy: Overseas Commercial Policy in the 1930s* (Cambridge, 1992), pp. 133–4; Henry J. Richardson, *British Economic Foreign Policy* (London, 1936), pp. 69–75; Robert B. Stewart, 'Great Britain's Foreign Loan Policy', *Economica*, new series, 5 (1938), pp. 45–60.

[19] Richardson, *British Economic Foreign Policy*, p. 75.

[20] E.g. memoranda by Cameron Cobbold, 'Scandinavian Issues in London', 18 January 1935, BEA, OV 26/2, and 'Foreign Lending: Issues "To increase the sterling assets of countries within the sterling bloc"', 9 April 1936, OV 26/3.

[21] Correspondence in BEA, OV 27/3 and OV 27/24–5, esp. memorandum by N. P. Grafftey-Smith, 26 October 1934, OV 27/3, and draft Treasury note for BT, sent to Bank of England, 22 July 1935, ibid.

[22] Cobbold minute of 8 July 1937 (for deputy governor), BEA, OV 26/3.

[23] 'Monetary Policy in Europe', part II, January–February 1937.

presided over the development of a far closer and more equitable relationship than had existed in the 1920s. Contacts with Danish bankers, which had been fitful before 1931, became much closer with the appointment of Oluf Berntsen as Danish currency controller, and still more so when the former finance minister C. V. Bramsnæs was appointed governor of Danmarks Nationalbank in 1934. Perhaps the most notable change was in relations with Sveriges Riksbank. When Ivar Rooth 'as a very new and very young Governor [he was appointed in 1929] came from the Riksbank, he was made to feel that he was in Threadneedle Street for mutual benefit'.[24] Rooth returned the compliment by keeping the Bank of England regularly informed of economic and financial developments in Sweden and the other Nordic countries.

But Sweden's growing economic success enhanced Rooth's self-confidence in his relations with the Bank of England, as well as his ability to act, in certain circumstances, as a spokesman for the interests of Scandinavia as a whole. At the beginning of 1937 he discreetly added his voice to Swedish criticisms of British commercial policy towards Denmark.[25] He was also identified (falsely, as the Bank of England later concluded) with the demand made by influential Swedish economists, led by Professor Gustav Cassel, that the Swedish government should 'separate the Swedish krone from the sterling group and . . . revalue it on a higher rate in view of the great prosperity of Sweden'.[26] This, a City banker warned, 'would presumably involve a serious breach in the sterling group since it was probable that Finland would follow in the wake of Sweden'.[27] The threat did not materialise, but it indicated Britain's growing difficulties in maintaining its leadership role. There were also signs that Scandinavians were becoming resentful of British tutelage in the monetary sphere. In September 1937 Rooth warned Cobbold that his presence in Helsinki at the same time as a meeting of Nordic central bankers was taking place (despite an invitation from the governor of the Bank of Finland, Risto Ryti) might be misinterpreted.[28] 'Our friends in Denmark', he wrote, 'feared that in certain political circles in Denmark it would be said that you are supervising us and that we are not even allowed to get together and discuss things alone but have to be under your control the whole time.' Nor, a year later, did Rooth's friendly relations with the Bank of England deter him from selling sterling during the Munich crisis.[29] The bonds of sympathy and mutual understanding extended only so far.

The Bank of England's increasingly active role in Scandinavia also had

---

[24] R. S. Sayers, *The Bank of England 1891–1944* (3 vols., Cambridge, 1976), vol. I, p. 332.

[25] Rooth to Cobbold, 11 January 1937, BEA, OV 29/27.

[26] Minute by Oliver Harvey, 10 March 1937, FO 371/21109, N1237/27/42; Palairet (Stockholm) telegram to FO, 1 February 1937, ibid., N570/27/42; Cobbold note recording telephone conversation with Rooth, 2 February 1937, BEA, OV 29/4.

[27] Samuel Guinness of Guinness Mahon & Co., reported in Harvey minute, 10 March 1937, FO 371/21109, N1237/27/42.

[28] Rooth to Cobbold, 20 September 1937, BEA, OV 26/25.

[29] Rooth to Cobbold, 26 September 1938; minute by H. A. Siepmann, 30 September 1938, BEA, OV 29/5.

repercussions for British trade. Throughout the 1930s Bank officials criticised the relentlessly bilateralist character of British commercial policy in Scandinavia as well as the Ministry of Agriculture's determination to restrict agricultural imports. They sympathised with Scandinavian complaints and cooperated with the Treasury in devising arguments with which to counter those of the Board of Trade and the Foreign Office.[30] In 1934–5 the Bank intervened directly, advising Denmark to reduce its imports, including those from Britain, out of concern for the balance of payments and the stability of the krone.[31] British diplomats and businessmen naturally resented the intrusion, but the Bank's intervention pointed to the existence of genuine conflicts of national economic interest which militated against the pursuit of purely commercial objectives. The Bank of England was not entirely mistaken in its view that Denmark's financial integrity reflected on that of the United Kingdom.

The clearest and most explicit acknowledgement of the relationship between Britain's enhanced economic role in Scandinavia and British political influence came from within the Foreign Office. The adoption of tariff protection and imperial preference had underlined the Foreign Office's isolation from the mainstream of economic policy making. In the aftermath of Ottawa a number of officials attempted to salvage something from the wreckage of internationalism. One consolation lay in the destructive impact of German protectionism on Germany's economic and political relations with its European neighbours, especially in Scandinavia. If international solutions were no longer possible, at least in the foreseeable future, might this not provide an opportunity to enhance Britain's influence on a regional basis? During the winter of 1932–3 the Foreign Office attempted to influence the course of the Anglo-Scandinavian trade negotiations in order to achieve worthwhile concessions on products of vital interest to the Scandinavian countries. It also tried to persuade the Board of Trade to extend the scope of the negotiations as quickly as possible to include Finland and the three Baltic states. This, it was hoped, might draw all of these countries into a close and profitable trading relationship with the United Kingdom and, together with the turbulent political situation in Germany, persuade them to look to Great Britain for political leadership.

In challenging, for example, the protectionist claims of Sheffield steel manufacturers against their Swedish competitors, or New Zealand butter producers against those of Denmark, the Foreign Office stressed the 'favourable chance of establishing our influence over those countries which are now

---

[30] E.g. Cobbold correspondence with Waley (Treasury), 12 and 22 February 1937, BEA, OV 27/5.

[31] Cobbold to Colville (DOT), 19 April 1934, FO 371/18268, N2419/481/15; Collier minute of conversation with E. G. Cable (commercial secretary, Copenhagen), 25 April 1934, FO 371/18265, N2520/188/15; minute by Sigismund Waley (Treasury) for Sir Richard Hopkins, 23 September 1935, T 160/921/F.12659/08/5; Ashton Gwatkin minute of conversation with Francis Rodd, 9 October 1935, FO 371/19429, N5269/516/15.

being injured and antagonised by our principal competitor' and which, 'as uncertainty increases in Germany and Central Europe', were 'at present . . . looking towards London rather than Berlin or Moscow'.[32] When the Foreign Office thus intervened the results were generally favourable, though this owed less to the advocacy of the foreign secretary than to the fact that, on these occasions, its political priorities coincided with the commercial priorities of the Board of Trade.[33]

To a large extent the Foreign Office's efforts reflected the views of one man: Frank Ashton Gwatkin, head of the Economic Relations Section which had been founded in 1930 in an attempt to restore something of the economic expertise that had been lacking since the end of the First World War.[34] Ashton Gwatkin's ideas were an interesting amalgam of economic internationalism, political idealism and strategic considerations, with strong geopolitical overtones deriving from the influence of Sir Halford Mackinder's *Democratic Ideals and Reality* (1919).[35] Two of Mackinder's lessons had made a particular impression: that the existing nation-states had no future except as components of larger economic groups; and that Britain's greatest potential danger lay in the joint domination of the Eurasian land-mass by Germany and Russia, whose technical advancement on the one side and material resources on the other made them naturally complementary. Hence Ashton Gwatkin's scepticism towards the empire, and his concern to strengthen Scandinavia and the Baltic against Soviet as much as German influence. His advocacy of 'economic appeasement' in the mid-1930s can also be seen as a means of preventing Soviet–German rapprochement through an Anglo-German understanding.[36]

By 1935 Ashton Gwatkin was persuaded that a British sphere of influence had evolved out of the Scandinavian and Baltic trade agreements. Following a visit to the region he wrote, echoing Canning:

The purely commercial objectives of the 1933 Agreements have developed into something more, into something like an imprecise and pacific alliance over the whole political, financial, commercial and cultural field. The United Kingdom has called the Baltic into existence to rectify the lack of equilibrium elsewhere.[37]

This was a rash statement to make on the day of the signature of the Anglo-

---

[32] Simon to Runciman, 7 March 1933 (drafted by Ashton Gwatkin), FO 371/17212, N1141/1/63.

[33] See, e.g., the discussion on butter in the Cabinet Committee on Commercial Negotiations with Foreign Countries on 8 February 1933, in which Simon took virtually no part, leaving Runciman to confront the Dominions Office and Ministry of Agriculture (quite effectively) on purely economic grounds: CAB 27/489.

[34] D. G. Boadle, 'The Formation of the Foreign Office Economic Relations Section 1930–1937', *Historical Journal* 20 (1977), pp. 919–36; R. P. T. Davenport-Hines, *Dudley Docker: The Life and Times of a Trade Warrior* (Cambridge, 1984), pp. 194–7.

[35] Martin Gilbert, *The Roots of Appeasement* (London, 1966), ch. 15.

[36] Ibid., pp. 153–4; Gustav Schmidt, *The Politics and Economics of Appeasement: British Foreign Policy in the 1930s* (Leamington Spa, 1986), pp. 31–225.

[37] 'Notes on a Visit to Denmark, Sweden and Norway', 18 June 1935, FO 371/19439, N3107/1967/63.

German naval agreement (18 June 1935).[38] Ashton Gwatkin nevertheless believed that Britain's position of strength in northern Europe was something which could be exploited as a bargaining counter in the process of Anglo-German economic appeasement. He proposed that Britain should acknowledge central and south-eastern Europe as a German sphere of economic interest by renouncing its most-favoured-nation rights in the region, in return for a corresponding German undertaking in respect of Scandinavia and the Baltic.[39] As he and his colleague Gladwyn Jebb wrote in August 1936,

North-East Europe is a much more prosperous trading area . . . and a much more promising market for United Kingdom trade than South-East Europe can ever be. German competition is a much less formidable danger to United Kingdom trade than it may become in the former; and so long as we can be predominant in the Baltic, we should not begrudge Germany the extension of her trade in the Danubian and Balkan countries.[40]

Even in this confident statement there was a hint of anxiety. It was well founded. By the mid-1930s Germany was regaining lost ground in Scandinavia which it had no intention of giving up, while British policy offered neither sufficient incentive nor any compulsion for Germany to do so.

Nordische Schicksalsgemeinschaft

In a lengthy memorandum on 'Germany, Denmark and the Border Question' written in May 1934, a National Socialist 'expert' on the Nordic countries expressed the change which, he believed, had come about in Germany's relationship with Scandinavia since the Nazi seizure of power. The importance of friendly relations with the Nordic states, formerly a matter of expediency, had now, 'through the emphasis of the Führer and his colleagues on the importance of blood and race . . . been given by National Socialism a deeper ideological justification'.[41] After 1933 the Nordic countries found themselves faced by 'an officially inspired wave of enthusiasm for the North'.[42] At best embarrassing, this display of German interest was also potentially menacing

---

[38] See pp. 298–300 in this volume.

[39] Ashton Gwatkin, 'Report on Trade Relations and Economic Conditions in the Baltic Area, Summer 1935', 12 September 1935, FO 419/29, N4653/1967/63; 'Memorandum by Messrs F. T. A. Ashton Gwatkin and H. M. G. Jebb Respecting German "Expansion"', 31 January 1936, *DBFP*, 2, XV, pp. 762–8.

[40] 'Memorandum Respecting German Economic Penetration in Central Europe, the Balkans and Turkey', 17 August 1936, FO 433/3, R4969/1167/67. For the south-east European context of the Ashton Gwatkin/Jebb proposals, see David E. Kaiser, *Economic Diplomacy and the Origins of the Second World War: Germany, Britain, France and Eastern Europe 1930–1939* (Princeton, N. J., 1980), pp. 170–5.

[41] Memorandum by Hans Clausen-Korff, 31 May 1934, PA, AA Abt. IV Dänemark, Po. 5, Bd 4.

[42] Seppo Kuusisto, *Alfred Rosenberg in der nationalsozialistischen Aussenpolitik 1933–1939* (Helsinki, 1984), p. 295. For critical contemporary discussions, see Joachim Joesten, 'The Nazis in Scandinavia', *Foreign Affairs* 15 (1937), pp. 720–8; Paul Olberg, 'Scandinavia and the Nazis', *Contemporary Review* 156 (1939), pp. 27–34.

since it clearly had nothing to do with the attractions of Scandinavian democracy. At the outset the implications of Alfred Rosenberg's 'Nordic community of fate' (*Nordische Schicksalsgemeinschaft*) were not necessarily anti-British. Indeed Rosenberg's 'German–Scandinavian bloc' was to be allied with Great Britain and the white races of North America.[43] Once Nazism had come to power, however, it became increasingly clear that, in the new relationship between Germany and northern Europe, Germany would be the dominant partner. The British alliance, moreover, failed to materialise.

Some of the manifestations of German interest seemed innocuous enough. There were, for instance, the Nordische Gesellschaft's efforts to build cultural bridges between Germany and the North. With some notable exceptions, such as the Norwegian novelist Knut Hamsun, only the more undistinguished of the numerous Scandinavian writers and artists targeted by the society proved sympathetic to the ideals of the new Germany. At least two of those who were invited to the 'Scandinavian writers' centre' at Travemünde repaid the compliment by returning home to write damaging books and articles.[44] On Scandinavian soil, such endeavours proved equally unproductive. Study tours made by Nordic zealots revealed the limited degree of Scandinavian sympathy for Nazi Germany and the fact that Scandinavian national socialist movements were only pallid derivatives of the German original. It was possible, one such visitor asserted, to believe that 'the North will one day be ripe for us. But the right man must come first.'[45] Rosenberg himself was fully aware of the limited appeal of Nazism in Scandinavia, though he naturally shifted the blame away from himself and the Nordische Gesellschaft: 'Scandinavia has done too well; it has become fat and lazy. The Vikings have gone; the burghers remain.'[46]

However, German displays of interest took on an increasingly menacing character. Many 'study tours' were undertaken under the auspices of the security authorities and one of the tasks of such travellers was to make political reports to the SD.[47] Anti-Semitism intruded on German–Scandinavian relations in forms ranging from the apparently trivial to the sinister. In 1935, for example, the Nordische Gesellschaft complained to the Ministry of Economics that, as a result of a recently concluded tourist agreement, Danish resorts were being 'swamped' by Jewish holiday-makers from Germany – an

---

[43] Alfred Rosenberg, *Der Mythus des 20. Jahrhunderts* (Munich, 1930), p. 676, quoted in Hans-Dietrich Loock, *Quisling, Rosenberg und Terboven. Zur Vorgeschichte und Geschichte der nationalsozialistischen Revolution in Norwegen* (Stuttgart, 1970), p. 161.

[44] Blücher to AA, 28 May 1938, *DGFP*, D, V, pp. 560–3 (p. 562); Below (Stockholm) to AA, 2 June 1938, ibid., pp. 565–71 (pp. 567–8). On the activities of the Travemünde centre, see Loock, *Quisling*, pp. 189–92.

[45] Memorandum by Cand. Phil. Paul Koopman, 'Volkliche Eindrucke einer Schweden–Norwegen Fahrt', 21 June 1934, PA, AA Abt. IV Norden, Politik 5 Dänemark, Bd 4.

[46] Diary entry for 5 June 1934, quoted in Loock, *Quisling*, p. 187.

[47] Hans-Dietrich Loock, 'Nordeuropa zwischen Aussenpolitik und "grossgermanischer" Innenpolitik', in Manfred Funke (ed.), *Hitler, Deutschland und die Mächte. Materialen zur Aussenpolitik des Dritten Reiches* (Düsseldorf, 1978), pp. 684–706 (p. 691).

outrage which German *Volksgenossen* could not be expected to tolerate.[48] If bureaucrats could ignore or neutralise such interventions in the early years of the regime,[49] they appear to have been neither willing nor able to do so by 1938. With Göring's drive to 'Aryanise' the German economy, Party and state organs worked together to enforce 'the will of the National Socialist German people' to exclude Jewish interests from participation in German–Scandinavian trade.[50]

The Nordic countries were made aware from an early stage of the Nazi regime's intolerance of foreign criticism. It employed a number of methods to influence press comment, including subsidies for pro-German newspapers and periodicals, orchestrated campaigns in the German press and direct diplomatic intimidation of Nordic governments.[51] Those governments were also placed under pressure to curb the activities of the many anti-Nazi émigrés for whom the Nordic countries had become a place of refuge. They became aware, on the other hand, that Nazi activists were seeking to Nazify local German colonies and spread propaganda among the population at large. Such activities led the Swedish government in 1936 to expel the local leader of the Auslands-Organisation, Heinrich Bartels, together with three others.[52] The decision of the Norwegian Nobel Committee to award the Peace Prize for 1935 to the German dissident and concentration camp inmate Carl von Ossietzky aroused Hitler's particular displeasure. That it did not lead to a major diplomatic incident between Norway and Germany was due to the moderating influence of the Auswärtiges Amt and the Norwegian government, as well as Germany's dependence on the import of Norwegian raw materials.[53]

The handling of this episode, with German–Norwegian trade remaining undisturbed while diplomatic relations were encumbered by a tiresome dispute which resulted from Hitler's insistence on banning the mutual exchange of decorations, provides an important clue to the nature of German–Scandinavian relations after 1933. Nordic enthusiasm on the one hand, and direct criticism or intimidation on the other, were kept within bounds in the interest of maintaining normal diplomatic and economic relations between Germany and the Nordic countries. Despite the increasingly domineering attitude of the German government, even the most dogmatic ideologists could generally be

---

[48] NG to RWM, 8 July 1935, PA, AA Sonderreferat Wirtschaft, Finanzwesen 16, Dänemark, Bd 4.

[49] See ch. 7, pp. 267–8.

[50] Ministerialdirektor Walter (RWM) in meeting of German–Danish inter-governmental trade committee, 16 August 1938, ZSta, AA 67777. For arrangements to check the non-Jewish credentials of firms trading with Germany, see Scherpenberg to Copenhagen and Helsinki legations, 16 February 1939, ZSta, AA 67973.

[51] On German efforts to influence the Swedish press, see Erik Lönnroth, *Den svenska utrikespolitikens historia*, vol. V, *1919–1939* (Stockholm, 1959), pp. 157–6.

[52] Ibid., pp. 167–9; Donald M. McKale, *The Swastika Outside Germany* (Kent, Ohio, 1977), pp. 99–100.

[53] Elisabeth Thue, *Nobels fredspris – og diplomatiske forviklinger. Tysk–norske forbindelser i kjølvannet av Ossietzky-saken* (Oslo, 1994).

persuaded of the need for moderation. In January 1938 the head of the northern European department at the Wilhelmstrasse, Werner von Grundherr, persuaded Gauleiter Hinrich Lohse of Schleswig-Holstein that to reopen the German–Danish frontier question would have 'serious consequences for our foreign and economic policies', while Alfred Rosenberg agreed some months later that it was necessary to restrain the activities of the Nordische Gesellschaft.[54]

Indeed, apart from those, like Lohse, who had local interests, Rosenberg and Darré were the only prominent Nazis who displayed a consistent interest in the Nordic countries during the pre-war years. And in the case of both men it is difficult to avoid the suspicion that the channelling of their energies in a northerly direction was a form of compensation for their failure to achieve more substantial objectives: Rosenberg, the Party's 'foreign policy expert', for his exclusion from the Wilhelmstrasse; Darré for his growing marginalisation in the sphere of agricultural and economic policy making.[55] Yet their efforts were not wasted. If National Socialism and its Nordic variants lacked mass appeal, as their dwindling electoral success seemed to prove, this, for a revolutionary movement, might be no bad thing. Nazism, after all, had begun as a radical political sect, and Hitler had insisted that he wished to recruit only dedicated revolutionaries and that his 'radical and inflammatory' propaganda was designed to repel 'weaklings and hesitant characters'.[56]

By the late 1930s there were sufficient Nazi sympathisers in each of the Nordic countries – some in relatively influential positions in business, academic life or the armed forces – to form a core of potential conspirators which might be activated if German interest turned towards the north. The best-documented case is of course that of Vidkun Quisling and his associates. Ideologically, there was a close affinity between Rosenberg's 'Nordic' state system and Quisling's '*Northern Coalition . . .* beginning with Scandinavia and Great Britain – and with the inclusion of Finland and Holland – which might attract Germany next, and possibly the British Dominions and America later on'.[57] In practical terms, the activities of the Nordische Gesellschaft bore fruit as the failure of Quisling's Nasjonal Samling as a mass movement provided the stimulus for his search for external allies in Germany to replace the support which he lacked at home.[58] Quisling's conspiratorial role in the background to the German invasion of Norway in 1940 was to provide belated justification for Rosenberg's long years of preparation and frustration in Scandinavia.

[54] Memorandum by Grundherr, 21 January 1938, *DGFP*, D, V, pp. 546–8; Grundherr to Renthe-Fink, 5 May 1938, ibid., pp. 556–8.
[55] Gustavo Corni, *Hitler and the Peasants: Agrarian Policy of the Third Reich 1930–1939* (New York, Oxford and Munich, 1990), pp. 245–9.
[56] Adolf Hitler, *Mein Kampf* (trans. Ralph Manheim, London, 1969), p. 533.
[57] Vidkun Quisling, *Russia and Ourselves* (London, 1931), pp. 275–6.
[58] Loock, *Quisling*, pp. 192–204; Paul M. Hayes, *Quisling: The Career and Political Ideas of Vidkun Quisling 1887–1945* (Newton Abbot, 1971), ch. 4; Oddvar K. Hoidal, *Quisling: A Study in Treason* (Oxford, 1989), chs. 9–10.

It would thus be a mistake to discount the force of ideology in Nazi Germany's attitudes towards Scandinavia and the Baltic. Of none was this more true than Hitler himself. Herman Rauschning asserted, on the basis of conversations supposed to have taken place with Hitler in the early 1930s, that 'Hitler is not interested in the pure Aryan blood of the Scandinavian, nor in the northern myths of Viking heroism. He is interested in the iron-ore mines.'[59] The truth was more complex. Hitler rarely wrote or spoke publicly on the subject of Scandinavia, and the evidence for his private opinions is patchy and not always reliable.[60] It suggests, however, that, although Hitler was cynical about Rosenberg's Nordic fervour, Scandinavia did occupy a distinctive niche in his thinking. In this sphere as in others, racist, geopolitical and strategic considerations were intimately linked in Hitler's mind.[61]

Scandinavia barely figured in Hitler's programmatic works of the 1920s, *Mein Kampf* (1925–6) and the 'second', or 'secret' book of 1928; but there are several indications from the early 1930s onwards that Hitler envisaged the incorporation of the Nordic countries into a German-dominated sphere. In discussion with Otto Wagener, one of the Nazi Party's economic experts, probably in 1931, Hitler declared that Denmark would be one of the components of a 'Central European economic bloc' which would eventually form the core of a union comprising all European states apart from the Soviet Union.[62] Rauschning's testimony from 1934 emphasises military considerations. He reports conversations in which Hitler allegedly referred to the formation of 'a Northern Union of Denmark, Sweden and Norway' and insisted that 'In the next war, one of his first measures must be to occupy Sweden. He could not leave the Scandinavian countries either to British or Russian influence.' In order to achieve this goal, Hitler envisaged a series of daring strikes aimed not at 'occupying the entire country, but only the important ports and industrial centres, above all the iron-ore mines . . . Such a *coup* would lead to the permanent incorporation of the Northern States into the Greater German system of alliances.'[63]

---

[59] Hermann Rauschning, *Hitler Speaks: A Series of Political Conversations with Adolf Hitler on His Real Aims* (London, 1939), p. 144.

[60] This stricture applies in particular to Edouard Calic (ed.), *Unmasked: Two Confidential Interviews with Hitler in 1931* (London, 1971) (see *Der Spiegel*, 4 September 1972, pp. 62–5), despite interesting remarks (pp. 65–6) on rural conditions in the Netherlands and Denmark and the suggestion (echoed in Hitler's wartime 'table-talk') that 'The young Dutchmen and Danes would count themselves lucky to be able to go off to the East as colonisers along with the Germans.' See H. R. Trevor-Roper (ed.), *Hitler's Table-Talk 1941–1944* (London, 1953; repr. Oxford, 1988), pp. 16, 55, 128, 326–8. There are also doubts about Rauschning, but Theodor Schieder, *Hermann Rauschnings 'Gespräche mit Hitler' als Geschichtsquelle* (Opladen, 1972), concludes that, although Rauschning does not provide a literal record of Hitler's words, he does convey their essence.

[61] For an interesting discussion of the relationship between Hitler's and Rosenberg's conceptions, see Loock, 'Nordeuropa', pp. 688–9.

[62] Otto Wagener (ed. Henry Ashby Turner Jr), *Hitler aus nächster Nähe. Aufzeichnungen eines Vertrauten 1929–1932* (Frankfurt am Main, Berlin and Vienna, 1978), pp. 281–6.

[63] Rauschning, *Hitler Speaks*, pp. 128–9, 141–4.

The necessity of expansion towards the north and east was also Hitler's theme when Wipert von Blücher, newly appointed minister to Finland, had his 'first and last' conversation with the Führer in November 1935. Since other parts of the world were closed to Germany, Hitler said, it could not send its surplus population to Canada or Brazil, while Africa offered raw materials but no living space. 'We must direct our expansion towards the Baltic sphere. The Baltic was a bottle which we could seal off. The English could exert no control there. We were masters of the Baltic.'[64]

In this context the most contentious issue in German–Scandinavian relations, the question of North Slesvig, was of only secondary importance. From the start, the position of the Nazi regime was consistent with that of its Weimar predecessor: no official recognition of the frontier, but no unnecessary agitation for its revision. In pursuit of this goal the regime was quite prepared to clamp down on the activities of local National Socialists, notably at the time of the 'Easter Storm' on the frontier in the spring of 1933.[65] In conversation with Renthe-Fink in 1936, Hitler was critical of the Danish government and the 1920 plebiscite, but declared that the frontier question was secondary to maintaining good relations with Denmark.[66] Hitler, indeed, was ultimately to go further in acknowledging the post-Versailles status quo than any previous German government when, in his Reichstag speech of 6 October 1939, he publicly recognised the existing frontier for the first time.[67]

The fact that Hitler could make such an assurance, ostensibly given in the light of the German–Danish non-aggression pact of May 1939, merely reflected the insignificance of the Slesvig question in his grand scheme. There are signs that by early 1939 German pragmatism over Slesvig was becoming merged into a more interventionist, more overtly geo-strategic and racist approach to the Nordic region.[68] According to Lohse's post-war testimony, Hitler spoke in the spring of 1939 in favour of a peaceful solution to the Slesvig question, with a possible exchange of minorities on both sides of the border. This approach (envisaged by Rosenberg as early as 1933)[69] would, Hitler said, fit in well with his 'Greater German' (*grossgermanisch*) conception.[70] Contemporary notes made by Renthe-Fink of a conversation between Hitler and Lohse in June 1939 confirm that Hitler was 'not – at least at present – in favour of the reunification of North Schleswig with Germany'. Only one-third of its

[64] Wipert von Blücher, *Gesandter zwischen Diktatur und Demokratie. Erinnerungen aus den Jahren 1935–1944* (Wiesbaden, 1951), p. 43.

[65] Sven Tägil, *Deutschland und die deutsche Minderheit in Nordschleswig. Eine Studie zur deutschen Grenzpolitik 1933–1939* (Lund, 1970), chs. 1–2.

[66] Testimony to the Danish post-war committee of inquiry, 23 July 1946, *Betænkninger og bilag til folketinget afgivet af den parlamentariske kommission* (Copenhagen, 1945), vol. II, pp. 5–7.

[67] Tägil, *Deutschland und die deutsche Minderheit*, pp. 138–9.

[68] Vadis O. Lumans, 'The Nordic Destiny: The Peculiar Role of the German Minority in North Schleswig in Hitler's Plans and Policies for Denmark', *Scandinavian Journal of History* 15 (1990), pp. 109–23.

[69] Tägil, *Deutschland und die deutsche Minderheit*, pp. 110–11.   [70] Ibid., p. 137.

people were German, and Hitler 'did not want any alien population in the Reich'. Rather than going to war over North Slesvig, Hitler envisaged a 'North-East European Confederation' (*Nordosteuropabund*) comprising Germany and the Scandinavian states.[71] In the same month Reichsminister Hans Frank told Renthe-Fink that Germany's policy in Scandinavia must be 'to cut the ground from under England's feet. Therefore as friendly as possible to Denmark and its government, in order to do England harm [*um England Tort anzutun*].'[72] The explicitly anti-British thrust of Hitler's thinking and the idea of merging the Nordic countries in a German-controlled sphere thus anticipated the 'Greater Germanic Reich' the foundation of which Hitler, less than a year later, was to claim as the outcome of Germany's conquest of Denmark and Norway.[73]

Great Britain and the German challenge in Scandinavia

Commercial policy and cartels

The Anglo-Scandinavian trade agreements of 1933 largely fulfilled the limited expectations placed in them by senior politicians. Commercial policy was 'taken out of politics'.[74] But they proved ineffective in the face of the intensification of German competition in the late 1930s. Britain was unable either to offer sufficiently generous market opportunities to Scandinavian exporters, or to exert sufficient pressure to make the Scandinavian countries buy more British goods.

It was precisely at the time, in the autumn of 1933, when Germany's policy of agricultural protectionism began to be reversed that the Ministry of Agriculture's policy of restricting agricultural imports started to take effect with a unilateral cut in bacon imports. Between 1933 and 1937 agricultural policy and commercial policy were perpetually in conflict, with the Foreign Office warning repeatedly that import restrictions would 'profoundly affect our trade and our political influence' over the Scandinavian and Baltic countries whose economic alignment with Great Britain was 'an important interest of the United Kingdom in time of peace, and might well be vital in the event of war'.[75] Though the more extreme demands of the Ministry were forestalled, the relative stagnation of the British market encouraged Scandinavian producers to look to the more dynamic, if still much smaller German market as

---

[71] Quoted ibid., p. 138.
[72] Quoted ibid. See also Viggo Sjøqvist, *Danmarks udenrigspolitik 1933–1940* (Copenhagen, 1966), p. 49.
[73] Loock, *Quisling*, pp. 263–70.
[74] John S. Eyers, 'Government Direction of Britain's Overseas Trade Policy 1932–1937' (DPhil. thesis, University of Oxford, 1977), p. 22. See also Clemens Wurm, *Business, Politics and International Relations: Steel, Cotton and International Cartels in British Politics 1924–1939* (Cambridge, 1993), pp. 70–1.
[75] Simon to Baldwin, 9 January 1935, FO 371/19628, W425/422/50. See also Eyers, 'Government Direction', and Rooth, *British Protectionism*, ch. 8.

an alternative. This tendency was encouraged by Darré and his 'Reich Peasant Office' (Reichsbauernkontor) at Goslar, who stressed the idea of cooperation between the 'Nordic' farmers of Germany and Scandinavia; and in at least one case, that of the Danish Landbrugernes Sammenslutning, an influential pro-German pressure group emerged.[76]

If the British were unable to dangle a sufficiently attractive carrot in front of the Scandinavians, they also lacked a large enough stick. British commercial policy provided no systematic means of compelling the Scandinavian countries to buy more British goods, or of retaliating when they failed to do so. The trade agreements contained no guarantee, apart from vague undertakings, that devices adopted by the Scandinavian countries under British pressure, like the Danish Valutacentral, would continue to operate in Britain's favour. The British had not foreseen that such a mechanism, introduced at a time when their bargaining position was strong, might come to be employed against them and in favour of Danish or German competitors, as was to occur within months of the signature of the Anglo-Danish agreement. British officials and businessmen were embittered in 1934–5 by what they regarded as Denmark's breach of faith in cutting back the issue of import licences for British goods.[77] Pressure for larger allocations could be exerted intermittently through diplomatic channels or by the threat to impose a clearing on Anglo-Danish trade, but the effects of such efforts were short-lived.

By the time the Anglo-Danish agreement came up for renewal in 1936, the Board of Trade had come to the conclusion that 'the Danish policy has been one of granting facilities for United Kingdom trade only so far as they felt compelled to do so. Once they decided that they had nothing to fear they did not hesitate to cut down United Kingdom trade.'[78] In the negotiations of 1936 the Board therefore sought, despite its economic orthodoxy, to bring the Anglo-Danish agreement closer to the German model. The changes envisaged included the establishment of a fixed ratio between the imports and exports of the two countries; fewer opportunities for evasion (i.e. a stricter allocation of import licences); and the establishment of an inter-governmental expert

---

[76] Speech by Dr Erich Winter (Hauptabteilungsleiter im Stabsamt des Reichsbauernführers), reported in *Berliner Börsen-Zeitung*, 6 March 1934; article by A. P. Jacobsen, 'Darré og Danmark', in *Dagens Nyheder*, 6 July 1933; Joachim Joesten, *Denmark's Day of Doom* (London, 1939), pp. 146–52. See also report by Metzger (Stabsamt des Reichsbauernführers), on discussions with the Norwegian farmers' organisation Norges Bondelag, 23 March 1939, ZSta, AA 68133.

[77] Raymond Streat (secretary, Manchester Chamber of Commerce) to BT, 12 February 1934, BT 11/296, CRT 259; 1934 correspondence in FO 371/18264, N188, and FO 371/18268, N481; 1935 correspondence in FO 371/19428-9, N324; and Susan Seymour, *Anglo-Danish Relations and Germany 1933–1945* (Odense, 1982), pp. 32–3, 40–1; Tim Rooth, 'Limits of Leverage: The Anglo-Danish Trade Agreement of 1933', *Economic History Review* 37 (1984), pp. 211–28 (p. 223).

[78] R. Kelf-Cohen, 'Review of the Working of the Anglo-Danish Agreement of 1933', 11 March 1936, FO 371/20322, N1487/73/15. See also Seymour, *Anglo-Danish Relations*, pp. 41–2.

committee.[79] Some of these provisions were contained in the supplementary commercial agreement but a ratio – the most important – was not. The Danish foreign minister described the outcome of the negotiations as 'better than one might have dared to expect'.[80] Certainly the British negotiators proved less skilled and less tenacious than their Danish counterparts.[81] However, the fact that British complaints about the Danish import licensing system diminished after 1936 suggests that the size of the British market continued to exert a significant influence on Danish policy despite the absence of formal guarantees. In some quarters British officials wished to go much further in emulating the German example. At the Foreign Office Collier repeatedly advocated 'taking a leaf out of the German book' by imposing clearings on Anglo-Scandinavian trade.[82] His arguments were contested by Ashton Gwatkin and Gladwyn Jebb and, more importantly, rejected by the Treasury and the Board of Trade, which refused to consider clearings for anything other than debt collection.[83] Collier's renewed demand for clearings in the summer of 1936 was effectively ruled out by Runciman in Parliament on 15 July.[84] His initiative came at a time when Whitehall had been debating for several months the merits of channelling German economic interests in the direction of south-eastern Europe.[85]

Economic appeasement, too, was opposed by Chamberlain at the Treasury and Runciman at the Board of Trade, and made little headway in the aftermath of Hitler's remilitarisation of the Rhineland in March 1936. But it continued to be promoted by the Foreign Office. One variant, as noted in the last chapter, was the proposal put forward by Ashton Gwatkin and Jebb by which Britain would renounce its most-favoured-nation rights in south-eastern Europe in

---

[79] Danish Foreign Ministry meeting, 30 April 1936, RA, UM 64 Dan. 73a, Bd 21; BT memorandum, 'United Kingdom–Danish Commercial Negotiations', 26 May 1936, FO 371/20322, N2843/73/15.

[80] Danish Foreign Ministry meeting, 22 June 1936, RA, UM 64 Dan. 73a, Bd 23.

[81] The chief Danish negotiators, Otto Carl Mohr and Einar Wærum, were described by Ashton Gwatkin as 'a tough pair': minute of 7 September 1936, FO 371/20325, N4397/237/15. The other agreements with the Scandinavian and Baltic states were renewed in 1936 without serious modification.

[82] Collier minute, 19 April 1934, FO 371/18265, N2352/188/15.

[83] See e.g. Ashton Gwatkin's minutes on Collier memorandum, 'Clearing Agreements', 8 June 1936, FO 371/20460, W5149/299/50; and Jebb's minutes of November 1937 on the 'Annual Economic Report (B) for Latvia', sent by Monson (Riga) to FO, 19 October 1937, FO 371/21055, N5351/66/59. The Whitehall debate on clearings in 1936 has been discussed from the Scandinavian perspective in Rooth, British Protectionism, pp. 275–8; Bengt Nilson, Handelspolitik under skärpt konkurrens. England och Sverige 1929–1939 (Lund, 1983), pp. 88–9; and Seymour, Anglo-Danish Relations, pp. 42–4; from that of eastern and south-eastern Europe in Kaiser, Economic Diplomacy, pp. 184–6; and from that of the Baltic states in Merja-Liisa Hinkkanen-Lievonen, 'Britain as Germany's Commercial Rival in the Baltic States 1919–1939', in Marie-Luise Recker (ed.), Von der Konkurrenz zur Rivalität. Das britisch–deutsche Verhältnis in den Ländern der europäischen Peripherie 1919–1939 (Stuttgart, 1986), pp. 15–49 (pp. 40–2).

[84] Collier memorandum, 8 June 1936, FO 371/20460, W5149/299/50; Hill (BT) to Collier, 18 July 1936, FO 371/20331, N3666/40/63.

[85] Gustav Schmidt, Politics and Economics of Appeasement, pp. 84–104.

exchange for a German agreement to limit competition in Scandinavia and the Baltic. It was an idea which found support elsewhere in Whitehall. In the words of a senior Treasury official, 'the effect of our own Agreements with the Scandinavian and Baltic States has no doubt been to deprive Germany to some extent of markets which she would otherwise have obtained and probably on the whole it suits us pretty well to develop those markets and to leave the thorny path of Central and Eastern Europe for Germany'.[86] But such an offer would lose much of its credibility if, as a report from Copenhagen in July 1936 suggested, the thrust of German commercial policy was turning towards northern Europe.[87]

At Ashton Gwatkin's suggestion, the Foreign Office therefore asked the legations in the other Scandinavian and Baltic capitals whether there were 'any signs of a German commercial offensive . . . in connexion with the general question of German economic penetration and with special reference to "clearing" agreements'.[88] None of the replies reported any systematic attempt to employ clearings as instruments of economic penetration, but there were several references to increased German competition as well as to the inherent tendency of the clearing system to increase bilateral trade.[89] The commercial secretary in Stockholm, for example, noted that

By buying more raw materials and semi-finished goods of Swedish origin, Germany is forcing up her export of manufactured goods to Sweden. The significance of such a development, and its disadvantages to local manufacturers as well as to the happy commercial relations existing between Sweden and the United Kingdom, do not appear to be fully realised here.[90]

The situation in northern Europe therefore posed no immediate threat to British interests but contained worrying indications for the future. This might have been the time to take an initiative of the kind proposed by Ashton Gwatkin – to have attempted it any later would certainly have been too late – but it never penetrated to ministerial level.[91]

Instead, 1936 saw the inception of a second approach to economic appease-

---

[86] Sir Sigismund Waley to Sir Edward Crowe (DOT), 15 June 1936, quoted in Nilson, *Handelspolitik*, pp. 93–4.

[87] Ramsay to FO, 2 July 1936, FO 371/20323, N3841/110/15. See also ch. 7, pp. 271–3.

[88] FO to ministers in Oslo, Stockholm, Helsinki, Riga and Warsaw, 8 September 1936, FO 371/20323, N3481/110/15.

[89] The replies can be read most conveniently in the FO Confidential Print, FO 419/30. In one case, that of Finland, the commercial secretary (Keith Jopson) had already undertaken such an investigation on his own initiative: 'Memorandum on the German–Finnish Clearing Agreements', 5 August 1936, enclosure in Grant Watson (Helsinki) to Eden, 7 August 1936, N4031/111/56. See also despatches from Palairet (Stockholm), 28 September 1936, N5047/109/42; Dormer (Oslo), 6 October 1936, N5071/2253/30; Monson (Riga), 15 October 1936, N5262/163/59.

[90] H. A. N. Bluett, 'Interim Report on Economic Commercial Conditions in Sweden', enclosure in Palairet despatch, FO 419/30, N5047/109/42.

[91] Gustav Schmidt, *Politics and Economics of Appeasement*, pp. 223–5.

ment, based on encouraging British industries to enter into cartel agreements with their German counterparts. The atmosphere of the time was conducive to suggestions that international agreements between major industries, such as that concluded between the British iron and steel industry and the International Steel Cartel in July 1935, might constitute a first step towards defusing political conflicts.[92] Favoured by influential figures such as Sir Frederick Leith-Ross, the government's chief economic adviser, as well as by the Federation of British Industries (FBI), this approach did not begin to show results until the middle of 1938, by which time Britain's competitive position had weakened and the political situation had altered very much to Britain's disadvantage.[93]

Cartel agreements, both open and concealed, played an important role in the relationship between British and German industries in Scandinavian markets, but did not lend themselves easily to those who wished to use them as means of promoting exports or Anglo-German political understanding. Such agreements came into existence only when the industries of each country were sufficiently organised to enable them to make firm commitments, and when the two sides recognised, or were forced to recognise, that they stood to gain more from cooperation than from unrestrained competition.

In the case of coal, this situation was not reached until 1938–9.[94] Britain had secured a predominant share of Scandinavian markets through the trade agreements and a cartel agreement with Poland, its leading competitor, which had been concluded in December 1934.[95] The German coal industry had not hitherto made special efforts to increase its exports to Scandinavia, but had been stimulated to do so by the price increase that followed the Anglo-Polish agreement. Between 1935 and 1938, the value of German coal exports to Scandinavia increased five-fold, from RM 3.9 million to RM 19 million. Since sales of coal were an important source of foreign exchange, they were actively promoted by German commercial diplomacy: as in the case of Denmark noted earlier (ch. 7, p. 272), increased coal purchases were frequently made a precondition for the renewal of trade and clearing agreements with the Nordic countries.

Initiatives for an Anglo-German coal agreement came primarily from the British government, but the German coal industry showed little interest in negotiations until 1938. The conclusion of an international coke convention in June 1937 was widely regarded as paving the way for a comprehensive European coal cartel, and at the end of 1937 the British coal industry was

[92] Wurm, *Business, Politics and International Relations*, pp. 181–9.

[93] Kaiser, *Economic Diplomacy*, pp. 187–8; Rooth, *British Protectionism*, pp. 278–81.

[94] Except where otherwise indicated, this paragraph and the next are based on Schröter, *Aussenpolitik und Wirtschaftsinteresse*, pp. 205–47, and Schröter, 'Risk and Control in Multinational Enterprise: German Businesses in Scandinavia 1918–1939', *Business History Review* 62 (1988), pp. 420–43 (pp. 431–2).

[95] Patrick Salmon, 'Polish–British Competition in the Coal Markets of Northern Europe 1927–1934', *Studia historiae oeconomicae* 16 (1981), pp. 217–43.

placed under more direct government control, making it a more realistic negotiating partner. By 1938, too, it was clear that commercial diplomacy could do little more to increase Germany's market share. Even then, political pressure on the part of both the British and the German governments was required before the German coal industry would agree to the terms of the Anglo-German coal agreement which was finally concluded in January 1939.[96] Cartels in the chemical industry were far less amenable to government intervention. The relationship between the two great chemical combines, IG Farben and Imperial Chemical Industries (ICI) was overwhelmingly one of cooperation rather than conflict.[97] Secure in its command of empire markets, ICI was content to leave IG Farben's dominant position in Scandinavia undisturbed.[98] In view, moreover, of world-wide over-capacity in the chemical industry, the two firms worked closely together in order to prevent the establishment of chemical works in the Nordic countries.[99] Ostensibly acting on its own account, but in fact on behalf of its German and Belgian partners in a chlorine export cartel, ICI succeeded in delaying for several years the construction of a chlorine factory in Finland; 'and when it was finally completed it was not ICI, the official contractor of the Finnish government, that owned it, but the members of the chlorine cartel'.[100] In a similar way, IG Farben hindered the establishment of indigenous nitrogen industries in Denmark and Finland, in accordance with an agreement with British chemical firms and Norsk Hydro.

Propaganda and arms sales

There is always a tendency for those demanding more activity on the part of their own government to attribute greater energy to their rivals. It is nevertheless difficult to discount the frequency and consistency with which German commentators contrasted the ineffectiveness of the German government's propaganda efforts in Scandinavia in the mid-1930s with those of Great Britain. There was a reluctant acknowledgement that 'the Nordic idea, as represented by the new Germany' and 'the German racial idea' had met with little sympathy in the Nordic countries.[101] Germany's policy towards the

---

[96] Rooth, *British Protectionism*, p. 280; C. A. MacDonald, 'Economic Appeasement and the German "Moderates" 1937–1939', *Past and Present* 56 (1972), pp. 105–35 (pp. 119–20, 123); Simon Newman, *March 1939: The British Guarantee to Poland* (Oxford, 1976), pp. 57–8, 79; Berndt-Jürgen Wendt, *Economic Appeasement. Handel und Finanz in der britischen Deutschland-Politik 1933–1939* (Düsseldorf, 1971), pp. 545–6.

[97] Schröter, *Aussenpolitik und Wirtschaftsinteresse*, pp. 247–322; Schröter, 'Risk and Control'.

[98] Ashton Gwatkin remarked: 'The ICI are well content, I know, with the working of their cartel . . . which I heard described the other day as an oasis of sanity in a world of international madness' (minute of 4 November 1938, FO 371/22268, N5136/495/56).

[99] Attempts to hinder the growth of competition by preventing establishment of new plant were also characteristic of the iron and steel industry: see Wurm, *Business, Politics and International Relations*, pp. 186–7.

[100] Schröter, 'Risk and Control', p. 439. See also correspondence in ZSta., AA 68078.

[101] 'Englischer Kurs in Schweden? Folgen der britischen Propaganda', *Kreuz-Zeitung*, 1 September 1934 (copy in PA, AA Pol. Abt. IV Schweden, Politik 3 – England).

Nordic countries was also criticised for merely dealing with problems as they arose rather than being guided by 'one unifying idea . . . one basic conception'.[102] Britain, on the other hand, seemed to be adopting an increasingly high profile. It was difficult to judge, the Copenhagen representative of the Deutscher Akademischer Austauschdienst observed, whether this was a matter of coincidence, or whether it resulted from 'a systematic activity in the political, economic and cultural fields'.[103]

In fact British policy, just as much as German, lacked a 'unifying idea'. There is no doubt, however, that British officialdom was beginning to regard Scandinavia in a more favourable light. Nothing had come of the tentative suggestions made in 1931–2 that Britain's strengthened economic ties with the Nordic countries should form the basis of a new political alignment. But after Ottawa, when hopes placed in the empire began to dissipate, and after the Nazi seizure of power, as the European situation became more menacing, British attitudes towards the Nordic countries became more positive. If the sterling area and the Anglo-Scandinavian trade agreements constituted the initial point of contact, the impetus came from a mutual interest in preserving peace. A close rapport developed between Sandler, the Swedish foreign minister, and Anthony Eden, lord privy seal and minister for League of Nations affairs, as they worked together on the disarmament question at Geneva in 1933–4. In October 1934, following an invitation from Sandler, Eden visited the three Scandinavian capitals. His visit represented the high point of British influence in northern Europe between the wars.

It is easy to be misled by the brief and diffident account of his Scandinavian tour in Eden's memoirs, as well as by the supercilious tone of Foreign Office officials when the visit was first proposed.[104] It would be equally mistaken to take seriously all the ulterior motives ascribed to the visit by some German and Soviet observers.[105] The latter were nevertheless correct in their assessment of its symbolic importance. With the assassinations of Chancellor Dollfuss in Austria and of King Alexander of Yugoslavia and Louis Barthou at Marseilles, and Hitler's purge of 30 June, 1934 was a year of violence. There was an increasingly marked distinction between those states which had succumbed to dictatorship and those which had not. In this climate the values shared by

---

[102] Prof. Dr Wolgast to Hasso von Etzdorf, 22 December 1934, PA, AA Pol. Abt. IV Norden, Politik 2.
[103] Rudolf von Wistinghausen to DAAD, 11 April 1935, AA, Parteidienststellen, 3/2 (copy in BA, ZSg 133/51).
[104] Earl of Avon, *The Eden Memoirs*, vol. I, *Facing the Dictators* (London, 1962), pp. 121–2; FO minutes on Eden minute of 5 June 1934, FO 371/18337, N3391/3391/42.
[105] E.g. Behr (Oslo) to AA, 20 October 1934, PA, AA Pol. Abt. IV Norwegen, Politik 3 – England; Wied (Stockholm) to AA, 23 October 1934, PA, AA Pol. Abt. IV Schweden, Politik 3 – England; Steffan (naval attaché, Stockholm) to Marineleitung, 22 October 1934, PA, AA Geheimakten Schweden II, FM 24, Bd 1; *Pravda* article of 19 October cited in Coote (Moscow) to FO, 20 October 1934, FO 371/18337, N6097/3391/42. Contrast the far more balanced assessment in Meynen (Stockholm) to AA, 19 October 1934, PA, AA Pol. Abt. IV Norden, Politik 3 – England.

Great Britain and the Nordic countries became more visible than the issues which divided them. As *The Times* put it,

The contrast between the British method of facing the difficulties of the last few years, without any abandonment of our democratic heritage, and the repressions of Hitlerism, the 'clean-up' of June 30, and the coercion of the German Church, has greatly strengthened faith in government by democracy in the Northern countries. Moreover, our mutual commercial interests have been advanced by the trading agreements concluded last year . . . so that both politically and commercially there is every reason why we should understand our Northern friends and be understood by them.[106]

A further indication of British interest in Scandinavia was the programme of the British Council for Relations with Other Countries (later known simply as the British Council), founded in November 1934 as the first British organisation devoted to cultural propaganda in peacetime.[107] The product of a belated recognition that Britain needed to match the propaganda efforts of the totalitarian states, the British Council represented, on the one hand, confidence in what its second head, Lord Eustace Percy, identified as a new spirit of national unity in the face of an increasingly ominous international situation, but on the other a tacit recognition of the limits of British power: 'if one could do little . . . to "project" British policy acceptably to foreign eyes and ears, it was beginning to be possible to "project" the British people'.[108] The comfortingly like-minded Scandinavians were to be the first recipients of the reassuring message that 'British society still had much to offer the world.'[109] According to the guidelines laid down in December 1934 by Lord Tyrrell's preparatory committee,

An initial effort will be made in Scandinavia, partly because the recent commercial treaties have increased trade prospects and aroused interest in Great Britain, partly because Germany is making a great effort to influence opinion in these countries for political and commercial reasons.[110]

The record of Britain's heightened profile can be traced most conveniently in the annual reports compiled by the British legations in the Nordic capitals. The report on Denmark for 1934 shows how much headway had been made even before the establishment of the British Council. The British minister emphasised that the spontaneous 'Danish interest in England and things English', enhanced by recent developments which had 'brought home to the Danes how important a part England plays in their economic life', was 'more effective than any propaganda, as such, could ever have been'.[111] He was

---

[106] Leading article in *The Times*, 'Mr Eden's Tour', 13 October 1934.
[107] Philip M. Taylor, 'Cultural Diplomacy and the British Council: 1934–1939', *British Journal of International Studies* 4 (1978), pp. 244–65.
[108] Lord Percy of Newcastle, *Some Memories* (London, 1958), pp. 159–60.
[109] Philip M. Taylor, 'Cultural Diplomacy', p. 265.
[110] Memoranda by the British Committee for Relations with Other Countries, sent to Baldwin, 20 December 1934, CUL, Baldwin Papers, vol. 122.
[111] Hugh Gurney, 'Denmark and Iceland. Annual Report, 1934', 19 January 1935, FO 371/ 19429, N475/475/15, pp. 31–2.

nevertheless able to report a number of positive developments. Rowland Kenney of the Foreign Office Press Department had visited Copenhagen in order to 'establish more personal contact with the Copenhagen press', and a leading daily, *Berlingske Tidende*, had 'become markedly more willing to devote space to British ideas and British news and views during the latter part of the year'. The teaching of English had continued to expand; English books were in strong demand both in the original and in translation; a British theatre company had paid two visits to Copenhagen; several British films had been shown in Denmark and all had been well received; a number of lectures had been given under the auspices of the Danish–British Association; and the BBC's Christmas empire broadcast had been heard in Denmark. 'It clearly brought home to all who heard it the extent and the family unity of the British Commonwealth of Nations, and was probably one of the most effective single items of cultural propaganda during the year.'[112]

By 1935 British Council funding was beginning to bear fruit. In Finland, its grants paid for the reorganisation of the Finnish–British Society and for visits to Britain by Finnish school-teachers and students. The moment, the British minister to Finland noted, was 'an opportune one for taking advantage of her reluctance to be swept into the German orbit and to enjoy the doubtful blessings of German "kultur"'.[113] In Norway the bulk of the funding went into assisting Norwegian teachers and students of English to visit the United Kingdom; in Sweden, support went to the Swedish–British Society and into book prizes to schools.[114]

Useful as they undoubtedly were, such activities could do little to counteract the growing impression of British weakness in the face of the international challenge of the totalitarian states. Disarmament had been a cause with particular appeal to Scandinavians, being long on idealism and short on substance. Eden's initiative on the issue had thus helped to boost Britain's prestige. Its decline began with an event which touched the Nordic countries much more directly: the Anglo-German naval agreement of 18 June 1935.[115]

Britain's defection from the 'Stresa Front' of April 1935 undermined Scandinavian faith in British principle and resolve; its acknowledgement of Germany's right to build a navy strong enough to dominate the Baltic seemed to consign the smaller states of the region to a German sphere of influence. Even in Finland, where the outcome was welcomed as a means of holding the Soviet fleet in check, there was apprehension that the Soviet Union might

---

[112] Ibid., pp. 32–6.
[113] Grant Watson, 'Finland. Annual Report, 1935', 8 January 1936, FO 371/20330, N404/404/56, p. 10.
[114] Cecil Dormer, 'Norway. Annual Report, 1935', 21 February 1936, FO 371/20336, N1261/1261/30, p. 17; Sir Michael Palairet, 'Sweden. Annual Report, 1935', 13 February 1936, FO 371/20356, N1229/1229/42, pp. 8–9.
[115] Donald Cameron Watt, 'The Anglo-German Naval Agreement of 1935: An Interim Judgment', *Journal of Modern History* 28 (1956), pp. 155–76.

respond by increasing its armaments and engaging in a struggle for supremacy in the Baltic.[116] The implications of the agreement were discussed in an article by the Scandinavian correspondent of *The Times* which attracted wide attention in northern Europe.[117] The emergence of Germany as a strong naval power was, he wrote, more significant than the prevention of Anglo-German naval rivalry in the future. Moreover, far from conceding German supremacy in the Baltic so as to maintain British superiority elsewhere, Britain had effectively permitted Germany to attain a position of equality in the North Sea.[118] Commenting on the article, Collier of the Foreign Office deplored the effect of the naval agreement on Britain's position: above all, 'the profound psychological impression of a complete *volte-face* in British policy, produced both by the contents of the Agreement and by the manner of negotiation – an impression which seems to be still deepening and spreading'.[119]

Most of all, however, the agreement reflected the low priority attached to the region by British policy makers. It was an example of Holtsmark's 'asymmetry of expectations' at work.[120] Whilst the Nordic countries regarded the naval agreement as a conscious abandonment of Britain's Baltic position, the British, in their pursuit of appeasement and the limitation of naval armaments, were scarcely thinking about the Baltic at all. Such decisions were not taken 'with the impact on morale in the smaller European states in mind'.[121] If challenged, the British could respond with the unanswerable argument that, if appeasement worked, all European states would benefit. Indeed the king of Denmark was prepared to acknowledge 'the view that any understanding between ourselves and Germany tended to safeguard the position of Denmark'.[122] The problem, however, was that both the naval agreement and the subsequent record of Britain and France – above all, the Hoare–Laval pact and the abandonment of sanctions against Italy over Abyssinia – seemed merely to demonstrate weakness rather than a coherent strategy of preserving of peace through the settlement of legitimate grievances. The Northern Department, dealing with countries whose commitment to collective security it had regarded

---

[116] Grant Watson (Helsinki) to FO, 28 June 1935, FO 419/29, N3705/231/63; Blücher (Helsinki) to AA, 24 July 1935, PA, AA Pol. Abt. IV Finnland, Politik 1, Bd 2; Steffan to Kriegsmarine, 8 August 1935, PA, AA Geheimakten Schweden II, FM 24, Bd 2.

[117] 'Sea Power in the Baltic', *The Times*, 6 July 1935.

[118] The article, which also contained the controversial suggestion that Finnish nationalists would be encouraged to seek expansion at the expense of the Soviet Union, had, according to the German minister in Helsinki, been toned down by the editors of *The Times* in London. A copy of the original had been sent by the author (Thomas Barman) to the editor of the Helsinki paper *Helsingin Sanomat* (Eljas Erkko): Blücher to AA, PA, AA Pol. Abt. IV Finnland, Politik 1, Bd 2. Barman's memoirs do not mention the episode but do refer to the damaging effect of the naval agreement on Scandinavian opinion: Thomas Barman, *Diplomatic Correspondent* (London, 1968), p. 19.

[119] Minute of 11 July 1935, FO 371/19438, N3444/231/63.

[120] Sven G. Holtsmark, *Enemy Springboard or Benevolent Buffer? Soviet Attitudes to Nordic Cooperation 1920–1955* (Oslo, 1992), pp. 74–5. See also pp. 15–16 in this volume.

[121] Seymour, *Anglo-Danish Relations*, p. 81.

[122] Gurney to FO, 20 June 1935, FO 371/19424, N3217/61/15.

throughout as more or less suspect, was fully aware of the impact of Britain's failures on Scandinavian attitudes. Collier wrote: 'Denmark was never willing to do very much for the League until the Abyssinian crisis. Had that crisis been handled resolutely in London and Paris, she might have done more in future; but now she makes it clear that she will, in practice, do nothing.'[123]

Quite rapidly, in 1935–6, the contrast between British energy and German ineffectiveness which had characterised the earlier part of the decade was reversed. Now, it was suggested, Scandinavians had 'a latent feeling' that, however unwelcome German attentions might be, 'the Germans do seem to care, and that the British do not'.[124] It was perhaps symptomatic that the most sustained attempt in the late 1930s to make Britain care more about Scandinavia was a one-man campaign. George Soloveytchik, a freelance journalist of Russian extraction, who became foreign editor of the *Financial Times* in 1938–9, travelled extensively in Scandinavia and the Baltic, making many contacts in business and government circles.[125] Regarded with some ambivalence by both British and Scandinavian officials,[126] Soloveytchik found an outlet for his views in the pages of the *Contemporary Review* and the *Financial Times*, as well as in a well-received address given at Chatham House in July 1937.[127] The message, constantly reiterated, was that Britain had squandered the immense reserves of political goodwill and commercial success which it had built up through its support for the League and through the Anglo-Scandinavian trade agreements. Soloveytchik accused Britain of taking Scandinavia for granted and failing to appreciate the importance of Scandinavian markets, and criticised it for its short-sighted attempts to 'balance' Anglo-Scandinavian trade. More importantly, Britain lacked vision and was guilty, above all, of a profound moral failure in its abandonment of sanctions over Abyssinia. Although he was able on one occasion to prompt a slight shift of British policy in a more resolute direction (see pp. 313–15), Soloveytchik was, as he subsequently acknowledged, a 'hopelessly unheeded Cassandra'.[128] Yet British officialdom was less lethargic than he allowed and, in one important respect, did try to make up lost ground.

Finland had been a conspicuous omission – ostensibly for lack of time – from

[123] Minute of 31 October 1936, FO 371/20325, N5288/213/15.

[124] Soloveytchik, 'Fears and Realities in Scandinavia', p. 912.

[125] For an indication of the range of Soloveytchik's activities and interests, see his entry in *Who Was Who 1981–1990* (London, 1991), p. 707.

[126] See e.g. Collier to Palairet (Stockholm), 12 January 1937, FO 371/21078, N197/59/63; Reventlow (London) to UM, 2 February 1939, RA, UM 5 D 26.

[127] 'The Lost Key', *Contemporary Review* 150 (August 1936), pp. 172–81; 'Who Threatens Scandinavia?', *Contemporary Review* 155 (February 1939), pp. 169–78; 'The Scandinavian *Débâcle*', *Contemporary Review* 157 (June 1940), pp. 659–69; four articles on 'The Scandinavian Scene', *Financial Times*, 29 and 30 July, 3 and 4 August 1937; Chatham House address printed in Soloveytchik, 'Fears and Realities', pp. 894–913; discussion summarised ibid., pp. 913–19.

[128] Soloveytchik, 'Scandinavian *Débâcle*', p. 663.

Eden's 1934 tour of Scandinavia. By 1935 the Northern Department was becoming worried about the growth of German influence in Finland and thus responded positively when the minister in Helsinki, having warned that the country was 'drifting into the German orbit', suggested that 'an expression of interest from Great Britain would perhaps stay the drift to some extent, and give fresh heart to those people in Finland who feel that she should look West, and not South'.[129] British efforts were focused on the area most susceptible to competing foreign influences because most divided in its allegiances – the Finnish armed forces – and upon the supply of military hardware, especially aircraft. German equipment had long been favoured by the Finnish military authorities for its cheapness and because its specifications were compatible with existing Finnish armaments.[130] The shift of German policy in an explicitly anti-Soviet direction had seen the strengthening of Germany's diplomatic presence in Finland and the other border states. One indication was the appointment of the capable Blücher as minister; another was the creation of a new military attaché post at Helsinki. Germany could capitalise on the traditional friendship of Finnish Jäger officers and on Finnish fears of the Soviet Union. Yet most Finns disliked Nazism. Britain, it was suggested, could counter German influence most effectively by cultivating Finnish officers and persuading them to look to Britain as an alternative source of supply.[131]

The Finns were in the market for all types of equipment, including artillery and tanks, but were engaged above all in a major modernisation programme for the air force. Since Finnish preferences were determined by both technical and political considerations, it was often difficult for prospective suppliers to assess the nature of the market. Technologically, 'neutral' suppliers sometimes had the edge: in 1936 the Finns chose to buy dive-bombers and fighter aircraft from the Dutch Fokker Company rather than from Germany.[132] Nor were political considerations confined to a simple preference for either Britain or Germany but included, for example, trying to ensure some degree of coordination with Swedish purchases so as to facilitate military cooperation with Scandinavia.[133] In 1936 the Finns went so far as to exclude the British firm of Vickers from a competition to supply artillery in order to enable the entire order to be placed with Bofors in Sweden and thus 'to co-ordinate completely their own artillery and that of the Swedish army'.[134] Britain and Germany, for their part, attempted to influence Finnish decision making but,

---

[129] Henderson to Collier, 29 March 1935, FO 371/19436, N1686/573/56.
[130] Martti Turtola, 'Die militärischen Beziehungen zwischen Deutschland und Finnland 1919–1939', in Hannes Saarinen (ed.), *Referate des vierten Seminars von Historikern aus der DDR und Finnland (5.–8.5.1977 in Hanasaari)* (Helsinki, 1978), pp. 223–41 (p. 231).
[131] See the extensive correspondence in FO 371/19432, N13/56 (1935), esp. letter from Godfrey (military attaché to Finland, the Baltic states and Poland) of 2 December 1935, N6644/13/56.
[132] Turtola, 'Deutschland und Finnland', p. 237.
[133] Col. Lundqvist's views on Swedish and Finnish purchases of aircraft, as reported in Henderson to FO, 29 May 1935, FO 371/19437, N2937/231/63.
[134] FO to Grant Watson (Helsinki), 3 June 1936, FO 371/20328, N 2727/52/56.

at a time when they were trying to build up their own air forces, both were constrained by limited manufacturing capacity. Indeed Göring advised Field-Marshal Mannerheim, when the latter visited Germany in the autumn of 1934, that if the Finns wanted large numbers of aircraft quickly they should place their orders in Britain.[135] In Britain, meanwhile, the Bristol Aircraft Company's reluctance to modify Blenheim bombers to meet Finnish requirements provoked a vigorous complaint from the Foreign Office:

We are now on the point of issuing an invitation to visit this country to Field-Marshal Mannerheim, the most influential personality in Finland, who has hitherto been inclined to favour a German rather than a British orientation for his Government's policy both in political and commercial matters; and if this question is not satisfactorily settled in the near future, the trouble and expenditure which we are about to incur in connexion with his visit will, I fear, be largely wasted.[136]

Mannerheim was the most distinguished, but not the only Finnish officer to visit Britain.[137] An early contact was with Colonel Paasonen, formerly military attaché in Moscow and Berlin, who came to London in 1935 to share intelligence on the Soviet Union with the War Office.[138] Others included Colonel (later General) Lundqvist, the conspicuously pro-British and anti-Nazi head of the air force, and General Österman, chief of the general staff. Mannerheim, who had been impressed by what he had seen at the Hendon air show in 1934, met Eden on the occasion of King George V's funeral in January 1936, and returned to Britain in September for specially arranged tank manoeuvres and visits to Vickers-Armstrong and the Bristol Aircraft Company.[139] Further evidence of British activity was provided by the appointment in 1936 of an air attaché to Finland and the Baltic states (the proposal having been turned down by the Air Ministry in 1935). The first holder of the post, Wing-Commander West, proved an exceptionally able salesman.[140]

The Finnish decision to rely very largely on Bristol Blenheims for their bomber fleet was the most conspicuous British success in the sphere of arms supply. Resulting from a combination of direct political pressure, the good relations established by the air attaché and technical considerations, the

---

[135] Turtola, 'Deutschland und Finnland', pp. 233–4; Stig Jägerskiöld, *Mannerheim mellan världskrigen* (Helsinki, 1972), p. 169.

[136] Eden to Lord Swinton (secretary of state for air), 25 July 1936, FO 371/20328, N3311/52/56.

[137] Jägerskiöld, *Mannerheim mellan världskrigen*, pp. 159–80.

[138] Henderson to Collier, 25 May 1935, FO 371/19436, N2659/573/56. Paasonen was to play an important role in Paris in 1939–40 in promoting plans for Allied intervention in the Soviet–Finnish Winter War.

[139] Baron C. G. E. Mannerheim, *The Memoirs of Marshal Mannerheim* (London, 1953), pp. 281–2, 286–9; Mannerheim–Eden conversation, 31 January 1936, FO 371/20330, N623/623/56; correspondence on September visit in FO 371/20328, 52/56. Mannerheim's visit was used by D. N. Pritt to confirm Finland's status as a British 'client state': *Must the War Spread?* (London, 1940), pp. 131–2 ('The Baron dines in London').

[140] P. R. Reid, *Winged Diplomat: The Life Story of Air Commodore Freddie West* (London, 1962), pp. 133–42.

decision was justified in that it provided Finland with a relatively large supply of modern aircraft, either imported directly from Britain or built under licence, with which to face the Soviet air force in the Winter War of 1939–40.[141] From the British point of view, the function of supplying arms to Finland was wholly political and commercial rather than strategic. A priority list for British arms exports drawn up in 1937 placed Finland in a remarkably high position: eleventh out of a total of thirty-seven countries, immediately followed by Estonia, Latvia and Lithuania.[142] The three Scandinavian countries did not figure on the list at all. This priority did not represent any suggestion that Finland could be of direct military value to Britain, or that Britain could afford any assistance to Finland in time of war; it was, rather, a tribute to the determination of the Foreign Office to keep Britain in the running in the contest for political influence in the eastern Baltic.

A more public expression of British interest in the region was the visit of Lord Plymouth, the under-secretary of state for foreign affairs, to Finland and the Baltic states in May 1937. Conceived as a counterpart to Eden's tour of the three Scandinavian capitals in 1934, it is significant that on this occasion the initiative came from the British side – and indeed from the head of the Foreign Office, Sir Robert Vansittart. His suggestion that a 'fairly well-known British personage' should visit Finland was made immediately after Mannerheim's departure from London in October 1936. Vansittart was, he said, 'strongly in favour of such a visit to Finland. It is an important country and gets few important British visitors. It needs something of this kind, for we have a willing public there; but our position has been let down of late years, and we have to face increasing German competition.'[143]

Lord Plymouth was a much less charismatic figure than Eden, but his presence in Helsinki gave welcome support to the efforts of the new centre–left coalition government, and particularly of Foreign Minister Holsti, to strengthen Finland's relations with 'the Anglo-Saxon world'.[144] Coming only a few months after Holsti's successful visit to Moscow, his tour of the Baltic prompted considerable German annoyance while being greeted by *Izvestia* as part of a policy which was 'proving a severe obstacle to the aggressive policy of the fascist powers'.[145] The Plymouth visit should also be seen in the context of

[141] Turtola, 'Deutschland und Finnland', p. 235.
[142] Kaiser, *Economic Diplomacy*, p. 182. The first ten countries, in order, were: Egypt, Afghanistan, Belgium, Portugal, Turkey, Saudi Arabia, Yugoslavia, Greece, Argentina and the Netherlands.
[143] Collier to Gurney (Helsinki), 3 October 1936, FO 371/20328, N3967/52/56.
[144] Gurney to Collier, 25 January 1937, FO 371/21083, N603/603/63.
[145] On German and Soviet reactions, see Snow (Helsinki) telegram to FO, 31 May 1937, and FO minutes, ibid., N2387/603/63; Mackillop (Moscow) to FO, 8 June 1937, ibid., N3164/603/63. Collier minuted (22 June 1937): 'The description of what was in our minds when planning Lord Plymouth's visit is, though exaggerated, not altogether untrue!' Contrast the contemporary Soviet reaction to the visit with that of D. N. Pritt, a Soviet sympathiser, in 1940: *Must the War Spread?*, pp. 128–31.

the renewed commercial offensive – directed, as we shall see, principally towards Finland – which was undertaken by Britain in the late 1930s. The *Economist*'s account of the visit contained an echo of the sentiments expressed by Ashton Gwatkin in 1935, with its suggestion that, for Finland and the Baltic states, Britain was 'their commercial – and in many ways their political – metropolis'.[146]

It is obvious in retrospect – and it was becoming clear at the time – that none of these measures was sufficient to arrest the decline of Britain's political influence in northern Europe, any more than Britain could sustain the commercial pre-eminence it had enjoyed in the early 1930s. Yet just as the Germans were wary of underrating Great Britain as a commercial competitor, so they were not inclined to write Britain off as a political presence in the region.

A memorandum written by Grundherr on the occasion of Sandler's visit to Berlin in May 1937 provides a corrective to the familiar picture of British weakness and incapacity.[147] Much of what he had to say about British policy was either inaccurate or misconceived. Britain had not offered to buy up the entire production of Swedish iron ore if Sweden agreed to place an embargo on its export; it was not promoting Soviet interests under the guise of working for peace; nor was it consciously engaged in the 'political and economic encirclement' of Germany. Yet Grundherr grasped something of the way in which Britain and Scandinavia had gravitated towards each other ideologically, producing a situation in which Germany could not regard the prospect of Scandinavian neutrality in a future war with as much confidence as it had been able to do in 1914–18:

The present *rapprochement* in Scandinavia, which is essentially under Social Democratic rule, with Sweden taking the lead, and democratic Britain, whereby Scandinavia is drawn into at least the intellectual realm of British politics, is hardly reconcilable any longer with the spirit of real neutrality . . . Against this background, any of M. Sandler's assurances that Sweden is carrying out a policy of strict neutrality will have to be regarded with some scepticism. At any rate Sweden would not adopt, in a parallel situation today, so benevolent a neutrality towards Germany as she did in 1914, and, perhaps, under British pressure she would not be in a position to do so.[148]

Within little more than a year the situation had been transformed. In the summer of 1938 the Nordic countries returned to a position of strict neutrality; in September the Munich conference demonstrated the fate of small countries which relied too heavily on the support of the Western powers. After Munich the editor of *The Times*, Geoffrey Dawson, passed on to the foreign secretary, Lord Halifax, a suggestion that the Swedish foreign minister should be invited to Britain in order to counteract 'the idea that Britain has gone defeatist'.[149] Cadogan, the permanent under-secretary, minuted:

---

[146] 'Lord Plymouth Flies to the Baltic', *Economist*, 29 May 1937.
[147] Memorandum of 20 May 1937, *DGFP*, D, VI, pp. 768–70.
[148] Ibid., p. 770.   [149] Dawson to Halifax, 24 November 1938, FO 800/322.

But I don't quite know what encouragement we *can* give Herr Sandler. M. Boheman, the Head of the Swedish FO, told me, three or four weeks ago, that the *feeling* against Germany in Sweden was marked and almost universal. If, with such a feeling, the Swedes are trying to placate Germany, that means they are conscious of being in the grip of Germany's superior power, and unless we can convince them that Germany is *not* in a position to dominate their part of the continent, I don't know what we can say that will do much good.[150]

The contest for markets and influence in Scandinavia 1937–1939

The serious recession in the world economy between late 1937 and early 1939 put Britain's balance of payments under pressure. It was a time when British production was heavily committed to rearmament, and when exports were meeting with increased competition from a German economy which had been largely sealed off from the recessionary forces in the outside world. The renewed economic policy debate within government and industry revolved around three main options. One was to return to multilateralism. The tripartite monetary agreement of September 1936 between the United States, Great Britain and France pointed in this direction. So too did the trade liberalisation programme of the American secretary of state Cordell Hull, and the tariff-reduction proposals put forward in 1937, on behalf of the Oslo Group, by the Dutch and Belgian prime ministers Hendrik Colijn and Paul Van Zeeland.[151] With extreme reluctance and partly for political reasons, the British government was pushed into a partial dismantlement of imperial preference in the trade agreement concluded with the United States in November 1938, but that was as far as it was prepared to go.[152] A second option was to head off the threat of German competition through cartel agreements; the third was to return to the bilateralist methods of export promotion which had worked in the early 1930s. The two latter approaches had serious implications for the Nordic countries. In some respects diametrically opposed, they were linked by the enigmatic figure of Robert Hudson, secretary of state for overseas trade, who emerged in 1938–9 as a leading advocate of an economic and political rapprochement with Germany, and as a vigorous bilateralist in Anglo-Scandinavian trade.[153]

---

[150] Minute of 28 November 1938, ibid.
[151] Cordell Hull, *Memoirs*, vol. I (London, 1948), chs. 26–7; Ger van Roon, *Small States in Years of Depression: The Oslo Alliance 1930–1940* (Assen and Maastricht, 1989), ch. 7.
[152] Carl Kreider, *The Anglo-American Trade Agreement: A Study of British and American Commercial Policies 1934–1939* (Princeton, N. J., 1942); C. A. MacDonald, *The United States, Britain and Appeasement 1936–1939* (London, 1981), pp. 110–11; R. A. C. Parker, *Chamberlain and Appeasement: British Policy and the Coming of the Second World War* (London, 1993), pp. 299–301.
[153] Hudson was particularly disliked by American anti-appeasers. One State Department official wrote: 'He is ready to sacrifice people to pounds sterling' (quoted in Donald Cameron Watt, *How War Came: The Immediate Origins of the Second World War* (London,

The attempt to maximise exports led attention to be focused once again on countries with which Britain had very large adverse trade balances, among which those of Scandinavia still figured prominently. British officials were becoming worried by the evidence of Britain's growing uncompetitiveness in Nordic markets. In a comprehensive report on Denmark written at the beginning of 1939 the commercial secretary in Copenhagen, E. G. Cable, identified a number of weaknesses.[154] In some respects, he suggested, the Anglo-Scandinavian trade agreements had been almost too successful in that they had encouraged British commerce to look to Scandinavia without fundamentally altering its practices. The size of the Danish market had tended to 'blind some United Kingdom manufacturers to the actual limitations of the market'. Of British exports, 36 per cent were taken up by coal, oil and certain iron and steel products; the rest of the market was shared by up to 3,000 British manufacturers, 'each doing a very small amount of business'. The result of unrestrained export competition – which Cable contrasted with both Danish and German practice – was that new business openings did 'not mean an extension of trade but merely increased competition for firms already established on the market'. Many of the reasons cited for the failure of British industry to secure export orders in the late 1930s were familiar ones. They included high prices, international cartel arrangements and general lack of enterprise.[155] Others, such as delivery delays, were specific to the immediate pre-war period and affected German exports as well: in both cases the internal demand generated by rearmament was a primary cause.[156]

Dominated by a preoccupation with the balance of trade, the renewed British export offensive of the late 1930s largely bypassed Norway, with which Britain's deficit was not unduly great. Denmark again came under pressure through its dependence on the British market for the sale of butter, eggs and bacon, which Britain could obtain without too much difficulty from other sources. In the spring of 1938 and again in 1939, Denmark was obliged to agree to buy extra goods to the value of £1 million.[157] Finland was a particular object of attention. By 1937, Britain's adverse balance of trade with Finland amounted to over £16 million, one of the largest with any country in the world.[158] Finally Sweden, having been left relatively undisturbed, began to feel

1989), p. 139). But Hudson was also in favour of government intervention to block German commercial expansion in south-east Europe. He also (during his visit to Moscow in March 1939) favoured an Anglo-Soviet agreement. The element common to these disparate objectives appears to have been personal ambition: ibid., pp. 90, 219–20.

[154] 'Report on Expansion of United Kingdom Exports to Denmark', 11 January 1939, FO 371/23635, N323/310/15.

[155] Memorandum by E. R. Lingeman (commercial secretary, Helsinki), 24 October 1938, FO 371/22268, N5386/495/56 (and numerous other complaints from Finland in this volume and the next, FO 371/22269).

[156] E.g. report from Finland in RfdA, 'Vertraulicher Sonderdienst der Nachrichten für Aussenhandel', 5 March 1937, ZSta., AA 67803.

[157] Ramsay to FO, 6 January 1938, FO 419/32, N107/107/15; Nilson, *Handelspolitik*, pp. 141–2.

[158] Board of Trade to FO, 14 December 1938, FO 371/22269, N6169/495/56.

the full force of British commercial pressure at the beginning of 1939. British efforts were hampered by the constraints which had operated since the early 1930s: the resistance of agricultural interests to any weakening of protection, and the Board of Trade's refusal to go further down the bilateralist path through the imposition of clearing arrangements on Anglo-Scandinavian trade. Yet it was becoming more difficult to reject the Board's objections as mere dogma when they were endorsed by an increasingly powerful United States.[159] British policy therefore relied on the methods that had worked at the beginning of the decade. There was the same stress on a 'moral' obligation to reduce excessively favourable trade balances and, in the absence of radical solutions such as clearings, the same reliance on increased purchases of British goods by state and municipal authorities.

Three hundred businessmen and advertisers visited Finland in July 1936 to investigate the prospects for British trade, and a delegation of leading Finnish industrialists, together with the trade minister, visited Britain in February 1937. In August Hudson held talks with the Finnish foreign minister and prime minister in which he stressed the need for Finland to buy more British goods. The pressure was resumed in 1938, with a trade delegation to Finland led by Sir Norman Vernon, chairman of the Finnish section of the London Chamber of Commerce.[160] Britain's efforts were watched closely by the German authorities.[161] From the German point of view, the Finns stood up well to British pressure. Even businessmen closely connected with British trade, like Sir Henrik Ramsay, referred to high prices and delivery delays as the main obstacles to increased sales, rather than any reluctance on the part of potential customers or the policies of the Finnish government. There was no reason to expect any immediate results from the visit of Vernon's delegation:

The English tone and England's insistence on increased Finnish purchases in England are, however, becoming ever clearer, probably in consequence of the fact that the English rearmament programme is gradually nearing completion. The Finns have, however, managed to avoid making any binding commitments.[162]

Recognition of the limits of British competitiveness on the part of both business and government led to a renewed export offensive in the autumn of 1938. The Association of British Chambers of Commerce demanded action to promote British exports to Finland on the part of the DOT, and talk of clearings was again in the air.[163] The British legation and the commercial secretary, E. R.

---

[159] On Cordell Hull's objection to clearings, see Rooth, *British Protectionism*, p. 305 (n. 87).

[160] Report of delegation in FO 371/22269, N6169/495/56.

[161] E.g. Blücher (Helsinki) to AA, 19 February 1937, ZSta., AA 67803, and other reports in this file.

[162] Scherpenberg to London embassy, 29 June 1938, ibid.

[163] Memoranda in FO 371/22269, N6169/495/56. See also: conversation between Collier and Finnish minister (Georg Gripenberg), 3 November 1938, FO 371/22268, N5406/495/56; Blücher to AA, 25 October 1938, ZSta., AA 67803; A. R. Ilersic, *Parliament of Commerce: The Story of the Association of British Chambers of Commerce 1860–1960* (London, 1960), pp. 210–12.

Lingeman, were fully alive to the deficiencies of British business methods, but nevertheless made strenuous efforts to persuade government departments, municipalities and state-controlled munitions factories to place orders in Britain. By the time the Board of Trade wrote to the Foreign Office in December 1938 suggesting 'the direction to this country of the orders of the State Purchasing Departments, and of the Finnish municipalities' in accordance with the terms of the 1933 trade agreement, orders worth over £350,000 had already been placed in a little over two months.[164] Meanwhile, the state-controlled Enso-Gutzeit company had placed an order for generators for a new power station with Metropolitan Vickers, the largest order for electrical machinery hitherto obtained by a British firm in Finland.[165] Additional pressure was exerted by Hudson, who was rapidly emerging as the leading exponent of bilateralism in government circles. Whilst talking about cartels to the Germans, he threatened the Finns with the imposition of a clearing.[166]

It was understandable that the German authorities should have interpreted these efforts as part of a wider strategy aimed at maintaining and extending Britain's commercial position in the Baltic 'as a counterweight to German commercial policy in south-east Europe'.[167] Something like this was indeed being advocated by the Foreign Office (see pp. 313–15). But for the Board of Trade the primary consideration was the need to reduce Britain's adverse balance of trade with Finland. And if the Board's preoccupations were orthodox, so too were its remedies. It recognised that there were limits to what could be achieved by Finnish government action but was not prepared to consider a clearing or even an import licensing system on the Danish model. As Collier pointed out, this made it difficult for the British minister in Helsinki to make representations on behalf of British trade.[168]

Yet in 1939 Britain unquestionably intensified its demands on Finland and, increasingly, on Sweden as well; and there is little doubt that the pressure would have been maintained if war had not broken out. As the German embassy in London noted, Britain was 'emphasising to an increasing extent the bilateral character of its commercial relations with countries outside the empire, by equalising imports and exports as much as possible'.[169] The clearest expression of this approach was the visit of Robert Hudson (accompanied by Ashton Gwatkin and officials from the Board of Trade and DOT) to Helsinki and Stockholm in late March and early April 1939.[170] In

---

[164] BT to FO, 14 December 1938, FO 371/22269, N6169/495/56; Gurney (Helsinki) to FO, 19 December 1938, ibid., N6360/495/56.

[165] Blücher to AA, 28 November 1938, ZSta., AA 67803.

[166] Conversation with Sir Henrik Ramsay and the Finnish minister, 17 November 1938, FO 371/22268, N5670/495/56. Ashton Gwatkin minuted (24 November 1938, ibid.): 'The B. of T. are alarmed at Mr Hudson's bilateralism.'

[167] RfdA to AA, 28 October 1938, ZSta., AA 67803.

[168] Collier to Kelf-Cohen (Board of Trade), 4 January 1939, FO 371/22269, N6169/495/56.

[169] London embassy to AA, 29 March 1939, ZSta., AA 67803.

[170] Hudson report on visit to northern capitals, 18 March–4 April 1939, FO 371/23654, N1907/64/63.

both capitals Hudson made it clear that he expected government and industry to find ways of increasing the purchase of British goods. He proposed that this should be done by sending delegations of industrialists to London. As far as Finland was concerned, such a visit would build on the significant efforts already made by the Finns. Hudson's tone was therefore conciliatory and unthreatening.[171] A Finnish industrial delegation duly negotiated with the London Chamber of Commerce in April and agreed to substantial purchases of British electrical and iron and steel products (though the DOT noted that the Finns were 'undoubtedly hard bargainers').[172]

The Swedes were not prepared to give way so readily.[173] They argued that the British demand for a greater equalisation of the trade balance between the two countries would oblige Sweden to introduce a state-controlled foreign trade system, and that 'If Sweden was forced to adopt a closed economy or regulated economy it would throw her increasingly into the arms of Germany.'[174] Swedish officials and industrialists also alleged (tendentiously) that Anglo-German cartel agreements prevented the sale of British goods in Sweden and (incorrectly) that they were prevented by the terms of the Swedish–American trade agreement from entering into purchase agreements with British industries. Hudson was irritated by the unforthcoming attitude of the Swedish government and warned the industrialists that, if they did not conclude preferential agreements, Britain would be obliged to consider adopting drastic measures against Swedish trade. The implicit threat to impose a clearing had some effect. The Swedes agreed to send an industrial delegation, which ultimately arrived in London at the beginning of July 1939.

The British were alarmed at the thoroughness with which the Swedes had prepared for the negotiations, since this implied that they had hoped to establish 'the reasons why, in a number of branches of trade, we are unable to compete'. The impression was that they were 'preparing a destructive criticism of UK export methods, rather than searching for any constructive suggestions for the improvement of our position in Swedish trade'.[175] More disturbingly, the size of the delegation, the largest ever to have left the country, and the presence on it of some of the most prominent figures in Swedish industrial life suggested 'that on the report issued by the Mission will largely depend the attitude of Swedish industrialists, exporters and merchants towards the United Kingdom in the event of war'.[176]

---

[171] Snow to FO, 10 April 1939, FO 433/6, N2002/429/56.
[172] Circular letter summarised in London embassy to AA, 10 May 1939, ZSta., AA 67803. For details of the discussions, see BT 59/25/625; Schröter, *Aussenpolitik und Wirtschaftsinteresse*, pp. 106–7.
[173] Schröter, *Aussenpolitik und Wirtschaftsinteresse*, pp. 107–8; Nilson, *Handelspolitik*, pp. 143–9.
[174] Sandler in conversation with Hudson, 1 April 1939, quoted in Nilson, *Handelspolitik*, pp. 145–6.
[175] Minute by L. C. S. Barber (assistant commercial secretary, Stockholm), 4 May 1939, BT 59/27/634.
[176] Bluett (Stockholm) to Jopson (DOT), 13 June 1939, ibid.

The negotiations between the FBI and Swedish business representatives from 4 to 7 July, covering forty different groups of products, proved reassuringly amicable.[177] The atmosphere of the talks was generally friendly, and the Swedes showed a 'desire to obtain positive results' without, however, wishing to make concrete commitments. Serious controversy arose in only one case, when the British textile industry, suffering severely from Japanese competition in the Swedish market, demanded guaranteed import quotas on the model of the coal agreements of 1933. The Swedish delegates rejected the proposal, and indeed the only positive result of the discussions was an agreement to establish a British–Swedish chamber of commerce in Stockholm. However, the Swedes left London with the very clear understanding that, if they did not do more to increase imports, they must expect a clearing to be imposed on Anglo-Swedish trade.

There is an interesting difference of emphasis among historians as to the significance of the Anglo-Swedish discussions. For Schröter, they demonstrate the continuing structural defects which rendered British exports uncompetitive despite the efforts of both sides to open up new market opportunities. For Nilson, they mark a stage in the increasing bilateralism of British policy in the course of 1939. The Treasury's resistance to clearings had weakened; only the Board of Trade remained firmly opposed to their introduction. The threat did not materialise in the summer of 1939 because Britain's dependence on imports of strategic raw materials such as iron ore, pulp and timber meant that it could not risk a trade war with Sweden. In this sense, Nilson suggests, Sweden benefited from Anglo-German confrontation. Détente between London and Berlin 'might open the door to a renewed British commercial offensive against Sweden'.[178] The fact that an Anglo-German cartel agreement had been successfully concluded in March 1939 was thus more significant than its subsequent shipwreck in the aftermath of the German occupation of Prague. It was an indication that countries like Sweden stood to lose at least as much through cooperation between the two powers as through conflict. From a British perspective, however, one of the most notable aspects of the discussions is the respect, even deference, shown by British officials and businessmen towards their Swedish counterparts. In the British anxiety to make a good impression and to ensure that their negotiators were well prepared lay a tacit recognition that Sweden was a formidable economic power in its own right.

With the renewed foreign exchange crisis of 1936, followed by the adoption in the autumn of the Four-Year Plan under Göring's direction, the function of German foreign trade came increasingly to be defined in strategic terms. In the short term it was to serve what Posse termed 'the primacy of imports': enabling

---

[177] Schröter, *Aussenpolitik und Wirtschaftsinteresse*, pp. 110–11; Nilson, *Handelspolitik*, pp. 150–3.
[178] Nilson, *Handelspolitik*, p. 153.

Germany to maintain the import of strategic raw materials that would be indispensable until it achieved self-sufficiency, or acquired the necessary resources by territorial expansion.[179] In the longer term the aim was to achieve German economic and political hegemony over continental Europe, including Scandinavia. A study of 'the prospects for a *Grossraumwirtschaft* under German leadership' produced by the Reichsamt für Wirtschaftsausbau (Reich Office for Economic Development) in July 1939 concluded that 'the inclusion of the Northern sphere is indispensable for the *Grosswirtschaftsraum*'.[180]

This required a more direct challenge to the British position in Scandinavia than had hitherto been attempted. In August 1936 Ritter spoke merely of 'catching up with Britain's economic lead' in Scandinavia.[181] By the beginning of 1937 he was hinting at a more systematic effort, informing the German minister in Oslo that he had been considering for some time the idea of 'directing our commercial activity rather more strongly towards the Scandinavian region', following the successful cultivation of trading relations with south-east Europe, South America and the Far East.[182]

But it was increasingly difficult to maintain the momentum of German exports in the face of raw material and labour shortages, and at a time when domestic consumption was claiming a growing share of production. Scandinavian complaints about high prices (despite export subsidies), delivery delays and the reduced quality of German goods resulting from the increased use of substitute materials were indications of the strain imposed on Germany's export capacity by rearmament.[183] Sustaining the flow of exports, however, was essential not only to secure raw material supplies but also to retain the political influence that would be of vital importance in wartime. The problem was exemplified by the case of Denmark where, in the view of the German minister, German influence derived largely from the market offered by Germany to Danish agricultural produce, but where the clearing mechanism dictated that the size of this market depended on the amount Germany was able to sell to Denmark. If German exports were not maintained, 'it would not only mean a loss of sympathy, but we would thereby cause Denmark to intensify her relations with other countries and thus undermine our own political influence'.[184] To an increasing degree, therefore, the dependence induced by bilateral trade was mutual.

This was the background to the German 'export offensive' from 1937 onwards, aimed in the first instance at securing supplies of iron ore from

[179] Hans Ernst Posse, 'Die Hauptlinien der deutschen Handelspolitik', in Deutsches Institut für Bankwissenschaft und Bankwesen (ed.), *Probleme des deutschen Wirtschaftslebens. Erstrebtes und Erreichtes* (Leipzig, 1937), pp. 481–513 (p. 503).
[180] Quoted in Schröter, *Aussenpolitik und Wirtschaftsinteresse*, p. 114.
[181] Foreign ministry circular, 17 August 1936, *DGFP*, C, V, pp. 901–12.
[182] Ritter to Sahm, 27 January 1937, PA, AA Handakten Wiehl, Norwegen, Bd 2.
[183] E.g. Swedish complaints detailed in German chamber of commerce in Sweden to Aussenhandelsamt der AO, 11 February 1939, ZSta., AA 67969.
[184] Renthe-Fink to AA, 24 February 1937, ZSta., AA 67734.

Sweden, but also directed towards Norway and Finland, both of which were of growing importance to Germany as raw material suppliers.[185] However, Denmark was not neglected. A Danish official noted in October 1937 that the Germans had carried out in full the promises made earlier in the year that Denmark would be given preferential treatment in the supply of raw materials and finished goods from Germany.[186] The combined efforts of the German legations and chambers of commerce in Scandinavia, of the Reichsgruppe Industrie (RI)[187] and of the authorities in Berlin led to a marked increase in German exports in 1938, at a time when the more open British economy was suffering from recession.

German attitudes displayed an increasing self-confidence. In the course of 1938 German officials intensified their drive to 'Aryanise' the business connections of German firms in Scandinavia.[188] The cartel discussions between the RI and the FBI early in 1939 showed that the German side had no intention of compromising its position in Scandinavia, and in December 1938 Schacht went so far as to 'intimate that there could be no Anglo-German arrangements of this sort unless His Majesty's Government dropped their present policy of making purchase agreements for the Scandinavian and Baltic countries and returned to a strict most-favoured-nation policy'.[189] Above all, despite occasional hints to the contrary, there was no intention that Germany should abandon or modify its existing commercial practices in order to bring them into line with those of Britain or the United States.

In the period after the Munich conference in September 1938 the British Foreign Office detected increasing 'evidence of an impending German drive, both political and economic, in Scandinavia and the Baltic countries'.[190] It took several forms. Indications of a German commercial offensive continued to accumulate. Ashton Gwatkin, not a man inclined to overrate the threat of German competition, noted in November 1938: 'I think our commercial policy will soon have trouble in the Baltic.'[191] More disquietingly, the German government started to intervene with unprecedented directness in Scandinavian internal affairs. The foreign editor of the Danish paper *Berlingske Tidende*,

---

[185] Schröter, *Aussenpolitik und Wirtschaftsinteresse*, pp. 90–1, 94–6.
[186] Memorandum by Nils Svenningsen, 18 October 1937, RA, Munch arkiv III, Pakke 76. See also the memorandum by the RfdA of 3 December 1938, quoted in Schröter, *Aussenpolitik und Wirtschaftsinteresse*, p. 94.
[187] Successor to the Reichsverband der Deutschen Industrie (RDI).
[188] Danish objections to the exclusion of Jewish agents were expressed in the trade discussions of 1–6 July 1938: Danish Foreign Ministry memorandum, 'Anvendelse af jødiske Agenter i den dansk–tyske Samhandel', 20 July 1938, RA, Munch arkiv III, Pakke 73. The German counter-arguments are recorded in a memorandum by Ludwig, 16 August 1938, ZSta., AA 67777. For evidence of pressure on Norwegian firms, see Dormer (Oslo) to FO, 28 December 1938, FO 371/23653, N74/64/63.
[189] *DGFP*, D, IV, pp. 423–6; conversation between Collier and Finnish minister, 21 December 1938, FO 371/22277, N6307/5766/63.
[190] Lord Halifax (foreign secretary) to Oliver Stanley (president of the Board of Trade), 1 February 1939, FO 371/23653, N260/64/63.
[191] Minute of 9 November 1938, FO 371/22268, N5406/495/56.

Nicolaj Blædel, was dismissed following a complaint by the German minister about an editorial which was critical of German actions in the Sudetenland; and pressure was successfully brought to bear on the Swedish government to curb unfavourable comment in the press.[192] The German minister in Helsinki complained about a speech in which the Finnish prime minister, Cajander, had suggested a greater use of English and French in Finnish schools and advocated increased purchases of British goods. Germany, Blücher declared, was an expanding state to which others must give way.[193] In November the Finnish foreign minister Holsti was forced to resign following an alleged remark that 'Herr Hitler was a mad dog and should be destroyed'.[194]

To an increasing extent, it appeared that Germany intended to establish an economic and political sphere of influence in Scandinavia and the Baltic. Moreover, in the aftermath of the Anglo-French capitulation at Munich, it was being suggested that Britain might acquiesce in this development. Blædel told Collier in November that it was being asked in Denmark 'whether the present British Government were not deliberately conniving at Herr Hitler's ambitions in order to protect their own interests elsewhere, and planning to divide up the world with him, as Napoleon and Alexander of Russia had done at Tilsit'.[195] A few days later Soloveytchik said that the German press was suggesting that Britain 'had recognised the Continent of Europe, and particularly Eastern and Northern Europe, as a German economic preserve, and latterly quoting in support of this contention the prime minister's words in the House of Commons about recognising Germany's right to economic expansion in the Balkans etc.'.[196]

Both Blædel and Soloveytchik advised, and Collier agreed, that there should be 'a public statement by a prominent member of His Majesty's Government – if possible, the prime minister himself – denying explicitly any intention of abdicating our commercial or cultural position in that part of the world'.[197] Early in December the Foreign Office asked the legations in the Scandinavian and Baltic capitals and the Berlin embassy if there was any evidence to support the two journalists' statements, while Ashton Gwatkin asked Leith-Ross to

---

[192] 'Memorandum by the Head of Political Division VI', c. 8 November 1938, *DGFP*, D, V, pp. 604–7; Collier minute, recording conversation with the British journalist George Soloveytchik, 12 November 1938, FO 371/22277, N5567/5567/63; Yngve Möller, *Rickard Sandler. Folkbildare. Utrikesminister* (Stockholm, 1990), p. 348. Blædel was reinstated in December, so that it was 'only a half-victory for Renthe-Fink': Sjøqvist, *Danmarks udenrigspolitik*, pp. 250–1.

[193] Snow to FO, reporting conversation with Holsti, 27 October 1938, FO 371/22265, N5489/64/56.

[194] Gurney (Helsinki) to FO, 14 November 1938, ibid., N5586/64/56. In a later despatch Gurney (22 November 1938, ibid., N5864/64/56) reported that German pressure was not the only reason for Holsti's departure but had been seized on by the latter's enemies as a pretext – on which Collier remarked (minute of 3 December 1938) that this could not have happened before Munich.

[195] Collier minute, 9 November 1938, FO 371/22262, N5566/253/15.

[196] Collier minute, 12 November 1938, FO 371/22277, N5567/5567/63.

[197] Collier minute, 14 November 1938, FO 371/22265, N5489/64/56.

investigate the extent of German commercial competition in the region.[198] The replies to the Foreign Office's enquiry were inconclusive.[199] There was no doubt about Germany's overbearing behaviour, but little sign of a German propaganda drive. The most perceptive comments came from Berlin. Solo-veytchik was quite wrong, wrote Sir George Ogilvie-Forbes, to suggest that Germany assumed Britain to have renounced its interest in south-eastern, let alone northern Europe.[200] On the contrary, 'every incident which can be connected with a British commercial offensive in Central and Eastern Europe is used to substantiate the theory of British opposition to legitimate German interests'. Ogilvie-Forbes was quite prepared to believe that a German commercial drive in northern Europe was impending,

but I would incline to ascribe it . . . to the urgent necessity with which the German Government find themselves faced at present of increasing their exports and of thus securing foreign exchange. As the Scandinavian countries possess free currencies, whereas few of Germany's other neighbours do, they are all the more desirable customers and are accordingly among the first to be singled out as objects of this increased activity.

There was nevertheless no doubt that Germany's political prestige had been vastly enhanced, and that the regime's recent actions displayed 'a complete intolerance of criticism on the part of Germany towards her weaker neighbours'.[201]

On 21 December 1938 (before most of the replies had been received), Collier wrote the first draft of a memorandum on 'German Aims in Northern Europe'.[202] By the end of January, having been redrafted several times by Collier and Ashton Gwatkin, the memorandum comprised a compendium of examples of German pressure on the Scandinavian and Baltic countries together with two proposals for action: first a ministerial statement of British interest in northern Europe; second an enquiry into whether clearings should be imposed on Britain's trade with the countries of the region.[203]

The timing of the initiative was unfortunate. It originated at a time when the government was expressing strong support for economic appeasement, in the form of high-level discussions between British and German industrial organisa-tions (the Anglo-German coal agreement was signed in January 1939 as a preliminary to the more wide-ranging negotiations to be held in March between the FBI and the RI). Collier was anxious lest, despite the FBI's

---

[198] FO despatch, 6 December 1938, FO 371/22262, N5566/253/15; Ashton Gwatkin to Leith Ross, 30 November 1938, FO 371/21706, C14456/772/18.

[199] Ramsay to FO, 15 December 1938, FO 371/22262, N6276/253/15; Dormer to FO, 17 December 1939, FO 371/23653, N64/64/63; Monson (Stockholm) to FO, 3 January 1939, ibid., N282/64/63.

[200] Ogilvie-Forbes to FO, 29 December 1938, FO 371/22277, N6383/5766/63.

[201] The British government did in fact take steps to increase British purchases from the countries of south-east Europe in the period after Munich: see Kaiser, *Economic Diplomacy*, pp. 286–95.

[202] FO 371/22277, N6261/5766/63.

[203] Undated draft memorandum, FO 371/23653, N260/64/63.

assurances to the contrary, British economic interests in Scandinavia might be sacrificed.[204] The proposal also suffered from the decision by Halifax and senior Foreign Office officials that no public statement should be made until the results of the enquiry into clearings became known.[205] It soon became apparent that the Board of Trade under Oliver Stanley was no more prepared to consider the adoption of clearings than it had been under his predecessor Runciman.[206] The Foreign Office's exchanges with the Board lasted until March 1939; the situation was then transformed by the German occupation of Bohemia, followed at the end of the month by rumours of German pressure on Romania.[207] Whitehall's shift from appeasement to containment was expressed in the British guarantee to Poland of 31 March.[208] The change was welcome in itself to anti-appeasers like Collier, but in the administrative confusion of late March his Scandinavian proposal was first submerged and then abandoned.[209]

As to the accuracy of Collier's analysis of German intentions, there is no doubt, as we have seen, of the intensification of German export activity in Scandinavia and the Baltic. On the other hand, as Ogilvie-Forbes pointed out, there was little sign of complacency about the likely British response. The German press did not speak with one voice. The German chamber of commerce in Sweden noted in February 1939 that there were two distinct opinions among German journalists: one, that the press should publicise every German success; the other, 'with which we are in total agreement, that such publications should be avoided in all circumstances' lest they provoke a reaction from Germany's competitors.[210] The Nazi Party's Auslands-Organisa-tion, an increasingly influential voice in Germany's foreign relations, shared the chamber of commerce's concern.[211] So too did the Ministry of Economics and the Auswärtiges Amt.[212] On 4 March 1939 the latter issued a detailed directive to the press, urging it to take a united line and warning it against drawing attention to German success in Scandinavia at Britain's expense: 'In contrast to certain other markets, we do not enjoy any kind of monopoly position in Scandinavia, but rather find ourselves in constant sharp competi-

---

[204] Conversation with Lithuanian minister, 7 January 1939, ibid., N151/64/63; conversation between Ashton Gwatkin and Guy Locock (FBI), 12 January 1939, ibid., N260/64/63; Collier minute, 7 March 1939, ibid., N1261/64/63.

[205] Minutes by Oliphant and Cadogan, 17 January 1939, and by Halifax, 18 January 1939, ibid., N260/64/63.

[206] Stanley to Halifax, 6 February 1939, ibid., N702/64/63; Stanley to Halifax, 7 March 1939, ibid., N1308/64/63.

[207] Watt, *How War Came*, pp. 169–76.

[208] Anita Prazmowska, *Britain, Poland and the Eastern Front 1939* (Cambridge, 1987), chs. 2–3.

[209] Minute by Sir Laurence Oliphant, 20 March 1939, FO 371/23653, N1308/64/63.

[210] German chamber of commerce in Sweden to Aussenhandelsamt der AO, 11 February 1939, ZSta., AA 67969.

[211] E. A. Schwartz (AO) to Ludwig (Ministry of Economics), 15 February 1939, ibid. On the role of the AO, see Peter Hayes, *Industry and Ideology*, pp. 197–8.

[212] Ludwig to Scherpenberg, 27 February 1939, ZSta., AA 67969.

tion with England.' Virtually every optimistic or incautious remark was liable to be picked up and exploited by 'English economic propaganda'.[213]

Britain thus remained a formidable economic presence in northern Europe, and one which German officials were in no way inclined to underestimate. A survey of 'German Competition in Denmark, Sweden, Norway and Holland' completed by the DOT in July 1939 suggested that it was still possible to view the situation without undue alarm:

> The broad conclusion of this investigation is that though during the period 1935–8 we have lost ground compared with Germany in Scandinavia we have least to fear from German competition in Denmark, where we hold special advantages so long as the present licensing system remains in force; Sweden and Norway are countries where, owing to the absence of trade restrictions, both the United Kingdom and Germany can compete on comparatively equal terms, apart from the operation of the subsidy system by Germany, while in the case of Holland, Germany possesses advantages owing to geographical and historical factors.[214]

Ashton Gwatkin, for one, was reassured: 'Although the situation wants constant watching, it cannot be regarded as catastrophic; nor is it such as at present to justify a major change in commercial policy such as the adoption of a clearing system.'[215]

Since 1936 the Foreign Office had been on its guard against a German politico-economic offensive in northern Europe which had never quite materialised. Though it had been steadily undermined since 1933, Britain's economic presence in the region remained substantially stronger in 1939 than it had been ten years earlier. Moreover, Scandinavia's incorporation into the *Grossraumwirtschaft* was still far from realisation: indeed a practical basis for its economic integration in the German New Order was created only by the military victories of 1940.[216] What Britain had never managed to do was to build a relationship with Scandinavian businessmen and officials which did not rely primarily on compulsion or threats, or on the constant repetition of an alleged moral obligation to buy British goods. It is true that the Bank of England was notably successful in fostering friendly relations and genuine cooperation with the Nordic central banks, while private banks such as Hambros remained intimately involved with Scandinavian finance; but these achievements did not penetrate far beyond the relatively closed world of banking. German practices were very different. On the whole Germany sold goods which the Nordic countries wished to buy, and gradually eased market opportunities for Scandinavian goods rather than restricting them. Politically, the Nordic countries had more in common with Great Britain than with Nazi Germany. The ties that bound them to Germany were those of bureaucratic routine and economic self-interest. In time of war these were to prove durable enough.

---

[213] Scherpenberg to AA Press Division, 4 March 1939, ibid. (copy in PA, AA Handakten Wiehl, Norwegen, Bd 2).

[214] DOT memorandum, 25 July 1939, FO 371/23656, N3598/64/63.

[215] Minute of 26 July 1939, ibid.   [216] See pp. 365–6 in this volume.

9   Scandinavia and the coming of the Second World War 1933–1940

The strategic plans produced by the great powers before the First World War were abstract, ambitious and largely unrealistic. When British, German and Soviet strategists returned after 1933 to consider the role of Scandinavia in a future war, they did so in the light of experience which their predecessors had lacked. There appear to have been no serious examinations of the possibility of military operations on Scandinavian territory of the kind which loomed so large in pre-1914 deliberations. The primary focus was on economic and naval warfare. For both Great Britain and Germany, the lesson of the last war was that economic pressure on Germany had been of decisive importance. Moreover, in the light of Germany's territorial losses after Versailles and the exploitation of new mineral resources in Scandinavia, it was reasonable to assume that Germany's economic dependence on indigenous Scandinavian products would be greater in both relative and absolute terms than it had been in 1914–18. Scandinavian resources would also be of great importance to Great Britain, but its geographical position, naval superiority, financial resources and world-wide empire would give Britain access to alternative sources of supply and the capacity to deny such access to Germany. Britain's principal aim in wartime would therefore be to enlist the Scandinavian countries in an economic blockade. Germany, by contrast, would require only business as usual.

The logic of British strategy meant not only that the machinery of economic warfare, with all that this implied for the Scandinavian neutrals, must be applied from the very outset, but also that neutrality itself was dispensable. As Winston Churchill expressed it when advocating naval action against the Narvik iron ore traffic in December 1939, 'we have a right, and indeed are bound in duty, to abrogate for a space some of the conventions of the very laws we seek to consolidate and reaffirm. Small nations must not tie our hands when we are fighting for their rights and freedom.'[1] Even before the outbreak of war there were some in Whitehall who had concluded that one economic warfare objective – that of depriving Germany of supplies of Swedish iron ore – was of such vital importance that direct action must be taken on neutral

---

[1] Memorandum of 16 December 1939, printed in Winston S. Churchill, *The Second World War*, vol. I, *The Gathering Storm* (2nd edn, London, 1949), pp. 490–2.

territory to prevent the ore from reaching Germany. But this growing, though tentative, activism was confined to the fringes of the policy-making establishment. The Admiralty remained central to any discussion of the strategic role of Scandinavia in wartime, and here pre-war and wartime orthodoxies continued to flourish. After a brief burst of confidence at the end of the First World War, the Admiralty had returned to its pre-war pessimism about the possibility of naval operations in Danish and Baltic waters – a pessimism reinforced by the development of German air power in the 1930s. On the other hand, the Admiralty remained untroubled in its assumption of naval superiority in the North Sea and the North Atlantic, rendering the possibility of German naval action against Norway virtually unthinkable.

For Nazi Germany, Scandinavian neutrality was of value as long as it ensured that German wartime trade equalled or, if possible, exceeded peacetime levels. The logic of German strategy was thus the maintenance of the status quo. In these circumstances the peacetime patterns of trade discussed in the previous two chapters acquired decisive importance. Not only economic but also military advantage would lie with the power that had mastered most effectively the machinery of bilateralism, for once trade had been diverted into bilateral channels, economic self-interest and institutional inertia tended to keep it there. In Scandinavia, as we have seen, Germany became that power. Yet some German naval strategists drew a different lesson from the First World War. For them, the capacity to mount a sustained resistance to British economic pressure carried less weight than the priority of going on to the offensive in naval warfare against Great Britain. If, as Admiral Wegener and his disciples argued, this required establishing bases in Norway to circumvent Britain's naval stranglehold, Scandinavian neutrality was an irrelevance.

Until December 1939 this view made little headway against the arguments in favour of respecting Scandinavian neutrality. The Soviet invasion of Finland on 30 November 1939 transformed the strategic debate in both Britain and Germany. From December 1939 onward, Britain and France on the one hand, and Germany on the other, developed plans for military intervention in the Scandinavian peninsula which were to culminate in the abortive Anglo-French military expedition to Finland in March 1940 and the successful German invasion of Denmark and Norway in April. But if the British and Germans were increasingly prepared to contemplate violating Scandinavian neutrality, the Soviet Union was the first power actually to do so. The decision to attack Finland, improvised and ill-thought-out though it may have been, also derived from expectations about the nature of a future war which were drawn from past experience. In the Soviet case this encompassed not only the First World War but also, perhaps more importantly, a civil war which had seen both German and British intervention on the side of the enemies of Bolshevism. The Gulf of Finland had been a particularly vulnerable point, and it was hardly surprising that the Soviet leadership should have sought to avert the danger of attack by attempting to reconstitute the tsarist system of land-based and island defences. The problem was that those defensive positions now lay on the territories of independent states: Estonia, Latvia and Finland. In the negotiations which preceded the Soviet invasion, the Soviet Union made clear its scepticism about Finnish declarations of neutrality which were not supported by concrete guarantees. In the last resort the integrity of small neighbouring states must give way to the imperatives of Soviet security.

The Finnish experience, like that of Denmark and Norway, exemplified the 'decline of neutrality' in the inter-war period. The Soviet attack – unprovoked but with a border incident staged to provide a veneer of legality, and accompanied by the establishment of a puppet 'people's government' – drew on Nazi precedents but added refinements of its own. The German plans for Operation Weserübung, the invasion of Denmark and Norway, also contained a characteristic mixture of military and politico-ideological elements. In its earliest (though not its final) form the German occupation of Norway was to be accomplished through a peaceful seizure of power by Quisling. The invasion as ultimately carried out relied for its success on deception and a significant measure of treachery.

The blurring of the distinction between war and peace is reflected in the structure of this chapter. In each section the outbreak of war is treated more as an incident than as a decisive break. This is partly in order to demonstrate the continuity in strategic debate between the pre-war and wartime periods. It is also designed to reflect the experience of the Nordic countries themselves. In the Nordic context the decisive events came before and after September 1939: not, in other words, with the outbreak of a long-anticipated European war, but with the Nazi–Soviet pact of 23 August and with the Soviet attack on Finland at the end of November. The first event destroyed the balance of power in northern Europe; the second ensured that the attention of the great powers would be fixed more firmly on Scandinavia, and with more disastrous consequences, than at any other time in the twentieth century.

Raw materials and naval strategy: Germany and the role of Scandinavia in a future war

As we turn to examine the role of Scandinavia in Nazi Germany's preparations for war, it is important to emphasise that the distinctions drawn in this and earlier chapters between the economic and political, the ideological and the strategic aspects of German policy are there partly as a matter of convenience. They do not reflect clear-cut divisions; indeed, the longer the Nazi regime was in power, the more such divisions ceased to have meaning. The extent to which the various categories of thought had merged becomes clear in the contorted prose of an otherwise lucid and highly professional naval officer, Captain Heinz Assmann, in a study of the strategic problem of the Baltic entrances completed in May 1939:

More and more, under the economic influence of Germany, there will develop, also in the Nordic sphere [*im nordischen Raum*] the recognition of a northern European community of fate [*nordeuropäische Schicksalsgemeinschaft*], from which there is no escape. On the contrary, it will be dependent, through the closest possible political and cultural alignment, on the weal and woe [*Wohl und Wehe*] of a dominant Germany.[2]

If the language is obscure, the meaning is clear enough. The Nordic countries were not only to be incorporated into the German sphere of influence, but would also be of vital importance both as a source of supply and for German naval warfare.

The importance of Scandinavian resources for the German war economy, amply demonstrated in the First World War, was reinforced by a number of developments during the inter-war period. New sources of supply for non-ferrous minerals became available. In Finland the mining of copper ore by the state-owned Outokumpu Company began in 1925, with production going almost exclusively to Germany.[3] Norway was the source of a number of metal ores, including pyrites and nickel, and also used its imports of manganese and chromium ores for the manufacture of ferro-manganese and ferrochrome which were exported to Germany.[4] Europe's largest nickel deposit, discovered in 1924 in the Petsamo district of northern Finland, became an object of British–German competition when it became clear that the reserves were too large to be exploited by Finnish capital alone.[5] Rivalry between the German chemical combine IG Farben and the Mond Nickel Company of London, a wholly owned subsidiary of the International Nickel Company of Canada, was resolved in favour of the latter in 1934.[6] However, production did not begin until 1941, by which time Petsamo nickel had become the focus of a diplomatic contest between Germany, Great Britain and the Soviet Union which helped to precipitate Finland's involvement in the war on Germany's side.[7]

Petsamo attracted German attention for other reasons. A plan to establish a fish-meal factory at Petsamo was supported by the Ministries of Economics and Agriculture, as well as by Göring's Four-Year Plan office, in 1936–7, but met with widespread opposition in Finland both for economic reasons and on the ground that 'the establishment of a German observation post in Arctic

---

[2] 'Studie Ostseezugänge', quoted in Jost Dülffer, *Weimar, Hitler und die Marine. Reichspolitik und Flottenbau 1920–1939* (Düsseldorf, 1973), p. 520. For an assessment of Assmann's talents (with the observation that he was sometimes guilty of stylistic excess), see Michael Salewski, *Die deutsche Seekriegsleitung 1935–1945* (2 vols., Frankfurt am Main, 1970), vol. I, pp. 103–4.

[3] Manfred Menger, *Deutschland und Finnland im Zweiten Weltkrieg. Genesis und Scheitern einer Militärallianz* (Berlin, 1988), p. 27.

[4] Alan S. Milward, *The Fascist Economy in Norway* (Oxford, 1972), pp. 57–9.

[5] H. Peter Krosby, *Finland, Germany and the Soviet Union 1940–1941: The Petsamo Dispute* (Madison, Milwaukee and London, 1968), pp. 4–5.

[6] Gerd R. Ueberschär, *Hitler und Finnland. Die deutsch–finnischen Beziehungen während des Hitler–Stalin-Paktes* (Wiesbaden, 1978), p. 31; Menger, *Deutschland und Finnland*, pp. 27–8.

[7] Krosby, *Finland, Germany and the Soviet Union*.

waters was not desirable'.[8] The British were equally suspicious of the proposal, which was duly vetoed by the Finnish government.[9] The German navy was certainly aware of the strategic potential of Petsamo, yet there is no reason to assume that German interest in Scandinavian fisheries was merely a cover. Norway's importance as a supplier of fish to Germany had been amply demonstrated in the First World War. The expansion of the Norwegian pelagic whaling industry during the inter-war period offered a solution to Germany's chronic deficiency in fats.[10] Germany's dependence on imports of whale oil, despite the expansion of its own whaling fleet through the hiring of Norwegian crews and ships, led a prominent official of the Four-Year Plan, Helmut Wohlthat, to declare early in 1939 that the long-term survival of the Norwegian whaling industry was a matter of vital interest to Germany. It would, he said, be secured by the conclusion of long-term contracts on generous terms.[11]

Since Germany's drive for agricultural self-sufficiency was still far from realisation by the late 1930s, it was clear that Denmark would remain an important source of supply for foodstuffs in wartime. IG Farben's economic experts, who played an increasingly significant role as advisers to government departments and military planners, were uncertain about the extent to which Danish agricultural production would be affected by a British blockade.[12] At first they were extremely pessimistic, concluding that Denmark's export potential in the event of blockade would be reduced to 'practically zero'.[13] By the autumn of 1939 they had arrived at a far more positive assessment.[14] Even if the import of fodder was completely halted, there would be no immediate drop in milk production, partly because the Danes had made considerable progress in meeting their fodder requirements from their own resources. No serious fall in production need be expected before the winter of 1940–1, and

---

[8] Correspondence in BA, R 43 11/810; memorandum by Scherpenberg, 16 October 1937, PA, Handakten Clodius, Finnland, Bd 5 (summarised in *DGFP*, D, V, p. 535); quotation from the Agrarian newspaper *Ilkka*, in K. T. Gurney (Helsinki) to FO, 6 October 1937, FO 419/31, N5119/24/56. By 1937 Petsamo had become a haven for disgruntled Finnish right-wingers: J. Hampden Jackson, *Finland* (London, 1938), p. 185.

[9] Berlin chancery to Northern Department, 12 April 1937, FO 371/21075, N2068/24/56; T. M. Snow (Helsinki) to FO, 9 August 1937, FO 419/31, N4207/24/56. A similar project for a fisheries base on the Faeroe Islands was proposed by a Danish–German consortium early in 1938. It was supported by the Four-Year Plan Office but rejected as unsound by the Copenhagen legation: Correspondence January–March 1938 in ZSta., AA 68318.

[10] Milward, *Fascist Economy in Norway*, pp. 48–9.

[11] Scherpenberg, 'Tagesmeldung vom 10. Januar 1939', ZSta., AA 67771.

[12] On the role of IG Farben's Volkswirtschaftliche Abteilung (Vowi), see Peter Hayes, *Industry and Ideology: IG Farben in the Nazi Era* (Cambridge, 1987), pp. 104, 127, 214–15. For examples of Vowi studies of the Nordic economies, see e.g. 'Wirtschaftsbericht Dänemark', 14 September 1939 (copy in PA, AA Handakten von Behr, Dänemark), as well as the reports included in ZSta., 80 IG 1: e.g. A415, 'Die Chemiewirtschaft Finnlands', 11 November 1938.

[13] Vowi 3729: 'Abweichungen des Gutachtens II vom Gutachten I', n.d. (c. November 1939), ZSta., 80 IG 1, A761.

[14] 'Dänemarks Ausführmöglichkeiten an tierischen Veredlungserzeugnissen bei Beschränkung bezw. Fortfall der Einfuhr von Futtermitteln', 2 November 1939, ibid. This is presumably the 'Gutachten II' referred to in the previous footnote.

even then it would not be on a scale comparable with the latter part of the First World War. And the export surplus of butter, pork products and eggs, which would normally go mainly to Britain, would be almost entirely available for sale to Germany instead.

Above all, however, Germany depended on Scandinavia for supplies of iron ore. A small but significant proportion came from Norway. Germany was the biggest customer for the iron ore – low in ferrous content, but also low in phosphorus and accessible from the sea – which had been mined at Sydvaranger in the far north of Norway since 1906, and of which production increased greatly between the wars.[15] But Swedish iron ore remained far more important in terms of both quality and quantity.[16] Germany's dependence on supplies from Sweden had been greatly enhanced by the loss of the Lorraine ore fields at the end of the First World War. Formerly 60 per cent self-sufficient in iron ore, Germany was now dependent on foreign sources for 75–80 per cent of its supply. In terms of iron content, Sweden accounted by the late 1930s for almost 60 per cent of Germany's iron ore imports, which represented about 45 per cent of its total requirements. Germany was by far the largest purchaser of Swedish ore, taking in most years about 75 per cent of the total export. Britain, Sweden's second largest customer, rarely took more than 12 per cent.

In 1927 Swedish iron ore exports had been fixed by the 'Grängesberg law' at 9 million tons per annum from the northern ore fields and 1.5 million tons from central Sweden.[17] Exports had fallen drastically during the depression years, but German demand picked up sharply in 1934–5. From 1936 British purchases, too, increased rapidly with the beginning of the rearmament programme and the construction of new steelworks such as Corby which were capable of utilising phosphoric ore. For Germany, whose iron ore imports had already imposed a severe strain on the Swedish–German clearing, the rise of British competition, offering better prices and more reliable payment methods, was disturbing.[18] The situation was complicated by the Four-Year Plan proclaimed by Hitler in October 1936. A key element of the plan, in which Göring was the dominant figure, was the increased exploitation of low-grade domestic ores.[19] This was opposed by the German steel industry on economic

---

[15] Milward, *Fascist Economy in Norway*, pp. 54–6; for British interest in German supplies of iron ore from Sydvaranger in 1939, see FO 371/23675, N3014/30. For a German assessment of the strategic significance of the Sydvaranger ore, see Steffan (naval attaché, Stockholm) to Marineleitung, 20 February 1934, PA, AA Geheimakten Schweden II, FM 24, Bd 1.

[16] For the significance of iron ore in Swedish–German economic relations, see Klaus Wittmann, *Schwedens Wirtschaftsbeziehungen zum Dritten Reich 1933–1945* (Munich and Vienna, 1978), pp. 113–28.

[17] These quantities could be raised by 10 per cent in any one year, so long as the total export in three consecutive years did not exceed 27 million tons and 4.5 million tons respectively.

[18] Prof. Dr E. Haarmann to Göring, 13 July 1936; comments on Haarmann memorandum by Stockholm legation in Meynen to AA, 6 October 1936, PA, AA HaPol. VI, Schweden, Rohstoffe und Waren, Eisenerz, Bd 1; Wittmann, *Schwedens Wirtschaftsbeziehungen*, p. 118.

[19] R. J. Overy, *Goering: The 'Iron Man'* (London, 1984), pp. 62–8.

grounds, while Swedish exporters were worried by the suggestion that Germany might become less dependent on Swedish ore. In fact Göring had no intention of renouncing Germany's interest, and informed directors of the TGO categorically in April 1937 that 'the Four-Year Plan aimed only at increasing the inadequate German production, and would never lead to a reduction in ore imports from Sweden'.[20]

Given Germany's continuing dependence on Swedish iron ore, the question of maintaining and, if possible, increasing imports in both peace and war assumed major significance. The most immediate problem was that the limit set by the Grängesberg law might soon be reached. It was clear that any German initiative to have the limit raised stood little chance of success in view of the opposition it would arouse in the Swedish Riksdag.[21] In this context British competition proved less disadvantageous than it appeared at first sight.[22] For in the spring of 1937 the Board of Trade launched a diplomatic initiative, on behalf of the British iron and steel industry, aimed at an upward revision of the Grängesberg law.[23] Both Runciman and Sir Andrew Duncan of the British Iron and Steel Federation acknowledged that Britain's heightened interest was due in part to the reduction in supplies of ore from Spain owing to the civil war, but assured the Swedes that British demand would outlast the current boom.[24] From the point of view of the TGO, any increase in sales to Great Britain was advantageous since it would enable them to spread their risks, both economic and political.[25] The directors of the TGO, furthermore, were notably reserved in their attitude towards 'the new Germany'.[26] They nevertheless hinted that, in view of the 'careful parliamentary preparation' that would be required, it would be to Germany's advantage if the request for increased supplies came mainly from 'other countries (England, Czechoslovakia etc.)'.[27]

Britain was thus allowed to make the running, and the 'scramble for Swedish iron ore' which aroused so much public attention in Scandinavia in

---

[20] Memorandum by Scherpenberg, 15 April 1937, PA, AA HaPol. VI, Schweden, Rohstoffe und Waren, Eisenerz, Bd 1; Gunnar Hägglöf, *Svensk krigshandelspolitik under andra världskriget* (Stockholm, 1958), pp. 21–2.

[21] Scherpenberg memorandum, 27 February 1937, PA, AA HaPol. VI, Schweden, Rohstoffe und Waren, Eisenerz, Bd 1.

[22] For German anxiety about increased British purchases, see e.g. Generalleutnant Liese (head of Heereswaffenamt) to J. W. Reichert (managing director of Wirtschaftsgruppe Eisenschaffende Industrie), 23 February 1937, BA, R 13 I/602.

[23] Runciman conversation with Sandler and Palmstierna, 18 March 1937, FO 371/21082, N1829/230/42; BT–FO correspondence, April 1937, FO 371/2110, N1509/42; Runciman to Sandler, 11 May 1937, SUD, H 40 Ct., Bd XIII; Hägglöf, *Svensk krigshandelspolitik*, pp. 22–4.

[24] Frisell (London representative of TGO) to Waldenström (managing director, TGO), reporting conversation with Duncan, 17 April 1937, SUD, H 40 Ba., Bd VII.

[25] Scherpenberg memorandum, 'Die deutschen Erzbezüge aus Schweden', 19 January 1938, PA, AA HaPol. VI, Schweden, Rohstoffe und Waren, Eisenerz, Bd 1.

[26] Meynen to AA, 6 October 1936, ibid.

[27] Scherpenberg memorandum, 15 April 1937, PA, AA HaPol. VI, Schweden, Rohstoffe und Waren, Eisenerz, Bd 1.

1937 had a largely deceptive character.[28] British efforts were rewarded in the autumn of 1937 when the Riksdag agreed to increase the export limit by 2.2 million tons per annum, of which the bulk was expected to go to Britain. In fact, although a demand for 3.5 million tons of Swedish ore had been predicted for 1938, a recession-hit British steel industry was able to absorb only 1.5 million tons. Most of the enlarged quota went to Germany instead.

This increased import was not achieved without difficulty. At a time when domestic demand was restricting German export capacity, the Ministry of Economics warned that it would be necessary to export extra goods to the value of RM 20 to 30 million in order to pay for the projected increase in iron ore imports.[29] Similar obstacles, together with the likelihood of political opposition in Sweden, ruled out ideas of stockpiling iron ore, either in Germany or Sweden, or of purchasing iron ore mines in central Sweden.[30] Assuming, however, that payments continued to be made, and that the Swedish government allowed the existing clearing arrangements to continue, it was possible at the beginning of 1938 to look forward to an annual peacetime import of up to 11 million tons.[31]

The wartime position appeared much less certain. It was possible that Sweden might ban iron ore exports to Germany outright, either through participation in League sanctions or as a result of 'left-wing' influence on the government.[32] Even if this did not happen, there was a danger that shipments might be disrupted by strike activity either at the mines or among the dock workers at Narvik. A Wehrmacht warning in November 1938 of Soviet intentions to foment strikes and sabotage at the mines, on the railway and at Narvik may have been well founded in view of what is known of Comintern activity in northern Scandinavia at the time.[33] The German authorities were less worried about the Swedish miners than about the Norwegian workers, who were reckoned to be far more radical.[34] But what was known about the disaffection of the population of northern Scandinavia gave rise to more general fears about the extent to which such attitudes could be exploited by Germany's enemies in time of war. Dr Sahm, the German minister in Oslo, was so concerned about the situation in northern Norway that in December 1936 he sent a 'reliable' Norwegian – a former senior officer and 'a Norwegian

[28] Joachim Joesten, 'The Scramble for Swedish Iron Ore', *Political Quarterly* 1938, 1, pp. 58–67.

[29] 'Besprechungen im RWM über grundsätzliche Fragen der Eisenschaffenden Industrie', 4 March 1938, BA, R 13 I/106. See also Clodius to Stockholm legation, 10 February 1938, PA, AA Handakten Wiehl, Schweden, Bd 2.

[30] On stockpiles, see Scherpenberg memorandum, 10 May 1938, PA, AA HaPol. VI, Schweden, Rohstoffe und Waren, Eisenerz, Bd 1. On possible purchases of mines, see Meynen to AA, 6 July 1937, Wied to AA, 22 July 1937 and 14 October 1937, ibid.

[31] Scherpenberg memorandum, 'Die deutschen Erzbezüge aus Schweden', 19 January 1938, ibid.

[32] Ibid.   [33] OKW to AA, 23 November 1938, ibid.

[34] E.g. Haarmann to Göring, 13 July 1936; Meynen to AA, 6 October 1936; Below (Stockholm) to AA, 12 May 1938, all ibid.

patriot and declared enemy of communism' – to investigate the situation.[35] His informant concluded that the 'proletariat', partly of Finnish and Lapp extraction, was notably receptive to Marxist propaganda, and that the Soviet Union, while dreaming the old tsarist dream of ice-free ports in Norway, was also interested in Swedish iron ore and its export route through Narvik.

With the apparent likelihood of a Soviet–German war, there was much public discussion in Scandinavia in 1937 of 'ghost' flights – supposedly made by Soviet aircraft – over the far north, and of the arrest of Soviet spies in northern Norway and Finland.[36] War with the USSR would threaten Germany's supplies from the Swedish Baltic ports, a problem which, as we shall see, was of persistent concern to the German navy. But the danger resulting from a conflict with Great Britain would be much greater.[37] The German authorities expected Britain to apply pressure on Sweden to reduce iron ore exports to Germany; and indeed such pressure was widely reported to have been exercised at the time of Munich.[38] It was assumed, too, that shipments from Narvik would largely cease.[39]

If Germany could do little to avert the latter danger, it could hope to stiffen the attitude of the Swedish government towards Britain's demands. Here the Germans were working with the grain. The Swedes wanted to continue earning money and the Swedish Foreign Ministry was engaged in formulating a neutrality policy which would enable Sweden as far as possible to continue to trade with both sides in time of war. They were, however, left in no doubt as to Germany's wishes. During the Munich crisis Grundherr warned the Swedish naval attaché that the question of maintaining Swedish iron ore exports in wartime was the one 'neuralgic point' in German–Swedish relations, 'one which, I thought, Sweden ought not to open up at all'.[40] In January 1939 Ribbentrop agreed that Sweden's interest in securing a revision of the Åland convention should be exploited in order to obtain an assurance that Sweden would continue to supply Germany in time of war.[41] The Wilhelmstrasse noted: 'We are to avoid the impression that our approval is conditional on a

---

[35] Sahm to AA, 2 February 1937: 'Nord-Norwegen in militär-politischer Hinsicht', enclosing 'Nemo': 'Bericht über Russlands Interessen in Nord-Norwegen', 23 December 1936, PA, AA Pol. Abt. VI, Norwegen, Politik 13.

[36] 'Scandinavia on Guard', *The Times*, 9 September 1937; 'Soviet Threat to Scandinavia', *Observer*, 12 December 1937.

[37] See e.g. the opinions expressed in an inter-departmental conference on the fortification of the Åland Islands, 17 January 1939, *DGFP*, D, V, pp. 610–13.

[38] Ibid.; Grundherr to London embassy, 23 January 1939, and Wied to AA, 24 January 1939, PA, AA Abt. Pol. VI, Politik 2, Schweden.

[39] Scherpenberg minute, 20 January 1939, *DGFP*, D, V, pp. 619–20.

[40] Grundherr memorandum, 21 September 1938, ibid., pp. 595–6; memorandum by naval attaché (Captain Muhl), sent by Richert to SUD, 21 September 1938, SUD, H 40 Ct., Bd XIV.

[41] Inter-departmental conference on Åland question, 17 January 1939, *DGFP*, D, V, pp. 610–13; note for Scherpenberg, 24 January 1939, PA, AA HaPol. VI, Schweden, Rohstoffe und Waren, Eisenerz, Bd 2; minute by Weizsäcker (state secretary), 26 January 1939, PA, AA Handakten Wiehl, Schweden, Bd 2.

settlement of this question.'[42] The Swedes nevertheless understood the message. A formal undertaking that Sweden would not take part in any measures aimed at cutting off Germany's ore supplies was duly delivered by the Swedish minister in April 1939.[43]

Germany's dependence on Swedish iron ore, together with the importance of the northern sphere in a war against either the Soviet Union or Britain, brought Scandinavia to the forefront of German naval interest in the late 1930s.[44] In many respects German naval thinking between the wars recalled that of the pre-1914 era. There was the same emphasis on building a battleship fleet – sometimes questioned but never fundamentally challenged – as opposed to relying on less prestigious but potentially cheaper and more effective strategies based on cruiser or U-boat warfare.[45] There was a similar ambivalence towards Great Britain: on the one hand the assumption that Germany would one day have to fight Britain for naval supremacy; on the other admiration for Britain as a 'leader of Western culture' and a role for Britain as a potential partner of Germany (which, of course, echoed the policy laid down by Hitler in *Mein Kampf*).[46]

One important difference from the period before 1914 was that Raeder's navy was far weaker than Tirpitz's, and could thus look forward to a conflict with Great Britain with even less optimism than Tirpitz had done. Another feature of the inter-war period was a persistent critique of the strategy pursued by Germany's naval leadership in the First World War. It was associated in particular with the name of Vice-Admiral Wolfgang Wegener, who had criticised Germany's naval strategy during the war itself, and who developed his ideas first in a memorandum of 1925 and later in a book, *Die Seestrategie des Weltkrieges*, published in 1929.[47] Although Raeder remained loyal to Tirpitz's memory (and indeed tried to suppress the public expression of Wegener's views),[48] Wegener's ideas came to permeate German naval planning and were absorbed by Raeder himself. It had been wrong, Wegener declared, to adopt a defensive naval strategy during the war. This had merely accentuated Germany's disadvantageous strategic position, hemmed in by the British Isles.

---

[42] Under State Secretary Woermann, in inter-departmental conference, 17 January 1939, *DGFP*, D, V, pp. 610–13.

[43] Note of 18 April 1939, SUD, H 40 Ct., Bd XV.

[44] Dülffer, *Weimar, Hitler und die Marine*, p. 520.

[45] Hans-Martin Ottmer, 'Skandinavien in den marinestrategischen Planungen des Reichs- bzw. Kriegsmarine', in Robert Bohn et al. (eds.), *Neutralität und totalitäre Aggression. Nordeuropa und die Grossmächte im Zweiten Weltkrieg* (Stuttgart, 1991), pp. 49–72 (p. 52).

[46] Dülffer, *Weimar, Hitler und die Marine*, pp. 75–6, 87–90; quotation from memorandum of 22 July 1926, printed in Gerhard Schreiber, 'Zur Kontinuität des Gross- und Weltmacht- strebens der deutschen Marineführung', *Militärgeschichtliche Mitteilungen* 26 (1979), pp. 101–71 (p. 136).

[47] Carl-Axel Gemzell, *Raeder, Hitler und Skandinavien. Der Kampf für einen maritimen Operationsplan* (Lund, 1965), pp. 15–25; Gemzell, *Organization, Conflict and Innovation: A Study of German Naval Strategic Planning 1888–1940* (Lund, 1973), pp. 215–22, 266–71.

[48] Ottmer, 'Skandinavien', pp. 54–5.

Strategy should instead have been directed towards solving the problem created by geography: in other words, towards the acquisition of bases which would enable the navy to outflank Great Britain and secure direct access to the Atlantic Ocean. For Wegener, this imperative pointed in two directions: the French Atlantic coast and Norway.

Such ideas were of largely theoretical interest as long as Britain was not identified as a potential enemy. For a long time the navy was reluctant to contemplate the prospect of hostilities with Great Britain. German naval planning was not directed explicitly towards war with Britain until as late as the spring of 1938 and, even on the basis of the high-priority 'Z-Plan' of January 1939, 1943 was the earliest point at which the navy could confront the British fleet with any hope of success. For the navy, the accelerating pace of Hitler's foreign policy therefore threatened disaster. Raeder nevertheless placed a blind trust in the Führer's ability to avert a confrontation with Britain.[49] Many of the contradictions and uncertainties underlying the navy's strategic debate thus remained unresolved up to the outbreak of war. In particular there remained an irreconcilable tension between the demand for bases in Scandinavia and the acknowledged advantages of Scandinavian neutrality.[50] If acquiring bases threatened the supply of Swedish iron ore, was the enterprise worth attempting?

There was a further conflict between those who favoured concentrating Germany's limited resources in the Baltic for a war against Poland or the Soviet Union and those who looked to the North Sea and the Atlantic in a confrontation with Great Britain. The strategic importance of the Baltic was heightened by the expansion of the Soviet navy following the Anglo-German naval agreement of 1935, but the growing likelihood that Britain would have to be added to the number of Germany's enemies complicated the task of planning Baltic operations. From the start, iron ore loomed large in the navy's calculations. In the light of the reported expansion of the Red Fleet in the Baltic and at Murmansk, the navy concluded in 1936–7 that the security of ore shipments from both Luleå and Narvik would be seriously endangered in the event of war.[51] The need to protect ore transports and defend the German coast would tie up a large proportion of Germany's limited naval resources in the Baltic. In 1938 – now contemplating a war against both Britain and the USSR – the navy demanded that ore shipments should be transferred to the ports of central and southern Sweden, and that iron ore should be stockpiled in the southern part of the country, so as to avoid the risk of Soviet interception.[52] Owing to high costs and lack of time, neither demand was fulfilled.

The German navy's plans for war against the Soviet Union also had an offensive aspect. Between 1936 and 1938, planning was based on the

[49] Salewski, *Deutsche Seekriegsleitung* I, p. 40.
[50] Expressed e.g. in Heye's important 'England Memorandum' of May 1938: ibid., pp. 50–1.
[51] Dülffer, *Weimar, Hitler und die Marine*, pp. 377–8.   [52] Ibid., pp. 521–4.

assumption that it would be necessary to establish bases on the Åland Islands and at Petsamo.[53] In February 1937 Raeder drew Hitler's attention to the strategic importance of the islands at the entrance to the Gulf of Finland, both for protecting the iron ore route from northern Sweden and for launching an assault on the Soviet base at Kronstadt.[54] In the light of the increasing likelihood of conflict with Britain (but possibly also influenced by changes in Finnish domestic politics in 1937), Raeder moved away from the idea of Baltic bases.[55] In August 1938 he declared himself in favour of remaining on the defensive against the Soviet Union in the Baltic. In these circumstances it was more desirable that Finland and Estonia should remain neutral than that they should intervene on Germany's side and risk being quickly overrun.[56]

By 1939 Baltic operations were again being viewed in a more positive light. Abandoning its plan to lay a minefield between the Swedish island of Öland and the Hela peninsula (near Danzig), which would have left the eastern Baltic largely free for Soviet naval operations, the navy decided instead to block the Gulf of Finland with mines in order to confine the Red Fleet in its Kronstadt base. Orders to this effect were issued on 18 August 1939, only five days before the Nazi–Soviet pact. Already, however, much more ambitious options were under discussion. Most of these centred on carrying the offensive into the Gulf of Finland and beyond, not merely to destroy the Red Fleet but also to occupy territory. Conquest of the Leningrad region would open up the possibility of gaining access to the Arctic Ocean. This in turn would enable Germany to outflank Great Britain. A French Atlantic port such as Brest was still the most desirable goal, but since it was expected to be several years before the German army was strong enough to break through the Maginot line, the establishment of an Arctic base on the Kola peninsula was regarded as a possible alternative.[57]

The linkage between Baltic operations against the Soviet Union and more far-reaching objectives in a war against Great Britain was also present in German discussions of Denmark and the Baltic approaches. In a war against either Poland or the Soviet Union, control of the entrance to the Baltic would be essential in order to prevent supplies and naval support from reaching the enemy. But Germany's naval weakness meant that the possibility of an enemy breakthrough into the Baltic had to be taken into account.[58] As late as May 1938 there was still thought to be some danger of a British Baltic offensive.[59]

[53] Gemzell, *Raeder, Hitler und Skandinavien*, p. 46; Ueberschär, *Hitler und Finnland*, pp. 39–40.

[54] Gemzell, *Raeder, Hitler und Skandinavien*, p. 67.

[55] Menger, *Deutschland und Finnland*, p. 68.

[56] Gemzell, *Raeder, Hitler und Skandinavien*, p. 112.

[57] The strategic and economic advantages of establishing a base at Petsamo were also acknowledged, and had been mentioned by Raeder as early as 1936: Dülffer, *Weimar, Hitler und die Marine*, p. 522; Gemzell, *Organization*, p. 278.

[58] Gemzell, *Organization*, pp. 275–6; Dülffer, *Weimar, Hitler und die Marine*, pp. 189–90; Salewski, *Deutsche Seekriegsleitung* I, p. 31.

[59] Salewski, *Deutsche Seekriegsleitung* I, p. 71.

However, the risk of an enemy incursion – reduced in any case by the development of air power[60] – was outweighed by the importance of the Baltic approaches for German offensive operations. Raeder agreed with the critics of German policy in the last war that the mining of Danish territorial waters had been a fundamental error. In 1935 he demanded that the Auswärtiges Amt should make clear to the Danish and Swedish governments that the Baltic approaches must be kept open in time of war.[61]

There was disagreement as to whether it would be necessary to occupy Danish territory. For Admiral Carls, the most ruthless of the navy's strategists, an occupation of Denmark was essential both to secure command of the Baltic and to create a jumping-off point for expansion towards the Atlantic.[62] While agreeing with Carls that 'the Danish question is a matter of life and death for us', Raeder remained non-committal about the merits of violating Danish neutrality.[63] A study produced on Raeder's orders in 1938 stressed the advantages of Danish neutrality and the risks involved in occupying the country, though it added significantly that, if Denmark was occupied, Norway must be occupied at the same time.[64] This view was reinforced by studies produced by the Operations Department later in the year, which pointed out that, whilst bases in Denmark, the Netherlands or southern Norway might improve Germany's tactical position, only an occupation of the Channel coast as far as Brest would be of *decisive* strategic value.[65]

With the French option ruled out by the apparent strength of France's defences, attention thus turned increasingly towards the north: to the Russian Arctic coast and to Norway. But the debate on bases retained its largely theoretical character. Raeder warned his officers in April 1938 against relying on the assumption that Germany could radically improve its strategic position through the acquisition of bases in the immediate future.[66] German naval planners still reckoned on a very long time-scale, paralleling the naval construction programme. Some, like Heinz Assmann, apparently believed as late as the spring of 1939 that it would be possible to obtain bases in Scandinavia by peaceful means, merely by the exercise of German economic, political and cultural influence.[67] For others, however, the imminence of war against Britain, combined with the inferiority of the German fleet, made the question a matter of urgency. Admiral Boehm, the commander-in-chief of the fleet, was clearly looking to the immediate future in a plan (nominally for a war to begin in 1942) prepared in April 1939.[68] An attempt must be made, 'at the latest immediately after the outbreak of war', to improve Germany's unfavourable geographical position. In March 1939 the North Sea Station openly advised the Seekriegsleitung (Naval Command) that Germany should consider

---

[60] Gemzell, *Organization*, p. 361.   [61] Ibid., p. 276.   [62] Ibid., p. 282.
[63] Ibid., p. 302.   [64] Ibid.; Dülffer, *Weimar, Hitler und die Marine*, pp. 442–3.
[65] Dülffer, *Weimar, Hitler und die Marine*, p. 478.
[66] Ibid., pp. 461–2.   [67] See n. 2 in this ch.
[68] Dülffer, *Weimar, Hitler und die Marine*, pp. 526–7; Gemzell, *Organization*, pp. 285–6.

occupying Norwegian territory in order to prevent Britain from blocking the approaches to the North Atlantic.[69]

Raeder still tried to confine the debate to 'realistic' options. At the conclusion of the 1938–9 war game in early March 1939 he conceded that it might be possible to establish bases in Spain, while ridiculing the suggestion that a base in Iceland, for example, was a feasible option.[70] But, as Gemzell points out, it is intriguing that the latter possibility was raised at all. Wegener, after all, had never regarded Norway as an end in itself but as a means to the conquest of the Shetlands, the Faeroes and Iceland. Only then would Germany have unrestricted access to the open seas. That control of Norway was not sufficient to guarantee this was shown in May 1940, when Britain responded to the German invasion by occupying Iceland, and thus 'again locked the gate to the Atlantic Ocean'.[71] Raeder went on to dismiss the value of bases in the Netherlands, Belgium or southern Norway since they would lie within the scope of the British blockade, and stated that bases in central or northern Norway would be difficult to supply and exposed to British attack. He acknowledged, however, that control of the French coast as far as Brest, if it could be achieved, would be of great value for both the naval and the air war against Great Britain. Raeder may subsequently have spoken to Hitler on the subject: there is certainly a strong similarity with the views expressed by Hitler in his meeting with the commanders of the armed forces on 23 May 1939.[72] The main difference was Hitler's addition of a point not mentioned by Raeder: the suitability of such a base for submarine warfare.

At the outbreak of war the naval strategic debate remained inconclusive. Bases were still discussed in the context of a war beginning no earlier than 1943; France was consistently preferred to Norway; the SKL acknowledged the value to Germany of Scandinavian neutrality. But if there was no 'maritime operation plan' directed towards Norway in the sense postulated by Gemzell, it is equally misleading to suggest that Norwegian bases would have been of value only to 'the fleet of 1945' and that 'the navy of 1939 had no interest in an occupation of the Scandinavian countries'.[73] In fact, as Dülffer emphasises, it was precisely in the circumstances of 1939 – in a 'premature' war – that the question of Norway acquired urgency.[74] For the navy, the war had indeed come too soon. As Raeder put it on the day Britain declared war, 'The surface forces . . . are so inferior in number and strength to those of the British fleet that, even at full strength, they can do no more than show that they know how to die gallantly

[69] Gemzell, *Organization*, pp. 286–7.
[70] Ibid., pp. 287–8; Dülffer, *Weimar, Hitler und die Marine*, pp. 527–9.
[71] Walther Hubatsch, 'Problems of the Norwegian Campaign 1940', *Journal of the Royal United Service Institution* 103 (1958), pp. 336–45 (pp. 343–4).
[72] Dülffer, *Weimar, Hitler und die Marine*, pp. 529–30.
[73] Salewski, *Deutsche Seekriegsleitung* I, p. 72.
[74] Dülffer, *Weimar, Hitler und die Marine*, p. 530.

and thus are willing to create the foundations for later reconstruction.'[75] Nor was there any confidence in the capacity of the Wehrmacht to break through France's defences and secure control of the French Atlantic coast.

Yet it was by no means obvious that Norway was the answer to the navy's strategic dilemma. There was a consensus within the German government that Scandinavian neutrality must be preserved: this was the message forcefully delivered by Ambassador von Hassell when he toured the Scandinavian capitals at the beginning of September 1939.[76] On the other hand, there was no certainty that any substantial quantity of iron ore could be obtained via the Narvik route. The minister in Oslo warned that Britain would exert pressure on Norway and that only small ships would be able to negotiate the Norwegian coast within territorial waters.[77] The iron and steel manufacturers advised that the only safe route, via Luleå, was far from satisfactory since the port was of smaller capacity and icebound throughout the winter.[78] Ore shipments from Narvik fell off drastically in September and October, and started to pick up only when German ship-owners challenged the navy's pessimism about the feasibility of safe passage in Norwegian waters for larger merchant ships.[79]

In one important respect, moreover, the strategic position was better than the navy had anticipated. The non-aggression pact with the Soviet Union enabled naval forces to be diverted from the Baltic to the North Sea and Atlantic.[80] It also offered an opportunity to realise one of the options discussed before the war: a base on the Russian Arctic coast.[81] Raeder raised the possibility of using Murmansk as a base for cruisers with Hitler on 23 September 1939.[82] Following Ribbentrop's negotiations in Moscow, the Soviets offered Germany a naval base at Zapadnaya Litsa to the west of Murmansk.[83] Although this base – 'Basis Nord' – was later to prove of importance during the German invasion of Norway, the navy's initial assessment was that lack of capacity and facilities limited its practical value.[84] At the

---

[75] Führer Conferences on Naval Affairs, 1939–1945, printed in *Brassey's Naval Annual* 1948, pp. 25–496 (p. 38); Salewski, *Deutsche Seekriegsleitung* I, p. 37.
[76] Hassell memorandum, 9 September 1939, *DGFP*, D, VIII, pp. 39–40.
[77] Sahm to AA, 29 August 1939, PA, AA Handakten Clodius, Norwegen, Bd 3.
[78] Meeting at Ministry of Economics, 12 September 1939, BA, R 13 I/607.
[79] 'Vermerk über die Besprechungen über Fragen des deutsch–norwegischen Warenverkehrs unter besonderer Berücksichtigung der Fragen des Seetransportes zwischen Deutschland und Norwegen', 9 October 1939, PA, AA HaPol. VI Norwegen, Handel 11.
[80] Führer Conference on Naval Affairs, 10 October 1939, *Brassey's Naval Annual* 1948, pp. 45–7; Gerhard L. Weinberg, *A World At Arms: A Global History of World War II* (Cambridge, 1994), p. 951 (n. 47).
[81] For a thorough discussion of 'Basis Nord', see Tobias R. Philbin III, *The Lure of Neptune: German–Soviet Naval Collaboration and Ambitions 1919–1941* (Columbia, S. C., 1994), ch. 5.
[82] Führer Conference on Naval Affairs, *Brassey's Naval Annual* 1948, pp. 41–3; Gemzell, *Raeder, Hitler und Skandinavien*, pp. 214–16.
[83] Gerhard L. Weinberg, *Germany and the Soviet Union 1939–1941* (Leiden, 1954), p. 80.
[84] Gemzell, *Raeder, Hitler und Skandinavien*, pp. 242–4. Raeder told Hitler on 16 October that the base was well situated and that a repair ship was to be stationed there: *Brassey's Naval Annual* 1948, pp. 51–2. For the role of the supply ship *Jan Wellem*, sent from 'Basis

meeting on 10 October during which Raeder informed Hitler of the Soviet offer, the grand admiral also pointed out 'how important it would be for submarine warfare to obtain bases on the Norwegian coast, e.g. Trondheim, with the help of Russian pressure'.[85]

This was the first mention of Norway at the highest level, and on this occasion Raeder was able to obtain no more than an assurance that the Führer would 'consider' the matter. It is no longer possible to accept the interpretation that Raeder's initiative was based on reliable intelligence of Allied aggressive intentions towards Scandinavia: this was a fabrication concocted by Raeder and his former adjutant Schulte-Mönting at Nuremberg in 1946.[86] The initiative derived rather from an aspect of naval warfare which had been relatively neglected in the pre-war discussions but had acquired urgency after the outbreak of war: submarines.

On 23 September and again on 10 October, Raeder obtained Hitler's authorisation to intensify submarine warfare against Great Britain and to promote the submarine construction programme. In contrast to his pre-war position, Raeder's view was now that only U-boats and the air force could secure 'a lasting and probably decisive effect' in the war against England.[87] At a meeting of the SKL on 3 October, the U-boat commander, Admiral Dönitz, expressed his worries about the slow rate at which submarine losses were likely to be replaced, and made it clear that the submarine weapon could only be brought to bear effectively if submarines avoided the waters close to the British Isles and concentrated on attacking convoys in the Atlantic.[88] He also declared that bases in Norway would be of immense value for the repair and supply of U-boats operating in the Atlantic.[89] Among the measures proposed by Raeder to meet Dönitz's concerns was that the Führer should be informed of the navy's interest in securing a Norwegian base and that the SKL should investigate the implications of obtaining and securing such a base either peacefully or by force.

The first proposal led, as we have seen, to Raeder's initiative of 10 October. He was, apparently, undeterred by the rather cautious response to his second

Nord' to Narvik shortly before the German invasion, see Magne Skodvin, 'Norwegian Neutrality and the Question of Credibility', *Scandinavian Journal of History* 2 (1977), pp. 123–45 (pp. 134–5); Philbin, *Lure of Neptune*, pp. 112–14.

[85] Führer Conference on Naval Affairs, 10 October 1939, *Brassey's Naval Annual* 1948, pp. 45–7.

[86] Patrick Salmon, 'Crimes Against Peace: The Case of the Invasion of Norway at the Nuremberg Trials', in Richard Langhorne (ed.), *Diplomacy and Intelligence During the Second World War: Essays in Honour of F. H. Hinsley* (Cambridge, 1985), pp. 245–69 (pp. 258–9); Ottmer, 'Skandinavien', pp. 65–6. For 'evidence' of British interest in Norway, see Walther Hubatsch, *Weserübung. Die deutsche Besetzung von Dänemark und Norwegen 1940* (Göttingen, 1960), pp. 14, 28; Salewski, *Deutsche Seekriegsleitung* I, p. 176 (based on Raeder's memoirs).

[87] Conversation between Schniewind, the naval chief of staff, and General Halder, the chief of the general staff, 5 October 1939, quoted in *Deutsche Seekriegsleitung* I, p. 122.

[88] Gemzell, *Raeder, Hitler und Skandinavien*, pp. 218–19; Ottmer, 'Skandinavien', p. 64.

[89] Gemzell, *Raeder, Hitler und Skandinavien*, p. 223.

proposal, in the form of an SKL memorandum of 9 October.[90] This came to the conclusion that the most suitable base would be Trondheim since it lay beyond the main British blockade line and offered direct access to the Atlantic. It might be possible to seize the port in the face of Norwegian resistance, but prolonged Norwegian opposition would jeopardise communications over land, and sea communications could also be easily disrupted by the enemy. The value of such a base would, in present circumstances, be outweighed by the political disadvantages entailed even if it was secured solely by political pressure. If it were to be obtained by force, a combined operation of all three armed services would be required. A second response to Raeder's enquiry of 3 October, from Dönitz, was much more positive. In a memorandum of 9 October which Raeder did not see before his meeting with Hitler on the 10th, Dönitz advocated the establishment of a submarine base at Trondheim, supplemented by a fuel depot at Narvik.[91] However, consultations with the General Staff and the air force in October made it clear that the navy could expect no support from either quarter.[92]

Although Raeder and Hitler discussed the possibility of exerting 'pressure on the Nordic states' on 23 October, they did so in the context of economic warfare and made no mention of acquiring bases.[93] On 25 November Raeder ordered the SKL to consider how Germany might respond to a British surprise landing on the Norwegian coast which, he suggested, might follow a German attack on the Netherlands as part of a western offensive.[94] Again, there was no evidence of aggressive intentions towards Norway on Britain's part. Raeder may thus, as Gemzell suggests, have been trying to win a recalcitrant SKL round to a Norwegian enterprise by emphasising defensive considerations. It is just as likely that, aware of Hitler's determination to attack in the west (delayed in early November but reiterated to a gathering of 200 officers on the 23rd), he wished to make provision for a British counter-move against Germany's northern flank. This, after all, was among the considerations which eventually persuaded Hitler to launch an invasion of Denmark and Norway in advance of his attack on the Low Countries and France. In the short term, however, there was no compelling reason to act against Norway.

By December 1939 the situation had changed dramatically. The Soviet–Finnish Winter War broke out on 30 November; in mid-December Quisling arrived in Berlin with what appeared to be, for the first time, firm evidence of British intentions to land in Norway. At this point ideological ambition and conspiratorial activity became fused with narrower considerations of naval strategy, as well as fears that the Allies might seek to extend the war into Scandinavia. Rosenberg's protégé Quisling offered a new possibility – that of gaining control of Norway by peaceful means – which for a time ran alongside

[90] Printed in Salewski, *Deutsche Seekriegsleitung* I, pp. 563–5.
[91] Gemzell, *Raeder, Hitler und Skandinavien*, p. 223.
[92] Salewski, *Deutsche Seekriegsleitung* I, p. 176.
[93] Gemzell, *Raeder, Hitler und Skandinavien*, pp. 244–5.   [94] Ibid., pp. 245–9.

the military planning for an invasion ordered by Hitler on 14 December. From this point onwards Norway never dropped out of sight. Eventually, in April 1940, the occupation of Norway was achieved through an operation of unprecedented daring, and with a degree of cooperation among the three armed services which the Third Reich was never to attain again.

Raeder declared rightly that Operation Weserübung was 'contrary to all principles in the theory of naval warfare', and the navy, above all, paid for the operation's success through the decimation of its ships in the Norwegian fjords.[95] Yet the alternative would have been to condemn the fleet to inaction: to a repetition of its fate in the First World War.[96] It was this that impelled Raeder to act at a time, in late March 1940, when he was fully aware that there was no immediate threat of British action against Norway. It is worth recalling once again Raeder's love–hate relationship with Wegener, born of the conflict between his loyalty to Tirpitz and his attraction to the ideas of the latter's most articulate critic.[97] It is also worth noting Raeder's fascination with the Dardanelles as an imaginatively conceived combined operation which might have succeeded had there been greater understanding of what was at stake and more willingness to cooperate among the armed services involved.[98]

Scandinavia and the Baltic in British strategy

Whilst the Baltic had retained a tenuous hold on British naval strategic thinking until the early 1930s, its importance dropped away rapidly after Hitler came to power. The remote prospect of a British Baltic intervention against the USSR was replaced after 1933 by a scenario in which any Baltic conflict would be fought between Germany and the Soviet Union, with the latter on the defensive rather than seeking to revolutionise northern Europe. By 1936 Mannerheim, returning from London, was able to inform the German minister in Helsinki that 'Russia and Bolshevism were no longer regarded as a danger threatening England. Only in military circles was a differing opinion still to be found.'[99] At the Foreign Office, Collier dismissed suggestions that the Soviet Union might still be 'seeking an ice-free port in Scandinavia'. For the next five years at least, he believed, 'it seems much more likely . . . that Germany will be the aggressor, indirectly if not directly, and that Russia will be on the defensive; and the Governments of other countries will have to shape their policies accordingly'.[100]

The assumption that the Baltic would be the setting for a German–Soviet war led all too readily to the conclusion that German naval interests were confined to that sea. It suited the Admiralty to emphasise the small size of the

---

[95] Führer Naval Conference, 9 March 1940, *Brassey's Naval Annual* 1948, pp. 84–7.
[96] Michael Salewski, 'Das Wesentliche von "Weserübung"', in Bohn et al., *Neutralität und totalitäre Aggression*, pp. 117–26.
[97] Ibid., p. 121.   [98] Salewski, *Deutsche Seekriegsleitung* I, pp. 32–3.
[99] Blücher to AA, 22 February 1936, PA, AA Pol. Abt. IV, Finnland, Politik 1, Bd 3.
[100] Collier to Torr (Riga), 11 January 1934, FO 371/18231, N7122/131/59.

German navy in comparison with what it regarded as the main strategic danger: the Japanese threat to the British empire in the Far East. The Admiralty was also willing to believe the Germans when they declared that their navy was not being built against Great Britain.[101] It was therefore convenient to assume that Germany would seek no more than 'to have a navy equal to that of the strongest power in the Baltic' – in other words, the Soviet Union.[102] On the other hand, as we have seen, the German navy remained acutely conscious of its inferiority in relation to Great Britain and did not openly acknowledge the possibility of a war against Britain until very late in the day.

The hypothesis that German naval ambitions were confined to the Baltic, combined with the Admiralty's obsession with preventing a repetition of the pre-1914 naval arms race, contributed in 1935 to an agreement which, as we have seen, crucially undermined Britain's standing in the region. The Admiralty's strategic assessments, by no means wholly invalid up to 1935, underwent little subsequent modification. Its handbook on the German navy, revised in 1936 and remaining in force up to the outbreak of war, reiterated the assertion that 'The keynote of Germany's Naval policy is "Supremacy in the Baltic"' and accepted the assurance which had been repeatedly given by Admiral Raeder to the British naval attaché in Berlin, 'that the "Tirpitz" tradition is dead and that never again will Germany challenge Great Britain's supremacy on the seas'.[103] Britain's indifference to the Baltic went so far that between 1936 and 1938 the Admiralty and Foreign Office were engaged in negotiations for an Anglo-Scandinavian naval agreement which, if it had been ratified, would have merely enhanced Germany's preponderance.[104] Fortunately Sweden refused in 1939 to ratify a treaty which would have reduced its capacity to meet either a German or a Soviet naval threat; and by 1939 the Admiralty had belatedly come round to the view that it would not be 'desirable at this stage to bring any pressure to bear on Sweden to force her to ratify an unwelcome treaty . . . From the strategical point of view a strengthening of the Swedish navy is to our advantage.'[105]

The Admiralty's 1936 assessment suggested that in time of war Germany would seek to gain control of the entrances to the Baltic. For this purpose it

---

[101] Wesley K. Wark, 'Baltic Myths and Submarine Bogeys: British Naval Intelligence and Nazi Germany 1933–1939', *Journal of Strategic Studies* 6 (1983), pp. 60–81.

[102] Memorandum by director of plans (Captain King), 29 June 1934, ADM 116/3373.

[103] Germany – Naval Intelligence Report, Section 2 – Strategy and Tactics (revised draft of 28 August 1936), ADM 178/137; Wark, 'Baltic Myths', pp. 72–3. On the ambivalence which lay behind such statements, see Dülffer, *Weimar, Hitler und die Marine*, pp. 342–5.

[104] Details in ADM 116/3928. The treaty was signed on 21 December 1938 by Lord Halifax and Lord Stanhope (first lord of the Admiralty) for Great Britain, and by the ministers of Denmark, Finland, Norway and Sweden.

[105] Minute by director of plans (Captain Danckwerts), 12 May 1939, ADM 116/3928. The Norwegian attitude, in contrast to that of Sweden, was enthusiastic, and Norway became the only country to ratify the agreement: Halvdan Koht, *Norway Neutral and Invaded* (London, 1941), pp. 19–21.

might lay mines in Danish waters, as in the last war, or even occupy certain strategic points on Danish territory such as the island of Langeland.[106] The assumption – again, valid as far as it went – was that the purpose of such action would be to reinforce German supremacy in the Baltic, by preventing seaborne supplies or French naval reinforcements from reaching either Poland or the Soviet Union. Denmark was coming to be viewed to an increasing extent as an aspect of Baltic strategy – a strategy in which, as we have seen, Britain no longer expected to play an active part. By the mid-1930s the principle of keeping the Baltic Straits open to British warships in time of war was one to which the British barely paid lip-service. The only suggestion that Britain might seek to conduct naval operations in the Baltic (in alliance with the Soviet Union) came from an amateur strategist and political outsider: Winston Churchill.[107]

On a number of occasions the first sea lord, Sir Ernle Chatfield, reassured the Danish minister that the Admiralty had not lost sight of the danger to Britain's strategic position if Germany were to establish naval and air bases on the west coast of Jutland.[108] However, bases in Denmark would not shorten the distance which German aircraft would have to fly in order to bomb the United Kingdom. Count Ahlefeldt-Laurvig was thus to be disappointed when he placed an optimistic interpretation on a statement in the 1935 defence white paper that 'the importance of the integrity of certain territories on the other side of the Channel and North Sea, which for centuries has been, and still remains, a vital interest to this country from a Naval point of view, looms larger than ever when air defence is also taken into consideration'. Hoping to secure the explicit commitment to Denmark's territorial integrity which the British had always been careful not to make, Ahlefeldt-Laurvig approached Eden and was 'crestfallen' to learn that Denmark was still not included among the countries in which Britain took a 'vital interest'.[109]

In June 1938 the Admiralty still held the view that, although an occupation of Denmark would extend Germany's naval and air operational range by up to two hundred miles, it was 'doubtful whether it would noticeably influence the course of a war between the United Kingdom and Germany'.[110] Its assessment was based on the assumption that German naval and air superiority were already so great that an occupation of Denmark would bring only minor advantages in comparison with the economic losses which would result from antagonising the Scandinavian countries. Once again, the Admiralty assumed

---

[106] Germany – Naval Intelligence Report, Section 2 – Strategy and Tactics (draft of c. 13 June 1936), ADM 178/137.

[107] Conversation with Sir Maurice Hankey, 19 April 1936, CAC, Hankey Papers, HNKY 5/ 1; Martin Gilbert, *Winston S. Churchill*, vol. V, *1922–1939* (London, 1976), p. 723.

[108] Susan Seymour, *Anglo-Danish Relations and Germany 1933–1945* (Odense, 1982), pp. 79–80.

[109] Eden minute, 12 March 1935, FO 371/19426, N1263/148/15.

[110] 'Note by the Admiralty on Possible German Penetration into Denmark', n.d. (c. June 1938), CAB 104/37.

that the principal German aim was to control trade within the Baltic, rather than to interrupt trade between Scandinavia and the United Kingdom.[111] Indeed, the assistant secretary to the CID, supporting the Admiralty view, suggested that an occupation of Denmark might be to Britain's advantage since it would make the German navy 'more venturesome in the North Sea' and thus 'increase our chances of bringing the Germans to action. In any event, we should be able to prevent German control of the west coast of Norway.'[112]

The downgrading of Denmark in British naval strategy was paralleled in the political sphere. The Danes were repeatedly assured, most authoritatively when Eden met Stauning in April 1937, that, apart from its commitments under the Locarno treaties, Britain had no European obligations 'beyond those contained in the Covenant of the League'.[113] Britain's attitude, to the extent that it was not based on ignorance and indifference, was a compound of realism and political calculation. It was realistic to make no specific promises in the light of Britain's inability to defend Denmark against German attack, as well as the Foreign Office's diminishing faith in Denmark's own defence capacity and resolve.[114] Moreover, the Danish government (as opposed to the Danish minister) would not welcome any public declaration of British support. It was thus advisable to leave both the Danes and the Germans guessing as to what Britain's attitude might be in the event of a German act of aggression.[115] On the other hand, there should be no hint that Britain might accept a 'voluntary' revision of the German–Danish frontier:

We do not want the Germans to be encouraged to think that they can upset a perfectly good frontier simply because it was 'imposed upon them' as the result of a plebiscite or to start a process of destroying the results of the Versailles Treaty by terrorising their weaker neighbours . . . nor do we wish Denmark to be drawn definitely into Germany's political and commercial orbit . . . for – to put it brutally – we are not concerned with Denmark's interests except in so far as they are also our own; and while it is not to our interest to see Danish–German relations definitely bad, it is equally against our interest to see them too close.[116]

Such attitudes were relatively easy to maintain as long as there was no immediate German threat to Danish integrity. The Foreign Office remained largely confident that the reoccupation of South Jutland was a low priority for Hitler, despite the agitation of local activists.[117] When Britain was eventually

---

[111] It was an enquiry regarding this contingency from the Industrial Intelligence Centre (IIC) which had led to the Admiralty's investigation: R. H. Owen (IIC) to Leslie Hollis (CID), 17 June 1936, ibid.

[112] Hollis to Owen, 29 June 1938, ibid.

[113] Eden–Stauning conversation, 8 April 1937, FO 371/21075, N1937/1380/15. For a summary of statements on Britain's attitude towards the questions of Danish integrity in general and of South Jutland in particular, see memorandum by P. S. Falla, 'South Jutland, 1934–1937', 13 April 1937, FO 371/21072, N1981/26/15 (paras. 10–14).

[114] Seymour, *Anglo-Danish Relations*, pp. 80–3.

[115] Collier to Ramsay, 10 February 1937, FO 371/21072, N330/26/15.

[116] Collier to Gurney, 27 February 1935, FO 371/19430, N817/807/15.

[117] Minutes by Vereker and Collier, 26–7 January 1937, FO 371/21072, N330/26/15.

obliged to consider the implications of a German attack on Denmark it was in quite different circumstances: not in response to any immediate threat or for any direct bearing it might have on Britain's strategic position, but as a theoretical *casus belli*.

The question arose as a by-product of the negotiations which surrounded the British guarantee to Poland of 30 March 1939. Denmark emerged in late March, along with Belgium, the Netherlands and Switzerland, as one of a number of west European countries for which Polish assistance might be expected in the event of German aggression.[118] For the first time, therefore, it appeared that Denmark was to be defined as part of western Europe and the security of Denmark as a matter of vital interest to the United Kingdom. The suggestion was evidently regarded as something of a novelty. The Foreign Office admitted that 'HMG have not reached any definite conclusion as to the action they would take in the event of a German attack upon Denmark, but they think that they would have no alternative but to regard it in much the same light as an attack on the Netherlands.'[119] However, when the Poles agreed to support Britain if it became involved in war over Denmark and the other countries named, the British government had to decide whether it would, in fact, defend Denmark against a German attack.[120]

The Foreign Office consulted the chiefs of staff on 18 April 1939.[121] Reminding them that Britain had no treaty obligations towards Denmark, the Foreign Office expressed doubts about Danish military resolve, and whether the Danes would welcome a public assurance of eventual British support. The opinion of the Industrial Intelligence Centre (IIC), also transmitted to the chiefs of staff, was that an occupation of Denmark would not be to Germany's advantage except in a very short war, 'since Danish agriculture is absolutely dependent on imports of fodder, which His Majesty's Government would be in a position to cut off'.[122] (The view of the German economic experts, as we have seen, was precisely the opposite.) In their report of 1 May the chiefs of staff considered that Denmark would be incapable of resisting a German attack and that Germany would gain complete control over the entrances to the Baltic, enhance the scope for naval and air operations in northern waters and, though without shortening the distance, acquire a broader base for air attacks on Great Britain. However, these 'slight strategic advantages . . . would be offset by the economic disadvantages, unless she [Germany] could be certain of a short war'. As far as British support was concerned, the conclusion of the report was overwhelmingly negative: 'In any event no military action which we

---

[118] There is a full account of the British deliberations on this question in Seymour, *Anglo-Danish Relations*, pp. 89–94.

[119] Draft telegram (not sent) to Sir E. Phipps (Paris), 14 April 1939, FO 371/23654, N2216/64/63.

[120] For the negotiations between British ministers and Col. Beck, see Anita Prazmowska, *Britain, Poland and the Eastern Front 1939* (Cambridge, 1987), pp. 59–61.

[121] D. W. Lascelles to secretary of CID, 18 April 1939, FO 371/23654, N2216/64/63.

[122] 'Brief Economic Appreciation of Denmark', 27 April 1939, ibid.

could take would prevent Germany gaining control of Denmark if she wished to do so, and anything we might attempt would only result in a useless dispersion of force.'[123]

Though the logic might be indisputable, the Foreign Office was not prepared to accept this conclusion. Cadogan minuted: 'The strategic and economic considerations may well be as represented. On the other hand, I should have thought it desirable that, if ever Germany did resort to such an act of wanton brigandage, the time would have come for a crusade.'[124] Halifax agreed and brought the matter to the Cabinet's Foreign Policy Committee for further consideration.[125] In the meantime a further element of uncertainty was created by the signature of the German–Danish non-aggression treaty on 31 May. While the British government understood the reasons why Denmark had felt obliged to sign, the treaty did little to clarify Germany's intentions.[126] When the Foreign Policy Committee met on 13 June Halifax attempted to keep open the possibility of assistance to Denmark by suggesting that the question might arise in the forthcoming negotiations with the Soviet Union.[127] His case was weakened by Runciman's insistence that 'nothing would induce the present Danish Government to fight Germany or resist German aggression', and by the declaration of Lord Chatfield, minister for coordination of defence, that an occupation of Denmark would do little to enhance Germany's position in relation either to the Soviet Union or to operations in the North Sea. But it was undermined most effectively by Chamberlain's trenchant recapitulation of the policy which had been initiated by the guarantee to Poland at the end of March:

THE PRIME MINISTER recalled that our general policy towards Germany was directed not to protecting individual States which might be threatened by Germany but to preventing German domination of the Continent resulting in Germany becoming so powerful as to be able to menace our security. German domination of Poland or Roumania would increase her military strength and it was for this reason that we had given guarantees to those countries. German domination of Denmark would not increase Germany's military strength and this therefore was not a case in which we should be bound to intervene forcibly to restore the status quo.

No decision was taken on this occasion or at a further meeting a week later, but Chamberlain evidently considered the matter settled. Denmark was not included among the states which Britain wished the Soviet Union to guarantee in its abortive alliance negotiations, and it was omitted (together with Switzerland) from the states specified in the secret protocol to the Anglo-Polish alliance of 25 August 1939.[128] 'The British excluded Denmark, partly because

---

[123] 'Denmark: Strategic Importance to the United Kingdom in the Light of Possible German Aggression', ibid.
[124] Minute of 5 May 1939, ibid.   [125] Minute of 5 May 1939, ibid.
[126] Eduard Reventlow, *I dansk tjeneste* (Copenhagen, 1956), pp. 112–13.
[127] FP(36) 51st meeting, CAB 27/625.
[128] Seymour, *Anglo-Danish Relations*, pp. 92–3; Prazmowska, *Britain, Poland and the Eastern Front*, pp. 161–4 (text of secret protocol printed in Appendix 4, pp. 201–4).

they concluded that the Danish Government would not want British assistance and because Denmark was considered dispensable.'[129]

The renunciation of an active role in the Baltic and the *de facto* assignment of Denmark to the German sphere of operations marked a reversion to the essentially passive stance adopted by Britain both before and during the First World War. By the late 1930s the naval pre-eminence in the Baltic enjoyed by Britain after the war had been revealed as artificial, sustainable only while Germany remained deprived of a navy. Any thought of forcing an entry through the Danish Straits had been rendered still more improbable by the development of German air power. Under the pressure of trying to construct a military alliance, first with France and later with the Soviet Union, the theoretical possibility of Baltic operations surfaced intermittently in the last months of peace.[130] Again, however, only Churchill appears to have retained a serious belief in the practicability of such operations – one which he was to force on a reluctant Admiralty, in the guise of Operation Catherine, when he returned to the post of first lord in September 1939.[131]

In other respects, too, the development of British strategic planning either involuntarily recalled or deliberately built upon the lessons of the war years. Economic warfare, above all, had been transformed from Hankey's revolutionary concept of the pre-1914 period into one of the key orthodoxies of British strategy. In February 1939 the chiefs of staff concluded that a future war would begin with Britain and France on the defensive and that 'Our subsequent policy should be directed to weakening Germany and Italy by the exercise of economic pressure and propaganda, while at the same time building up our major strength until we can adopt an offensive strategy.'[132] The Scandinavian countries would thus be expected to comply from the outset with the requirements of a strategy which it had taken four years of trial and error to establish between 1914 and 1918.

The experience of the First World War had inculcated an exaggerated belief in the effectiveness of the blockade in bringing about Germany's defeat, as well as a determination to avoid repeating the horrors of trench warfare. In the post-war period Britain's commitment to the League had strengthened these inclinations with the latter's emphasis on economic rather than military sanctions. Ashton Gwatkin was typical of informed opinion when he assured Swedish officials in April 1939 (during Hudson's visit to Stockholm) that the

---

[129] Seymour, *Anglo-Danish Relations*, p. 93.

[130] 'Anglo-French Staff Conversations 1939: British Strategical Memorandum', 14 March 1939, AFC(39)1, CAB 16/209; 'Staff Conversations with Russia. Instructions for Guidance of United Kingdom Delegation', 31 July 1939, DP(P)71, CAB 16/183B.

[131] Churchill, 'Memorandum on Sea Power', 25 March 1939, PREM 1/345; conversation with General Ironside, 25 July 1939, recorded in Roderick Macleod and Denis Kelly (eds.), *The Ironside Diaries 1937–1940* (London, 1962), pp. 83–4; Gilbert, *Churchill* V, pp. 1051, 1093–4.

[132] Quoted in Michael Howard, *The Continental Commitment: The Dilemma of British Defence Policy in the Era of the Two World Wars* (London, 1972), p. 135.

next war would be 'an air and blockade war'.[133] The establishment by the CID in 1929–30 of what was later to become the Industrial Intelligence Centre was a product of such assumptions, and its subsequent activities did much to reinforce them.[134] Headed by Major Desmond Morton, a close associate of Churchill,[135] the IIC soon moved beyond its original terms of reference, to report on 'the state of industrial and economic preparedness of foreign countries to make war', towards active cooperation with the Foreign Office and the intelligence branches of the armed forces in the formulation of policy. In 1938 it took a leading part in planning for the Ministry of Economic Warfare which was to come into existence on the outbreak of war; and when this materialised a year later the IIC formed the nucleus of MEW's Intelligence Division. The term 'economic warfare', apparently coined by the IIC, had implications which were deliberately much wider than its predecessor, 'blockade'. 'Blockade was a familiar enough thing in European warfare; but, adorned and transmogrified with a new name and an ill-defined promise, it had become in 1939 Britain's secret weapon.'[136]

When Ashton Gwatkin and other members of Hudson's delegation told the Swedes that neutrality would be impossible in wartime for the states bordering the Baltic, they underlined the difference between the British and German positions. As the IIC emphasised, the economic value of northern Europe to Britain in war, though very great, would be smaller than its value to Germany.[137] For Britain, most Scandinavian supplies were replaceable in the last resort from other sources. It might be more inconvenient, more dangerous or more costly to import timber from Canada instead of Finland, or iron ore from Newfoundland instead of Sweden; but Britain had some choice while Germany generally had none. Strict neutrality of the kind to which the Nordic countries had returned by the late 1930s was therefore of greater advantage to Germany than to Britain, since it meant the maintenance as far as possible of normal trading relations with all belligerents. If British economic warfare was to have any effect, trade between these countries and Germany would have to be substantially reduced. The onus was therefore on Great Britain to persuade them to adopt a more flexible interpretation of neutrality.

In April 1938, when there was a threat of war over Czechoslovakia, a blockade of Germany by the Nordic countries was already regarded in the Foreign Office as being 'in the highest degree unlikely'.[138] This pessimistic

---

[133] Memoranda by G. Hägglöf (head of Economic Section, Swedish Foreign Ministry) and R. Kumlin, 15 April 1939, SUD, H 40 Ct., Bd XV; Hägglöf, *Svensk krigshandelspolitik*, pp. 26–7.

[134] Robert J. Young, 'Spokesmen for Economic Warfare: The Industrial Intelligence Centre in the 1930s', *European Studies Review* 6 (1976), pp. 473–89.

[135] R. W. Thompson, *Churchill and Morton* (London, 1976).

[136] W. N. Medlicott, *The Economic Blockade* (2 vols., London, 1952), vol. I, p. xi.

[137] IIC to Joint Planning Committee, CID, 30 August 1939, FO 371/23657, N4041/64/63.

[138] Memorandum by R. H. Hadow, 'Possible Opposition to a German Attack on Czechoslovakia by Soviet Union, Baltic States and Scandinavian Countries', 26 April 1938, FO 371/22276, N2072/533/63.

assessment was reinforced by the results of a circular enquiry sent in May to the legations in Copenhagen, Oslo and Stockholm, as part of the detailed preparations for economic warfare begun at this time.[139] Recalling that in the last war the northern neutrals had in practice favoured the belligerents 'according to the degree of pressure which each was able to bring to bear upon them', and assuming that in a future war 'the position of the Scandinavian countries will again be of paramount importance', the Foreign Office asked how far and in what ways they might respond to similar pressure from Britain and Germany in a future war. The three replies were depressingly similar. The minister in Oslo quoted a Norwegian officer to the effect that Norway felt like a 'louse between two nails': 'She fears both sides, but Germany most on account of her general ruthlessness.' None of the three countries was likely to take active steps to discourage 'the establishment of a transit trade designed to frustrate the British contraband control'; all would claim the right to continue trading with both belligerents and would go to extreme lengths to placate Germany. In Sweden's case it was suggested that 'if Germany has control of the Baltic it is probable that Sweden will supply Germany with all the foodstuffs and raw materials demanded, even if it meant starving her people and industries'.[140]

In fact the war trade policy formulated in Sweden between the summer of 1938 and the outbreak of war belied this bleak prediction. It was designed to avoid just such a one-sided interpretation of neutrality, since the excessive favour shown to Germany by the Hammarskjöld government in the last war had exposed Sweden to such devastating Allied reprisals.[141] On the other hand there was an equally firm resolve to avoid entanglement in a blockade of Germany. Following the lines laid down during the crisis of September 1938 by Östen Undén, Swedish policy sought to avoid both extremes and to take account only of Sweden's national interests.[142] Trade relations would be maintained with all sides, as far as possible in the same proportions and at the same level as in peacetime, as long as the belligerents continued to supply Sweden's needs and respect its neutrality. For the Germans this situation was tolerable if not ideal, especially in the light of the formal assurance given by Sweden in April 1939 that it would take no part in any attempt to cut off supplies of iron ore.[143]

For the British such an attitude was not sufficient. When Hudson visited Stockholm he was disturbed by the apparent complacency with which the Swedes declared their intention of doing business with both sides while

[139] FO to ministers in Scandinavian capitals, 16 May 1938, ibid., N1446/533/63.
[140] Ibid.: Ramsay to FO, 26 May 1938, N2670/533/63; Dormer to FO, 8 July, N3580/533/63; Monson (Stockholm), 19 July, N3863/533/63.
[141] Hägglöf, *Svensk krigshandelspolitik*, ch. 1; Erik Boheman, *På vakt*, vol. II, *Kabinettsekreterare under andra världskriget* (Stockholm, 1964), pp. 78–80.
[142] Hägglöf, *Svensk krigshandelspolitik*, pp. 18–20; Erik Lönnroth, *Den svenska utrikespolitikens historia*, vol. V, *1919–1939* (Stockholm, 1959), pp. 170–2.
[143] See note 43 above.

acknowledging that, since the Germans would control the Baltic, most of that business would be with them.[144] Both before and after the outbreak of war, therefore, the British were faced with a dilemma. Should they accept the logic of the Swedish position and agree that Scandinavian–German trade should remain at its peacetime level? This would at least prevent the sudden explosion of German imports which had occurred in the last war. Or should they take steps to reduce or cut off that trade by peaceful, or possibly military, means? The problem was posed most acutely in the case of Swedish iron ore.

Iron ore had been identified at an early stage by the IIC as one of the German war economy's key deficiency commodities.[145] By 1938, however, British strategic planners were having to face the consequence of the successful British campaign to secure an upward revision of the export limit set by the 'Grängesberg law'. A partial solution to the problem was achieved in the summer of 1939 when, at Swedish prompting, it was agreed that a war reserve of 500,000 tons of Swedish ore should be created. Morton, however, sought more radical solutions. In 1937 he suggested that bombing Germany's internal transport system would have a 'catastrophic' effect on the steel output of the Ruhr.[146] Between 1937 and the spring of 1939 the planners at the IIC and the Foreign Office moved away from action on German territory towards various kinds of covert action aimed at disruption of mining operations or the interruption of communications closer to source – in other words on Scandinavian territory. Morton spoke of fomenting strike action at the mines of northern Sweden and appears to have been involved in plans for sabotaging the Narvik–Luleå railway or the port installations at Narvik itself. He also suggested that some form of military guarantee should be offered to Sweden as an inducement to resist German pressure, though this idea was not taken up by his superiors.[147] A further option, that of interception within Norwegian territorial waters, was under discussion by a small unofficial planning group at the Admiralty early in 1939.[148]

These tentative schemes were to re-emerge in one guise or other during the first months of the war. Sabotage – directed not at Narvik or the northern ore fields but at the Swedish Baltic port of Oxelösund – was attempted early in 1940, with disastrous incompetence, by the SIS agent Alfred Rickman and his associates.[149] Interrupting the supply of Swedish iron ore in Norwegian waters,

---

[144] Conversations with Sandler, 1 April 1939, FO 371/23709, N1842/1818/42, and with Marcus Wallenberg Jr, 2 April 1939, FO 371/23652, N1910/31/63.

[145] IIC memorandum, 'Sweden', 13 December 1934, FO 419/29, N1525/18/42; Patrick Salmon, 'British Plans for Economic Warfare Against Germany 1937–1939: The Problem of Swedish Iron Ore', *Journal of Contemporary History* 16 (1981), pp. 53–72.

[146] 'Germany. Supplies of Iron Ore in War', 25 June 1937, ATB(EPG)6, CAB 47/13.

[147] Salmon, 'British Plans', pp. 63–7.

[148] Patrick Salmon, 'Churchill, the Admiralty and the Narvik Traffic September–November 1939', *Scandinavian Journal of History* 4 (1979), pp. 305–36.

[149] The most authoritative accounts of this episode are now to be found in Thomas Munch-Petersen, 'Confessions of a British Agent: Section D in Sweden 1938–1940', in *Utrikespolitik och historia. Studier tillägnade Wilhelm M. Carlgren den 6 maj 1987* (Stock-

either by interception or by laying mines, was one of Winston Churchill's earliest initiatives as first lord of the Admiralty.[150] First proposed to the War Cabinet on 19 September 1939, it remained on the agenda throughout the Anglo-French deliberations on intervention in Scandinavia, ultimately to be put into effect twenty-four hours before the Germans landed in Norway. All such efforts represented a growing belief in the necessity of 'stoppage at source' whatever that might entail for the neutrality of the country concerned. They were also a measure of the frustration experienced by British strategists in the face of the progressive incorporation of the Nordic countries into the German sphere.

In one important respect British strategic assumptions remained unchanged up to the outbreak of war. Norway, so it was presumed, still lay comfortably within the British sphere of influence. Britain's naval superiority off the coast of Norway was unquestioned, and the possibility of either British or German naval operations in Norwegian waters was given less attention between the wars than in the pre-1914 period. Admiral Godfrey, the wartime director of naval intelligence, wrote that

In all my four years in Plans Division, and another four years as a teacher at the Staff College, no-one ever suggested that we should carry the war into Norwegian waters. There was no demand and this essentially secret job (in peacetime) never got on to any priority list at all.[151]

The Admiralty apparently remained unaware of German interest in naval bases in Norway until Vansittart drew its attention to the existence of Admiral Wegener's book in April 1939.[152]

Yet the position of Norway was less reassuring than it appeared. There was a growing dichotomy, not fully appreciated in Britain, between Norway's actual dependence on Britain and the determination of its government to avoid involvement in a British blockade of Germany. Norwegians were also beginning to doubt whether the comfortable assumption of British naval superiority would be borne out in wartime. This doubt was never shared by

holm, 1987), pp. 175–88; C. G. McKay, *From Information to Intrigue: Studies in Secret Service Based on the Swedish Experience 1939–1945* (London, 1993), pp. 44–62; and Sir Peter Tennant, *Touchlines of War* (Hull, 1992), pp. 126–32. Nominally, at least, Rickman was the author of the respectable study, *Swedish Iron Ore* (London, 1939), for which he conducted 'research' in Sweden in 1938. In fact the book was written for him by Col. Laurence Grand, the head of Section D of SIS.

[150] Churchill, *The Second World War* I, pp. 478–9.

[151] J. H. Godfrey, *Naval Memoirs of Admiral J. H. Godfrey* (8 vols. in 11, privately printed, 1964–6; copy in Churchill College Archive Centre, Cambridge), vol. VIII, ch. 13.

[152] Vansittart to Backhouse (first sea lord), 14 April 1939, ADM 1/9956. Godfrey commented: 'Reports of German intentions to seize Skagen and Lacso [i.e. the Danish island of Læsø], and the Norwegian fears concerning Stavanger aerodrome give colour to the views expressed.' Given the importance attached by Admiral Carls to acquiring strategic points on Danish territory (including Læsø), Godfrey's comment suggests that the Admiralty may have had some inkling of the content of the strategic debate within the German naval command: Gemzell, *Raeder, Hitler und Skandinavien*, pp. 97–102.

Foreign Office officials, but in 1938–9 they began to realise that the Norwegians were worried and came round to the view that it was necessary to provide some form of reassurance. This ultimately took the form of a military guarantee. A report by the chiefs of staff on Norwegian neutrality of 4 September 1939 represented the first high-level examination in wartime of the military significance of Scandinavia, and led on 16 September to Britain's first formal commitment to the defence of one of the Nordic countries. It was a small but significant step towards the military disaster into which both Britain and Norway were to be plunged eight months later.

The process began shortly after the Munich crisis when Colonel Gulliksen, the strongly pro-British head of the Norwegian military air service, suggested to the British air attaché that if war had broken out the Germans might have seized the new aerodrome of Sola near Stavanger, owing to its importance as an advanced base for attacking British shipping or the British Isles.[153] The intention behind Gulliksen's suggestion was unclear: he might have been trying to find out whether, in the event of war, Britain would occupy the aerodrome in order to forestall the Germans, or seeking to coordinate defence measures between Britain and Norway in peacetime.[154] The second alternative was so out of line with his government's neutrality policy that the Foreign Office, War Office and Admiralty were wary of following up Gulliksen's approach.[155] However, it was decided in March 1939 that he should be sounded unofficially, partly to discover whether the Norwegian government was in any way involved, and partly because in the Air Ministry's view the aerodrome at Sola 'was so vital that we should have to try to recover it, whatever the situation'.[156]

A statement to the effect that Britain would 'attempt to dislodge' the Germans would represent no commitment, but it would be a realistic estimate of British intentions which might help the Norwegians in their defence preparations. It might also be of great political value, in the aftermath of Prague, in restoring Norwegian faith in Britain's resolve. This was now, in Collier's view, dangerously weak:

The assumption of the 'defeatists' – that this country would not defend Norway against Germany – is of course wrong; and a glance at the map ought to show them that we could never allow so vital a strategic position for attack on Great Britain to fall into German hands without a fight.

It is thus all the more significant, as a measure of the disrepute into which we have fallen, that even a German attack on Norway is not thought, in that country itself, to be enough to rouse us.[157]

[153] Dormer to Collier, 3 October 1938, FO 371/22283, N4973/4973/30; P. Davis (air attaché) to Freese-Pennefather (Oslo), 19 October 1938, ibid., N5357/5973/30.
[154] Minutes by Lascelles and Collier, 7 November 1938, ibid.
[155] Brownjohn (WO) to Collier, 20 December 1938, FO 371/23654, N6296/4974/30; Jones (Admiralty) to Collier, 23 December 1938, N6367/4973/30, ibid.
[156] Lascelles minute, 31 March 1939, FO 371/23674, N1661/849/30; Collier minute, 5 April 1939 (recording Air Ministry view), ibid.
[157] Collier minute, 29 March 1939, FO 371/23652, N1674/31/63.

The Oslo legation was therefore authorised on 11 April to give Gulliksen a specific assurance on Sola, find out whether the Norwegians intended to defend the aerodrome themselves, and 'tell the Norwegians to look at the map and realize that we *must* defend Norway'.[158] Together with the guarantee to Poland, the adoption of conscription and a Commons statement of 26 April that the British government would be 'by no means indifferent' to a threat to the integrity of Norway, Sweden or Finland, such statements might help to prop up British prestige in Norway and elsewhere in northern Europe.[159]

Apart from the assurance on Sola they remained the 'private' opinions of the British minister and his staff: Cadogan had warned that 'we can't take explicit commitments to defend every country on earth'.[160] But between April and July 1939 the Northern Department came to the conclusion that precisely this kind of commitment was essential if the Norwegians were to be persuaded to lend any assistance to a future blockade of Germany. It now seemed clear that, although the Norwegians intended to offer some resistance to a German attack on the aerodrome, it was unlikely to amount to much and there were 'serious chances of a complete German domination of Norway'.[161]

Collier suggested that the Norwegian fear that, 'while expecting them to help us in our blockade of Germany, we shall not protect them against German reprisals', could be 'largely exorcised by letting it be known in Norway that, without giving that country an actual guarantee (which it does not want), we are in fact, in our own interests, obliged to regard an attack on Norway as an attack on ourselves'.[162] The proposal was unorthodox. Cadogan was suspicious because, while falling short of a formal guarantee, such an assurance would in fact commit Britain to war with Germany if the latter attacked Norway; but Halifax thought the matter serious enough to merit investigation by the CID.[163] On 24 August the chiefs of staff were therefore requested to consider

the commitments involved in the issue of instructions to His Majesty's Minister at Oslo to speak to the Norwegian authorities on these lines, intimating confidentially but formally that His Majesty's Government would regard a German attack on Norway as tantamount to an attack on this country.[164]

Owing partly to the wording of this request and partly to the advice of the IIC, the chiefs of staff read more into the proposal than Collier had intended.

Dormer's recent reports from Oslo seem to have dispelled much of the

---

[158] Collier minute, 1 April 1939, ibid.; telegram to Freese-Pennefather, 11 April 1939, FO 371/23674, N1661/849/30.
[159] Cadogan minute, 31 March 1939, FO 371/23652, N1674/31/63; Lascelles minute, 21 April 1939, FO 371/23654, N2132/64/63.
[160] Cadogan minute, 31 March 1939, FO 371/23652, N1674/31/63.
[161] Freese-Pennefather to FO, 22 April 1939, FO 371/23674, N2207/849/30; Dormer to Sir L. Oliphant, 25 April 1939, FO 371/23654, N22162/64/63; Collier minute, 4 May 1939, ibid.
[162] Draft memorandum (written between 30 June and 10 July 1939), ibid., N1764/64/63.
[163] Minutes of 16 and 18 August 1939, ibid.
[164] Lascelles to secretary of CID, ibid.

Northern Department's earlier pessimism about Norwegian attitudes. When he asked Koht in April how the Norwegian government would respond to a German ultimatum, the latter declined to give a direct answer; 'but, he added, putting on his most determined and fierce expression, "I know very well myself what my answer would be"'.[165] Apart from his formal interviews with the foreign minister, Dormer's contacts were mainly with the king, and with members of the armed forces and business community whose inclinations were conspicuously pro-British.[166] The views of the latter, together with Koht's encouraging response, may have led the British minister to underestimate the extent to which isolationism, neutralism and simple fear of Nazi Germany had come to prevail among members of the government, as well as in political circles by no means exclusively socialist, with whom he had little professional or social contact.[167]

The chiefs of staff were thus informed that 'The sympathies both of the Government and of the people would be likely to favour the British cause, to a greater extent perhaps than in any other neutral country', and that, without wanting a formal guarantee, individual members of the government 'would be by no means averse from learning privately' that Britain would regard an attack on Norway as an attack on itself.[168] Given the strength of Koht's views on neutrality and great-power politics, this advice represented a serious misjudgement. But the fault did not lie exclusively with the Northern Department. Collier, after all, had been thinking only in terms of 'benevolent neutrality' in 'such matters as the collection of blockade information'; and this, given the pro-British sympathies of the Norwegian naval authorities and some Norwegian businessmen, was not an unrealistic expectation.[169] The IIC bore a larger responsibility, for, in its advice to the chiefs of staff on the importance of Norway from the point of view of economic warfare, it contemplated forcing Norway 'into taking action which would be construed by Germany as directly hostile, as would most certainly be a refusal to export iron ore from Narvik'.[170]

---

[165] Dormer to FO, 26 April 1939, FO 371/23654, N2251/64/63. See also the accurate account of the conversation in Weizsäcker telegram to Oslo legation, 11 May 1939, *DGFP*, D, VI, p. 474. It was on this occasion that Koht made the subsequently much-criticised statement that he believed that the development of military technology no longer made it so necessary for the belligerents to acquire a base in Norway: Arne Bergsgård, 'Utrikspolitikk', in *Innstilling fra undersøkelsekommisjonen av 1945. Bilag*, vol. I (Oslo, 1947), pp. 117–264 (p. 178); Halvdan Koht, *For fred og fridom i krigstid 1939–1940* (Oslo, 1957), p. 24.

[166] Collier minute, 12 August 1939, FO 371/23656, N3660/64/63.

[167] In 1937 Collier had advised against ascribing anti-British sentiments solely to the Norwegian Labour Party: 'On the contrary, the chief anti-British force in Norway is M. Hambro, the Conservative leader, whose attitude in the fishery question, for example, has been one of the chief obstacles to an agreement and appears inspired partly by chauvinism and partly by personal rancour' (extract from passage added to Admiralty Intelligence Report on Scandinavia, sent to DNI on 21 January 1937, FO 371/21225, W531/531/50).

[168] Lascelles to secretary of CID, FO 371/23654, N2200/64/63.

[169] Collier minute, 1 September 1939, FO 371/23657, N4041/64/63.

[170] IIC to Joint Planning Committee, CID, 30 August 1939, FO 371/23657, N4041/64/63.

In the view of the IIC, the importance of Norway to Britain would on balance be less, in spite of the great value of its merchant fleet, than the benefit derived by Germany from a neutral Norway as the most important export route for Swedish iron ore. Economic pressure would not be sufficient to persuade the Norwegians to ban iron ore exports, but military guarantees might be offered 'in exchange for an undertaking on the part of Norway to take certain action favouring the Allies, in excess of that which she could be persuaded to take by the exercise or threat of economic pressure alone'.[171] Collier's original idea of strengthening Norwegian morale by making a statement of the obvious – that Britain could never allow Norway to fall into enemy hands – had thus been transformed into a bargain by which Norway was to be induced to take conspicuously unneutral action on Britain's behalf.

This new emphasis was reflected in the chiefs of staff report of 4 September, which recognised that Britain might exert economic pressure to the 'fullest extent compatible with international law in order to compel Norway to stop exporting Swedish iron ore'. The report anticipated German reprisals following such action – probably economic or diplomatic rather than military – but concluded that if Norway were attacked, 'it would be in our interest to come to Norway's assistance, except that as regards direct air attack by Germany our assistance could only be indirect'.[172] With this one reservation, the chiefs of staff thus endorsed Collier's proposal and implicitly rejected a bargain of the kind proposed by the IIC. The members of the Joint Planning Committee, who actually composed the report, were too cautious and too realistic to contemplate any unnecessary dispersion of Britain's limited military resources. They accepted that such an assurance could be given to Norway solely because they saw it as a morale-booster rather than a new commitment. Indeed the Air Ministry's director of plans subsequently described the assurance to Norway as 'unexceptionable in theory', but 'precisely nil' in practical value.[173]

Nevertheless the report acknowledged the possibility of bringing pressure to bear on Norway on the iron ore question, and it was this aspect – now that war had actually broken out – which was taken up with greatest interest in the Northern Department. Collier was not sure that it would work, but a junior official, Daniel Lascelles, argued in favour of applying rigorous pressure in the forthright terms which were typical of his robust approach to Scandinavian questions during the few months he spent in the department in 1939:

If we succeed without provoking German military reprisals against Norway, our main objective will have been achieved. If, on the other hand, Germany resorts to such reprisals, infringing Norwegian neutrality and enabling us to intervene in a 'protective' capacity, we need not fear the outcome. At present one of our main difficulties is to find

[171] Ibid.
[172] 'Norwegian Neutrality. Report by the Chiefs of Staff Committee', 4 September 1939, WP(39)5, CAB 66/1.
[173] Sir John Slessor, *The Central Blue* (London, 1956), p. 260.

the means of attacking Germany on relatively undefended sectors. Operations against her in Norway would enable us to exploit our immense naval superiority to the full; they would hamper her at a moment when she wishes to concentrate her forces elsewhere; and as Germany would have been the first to infringe Norwegian neutrality, the reactions of the other Scandinavian states would be extremely unfavourable to her.

The real moral of this report is, in fact, that we should do all in our power to provoke a German infringement of Norwegian neutrality and be prepared to intervene vigorously as soon as this is brought about.[174]

This was a remarkable anticipation of most of the arguments for a 'flanking strategy' in Scandinavia which were to be employed by Churchill and other members of the British and French governments during the winter of 1939–40.

In the short term, however, it could have no effect on policy beyond reinforcing the Foreign Office's conviction that an approach to the Norwegian foreign minister would be opportune.[175] The assurance was duly made on 16 September. According to Dormer's report, Koht 'made no remark but it will probably have a good effect'.[176] Koht's own account confirms that he was glad to hear that Britain would regard an attack on Norway as an attack on itself, but was determined that this assurance should not lead to anything resembling an alliance.[177] He tried to deflect that possibility by replying that he did not believe that Germany would attack Norway because he could not see that it would gain any advantage from doing so.

Indeed nothing could have been more unwelcome to Koht than a closer relationship with Great Britain. Much of his activity over the previous months had been devoted to maintaining a distance between Britain and Norway. He had put off a planned visit to London in May 1939 because it might have given the impression that Norway was on the verge of concluding an alliance, as the recent visit of the Polish foreign minister had done. If Norway were allied with Britain, he believed, it would immediately be attacked by Germany.[178] It is hardly surprising that Koht was unimpressed by an offer of support which excluded German air attack, and which must merely have reinforced his doubts about the preparedness of the British army and air force. A measure of Koht's alarm was the fact that he said nothing about the British approach to the Storting's foreign affairs committee, where the idea of an alliance might have received a measure of support.[179] For Koht, a rigorous adherence to neutrality was the only hope of escaping involvement in the war. As he stated in his post-war apologia, 'Norway could not have chosen a more risky course

[174] Minute of 8 September 1939, FO 371/23658, N4218/64/63. In January 1940 Lascelles was appointed first secretary to the Oslo legation.

[175] Collier minute, 8 September 1939, FO 371/23658, N4218/64/63.

[176] Dormer telegram to FO, 16 September 1939, FO 371/23049, C14318/454/18.

[177] Koht, For fred og fridom i krigstid, pp. 65–6; Bergsgård, 'Utrikspolitikk', p. 184.

[178] Halvdan Koht, Norsk utanrikspolitikk fram til 9. april 1940. Synspunkt frå hendings-tida (Oslo, 1947), p. 12.

[179] Odd-Bjørn Fure, Norsk utenrikspolitikks historie, vol. III, Mellomkrigstid 1920–1940 (Oslo, 1996), p. 341.

than to abandon neutrality in September 1939.'[180] It is a reflection of the extent to which British and Norwegian attitudes had diverged that British officials had so little appreciation of the depth of Koht's convictions, and the extent to which faith in Britain's military capacity had declined, that his subsequent suspicion and obstructiveness towards Great Britain came as a surprise and a disappointment.

The Soviet Union, Finland and the defence of Leningrad

The defence of Leningrad posed a more serious problem for the Soviet government than had been faced by its tsarist predecessor before 1914.[181] At that time Russia's strategic frontier had encompassed Finland (including the Åland Islands) and the Baltic provinces, stretching as far west as the River Niemen. Now the Soviet Union's Baltic coastline was confined to a small area around Leningrad, hemmed in by independent states on both sides of the Gulf of Finland. To the north, Finland was no longer an intermittently restive province but a sovereign state. It owed its origins to a bitter civil war which had instilled a deep hatred of Russia and of Bolshevism in large sections of the Finnish people. Important sections of the political and military leadership still looked to Germany as the country which had saved Finland in 1918 and might do so again in the future. To the south, Estonia, Latvia and Lithuania were small states which had succumbed to various brands of right-wing dictatorship and were also linked in various ways to Germany, notably through trade, but also through collaboration with the German armed forces and intelligence services. Formal defence cooperation between Finland and the Baltic states and their neighbours to the south had made little progress, but there were informal links between the Finnish and Estonian armed forces.[182] Even in the absence of such contacts, the fact that both shores of the Gulf of Finland, and all the islands in the Gulf (with their tsarist defences still intact), were in the hands of weakly armed and potentially hostile states represented an invitation which, it seemed, a power like Germany could scarcely ignore. The USSR for its part was determined to move forward its strategic defence line so as to ensure that any German attack would not have to be met on Soviet soil.[183]

As the danger of war grew, the USSR sought to obtain reassurance about Finland's attitude.[184] To some extent this requirement was met by Finland's explicit commitment to a policy of neutrality and Scandinavian cooperation, as

---

[180] Koht, *Norsk utanrikspolitikk*, p. 28.

[181] Patrick Salmon, 'Great Britain, the Soviet Union and Finland at the Beginning of the Second World War', in John Hiden and Thomas Lane (eds.), *The Baltic and the Outbreak of the Second World War* (Cambridge, 1992), pp. 95–123.

[182] Martti Turtola, 'Aspects of Finnish–Estonian Military Relations in the 1920s and 1930s', in John Hiden and Aleksander Loit (eds.), *The Baltic in International Relations Between the Two World Wars* (Stockholm, 1988), pp. 101–10.

[183] Seppo Myllyniemi, *Die baltische Krise 1938–1941* (Stuttgart, 1979), p. 18.

[184] The most authoritative account of the Soviet–Finnish exchanges in 1938–9 remains that of Max Jakobson, *The Diplomacy of the Winter War* (Cambridge, Mass., 1961). It should

well as by the leftward shift of Finnish politics reflected in the formation of the Cajander government in 1937. But protestations were not enough. As Litvinov told Holsti during the latter's visit to Moscow in October 1937, the Soviets did not fear that Finland would attack them, but there was nevertheless a danger that in time of war Finland might suddenly find itself in the camp of the USSR's enemies. They needed to know what Finland was prepared to do in order to prevent its territory from being used by a third party to launch an attack on the Soviet Union.[185] The same message was conveyed in the secret exchanges initiated by Boris Yartsev in April 1938. The Finns, unable to divine the complexities of the Soviet power structure, failed to grasp the significance of Yartsev's role as 'the agent of the Politburo itself or perhaps of a powerful group within it'.[186] Since the Finns proved unable or unwilling to do more than state their determination to resist the use of their territory for an attack on the USSR, the Soviets became increasingly insistent upon the need for concrete guarantees. These centred on the Gulf of Finland. In August 1938 they requested base facilities on the island of Suursaari (Hogland). During further discussions in October Yartsev suggested that Finland should itself fortify Suursaari with Soviet cooperation. In March 1939 Litvinov proposed that Suursaari, along with a number of smaller islands (Lavansaari, Seiskaari and the Tytärsaari Islands), should be leased to the Soviet Union for thirty years – a request repeated by the former minister to Finland, Boris Shtein, who visited Helsinki on a special mission later in the month. On each occasion the Soviet Union offered compensation, including the conclusion of a trade agreement on favourable terms and, finally, the cession to Finland of territory in Soviet Karelia (long coveted by Finnish irredentists).

Consulted for the first time by the Finnish government, Mannerheim urged that Shtein should not be allowed to leave Helsinki empty-handed. In his opinion the islands were of no military use to Finland and could not be defended, but were of real importance to the Soviet Union. He even suggested that Finland should offer to move the frontier on the Karelian Isthmus farther away from Leningrad.[187] The Finnish refusal to accede to the Soviet requests (while seeking Soviet approval for the refortification of the Åland Islands) was thus not due to lack of authoritative advice. It derived in part from a simple refusal to contemplate the cession of any part of Finnish territory, least of all to the hereditary enemy. This disinclination was reinforced by the knowledge that no government could take such a step without unleashing a storm of public disapproval. Perhaps, too, the Finnish government had been sufficiently

be supplemented by the important article by D. W. Spring, 'The Soviet Decision for War Against Finland 30 November 1939', *Soviet Studies* 38 (1986), pp. 207–26.
[185] Menger, *Deutschland und Finnland*, pp. 37–8.
[186] Jakobson, *Diplomacy of the Winter War*, p. 51.
[187] Baron C. G. E. Mannerheim, *The Memoirs of Marshal Mannerheim* (London, 1953), pp. 299–301. The view that Finland should hand over the islands in advance of a Soviet seizure was also conveyed to the British during General Kirke's visit (see p. 354): Col. Beaumont-Nesbitt to FO, FO 371/23648, N3199/698/56.

encouraged by the progress of Swedish–Finnish military cooperation to believe that Sweden might come to Finland's aid in time of crisis.[188] But the Finnish attitude was also based on a serious underestimate of Soviet military capacity. In the light of the purges 'the conviction [had] taken root in the Government and the parties supporting it, as well as in the top military command, that Russia [was] incapable of waging a war for years to come'.[189]

In fact, although the Soviet armed forces had undoubtedly been gravely weakened by the purges, Stalin was already considering a military solution to the Finnish problem. The earliest preparations appear to date from the end of 1938, a time when Finnish stubbornness had already been made clear.[190] In April 1939 B. M. Shaposhnikov, chief of the general staff and former commander of the Leningrad military district, was ordered to prepare plans for a campaign against Finland.[191] He concluded that it would be 'far from a simple matter and expected that it would require not less than several months of intense and difficult war, even in the event that the great imperialist powers did not intervene directly in the conflict'.[192] Similar conclusions were reached by K. A. Meretskov, commander of the Leningrad military district, when he was ordered in June to prepare plans for a campaign against Finland using the resources of his own district alone.[193]

Both commanders were overruled by the Chief Military Council, a body set up after the purges which included both Stalin and Zhdanov, the Leningrad party chief, but few competent military specialists, on the grounds that they underestimated the strength of the Red Army and, rather perversely in the light of its own instructions, did not take into account the strength of the Soviet Union as a whole. Khrushchev's posthumous memoirs suggest, on the one hand, that neither Stalin nor Marshal Voroshilov, the people's commissar for defence, fully appreciated the underpreparedness of the Red Army; and on the other that, when the attack on Finland was finally launched on 30 November 1939, Stalin did not expect to meet serious resistance. 'All we had to do was raise our voice a little bit, and the Finns would obey. If that didn't work, we could fire one shot and the Finns would put up their hands and surrender. Or so we thought.'[194] Under the influence of Zhdanov and Kuusinen, Stalin probably also expected class conflict to weaken Finland's will to fight.[195]

By the summer of 1939 Finland had become the centre of a three-way struggle for influence. The Soviet overtures remained largely secret, though both the

[188] Martti Turtola, *Från Torne älv till Systerbäck. Hemligt försvarssamarbete mellan Finland och Sverige 1923–1940* (Stockholm, 1987), pp. 13–14, 207–13.
[189] Blücher to AA, 1 August 1938, *DGFP*, D, V, pp. 589–93 (p. 591).
[190] Anthony F. Upton, *Finland 1939–1940* (London, 1974), pp. 22–3.
[191] Spring, 'Soviet Decision', p. 212.   [192] Quoted ibid.
[193] Ibid., p. 213; Upton, *Finland 1939–1940*, pp. 22–3.
[194] Nikita Khrushchev, *Khrushchev Remembers* (London, 1971), pp. 152, 159–60.
[195] Jakobson, *Diplomacy of the Winter War*, pp. 145–6; Spring, 'Soviet Decision', pp. 217–19.

Finnish foreign minister Eljas Erkko (Holsti's successor) and Mannerheim allowed details of Shtein's proposals to percolate through to foreign contacts.[196] German and British efforts were much more visible. While Blücher, the German minister, was wholly realistic in his assessment that even the pro-German sympathies of the armed forces would not counteract the overwhelming desire in the country for peace, Germany could still exploit those sympathies in order to impede rapprochement between Finland and the Soviet Union.[197] The ostentatious displays of German military interest from 1937 onwards certainly helped to reinforce the Soviet belief that Finland must be acting with German encouragement. A delegation of officers led by General von Falkenhorst visited Finland on the occasion of Mannerheim's seventieth birthday in June 1937. In the summer of 1937 the creation of a new naval attaché's post at Helsinki was followed by the visit of a U-boat squadron. In October 1937, at almost the same time as Holsti was pursuing his peace policy in Moscow, former president Svinhufvud was assuring German listeners, including Himmler and General von der Goltz, that Russia's enemy must always be Finland's friend. In March 1938 the commander-in-chief of the Finnish army, General Österman, was received by Hitler during a visit to Germany; in April von der Goltz led a delegation to celebrate the twentieth anniversary of the liberation of Helsinki. Finnish–German contacts culminated in June 1939 with visits from the chief of German counter-intelligence, Admiral Canaris, and the chief of the general staff, General Halder.

In Britain, the growing intensity of the Finnish–German military relationship tended to confirm Foreign Office suspicions of the Finnish General Staff's 'habit of conducting a policy of its own, independent of the Government'.[198] It also threatened to undermine British influence since, although the Finnish armed forces by now purchased much of their military hardware from Great Britain, they still relied on Germany for training. From 1937 onwards increasing numbers of officers from both countries participated in the Finnish–German military exchange programme.[199] By the spring of 1939, however, Britain had a more immediate concern: to dispel well-founded Finnish fears concerning Finland's role in the British–French–Soviet negotiations for a military alliance. The Soviets certainly expected the British and French to deliver the strategic strong points which the Finns had refused to volunteer. When the Soviet plans were finally revealed to the Anglo-French delegation in Moscow in August 1939, they included the stipulation that Britain and France '*must* obtain from the Governments of the Baltic States and of Finland their permission for the temporary occupation by the Franco-British Fleets', with the participation of the Soviet Baltic Fleet, of a number of

---

[196] Jakobson, *Diplomacy of the Winter War*, p. 64; Snow to FO, 19 June 1939, FO 419/33, N3150/26/63.
[197] Blücher to AA, 1 August 1938, *DGFP*, D, V, pp. 589–93; Menger, *Deutschland und Finnland*, pp. 40–7; Ueberschär, *Hitler und Finnland*, pp. 24–7, 59–60.
[198] Collier minute, 8 July 1939, FO 371/23663, N3234/3076/63.
[199] Menger, *Deutschland und Finnland*, p. 41.

islands, including the Ålands, as well as the peninsula of Hanko on the Finnish mainland.[200]

Well before these specific requirements were made known, the Soviets demanded that in order to guard against the danger of 'indirect aggression', the alliance must include an explicit guarantee of the 'Baltic states' (among which, in this context, they included Finland), with or without their consent.[201] In these circumstances a planned visit to Finland by General Sir Walter Kirke, originally viewed as a means of countering German influence, acquired heightened significance. It would now serve to reassure the Finns that Britain was not 'prepared to sacrifice their interests in order to come to terms with the Soviet Union'.[202] General Kirke's visit in June 1939, his first to the country since his advisory mission in 1924, made a very positive impression: the Foreign Office noted with satisfaction that he had been more warmly welcomed than General Halder.[203] Ultimately, moreover, Great Britain was not prepared to consign Finland and the Baltic states unconditionally to the Soviet sphere of influence. 'Quite apart from the immorality of the whole proceeding', Halifax pointed out, 'We shall not be furthering our ends if we gratuitously drive Finland and the Baltic States into the arms of Germany.'[204]

Germany, of course, had no such scruples. The Soviet sphere of influence demarcated in the secret protocol to the German–Soviet non-aggression pact of 23 August 1939 included Finland, Estonia and Latvia (Lithuania, along with half of Poland, was added in a second secret protocol of 28 September). With the conclusion of the Nazi–Soviet pact Finland was left wholly isolated. The Soviet Union soon initiated negotiations to move forward its strategic frontier in the Baltic. Between 28 September and 10 October it concluded non-aggression pacts with the three Baltic states. On 5 October Molotov issued an invitation to the Finnish government to enter into talks in Moscow. The first round of negotiations began on 12 October; the third and final round ended on 13 November. On 26 November an incident was staged at the frontier village of Mainila to provide the pretext for the attack on Finland which began four days later.

Throughout the negotiations the Soviets seemed genuinely interested in reaching agreement. Their demands were more far-reaching than before the war. They now included a thirty-year lease of the Hanko peninsula; a shift of the frontier on the Karelian Isthmus; the cession of the Finnish part of the

---

[200] British–French–Soviet military delegation meetings, August 1939 (meeting of 15 August), CAB 16/183B.

[201] For details of the negotiations, see Donald Cameron Watt, *How War Came: The Immediate Origins of the Second World War* (London, 1989), pp. 361–84.

[202] Halifax to Hore-Belisha (secretary of state for war), 26 May 1939, FO 371/23648, N2496/698/56.

[203] Snow to FO, 3 July 1939; minute by D. W. Lascelles, 13 July 1939, ibid., N3310/698/56. See also General Sir Walter Kirke, 'Autobiographical Notes', WMK 13 (Kirke Papers, vol. VII), p. 19.

[204] Halifax to Sir Bernard Pares, 19 July 1939, FO 800/309.

Rybachi peninsula near Petsamo in the far north; and the addition of Koivusaari (Björkö) to the islands required in the Gulf of Finland. In return they offered a large area of territory in Karelia, as well as consent to the fortification of the Åland Islands on condition that it was carried out by Finland alone. They were ready to make at least token modifications to these demands but not to compromise on the essentials. However, the Finnish government responded with only minor concessions which fell far short of the minimum Soviet demands. Again their refusal to compromise was made in the face of authoritative advice: from both Mannerheim and the veteran politician J. K. Paasikivi, the leader of the Finnish delegation to Moscow. The government lacked insight into the Soviet Union's fears while remaining suspicious of its motives – and yet it overlooked the vast imbalance in capacity between the two countries. Erkko told Paasikivi to 'forget that Russia is a great power'.[205]

The Finnish government was misled by the archaic nature of the Soviet demands. As one of its military advisers put it, 'No officer with a modern training could take really seriously the grounds for the demands they have put to us. More likely what they are demanding is only the preparation for further, much more far-reaching demands.'[206] Such experts failed to take account of the conservative nature of Soviet military planning, which envisaged no more than a reconstitution of the plans worked out by the Russian General Staff before 1914. In July 1939 Zhdanov and Admiral Kuznetsov, the naval commissar, had taken a cruise along the Gulf of Finland during which 'the strategic problems created for the navy bottled up in Kronstadt were discussed and compared with 1914'.[207] This conservatism was reinforced by the preoccupation of Stalin and other Soviet leaders with British intervention during the Russian civil war. Stalin told the Finnish negotiators in October that once the war between Britain and Germany was over, 'the fleet of the victor will sail into the Gulf of Finland. Yudenitch attacked along the Gulf, and later the British did the same.'[208] However, Paasikivi never doubted that Germany was the only enemy the Soviets had seriously in mind.[209] Misguided though the Soviet analysis of Finland's position may have been, it was, Paasikivi reflected, simply in the nature of the great powers that they should claim the right to strengthen their security, whatever the consequences for the

---

[205] Quoted in Upton, *Finland 1939–1940*, p. 33.

[206] Quoted ibid., pp. 31–2.

[207] Spring, 'Soviet Decision', p. 217. See also a statement by Admiral Kuznetsov dating from August 1940 (by which time, of course, Finland's defeat in the Winter War had made the assumption of Finnish hostility a self-fulfilling prophecy) to the effect that 'our defences in the Gulf of Finland were patterned on those of World War I, but we had a weak spot – a point on which the mine position was pivoted in World War I belonged to Finland . . . it became obvious [that] in the event of war with Germany, Finland would side with her': quoted (without indication of source) in Philbin, *Lure of Neptune*, p. xviii.

[208] Quoted in Jakobson, *Diplomacy of the Winter War*, p. 117.

[209] J. K. Paasikivi, *Meine Moskauer Mission 1939–1941* (Hamburg, 1966), p. 236.

small states concerned. If Finland would not submit voluntarily to the Soviet Union's strategic demands, it must be compelled to do so by force.[210] In this respect Soviet behaviour towards Finland was little different from that of Great Britain, France and Germany towards the other Nordic states in the winter of 1939–40.

[210] Ibid., p. 238.

Epilogue

1939–1940: Looking backward

It was inevitable that at the beginning of the Second World War belligerents and neutrals alike should have looked to the past for guidance. The Allies entered the war committed to a strategy of 'containment'. Over a period of up to three years, Germany would be worn down by 'economic pressure combined with anti-Hitler propaganda' while the Allies gradually built up their armaments to the point at which they could challenge the enemy in the field.[1] As part of this strategy they began to negotiate war trade agreements with neutral governments.[2] The Nordic countries, for their part, set in motion the machinery which would enable them either individually or – to a limited extent – collectively to resist economic pressure, while some of their citizens – a much larger and more heterogeneous group than in the last war – attempted to mediate between the belligerents.[3] But the war did not develop as expected. There was no German offensive in the west, no aerial bombardment of the British Isles and no peace. This should have given the British and French governments confidence in their frequently repeated claim that 'time was on our side'.[4] In fact, by the end of 1939 their faith had begun to waver. Faced with no great military crises, the Allied governments' main task had become the irksome one of maintaining morale at home and prestige abroad while waiting for an increasingly improbable 'collapse of the German home front'.[5] They were thus susceptible to any suggestions – short of a direct assault on Germany – which might promise a speedy end to the war. As we have seen, the Soviet attack on Finland at the end of 1939, together with a growing belief in

---

[1] Memorandum by Lord Hankey, 'War Policy', 12 September 1939, CAC, Hankey Papers, HNKY 11/1.
[2] W. N. Medlicott, *The Economic Blockade* (2 vols., London, 1952–9), vol. I, ch. 4.
[3] Peter W. Ludlow, 'Scandinavia Between the Great Powers: Attempts at Mediation in the First Year of the Second World War', *Historisk tidskrift* (Sweden) 94 (1974), pp. 1–58.
[4] E.g. first meeting of the Supreme War Council, 12 September 1939, printed in François Bédarida (ed.), *La stratégie secrète de la drôle de guerre. Le Conseil Suprême Interallié septembre 1939–avril 1940* (Paris, 1979), pp. 89–105 (p. 94, n. H); Churchill's wireless broadcast, 'Ten Weeks of War' of 12 November 1939, printed in Randolph S. Churchill (comp.), *Into Battle: Speeches by the Right Hon. Winston S. Churchill* (London, 1941), pp. 142–6.
[5] Neville Chamberlain to Hilda Chamberlain, 10 September 1939, BUL, Neville Chamberlain Papers, NC 18/1/116.

the importance of Swedish iron ore to the German war economy, ensured that the most plausible of such suggestions came to converge on Scandinavia.

The Allies might have been more encouraged had they realised that Hitler shared their view that Germany did not have time on its side.[6] His deduction, however, was that Germany must launch a western offensive as soon as possible. In this context, Scandinavia was an unwelcome distraction. Promoted by Raeder for reasons of naval strategy and by Rosenberg on grounds of racial imperialism, Operation Weserübung was intended by Hitler to pre-empt the possibility of Allied action in Scandinavia as a counter-move to the German offensive in the west. In that it broke all the recognised rules of naval warfare, Weserübung represented a break with the past; but Quisling's role, as we have seen, appealed to the conspiratorial tradition of the Nazi movement, while for the navy the operation offered a chance to avoid repeating mistakes of the last war.

On the Allied side in particular, the winter of 1939–40 thus witnessed an odd telescoping of the events and preoccupations of 1914–18. Not only did the Allies apply the blockade systematically from the outset, but they seriously contemplated the kinds of drastic action which had been largely a matter of fantasy or speculation throughout the First World War. The Northern Barrage, which had been one of the last naval expedients of the war in 1918, became one of the first projects which Churchill sought to initiate on his return to the Admiralty in 1939.[7] He also reverted to his old dream of sending a naval expedition into the Baltic.[8] Just as the Allies' static conception of warfare was a rationalisation of the stalemate that had developed in 1914, so there emerged, as in 1915, an interest in the periphery. Churchill made the parallel explicit when he noted on Christmas Day 1939: 'The great question for 1940, as for 1915, is whether and how the Navy can make its surplus force tell in shortening the war, and of course the amphibious operations to seize Narvik and the great ironfield present themselves in the light of decisive action.'[9] Under Churchill's influence the possibility of taking action in Norwegian waters or seizing Norwegian bases, as well as the danger that Germany might get there first, discussed in 1916–17, remained a recurrent topic of debate in the War Cabinet, before both became a reality in April 1940.[10] An Allied expedition to Narvik, which the Swedish General Staff had

---

[6] Memorandum of 9 October 1939, printed in Jeremy Noakes and Geoffrey Pridham (eds.), *Nazism 1919–1945: A Documentary Reader*, vol. III, *Foreign Policy, War and Racial Extermination* (Exeter, 1988), pp. 760–2.

[7] Winston S. Churchill, *The Second World War*, vol. I, *The Gathering Storm* (2nd edn, 1949), pp. 478–9.

[8] Ibid., pp. 415–16; Arthur J. Marder, '"Winston is Back": Churchill at the Admiralty 1939–1940', in Marder, *From the Dardanelles to Oran: Studies of the Royal Navy in War and Peace 1915–1940* (London, 1974), pp. 105–78.

[9] 'A Note on the War in 1940', 25 December 1939, ADM 199/1929.

[10] Thomas Munch-Petersen, *The Strategy of Phoney War: Britain, Sweden and the Iron Ore Question 1939–1940* (Stockholm, 1981).

feared in 1915–16, nearly materialised in March 1940 under the pretext of assistance to Finland.[11]

There were echoes not only from the First World War but also from many smaller wars of the early twentieth century. Leo Amery, an advocate of action in Finland against Russia in 1904, became one of the leading members of the Finnish Aid Bureau, set up in January 1940 to coordinate material assistance and the recruitment of volunteers for Finland.[12] General Sir Ormonde Winter, director of intelligence at Dublin Castle during the Troubles in 1920–2 and director of communications for the Spanish Non-Intervention Board in 1938–9, materialised at the end of January 1940 as base commander of the British volunteer force.[13] Many in Britain who had supported Franco now devoted themselves to the Finnish cause.[14] General Ironside, the CIGS and one of the leading proponents of British intervention in Scandinavia, drew on his experiences as commander of the British expeditionary force in North Russia in 1918–19 to promote, in words quoted by one of his most scathing critics, an operation whose ultimate aim would be to 'shove the Russians out of Murmansk'.[15]

Churchill was not the only one who took the opportunity of the Christmas break to reflect upon the lessons of the past. At meetings of the Supreme War Council on 19 December and of the Military Co-ordination Committee the following day, the Allies had taken the first steps towards military intervention in Scandinavia, Ironside informing his colleagues that 'here was a legitimate side-show, unlike Salonika, Archangel and Mesopotamia'.[16] Now the thoughts of amateur strategists both inside and outside the government turned in the same direction. Leo Amery spent Christmas plotting to bring Norway and Sweden into the war.[17] On 24 December Sir Francis Lindley, formerly British high commissioner in North Russia and a minister to Norway in the 1920s, wrote to the foreign secretary that it was 'absolutely vital that we should help the Finns who really are an outpost of European civilisation', and that the best means of doing so was a naval attack on the Arctic port of Petsamo.[18] Lord Hankey, now minister without portfolio, wrote on Christmas Day to General

---

[11] Jukka Nevakivi, *The Appeal that Was Never Made: The Allies, Scandinavia and the Finnish Winter War 1939–1940* (London, 1976).

[12] The Amery Papers, Box 159B, contain extensive correspondence, together with complete minutes of the committee of the Finnish Aid Bureau from January 1940 to its winding-up in September 1941.

[13] Sir Ormonde Winter, *Winter's Tale: An Autobiography* (London, 1955), pp. 354–8.

[14] E.g. Lord Phillimore, chairman of 'The Friends of Spain', who was also chairman of the executive committee of 'The Finland Fund'.

[15] Brian Bond (ed.), *Chief of Staff: The Diaries of Lieutenant-General Sir Henry Pownall* (2 vols., London, 1972), vol. I, p. 281 (entry for 9 February 1940). Parallels between the intervention of 1918–19 and the Winter War are explicitly drawn in Andrew Soutar, *With Ironside in North Russia* (London, 1940), esp. pp. ix–x, 19–20.

[16] Roderick Macleod and Denis Kelly (eds.), *The Ironside Diaries 1937–1940* (London, 1962), pp. 186–7 (entry for 21 December 1939).

[17] Amery diary, 20 December 1939, Amery Papers.

[18] Lindley to Halifax, 24 December 1939, FO 371/23646, N7893/194/56.

Smuts in South Africa: 'if I had to see an extension of the war to Scandinavia or the Balkans, I would choose the former every time. It is nearer to us, better adapted to sea-power (which might even be brought to bear with air-power in the Baltic); Germany herself has to cross the sea to reach Scandinavia; and the Scandinavians are real live he-men to have as allies.'[19]

All this was fantasy. The hopes placed in the strategic potential of Scandinavia in 1939–40 were inherently unrealisable. The Allies had neither the manpower nor the material resources to sustain a campaign on the scale contemplated in the plans for Operation Stratford, authorised by the Supreme War Council on 5 February 1940, by which 100,000 men and 11,000 vehicles would ultimately find themselves entrenched in central Sweden awaiting a German invasion. Nor could operations in Scandinavia ever have delivered a decisive blow to Germany. Climate and terrain posed formidable obstacles. Neither the Soviet Union in Finland nor Britain and France in Norway were adequately equipped, either materially or mentally, to fight such determined opponents as the Finns or the Germans in such conditions. And it was only after 1941 that the Germans themselves, under General Dietl, became fully acclimatised to Arctic warfare.

More fundamentally, the promise offered by a flanking strategy in Scandinavia was a false one. The outcome of the two great wars of the twentieth century was decided not in the north but in the south, the west and, above all, the east. This is not to deny that the apparent strategic potential of the vast spaces of northern Europe continued to exert a fascination. Both Hitler and Churchill remained preoccupied with the idea of an Allied landing in Scandinavia. Churchill declared that 'Hitler had unrolled the map of Europe starting with Norway and he would start rolling it up again with Norway.'[20] In the guise of Operation Jupiter the prospect of returning to Scandinavia served to distract the prime minister's attention from areas where his advisers feared his meddling could do greater damage.[21] It also represented an important deception – eventually evolving into the Fortitude North plans in connection with Operation Overlord – which helped to keep over 300,000 German troops tied down in Norway for the duration of the war.[22] But Norway could never realistically be regarded as the launch-pad for the liberation of Europe.[23]

---

[19] Hankey to Smuts, dated 'Xmas 1939', CAC, Hankey Papers, HNKY 4/31 (original in Smuts Archive, University of Cape Town).

[20] Quoted in Sir Arthur Bryant, *The Turn of the Tide 1939–1943: A Study Based on the Diaries and Autobiographical Notes of Field Marshal the Viscount Alanbrooke KG, OM* (London, 1957), pp. 340–1.

[21] H. P. Willmott, 'Operation *Jupiter* and Possible Landings in Norway', in Patrick Salmon (ed.), *Britain and Norway in the Second World War* (London, 1995), pp. 97–108.

[22] Einar Grannes, 'Operation *Jupiter*: A Norwegian Perspective', in Salmon, *Britain and Norway*, pp. 109–16; Sir Peter Thorne, 'Andrew Thorne and the Liberation of Norway', in Salmon, *Britain and Norway*, pp. 206–20; Michael Howard, *Strategic Deception in the Second World War* (London, 1990), ch. 6.

[23] Howard notes, in *Strategic Deception*, p. 117, that 'although the deception was successful

Moreover, Scandinavia in 1939–40 was not a *tabula rasa*. It was made up of peoples and governments whose attitudes had been shaped in part by their dealings with the great powers: those powers whose leaders now chose for the first time to pay them close attention. Thus the credibility of Allied offers of assistance, or of Allied threats, was fatally undermined by the widespread perception of their military weakness and by their abject record in the face of Japanese, Italian and German aggression. In matters of war trade, the negotiating teams hastily improvised by the new Ministry of Economic Warfare proved barely a match for Swedish officials schooled by years of hard bargaining with Nazi Germany.[24] Within limits, moreover, the Nordic countries could influence the actions of the belligerents. They could exploit their dependence on Scandinavian resources – Britain's on Norwegian tankers, Germany's on Swedish iron ore – as a bargaining counter in war trade negotiations. They could portray themselves as sympathetic to the Allied cause while exploiting British doubts about the morality and expediency of the actions they were contemplating. Thus, for example, Boheman's robust advice that 'It would be better for you to slip in and sink the ships on the quiet than for you to declare that you were justified in so doing.'[25] With the Allies such tactics worked. British scruples about violating neutrality crippled the entire Scandinavian enterprise, up to and including the final decision to lay mines in Norwegian waters at the beginning of April 1940.

Yet at the same time past experience vitiated Scandinavian capacity to meet the catastrophe of 1940. Both the Norwegian and Danish governments were preoccupied with the danger of a British violation of their neutrality because the actions of the Royal Navy and the rhetoric of British politicians in the winter of 1939–40 – the *Altmark* incident and Churchill's wireless broadcasts – rightly led them to the conclusion that Britain was resuming the naval and blockade war where it had been left off in 1918. The resulting tendency to ignore evidence of impending German aggression was reinforced by the experience of the First World War in which Germany had demonstrated its paramount interest in Scandinavian neutrality. Again, they were correct in their assumption that neutrality was in Germany's interest; what they could not grasp (any more than the British or the French) was the extent to which this assumption had been subverted and ultimately overthrown by new strategic imperatives: the navy's search for naval bases and Hitler's conviction that the northern flank must be secured before a western offensive could be launched. Thus, for example, the perception of the Danish government and the opposition parties on the eve of the German invasion was dominated by the experience of August 1914, when judicious compliance with a limited German demand – closing the Belts by laying mines – had preserved Danish neutrality.

. . . it failed substantially to affect enemy dispositions. The size of the German garrison in Norway remained at twelve divisions.'
[24] Munch-Petersen, *Strategy of Phoney War*, pp. 47–53.
[25] Montagu-Pollock (Stockholm) to FO, 7 January 1940, FO 371/24820, N295/19/63.

'It's 5 August 1914 all over again!', the Social Democrats' chairman exclaimed.[26] Danish politicians could not comprehend the occupation of the entire country with virtually no warning and for no reason other than that it was a stepping-stone to Norway.

Finally, neither Allied nor Scandinavian actions could surmount the fact that after 23 August 1939 Scandinavia's fate lay almost entirely in the hands of Germany and the Soviet Union. Hitherto, Nordic foreign and security policies had been based either explicitly or implicitly on the existence of an approximate balance between two or possibly three countervailing forces: Britain and Germany, Germany and the Soviet Union, or all three powers together. It was, after all, the existence of a balance of power which had made neutrality possible.[27] The Nazi–Soviet pact belatedly fulfilled the northern European condominium envisaged by German and Russian statesmen at Swinemünde in 1907. It consigned British influence to the western margin of Scandinavia, from which it was to be eliminated entirely in April 1940. Thereafter, Scandinavia's release from the German–Soviet grip had to await the outcome of the war between the two powers, begun when Hitler launched Operation Barbarossa in June 1941.

1940–1949: Looking forward

By 1939 the Nordic countries had solved, or were on the way towards solving, some of the most pressing problems affecting the material well-being of their citizens. The one issue which remained unresolved was that of national security. In 1939–40 neutrality failed Finland, Denmark and Norway in turn, while Swedish neutrality was preserved largely by default. Yet to speak merely of the decline of neutrality or the bankruptcy of small nations is inappropriate.[28] The year 1940 saw the collapse of the nation-state throughout Europe.[29] Virtually every European society succumbed to the Nazi challenge – and in this context Nordic societies were more resilient than most.[30] It is true that military defeat was followed by bitter recrimination directed mainly at the governments in power in April 1940, but also at the political and social establishments of which they formed a part. This critique in turn fuelled the growth of resistance to Nazi rule and opposition to those elements in

---

[26] Quoted in Hans Kirchhoff, 'Foreign Policy and Rationality – The Danish Capitulation of 9 April 1940: An Outline of a Pattern of Action', *Scandinavian Journal of History* 16 (1991), pp. 237–68 (p. 256).

[27] This point was emphasised by a noted practitioner of Swedish neutrality: Gunnar Hägglöf, 'A Test of Neutrality: Sweden in the Second World War', *International Affairs* 36 (1960), pp. 153–67 (p. 166).

[28] Nils Ørvik, *The Decline of Neutrality 1914–1941* (2nd edn, London, 1971), pp. 277–8.

[29] Alan S. Milward, *The European Rescue of the Nation-State* (London, 1992), p. 4.

[30] On the variety of European responses to Germany's victory (many of them positive), see John Lukacs, *The Last European War: September 1939–December 1941* (London, 1977), esp. pp. 201–24, 282–326, 383–414.

Scandinavian society – in politics, administration and business – which, for whatever reason, had reached an accommodation with it.

Such conflict was barely present in Norway where, after the brief experiment of the summer of 1940, 'administrative' collaboration was totally discredited and the leading elements in the pre-war establishment both inside the country and in exile – king, Storting and Supreme Court – shared a common commitment to resistance. But it was expressed in the Danish 'August uprising' of 1943, in which young people on the streets, communists and oppositional elements within the constitutional political parties forced not merely the government but the entire political system to end its collaboration with the German authorities.[31] Despite such antagonisms, however, and notwithstanding the 'necessary myths' with which each Nordic society subsequently justified its wartime role – occupied (Denmark and Norway); reluctant or willing co-belligerent (Finland and Norway); or neutral (Sweden) – Nordic societies were more cohesive and less divided in 1945 than they had been in 1939.[32] The experience of war helped to erode class antagonisms and to consolidate the process of national regeneration which had begun during the 1930s.

War and defeat, exile and resistance nevertheless encouraged and indeed necessitated a fundamental reassessment of the security policies that had foundered in 1939–40. Some drew the lesson that, whilst isolated neutrality had failed three out of the four Nordic states, cooperation with other states might enhance their prospect of staying outside a future conflict. 'Small-state' cooperation, either within the Nordic sphere or in a wider European context, was one option but in the end it did not develop very far.[33] At the end of the Winter War the Finnish government's proposal for a defence alliance with Norway and Sweden found some support within the Swedish Cabinet but none in Norway, before being decisively vetoed by the Soviet Union.[34] Such an alliance, Molotov warned, could only be directed against Russia. Since the

---

[31] See the discussion of Hans Kirchhoff's *Augustoprøret 1943* (Copenhagen, 1979) in Henrik Dethlefsen, 'Denmark and the German Occupation: Cooperation, Negotiation or Collaboration?', *Scandinavian Journal of History* 15 (1990), pp. 193–206 (p. 197).

[32] Ways of coming to terms with the past included: retribution (e.g. the trial and execution of Quisling); the search for culprits (official investigations into the background to the events of 1940 in Denmark and Norway); and self-justification (e.g. the 'white books' on Sweden's wartime diplomacy published by the Swedish Foreign Ministry). Important insights into these issues were provided by contributions to the conference 'War Experience, Self-Image and National Identity: The Second World War as Myth and History' in Stockholm in August 1995, by Ole Kristian Grimnes (Norway), Matti Klinge (Finland) and Henning Poulsen (Denmark), and most of all by Alf W. Johansson's startling reassessment of Swedish neutrality policy, 'Neutrality and Modernity: The Second World War as Non-Experience'.

[33] For Norwegian reactions to Polish plans for post-war small-state cooperation in central and eastern Europe, see Sven G. Holtsmark, 'Atlantic Orientation or Regional Groupings: Elements of Norwegian Foreign Policy Discussions During the Second World War', *Scandinavian Journal of History* 14 (1989), pp. 311–24.

[34] W. M. Carlgren, *Svensk utrikespolitik 1939–1945* (Stockholm, 1971), pp. 132–6; Arne Bergsgård, 'Utrikspolitikk', in *Innstilling fra Undersøkelsekommisjonen av 1945. Bilag*, vol. I

Soviet Union had demonstrated its desire to see an independent Finland and wished to have only the best of relations with the Scandinavian states, what purpose could an alliance serve?

Great Britain too remained hostile to the idea of a Scandinavian or Nordic union, albeit more discreetly. British reactions to the post-war plans emanating from Stockholm in 1942 – from Swedish enthusiasts, and from the group of Norwegian exiles centred around the veteran Labour leader Martin Tranmæl – echoed those of Findlay and Howard during and immediately after the First World War.[35] Whilst Victor Mallet, the minister in Stockholm, felt that discussion of a future Nordic bloc should not be discouraged, Laurence Collier, minister to the Norwegian government in London, and G. M. Gathorne-Hardy of the Political Intelligence Department argued that Scandinavian interests were so divergent as to make such a bloc a remote prospect.[36] Norway remained the key to British interest in Scandinavia. It was therefore desirable, Collier argued, 'to draw Norway into the Atlantic orbit rather than to urge her against her will to become a minor partner in a *bloc* which would inevitably concern itself mainly with the Baltic'.[37]

There was, however, little danger of Norwegian involvement. The deepest opposition to Scandinavian cooperation came, as so often, from Norway itself. This was not merely a negative reaction. On the contrary, Norway set the agenda for discussion of post-war security arrangements not only in Scandinavia but in the entire Western alliance. The new 'Atlantic' conception which replaced the old isolationism was symbolised by the replacement of Koht by Trygve Lie as Norwegian foreign minister in November 1940. A group of exiled intellectuals in London had argued as early as July 1940 that Norway's interests would be best served by the closest possible association with Great Britain: 'Only by effectively supporting our British ally will the government be able to assert Norwegian sovereignty as well as their own authority towards the British government during the war.'[38] Under their influence Lie developed this idea into one of post-war cooperation with both Great Britain and the United States in a new Atlantic community.[39] Norway's Atlantic orientation was the most explicit expression of a security solution based not on Scandinavian

(Oslo, 1947), pp. 117–264 (pp. 225–30); Halvdan Koht, *For fred og fridom i krigstid 1939–1940* (Oslo, 1957), pp. 183–6.

[35] Karl Petander, W. Kleen and Anders Örne, *Nordens förenta stater* (Stockholm, 1942); Holtsmark, 'Atlantic Orientation or Regional Groupings'; Peter Ludlow, 'Britain and Northern Europe 1940–1945', *Scandinavian Journal of History* 4 (1979), pp. 123–62 (pp. 143–5).

[36] Gathorne Hardy memorandum, 'Possibilities of a Post-War Northern *Bloc*', 6 July 1942, enclosed in FO to Mallet, 22 July 1942, FO 371/3208, N3523/2954/63; Mallet to FO, 9 October 1942, ibid., N5441/2954/63.

[37] Collier to FO, 31 March 1942, FO 371/33062, N1756/282/42.

[38] Letter to the Norwegian government of 5 July 1940, quoted in Olav Riste, 'Relations Between the Norwegian Government in Exile and the British Government', in Salmon, *Britain and Norway*, pp. 41–50 (p. 42).

[39] Olav Riste, *'London-regjeringa'. Norge i krigsalliansen 1940–1945* (2 vols., Oslo, 1973–9), vol. I, *1940–1942. Prøvetid*, ch. 4. For positive British reactions (as well as resentment at

resources alone but on cooperation with one or more great powers. However, it did not go unchallenged. Even among Norwegians, 'small-power' and 'Scandinavian' preferences remained strong. Reservations about too one-sided an orientation towards the Western powers increased in the latter part of the war with the growth of Soviet–Western discord and when it became evident that the Soviet Union would play a significant (and, as it turned out, exclusive) role in the liberation of north Norway.[40]

Nor was Lie's vision the only variety of small-power/great-power cooperation on offer during the war. Nazi Germany proposed its own vision for the future, one in which the Nordic countries were destined to play an active part, and which might attract support from a significant minority of their populations. Racial affinity was of course a prime consideration. As early as 3 May 1940 Hitler ordered that Danish volunteers should be recruited to the SS in order to 'influence them for the idea of a community of Germanic peoples, and gradually to win them away from their connections with the Western Powers'.[41] By the end of the war some 6,000 Danes had joined the Waffen SS. The Nordic peoples were invited to share in the colonisation and exploitation of the new territories in the east.[42] Finland's partnership in Germany's offensive against the Soviet Union in June 1941 resulted in the temporary fulfilment of Finnish claims to a 'greater Finland' in Soviet Karelia. In the autumn of 1941 territorial expansion, in the guise of 'secure frontiers' or *Lebensraum* came to be accepted as a war aim by all the political parties, while Finnish propaganda misleadingly claimed a 'Nordic' racial character for the Finns.[43] In Norway, Quisling sought first to achieve territorial expansion in north Russia and, when this failed, tried to bring about Norwegian collaboration in the economic development of Ukraine and Belorussia.[44]

The Nordic countries were expected to become an integral part of the German New Order in Europe. On 11 May 1940 Karl Ritter wrote of the opportunity provided by military victory in Denmark and Norway to 'correct'

being told what to do by small allies), see Ludlow, 'Britain and Northern Europe', pp. 137–8.

[40] Sven G. Holtsmark, 'Om Den røde hær rykker inn i Norge . . . Spørsmålet om sovjetisk deltagelse i frigjøringen av Norge 1941–1944' (IFS Info No. 6, Oslo, 1994).

[41] *DGFP*, D, VI, p. 287. The task of the Danes recruited to these units would be 'a purely political one' and would have 'nothing to do with military duties'. For a thorough discussion of the role of Scandinavian volunteers in the German campaign against the Soviet Union after 1941, see Horst Boog et al., *Das Deutsche Reich und der Zweite Weltkrieg*, vol. IV, *Der Angriff auf die Sowjetunion* (Stuttgart, 1983), pp. 926–35.

[42] For details of the specific contributions which each country might be expected to make, see extracts from a memorandum by Karl Clodius of 23 November 1941, printed in Manfred Menger, Fritz Petrick and Wolfgang Wilhelmus (eds.), *Expansionsrichtung Nordeuropa. Dokumente zur Nordeuropapolitik des faschistischen deutschen Imperialismus 1939 bis 1945* (Berlin, 1987), pp. 120–2.

[43] Boog et al., *Das Deutsche Reich und der Zweite Weltkrieg* IV, pp. 852–5.

[44] Ole Kolsrud, 'Kollaborasjon og imperialisme. Quisling-regjeringens "Austrveg"-drøm 1941–1944', *Historisk tidsskrift* (Norway) 67 (1988), pp. 241–70.

the orientation of the Nordic economies towards Great Britain and to incorporate them in the *Grossraumpolitik* which had already been directed towards the Danubian region.[45] In pursuit of this policy there was a calculated appeal to economic self-interest. In June 1940 the Ministry of Agriculture took the lead in raising the export prices for Danish agricultural products above world market prices in order to 'strengthen Denmark's economic integration [*Verflechtung*] with Germany'.[46] This policy clearly worked. The production record of Danish farmers during the war was 'one of the most remarkable in the annals of world agriculture'.[47] Even Denmark, however, needed careful handling. Walter, still chairman of the German–Danish inter-governmental committee, warned that Danish discontent would grow if prices for German export goods continued to rise, and that 'our pricing policy' was 'not very useful propaganda for the future *Grossraum*'.[48]

For Norway the implications of the German New Order were far more drastic. One of Europe's least self-sufficient economies was to be wrenched away from the outside world in which its trade and shipping had prospered, and wholly subordinated to German strategic and economic imperatives.[49] This was not exploitation in the strict sense. On the contrary, it meant huge investment in the aluminium and shipbuilding industries (to meet the needs, respectively, of the German air force and navy), in electrification (Hitler declared that Norway would 'at last find a European mission to fulfil' in becoming 'the electrical centre of Northern Europe'), as well as in roads and, above all, railways.[50] But the corollary of development in the industrial sector was arrested development in the primary sectors – in fisheries and agriculture – and a drastic reduction in the living standards of the entire population, which again reflected the subordinate role decreed for peripheral primary-producing countries in the German *Grosswirtschaftsraum*.[51]

As these ambitious long-term objectives gave way after 1942 to the more immediate priority of military survival, the attractions of the German New Order diminished still further. Norwegian and Danish resistance gained in strength and became more active; Swedish neutrality became more accommodating to Western demands and Swedish humanitarian efforts on behalf of

[45] Circular despatch to legations in Baltic states, Sweden and Denmark, and Reichskommissar for occupied Norwegian territories, ZSta., AA 68314, part printed in Menger et al., *Expansionsrichtung Nordeuropa*, pp. 73–4. See also memoranda by Clodius, 30 May 1940, and Ritter, 1 June 1940, *DGFP*, D, VI, pp. 476–82, 496–501.

[46] Memorandum by Regierungsrat Meyer-Burckhardt, 'Preispolitik bei der Einfuhr landwirtschaftlicher Erzeugnisse aus Dänemark', 19 June 1940, ZSta., AA 67771.

[47] Karl Brandt, *Management of Agriculture and Food in the German-Occupied and Other Areas of Fortress Europe: A Study in Military Government* (Stanford, Calif., 1953), p. 301.

[48] Walter memorandum, 'Bemerkungen zur Wirtschaftslage Dänemarks', 18 February 1941, ZSta., AA 68311.

[49] Alan S. Milward, *The Fascist Economy in Norway* (Oxford, 1972).

[50] H. R. Trevor-Roper (ed.), *Hitler's Table Talk 1941–1944* (London, 1953; repr. Oxford, 1988), pp. 22–3.

[51] Milward, *Fascist Economy in Norway*, pp. 291–300.

Denmark and Norway were intensified; the Finnish government sought to extricate itself from Germany's war against the Soviet Union. All four countries began to come to terms with the prospect of a post-war world dominated by the victors, though the victors themselves still had no clear idea of what form this world might take. Soviet intentions towards Scandinavia remained impenetrable and the available evidence ambiguous. Long-term security preoccupations were revealed in Molotov's discussions with Ribbentrop and Hitler in Berlin in 1940, and later in exchanges with Great Britain and the United States, when the Soviets indicated their interest in control of the Danish Straits.[52] A similar concern probably motivated Molotov's proposal to Trygve Lie in November 1944 for a revision of the Svalbard treaty of 1920 to allow joint Norwegian–Soviet sovereignty over the archipelago.[53] Both issues were clearly linked to one of much greater importance to the Soviet Union: the demand for a revision of the Montreux convention of 1936, which governed the international status of the Black Sea Straits. If such connections were difficult for Scandinavian governments to discern, concrete evidence of Soviet power in northern Europe was provided by the liberation of northern Norway by the Red Army in the autumn of 1944, by the rapid occupation of the Danish island of Bornholm in May 1945 – a move clearly designed to forestall the West – and by the harsh terms imposed on Finland in the armistice of 19 September 1944.

By contrast the West – Great Britain and, still more, the United States – seemed remote and even indifferent towards Scandinavia. The Foreign Office was fatalistic about Finland and felt unable to dissuade Norway from concluding a civil affairs agreement with the Soviet Union in May 1944, in advance of the Soviet occupation of north Norway.[54] It was not fully aware of the extent to which, in the absence of 'a cut and dried scheme' for western European cooperation, and under the shadow of Soviet power, the Norwegian government, Britain's most loyal wartime ally, was drifting back towards neutralism and even 'a Scandinavian neutrality bloc'.[55] The one post-war vision offered by the West at the end of the Second World War was a new form of international organisation, the United Nations. It would be dominated by a great-power directorate in the form of the Security Council and was thus unlikely to restore the status enjoyed by the smaller powers at Geneva in the 1920s. Nevertheless, Denmark and Sweden, the two Scandinavian states outside the wartime alliance, were under pressure to establish their credentials

---

[52] *DGFP*, D, XI, pp. 562–70; Vojtech Mastny, *Russia's Road to the Cold War: Diplomacy, Warfare and the Politics of Communism 1941–1945* (New York, 1979), pp. 31, 52–3, 269–70.

[53] Riste, *'London-regjeringa'* II, pp. 315–39.

[54] FO brief on Scandinavia for secretary of state, 6 October 1944, FO 371/43213, N6163/6163/63; Ludlow, 'Britain and Northern Europe', p. 159.

[55] Minute by Sir Orme Sargent of August 1944, quoted in Ludlow, 'Britain and Northern Europe', p. 160.

as authentic opponents of Nazism and thus win membership of an organisation which would be the foundation of the post-war international order.

One thing was clear: that Scandinavia *would* form part of the new world order and that it could not revert to isolation. But in the immediate post-war years the division between East and West did not yet appear irrevocable. The Soviet Union withdrew from the territory it had occupied in north Norway and from Bornholm. Its policy towards Finland was relatively restrained – though it has been suggested that the long-term aim of Zhdanov, the chairman of the Allied Control Commission, was 'to test Finland as a model for Soviet satellites'.[56] The United States still took little active interest in northern Europe, preferring to regard it as a British sphere of influence. Great Britain, for its part, enjoyed a position of unprecedented prestige. It had close ties with both the Norwegian and Danish armed forces and was recovering its position as a major trading partner of the Nordic countries. Initially, however, the British adopted a notably detached attitude towards the Soviet presence in the region. Nothing could be done to contest Soviet influence in Finland nor, in the view of the Foreign Office, 'would it serve any important British interests' to do so.[57] In the opinion of the chiefs of staff, bases on Svalbard and Bornholm would be of little strategic value to the Soviets, and Britain offered no diplomatic support to the Norwegian and Danish governments in their negotiations with the USSR on these questions.[58]

It was thus understandable that both Norway and Denmark should have reverted to a policy of 'bridge-building' which in part reflected recognition of Soviet power and the absence of a Western alliance but was also meant to be, in its Norwegian variant, an active peace policy which recalled Koht's diplomacy of the late 1930s. Their tendency to gravitate towards Swedish-style neutralism was also natural given Sweden's economic and military strength: among European states it was, after Great Britain, 'probably the strongest military power outside the iron curtain'.[59] But in fact no 'Scandinavian option' was available.[60] The proposal for a Scandinavian defence alliance made by Sweden in May 1948 was ostensibly a radical departure from Sweden's traditional policy of isolated neutrality, a belated vindication of Sandler's pre-war efforts made all the more remarkable because it emanated from one of his severest critics, Foreign Minister Östen Undén.[61] In fact the idea of an isolated

---

[56] Jukka Nevakivi, 'The Control Commission in Helsinki – A Finnish View', in Nevakivi (ed.), *Finnish–Soviet Relations 1944–1948* (Helsinki, 1994), pp. 67–79 (p. 74).

[57] FO memorandum of 9 August 1944, quoted in Tuomo Polvinen, *Between East and West: Finland in International Politics 1944–1947* (Minneapolis, 1986), pp. 14–15.

[58] Knut Einar Eriksen, 'Great Britain and the Problem of Bases in the Nordic Area 1945–1947', *Scandinavian Journal of History* 7 (1982), pp. 135–63.

[59] Knut Einar Eriksen and Helge Pharo, 'Norway and the Early Cold War: Conditional Atlantic Cooperation' (IFS Info No. 5, Oslo, 1993), p. 11.

[60] Barbara G. Haskel, *The Scandinavian Option: Opportunities and Opportunity Costs in Postwar Scandinavian Foreign Policies* (Oslo, 1976).

[61] For discussions of the origin of the Swedish proposal, see Gerard Aalders, 'The Failure of the Scandinavian Defence Union 1948–1949', *Scandinavian Journal of History* 15 (1990),

neutral Scandinavian bloc was doomed from the outset. By 1948 the early Cold War was approaching its height, with both the West (now led by the United States) and the Soviet Union shifting their attention to the northern sphere and demanding that the Nordic countries choose sides. The Swedish initiative was largely a blocking exercise, designed to arrest the drift of Norway and Denmark towards a North Atlantic alliance – something of which the Norwegians in particular were only too well aware.[62] Moreover, Sweden was unable to offer sufficient military support to its neighbours to tempt them away from reliance on Great Britain and the United States. Above all, a neutral Scandinavian bloc was impossible because it would not be neutral. Its proponents (and especially the Swedish armed forces) never doubted that the Soviet Union was the only likely aggressor and that in the last resort any Scandinavian arrangement must be Westward-leaning. The function of a Scandinavian alliance was to enable the Scandinavian countries to hold out until Western support arrived. It is hardly surprising that Norway and Denmark preferred the security offered by a North Atlantic alliance to Swedish tutelage.

Since the new world order was a divided one, Scandinavia must be divided too. This was in keeping with the lessons of Scandinavian history and geography, with the divisions imposed by war and occupation, and with the competing interests of the superpowers. Neither the United States nor the Soviet Union placed any credence in Scandinavian neutrality; if Scandinavia, like Europe as a whole, could not be won for one superpower bloc or the other, it must be split apart. In these circumstances the priority was to strengthen their hold on the parts of Scandinavia which mattered – for the West, this meant Norway and Denmark, but also Iceland and Danish-controlled Greenland whose strategic importance had been demonstrated during the war. In April 1949 Norway, Denmark and Iceland became founder signatories of the North Atlantic treaty. For the Soviet Union, it meant Finland, though a Finland which was rapidly becoming a strategic backwater. In 1948 the two countries concluded a treaty of friendship and mutual assistance. But Soviet interests were served more directly by the extension of Soviet territory in the far north, at Finland's expense, and, above all, by the pushing forward of the USSR's strategic frontier on the southern shore of the Baltic (though this gain, too, had been negated by the detonation of the first atomic bomb). Sweden was left non-aligned, neutral and isolated. In one sense this was a vindication of Swedish policy; in another it was a tribute to Sweden's relative unimportance once the western, eastern, northern and southern flanks of Scandinavia had been secured by the respective superpowers. Both sides were content to let

---

pp. 125–53; Karl Molin, *Omstridd neutralitet. Experternas kritik av svensk utrikespolitik 1948–1950* (Angered, 1991).

[62] For Swedish bitterness about Norway's role in the negotiations, see Aalders, 'Failure of the Scandinavian Defence Union', pp. 148–53.

the Swedes perpetuate the myth of neutrality, while being in no doubt as to where Sweden' s security interests ultimately lay.[63]

Scandinavia's involvement in the Cold War order remained incomplete. Both Denmark and Norway limited their commitment to the Western alliance by preventing the stationing of NATO forces on their territories in peacetime, while Norway carefully pursued a policy of 'reassurance' towards the Soviet Union.[64] The Cold War era also saw the gradual establishment of an autonomous Finnish neutrality policy in the shadow of Soviet power (in other words, the reverse of 'Finlandisation'), while the existence of a 'Nordic balance' helped to preserve Scandinavia from becoming an area of direct superpower confrontation. At the same time Scandinavian autonomy was threatened by the build-up of Soviet nuclear forces on the Kola Peninsula, which made the region decidedly unbalanced in strategic terms. For a time in the 1980s the situation seemed still more ominous as Soviet submarines were discovered in Swedish waters and President Reagan's navy secretary spoke of 'steaming into the Kola Peninsula' and fighting a major naval battle in the Norwegian Sea.[65] By the 1990s Scandinavians were more preoccupied with the challenge of European integration – yet another issue on which they were divided (though Norway was now in a minority of one) – while nuclear submarines rotted at their jetties in Murmansk or disintegrated at the bottom of the Arctic Ocean. If there was a threat to their existence, it was now environmental rather than military, with the problems of acid rain and the fall-out from Chernobyl, and with the degradation of the North Sea and the Baltic. This was a reminder, however, of the extent to which the fate of the Nordic countries was still determined by the priorities – and the negligence – of larger powers.

[63] Sweden's security links with the West are documented in the report of a committee of inquiry: *Om kriget kommit . . . Förberedelser för mottagande av militärt bistand 1949–1969. Betänkande av Neutralitetspolitikkommissionen* (Stockholm, 1994).

[64] Rolf Tamnes, *Integration and Screening: The Two Faces of Norwegian Alliance Policy 1945–1986* (Oslo, 1986); Geir Lundestad, 'The Evolution of Norwegian Security Policy: Alliance with the West and Reassurance in the East', *Scandinavian Journal of History* 17 (1992), pp. 227–56.

[65] Quoted in Steven Miller, 'The Maritime Strategy and Geopolitics in the High North', in Clive Archer (ed.), *The Soviet Union and Northern Waters* (London, 1988), pp. 205–38 (p. 206).

Bibliography

I UNPUBLISHED SOURCES

All documentary references in the footnotes are to material in the PRO unless otherwise stated.

I GREAT BRITAIN

Public Record Office, London (PRO)
Admiralty
ADM 1   Admiralty and Secretariat Papers
ADM 116 Admiralty and Secretariat Cases
ADM 137 War of 1914–1918: War History Cases
ADM 178 Admiralty and Secretariat Papers and Cases, Supplementary Series
ADM 199 War of 1939–1945: War History Cases and Papers

Board of Trade
BT 11   Commercial Department: Correspondence and Papers
BT 90   Advisory Committee to the DOT 1918–1930: Minutes and Papers
BT 198   Board of Trade Council, Minutes and Papers 1917–1927

Cabinet Office
CAB 2   CID: Minutes
CAB 16   CID: *Ad Hoc* Sub-Committees of Enquiry: Proceedings and Memoranda
CAB 17   CID: Correspondence and Miscellaneous Papers
CAB 23   War Cabinet and Cabinet Minutes 1916–1939
CAB 24   War Cabinet and Cabinet Memoranda 1916–1939
CAB 27   Cabinet Committees: General Series 1915–1939
CAB 37   Cabinet Papers 1880–1916
CAB 42   Papers of the War Council, Dardanelles Committee and War Committee 1914–1916
CAB 47   CID: Advisory Committee on Trade Questions in Time of War
CAB 53   CID: Chiefs of Staff Committee
CAB 104   Cabinet Registered Files: Supplementary

Department of Overseas Trade
BT 59   Development Council

Foreign Office
FO 368   Commercial Department

FO 371   General Correspondence: Political
FO 372   Treaty Department
FO 382   Contraband Department
FO 419   Confidential Print: Scandinavia and the Baltic States
FO 425   Confidential Print: Western Europe
FO 433   Confidential Print: Economic Affairs, General
FO 800   Private Collections: Ministers and Officials
HD 3/133 Permanent Under Secretary's Department: Correspondence and Papers
          (Intelligence Service)

Prime Minister's Office
PREM 1   Correspondence and Papers 1916–1940

Treasury
T 160   Finance Files

War Office
WO 106   Directorate of Military Operations and Intelligence

Business Archives
Bank of England Archive (BEA)
Overseas Department
OV 26   Norway 1875–1977
OV 27   Denmark and Faeroes 1926–1977
OV 29   Sweden 1926–1977
OV 30   Finland 1922–1973

Private papers
Leo Amery (in the possession of the late Lord Amery)
Earl Baldwin of Bewdley (Cambridge University Library (CUL))
Neville Chamberlain (Birmingham University Library (BUL))
Lord Hankey (Churchill Archives Centre, Churchill College, Cambridge (CAC))
Sir Thomas Hohler (in the possession of Mr George Hohler; material bound in volumes
          denoted by year)
General Sir Walter Kirke (Imperial War Museum, London (IWM))
Lord Runciman (Robinson Library, University of Newcastle upon Tyne (RL))

2 GERMANY

Bundesarchiv, Koblenz (BA)
R 13 I   Verein Deutscher Eisen- und Stahlindustrieller/Wirtschaftsgruppe Eisen
           schaffende Industrie
R 43 I   'Alte' Reichskanzlei 1917–1933
R 43 II   'Neue' Reichskanzlei 1933–1945
ZSg 133   Sammlung Jacobsen (material collected by Prof. H.-A. Jacobsen for his book
           Nationalsozialistische Aussenpolitik)

Nachlässe
NL 94 Nachlass Darré

Bibliography 373

Politisches Archiv des Auswärtigen Amtes, Bonn (PA)
Abteilung III 1920–1936
England
Politik 3 – Finnland
Abteilung IV 1920–1936
Norden – Dänemark
Politik 2
Politik 5
Norden – Finnland
Politik 1
Norden – Norwegen
Politik 2
Politik 3 – England
Norden – Schweden
Politik 3 – England
Wirtschaft – Dänemark
Handel 11
Handel 12
Handel 13
Abteilung Pol. VI 1936–1945
Po 2 Dänemark
Po 2 Schweden
Po 13 Norwegen
Geheimakten 1920–1936
Länder IV – Norden
Schweden II, FM 24
Gesandtschaft Kopenhagen
Das Ostseeproblem
Handelspolitische Abteilung (HaPol.) 1936–1945
VI Norwegen, Handel 11
VI Schweden, Handel 13A
VI Schweden, Rohstoffe und Waren, Eisenerz
Sonderreferat Wirtschaft
Finanzwesen 16 – Dänemark
Handel 11
Handel 12
Handakten
Behr
Clodius
Eisenlohr
Wiehl
Nachlässe
Gesandter Cecil von Renthe-Fink

Former Zentrales Staatsarchiv, Potsdam (ZSta.)
09.01 Auswärtiges Amt
Abteilung IV 1920–1936
Handel
AA 63850 Finnland 13 – Handelsvertragsverhältnis zu Deutschland
AA 65155 Finnland 13 – Handelsvertragsverhältnis zu Deutschland

AA 64078   Schleswig – Handelssachen Rohstoffe und Waren
AA 66019   Dänemark – Kohle
Handelspolitische Abteilung (HaPol.) 1936–1945
AA 67734   Dänemark – Handelsbeziehungen zu Deutschland
AA 67771   Dänemark – Handelsvertragsverhältnis zu Deutschland
AA 67777   Dänemark – Handelsvertragsverhältnis zu Deutschland
AA 67803   Finnland – Handelsbeziehungen zu Grossbritannien
AA 67969   Nordeuropa – Handel
AA 67973   Nordeuropa – Handel
AA 68078   Nordeuropa – Industrie
AA 68133   Nordeuropa – Landwirtschaftliche Beziehungen zu Deutschland
AA 68311   Dänemark – Wirtschaft
AA 68314   Dänemark – Wirtschaft
AA 68318   Dänemark – Wirtschaft

80 IG 1 IG Farben
Volkswirtschaftliche Abteilung
A415-761   Wirtschaftsberichte 1938–1939

3 DENMARK

Rigsarkivet, Copenhagen (RA)
Udenrigsministeriet (UM)
5 D 26a   Denmark – England: Politiske forhold 1914–1945
64 Dan. 73a Danmark – Storbritannien: Handelsforhold 1933–1940
64 Dan. 80a Danmark – Tyskland: Handelsforhold 1933–1940
72 Stb. 1   Storbritannien: Toldtarif – Toldpolitik 1931–1940
72 Tys. 1   Tyskland: Toldtarif – Toldpolitik 1926–1940

Privatarkiver
6663   P. Munchs arkiv

4 NORWAY

Riksarkivet, Oslo (RA)
Privatarkiver
258   Halvdan Koht

Utenriksdepartementet (NUD)
H 62 B 1/25   Norges forsvarsordning, utenriks- og krigspolitiske stilling 1912–1935
52 D 1   Norges forsvar 1936–1940
H 62 C 5/29   Norge – Tyskland: politiske forhold i sin alm.het 1931–1936
P 10 A 3/17   Rusland. Anerkjendelse av nye regjering 1917–1924

Stortingets arkiv, Oslo (SA)
Ekstrakt – Forhandlings – og Ekspeditions-Protokol for Stortinget
96   Referater fra møter for lukkede dører i sesjonen 1923

5 SWEDEN

Utrikesdepartementet (SUD) (now in Riksarkiv, Stockholm)
H 40 Ct. Järn och stål: Tyskland
H 40 Ba. Järn och stål: Storbritannien

II PUBLISHED SOURCES

I OFFICIAL DOCUMENTS

Akten zur Deutschen Auswärtigen Politik, series B (21 vols., Göttingen, 1966–83)
  (*ADAP*)
Bédarida, François (ed.), *La stratégie secrète de la drôle de guerre. Le Conseil Suprême
  Interallié septembre 1939–avril 1940* (Paris, 1979)
Betænkninger og bilag til folketinget afgivet af den parlamentariske kommission (Copenhagen,
  1945), vol. II
Bourne, Kenneth, and Donald Cameron Watt (eds.) *British Documents on Foreign
  Affairs*, part I, series F, vol. III (Bethesda, Md., 1987) (*BDFA*)
Documents on British Foreign Policy, series 1–3 (London, 1949 *et seq.*) (*DBFP*)
Documents diplomatiques français, series 2 and 3 (Paris, 1930–53) (*DDF*)
Documents on German Foreign Policy, series C and D (London, 1954 *et seq.*) (*DGFP*)
Fält, Olavi K., and Antti Kujala (eds.), *Rakka Ryusui: Colonel Akashi's Report on His
  Secret Activities During the Russo-Japanese War* (Helsinki, 1988)
Führer Conferences on Naval Affairs 1939–1945, Brassey's Naval Annual 1948,
  pp. 25–496
Gooch, G. P., and H. W. V. Temperley (eds.), *British Documents on the Origins of the War
  1898–1914* (11 vols. in 13, London, 1926–38) (*BD*)
Gøtke, E., *Forudsætningerne for 9. april 1940. Danmarks strategiske situation før 2.
  verdenskrig belyst ved to studier udarbejdet 1936 af adjutanten ved Sjællandske Division*
  (Copenhagen, 1979)
Holtsmark, Sven (ed.), *Norge og Sovjetunionen 1917–1955. En utenrikspolitisk dokumen-
  tasjon* (Oslo, 1995)
Innstilling fra undersøkelseskommisjonen av 1945 (Oslo, 1947)
Knaplund, Paul (ed.), *British Views on Norwegian–Swedish Problems 1880–1895:
  Selections from Diplomatic Correspondence* (Oslo, 1952)
Lepsius, J., A. Mendelssohn-Bartholdy and F. Thimme (eds.), *Die grosse Politik der
  europäischen Kabinette 1871–1914* (40 vols. in 54, Berlin, 1922–7) (*GP*)
Menger, Manfred, Fritz Petrick and Wolfgang Wilhelmus (eds.), *Expansionsrichtung
  Nordeuropa. Dokumente zur Nordeuropapolitik des faschistischen deutschen Imperia-
  lismus 1939 bis 1945* (Berlin, 1987)
Noakes, Jeremy, and Geoffrey Pridham (eds.), *Nazism 1919–1945: A Documentary
  Reader*, vol. III, *Foreign Policy, War and Racial Extermination* (Exeter, 1988)
*Om kriget kommit . . . Förberedelser för mottagande av militärt bistand 1949–1969.
  Betänkande av Neutralitetspolitikkommissionen* (Stockholm, 1994)
Omang, Reidar (ed.), *Norge og stormaktene 1906–1914*, vol. I (Oslo, 1957)
Schreiber, Gerhard, 'Zur Kontinuität des Gross- und Weltmachtstrebens der deutschen
  Marineführung', *Militärgeschichtliche Mitteilungen* 26 (1979), pp. 101–71
'The Winter War (Documents on Soviet–Finnish Relations in 1939–1940)', *Inter-
  national Affairs* (Moscow) 1989, No. 9, pp. 49–71

2 DIARIES, PAPERS AND SPEECHES

Amery, Leo: John Barnes and David Nicholson (eds.), *The Leo Amery Diaries*, vol. I, *1896–1929* (London, 1980)

Brooke, Sir Alan: Sir Arthur Bryant, *The Turn of the Tide 1939–1943: A Study Based on the Diaries and Autobiographical Notes of Field Marshal the Viscount Alanbrooke KG, OM* (London, 1957)

Churchill, Winston: Randolph S. Churchill (comp.), *Into Battle: Speeches by the Right Hon. Winston S. Churchill* (London, 1941)

Fisher, Sir John: P. K. Kemp (ed.), *The Papers of Admiral Sir John Fisher* (2 vols., London, 1964)

   Arthur J. Marder (ed.), *Fear God and Dread Nought: The Correspondence of Admiral of the Fleet Lord Fisher of Kilverstone* (2 vols., London, 1956)

Hitler, Adolf: Edouard Calic (ed.), *Unmasked: Two Confidential Interviews with Hitler in 1931* (London, 1971)

   Hermann Rauschning, *Hitler Speaks: A Series of Political Conversations with Adolf Hitler on His Real Aims* (London, 1939)

   H. R. Trevor-Roper (ed.), *Hitler's Table-Talk 1941–1944* (London, 1953; repr. Oxford, 1988)

   Otto Wagener (ed. Henry Ashby Turner Jr), *Hitler aus nächster Nähe. Aufzeichnungen eines Vertrauten 1929–1932* (Frankfurt am Main, Berlin and Vienna, 1978)

Holstein, Friedrich von: Norman Rich and M. H. Fisher (eds.), *The Holstein Papers* (4 vols., Cambridge, 1955–63)

Ironside, Sir Edmund: Roderick Macleod and Denis Kelly (eds.), *The Ironside Diaries 1937–1940* (London, 1962)

Jellicoe, Sir John: A. Temple Patterson (ed.), *The Jellicoe Papers* (2 vols., London, 1966)

Jones, Thomas, *A Diary with Letters 1931–1950* (London, 1954)

Koht, Halvdan (ed. Steinar Kjærheim), *Rikspolitisk dagbok 1933–1940* (Oslo, 1985)

Kollontai, Aleksandra, 'Diplomatic Diary: A Record of Twenty-Three Years', *International Affairs* (Moscow) 1988, No. 10, pp. 117–27; No. 11, pp. 127–36; No. 12, 107–18; 1989, No. 1, pp. 106–22

Lindman, Arvid (ed. Nils F. Holm), *Dagbocksanteckningar* (Stockholm, 1972)

Nansen, Fridtjof: Steinar Kjærheim (ed.), *Fridtjof Nansen. Brev* (4 vols., Oslo, 1961–6)

Palmstierna, Erik, *Orostid. Politiska dagbocksanteckningar* (2 vols., Stockholm, 1952–3)

Pownall, Sir Henry: Brian Bond (ed.), *Chief of Staff: The Diaries of Lieutenant-General Sir Henry Pownall* (2 vols., London, 1972)

Spring Rice, Sir Cecil: Stephen Gwynn (ed.), *The Letters and Friendships of Sir Cecil Spring Rice* (2 vols., London, 1929)

Wedel Jarlsberg, F., *Reisen gjennem livet* (Oslo, 1932)

Weizsäcker, Ernst von: Leonidas E. Hill (ed.), *Die Weizsäcker-Papiere: 1900–1932* (Berlin, 1982)

   Leonidas E. Hill (ed.), *Die Weizsäcker-Papiere: 1933–1950* (Berlin, 1974)

Westman, K. G. (ed. W. M. Carlgren), *Politiska anteckningar april 1917–augusti 1939* (Stockholm, 1987)

Wilhelm II, Kaiser: Herman Bernstein (ed.), *The Willy–Nicky Correspondence: Being the Secret and Intimate Telegrams Exchanged Between the Kaiser and the Tsar* (New York, 1918)

Wilson, Sir Henry: C. E. Callwell, *Field-Marshal Sir Henry Wilson: His Life and Diaries* (2 vols., London, 1927)

3 MEMOIRS

Agar, Augustus, *Baltic Episode* (London, 1963)

Amery, L. S., *My Political Life* (3 vols., London, 1953–5)

Avon, Earl of, *The Eden Memoirs*, vol. I, *Facing the Dictators* (London, 1962)

Barman, Thomas, *Diplomatic Correspondent* (London, 1968)

Blücher, Wipert von, *Gesandter zwischen Diktatur und Demokratie. Erinnerungen aus den Jahren 1935–1944* (Wiesbaden, 1951)

Boheman, Erik, *På vakt*, vol. I, *Från attaché till sändebud*; vol. II, *Kabinettsekreterare under andra världskriget* (Stockholm, 1963–4)

Bülow, Bernhard Fürst von, *Denkwürdigkeiten* (4 vols., Berlin, 1930–1)

Castberg, Frede, *Minner om politik og vitenskap fra årene 1900–1970* (Oslo, 1971)

Churchill, Winston S., *The Second World War*, vol. I, *The Gathering Storm* (2nd edn, London, 1949)

The World Crisis 1911–1918 (new edn, 2 vols., London, 1938)

Egan, Maurice Francis, *Ten Years near the German Frontier: A Retrospect and a Warning* (London, 1918)

Godfrey, J. H., *Naval Memoirs of Admiral J. H. Godfrey* (8 vols. in 11, privately printed, 1964–6; copy in Churchill College Archive Centre, Cambridge)

Gregory, J. D., *On the Edge of Diplomacy: Rambles and Reflections 1902–1928* (London, 1928)

Grey of Falloden, Viscount, *Twenty-Five Years* (2 vols., London, 1925)

Günther, Ernst, *Minnen från ministertiden i Kristiania åren 1905–1908* (Stockholm, 1923)

Hägglöf, Gunnar, *Möte med Europa. Paris–London–Moskva–Genève–Berlin* (Stockholm, 1971)

Hankey, Lord, *The Supreme Command 1914–1918* (2 vols., London, 1961)

Hitler, Adolf, *Mein Kampf* (trans. Ralph Manheim, London, 1969)

Howard of Penrith, Lord, *Theatre of Life* (2 vols., London, 1935–6)

Hull, Cordell, *Memoirs*, vol. I (London, 1948)

Isvolsky, Alexander, *The Memoirs of Alexander Iswolsky* (London, n.d. [c. 1920])

Kenney, Rowland, *Westering* (London, 1939)

Khrushchev, Nikita, *Khrushchev Remembers* (London, 1971)

Krebs, Richard: see Valtin, Jan

Kroll, Hans, *Lebenserinnerungen eines Botschafters* (Cologne and Berlin, 1967)

Kuusinen, Aino, *Before and After Stalin* (London, 1974)

Lie, Trygve, *Leve eller dø. Norge i krig* (Oslo, 1955)

Ludendorff, Erich, *My War Memories 1914–1918* (2 vols., London, 1919)

Mannerheim, Baron C. G. E., *The Memoirs of Marshal Mannerheim* (London, 1953)

Munch, Peter, *Erindringer 1924–1933. Afrustningsforhandlinger og verdenskrise* (Copenhagen, 1964)

Nadolny, Rudolf (ed. Günter Wollstein), *Mein Beitrag. Erinnerungen eines Botschafters des Deutschen Reiches* (Cologne, 1985)

Nekludoff, A., *Diplomatic Reminiscences Before and During the World War 1911–1917* (London, 1920)

Paasikivi, J. K., *Meine Moskauer Mission 1939–1941* (Hamburg, 1966)

Percy of Newcastle, Lord, *Some Memories* (London, 1958)

Reventlow, Eduard, *I dansk tjeneste* (Copenhagen, 1956)

Rumbold, Sir Horace, *Further Recollections of a Diplomatist* (London, 1903)

Sazonov, Serge, *Fateful Years 1909–1916* (London, 1928)

Schoen, Freiherr von, *The Memoirs of an Ambassador* (London, 1922)
Sims, Rear-Admiral William Sowden, *The Victory at Sea* (London, 1921)
Slessor, Sir John, *The Central Blue* (London, 1956)
Taube, Dr Michael Freiherr von, *Der grossen Katastrophe entgegen. Die russische Politik der Vorkriegszeit und das Ende des Zarenreichs (1904–1917)* (2nd edn, Leipzig, 1937)
Tennant, Sir Peter, *Touchlines of War* (Hull, 1992)
Tirpitz, A. von, *My Memoirs* (2 vols., London, n.d. [1919])
Tuominen, Arvo, *The Bells of the Kremlin: An Experience in Communism* (Hanover and London, 1983)
Valtin, Jan (pseud. of Richard Krebs), *Out of the Night* (London, 1941; repr. London, 1988)
Vansittart, Lord, *The Mist Procession* (London, 1958)
Vogt, Johan, *Om fred og strid mellom hjerte og hode* (Oslo, 1975)
Weizsäcker, Ernst von, *Erinnerungen* (Munich, 1950)
Winter, Sir Ormonde, *Winter's Tale: An Autobiography* (London, 1955)

4 BIOGRAPHIES

Boyle, Andrew, *Montagu Norman* (London, 1967)
Bramwell, Anna, *Blood and Soil: Walther Darré and Hitler's 'Green Party'* (Bourne End, 1985)
Burton, David H., *Cecil Spring Rice: A Diplomat's Life* (London and Toronto, 1990)
Busch, Briton Cooper, *Hardinge of Penshurst: A Study in the Old Diplomacy* (Hamden, Conn., 1980)
Crowe, Sibyl, and Edward Corp, *Our Ablest Public Servant: Sir Eyre Crowe GCB, GCMG, KCB, KCMG 1864–1925* (Braunton, 1993)
Davenport-Hines, R. P. T., *Dudley Docker: The Life and Times of a Trade Warrior* (Cambridge, 1984)
Fasting, Kåre, *Nils Claus Ihlen* (Oslo, 1955)
Feiling, Keith, *The Life of Neville Chamberlain* (London, 1946)
Gilbert, Martin, *Winston S. Churchill*, vol. III, *1914–1916* (London, 1971); vol. V, *1922–1939* (London, 1976)
Greve, Tim, *Haakon VII of Norway* (London, 1983)
Hauge, Kaare, *Alexandra Mikhailovna Kollontai: The Scandinavian Period 1922–1945* (Ph.D thesis, University of Minnesota, 1971; published Ann Arbor, Mich., 1986)
Hayes, Paul M., *Quisling: The Career and Political Ideas of Vidkun Quisling 1887–1945* (Newton Abbot, 1971)
Hedegaard, Ole A., *En general og hans samtid. General Erik With mellem Stauning og kaos* (Frederikssund, 1990)
Heineman, John L., *Hitler's First Foreign Minister: Constantin Freiherr von Neurath* (Berkeley, New York and London, 1980)
Hildebrand, Karl, *Gustav V som människa och regent* (2 vols., Stockholm, 1948)
Hodgson, John H., *Den röda eminensen. O. W. Kuusinens politiska biografi* (Helsinki, 1974)
Hoidal, Oddvar K., *Quisling: A Study in Treason* (Oxford, 1989)
Jägerskiöld, Stig, *Mannerheim mellan världskrigen* (Helsinki, 1972)
Kessler, Count Harry, *Walther Rathenau: His Life and Work* (London, 1929)
Kohut, Thomas A., *Wilhelm II and the Germans: A Study in Leadership* (New York and Oxford, 1991)
Lee, Sir Sidney, *King Edward VII* (2 vols., London, 1925–7)

Lemberg, Magnus, *Hjalmar J. Procopé som aktivist, utrikesminister och svensk partiman. Procopés politiska verksamhet till år 1926* (Helsinki, 1985)

Leopold, John A., *Alfred Hugenberg: The Radical National Campaign Against the Weimar Republic* (New Haven, Conn., and London, 1977)

Mackay, Ruddock F., *Fisher of Kilverstone* (Oxford, 1973)

McKercher, B. J. C., *Esme Howard: A Diplomatic Biography* (Cambridge, 1989)

Möller, Yngve, Östen Undén. *En biografi* (Stockholm, 1986)

Rickard Sandler. Folkbildare. Utrikesminister (Stockholm, 1990)

Overy, R. J., *Goering: The 'Iron Man'* (London, 1984)

Reid, P. R., *Winged Diplomat: The Life Story of Air Commodore Freddie West* (London, 1962)

Rich, Norman, *Friedrich von Holstein: Politics and Diplomacy in the Era of Bismarck and Wilhelm II* (2 vols., Cambridge, 1965)

Schöllgen, Gregor, *A Conservative Against Hitler. Ulrich von Hassell: Diplomat in Imperial Germany, the Weimar Republic and the Third Reich 1881–1944* (London, 1991)

Sjøqvist, Viggo, *Erik Scavenius. Danmarks udenrigsminister under to verdenskrige. Statsminister 1942–1945* (2 vols., Copenhagen, 1973)

Peter Munch. Manden, politikeren, historikeren (Copenhagen, 1976)

Peter Vedel. Udenrigsministeriets direktør (2 vols., Århus, 1957–62)

Skard, Sigmund, *Mennesket Halvdan Koht* (Oslo, 1982)

Thompson, R. W., *Churchill and Morton* (London, 1976)

Trevelyan, G. M., *Grey of Falloden* (London, 1937)

5 SECONDARY WORKS

Aalders, Gerard, 'The Failure of the Scandinavian Defence Union 1948–1949', *Scandinavian Journal of History* 15 (1990), pp. 125–53

Adamson, O. G. (ed.), *Industries of Norway* (Oslo, 1952)

Åhlander, Olof, *Staat, Wirtschaft und Handelspolitik. Schweden und Deutschland 1918–1921* (Lund, 1983)

Alapuro, Risto, *State and Revolution in Finland* (Berkeley, Los Angeles and London, 1988)

Alexandersson, Gunnar, *The Baltic Straits* (The Hague, 1982)

Allason, Rupert: see West, Nigel

Anderson, Edgar, 'An Undeclared Naval War', *Journal of Central European Affairs* 22 (1962), pp. 43–78

Anderson, M. S., *The Rise of Modern Diplomacy 1450–1919* (London, 1993)

Andrew, Christopher, *Secret Service: The Making of the British Intelligence Community* (London, 1985)

Arup, Erik (ed. Thyge Svenstrup), 'Den danske Regerings Forhandlinger og Beslutninger 5. August 1914', *Historisk tidsskrift* (Denmark) 91 (1991), pp. 402–27

Åselius, Gunnar, 'Storbritannien, Tyskland och den svenska neutraliteten 1880–1914: en omvärdering', *Historisk tidskrift* (Sweden) 114 (1994), pp. 228–66

Bailey, Thomas A., *The Policy of the United States Toward the Neutrals 1917–1918* (Baltimore, Md., 1942)

Bairoch, Paul, 'Europe's Gross National Product: 1800–1975', *Journal of European Economic History* 5 (1976), pp. 273–340

Barkai, Avraham, *Nazi Economics: Ideology, Theory and Policy* (Oxford, New York and Munich, 1990)

Barros, James, *The Aland Islands Question: Its Settlement by the League of Nations* (New Haven, Conn., and London, 1968)

Basch, Antonin, *The Danube Basin and the German Economic Sphere* (New York, 1943)

Bell, A. C., *A History of the Blockade of Germany and of the Countries Associated with Her in the Great War* (London, 1937; declassified 1961)

Ben-Moshe, Tuvia, 'Churchill's Strategic Conception During the First World War', *Journal of Strategic Studies* 12 (1989), pp. 5–21

Bennett, Geoffrey, *Cowan's War: The Story of British Naval Operations in the Baltic 1918–1920* (London, 1964)

Berg, Roald, '"Det land vi venter hjælp af". England som Norges beskytter 1905–1908', in *Forsvarsstudier IV. Årbok for Forsvarshistorisk forskningssenter, Forsvarets høgskole 1985* (Oslo, 1985), pp. 111–68

Norsk utenrikspolitikks historie, vol. II, *Norge på egen hånd 1905–1920* (Oslo, 1995)

'Spitsbergen-saken 1905–1925', *Historisk tidsskrift* (Norway) 72 (1993), pp. 443–57

Bergh, T., T. J. Hanisch, E. Lange and H. Ø. Pharo, *Growth and Development: The Norwegian Experience 1830–1980* (Oslo, 1981)

Bergsgård, Arne, 'Utrikspolitikk', in *Innstilling fra Undersøkelsekommisjonen av 1945. Bilag*, vol. I (Oslo, 1947), pp. 117–264

Bergquist, Mats, Alf W. Johansson and Krister Wahlbäck (eds.), *Utrikespolitik och historia. Studier tillägnade Wilhelm M. Carlgren den 6 maj 1987* (Stockholm, 1987)

Bjørgo, Narve, Øystein Rian and Alf Kaartvedt, *Norsk utenrikspolitikks historie*, vol. I, *Selvstendighet og union. Fra middelalderen til 1905* (Oslo, 1995)

Blüdnikow, Bent, 'Denmark During the First World War', *Journal of Contemporary History* 24 (1989), pp. 683–703

Boadle, D. G., 'The Formation of the Foreign Office Economic Relations Section 1930–1937', *Historical Journal* 20 (1977), pp. 919–36

Böhme, Klaus-Richard, 'Huvuddragen i svensk försvarspolitik 1925–1945', in Huge-mark, *Neutralitet och försvar*, pp. 166–84

Bohn, Robert, et al. (eds.), *Neutralität und totalitäre Aggression. Nordeuropa und die Grossmächte im Zweiten Weltkrieg* (Stuttgart, 1991)

Bolsover, G. H., 'Izvol'sky and Reform of the Russian Ministry of Foreign Affairs', *Slavonic and East European Review* 63 (1985), pp. 21–40

Boog, Horst, et al., *Das Deutsche Reich und der Zweite Weltkrieg*, vol. IV, *Der Angriff auf die Sowjetunion* (Stuttgart, 1983)

Bourne, Kenneth, and D. C. Watt (eds.), *Studies in International History: Essays Presented to W. Norton Medlicott* (London, 1967)

Bower, Tom, *The Red Web: MI6 and the KGB Master Coup* (London, 1989)

Boyce, Robert W. D., 'British Capitalism and the Idea of European Unity Between the Wars', in Stirk, *European Unity in Context*, pp. 65–83

British Capitalism at the Crossroads 1919–1932: A Study in Politics, Economics and International Relations (Cambridge, 1987)

Bramsen, Bo, and Kathleen Wain, *The Hambros 1779–1979* (London, 1979)

Brandt, Karl, *Management of Agriculture and Food in the German-Occupied and Other Areas of Fortress Europe: A Study in Military Government* (Stanford, Calif., 1953)

Branner, Hans, 'Østersøen og de danske stræder i engelsk krigsplanlægning 1904–1914', *Historie. Jyske samlinger* 9 (1972), pp. 493–535

Småstat mellem stormagt. Beslutningen om mineudlægning august 1914 (Copenhagen and Århus, 1972)

Britannicus, 'The Northern Question', *North American Review* 188 (1908), pp. 237–47

Bunselmayer, Robert E., *The Cost of the War: British Economic War Aims and the Origins of Reparations* (Hamden, Conn., 1975)

Burchardt, Lothar, *Friedenswirtschaft und Kriegsvorsorge. Deutschlands wirtschaftliche Rüstungsbestrebungen vor 1914* (Boppard am Rhein, 1968)

Carlgren, Wilhelm M., 'Gustaf V och utrikespolitiken', in *Studier i modern historia*, pp. 41–57

Ministären Hammarskjöld. Tillkomst, söndring, fall. Studier i svensk politik 1914–1917 (Stockholm, 1967)

Neutralität oder Allianz. Deutschlands Beziehungen zu Schweden in den Anfangsjahren des Ersten Weltkrieges (Stockholm, 1962)

review of Yvonne-Maria Werner, *Svensk–tyska förbindelser kring sekelskiftet 1900* (Lund, 1989), in *Historisk tidskrift* (Sweden) 110 (1990), pp. 425–7

Svensk utrikespolitik 1939–1945 (Stockholm, 1971)

'Sweden: The Ministry for Foreign Affairs', in Steiner, *Times Survey of Foreign Ministries*, pp. 455–69

Varken – eller. Reflexioner kring Sveriges Ålandpolitik 1938–1939 (Stockholm, 1977)

Carr, E. H., *A History of Soviet Russia*, vol. IV, *The Interregnum 1923–1924* (London, 1954)

Carr, William, *Schleswig-Holstein 1815–1848: A Study in National Conflict* (Manchester, 1963)

Castles, Francis G., *The Social Democratic Image of Society: A Study of the Achievements and Origins of Scandinavian Social Democracy in Comparative Perspective* (London, 1978)

Cecil, Lamar, *The German Diplomatic Service 1871–1914* (Princeton, N. J., 1976)

Champonnois, Suzanne, 'The Baltic States as an Aspect of Franco-Soviet Relations 1919–1934: A Policy or Several Policies?', in Hiden and Loit, *Contact or Isolation?*, pp. 405–13

Childs, Marquis W., *Sweden: The Middle Way* (New Haven, Conn., 1936; revised and enlarged edn, 1938)

Christmas-Møller, Wilhelm, 'Forsvarsminister P. Munchs opfattelse af Danmarks stilling som militærmakt – belyst ved hans forvaltning af sit ressort 1913–1920', in Bertel Heurlin and Christian Thune (eds.), *Danmark og det internationale system. Festskrift til Ole Karup Pedersen* (Copenhagen, 1989), pp. 205–22

Cline, Peter, 'Winding Down the War Economy: British Plans for Peacetime Recovery 1916–1919', in Kathleen Burk (ed.), *War and the State: The Transformation of British Government 1914–1919* (London, 1982), pp. 157–81

Colban, Erik, *Stortinget og utenrikspolitikken* (Oslo, 1961)

Cole, Margaret, and Charles Smith (eds.), *Democratic Sweden: A Volume of Studies Prepared by Members of the New Fabian Research Bureau* (London, 1938)

Consett, Rear-Admiral M. W. W. P., *The Triumph of Unarmed Forces (1914–1918)* (London, 1923)

Coogan, John W., *The End of Neutrality: The United States, Britain and Maritime Rights 1899–1915* (Ithaca, N. Y., and London, 1981)

Corni, Gustavo, *Hitler and the Peasants: Agrarian Policy of the Third Reich 1930–1939* (New York, Oxford and Munich, 1990)

Cottrell, P. L., 'The Bank of England in Its International Setting 1918–1972', in Richard Roberts and David Kynaston (eds.), *The Bank of England: Money, Power and Influence 1694–1994* (Oxford, 1995), pp. 83–139

Crafts, N. F. R., 'Gross National Product in Europe 1870–1910: Some New Estimates', *Explorations in Economic History* 20 (1983), pp. 387–401

'Patterns of Development in Nineteenth-Century Europe', *Oxford Economic Papers* 36 (1984), pp. 438–58

Craig, Gordon A., and Felix Gilbert (eds.), *The Diplomats 1919–1939* (Princeton, N. J., 1953)

Cronenberg, Arvid, 'Kapplöpning med tiden. Svensk krigsorganisation och krigsplanering', in Bo Hugemark (ed.), *Stormvarning. Sverige inför andra världskriget* (Stockholm, 1989), pp. 91–122

Militär intressegrupp-politik. Kretsen kring Ny Militär Tidskrift och dess väg till inflytande i 1930 års forsvarskommission (Stockholm, 1977)

Dahl, Generalmajor A. D., 'Den britiske bedømmelse av Norges forsvarsberedskap', *Norges forsvar* 24 (1974), pp. 153–6

Danielsen, Egil, *Norge–Sovjetunionen. Norsk utenrikspolitikk overfor Sovjetunionen 1917–1940* (Oslo, 1964)

Danielsen, Rolf, 'Forsvarsforliket 1937', in Ottar Dahl et al. (eds.), *Makt og motiv. Et festskrift til Jens Arup Seip* (Oslo, 1975), pp. 166–81

Davis, Lance E., and Robert A. Huttenback, *Mammon and the Pursuit of Empire: The Economics of British Imperialism* (abridged edn, Cambridge, 1988)

Derry, T. K., *A History of Modern Norway 1814–1972* (Oxford, 1973)

Dethlefsen, Henrik, 'Denmark and the German Occupation: Cooperation, Negotiation or Collaboration?', *Scandinavian Journal of History* 15 (1990), pp. 193–206

Dillon, E. J., *The Eclipse of Russia* (New York, 1918)

Doering, Dörte, 'Deutsche Aussenwirtschaftspolitik 1933–1935. Die Gleichschaltung der Aussenwirtschaft in der Frühphase des nationalsozialistischen Regimes' (Doctoral dissertation, Free University of Berlin, 1969)

Döscher, Hans-Jürgen, *Das Auswärtige Amt im Dritten Reich. Diplomatie im Schatten der 'Endlösung'* (Berlin, 1987)

Doss, Kurt, *Das deutsche Auswärtige Amt im Übergang vom Kaiserreich zur Weimarer Republik. Die Schülersche Reform* (Düsseldorf, 1977)

Drachmann, Poul, *The Industrial Development and Commercial Policies of the Three Scandinavian Countries* (Oxford, 1915)

Drummond, Ian M., *The Floating Pound and the Sterling Area 1931–1939* (Cambridge, 1981)

Imperial Economic Policy 1917–1939: Studies in Expansion and Protection (London, 1974)

Due-Nielsen, Carsten, 'Denmark and the First World War', *Scandinavian Journal of History* 10 (1985), pp. 1–18

Dülffer, Jost, *Weimar, Hitler und die Marine. Reichspolitik und Flottenbau 1920–1939* (Düsseldorf, 1973)

Dyck, Harvey L., 'German–Soviet Relations and the Anglo-Soviet Break 1927', *Slavic Review* 25 (1966), pp. 67–83

Dyrbye, Martin, 'Dansk–tyske handelsforbindelser 1933–1934, med særligt henblik på afslutningen af den dansk–tyske overenskomst vedrørende den gensidige vareudveksling af 1. marts 1934' (Specialeafhandling i historie, University of Copenhagen, 1984)

Eichengreen, Barry, 'Sterling and the Tariff 1929–1932', in Eichengreen, *Elusive Stability: Essays in the History of International Finance 1919–1939* (Cambridge, 1990), pp. 180–214

Eichholz, Dietrich, 'Expansionsrichtung Nordeuropa', *Zeitschrift für Geschichtswissenschaft* 27 (1979), pp. 17–31

Einzig, Paul, *Bloodless Invasion: German Economic Penetration into the Danubian States and the Balkans* (London, 1938)

Eisenstadt, S. N., 'Reflections on Centre–Periphery Relations and Small European

States', in Risto Alapuro et al., *Small States in Comparative Perspective: Essays for Erik Allardt* (Oslo, 1985), pp. 41–9

Ellis, Havelock, Preface to *The Pillars of Society, and Other Plays by Henrik Ibsen* (London, 1888), pp. vii–xxx

Elvander, Nils, *Harald Hjärne och konservatismen. Konservativ idédebatt i Sverige 1865–1922* (Stockholm, 1961)

Elviken, Andreas, 'The Genesis of Norwegian Nationalism', *Journal of Modern History* 3 (1931), pp. 365–91

Erbe, René, *Die nationalsozialistische Wirtschaftspolitik 1933–1939 im Lichte der modernen Theorie* (Zurich, 1958)

Ericsson, Tom, *Mellan kapital och arbete. Småborgerligheten i Sverige 1850–1914* (Umeå, 1988)

Eriksen, Knut Einar, 'Great Britain and the Problem of Bases in the Nordic Area 1945–1947', *Scandinavian Journal of History* 7 (1982), pp. 135–63

Eriksen, Knut Einar, and Helge Pharo, 'Norway and the Early Cold War: Conditional Atlantic Cooperation' (IFS Info No. 5, Oslo, 1993)

Eyers, John S., 'Government Direction of Britain's Overseas Trade Policy 1932–1937' (DPhil. thesis, University of Oxford, 1977)

Facius, Friedrich, *Wirtschaft und Staat. Die Entwicklung der staatlichen Wirtschaftsverwaltung in Deutschland vom 17. Jahrhundert bis 1945* (Boppard am Rhein, 1959)

Farquarson, J. E., *The Plough and the Swastika: The NSDAP and Agriculture in Germany 1928–1945* (London and Beverly Hills, 1976)

Feldman, Gerald D., *Army, Industry and Labor in Germany 1914–1918* (2nd edn, Oxford, 1992)

Field, Geoffrey, 'Nordic Racism', *Journal of the History of Ideas* 38 (1977), pp. 523–40

Fink, Troels, *Da Sønderjylland blev delt 1918–1920* (3 vols., Åbenrå, 1979)
Estruptidens politiske historie 1875–1894 (2 vols., Odense, 1986)
Spillet om dansk neutralitetet 1905–1909. L. C. F. Lütken og dansk udenrigs- og forsvarspolitik (Århus, 1959)
Ustabil balance. Dansk udenrigs- og forsvarspolitik 1894–1905 (Århus, 1969)

Fischer, Fritz, *Germany's Aims in the First World War* (London, 1967)
Griff nach der Weltmacht. Die Kriegszielpolitik des kaiserlichen Deutschland 1914–1918 (revised edn, Düsseldorf, 1977)

Flinn, M., 'Scandinavian Iron Ore Mining and the British Steel Industry 1870–1914', *Scandinavian Economic History Review* 1 (1953), pp. 31–46

Floud, R., and D. McCloskey (eds.), *The Economic History of Britain Since 1700* (2 vols., Cambridge, 1981)

Francis, E. V., *Britain's Economic Strategy* (London, 1939)

French, David, *British Economic and Strategic Planning 1905–1915* (London, 1982)
British Strategy and War Aims 1914–1916 (London, 1986)

Freymond, Jean, *Le IIIe Reich et la réorganisation économique de l'Europe 1940–1942. Origines et projets* (Leiden, 1974)

Friis, Henning (ed.), *Scandinavia Between East and West* (Ithaca, N. Y., 1950)

Fritz, Martin, *Svensk järnmalmsexport 1883–1913* (Gothenburg, 1967)

Fure, Odd-Bjørn, *Norsk utenrikspolitikks historie*, vol. III, *Mellomkrigstid 1920–1940* (Oslo, 1996)

Furre, Berge, *Norsk historie 1905–1940* (Oslo, 1972)

Futrell, Michael, *Northern Underground: Episodes of Russian Revolutionary Transport and Communications Through Scandinavia and Finland 1863–1917* (London, 1963)

Gasslander, Olle, *History of Stockholms Enskilda Bank to 1914* (Stockholm, 1962)

Gathorne-Hardy, G. M., *Norway* (London, 1925)

Gatrell, Peter, 'After Tsushima: Economic and Administrative Aspects of Russian Naval Rearmament 1905–1913', *Economic History Review* 43 (1990), pp. 255–70

Gemzell, Carl-Axel, *Organization, Conflict and Innovation: A Study of German Naval Strategic Planning 1888–1940* (Lund, 1973)

  Raeder, Hitler und Skandinavien. Der Kampf für einen maritimen Operationsplan (Lund, 1965)

Gerhardt, M., and W. Hubatsch, *Deutschland und Skandinavien im Wandel der Jahrhunderte* (Bonn, 1977)

Gessner, Dieter, 'Agrarian Protectionism in the Weimar Republic', *Journal of Contemporary History* 12 (1977), pp. 759–78

  'The Dilemma of German Agriculture During the Weimar Republic', in Richard Bessel and E. J. Feuchtwanger (eds.), *Social Change and Political Development in Weimar Germany* (London, 1981), pp. 134–54

Gibbs, Norman, *Grand Strategy*, vol. I (London, 1976)

Gihl, Torsten, *Den svenska utrikespolitikens historia*, vol. IV, *1914–1919* (Stockholm, 1951)

Gilbert, Martin, *The Roots of Appeasement* (London, 1966)

Glaser-Schmidt, Elisabeth, 'German and American Concepts to Restore a Liberal World Trading System After World War I', in Schröder, *Confrontation and Cooperation*, pp. 353–76

Gooch, G. P., *Recent Revelations of European Diplomacy* (London, 1927)

Gorodetsky, Gabriel, *The Precarious Truce: Anglo-Soviet Relations 1924–1927* (Cambridge, 1977)

Graml, Hermann, 'Resistance Thinking on Foreign Policy', in Graml, Hans Mommsen, Hans-Joachim Reichhardt and Ernst Wolf, *The German Resistance to Hitler* (London, 1970), pp. 1–54

Grannes, Einar, 'Operation *Jupiter*: A Norwegian Perspective', in Salmon, *Britain and Norway*, pp. 109–16

Graubard, Stephen R. (ed.), *Norden – The Passion for Equality* (Oslo, 1986)

Greenhill, Basil, and Ann Giffard, *The British Assault on Finland 1854–1855: A Forgotten Naval War* (London, 1988)

Grell, Detlef, *Die Auflösung der Schwedisch–Norwegischen Union – 1905 – im Spiegel der europäischen Grossmachtspolitik. Unter besonderer Berücksichtigung der Akten des Auswärtigen Amtes* (Essen, 1984)

Greve, Tim, *Spionjakt i Norge* (Oslo, 1982)

Grimley, O. B., *The New Norway: A People with the Spirit of Cooperation* (Oslo, 1939)

Grohmann, Justus-Andreas, *Die deutsch–schwedische Auseinandersetzung um die Fahrstrassen des Öresunds im Ersten Weltkrieg* (Boppard am Rhein, 1974)

Grzybowski, K., 'The Soviet Doctrine of Mare Clausum and Policies in Black and Baltic Seas', *Journal of Central European Affairs* 14 (1954–5), pp. 339–53

Guichard, L., *The Naval Blockade 1914–1918* (London, 1930)

Gustafsson, Bo, 'A Perennial of Doctrinal History: Keynes and "The Stockholm School"', *Economy and History* 16 (1973), pp. 114–28

Gustavson, Carl G., *The Small Giant: Sweden Enters the Industrial Era* (Athens, Ohio, and London, 1986)

Haggie, Paul, 'The Royal Navy and War Planning in the Fisher Era', in Kennedy, *War Plans*, pp. 118–32

Hägglöf, Gunnar, *Svensk krigshandelspolitik under andra världskriget* (Stockholm, 1958)

  'A Test of Neutrality: Sweden in the Second World War', *International Affairs* 36 (1960), pp. 153–67

Hagtvedt, Bernt, and Erik Rudeng, 'Scandinavia: Achievements, Dilemmas, Challenges', in Graubard, *Norden*, pp. 283–308

Hambro, Carl J., *I Saw It Happen in Norway* (London, 1940)

Handel, Michael, *Weak States in the International System* (London, 1981)

Haskel, Barbara G., *The Scandinavian Option: Opportunities and Opportunity Costs in Postwar Scandinavian Foreign Policies* (Oslo, 1976)

Hatton, Ragnhild, 'Palmerston and "Scandinavian Union"', in Bourne and Watt, *Studies in International History*, pp. 119–44

Haugen, Einar, *Language Conflict and Language Planning: The Case of Modern Norwegian* (Cambridge, Mass., 1966)

Hayes, Paul, 'Britain, Germany and the Admiralty's Plans for Attacking German Territory 1906–1915', in Lawrence Freedman, Hayes and Robert O'Neill (eds.), *War, Strategy and International Politics: Essays in Honour of Sir Michael Howard* (Oxford, 1992), pp. 95–116

Hayes, Peter, *Industry and Ideology: IG Farben in the Nazi Era* (Cambridge, 1987)

Heckscher, Eli F., 'A Survey of Economic Thought in Sweden 1875–1950', *Scandinavian Economic History Review* 1 (1953), pp. 105–25

Heckscher, Eli F., Kurt Bergendal, Wilhelm Keilhau, Einar Cohn and Thorsteinn Thorsteinsson, *Sweden, Norway, Denmark and Iceland in the World War* (New Haven, Conn., 1930)

Herre, Paul, *Die kleinen Staaten Europas und die Entstehung des Weltkrieges* (Munich, 1937)

Hiden, John, *The Baltic States and Weimar Ostpolitik* (Cambridge, 1987)

Hiden, John, and Aleksander Loit (eds.), *The Baltic in International Relations Between the Two World Wars* (Stockholm, 1988)

Contact or Isolation? Soviet–Western Relations in the Interwar Period (Stockholm, 1991)

Hildebrand, Karl-Gustaf, 'Economic Policy in Scandinavia During the Inter-War Period', *Scandinavian Economic History Review* 23 (1975), pp. 99–115

'Labour and Capital in the Scandinavian Countries in the Nineteenth and Twentieth Centuries', in P. Mathias and M. M. Postan (eds.), *Cambridge Economic History of Europe*, vol. VII, part 1 (Cambridge, 1978), pp. 590–628

Hinkkanen-Lievonen, Merja-Liisa, 'Britain as Germany's Commercial Rival in the Baltic States 1919–1939', in Marie-Luise Recker (ed.), *Von der Konkurrenz zur Rivalität. Das britisch–deutsche Verhältnis in den Ländern der europäischen Peripherie 1919–1939* (Stuttgart, 1986), pp. 15–49

British Trade and Enterprise in the Baltic States 1919–1925 (Helsinki, 1984)

Hinsley, F. H. (ed.), *British Foreign Policy Under Sir Edward Grey* (Cambridge, 1977)

Hirschfeld, Gerhard, and Lothar Kettenacker (eds.), *Der 'Führerstaat'. Mythos und Realität* (Stuttgart, 1981)

Hirschman, Albert O., *National Power and the Structure of Foreign Trade* (Berkeley and Los Angeles, 1945)

Hodgson, John H., *Communism in Finland: A History and Interpretation* (Princeton, N. J., 1966)

Hodne, Fritz, *An Economic History of Norway 1815–1970* (Bergen, 1975)

The Norwegian Economy 1920–1980 (London and Canberra, 1983)

Hoffman, Ross J. S., *Great Britain and the German Trade Rivalry 1875–1914* (Philadelphia, 1933; repr. New York and London, 1983)

Holborn, Hajo, 'Diplomats and Diplomacy in the Early Weimar Republic', in Craig and Gilbert, *The Diplomats*, pp. 123–71

Holbraad, Carsten, *Danish Neutrality: A Study in the Foreign Policy of a Small State* (Oxford, 1991)

Holtsmark, Sven G., 'Atlantic Orientation or Regional Groupings: Elements of Norwegian Foreign Policy Discussions During the Second World War', *Scandinavian Journal of History* 14 (1989), pp. 311–24

Enemy Springboard or Benevolent Buffer? Soviet Attitudes to Nordic Cooperation 1920–1955 (Oslo, 1992)

'Om Den røde hær rykker inn i Norge . . . Spørsmålet om sovjetisk deltagelse i frigjøringen av Norge 1941–1944' (IFS Info No. 6, Oslo, 1994)

A Soviet Grab for the High North? USSR, Svalbard and Northern Norway 1920–1953 (Oslo, 1993)

'Spørsmålet om sovjetiske ikke-angrepsavtaler med de skandinaviske land' (unpublished manuscript)

Holtsmark, Sven G., and Tom Kristiansen, *En nordisk illusion? Norge og militært samarbeid i Nord 1918–1940* (Oslo, 1991)

Holtze, Bengt, 'Några militära bedömningar 1915 avseende Sverige', *Aktuellt och historiskt* 1969, pp. 95–116

'Sverige i brittiska bedömningar under första världskriget', *Aktuellt och historiskt* 1971, pp. 113–80

Hornborg, Eirik, *Sverige och Ryssland genom tiderna* (Stockholm, 1941)

Hovi, Kalervo, *Cordon Sanitaire or Barrière de l'Est? The Emergence of the New French Eastern Alliance Policy 1917–1919* (Turku, 1975)

Interessensphären im Baltikum. Finnland im Rahmen der Ostpolitik Polens 1919–1922 (Helsinki, 1984)

Hovi, Olavi, *The Baltic Area in British Policy 1918–1921*, vol. I, *From the Compiègne Armistice to the Implementation of the Versailles Treaty, 11.11.1918–20.1.1920* (Helsinki, 1980)

Howard, Michael, *The Continental Commitment: The Dilemma of British Defence Policy in the Era of the Two World Wars* (London, 1972)

Strategic Deception in the Second World War (London, 1990)

Howson, Susan, and Donald Winch, *The Economic Advisory Council 1930–1939: A Study in Economic Advice During Depression and Recovery* (Cambridge, 1977)

Hubatsch, Walther, *Der Admiralstab und die obersten Marinebehörden in Deutschland 1848–1945* (Frankfurt am Main, 1958)

'Deutschlands Seeflanke in Nordeuropa', in Hubatsch, *Kaiserliche Marine*, pp. 124–36

'Finnland in der deutschen Ostseepolitik 1914–1918', in Hubatsch, *Unruhe des Nordens. Studien zur deutsch–skandinavischen Geschichte* (Göttingen, Berlin and Frankfurt am Main, 1956), pp. 106–49

Kaiserliche Marine. Aufgaben und Leistungen (Munich, 1975)

'Problems of the Norwegian Campaign 1940', *Journal of the Royal United Service Institution* 103 (1958), pp. 336–45

'Die russische Marine im deutschen Urteil', in Hubatsch, *Kaiserliche Marine*, pp. 92–123

Weserübung. Die deutsche Besetzung von Dänemark und Norwegen 1940 (Göttingen, 1960)

'Zur deutschen Nordeuropa-Politik um das Jahr 1905', *Historische Zeitschrift* 188 (1959), pp. 594–605

Hugemark, Bo (ed.), *Neutralität och försvar. Perspektiv på svensk säkerhetspolitik 1809–1985* (Stockholm, 1986)

Ilersic, A. R., *Parliament of Commerce: The Story of the Association of British Chambers of Commerce 1860–1960* (London, 1960)

Jackson, J. Hampden, *Finland* (London, 1938)

Jacobsen, Hans-Adolf, *Nationalsozialistische Aussenpolitik 1933–1938* (Frankfurt am Main and Berlin, 1968)

Jakobson, Max, *The Diplomacy of the Winter War* (Cambridge, Mass., 1961)

James, Harold, *The German Slump: Politics and Economics 1924–1936* (Oxford, 1986)

Jensen, Bent, 'Denmark and the Russian Question 1917–1924: Private Interests, Official Policy and Great Power Pressure', in Hiden and Loit, *Contact or Isolation?*, pp. 43–55

Joesten, Joachim, *Denmark's Day of Doom* (London, 1939)

'The Nazis in Scandinavia', *Foreign Affairs* 15 (1937), pp. 720–8

'The Scramble for Swedish Iron Ore', *Political Quarterly* 1938, 1, pp. 58–67

Johansen, Hans Chr., et al., 'Hovedlinier in den økonomiske udvikling i de nordiske lande i mellemkrigstiden', in *Kriser och krispolitik i Norden i mellankrigstiden. Nordiska historikermötet in Uppsala 1974: Mötesrapport* (Uppsala, 1974), pp. 13–26

Johanson, Gösta, 'Efter borggårdstalet – nya kupp-planer', *Scandia* 59 (1993), pp. 71–111

Johansson, Alf W., and Torbjörn Norman, 'Den svenska neutralitetspolitiken i historiskt perspectiv', in Hugemark, *Neutralität och försvar*, pp. 11–43

Jones, Raymond A., *The British Diplomatic Service 1815–1914* (Waterloo, Ont., 1983)

Jones, S. Shepherd, *The Scandinavian States and the League of Nations* (Princeton, N. J., 1939; repr. New York, 1969)

Jonsson, B., *Staten och malmfälten. En studie i svensk malmfältpolitik omkring sekelskiftet* (Stockholm, 1969)

Jörberg, Lennart, 'The Nordic Countries 1850–1914', in Carlo M. Cipolla (ed.), *The Fontana Economic History of Europe*, vol. IV, part 2 (London, 1973), pp. 375–485

Jörberg, Lennart, and Olle Krantz, 'Scandinavia 1914–1970', in Carlo M. Cipolla (ed.), *The Fontana Economic History of Europe*, vol. VI, part 2 (London, 1976), pp. 377–459

Jordan, Nicole, *The Popular Front and Central Europe: The Dilemmas of French Impotence 1918–1940* (Cambridge, 1992)

Jorgensen, Theodore, *Norway's Relation to Scandinavian Unionism 1815–1871* (Northfield, Minn., 1935)

Jungar, Sune, 'Bolsjevikmissionen lämnar Stockholm. Sveriges brytning med sovjetregeringen 1918', in *Studier i modern historia*, pp. 151–67

Ryssland och den svensk–norska unionens upplösning (Turku, 1969)

'The XXth-Century Varangians: The Russian Policy of Sweden, Norway and Denmark After the Revolution. Some Comparative Observations', in Hiden and Loit, *Contact or Isolation?*, pp. 161–74

Kaarsted, Tage, *Great Britain and Denmark 1914–1920* (Odense, 1979)

Kahn, Alfred E., *Great Britain and the World Economy* (London, 1946)

Kaiser, David E., *Economic Diplomacy and the Origins of the Second World War: Germany, Britain, France and Eastern Europe 1930–1939* (Princeton, N. J., 1980)

Kalela, Jorma, *Grannar på skilda vägar. Den finländsk–svenska samarbetet i den finländska och svenska utrikespolitiken 1921–1923* (Helsinki, 1971)

Kennedy, Paul, 'The Development of German Naval Plans Against England 1896–1914', in Kennedy, *War Plans*, pp. 170–98

Kennedy, Paul (ed.), *The War Plans of the Great Powers 1880–1914* (London, 1979)

Kenney, Rowland, *The Northern Tangle: Scandinavia and the Post-War World* (London, 1946)

Kirby, David, *The Baltic World 1772–1993: Europe's Northern Periphery in an Age of Change* (London, 1995)

Northern Europe in the Early Modern Period: The Baltic World 1492–1772 (London, 1990)

Kirchhoff, Hans, *Augustoprøret 1943* (Copenhagen, 1979)

'Foreign Policy and Rationality – The Danish Capitulation of 9 April 1940: An Outline of a Pattern of Action', *Scandinavian Journal of History* 16 (1991), pp. 237–68

Kjellén, Rudolf, *Stormakterna. Konturer kring samtidens storpolitik* (2nd edn, 2 vols., Stockholm, 1911)

Kjølsen, Klaus, 'Denmark: The Royal Danish Ministry of Foreign Affairs', in Steiner, *Times Survey of Foreign Ministries*, pp. 163–83

Knaplund, Paul, 'Finmark in British Diplomacy 1836–1855', *American Historical Review* 30 (1925), pp. 478–502

Knorr, Klaus, *The Power of Nations: The Political Economy of International Relations* (New York, 1975)

Koblik, Steven, *Sweden: The Neutral Victor. Sweden and the Western Powers 1917–1918* (Lund, 1972)

Koht, Halvdan, *For fred og fridom i krigstid 1939–1940* (Oslo, 1957)

Norsk utanrikspolitikk fram til 9. april 1940. Synspunkt frå hendings-tida (Oslo, 1947)

Norway Neutral and Invaded (London, 1941)

Kolsrud, Ole, 'Kollaborasjon og imperialisme. Quisling-regjeringens "Austrveg"-drøm 1941–1944', *Historisk tidsskrift* (Norway) 67 (1988), pp. 241–70

Krasner, Stephen D., 'State Power and the Structure of International Trade', *World Politics* 28 (1976), pp. 317–47

Kreider, Carl, *The Anglo-American Trade Agreement: A Study of British and American Commercial Policies 1934–1939* (Princeton, N. J., 1942)

Kristiansen, Tom, 'Mellom landmakter og sjømakter. Norges plass i britisk forsvars- og utenrikspolitikk 1905–1914' (Hovedoppgave i historie, University of Oslo, 1988)

Kroll, Gerhard, *Von der Weltwirtschaftskrise zur Staatskonjunktur* (Berlin, 1958)

Krosby, H. Peter, *Finland, Germany and the Soviet Union 1940–1941: The Petsamo Dispute* (Madison, Milwaukee and London, 1968)

Krüger, Karl, *Deutsche Grossraumwirtschaft* (Hamburg, 1932)

Krüger, Peter, *Die Aussenpolitik der Republik von Weimar* (Darmstadt, 1985)

Kuuse, J., 'Foreign Trade and the Breakthrough of the Engineering Industry in Sweden 1890–1920', *Scandinavian Economic History Review* 25 (1977), pp. 1–36

Kuusisto, Seppo, *Alfred Rosenberg in der nationalsozialistischen Aussenpolitik 1933–1939* (Helsinki, 1984)

Lambert, Andrew, *The Crimean War: British Grand Strategy Against Russia 1853–1856* (Manchester, 1990)

'"Part of a Long Line of Circumvallation to Confine the Future Expansion of Russia": Great Britain and the Baltic 1809–1890', in Rystad, Böhme and Carlgren, *In Quest of Trade and Security* I, pp. 297–334

Lammers, Donald, 'Fascism, Communism and the Foreign Office 1937–1939', *Journal of Contemporary History* 6, 3 (1971), pp. 66–86

Lange, Even, 'The Concession Laws of 1906–1909 and Norwegian Industrial Development', *Scandinavian Journal of History* 2 (1977), pp. 311–30

Large, J. A., 'The Origins of Soviet Collective Security Policy 1930–1932', *Soviet Studies* 30 (1976), pp. 212–36

Larsen, Hans Kryger, 'Det nationale synspunkt på den økonomiske udvikling

1888–1914', in Ole Feldbæk (ed.), *Dansk identitetshistorie*, vol. III, *Folkets Danmark 1848–1940* (Copenhagen, 1992), pp. 468–511

Larsson, Jan, *Diplomati och industriellt genombrott. Svensk exportsträvanden på Kina 1906–1916* (Uppsala, 1977)

Laue, Theodore H. von, 'Soviet Diplomacy: G. V. Chicherin, People's Commissar for Foreign Affairs 1918–1930', in Craig and Gilbert, *The Diplomats*, pp. 234–81

Lerman, Katharine A., 'Bismarck's Heir: Chancellor Bernhard von Bülow and the National Idea 1890–1918', in John Breuilly (ed.), *The State of Germany: The National Idea in the Making, Unmaking and Remaking of a Modern Nation-State* (London, 1992), pp. 103–27

Lewin, Leif, *Ideology and Strategy: A Century of Swedish Politics* (Cambridge, 1988)

Lieven, Dominic, *Russia's Rulers Under the Old Regime* (New Haven, Conn., and London, 1989)

Lindberg, Anders, *Småstat mot stormakt. Beslutsystemet vid tillkomsten av 1911 års svensk–tyska handels- och sjöfartstraktat* (Lund, 1983)

Lindberg, Folke, *Kunglig utrikespolitik. Studier och essayer från Oskar II:s tid* (Stockholm, 1950)

  Scandinavia in Great Power Politics 1905–1908 (Stockholm, 1958)

  'De svensk–tyska generalstabsförhandlingarna år 1910', *Historisk tidskrift* (Sweden) 77 (1957), pp. 1–28

  Den svenska utrikespolitikens historia, vol. III, part 4, *1872–1914* (Stockholm, 1958)

Lindedahl, Ingemar, 'Alexandra Kollontaj och Norden', in Bergquist, Johansson and Wahlbäck, *Utrikespolitik och historia*, pp. 145–62

Lindgren, Raymond E., *Norway–Sweden: Union, Disunion and Scandinavian Integration* (Princeton, N. J., 1959)

Lönnroth, Erik, *Den svenska utrikespolitikens historia*, vol. V, *1919–1939* (Stockholm, 1959)

  'Sweden: The Diplomacy of Östen Undén', in Craig and Gilbert, *The Diplomats*, pp. 86–99

Loock, Hans-Dietrich, 'Nordeuropa zwischen Aussenpolitik und "grossgermanischer" Innenpolitik', in Manfred Funke (ed.), *Hitler, Deutschland und die Mächte. Materialen zur Aussenpolitik des Dritten Reiches* (Düsseldorf, 1978), pp. 684–706

  Quisling, Rosenberg und Terboven. Zur Vorgeschichte und Geschichte der nationalsozialistischen Revolution in Norwegen (Stuttgart, 1970)

Ludlow, Peter W., 'Britain and Northern Europe 1940–1945', *Scandinavian Journal of History* 4 (1979), pp. 123–62

  'Scandinavia Between the Great Powers: Attempts at Mediation in the First Year of the Second World War', *Historisk tidskrift* (Sweden) 94 (1974), pp. 1–58

Lukacs, John, *The Last European War: September 1939–December 1941* (London, 1977)

Lumans, Vadis O., 'The Nordic Destiny: The Peculiar Role of the German Minority in North Schleswig in Hitler's Plans and Policies for Denmark', *Scandinavian Journal of History* 15 (1990), pp. 109–23

Lundestad, Geir, 'The Evolution of Norwegian Security Policy: Alliance with the West and Reassurance in the East', *Scandinavian Journal of History* 17 (1992), pp. 227–56

Lundin, C. Leonard, 'Finland', in Edward C. Thaden (ed.), *Russification in the Baltic Provinces and Finland 1855–1914* (Princeton, N. J., 1981), pp. 355–457

Luntinen, Pertti, *The Baltic Question 1903–1908* (Helsinki, 1975)

  French Information on the Russian War Plans 1880–1914 (Helsinki, 1984)

  'Neutrality in Northern Europe Before the First World War', in Jukka Nevakivi (ed.), *Neutrality in History* (Helsinki, 1993), pp. 107–14

Lutzhöft, Hans-Jürgen, *Der Nordische Gedanke in Deutschland 1920–1940* (Stuttgart, 1971)

Lyytinen, Eino, *Finland in British Politics in the First World War* (Helsinki, 1980)

McDermott, J., 'The Revolution in British Military Thinking from the Boer War to the Moroccan Crisis', in Kennedy, *War Plans*, pp. 99–117

MacDonald, C. A., 'Economic Appeasement and the German "Moderates" 1937–1939', *Past and Present* 56 (1972), pp. 105–35

The United States, Britain and Appeasement 1936–1939 (London, 1981)

McDonald, David M., 'A Lever Without a Fulcrum: Domestic Factors and Russian Foreign Policy 1905–1914', in Hugh Ragsdale (ed.), *Imperial Russian Foreign Policy* (Cambridge, 1993), pp. 268–311

McKale, Donald M., *The Swastika Outside Germany* (Kent, Ohio, 1977)

McKay, C. G., *From Information to Intrigue: Studies in Secret Service Based on the Swedish Experience 1939–1945* (London, 1993)

'Our Man in Reval', *Intelligence and National Security* 9 (1994), pp. 88–111

McKercher, B. J. C., 'The Last Old Diplomat: Sir Robert Vansittart and British Foreign Policy', *Diplomacy and Statecraft* 6 (1995), pp. 1–38

McKercher, B. J. C., and Keith E. Neilson, '"The Triumph of Unarmed Forces": Sweden and the Allied Blockade of Germany 1914–1917', *Journal of Strategic Studies* 7 (1984), pp. 178–99

Maisel, Ephraim, *The Foreign Office and Foreign Policy 1919–1926* (Brighton, 1994)

'The Formation of the Department of Overseas Trade 1919–1926', *Journal of Contemporary History* 24 (1989), pp. 169–90

Manniche, Peter, *Denmark: A Social Laboratory* (Copenhagen, 1939)

Marder, Arthur J., *British Naval Policy 1880–1905: The Anatomy of British Sea Power* (London, 1940)

From the Dreadnought to Scapa Flow: The Royal Navy in the Fisher Era 1904–1919 (5 vols., London, 1961–70)

'"Winston is Back": Churchill at the Admiralty 1939–1940', in Marder, *From the Dardanelles to Oran: Studies of the Royal Navy in War and Peace 1915–1940* (London, 1974), pp. 105–78

Marschall, Birgit, *Reisen und Regieren. Die Nordlandfahrten Kaiser Wilhelms II* (Heidelberg, 1991)

Marsden, Arthur, 'The Blockade', in Hinsley, *British Foreign Policy*, pp. 488–515

Mastny, Vojtech, *Russia's Road to the Cold War: Diplomacy, Warfare and the Politics of Communism 1941–1945* (New York, 1979)

Mathisen, Trygve, *Svalbard i internasjonal politikk 1871–1925* (Oslo, 1951)

Maude, George, 'Finland in Anglo-Russian Diplomatic Relations 1899–1910', *Slavonic and East European Review* 48 (1970), pp. 557–81

'The Finnish Question in British Political Life 1899–1914', *Turun historiallinen arkisto* 28 (1973), pp. 325–44

Mead, W. R., 'Anglo-Finnish Commercial Relations Since 1918', *Baltic and Scandinavian Countries* 5 (1939), pp. 117–25

An Economic Geography of the Scandinavian States and Finland (London, 1958)

An Historical Geography of Scandinavia (London, 1981)

Medlicott, W. N., *The Economic Blockade* (2 vols., London, 1952–9)

Meinander, Nils, *Gränges. En kronika om svensk järnmalm* (Stockholm, 1968)

Menger, Manfred, *Deutschland und Finnland im Zweiten Weltkrieg. Genesis und Scheitern einer Militärallianz* (Berlin, 1988)

Meyer, Henry Cord, *'Mitteleuropa' in German Thought and Action 1815–1945* (The Hague, 1955)

Miller, Steven, 'The Maritime Strategy and Geopolitics in the High North', in Clive Archer (ed.), *The Soviet Union and Northern Waters* (London, 1988), pp. 205–38

Milward, Alan S., 'Der deutsche Handel und der Welthandel 1925–1939', in Hans Mommsen, Dietmar Petzina and Bernd Weisbrod (eds.), *Industrielles System und politische Entwicklung in der Weimarer Republik* (Düsseldorf, 1974), pp. 472–84

The European Rescue of the Nation-State (London, 1992)

The Fascist Economy in Norway (Oxford, 1972)

The New Order and the French Economy (Oxford, 1970)

'The Reichsmark Bloc and the International Economy', in Hirschfeld and Kettenacker, *Der 'Führerstaat'*, pp. 377–413

Milward, Alan S., and S. B. Saul, *The Economic Development of Continental Europe 1780–1870* (London, 1973)

Mitchell, B. R., *International Historical Statistics: Europe 1750–1988* (New York, 1992)

Mitchell, Donald W., *A History of Russian and Soviet Sea Power* (New York, 1974)

Mitchison, Rosalind (ed.), *The Roots of Nationalism: Studies in Northern Europe* (Edinburgh, 1980)

Molin, Karl, *Omstridd neutralitet. Experternas kritik av svensk utrikespolitik 1948–1950* (Angered, 1991)

Mommsen, Wolfgang J., *Imperial Germany 1867–1918: Politics, Culture and Society in an Authoritarian State* (London, 1995)

Mosse, W. E., 'Queen Victoria and Her Ministers in the Schleswig-Holstein Crisis 1863–1864' *English Historical Review* 78 (1963), pp. 263–83

Mousson-Lestang, Jean-Pierre, *Le parti social-démocrate et la politique étrangère de la Suède (1914–1918)* (Paris, 1988)

Munch-Petersen, Thomas, 'Confessions of a British Agent: Section D in Sweden 1938–1940', in Bergquist, Johansson and Wahlbäck, *Utrikespolitik och historia*, pp. 175–88

'Great Britain and the Revision of the Åland Convention', *Scandia* 41 (1975), pp. 67–86

The Strategy of Phoney War: Britain, Sweden and the Iron Ore Question 1939–1940 (Stockholm, 1981)

Munthe, Gerhard, '1905. Fred eller krig', *Historisk tidsskrift* (Norway) 59 (1980), pp. 164–75

Myllyniemi, Seppo, *Die baltische Krise 1938–1941* (Stuttgart, 1979)

Myllyntaus, Timo, *Electrifying Finland: The Transfer of a New Technology into a Late Industrialising Economy* (London, 1991)

The Gatecrashing Apprentice: Industrialising Finland as an Adopter of New Technology (Helsinki, 1990)

Neal, Larry, 'The Economics and Finance of Bilateral Exchange Clearing: Germany 1934–1938', *Economic History Review* 32 (1979), pp. 391–404

Neilson, Keith, '"A Dangerous Game of American Poker": The Russo-Japanese War and British Policy', *Journal of Strategic Studies* 12 (1989), pp. 62–87

Neumann, Franz L., *Behemoth: The Structure and Practice of National Socialism 1933–1944* (London, 1944; repr. New York, 1966)

Nevakivi, Jukka, *The Appeal that Was Never Made: The Allies, Scandinavia and the Finnish Winter War 1939–1940* (London, 1976)

'The Control Commission in Helsinki – A Finnish View', in Nevakivi (ed.), *Finnish–Soviet Relations 1944–1948* (Helsinki, 1994), pp. 67–79

'The Finnish Foreign Service', in Steiner, *Times Survey of Foreign Ministries*, pp. 185–99

Newbolt, Sir Henry, *History of the Great War: Naval Operations*, vol. V (London, 1931)

Newman, E. W. Polson, *Britain and the Baltic* (London, 1930)

Newman, Simon, *March 1939: The British Guarantee to Poland* (Oxford, 1976)

Nielsen, Henning, *Nordens enhed gennem tiderne* (3 vols., Copenhagen, 1938)

Nielsen, Jens Petter, 'Ønsket tsaren seg en isfri havn i nord?', *Historisk tidsskrift* (Norway) 70 (1991), pp. 604–21

Nilson, Bengt, *Handelspolitik under skärpt konkurrens. England och Sverige 1929–1939* (Lund, 1983)

Nissen, Henrik S., 'The Nordic Societies', in Nissen (ed.), *Scandinavia During the Second World War* (Minneapolis, 1983), pp. 3–52

Nordlund, Sven, *Upptäckten av Sverige. Utländska direktinvestingar i Sverige 1895–1945* (Umeå, 1989)

Norman, Erik-Wilhelm, 'Norway: The Royal Norwegian Ministry of Foreign Affairs', in Steiner, *Times Survey of Foreign Ministries*, pp. 391–408

Norman, L. Torbjörn, 'Drömmen om Fennoskandia. Alexis Gripenberg och det fria Finlands utrikespolitiska orientering', in *Studier i modern historia*, pp. 169–89

'"A Foreign Policy Other than the Old Neutrality" – Aspects of Swedish Foreign Policy After the First World War', in Hiden and Loit, *The Baltic*, pp. 235–501

'Right-Wing Scandinavianism and the Russian Menace', in Hiden and Loit, *Contact or Isolation?*, pp. 329–49

Nüchel Thomsen, Birgit, and Brinley Thomas, *Anglo-Danish Trade 1661–1963: A Historical Survey* (Århus, 1966)

O'Connor, Timothy Edward, *Diplomacy and Revolution: G. V. Chicherin and Soviet Foreign Affairs 1918–1930* (Ames, Iowa, 1988)

Offer, Avner, *The First World War: An Agrarian Interpretation* (Oxford, 1989)

Olberg, Paul, 'Scandinavia and the Nazis', *Contemporary Review* 156 (1939), pp. 27–34

Omang, Reidar, *Norsk utenrikstjeneste*, vol. I, *Grunnleggende år*; vol. II, *Stormfulle tider 1913–1928* (Oslo, 1955–9)

Ørvik, Nils, *The Decline of Neutrality 1914–1941* (Oslo, 1953; 2nd edn, London, 1971)

'From Collective Security to Neutrality: The Nordic Powers, the League of Nations, Britain and the Approach of War 1935–1939', in Bourne and Watt, *Studies in International History*, pp. 385–401

Sikkerhetspolitikken 1920–1939. Fra forhistorien til 9. april 1940 (2 vols., Oslo, 1960–1)

Ottmer, Hans-Martin, 'Skandinavien in den marinestrategischen Planungen des Reichs- bzw. Kriegsmarine', in Bohn et al., *Neutralität und totalitäre Aggression*, pp. 49–72

Overy, R. J., *The Nazi Economic Recovery 1932–1938* (London, 1982)

Paasivirta, Juhani, *Finland and Europe: The Early Years of Independence 1917–1939* (Helsinki, 1988)

Finland and Europe: The Period of Autonomy and the International Crises 1808–1914 (London, 1981)

The Victors in World War I and Finland (Helsinki, 1965)

Palmstierna, C. F., 'Sweden and the Russian Bogey: A New Light on Palmerston's Foreign Policy', *Nineteenth Century and After* 112 (1933), pp. 739–54

Parker, R. A. C., *Chamberlain and Appeasement: British Policy and the Coming of the Second World War* (London, 1993)

Parry, Clive, 'Foreign Policy and International Law', in Hinsley, *British Foreign Policy*, pp. 89–110

PEP (Political and Economic Planning), *Report on International Trade* (London, 1937)

Petander, Karl, W. Kleen and Anders Örne, *Nordens förenta stater* (Stockholm, 1942)

Petersen, Nikolaj, 'International Power and Foreign Policy Behavior: The Formulation of Danish Security Policy in the 1870–1914 Period', in Kjell Goldmann and Gunnar Sjöstedt (eds.), *Power, Capabilities, Interdependence: Problems in the Study of International Influence* (London and Beverly Hills, 1979), pp. 235–69

Petzina, Dietmar, *Autarkiepolitik im Dritten Reich. Der nationalsozialistische Vierjahresplan* (Stuttgart, 1968)

Philbin, Tobias R., III, *The Lure of Neptune: German–Soviet Naval Collaboration and Ambitions 1919–1941* (Columbia, S. C., 1994)

Pihkala, Erkki, 'Relations with Russia, Foreign Trade and the Development of the Finnish Economy 1860–1939', in Tapani Mauranen (ed.), *Economic Development in Hungary and Finland 1860–1939* (Helsinki, 1985), pp. 25–48

Platt, D. C. M., *Finance, Trade and Politics in British Foreign Policy 1815–1914* (Oxford, 1970)

Foreign Finance in Continental Europe and the United States 1815–1870 (London, 1984)

'The Role of the British Consular Service in Overseas Trade 1825–1914', *Economic History Review* 15 (1962–3), pp. 494–512

Pohl, Karl Heinrich, *Weimars Wirtschaft und die Aussenpolitik der Republik 1924–1926* (Düsseldorf, 1979)

Pollard, Sidney, *Peaceful Conquest: The Industrialization of Europe 1760–1970* (Oxford, 1981)

Polvinen, Tuomo, *Between East and West: Finland in International Politics 1944–1947* (Minneapolis, 1986)

Die finnischen Eisenbahnen in den militärischen und politischen Plänen Russlands vor dem Ersten Weltkrieg (Helsinki, 1962)

Imperial Borderland: Bobrikov and the Attempted Russification of Finland 1898–1904 (London, 1995)

Posse, Hans Ernst, 'Die Hauptlinien der deutschen Handelspolitik', in Deutsches Institut für Bankwissenschaft und Bankwesen (ed.), *Probleme des deutschen Wirtschaftslebens. Erstrebtes und Erreichtes* (Leipzig, 1937), pp. 481–513

Prazmowska, Anita, *Britain, Poland and the Eastern Front 1939* (Cambridge, 1987)

Prior, Robin, *Churchill's 'World Crisis' as History* (London, 1983)

Pritt, D. N., *Must the War Spread?* (London, 1940)

Quisling, Vidkun, *Russia and Ourselves* (London, 1931)

Radkau, Joachim, 'Entscheidungsprozesse und Entscheidungsdefizite in der deutschen Aussenwirtschaftspolitik 1933–1940', *Geschichte und Gesellschaft* 2 (1976), pp. 33–65

Ramsden, John, *A History of the Conservative Party: The Age of Balfour and Baldwin 1902–1940* (London, 1978)

Reunala, Aarne, 'The Forest and the Finns', in Max Engman and David Kirby (eds.), *Finland: People, Nation, State* (London, 1989), pp. 38–56

Richardson, Henry J., *British Economic Foreign Policy* (London, 1936)

Rickman, A. F., *Swedish Iron Ore* (London, 1939)

RIIA (Royal Institute of International Affairs), *The Scandinavian States and Finland: A Political and Economic Survey* (London, 1951)

World Agriculture: An International Survey (London, 1932)

Rislakki, Jukka, 'Finland som objekt och arena för underrättelseverksamhet', *Historisk tidskrift för Finland* 77 (1992), pp. 595–608

Riste, Olav, 'The Foreign Policy-Making Process in Norway: An Historical Perspective', in *Forsvarsstudier. Årbok for Forsvarshistorisk forskningssenter, Forsvarets høgskole 1982* (Oslo, 1983), pp. 232–45

Isolationism and Great Power Protection: The Historical Determinants of Norwegian Foreign Policy (Oslo, 1984)

'London-regjeringa'. Norge i krigsalliansen 1940–1945 (2 vols., Oslo, 1973–9)

The Neutral Ally: Norway's Relations with Belligerent Powers in the First World War (Oslo, 1965)

'Relations Between the Norwegian Government in Exile and the British Government', in Salmon, *Britain and Norway*, pp. 41–50

'Den svensk–norske nøytralitetsavtalen i august 1914', *Historisk tidsskrift* (Norway) 41 (1962), pp. 347–53

Röhl, John C. G., 'Germany', in Keith Wilson (ed.), *Decisions for War* (London, 1995), pp. 27–54

Rohwer, Jürgen, 'Alternating Russian and Soviet Naval Strategies', in Philip S. Gillette and Willard C. Frank Jr (eds.), *The Sources of Soviet Naval Conduct* (Lexington, Mass., 1990), pp. 95–120

Roon, Ger van, *Small States in Years of Depression: The Oslo Alliance 1930–1940* (Assen and Maastricht, 1989)

Rooth, Tim, *British Protectionism and the International Economy: Overseas Commercial Policy in the 1930s* (Cambridge, 1992)

'Limits of Leverage: The Anglo-Danish Trade Agreement of 1933', *Economic History Review* 37 (1984), pp. 211–28

Röpke, Wilhelm, *International Economic Disintegration* (London, 1942)

Rosenberg, Alfred, *Der Mythus des 20. Jahrhunderts* (Munich, 1930)

Rothstein, Robert L., *Alliances and Small States* (New York and London, 1968)

Ruth, Arne, 'The Second New Nation: The Mythology of Modern Sweden', in Graubard, *Norden*, pp. 240–82

Rystad, Göran, 'Die deutsche Monroedoktrin der Ostsee. Die Alandsfrage und die Entstehung des deutsch–schwedischen Geheimabkommens vom Mai 1918', in *Probleme deutscher Zeitgeschichte* (Stockholm, 1971), pp. 1–75

Rystad, Göran, Klaus-Richard Böhme and Wilhelm M. Carlgren (eds.), *In Quest of Trade and Security: The Baltic in Power Politics 1500–1990*, vol. I, *1500–1890* (Lund, 1994); vol. II, *1890–1990* (Lund, 1995)

Salewski, Michael, *Die deutsche Seekriegsleitung 1935–1945* (2 vols., Frankfurt am Main, 1970)

'Das Wesentliche von "Weserübung"', in Bohn et al., *Neutralität und totalitäre Aggression*, pp. 117–26

Salmon, Patrick, '"Between the Sea Power and the Land Power": Scandinavia and the Coming of the First World War', *Transactions of the Royal Historical Society*, 6th series, 3 (1993), pp. 23–49

'British Plans for Economic Warfare Against Germany 1937–1939: The Problem of Swedish Iron Ore' *Journal of Contemporary History* 16 (1981), pp. 53–72

'British Security Interests in Scandinavia and the Baltic 1918–1939', in Hiden and Loit, *The Baltic*, pp. 113–36

'Churchill, the Admiralty and the Narvik Traffic September–November 1939', *Scandinavian Journal of History* 4 (1979), pp. 305–36

'Crimes Against Peace: The Case of the Invasion of Norway at the Nuremberg Trials', in Richard Langhorne (ed.), *Diplomacy and Intelligence During the Second World War: Essays in Honour of F. H. Hinsley* (Cambridge, 1985), pp. 245–69

Foreign Policy and National Identity: The Norwegian Integrity Treaty 1907–1924 (Oslo, 1993)

'Great Britain, the Soviet Union and Finland at the Beginning of the Second World

War', in John Hiden and Thomas Lane (eds.), *The Baltic and the Outbreak of the Second World War* (Cambridge, 1992), pp. 95–123

'Perceptions and Misperceptions: Great Britain and the Soviet Union in Scandinavia and the Baltic Region 1918–1939', in Hiden and Loit, *Contact or Isolation?*, pp. 415–29

'Polish–British Competition in the Coal Markets of Northern Europe 1927–1934', *Scripta historiae oeconomicae* 16 (1981), pp. 217–43

Salmon, Patrick (ed.), *Britain and Norway in the Second World War* (London, 1995)

Sandberg, Lars G., 'Banking and Economic Growth in Sweden Before World War I', *Journal of Economic History* 38 (1978), pp. 650–80

'The Case of the Impoverished Sophisticate: Human Capital and Swedish Economic Growth Before World War I', *Journal of Economic History* 39 (1979), pp. 225–41

Sandiford, Keith A. P., 'The British Cabinet and the Schleswig-Holstein Crisis 1863–1864', *History* 58 (1973), pp. 360–83

Sarnow, Otto, 'Handelspolitische Aktivität in Europa', *Volk und Reich* 5 (1934), pp. 321–30

Sayers, R. S., *The Bank of England 1891–1944* (3 vols., Cambridge, 1976)

Schädlich, K., 'Wandlungen in der Aussenhandelsdiplomatie Grossbritanniens (1885–1910)', in F. Klein (ed.), *Neue Studien zum Imperialismus vor 1914* (Berlin, 1980), pp. 135–63

Schieder, Theodor, *Hermann Rauschnings 'Gespräche mit Hitler' als Geschichtsquelle* (Opladen, 1972)

Schmidt, Gustav, *The Politics and Economics of Appeasement: British Foreign Policy in the 1930s* (Leamington Spa, 1986)

Schmidt, Heide-Irene, 'Wirtschaftliche Kriegsziele Englands und interalliierte Kooperation. Die Pariser Wirtschaftskonferenz 1916', *Militärgeschichtliche Mitteilungen* 29 (1981), pp. 37–54

Schröder, Hans-Jürgen, 'Deutsche Südosteuropapolitik 1926–1936. Zur Kontinuität deutscher Aussenpolitik in der Weltwirtschaftskrise', *Geschichte und Gesellschaft* 2 (1976), pp. 5–32

'Südosteuropa als "Informal Empire" Deutschlands 1933–1939. Das Beispiel Jugoslawien', *Jahrbücher für Geschichte Osteuropas* 23 (1975), pp. 70–96

'Zur politischen Bedeutung der deutschen Handelspolitik nach dem Ersten Weltkrieg', in Gerald D. Feldman, Carl-Ludwig Holtfrerich, Gerhard A. Ritter and Peter-Christian Witt (eds.), *Die deutsche Inflation. Eine Zwischenbilanz* (Berlin and New York, 1982), pp. 235–51

Schröder, Hans-Jürgen (ed.), *Confrontation and Cooperation: Germany and the United States in the Era of World War I 1900–1924* (Providence, R. I., and Oxford, 1993)

Schröter, Harm, *Aussenpolitik und Wirtschaftsinteresse. Skandinavien im aussenwirtschaftlichen Kalkül Deutschlands und Grossbritanniens 1918–1939* (Frankfurt am Main, Berne and New York, 1983)

'Risk and Control in Multinational Enterprise: German Businesses in Scandinavia 1918–1939', *Business History Review* 62 (1988), pp. 420–43

Schuberth, Inger, *Schweden und das Deutsche Reich im Ersten Weltkrieg. Die Aktivistenbewegung 1914–1918* (Bonn, 1981)

Scott, Franklin D., 'Sweden's Constructive Opposition to Emigration', *Journal of Modern History* 37 (1965), pp. 307–35

Screen, J. E. O., 'The Finnish Army 1881–1901: A National Force in a Russian Context', *Slavonic and East European Review* 70 (1992), pp. 453–76

Seabury, Paul, *The Wilhelmstrasse: A Study of German Diplomats Under the Nazi Regime* (Berkeley and Los Angeles, 1954)

Sejersted, Francis, 'A Theory of Economic and Technological Development in Norway in the Nineteenth Century', *Scandinavian Economic History Review* 40 (1992), pp. 40–75

Selén, Kari, 'The Main Lines of Finnish Security Policy Between the World Wars', *Revue internationale d'histoire militaire* 62 (1985), pp. 15–35

Senghaas, Dieter, *The European Experience: A Historical Critique of Development Theory* (Leamington Spa, 1985)

Seymour, Susan, *Anglo-Danish Relations and Germany 1933–1945* (Odense, 1982)

Simon, Sir E. D., *The Smaller Democracies* (London, 1939)

Siney, Marion C., *The Allied Blockade of Germany 1914–1916* (Ann Arbor, Mich., 1954; repr. Westport, Conn., 1973)

Sjøqvist, Viggo, *Danmarks udenrigspolitik 1933–1940* (Copenhagen, 1966)

Skodvin, Magne, 'Norwegian Neutrality and the Question of Credibility', *Scandinavian Journal of History* 2 (1977), pp. 123–45

Smith, C. Jay, Jr, *Finland and the Russian Revolution 1917–1922* (Athens, Ga., 1958)

Snyder, Jack, *The Ideology of the Offensive: Military Decision Making and the Disasters of 1914* (Ithaca, N. Y., and London, 1984)

Søhr, Joh., *Spioner og bomber. Fra opdagelsespolitiets arbeidet under verdenskrigen* (Oslo, 1938)

Soloveytchik, George, 'Fears and Realities in Scandinavia', *International Affairs* 16 (1937), pp. 894–919

'The Lost Key', *Contemporary Review* 150 (August 1936), pp. 172–81

'The Scandinavian *Débâcle*', *Contemporary Review* 157 (June 1940), pp. 659–69

'Who Threatens Scandinavia?', *Contemporary Review* 155 (February 1939), pp. 169–78

Sontag, John P., 'The Soviet War Scare of 1926–1927', *Russian Review* 34 (1975), pp. 66–77

Sontag, R. J., 'German Foreign Policy 1904–1906', *American Historical Review* 33 (1928), pp. 278–301

Soutar, Andrew, *With Ironside in North Russia* (London, 1940)

Soutou, Georges-Henri, 'German Economic War Aims Reconsidered', in Schröder, *Confrontation and Cooperation*, pp. 315–21

L'or et le sang. Les buts de guerre économiques de la Première Guerre mondiale (Paris, 1989)

Spring, D. W., 'The Soviet Decision for War Against Finland 30 November 1939', *Soviet Studies* 38 (1986), pp. 207–26

Stegemann, Bernd, *Die deutsche Marinepolitik 1916–1918* (Berlin, 1970)

Stegmann, Dirk, 'Deutsche Zoll- und Handelspolitik 1924/5–1929 unter besonderer Berücksichtigung agrarischer und industrieller Interessen', in Hans Mommsen, Dietmar Petzina and Bernd Weisbrod (eds.), *Industrielles System und politische Entwicklung in der Weimarer Republik* (Düsseldorf, 1974), pp. 499–513

'"Mitteleuropa" 1925–1934. Zum Problem der Kontinuität deutscher Handelspolitik von Stresemann bis Hitler', in Stegmann, Bernd-Jürgen Wendt and Peter-Christian Witt (eds.), *Industrielle Gesellschaft und politisches System* (Bonn, 1978), pp. 203–21

Stein, Arthur A., 'The Hegemon's Dilemma: Great Britain, the United States and the International Economic Order', *International Organization* 38 (1984), pp. 355–86

Steinberg, John W., 'Russian General Staff Training and the Approach of War', in Frans Coetzee and Marilyn Shevin-Coetzee (eds.), *Authority, Identity and the Social History of the Great War* (Providence, R. I., and Oxford, 1995), pp. 275–303

Steinberg, Jonathan, 'Germany and the Russo-Japanese War', *American Historical Review* 75 (1970), pp. 1965–86

Steiner, Zara, *The Foreign Office and Foreign Policy 1898–1914* (Cambridge, 1969)

Steiner, Zara (ed.), *The Times Survey of Foreign Ministries of the World* (London, 1982)

Stenslund, Trond, 'Norges sjømilitære opprustning 1895–1902 og forholdet til Sverige', *Scandia* 61 (1995), pp. 29–44

Stewart, Robert B., 'Great Britain's Foreign Loan Policy', *Economica*, new series, 5 (1938), pp. 45–60

Stirk, Peter M. R., 'Authoritarian and National Socialist Conceptions of Nation, State and Europe', in Stirk, *European Unity in Context*, pp. 125–48

Stirk, Peter M. R. (ed.), *European Unity in Context: The Interwar Period* (London and New York, 1989)

Stonehill, Arthur, *Foreign Ownership in Norwegian Enterprises* (Oslo, 1965)

Studier i modern historia tillägnade Jarl Torbacke den 18 augusti 1990 (Stockholm, 1990)

Summerton, Neil W., 'The Development of British Military Planning for a War Against Germany 1904–1914' (Ph.D thesis, University of London, 1970)

Sundbäck, Esa, '"A Convenient Buffer Between Scandinavia and Russia": Great Britain, Scandinavia and the Birth of Finland After the First World War', *Jahrbücher für Geschichte Osteuropas* 42 (1994), pp. 355–75

Supple, Barry, *The History of the British Coal Industry*, vol. IV, *1913–1946: The Political Economy of Decline* (Oxford, 1987)

Susiluoto, Ilmari, 'The Origins and Development of Political Formations: The Political Science Practiced by Rudolf Holsti', in Jukka Kanerva and Kari Palonen (eds.), *Transformation of Ideas on a Periphery: Political Studies in Finnish History* (Helsinki, 1987), pp. 76–97

Svensson, Bjørn, *Tyskerkursen* (Copenhagen, 1983)

Sweet, David W., 'The Baltic in British Diplomacy Before the First World War', *Historical Journal* 13 (1970), pp. 451–90

Tägil, Sven, *Deutschland und die deutsche Minderheit in Nordschleswig. Eine Studie zur deutschen Grenzpolitik 1933–1939* (Lund, 1970)

Tamnes, Rolf, *Integration and Screening: The Two Faces of Norwegian Alliance Policy 1945–1986* (Oslo, 1986)

Svalbard og stormaktene. Fra ingenmannsland til Kald Krig 1870–1953 (Oslo, 1991)

Tasca, Henry J., *World Trading Systems: A Study of American and British Commercial Policies* (Paris, 1939)

Taylor, A. J. P., *The Struggle for Mastery in Europe 1848–1918* (Oxford, 1954)

Taylor, Philip M., 'Cultural Diplomacy and the British Council: 1934–1939', *British Journal of International Studies* 4 (1978), pp. 244–65

Teichert, Eckart, *Autarkie und Grossraumwirtschaft in Deutschland 1930–1939* (Munich, 1984)

Temperley, H. W. V. (ed.), *A History of the Peace Conference of Paris* (6 vols., London 1920–3)

Theiner, Peter, '"Mitteleuropa"-Pläne im Wilhelminischen Deutschland', in Helmut Berding (ed.), *Wirtschaftliche und politische Integration in Europa im 19. und 20. Jahrhundert* (Göttingen, 1984), pp. 128–48

Thorne, Sir Peter, 'Andrew Thorne and the Liberation of Norway', in Salmon, *Britain and Norway*, pp. 206–20

Thue, Elisabeth, *Nobels fredspris – og diplomatiske forviklinger. Tysk–norske forbindelser i kjølvannet av Ossietzky-saken* (Oslo, 1994)

Tillotson, H. M., *Finland at Peace and War 1918–1993* (Norwich, 1993)

Timm, Ernst, 'Warum Skandinavien?', *Ruhr und Rhein* 14 (1933), pp. 666–7

Tingsten, Herbert, *The Debate on the Foreign Policy of Sweden 1918–1939* (London, 1949)

Turner, John, *British Politics and the Great War: Coalition and Conflict 1915–1918* (New Haven, Conn., 1991)

Turtola, Martti, 'Aspects of Finnish–Estonian Military Relations in the 1920s and 1930s', in Hiden and Loit, *The Baltic*, pp. 101–10

Från Torne älv till Systerbäck. Hemligt försvarssamarbete mellan Finland och Sverige 1923–1940 (Stockholm, 1987)

'Die militärischen Beziehungen zwischen Deutschland und Finnland 1919–1939', in Hannes Saarinen (ed.), *Referate des vierten Seminars von Historikern aus der DDR und Finnland (5.–8.5.1977 in Hanasaari)* (Helsinki, 1978), pp. 223–41

Ueberschär, Gerd R., *Hitler und Finnland. Die deutsch–finnischen Beziehungen während des Hitler–Stalin-Paktes* (Wiesbaden, 1978)

Uldricks, Teddy J., *Diplomacy and Ideology: The Origins of Soviet Foreign Relations 1917–1930* (London and Beverly Hills, 1979)

'Russia and Europe: Diplomacy, Revolution and Economic Development in the 1920s', *International History Review* 1 (1979), pp. 55–83

Upton, Anthony F., *The Communist Parties of Scandinavia and Finland* (London, 1973)

'The Crisis of Scandinavia and the Collapse of Interwar Ideals 1938–1940', in Stirk, *European Unity in Context*, pp. 170–87

Finland 1939–1940 (London, 1974)

Vandenbosch, Amry, *The Neutrality of the Netherlands During the World War* (Grand Rapids, Mich., 1927)

Verney, Douglas V., *Parliamentary Reform in Sweden 1866–1921* (Oxford, 1957)

Vigness, Paul G., *The Neutrality of Norway in the World War* (Stanford, Calif., and London, 1932)

Vogel, Barbara, *Deutsche Russlandspolitik. Das Scheitern der deutschen Weltpolitik unter Bülow 1900–1906* (Düsseldorf, 1973)

Vogt, Johan, *Den tyske Indflydelse i Danmark* (Copenhagen, 1937)

Volkmann, Hans-Erich, 'Das aussenwirtschaftliche Programm der NSDAP 1930–1933', *Archiv für Sozialgeschichte* 17 (1977), pp. 251–74

Wahlbäck, Krister, *Finlandsfrågan i svensk politik 1937–1940* (Stockholm, 1964)

'The Nordic Region in Twentieth-Century European Politics', in Bengt Sundelius (ed.), *Foreign Policies of Northern Europe* (Boulder, Colo., 1982), pp. 9–32

The Roots of Swedish Neutrality (Stockholm, 1986)

'Svek Sverige Finland hösten 1939?', *Historisk tidskrift för Finland* 74 (1989), pp. 245–76

Wallace, William, *The Foreign Policy Process in Britain* (London, 1976)

Wark, Wesley K., 'Baltic Myths and Submarine Bogeys: British Naval Intelligence and Nazi Germany 1933–1939', *Journal of Strategic Studies* 6 (1983), pp. 60–81

Watt, Donald Cameron, 'The Anglo-German Naval Agreement of 1935: An Interim Judgment', *Journal of Modern History* 28 (1956), pp. 155–76

How War Came: The Immediate Origins of the Second World War (London, 1989)

Personalities and Policies (London, 1965)

'The Study of International History: Language and Reality', in Commission of History of International Relations, Cahier No. 1, *Problems and Discussions on the History of International Relations* (Madrid, 1990), pp. 20–1

Weinberg, Gerhard L., *Germany and the Soviet Union 1939–1941* (Leiden, 1954)

A World at Arms: A Global History of World War II (Cambridge, 1994)

Weir, Gary E., 'Tirpitz, Technology and Building U-boats 1897–1916', *International History Review* 6 (1984), pp. 174–90

Wendt, Bernd-Jürgen, *Economic Appeasement. Handel und Finanz in der britischen Deutschland-Politik 1933–1939* (Düsseldorf, 1971)

'Südosteuropa in der nationalsozialistischen Grossraumwirtschaft', in Hirschfeld and Kettenacker, *Der 'Führerstaat'*, pp. 414–55

Werner, Yvonne Maria, *Svensk–tyska förbindelser kring sekelskiftet 1900. Politik och ekonomi vid tillkomsten av 1906 års svensk–tyska handels- och sjöfartstraktat* (Lund, 1989)

West, Nigel (pseud. of Rupert Allason), *MI6* (London, 1983)

Wheeler-Bennett, John W., *Brest-Litovsk: The Forgotten Peace March 1918* (London, 1938)

White, Christine, '"Riches Have Wings": The Use of Russian Gold in Soviet Foreign Trade 1918–1922', in Hiden and Loit, *Contact or Isolation?*, pp. 117–36

White, Stephen, *Britain and the Bolshevik Revolution* (London, 1979)

Who Was Who 1981–1990 (London, 1991)

Wilhelmus, Wolfgang, 'Das schwedische Echo auf die faschistischen "Neuordnungspläne" im Zweiten Weltkrieg', *Jahrbuch für Wirtschaftsgeschichte* 1975, 1, pp. 35–46

Williamson, Philip, *National Crisis and National Government: British Politics, the Economy and Empire 1926–1932* (Cambridge, 1992)

Willmott, H. P., 'Operation *Jupiter* and Possible Landings in Norway', in Salmon, *Britain and Norway*, pp. 97–108

Wilson, Michael, *Baltic Assignment: British Submariners in Russia 1914–1919* (London, 1985)

Winterhager, Wilhelm Ernst, *Mission für den Frieden. Europäische Mächtepolitik und dänische Vermittlung im Ersten Weltkrieg. Vom August 1914 bis zum italienischen Kriegseintritt Mai 1915* (Stuttgart, 1984)

Winzen, Peter, 'Prince Bülow's *Weltmachtpolitik*', *Australian Journal of Politics and History* 22 (1976), pp. 227–42

Wittmann, Klaus, *Schwedens Wirtschaftsbeziehungen zum Dritten Reich 1933–1945* (Munich and Vienna, 1978)

Wurm, Clemens A., 'Britische Aussenwirtschaft 1919–1939. Exportverfall, Aussenhandelsorganisation und Unternehmerverhalten', *Scripta Mercuriae* 17 (1983), pp. 1–40

Business, Politics and International Relations: Steel, Cotton and International Cartels in British Politics 1924–1939 (Cambridge, 1993)

'Der Exporthandel und die britische Wirtschaft 1919–1939', *Vierteljahrsschrift für Sozial- und Wirtschaftsgeschichte* 68 (1981), pp. 191–224

Young, Robert J., 'Spokesmen for Economic Warfare: The Industrial Intelligence Centre in the 1930s', *European Studies Review* 6 (1976), pp. 473–89

Index